The Cambridge Companion to
English Renaissance Drama

The Cambridge Companion to
English Renaissance Drama

Edited by A. R. Braunmuller
and Michael Hattaway

CAMBRIDGE
UNIVERSITY PRESS

PUBLISHED BY THE PRESS SYNDICATE OF THE UNIVERSITY OF CAMBRIDGE
The Pitt Building, Trumpington Street, Cambridge, United Kingdom

CAMBRIDGE UNIVERSITY PRESS
The Edinburgh Building, Cambridge CB2 2RU, UK   www.cup.cam.ac.uk
40 West 20th Street, New York, NY 10011–4211, USA   www.cup.org
10 Stamford Road, Oakleigh, Melbourne 3166, Australia
Ruiz de Alarcón 13, 28014 Madrid, Spain

First published 1990
5th printing 1999

Printed in the United Kingdom at the University Press, Cambridge

British Library Cataloguing in Publication data
The Cambridge companion to English Renaissance drama.
1. Drama in English, 1558–1625. Critical studies
I. Braunmuller, A. R. 1945–   II. Hattaway, Michael 1941–
822'.3'09

Library of Congress Cataloguing in Publication data available

ISBN 0 521 34657 6 hardback
ISBN 0 521 38662 4 paperback

Contents

Plates

Nos 16–18 are in the Devonshire Collection, Chatsworth. Reproduced by permission of the Chatsworth Settlement Trustees. Prints by courtesy of the Courtauld Institute of Art.

Contributors

LEE BLISS, University of California, Santa Barbara
A. R. BRAUNMULLER, University of California, Los Angeles
JAMES BULMAN, Allegheny College, Meadville, Pennsylvania
MARTIN BUTLER, University of Leeds
R. A. FOAKES, University of California, Los Angeles
BRIAN GIBBONS, University of Zurich
MICHAEL HATTAWAY, University of Sheffield
MARGOT HEINEMANN, University of Cambridge
JILL LEVENSON, University of Toronto
ROBERT N. WATSON, University of California, Los Angeles

Preface

We know that there is no such thing as a 'neutral' organization for a book such as this, indeed, none for any book. Any shaping of material implies (pre)conceptions about that material; every system stipulates an order, any order accepts some values and ignores others. Still, a book must be ordered, and its order should have a phrasable rationale. Throughout, we have aimed for clarity combined with thought-provoking juxtapositions that convey the exciting multifariousness of the drama our contributors examine.

We considered two obvious ways of arranging this *Companion* – by author and by chronology. Our reasons for rejecting these arrangements will make clear the benefits and advantages of the pattern we did choose. Of all the nominally 'literary' arts, theatre involves the widest collaboration, requiring large numbers of people for its production and consumption. Renaissance English drama is, like classical Greek drama, heavily language-biased (and hence written texts provide, or preserve, more pleasure than texts of later drama); nevertheless, the source of these words, the author, is at best *primus inter pares*. For centuries, the act of preparing a play for production has changed the author's original text, and the Renaissance theatre was no different. Talking about plays in terms of their authors, like the common metonymy by which we use 'Milton' to refer to 'L'Allegro', *Arcades, Paradise Lost, Samson Agonistes*, etc., is a convenience, emphasizing some elements in our relation with a play or other literary work, but ignoring or minimizing others. Discourse about drama almost inevitably speaks of authors and authorship, but to make authors the exclusive basis of our approach to fifty or more years of intense activity ignores the theatre as a collaborative mass art (whether the 'mass' of responding spectators be several hundred at the 'private' Blackfriars or 2,500 at the 'public' Globe), disregards the creative and coercive power of convention, that necessary mediator of similarity and difference, and ignores the less visible but even more powerful forces of society and culture.

An arrangement in chronological terms is still more artificial, since it lacks even the basis in psychological identity provided by individual authors. Chronology's drawbacks are most simply illustrated in its grossest form, division by regnal periods. 'Elizabethan', 'Tudor', 'Jacobean', 'Stuart' ordinarily can point to the crudest of contrasts, even if we recognize how absurd it is to suppose, for example, that Jonson, Shakespeare, or Chapman, or their theatre companies, or their audiences, or their experiences and sensibilities changed detectably on that day in March 1603 when Queen Elizabeth died. (This absurdity is proved by the fact of revivals: placing prominence on only the first performance of any one play obscures the kinds of popularity and importance it may have enjoyed with different kinds of companies and at different periods – witness the early theatrical fortunes of Marston's *Malcontent*, originally a children's play, but soon performed by an adult, public theatre company in revenge for the children's producing an adult company's play at the Blackfriars.) Any chronological organization suffers from some form of the problem caused by regnal divisions – important theatrical events rarely march to the calendar's arbitrary metronome, and even when one could argue for an overall consistency or expository clarity offered by the plays, players, audiences, and social conditions of, e.g., the 1590s, what of the 1580s, or the half-decade 1615–20? Imprecise or unknown dates of composition, first performance, and revival also serve to make the dates of the volume's chronological range, 1580–1642, define an area of concentration and not set limits to a period.

The predominant organizing principle of this *Companion* is generic, but 'genre' conceived without neo-classical rigidity. Instead, our contributors have been asked to conceive of genre so as to catch some of the idea's Renaissance capaciousness: the mingle-mangle of clowns and kings, the variety of Bartholomew Fair, the social and musical expectations of a masque-audience. Occasionally, identifiable theatrical change does more or less coincide with a period neatly typified by some non-theatrical event, and we feel that Caroline drama is an example. Even here, however, we would claim no hard and fast temporal boundary, no throwing of switch or gears at the accession of Charles I. Rather, social and political changes rooted as far back as the economic and educational crises of the 1590s and parliamentary events of the later years of James's reign now appear forcefully in the plays produced during his son's reign.

Finally, we have made no attempt to be encyclopaedic. Our contributors were each assigned a list of representative plays appropriate to their topics, and were encouraged to offer accounts or analyses of particular passages or sequences. The general editors thus attempted to avoid duplicating material and to make certain that some account appeared of works by each major author, but they could not guarantee that a place would be found for *every* play commonly taken to rank among the period's masterpieces. Shakespeare was included but given no privileged treatment. Some contributors have ranged more widely from the agreed texts than others, and this was always the intention. The essays seek not to be definitive but perhaps to be paradigmatic: to offer the reader examples of recent ways of experiencing texts and performances, to provoke further reading and, above all, to add to the enjoyment of Renaissance dramatic texts in the study and the playhouse. The volume's apparatus does, however, attempt a conspectus of the best that has been written about the period and about authors. The Bibliography offers a selection of further reading on many of the topics covered in this volume – and many that could not be included in a book of this size. Major and some minor authors are there accorded a brief biography, a citation of the standard edition of their complete works (if there is one), and a brief list of relevant studies. Within the book, each essay is followed by a bibliographical note in which our expert contributors offer guidance on important past and recent work in their areas. The volume ends with a fairly comprehensive chronological table of plays and theatrical and political events. With these guides, and the volume's indices, we hope to match the curiosity and interest of both general and specialist readers.

Our contributors have graciously helped us and each other in shaping this volume. We thank Mary Jane Ross for her assistance in compiling many of the biographies and bibliographical materials and Sarah Stanton and Victoria Cooper for their patience and counsel in seeing the book through the press.

A note on dates, references, and quotations

The dates assigned to plays are those of composition and/or performance and derive from Alfred Harbage, *Annals of English Drama 975–1700*, rev. edn, S. Schoenbaum and Sylvia Wagonheim (London, 1989); these dates are often speculative or unreliable, and contributors have felt free to modify them.

Contributors have generally cited the following editions; divergences from and additions to this list are mentioned in the bibliographies to individual chapters.

The Dramatic Works in the Beaumont and Fletcher Canon, gen. ed., Fredson Bowers (Cambridge, 1966–   )

The Plays of George Chapman: The Comedies (Urbana, Illinois, 1970) and *The Tragedies* (Cambridge, 1987), gen. ed., Allan Holaday

The Dramatic Works of Thomas Dekker, ed. Fredson Bowers, 4 vols. (Cambridge, 1953–61)

The Complete Plays of Ben Jonson, ed. G. A. Wilkes, 4 vols. (Oxford, 1981–82)

The Complete Works of Christopher Marlowe, ed. Fredson Bowers, 2nd edn, 2 vols. (Cambridge, 1981)

The Plays and Poems of Philip Massinger, ed. Philip Edwards and Colin Gibson, 5 vols. (Oxford, 1976)

The Life and Works of George Peele, gen. ed. C. T. Prouty, 3 vols. (New Haven, 1952–71)

William Shakespeare: The Complete Works, ed. Peter Alexander (Glasgow and London, 1954)

The Complete Works of John Webster, ed. F. L. Lucas, 4 vols. (London, 1927)

In quoting these editions and other texts, contributors have modernized original spelling and punctuation where necessary.

Abbreviations

CL	*Comparative Literature*
CompD	*Comparative Drama*
CritQ	*Critical Quarterly*
DUJ	*Durham University Journal*
E&S	*Essays and Studies by Members of the English Association*
EIC	*Essays in Criticism*
ELH	*ELH: A Journal of English Literary History*
ELR	*English Literary Renaissance*
EM	*English Miscellany*
ES	*English Studies*
HLQ	*Huntington Library Quarterly*
JEGP	*Journal of English and Germanic Philology*
JWCI	*Journal of the Warburg and Courtauld Institutes*
MLN	*Modern Language Notes*
MLQ	*Modern Language Quarterly*
MLR	*Modern Language Review*
MP	*Modern Philology*
NLH	*New Literary History*
PMLA	*PMLA: Publications of the Modern Language Association of America*
PQ	*Philological Quarterly*
RenD	*Renaissance Drama*
RenQ	*Renaissance Quarterly* (formerly *Renaissance News*)
RES	*Review of English Studies*
RMS	*Renaissance and Modern Studies*
RORD	*Research Opportunities in Renaissance Drama*
SEL	*Studies in English Literature, 1500–1900*
ShakS	*Shakespeare Studies*
ShJ	*Shakespeare Jahrbuch (West)*
ShS	*Shakespeare Survey*
SP	*Studies in Philology*

SQ   *Shakespeare Quarterly*
TDR   *Tulane Drama Review*
TSLL   *Texas Studies in Language and Literature*
UTQ   *University of Toronto Quarterly*
YR   *Yale Review*

1   Playhouses and players

When we look back at a distant historical period, it is easy to succumb to two temptations; the first is to see a sudden, sharp break with the past taking place at some date such as the coming to the throne of Elizabeth I (1558), or James I (1603), as though a transformation in all aspects of society happened in those instants. The second is to telescope the passage of decades of change into a single, homogenized period like 'the age of Elizabeth', as though forty-five years could be focused in a single, unchanging image. In our own lives we are continually alert to shifts and changes that make what happened or was in vogue ten years, five years, or even one year ago seem curiously old-fashioned and different now. Perhaps it has always been so, even when change was slower technologically. The period from 1558 to the end of the reign of Charles I saw the passage of eighty-four years, during which the theatre was transformed, and the drama startlingly expanded and diversified. It is perhaps unfortunate that the great standard works on the theatres and drama in this period should be entitled *The Elizabethan Stage* and *The Jacobean and Caroline Stage*.[1] Yet any account of the period needs to begin with the recognition that there were many different stages as play-houses became more sophisticated, and that perhaps the only constant feature of the theatres up to 1642 was that all parts were normally played by men and boys; the professional companies in London had no actresses in them until after the restoration of the monarchy in 1660. The following account of playhouses and players in this period is especially concerned to illustrate the changes and developments that took place in the theatres during the passage of nearly a century. It is divided into four sections: the first deals with the growth of the 'public' or arena theatres; the second is concerned with the earlier 'private' or indoor playhouses; the third describes the later private theatres after 1615, and their relation to the surviving arena

---

[1] Chambers, *Elizabethan Stage*; Bentley, *Jacobean and Caroline Stage*.

stages; and the last focuses on the companies that played in the various theatres, and the business of acting.

The arena theatres

By the time Queen Elizabeth came to the throne a tradition of playing both by adult groups of players, and by companies of boys, was well established. A number of adult groups toured the major towns of England giving performances, without having any regular schedule or theatre buildings in which to play. A longstanding tradition of including the acting of plays in a humanist education for grammar-school boys led to boys' companies providing a major part of the entertainment at court during the Christmas season, and at Shrovetide. Plays had been staged at court for festive occasions since the reign of Henry VII, and Queen Elizabeth maintained the custom. During the early years of her reign up to 1576, performances at court by groups of boys drawn from choir-schools outnumbered those by adult groups. After 1576 professional companies of adult players became far more important, and began to establish their own permanent playhouses in London. I shall deal with these playhouses first.

In the early years of Elizabeth's reign groups of players performed where they could, occasionally indoors in halls to provide entertainment at court or in great houses, but more frequently in public in the square or rectangular yards of a number of inns in the city of London, the galleries round the yards being used by spectators. The companies were all licensed by the patronage of some great lord to travel and perform, for, if unlicensed, they were, according to a statute of 1598, technically deemed 'Rogues Vagabonds and Sturdy Beggars'.[2] The civic authorities of the city of London generally showed hostility to players, whom they saw as a nuisance, promoting crowds and disorder, and distracting people, especially apprentices, from their proper occupations, as well as from divine service on Sundays. Following a prohibition of 1559, which does not seem to have had much effect, the Common Council of London in December 1574 banned performances in taverns in the city unless innkeepers were licensed and the plays first subjected to strict supervision and censorship.[3]

We do not know how effective such prohibitions were, for they did not altogether stop playing at the Bull in Bishopsgate, or at the Bell in Gracechurch Street, where performances continued for another decade or more; however, they may have stimulated entrepreneurs to borrow money and

---

[2] Chambers, *Elizabethan Stage*, IV.324.
[3] *Ibid.*, IV.273–6.

build the first professional playhouses outside the jurisdiction of the city authorities. The earliest was the Red Lion, erected east of London in Stepney in 1567 by John Brayne, brother-in-law of James Burbage, who, with Brayne, built the Theatre in 1576. Not much is known about the Red Lion, except that it had a large stage, surrounded by galleries, and a 'turret' thirty feet high, with a floor made seven feet below the top.[4] James Burbage was father of the actor, Richard Burbage, who later played leading roles in many of Shakespeare's plays. The Theatre and the Curtain (built in 1577) were located to the north of the city limits (see pp. 4–5). Within a few years a fourth playhouse was built in Newington, well to the south of the Thames, and then a fifth with the erection of the Rose on Bankside in 1587. By this date it seems that performances were being offered daily, if the account of a German visitor to London in 1585 can be trusted.[5] The new theatres appeared sumptuous to visitors and to puritan critics of the stage, and they were evidently much more luxurious than the innyards which they superseded.

The city's attempt to restrain playing in innyards thus contributed to the development of fully professional companies playing regularly on most days, except in Lent, or in times of plague, in purpose-built theatres. The immediate success of the new theatres can be measured to some extent by the anxieties they provoked; indeed, by 1583, Philip Stubbes, disclaiming any hostility to theatres and plays in general, nevertheless voiced what had already become a regular complaint, that people flocked to 'Theatres and curtains' when 'the church of God shall be bare and empty'.[6] Stubbes's reference to the Theatre and the Curtain shows that the current centre of theatrical activity was Shoreditch, a north-east suburb. The playhouses here were a long way from the heart of the old city of London, which lay close to the River Thames. There had been arenas for bull- and bear-baiting south of the Thames on Bankside for many years, and the Beargarden there remained in business until 1613. So when the Rose was also built on Bankside in 1587, there were plenty of 'watermen' to ferry spectators over the river, and it may have been easier to cross the river by boat or by London Bridge, than to ride or walk out to the north. With the erection of the Swan on Bankside in 1595, this area became a major focus of theatrical activity. The river formed the southern boundary here of the city limits, so that the Bankside stages too were beyond the control of the city council.

A Flemish visitor to London in 1596 described the Swan as the largest

---

[4] See Loengard, 'An Elizabethan lawsuit'.
[5] Chambers, *Elizabethan Stage*, II.358.
[6] *Ibid.*, IV.223.

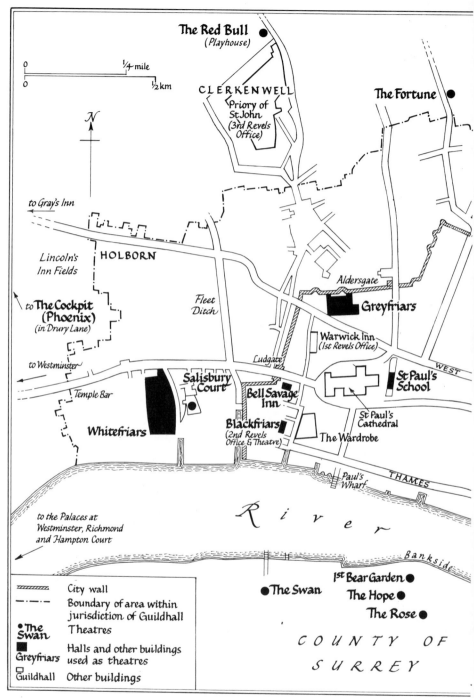

The Red Bull
(Playhouse)

The Fortune

CLERKENWELL
Priory of
St John
(3rd Revels
Office)

0 ¼ mile
0 ½ km

N

to Gray's Inn

Lincoln's
Inn Fields

HOLBORN

Fleet
Ditch

Aldersgate

Greyfriars

to The Cockpit
(Phoenix)
(in Drury Lane)

Warwick Inn
(1st Revels Office)

to Westminster

Ludgate

WEST

Temple Bar

Salisbury
Court

St Paul's
School

Bell Savage
Inn

St Paul's
Cathedral

Whitefriars

Blackfriars
(2nd Revels
Office & Theatre)

The Wardrobe

THAMES

Paul's
Wharf

to the Palaces at
Westminster, Richmond
and Hampton Court

R i v e r

Bankside

City wall
Boundary of area within
jurisdiction of Guildhall
Theatres

1st Bear Garden

The Swan

The Hope

●The Swan

The Rose

Halls and other buildings
Greyfriars used as theatres

COUNTY OF

□
Guildhall Other buildings

SURREY

1 Map showing principal public and private theatres, other locations important
to theatrical regulation and performance, and some main topographical features of
London, c. 1560–1640

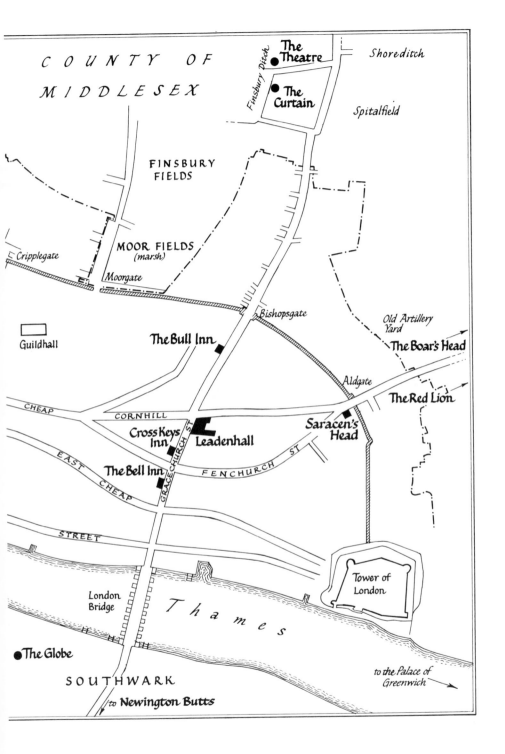

COUNTY OF
MIDDLESEX

The Theatre

Finsbury Ditch

The Curtain

Shoreditch

Spitalfield

FINSBURY
FIELDS

Cripplegate

MOOR FIELDS
(marsh)

Moorgate

Bishopsgate

Old Artillery
Yard

Guildhall

The Bull Inn

The Boar's Head

Aldgate

The Red Lion

CHEAP

CORNHILL

Cross Keys
Inn

GRACECHURCH ST.

Leadenhall

Saracen's
Head

The Bell Inn

EAST
CHEAP

FENCHURCH ST.

STREET

Tower of
London

London
Bridge

Thames

The Globe

SOUTHWARK

to the Palace of
Greenwich

to Newington Butts

2   Claude de Jongh's sketch of London Bridge, *1627*; detail showing the roof-lines and flags of the Hope or Beargarden and the Globe

and most splendid of the London theatres. In 1592 and again in 1595, the owner of the Rose, Philip Henslowe, spent substantial sums on repairing, improving, and extending his theatre (see p. 13). It is probable that the wooden Theatre and Curtain were in disrepair and obsolescent by this time, after nearly twenty years of use. Burbage had taken a lease on the site of the Theatre for twenty-one years in 1576, and had difficulty in his attempts to renew it. Foreseeing the need to make a move, in 1596 Burbage acquired space in the precinct of the old Blackfriars monastery, which, although it lay within the city walls (see pp. 4–5), retained certain privileges as a 'liberty' exempt from city control; but Burbage's idea of turning his newly acquired property into a 'common playhouse' was frustrated by the local inhabitants, who petitioned the Privy Council to prevent him. Burbage's way out was to take a lease on a site on Bankside, dismantle the Theatre, and use those timbers that could be salvaged in the construction there of a new playhouse, the Globe, which was in operation by 1599. In the summer of 1597, the performance at the Swan of a play (Thomas Nashe's *The Isle of Dogs*, now lost) containing lewd and seditious matters led to the arrest of three men, including Ben Jonson, who had been involved in the production, and provoked the Privy Council, according to Henslowe, to order a 'restraint' prohibiting the performance of plays within three miles of the city in the county of Middlesex.[7] A more serious effect of the affair of *The Isle of Dogs* was that Francis Langley, the owner of the Swan, could not obtain a licence to stage plays there when the restraint was lifted in the autumn; after this time the Swan never seems to have been able to attract and retain a regular company of players, though it continued to be used for other kinds of shows and entertainments.

For a brief period in 1599 the two most important companies of players operated on Bankside, where the Rose, the Globe, and the Swan drew audiences across the river. The most settled and prosperous companies were the Lord Chamberlain's Men, who played at the Globe, and the Lord Admiral's Men, who played at the Rose. The increased competition brought by the presence of the new Globe, the dilapidation of the Rose, now an ageing playhouse, and the fact that his lease was due to expire in 1605, drove Philip Henslowe to seek a replacement. In 1600 he opened his new theatre, the Fortune, in a northern suburb, just beyond Cripplegate (see pp. 4–5), but well to the west of the Shoreditch area where the old Theatre had stood, and where the Curtain was still operating in spite of the Privy Council order for its dismantling. The city was spreading west and north, and the

---

[7] *Ibid.*, IV.322–3; Foakes and Rickert, *Henslowe's Diary*, p. 240. But see also Ingram, *A London Life*, pp. 167–96.

Fortune stood within convenient walking distance for a growing population. A little earlier Robert Browne had established a company at the Boar's Head, in Whitechapel, outside the eastern limits of the city, where an inn was converted into a theatre in 1599, with a stage in the innyard, and galleries along each side of the rectangular yard. Here a strong company, formed by the amalgamation of the Earl of Worcester's Men and Lord Oxford's Men, was playing in 1602. Browne died of the plague in 1603, and was succeeded by Thomas Greene, but perhaps the venture was never a success; no plays can certainly be identified with this theatre, and the company moved in 1605 to a new playhouse, the Red Bull, in the same area as the Fortune, but a little further north-west, in Clerkenwell (see p. 4). The Red Bull had been an inn too, but it is always referred to as a playhouse or theatre after 1605, and perhaps what took place here was not, as Wickham believes, a conversion, in the manner of the Boar's Head,[8] but rather a virtual reconstruction.

The Red Bull was the last open-air arena theatre to be built, apart from the Hope. The Hope was designed as a dual-purpose place of entertainment, doubling as a bear-baiting arena and a theatre, and it replaced the old Beargarden on Bankside, torn down in 1613. Of the older theatres, that furthest south, at Newington Butts, seems to have fallen into disuse by 1595; the Theatre was dismantled in 1598, and the Rose demolished probably by 1606. The Boar's Head was effectively replaced by the Red Bull in 1605. After its brief period of success from about 1595 to 1597, the Swan, located furthest west of the Bankside theatres, and less accessible than the others from London Bridge, ceased to be in regular use as a theatre; although performances were revived there between 1611 and 1615, it seems thereafter to have been used only for 'feats of activity' (see below, p. 13), and had fallen into decay by 1632. The Hope opened with some éclat in the autumn of 1614, when Ben Jonson's *Bartholomew Fair* was presented there, but from about 1617 onwards it functioned mainly as a house for the baiting of bears and bulls, and for the exhibition of exotic animals. The history of the Curtain is obscure after 1607, apart from a few years between 1621 and 1625, when it was in use as a playhouse, but, as far as is known, no plays were staged there after 1625.

The remaining open-air theatres, the Globe (burned down in 1613 and rebuilt), the Fortune (burned down in 1621 and rebuilt), and the Red Bull, all continued in operation until Parliament closed the theatres in 1642. Throughout the period from 1576 to 1642, substantial audiences were

[8] Wickham, *Early English Stages*, II.2.108.

drawn to these large theatres. As far as we know, each of them had a stage projecting into an arena partly open to the skies, and surrounded by three tiers of galleries. According to Thomas Platter, a Swiss visitor who saw *Julius Caesar* performed at the Globe in October 1599, the spectator paid one penny to stand in the arena, another penny to sit in a gallery, and a penny more 'to sit on a cushion in the most comfortable place of all, where he not only sees everything well, but can also be seen'.[9] Prices of admission increased in later years, and the theatres were made more comfortable: the surviving contract for the Fortune called for 'gentlemen's rooms' and 'twopenny rooms' to be plastered.[10] These rooms were either in the gallery over the rear of the stage, or in sections of the main galleries – perhaps those sections closest to the stage were partitioned off to make 'twopenny rooms'. Wherever these rooms were (see below, p. 17), the evidence shows that the playhouses provided a hierarchy of accommodations in the expectation that the audience would be socially and economically diversified. There are a number of instances of dramatists joking with the 'understanding gentlemen o'the ground' (Ben Jonson, Induction to *Bartholomew Fair*), or sneering at them, as in Hamlet's snobbishly caustic comments on the 'groundlings' as capable only of 'inexplicable dumb-shows and noise'. It seems that arena spectators might also throw eggs or apples at players if they disliked the entertainment (Prologue to *The Hog hath Lost his Pearl*, 1613). However uneducated, and however much they may have preferred fights, noise, and clowning to serious drama, the groundlings remained an important part of the audience, and the arena theatres continued to cater to them.[11]

These playhouses were all similar in their basic conception, which is to say that all were relatively large arena theatres, accommodating probably between 2,000 and upwards of 3,000 spectators. Many of the detailed arrangements remain a matter of speculation, however, and not only did these theatres differ from one another in important ways, but over the years it seems that many structural changes were introduced. The early theatres were built of wood, probably, as the Fortune contract specifies, on piles and foundations of brick. Flint may have been used for the Swan, but the evidence is conflicting; and, like the others, this theatre appeared round, so that Johannes De Witt, visiting London in 1596, could describe all four theatres he saw (Theatre, Curtain, Rose, Swan) as 'amphiteatra'.[12] We now know that the Rose was multi-sided (see pp. 10–11), and no doubt the other

[9] Chambers, *Elizabethan Stage*, II.365.
[10] Foakes and Rickert, *Henslowe's Diary*, p. 308.
[11] Gurr, *Playgoing*, pp. 72–7.
[12] Chambers, *Elizabethan Stage*, II.362.

3   The Rose theatre excavation

The illustration shows the remains of the Rose theatre exposed when excavation halted in May 1989. Much of the groundplan of the playhouse can be seen, although parts of it to the east and south remain unexcavated, and some other features have been obliterated by the sets of piles driven through for a building put up in the 1950s. The Rose was built for Philip Henslowe in 1587 as a slightly irregular polygonal building. To the north-west only eight pilecaps survive to show the line of the original outer wall, but enough of the chalk and stone footings of the outer and inner walls of the theatre have been exposed to show that it had fourteen sides or bays. The straight sections of the outer wall measure between 15 feet and 16 feet 6 inches, those of the inner wall just over 11 feet, and the depth of each bay, i.e., the distance between the outer and inner walls, was 10 feet 6 inches. The playhouse had an external diameter of about 74 feet, was smaller than the Fortune, built to replace it in 1600 (4,500 square feet ground area, excluding the galleries, as against 6,400 square feet), and considerably smaller than the Globe, if that was as large as many now think (about 7,800 square feet ground area).

The open-air arena inside the inner walls was covered with impervious mortar, most of which is still in place. The northern section is confusing because the theatre was extended and partly rebuilt at some point, probably in 1592, when Henslowe recorded large expenses for work that included breaking up, buying bricks and chalk, putting in rafters, bricklaying, thatching, plastering, painting the stage, and setting up a penthouse shed at the tiring-house door (*Henslowe's Diary*, pp. 9–13). The extension involved erecting a new stage, and enlarged the capacity of the arena and galleries. The earlier stage is marked by a plinth running roughly east–west, and it tapered towards the front, where it was 24 feet 9 inches wide; at the rear it measured 37 feet 6 inches wide, and it had a maximum depth of 15 feet 6 inches. It was thus smaller than the stage at the Fortune, which the contract specified should be 43 feet wide and extend to the middle of the yard. The rear wall seems to have been the inner frame of the polygon, so that the stage was very different from the rectangular one depicted by De Witt at the Swan, with its straight rear screen or *frons scenae* (see p. 14).

North of the outline of the earlier stage can be seen the clunch or soft stone footings of a second stage of a similar shape, built when the theatre was extended. The front of it is set back 6 feet 6 inches from the earlier stage. A base, presumably for a column, has been found in the south-west corner of the later stage, and may be evidence of support for a cover over the stage. If so, the boards of the platform would need to have extended beyond the perimeter marked by the footings to allow an actor to pass in front of it. Both stages were oriented roughly south, so that they would have the even light of shade when plays were performed during the afternoon. An erosion trench visible in the mortar of the arena indicates where water fell from the thatched roof above the galleries. On the west side two parallel partition walls may mark a passage for access to the arena, but the main entrance may have been on the south side, opposite centre-stage. No evidence has yet been found of the tiring-house, which was probably located in the bays behind the stage.

Further analysis will no doubt reveal more details (see John Orrell and Andrew Gurr, 'What the Rose can tell us', *Times Literary Supplement*, 9–15 June, 1989, pp. 636, 649), but the basic information outlined here is already startling in many ways. The Rose was different from the Swan and the Globe, and its smaller auditorium requires us to think of a capacity of the order of 2,000 spectators rather than 3,000 or more as at the Globe. The new information is thus of great importance, for it is the first reliable evidence we have about the Elizabethan arena theatres, and it challenges some assumptions that have long been taken for granted.

wood-framed theatres were similarly constructed. This would explain why on some maps (none of them authoritative), they are represented as polygonal, usually hexagonal or octagonal. Current research suggests that the playhouses had many more sides: the Rose, with a diameter of about 74 feet, had fourteen, and the much larger Globe, thought to have had a diameter of about 100 feet, may have had twenty or twenty-four.[13] The design of the theatres can be related to the circular arenas for bear- and bull-baiting which had stood on Bankside for decades;[14] but they appeared to visitors to London to resemble the structure of ancient Roman amphitheatres.[15]

Only one drawing survives of the interior of an arena playhouse, a copy by Aernout van Buchell of a sketch of the Swan theatre made in 1596 by Johannes De Witt (see p. 14). This shows the large projecting rectangular stage, with a canopy over it supported by two columns. At the rear of the stage is the wall of the tiring-house, with two large, round-arched rustic doors in it providing entrances on to the stage. Above this wall is a gallery partitioned into six bays. The drawing also clumsily incorporates a hut apparently above and behind the canopy over the stage, with a trumpeter blowing as if to announce a performance, and a flag flying, with the house emblem on it. No spectators are shown in the galleries or the arena, and the only figures portrayed are three actors on stage and one or two persons in each bay of the gallery at the rear of the stage. The figures on stage and the bench drawn there could be an artist's invention to decorate that otherwise blank space, or they may have been recollected from some performance. The figures in the gallery may indicate gentlemen in the 'gentlemen's rooms', or, again, may be decorative. The stage itself seems to float above two openings where curtains have been partly drawn, but these could also be interpreted as columns supporting the stage. The drawing does not show a performance taking place; some have thought it depicts a rehearsal, but this is improbable, for there would be other persons at a rehearsal, the book-holder or prompter, other members of the company, and those who managed or directed productions. The details of the drawing are difficult to interpret, and of uncertain reliability, and I think the sketch needs to be treated with scepticism, not accepted 'at its face value',[16] or as 'generally reliable'.[17]

The Swan (1595) was the first of the second generation of purpose-built theatres, and may well have been the largest and most splendid of the play-

---

[13] Orrell, *Quest*, pp. 160–1.
[14] Foakes, *Illustrations*, pp. 2–3.
[15] Chambers, *Elizabethan Stage*, II.362, 366.
[16] Wickham, *Early English Stages*, II.1.204.
[17] Hosley, 'Playhouses', p. 136.

houses when it was erected, as De Witt observed,[18] but it was probably very different from the Globe and Fortune in important respects. The contract for the Fortune shows that it imitated the best features of the Globe,[19] but when Philip Henslowe went on to erect the Hope in 1613–14 as a replacement for the Beargarden, the contract he drew up for it specifically calls for a design similar to that of the Swan.[20] The explanation for this is probably that the Swan itself was a dual-purpose playhouse and game-house,[21] with a removable stage, which would have made possible the use of the entire arena for the 'feats of activity' one Peter Bromville was licensed to put on there in 1600. There is no evidence that the Swan was used for animal-baiting, but there is little evidence, either, that it was used for plays between 1597 and 1611. In February 1602 a man was accidentally killed while taking part in a fencing match held there.[22] A spectacular entertainment was advertised as taking place there in November 1602 by Richard Vennar (see below, p. 16), but this proved to be a hoax. The Swan, then, was little used after 1597; only one play (Thomas Middleton's *A Chaste Maid in Cheapside*, 1613; printed 1630) is certainly known to have been acted there, and the Hope, modelled on it, seems pretty well to have put it out of business. It is reasonable to infer that the Swan was more like the Hope than the other theatres on Bankside. The Hope itself proved to be more successful as a game-house than as a playhouse.

The simpler facilities of the dual-purpose houses may have made them less and less attractive as theatres during a period when the playhouses were gradually becoming more elaborate and comfortable. Accommodations in the early playhouses seem to have been spartan for most spectators, and probably for actors too. Henslowe plastered and put ceilings into the gentlemen's rooms at the Rose in 1592, and improved the tiring-house facilities by adding a penthouse. In 1595, he had a 'throne' made in the 'heavens',[23] presumably a machine to make it possible to lower a throne, and perhaps other properties, on to the stage; he also made substantial renovations at this time. The De Witt drawing of the Swan has perpetuated the idea of the Elizabethan theatres as having a bare stage and minimal facilities, but other evidence suggests rather that their accommodation and equipment were continually being improved. They were a tourist attraction for foreign

[18] Chambers, *Elizabethan Stage*, II.362.
[19] *Ibid.*, II.437.
[20] *Ibid.*, II.466–7.
[21] Wickham, *Early English Stages*, II.2.68–9.
[22] Chambers, *Elizabethan Stage*, II.413.
[23] Foakes and Rickert, *Henslowe's Diary*, p. 7.

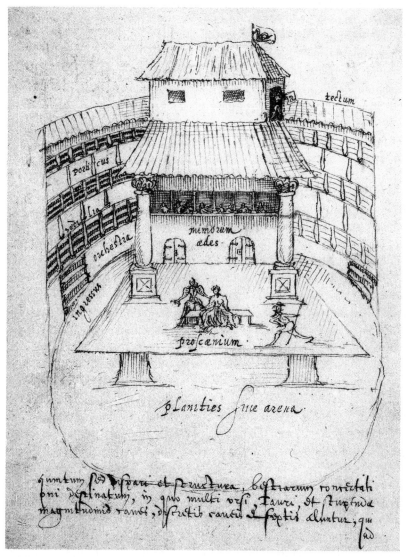

tectum

porticus

orchestra

mimorum
ædes

proscenium

planities siue arena

4 Johannes de Witt's sketch of the interior of the Swan Theatre about 1596, as copied by Aernout van Buchell; see p. 12

visitors, who, like the puritan critics of the stage, frequently remarked on the magnificence of the buildings. So De Witt himself noted the beauty ('pulchritudinis') of the four theatres in 1596, and Thomas Platter in 1599 observed that the players were 'most expensively and elegantly apparelled'.[24] In November 1602 Richard Vennar lured a large audience to the Swan on a Saturday by advertising an elaborate entertainment called 'England's Joy'; but, according to a letter written by John Chamberlain, 'the common people, when they saw themselves deluded, revenged themselves upon the hangings, curtains, chairs, stools, walls, and whatsoever came in their way'.[25] Apparently the 'great store of good company, and many noblemen' present did not take part in this riot. The curtains and hangings referred to by Chamberlain are not hinted at in De Witt's drawing.

The new Swan struck De Witt as the most splendid of the London theatres in 1596, apparently because it was more richly furnished and decorated than the earlier theatres. The Globe (1599) and Fortune (1600) were no doubt even more elaborate. At the Fortune the main posts of the frame of the theatre and the stage were to be wrought 'pilasterwise', with 'carved proportions called Satyrs' to be placed on the top of each;[26] in other words, the columns of the main frame and stage were to be carved so as to present the appearance of one of the classical orders, and to be decorated with figures, half-man, half-goat, drawn from classical mythology. So at the Fortune, not only were the stage posts classical in appearance (perhaps like the elaborate Corinthian columns supporting the canopy in the De Witt drawing), but also the main posts of the entire frame. These features could explain why foreign visitors like Thomas Platter thought of the Bankside playhouse he visited as constructed in the style of an ancient Roman amphitheatre. The internal façade of the stage and the whole theatre at the Fortune, built in emulation of the Globe, must have been imposing. The cover over the stage was perhaps initially a simple canopy, designed to protect actors, properties, and hangings from the worst of the weather; it was painted on the underside with a representation of the sun, moon, stars, and zodiac, and known as the heavens. The Swan seems to have had such a simple canopy, and a removable stage; but at the Globe and Fortune, the canopy was probably more substantial, and it may have ┗   ┛cticable to use the space between the sloping roof of the 'shadow oɪ   't is called in the Fortune contract,[27] and a flat ceiling laid under it, fᴜ   ..dlasses and

[24] Chambers, *Elizabethan Stage*, II.362, 365.
[25] *Ibid.*, III.501.
[26] *Ibid.*, II.437.
[27] Foakes and Rickert, *Henslowe's Diary*, p. 308.

THE PLOT OF THE PLAY, CALLED
ENGLANDS JOY.
To be Playd at the Swan this 6. of Nouember. 1602.

FIRST, there is induct by shew and in Action, the ciuill warres of England from *Edward* the third, to the end of Queene *Maries* raigne, with the ouerthrow of Vsurpation.

2 Secondly then the entrance of Englands Ioy by the Coronation of our Soueraigne Lady *Elizabeth*; her Throne attended with peace, Plenty, and ciuill Pollicy: A sacred Prelate standing at her right hand, betokening the Serenity of the Gospell: At her left hand Iustice: And at her feete Warre, with a Scarlet Roabe of peace vpon his Armour: A wreath of Bayes about his temples, and a braunch of Palme in his hand.

3 Thirdly is dragd in three Furies, presenting Dissention, Famine, and Bloudshed, which are throwne downe into hell.

4 Fourthly is exprest vnder the person of a Tyrant, the enuy of *Spayne*, who to shew his cruelty causeth his Souldiers dragge in a beautifull Lady, whome they mangle and wound, tearing her garments and Iewels from off her: And so leaue her bloudy, with her hayre about her shoulders, lying vpon the ground. To her come certaine Gentlemen, who seeing her pitious dispoylment, turne to the Throne of England, from whence one descendeth, taketh vp the Lady, wipeth her eyes, bindeth vp her woundes, giueth her treasure, and bringeth forth a band of Souldiers, who attend her forth: This Lady presenteth *Belgia*.

5 Fiftly, the Tyrant more enraged, taketh counsell, sends forth letters, priuie Spies, and secret vnderminers, taking their othes, and giuing them bagges of treasure. These signifie *Lopus*, and certaine Iesuites, who afterward, when the Tyrant lookes for an answere from them, are shewed to him in a glasse with halters about their neckes, which makes him mad with fury.

6 Sixtly, the Tyrant seeing all secret meanes to fayle him, intendeth open violence and inuasion by the hand of Warre, whereupon is set forth the battle at Sea in 88. with Englands victory.

7 Seuenthly, hee complotteth with the Irish rebelles, wherein is layd open the base ingratitude of *Tyrone*, the landing there of *Don Iohn de Aguila*, and their dissipation by the wisedome and valour of the Lord *Mountioy*.

8 Eightly, a great triumph is made with fighting of twelue Gentlemen at Barriers, and sundrie rewards sent from the Throne of England, to all sortes of well deseruers.

9 Lastly, the Nine Worthyes, with seuerall Coronets, present themselues before the Throne, which are put backe by certaine in the habite of Angels, who set vpon the Ladies head, which represents her Maiestie, an Emperiall Crowne, garnished with the *Sunne*, *Moone* and *Starres*; And so with Musicke both with voyce and Instruments shee is taken vp into Heauen, when presently appeares, a Throne of blessed Soules, and beneath vnder the Stage set forth with strange fireworkes, diuers blacke and damned Soules, wonderfully discribed in their seuerall torments.

5 The playbill for Richard Vennar's hoax entertainment *England's Joy*, 1602; see p. 15

machinery for lowering people and properties on to the stage.[28] Such machinery could easily have been accommodated at the second Globe, which had a cover surmounted by spacious twin-gabled roofs, and extending almost to the centre of the arena.[29]

The stage was 'paled in' with strong oak boards at the Fortune, and the area underneath was jocularly known as 'hell'. The use of at least one large trapdoor made possible various kinds of startling appearances, like the devil that rises from the stage in Scene 3 of Marlowe's *Doctor Faustus*; some idea of this stage effect can be gathered from the frontispiece of the 1616 quarto. George Chapman's *All Fools*, written probably in 1599 for performance by the Admiral's Men, was printed in 1605 with a prologue designed for the Fortune that calls attention to the startling nature of the stage effects made possible by the use of the stage-hell and stage-heavens:

> The fortune of a Stage (like Fortune's self)
> Amazeth greatest judgments; and none knows
> The hidden causes of those strange effects
> That rise from this Hell, or fall from this Heaven.

We know least about the appearance of the stage façade, i.e., the tiring-house wall at the rear of the stage. The drawing of the Swan shows two doors in an otherwise flat screen wall, and Richard Hosley has seen in this feature an echo of the two doors common in the screens in the domestic halls of colleges and private houses, from which he thinks the stage façade at the Swan was derived.[30] At the Rose, however, the polygonal inner frame of the playhouse served as the rear wall of the stage, and the evidence shows that the stage façades at the Globe and Fortune were more elaborate than that indicated in the Swan drawing. It is reasonable to suppose that the neo-classical moulding of the columns at the Fortune was carried through the stage façade, in imitation of the Globe. At these theatres there were three stage doors or openings; so, for instance, Thomas Heywood's play, *The Four Prentices of London* (Fortune, *c.*1600), begins with a prologue specifying 'Enter three in black cloaks, at three doors'.

At the Swan a gallery ran the width of the stage above the doors, and was partitioned into six 'rooms', if De Witt's drawing can be trusted. Here perhaps were the four 'gentlemen's rooms' specified in the Fortune contract; but at the Fortune and Globe, part of this space appears to have been set aside for musicians and for stage action requiring an upper level. The gallery overhung the stage, and hangings mounted on rods affixed to this projection

[28] Wickham, *Early English Stages*, II.1.304–5.

[29] Foakes, *Illustrations*, p. 37.

[30] Hosley, 'Playhouses', p. 131.

could be used to conceal actors as required behind the 'arras' (see below, p. 20). The tapestries or curtains hung on the stage could, of course, be decorative or symbolic, and there are several references to using black hangings for tragedies;[31] they could also be drawn across one of the doors or openings to make possible discovery scenes. Occasionally, as in Robert Greene's *Friar Bacon and Friar Bungay* (Rose, *c.*1590), a character in the play draws the curtain himself. The Fortune contract also calls for 'convenient windows and lights glazed' to the tiring-house;[32] and since the tiring-house was to be built within the frame of the theatre, these windows and lights may have been in the tiring-house wall facing the stage. Although there are many references to action taking place at windows, the question of their physical reality is part of a larger problem that has not been adequately studied, and may be unresolvable.

The problem, briefly stated, is this: for much of our knowledge about playhouses of the period we depend upon the evidence provided by the stage directions and action of the plays staged there; where the action refers to posts on the stage, or requires three men to enter at different doors, we take this as evidence about the posts and doors which we know must have been there. Beyond such requirements is a grey area where the objects or locations could have been real, or simply imagined; windows perhaps belong in this category. Then there are plays in which the rear wall of the stage serves as the battlements of a city under siege, or a castle, or houses and shops in a street, or a forest, a seashore, or whatever the dramatist declares it to be. I know of no way to establish a boundary between what was done in practice on the stages of the public playhouses, and what was left to the imagination. Many scholars take a minimalist view, and, believing the Swan to be typical, tend to assume that any feature mentioned in the text or stage directions of a play is to be imagined by the audience unless it is indicated in the Swan drawing. I think, for reasons already indicated, that the Swan was not typical, and was superseded by better-equipped theatres such as the Globe and Fortune. Later theatres certainly had practical windows at the rear or sides of the stage, and the Fortune contract would suggest that these were provided there, on the gallery level, along with 'lights' or gratings in the stage doors.

This problem reminds us that the evidence is not easy to interpret, and that all students of the Elizabethan theatres have to rely on some element of speculation. I believe myself that Elizabethan theatres, like modern ones, offered as lavish and brilliant spectacles as they could create. Certainly the

---

[31] Chambers, *Elizabethan Stage*, III.79.
[32] *Ibid.*, II.437.

costuming could be magnificent; Henslowe, for instance, spent £21, a huge sum then, on velvet, satin, and taffeta for a single play on Cardinal Wolsey (by Henry Chettle; now lost) in 1601.[33] His accounts for this period show that the Fortune company regularly spent large sums on new costumes and properties. An inventory of the costumes of this company made in 1598 confirms contemporary comments on how the players strutted in some splendour on their stages: the list includes numerous items of apparel in satin, taffeta, and cloth of gold; also cloaks, jerkins, breeches, and doublets of various colours, white, tawny, silver, red, black, green, yellow, orange, many of them trimmed with 'gold' (usually copper, as Henslowe's accounts show) or silver lace.[34] Henslowe's payments suggest that they had some concern for an appearance of historical authenticity in costuming plays on recent or contemporary themes (like the lost *Cardinal Wolsey*), but the players were less troubled by historical accuracy in presenting plays on topics drawn from earlier times. The drawing by Henry Peacham of characters in *Titus Andronicus* shows a mixture of costumes: soldiers are dressed in Elizabethan armour, and other figures in tunics appropriate to ancient Rome.[35] In general, it can be said that the costumes appeared sumptuous and were rich in a variety of colours.

The players also made use of an elaborate range of properties. Henslowe's 1598 inventory[36] includes tombs, a chariot, a bedstead, and other properties fairly often used, but also two steeples, several trees, two moss-banks, a hell-mouth, and the city of Rome. The last item may have been a painted hanging, but we do not know how other properties were managed, or to what extent the players tried to provide settings for their plays. The openings in the tiring-house wall could be made to serve as various locations, and some indications or representations of the scene were certainly employed. So, for instance, Thomas Middleton's *The Roaring Girl* (Fortune, *c.*1610) calls for three shops in a row, an apothecary's, a feather shop, and a sempster's shop.

Plain-coloured hangings were also used, and the stage was customarily 'hung with black' (Induction, *A Warning for Fair Women*; Theatre/Globe, printed 1599) for tragedies; but painted cloths adorned the stage for other plays, and Ben Jonson refers to the 'fresh pictures, that use to beautify the decay'd dead arras, in a public theatre' (*Cynthia's Revels*; Blackfriars, 1601). In a later play that mockingly alludes to the public theatres, Beaumont's *The Knight of the Burning Pestle* (?Blackfriars, 1607), a joke is made out of an

---

[33] Foakes and Rickert, *Henslowe's Diary*, p. 179.
[34] *Ibid.*, pp. 321–3; see also Gurr, *Shakespearean Stage*, pp. 178–83.
[35] Foakes, *Illustrations*, p. 50.
[36] Foakes and Rickert, *Henslowe's Diary*, pp. 319–21.

incongruous cloth painted with a representation of the rape of Lucrece. The Jonson allusion suggests that the 'arras' or heavy tapestry may have been a permanent feature, and that painted cloths were hung over this when desired. If scenes were generally unlocalized, the imagined locality being indicated in the text, hangings nevertheless could be used to provide an appropriate background; and the curtains could be parted to suggest interior scenes, and allow beds, tables, and other properties to be brought forth or revealed as necessary for the action of a play. Frequently a tableau discovered by opening the curtains dissolves as the participants move out on to the main stage. Remarkable effects could be obtained, as when, after a series of battle scenes, *Tamburlaine, Part 2*, 2.4 (Rose, 1588) opens with the direction: 'The Arras is drawn, and Zenocrate lies in her bed of state, Tamburlaine sitting by her; three Physicians about her bed, tempering potions. Theridamas, Techelles and Usumcasane, and the three sons'. The moment of stasis here at the beginning of the death scene of Tamburlaine's great love halts the flow of action, achieving a visual pathos.

The first part of Marlowe's *Tamburlaine* (Rose, 1587) is famous for its visual effects; Tamburlaine transforms himself from a shepherd into a king, and later changes his costume according to his mood and intentions, from white to scarlet to black, and in 4.4 hangs his 'bloody colours' on the tiring-house wall, which serves as the city walls of Damascus. There the citizens 'walk quivering on their city walls' (4.4.3), perhaps on the 'tarras' or narrow ledge or balcony projecting from the gallery at the rear of the stage. Many plays make use of the different levels of the stage, turning the tiring-house wall into battlements which could be scaled with ladders, or from which proclamations of victory could be announced. The text of *Tamburlaine, Part 1* also refers to Tamburlaine's 'tents of white' and 'vermilion Tent' (4.2.111, 117); it is not certain that these were shown on stage in this play (were the tents real or imagined?), though in *Part 2*, the stage direction for 4.1 calls for two characters to enter 'from the tent where Calyphas sits asleep'. Practical tents or pavilions were set up for many plays, with doors or openings allowing for display within, as the stage direction in *Edward I* (Theatre, 1591), 1.1932, suggests: 'the king sits in his Tent with his pages about him'. During the 1580s and 1590s battle scenes were very popular, and in some plays two or more tents were pitched, as most famously in Shakespeare's *Richard III* (Theatre, 1593) where the tents of the leaders of the opposing armies, Richard and Richmond, are set up on stage in 5.3.

Many different kinds of spectacular effect could be contrived by the use of hangings, of practicable tents, scaffolds, arbours, chairs of state, beds, ladders, trees, and other objects brought on stage, or thrust through the trapdoor. The use of fireworks also made possible such effects as the display of lightning, or the effect of a blazing star. The open-air theatres also made much use of loud noises, of trumpets and drums, and the shooting of guns. Processions and dumbshows enlivened scenes with visual effects that could often be striking; so in *Captain Thomas Stukeley* (Rose/Fortune, ?1595; printed 1605), a dumbshow or pantomime in which the hero dithers between joining forces with the Spanish or the Portuguese, then decides to ally himself with the Portuguese, ends 'and so both armie[s] meeting embrace, when with a sudden thunder-clap the sky is one fire, and the blazing star appears, which they prognosticating to be fortunate departed very joyful' (sig. K1r).[37] It is often said that 'Stage business and spectacle of this kind should not be allowed to obscure the fact that the stages themselves were essentially bare',[38] but I believe this claim, based on the Swan drawing, is misleading. The stage façade was highly decorated, and the Elizabethan playhouses offered their public colour, spectacle, and richness. The stage was anything but bare; even the platform itself was covered with rushes, probably in part to deaden the noise of the actors' movements.

The essential point is not that the stage was bare, but that no attempt at scenic illusion was made; the stage-location was whatever the dramatist made his actors say it was. This in itself marks an extraordinary development away from the 'simultaneous' staging of medieval theatre that lingered on into the 1590s, notably in plays by Lyly and Peele, mainly written for children to perform, and with presentation at court in mind. The use of three-dimensional structures or 'houses' placed in different parts of the stage, or along the rear, to represent different localities, gave way as a general principle to successive staging for audiences that loved romances, histories, and tragedies that ranged freely over the known world, like Marlowe's *Tamburlaine*, or John Day's *The Travels of the Three English Brothers* (Red Bull, 1607), or Thomas Heywood's *The Four Prentices of London, with the Siege of Jerusalem* (Rose, ?1594). Parts of the stage could, of course, be identified as particular locations when necessary, as in Dekker's *The Shoemaker's Holiday* (Rose, 1599), where Simon Eyre's shoemaker's shop is opened up in 1.4 ('open my shop windows!'), shut up at 3.2.149, and displayed in 4.1 with 'Hodge at his shop board' (stage direction). In 3.4 a 'sempster's shop' is the setting, and probably hinged shutters were made that could serve as windows, and also opened out to form a board or counter. But when the shops were closed up, the stage became a street, or a rural place, as at the opening of 1.2, where Rose sits 'upon this flow'ry bank' making a garland. It

---

[37] See Mehl, *Dumb Show*, pp. 102–3.
[38] Gurr, *Shakespearean Stage*, p. 175.

Arundel houſe

Ex houſe

Temple

Temple ſtayres

Black freyars

The Globe

The Globe

Beere bayting H

6 Hollar's 'Long View of London from Bankside', 1647; section showing the Globe and Beargarden – Hollar has reversed their designations

has been argued[39] that mansion staging 'was imported intact into the first permanent theatres of Elizabethan London', but I see little evidence to support this claim; indeed, by 1599 the free-ranging spectaculars of the public theatres were drawing the scorn of Ben Jonson, who preferred to observe the neo-classical unities of action and place. In *Every Man out of his Humour* (Globe, 1599), Jonson's commentators on the action pun on the playwright's 'travel':

MITIS ... how comes it then that in some one play we see so many seas, countries, and kingdoms passed over with such admirable dexterity?
CORDATUS Oh, that but shows how well the authors can travail in their vocation, and outrun the apprehension of their auditory. (Induction, 269–72)

As long as the open-air, public theatres had a virtual monopoly on playing, that is, up to about 1600, they may have paid less attention to the comfort of spectators in the arena and galleries than to improvements in the stage area. In the winter especially, the spectators must have been often exposed to cold and damp. If the first Globe had a diameter of about 100 feet,[40] then an area of more than 2,000 square feet would have been directly exposed to rain. The new design of the second Globe (1613), as shown in Hollar's 'Long View', included a large roofed area covering all the stage and at least half the arena. This modification reduced the area exposed directly to the sky, and made the galleries, especially those areas near the stage, less vulnerable to the wind and rain. The Fortune, being square and smaller (the sides were 80 feet long), had a much smaller area directly open to the sky, perhaps 1,500 square feet; probably the square or rectangular Red Bull had a similar design. The first Globe was thatched, the second, like the Fortune, tiled. When the Fortune burned down in 1621, it was replaced by a round brick building, 'partly open to the weather',[41] but no doubt much more enclosed than the early playhouses. There had, of course, to be sufficient daylight for the actors to perform, and some stages appear to have faced north-east, perhaps to ensure an even light without glare or strong contrasts in the stage area.[42]

In this respect the arena playhouses of the period 1576–1642 were radically different from modern theatres, in which actors usually appear behind a proscenium arch, under spotlights, in front of an audience sitting in a darkened auditorium. It is a matter of fundamental importance that actor and audience shared the same lighting, and, effectively therefore, the same space in the arena playhouses, since the stage projected into the middle of

---

[39] Wickham, *Early English Stages*, II.1.8–9.
[40] Orrell, *Quest*, pp. 99–104.
[41] Chambers, *Elizabethan Stage*, II.443.
[42] Foakes, *Illustrations*, pp. 37–8.

the building, and the actors spent much of their time in close contact with spectators who surrounded them. One reason these theatres stayed in business was that they provided an especially close relationship between actors and audience, with no visual barrier between them, allowing the actor to identify as intimately as he pleased with spectators, or to distance himself within the action. 'Awareness of the illusion as illusion was therefore much closer to the surface all the time.'[43] Dramatists continually exploited this awareness, in prologues, inductions, jokes, metaphors, and plays within the play, reminding their audiences of the fictive nature of what they were watching, and of the uncertain boundary between illusion and reality. Two devices used with especial brilliance were the aside, in which an actor could step out of his role for a moment to comment on the action, and the soliloquy, in which the actor could address the audience directly, seem to take it into his confidence, or, as in *The Revenger's Tragedy* (Globe, 1607), switch, in attacking vice, from commenting on the grotesque characters of the unnamed Italian court which is the play's setting, and involve the audience directly. Holding up his moral emblem of a skull in a woman's headdress, Vindice cries,

> See, ladies, with false forms,
> You deceive men, but cannot deceive worms.   (3.5.96–7)

There are no ladies on stage, and those in the audience are confronted momentarily with a frightening reality. It should not, after all, surprise us that so much of the greatest drama of the period was created in theatres that must have been, by modern standards, cold and uncomfortable.

The early private playhouses

By 1600 the public playhouses were beginning to face competition. In the early years of her reign, Queen Elizabeth had relied heavily for dramatic entertainment during the Christmas and Shrovetide festival seasons on performances at court by the boys of the choir and grammar schools associated with St Paul's cathedral, and the choirboys of the Chapel Royal at Windsor. Richard Farrant, an enterprising master of the choirboys at Windsor, and deputy master of the boys of the parallel Chapel Royal that served the court in London, had become well known as a presenter of plays at court when, in 1576, he took a lease on rooms in the old Blackfriars monastery in the city in order to establish a playhouse for his boys, perhaps in association with the Paul's boys. After Farrant's death in 1580, the lease passed to the dramatist

---

[43] Gurr, *Shakespearean Stage*, p. 163.

John Lyly, and under his guidance playing continued there until 1584. This was the first roofed, indoor playhouse in London. The space available was quite small, in all about 46 by 26 feet, and rectangular.[44] Probably the boys performed once or twice a week, and the audiences must have been small, so that their impact on the public arena playhouses was at first slight. Indeed, after 1576, professional adult companies increasingly displaced the boys in providing plays for court festivities.

Nevertheless, the establishment of the first Blackfriars playhouse between 1576 and 1584 marked a major innovation in offering to a select audience a sophisticated alternative to the dramatic fare provided at the adult theatres. The Paul's boys, under their new master, Thomas Giles, appointed in 1584, continued to present plays by Lyly at court, and they performed in the precincts of St Paul's cathedral until their activities were suppressed about 1590, when they gave offence by handling matters of divinity and state in connection with the Martin Marprelate controversy.[45] Much of the repertory of the boys' companies from this period is lost, but it included morality plays, classical pastorals like Peele's *The Arraignment of Paris* (1584), and the graceful court comedies of Lyly, usually based on classical themes, but laced with topical allegory, as in *Endymion* and *Midas*. These may have come to seem old-fashioned by the late 1580s, when the ascendancy of the professional adult players is indicated in the establishment of a select company of Queen's Men, under the direct patronage of the crown, in 1583. The dramatic activities of the boys up to 1590 depended, in any case, on the enthusiasm of particular masters, and it was not until 1599–1600 that another master of Paul's boys, Edward Pearce, launched a new period of quasi-professional playing in a hall within the precincts of St Paul's cathedral. The exact location of this hall has not certainly been identified; but if Reavley Gair is right, it was very small, polygonal in shape so that it could appear as 'round' (Prologue to *Antonio's Revenge*, 1600), and seated perhaps 100 spectators at most.[46] However, the small stage had three doors, with windows above the two side doors, and an alcove with curtains above the central double doors.[47] The boys were able to draw on some of the best new talent among emerging dramatists, staging plays by Marston, Chapman, and Middleton, and their instant success may have encouraged Henry Evans to take a lease in 1600 on the Blackfriars property James Burbage had bought in 1596 (see above, p. 7), in order to establish a professional

[44] This is Wickham's estimate, *Early English Stages*, II.2.127.
[45] Chambers, *Elizabethan Stage*, IV.229–33.
[46] Gair, *Paul's*, pp. 66–7.
[47] Gair, *Paul's*, pp. 58–9.

company of boys there. In this theatre, by an arrangement with Evans, Nathaniel Giles, Master of the choirboys of the Chapel Royal, began to stage plays regularly; he began with some old ones, including at least one by Lyly, but also introduced work by new dramatists, like Ben Jonson, whose *Poetaster* in 1601 poked fun at the adult players and their theatres.

The second Blackfriars playhouse was much larger than that at Paul's, and measured 66 by 46 feet; it had at least two galleries of seating for spectators, and could accommodate perhaps as many as 500. Nothing is known about the size and disposition of the stage area at Blackfriars, other than what can be gleaned from the stage directions and texts of plays put on there. Both the Paul's and Blackfriars playhouses were located within the boundaries of the city of London, but in precincts that retained ancient ecclesiastical liberties, and were not under the direct jurisdiction of civic authority. By 1608, when a new charter gave the city authority over the old liberties, the playhouses and their companies had been taken under royal protection.[48] The methods of operation of the indoor playhouses were presumably sufficiently different from those of the adult theatres, since they were able to ignore the restrictions imposed by the Privy Council in a minute of 1598 and reinforced in an order of 1600, proclaiming that 'there shall be about the City two houses [i.e., the Globe and Fortune] and no more allowed to serve for the use of common stage plays'.[49] Ben Jonson's *Cynthia's Revels* (1601) was published as 'privately acted' at Blackfriars, and from about this time the indoor playhouses at Paul's and Blackfriars became generally known as 'private' theatres, in contrast to 'public' playhouses like the Globe and Fortune. The private theatres staged plays less frequently; Frederic Gerschow, a German who recorded a visit to Blackfriars on 18 September 1602, said the boys there performed once a week on Saturdays.[50] They began performances at later times, 3 or 4 in the afternoon, as against 2 o'clock, the customary time at the public theatres. They may have had different arrangements for admission, with some system of advance booking rather than payment at the door; and they may have advertised merely by word of mouth or by handbills, rather than sticking 'playbills upon every post' (*A Warning for Fair Women*, Induction, 75; Theatre/Globe, printed 1599). But whatever differences in practice there may have been, the private and public theatres were all staging plays for the entertainment of a paying audience.

The private playhouses charged much higher prices; in 1599–1600, when standing-room cost a penny at the public theatres, and a seat in the galleries

[48] Chambers, *Elizabethan Stage*, II.480.
[49] *Ibid.*, IV.330.
[50] *Ibid.*, II.46–7.

twopence, the private playhouses were charging sixpence. All the audience were seated at the private houses, and higher prices meant that these theatres attracted gallants, 'select and most respected auditors' (Marston, Prologue to *Antonio and Mellida*; Paul's, 1599–1600), and gentlewomen, 'the female presence; the Genteletza' (Marston, Induction to *What You Will*; Paul's, 1604). The boys acted by candlelight; in this same induction, 'Before the Music sounds for the Act', three characters enter and 'sit a good while on the Stage before the Candles are lighted'. A reference in a poem of 1629 to the 'torchy Friars'[51] may indicate how the auditorium was lit. They apparently shuttered the playhouse windows for tragedies, if Thomas Dekker's simile in a pamphlet of 1606, *Seven Deadly Sins*, can be trusted: 'All the city looked like a private playhouse, when the windows are clapped down, as if some *nocturnal*, or dismal *tragedy* were to be presented.' Playing indoors, with artificial lighting, the companies of boys also provided music between the acts of a play.

This was an innovation, for act divisions do not, in general, appear to have been observed as intervals at the public theatres, and music was not played between the acts, as the Induction to Marston's *Malcontent* (Paul's; revised for the Globe, 1604) testifies. At Blackfriars music was played before the performance began, and sometimes there was dancing or singing too between the acts. Probably intervals were required because the candles needed to be trimmed; but music was a special feature of small, enclosed theatres, where soft sounds could be heard, and a range of instruments used. Blackfriars had an orchestra of 'organs [meaning pipes], lutes, pandores [ancestor of the modern banjo], violins, and flutes', as well as a double-bass, according to Gerschow.[52] The tiny Paul's theatre had two 'music-houses' above and on either side of the stage, for, in Marston's *Antonio's Revenge* (1600), the ghost of Andrugio is placed between them during a dance in 5.3, to look down on the final revenge of his murder, and comment on it before the curtains are drawn across the alcove in which he sits, and he is able to make his exit (5.3.115).

Not much is known about the stages and seating arrangements at the private theatres. The stages were small by comparison with those of the public playhouses. There were boxes or lords' rooms at Blackfriars, apparently at the sides of the stage. The evidence of stage directions shows that there were three doors for use by actors in entering and leaving the stage[53] at both the private houses. One innovation apparently introduced at

[51] Gurr, *Playgoing*, p. 237.
[52] Cited in Chambers, *Elizabethan Stage*, II.47.
[53] Chambers, *Elizabethan Stage*, III.132.

public theatres in the late 1590s became a feature of the private houses, especially Blackfriars; this was the practice of allowing members of the audience, who paid extra for the privilege, to have a stool and sit on the stage. If the stage at Blackfriars was at one end of the hall, and extended most of the width of the room, there may have been space both for boxes and also for gallants who wished to display themselves to sit on the sides of the stage, without interfering with the sightlines of other members of the audience, or the action of the play itself.[54] In his play *The Devil is an Ass* (Blackfriars, 1616), Ben Jonson offers a vivid glimpse of one kind of foolish gallant, a squire of Norfolk, Fitzdottrell, showing off to his friends, to his wife, and to the women in the audience:

> Today I go to the Blackfriars Playhouse
> Sit i'the view, salute all my acquaintance,
> Rise up between the acts, let fall my cloak,
> Publish a handsome man, and a rich suit
> (As that's a special end, why we go thither,
> All that pretend, to stand for't o'the stage)
> The ladies ask who's that? (For they do come
> To see us, love, as we do to see them).   (1.6.31–8)

The private theatres, then, offered several kinds of refinement not available at the public playhouses: a more select clientele; greater comfort, including cushions on the benches (at the public playhouses the audience at this time sat on benches 'not adorn'd with mats', according to William Davenant's Prologue to *The Unfortunate Lovers*; Blackfriars, 1638); protection from the weather; and music and songs between the acts.

The boys' companies specialized for some years after 1600 in satiric comedies, and their characteristic style of playing has been described as 'anti-mimetic' in contrast to what has been seen as the naïve illusionism of the adult theatres.[55] This seems too categorical an opposition, since the adult companies always seem to have practised a mode of self-conscious theatre, playing against the audience's awareness of the stage as only a stage (see Chapter 2 for fuller discussion of this matter). At the same time, it would appear that the boys, playing and mimicking adults, invited their audiences to be more continuously critical and detached, and were more stridently anti-mimetic in their frequent mockery of what they portrayed as old-fashioned public-theatre modes of drama or styles of verse. They

---

[54] Berry, 'The stage and boxes at Blackfriars'; Berry speculates about the location of the boxes, and guesses that they might have been at the rear of the stage. See also the mock advice in Dekker's *The Gull's Hornbook*, 1609, cited in Chambers, *Elizabethan Stage*, IV.365–9.

[55] Gurr, *Playgoing*, p. 153.

deliberately catered to a more select and homogeneous audience, seeking to create the consciousness of an in-group that would appreciate their railing, an audience drawn largely from gallants, gentlemen and gentlewomen, and the sons of gentlemen who thronged the nearby Inns of Court, treating these as finishing schools rather than as institutions for serious study of the law.

Initially the private theatres succeeded in drawing a 'good, gentle Audience' (*Jack Drum's Entertainment*, 1600, sig. H3v) to Paul's, and offering at Blackfriars 'a nest of boys able to ravish a man', according to Thomas Middleton's advice to a gallant in *Father Hubburd's Tales*, 1604.[56] So too in the bad Quarto of *Hamlet*, 1603, Gilderstone says in 2.2 'the principal public audience ... are turned to private plays'. However, the boys had a more limited range than the adult players, and the satirical comedies which they preferred were always liable to give offence either to civic authorities or to the court. Some authors of plays seem to have taken ever-increasing risks in order to impress and hold their audiences. Furthermore, boy actors grew out of their parts as they became adults, so it is not surprising that the companies tended to have brief and chequered careers. For a variety of reasons the fortunes of the Paul's boys declined after 1606,[57] and they ceased playing altogether by 1608. By 1603 Middleton had replaced Marston as their principal dramatist, and the ageing of the boys may be reflected in the tone of some later plays he wrote for them, targeting the corruptions of unscrupulous usurers or lawyers in London rather than the corruptions of a court. Like the adult companies, the boys at Blackfriars were given a measure of royal protection in 1603 with the title of Children of the Queen's Revels, but lost their privilege because of offence caused by what James took to be insults against the Scots in *Eastward Ho!* (1605); two of the authors (Chapman and Jonson) were imprisoned, and the third (Marston) fled. Then in 1607–8, more serious offence was given by topical comments on the French in Chapman's play *The Conspiracy of Charles, Duke of Byron*, and in some lost play which included criticism of James himself. The company survived, and the King seems quickly to have forgotten his vow that 'they should never play more';[58] indeed, they staged three plays at court for the Christmas festivities in 1608. Then in 1609, the King's Men, who had obtained a surrender of the lease Richard Burbage had inherited from his father on the Blackfriars theatre, took possession of it, and began to use it as a winter house, continuing to play at the Globe during the summer months.

The Blackfriars company of boys seems to have been absorbed into the

---

[56] Chambers, *Elizabethan Stage*, II.50.
[57] Gair, *Paul's*, pp. 172–3.
[58] Chambers, *Elizabethan Stage*, II.54.

THE
Hiſtory of the two Maids of More-clacke,
VVith the life and ſimple maner of IOHN
in the Hoſpitall.

Played by the Children of the Kings
Maieſties Reuels.

VVritten by ROBERT ARMIN, ſeruant to the Kings
moſt excellent Maieſtie.

LONDON,
Printed by N.O. for *Thomas Archer,* and is to be ſold at his
ſhop in Popes-head Pallace, 1 6 0 9.

7   Robert Armin, title-page of *The Two Maids of Moreclack*, performed by the
Children of the King's Revels, 1606–7

group playing at Whitefriars, another hall theatre converted before 1609 from some portion of the old monastic buildings situated between Fleet Street and the Thames. Here they continued to work as the Children of the Queen's Revels until 1613, when they amalgamated with an adult company, the Lady Elizabeth's Men, playing at the Swan, with the intention of using Whitefriars as a winter playhouse, and the Swan as a summer house, in emulation of the King's Men at Blackfriars and the Globe. However, the lease at Whitefriars ran out in 1614, and, with the building of the new Hope on Bankside, activity at the Swan was curtailed; almost nothing further is heard about the Whitefriars theatre. The boys' companies at the private theatres thus flourished for a relatively short period. It may be that they ran out of steam, exhausting for their audiences the variations that could be worked in the kinds of play they did best; but a more important factor may have been the ageing of the companies, as the boys began to turn into adults. Still, their impact during the period from 1599 to 1614 was enormous. They established the desirability of enclosed theatres for winter playing, and the idea of a winter season (at Whitefriars performances were given only from Michaelmas to Easter). They showed that small theatres, charging higher prices, could operate profitably for a select audience; and after 1614 no more public arena theatres were built, apart from the replacement of the Fortune after it burned down in 1621.

The development of the indoor playhouses at Paul's, Blackfriars, and Whitefriars points to an increasing concern not only for refinement, comfort, and sophistication, but also for a kind of naturalism. In these theatres the relation of the audience to the stage was fundamentally changed. At the public theatres the groundlings stood nearest to the stage, and spectators paid more to sit further away in the galleries; at the private playhouses, as in modern theatres, the expensive seats were those closest to the stage. At the public theatres, actors would literally play to the galleries, if they played to the most esteemed part of their audience, and in open-air theatres that would require bold and strong delivery of lines. At the private theatres, where for the players the most important part of the audience was seated nearest the stage, a more low-keyed and intimate style was possible. The idea of what is 'natural', of course, changes all the time. By the 1590s the playhouses of the previous two decades were noted for what had now come to seem bombast and strutting; so Robert Greene makes a player in his *Greene's Groatsworth of Wit* (1592) boast, 'The twelve labours of Hercules have I terribly thundered on the stage'. At the beginning of the seventeenth century the style of plays popular in the late 1580s and 1590s had come to seem unnatural or old-fashioned to the new dramatists like Jonson and

Marston; so, for instance, *The Spanish Tragedy* (Rose/Fortune, 1587) is mocked or parodied in several plays, such as Marston's *Antonio and Mellida* (Paul's, 1599), and Ben Jonson imagines a foolish playgoer in the induction to *Cynthia's Revels* (Blackfriars, 1601) swearing 'that the old Hieronimo, as it was first acted, was the only best, and judiciously penned play of Europe' (191–2). Then again, by 1610 or so Beaumont, writing for the now well-established private theatres, could, in *The Knight of the Burning Pestle*, mock not only old plays like *The Spanish Tragedy*, and Heywood's *Four Prentices of London* (Red Bull, published 1615, but an old play then), but also contemporary works that appealed to 'citizens', like Heywood's *If You Know not Me, You Know Nobody* (Curtain/Red Bull, 1605), and *The Travels of the Three English Brothers* by John Day, William Rowley, and George Wilkins (Curtain/Red Bull, 1607). If the choicest blank verse of one decade seemed mere bombast to the next, the private theatres brought a qualitative shift because of the change in the audience's relationship to the stage, and the greater intimacy of the space. This is seen most markedly in the new comedies, written in prose rather than blank verse, set in London, and concerned with such matters as the tricking of a miserly rich uncle by a poor but witty gentleman named Witgood (Middleton, *A Trick to Catch the Old One*; Paul's /Blackfriars, 1605); or with the outwitting of another difficult uncle by Truewit (Jonson, *Epicœne*; Whitefriars, 1609). In another play in which a usurer is punished (Chapman, Jonson, and Marston, *Eastward Ho!*; Blackfriars, 1605), an amusing in-joke is the reduction of Hamlet, the public-theatre prince, to a rather different role: the cast includes 'Hamlet, a footman'.

The later theatres

The three new theatres erected for public performances between 1615 and 1642 were all small, indoor playhouses. The first, the so-called Porter's Hall (1615–16), was probably never finished, because the inhabitants of the Blackfriars area where it was located successfully petitioned to have it suppressed. Playing ceased there by 1617, but the title-pages of two plays, Nathan Field's *Amends for Ladies* (1618), and Fletcher's *The Scornful Lady* (1618), state that these were performed there.[59] The second theatre, the Cockpit in Drury Lane, or Phoenix, as it came to be known, was situated to the west of the city limits, in an increasingly affluent suburb, convenient both for Westminster and the Inns of Court. This theatre was converted from a cockpit in 1616–17; the circular building was extended into a U-shaped auditorium, with two galleries for spectators, and probably measured 55 feet

[59] Bentley, *Jacobean and Caroline Stage*, VI.85.

by 40 feet.[60] The new playhouse at once became the 'favourite resort of the gentry' after Blackfriars.[61] The third playhouse, converted from a barn, was the Salisbury Court, built in 1629–30 in the Whitefriars area, between Fleet Street and the River Thames. This also was 40 feet wide, but nothing more is known about its dimensions. However, it was sometimes referred to in plays staged there as a 'little House' (Thomas Nabbes, Epilogue to *Tottenham Court*, 1633), and it was probably smaller and less well fitted up than the Blackfriars and Phoenix. It never seems to have enjoyed the same success and prestige as the other two. A fourth new theatre of some importance was built on the site of a cockpit at court in Whitehall in 1630; the building was 58 feet square, and the design, with two galleries of seating, and a painted stage façade, retained many features common to other playhouses. This theatre, however, planned by Inigo Jones for court performances, had an elaborate semi-circular stage façade with five doors in it.[62]

A new kind of private theatre thus achieved ascendancy after 1617, operated by adult companies; the Cockpit/Phoenix and Salisbury Court joined the Blackfriars, used as a winter playhouse by the King's Men since 1609, as theatres with an increasing appeal to the gentry. The early theatres were located either on Bankside, south of the Thames, or to the north and east of the city limits; the later theatres were all within the city in areas protected by the crown, or in the western and north-west suburbs, in areas of growing population and wealth. The population of London doubled between 1600 and 1650, rising from about 200,000 inhabitants to 400,000, a growth brought about by a massive influx of people from the provinces. This growth increasingly fostered a polarization of society that seems more and more marked through the reigns of James I and Charles I. Dramatists writing for the later private theatres were inclined to congratulate their audiences for their sophistication, and distance themselves from the fare provided at the arena playhouses.

For many years in an age that lacked newspapers, films, television, and all the numerous forms of commercial entertainment now available, the public playhouses of the sixteenth and seventeenth centuries were truly popular in that all ranks of society might be found there:

> For as we see at all the playhouse doors,
> When ended is the play, the dance, and song,
> A thousand townsmen, gentlemen, and whores
> Porters and serving-men together throng.
> (Sir John Davies, *Epigram* 17, 'In Cosmum', ?1593)[63]

---

[60] Foakes, *Illustrations*, pp. 64–7.
[61] Bentley, *Jacobean and Caroline Stage*, VI.47.
[62] Foakes, *Illustrations*, pp. 68–71.
[63] Gurr, *Playgoing*, pp. 65–6.

8   Drawings by Inigo Jones of about 1616, thought to be of the plan and stage
façade of the Cockpit or Phoenix Theatre, Drury Lane: (a) the plan

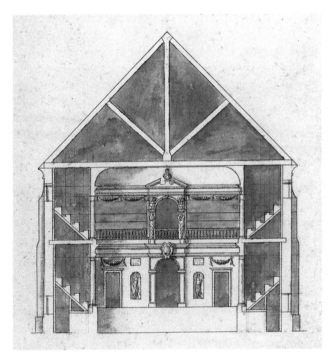

8(b) Stage façade of the Cockpit or Phoenix Theatre

Going to the theatre, moreover, did not demand literacy in an age when most of the population was illiterate. In later years there developed what became a well-established pecking order, as far as theatres were concerned, in the minds of those who wrote for and attended the private playhouses, especially the Blackfriars and Phoenix. Writers were ready to sneer at the competition of the Red Bull, and Thomas Carew, writing prefatory verses for Davenant's *The Just Italian* in 1630, was not alone in his contempt for

> that adulterate stage, where not a tongue
> Of th'untuned kennel, can a line repeat
> Of serious sense,

or in his praise of the 'natural, unstrained action' offered by 'the true brood of actors' at Blackfriars.[64] But if it was easy to take a lofty attitude towards the Red Bull or the Fortune, with their jigs, target-fights, clowning, and the 'shag-hair'd devils' (in the ever-popular *Doctor Faustus*) that ran 'roaring over the stage with squibs in their mouths, while drummers make thunder in the

[64] *Ibid.*, p. 237.

tiring-house, and the twelve-penny hirelings make artificial lightning in their heavens' (John Melton, *Astrologaster*, 1620, p. 31), this sensationalism of staging was paralleled by a new fashion on the private stages: for their refinement and sophistication included a taste for a sensationalism of content in plays that deal with sexual perversity or deviance, and toy with rape, incest, and adultery, like Beaumont and Fletcher's *A King and No King* (King's Men, Blackfriars, 1611), or Ford's *'Tis Pity She's a Whore* (Phoenix, 1632).

The professional companies had guarded their repertories, since it was customary for the company to buy a play outright from the author(s), and it was in the interest of each company not to allow too many of those which remained in the repertory to come into print. However, the private theatres sought to create a kind of collusion with their audience, as the increasing use of inductions, prologues, and epilogues suggests. During the reign of Charles 'a flourishing literary world was gradually being established'[65] around the leading private playhouses. Many plays were copied and circulated in manuscript, and many more were published within a year or two of first performance, often with prologues, epilogues, and commendatory verses, all creating a link between the play and its audience. It would appear that audiences at the private theatres were now in the main literate, and plays were being written to be read, not just performed. It may well be true that 'Plays by Brome, Shirley and Davenant offered the audience images of themselves in parks, squares, taverns and gaming houses, supplying standards against which forms and codes of behaviour could be established, scrutinized and adjusted'.[66] The decor and design of the private theatres also reflected a change in taste; for while the early large playhouses were round or square, and were related to bear-baiting rings and innyards, the later private playhouses were small and rectangular, and incorporated ideas borrowed from Renaissance Italian architectural treatises, like those of Andrea Palladio and Sebastiano Serlio, studied by Inigo Jones, who designed the Cockpit/Phoenix in 1616–17. The stage façade of this playhouse had an elegant elevation in the manner of Palladio, with a round-arched central opening, flanked by two square-headed niches with sculpted figures in them, and two square-headed doors surmounted by ornamental scrolls (see pp. 34–5). The railed gallery above also had a central, pedimented arch, opening into a space apparently reserved for actors or musicians, since seating continued through the galleries on either side.[67]

---

[65] Butler, *Theatre and Crisis*, p. 105.
[66] *Ibid.*, pp. 110–11.
[67] Foakes, *Illustrations*, p. 66.

The later theatres also had low rails around the outside of the stage; these are first mentioned in 1604.

It would be wrong to conclude from this account of the later private theatres that there was a clear-cut distinction between the audiences and the repertories at the indoor playhouses and those at the public theatres. Not only did the King's Men continue to play at the Blackfriars and the Globe, but there was considerable interchange of repertory between the Cockpit and the Red Bull. At the private theatres gentlemen and gentlewomen paid their shilling to sit in the pit, but the audience included 'the faeces or grounds of your people, that sit in the oblique caves and wedges of your house, your sinful sixpenny mechanics' (Ben Jonson, Induction to *The Magnetic Lady*; Blackfriars, 1632). There is evidence of gentry attending the Globe, while on one notable occasion, Count Gondomar, the Spanish ambassador, visited the rebuilt Fortune in 1621, and gave a feast for the players there. Although the King's Men had the lion's share of court performances, most of the other companies were also invited to play there from time to time. At the same time, the northern theatres, the Red Bull and Fortune, catered primarily to audiences who preferred old-fashioned kinds of drama, and the Red Bull especially offered a repertory largely drawn from the popular tradition of chivalry, romance, farce, history, and fantasy.[68]

The 'Praeludium' to Thomas Goffe's *The Careless Shepherdess* (Salisbury Court, 1638) consists of a debate between 'Spark', an Inns of Court man; 'Spruce', a courtier; 'Thrift', a citizen; and 'Landlord', a country gentleman. For Spark and Spruce, the 'Prerogative of the wits in Town' is to 'censure Poetry' according to the 'Laws of Comedy and Tragedy' (sig. B2r–B2v); but Landlord wants to see again the Fool in *The Changeling* (1622), an old play he once saw at this playhouse, while Thrift decides to recover the shilling he has paid:

> I'll go to the Bull, or Fortune, and there see
> A Play for two pence, with a Jig to boot.   (sig. B4v)

Thrift's remark implies that the other theatres had abandoned the practice, continued at the Red Bull and Fortune, of following the performance of a play with an afterpiece in the form of a jig, or brief farcical entertainment with songs or dances (but see below, pp. 45–6). To Spark and Spruce, both Thrift and Landlord appear fools; Spark dismisses them:

> 'Tis hard to tell which is the verier fool,
> The Country Gentleman, or Citizen:
> Your judgments are ridiculous and vain

---

[68] Butler, *Theatre and Crisis*, pp. 181–3.

As your Forefathers, whose dull intellect
Did nothing understand but fools and fighting.   (sig. B3r)

At the same time a different kind of drama was being played at the Phoenix and Salisbury Court, where 'the more popular end of the fashionable spectrum participated in the Elizabethan tradition too'.[69] In these theatres old patriotic plays on the reigns of Henry VIII or Queen Elizabeth were revived, and new political comedies were presented, most notably those of Richard Brome, perhaps the most important dramatist of the period. All these plays reflected growing dissatisfaction with the rule of Charles I, and show that audiences for them were interested in a 'drama that was sceptical, critical and levelling'.[70] It is arguable that much of the most significant drama of the period was being staged at these theatres, and it will not do to take the snobbish sentiments of a Spark or Spruce too literally.

Others who paid their shilling at the private theatres in the 1630s also looked for plays to please gentlewomen, plays that could be judged as 'matter for serious discussion'.[71] This was especially true of the Blackfriars playhouse, which drew on the talents of new dramatists like Sir William Davenant, whose links were with a court circle patronized by Queen Henrietta Maria; she attended special privately arranged performances at Blackfriars on at least three occasions between 1634 and 1638. Although old plays were revived by the King's Men, amongst them Chapman's *Bussy D'Ambois* (1607), Webster's *The Duchess of Malfi* (1613), and *Sir John Oldcastle*, a play written for the Admiral's Men in 1599 by Michael Drayton and others, the main repertory consisted of the plays of Shakespeare, Beaumont and Fletcher, and Ben Jonson, together with new work by Davenant, Massinger, Shirley, and others. The patrons who paid to sit in the pit no doubt were like these new dramatists in priding themselves on their wit and disdaining the 'Good easy judging souls' who used to 'expect a jig, or target fight' (Davenant, Prologue to *The Unfortunate Lovers*, printed 1643).

The new drama of the Blackfriars during the Caroline period shows a conscious rejection of the highly charged and often highly metaphorical dramatic verse exemplified in Marlowe's 'mighty line', in the energy of the old history plays, or in the fierce compression of plays like *The Revenger's Tragedy* (1607), in favour of a verse so limpid and quiet that it seems a much more naturalistic vehicle for the conversation of educated characters who are no longer quite different from the audience in being distanced by romance or history, made heroic, or heroically corrupt, and being further differentiated

[69] *Ibid.*, pp. 183–4.
[70] *Ibid.*, p. 185.
[71] Gurr, *Playgoing*, p. 179.

by a stylized speech in strongly marked verse; but rather speak a language much closer to that of the better patrons who prized ease and wit. The preference of the Blackfriars audience for sophistication and wit rather than vigorous action and clowning may mean that the old plays that survived in the repertories of the private theatres were adapted to some extent to a new style of playing. Certainly the Red Bull was noted for its noisy and vulgar audience,[72] and for plays full of fights and bombast, at a time when the private playhouses were accelerating a shift towards refinement, and appealing to more consciously critical audiences, including the 'noble Gentlewomen' who sat as 'high Commissioners of wit' (Shirley, Prologue to *The Coronation*; Phoenix, 1635).

Players and playing

In 1583, the Queen's Secretary, Sir Francis Walsingham, directed the Master of the Revels, Edmond Tylney, to select players from the dozen or more companies then operating mainly in the provinces: Edmond Howes, in his continuation of John Stow's *Annals* (1615), recorded what happened:[73]

Comedians and stage-players of former times were very poor and ignorant in respect of these of this time: but being now grown very skillful and exquisite actors for all matters, they were entertained into the service of divers great lords: out of which companies there were twelve of the best chosen, and, at the request of Sir Francis Walsingham, they were sworn the queen's servants and were allowed wages and liveries as grooms of the chamber: and until the year 1583, the queen had no players.

Howes went on to note that there were two 'rare men' among the actors, Robert Wilson and Richard Tarlton, both noted for their 'extemporal wit'. The establishment of this company under royal protection in London marked the beginning of a new and enhanced social stature for leading actors. It is an exaggeration to claim, as Gurr does, that Tarlton, 'the wonder of his time' as Howes called him, 'became the chief emblem of the emerging national consciousness at the end of the sixteenth century',[74] but he certainly acquired a legendary reputation by the time of his death in 1588. He was loved for his clowning, his impromptu songs and rhymes, and his repartee, though the collection of *Tarlton's Jests* published after his death (the earliest edition is of 1611) merely uses his name to sell what is largely a gathering of old chestnuts. He was equally popular at court and in the provinces, where he could make an audience laugh simply by sticking his head out 'The Tire-

---

[72] Bentley, *Jacobean and Caroline Stage*, VI.238–47.
[73] Chambers, *Elizabethan Stage*, II.104–5.
[74] Gurr, *Playgoing*, p. 121.

9   John Scottowe, drawing of the actor Richard Tarlton (?1588); see p. 39

house door and Tapistry between' (Henry Peacham, *Thalia's Banquet*, 1620, Epigram 94). Less is known about Robert Wilson, but, like Tarlton, he became conspicuous as an actor in the 1570s, and ended his career with the Queen's Men.

Tylney picked out twelve men to form the Queen's company, and perhaps already a norm was established of twelve sharers in the company: ten or twelve seems to have remained the usual number.[75] The sharers in the early companies were the principal players, and their shares constituted their investment in their joint stock of playing apparel, properties, and playbooks. The companies did not own theatre buildings, but normally made an arrangement with the owner of a theatre to perform there in return for a

75
   Bentley, *Profession of Player*, p. 42.

proportion of the takings, half the money collected in the galleries at their daily performances.[76] Before the erection of the first custom-built theatres in London in 1576, the companies had been used to a peripatetic life, and indeed, the Queen's Men spent much of their time in the 1580s on the road, visiting Norwich, Bristol, Leicester, Cambridge, Bath, Dover, and other towns.[77] The companies had no habit at this time of settling in one place and investing in a theatre building.

Even when the first professional theatres were established in London, life for most of the companies could at any moment become precarious. They might be forced to seek another theatre if relations with the current owner became strained. Other circumstances beyond their control might force a company to regroup, break up, move to the provinces, or go abroad to travel in northern Europe, where English players were in demand. After the death of Tarlton, the Queen's Men seem to have lost ground to the competition from the Lord Admiral's and Lord Strange's Men, who between 1588 and 1594 were using the Theatre and the Rose, and who had a new star actor in Edward Alleyn. The Queen's Men did not survive the great plague of 1593 as a London company; after they 'broke and went into the country to play'[78] in May 1593, they never returned as a group to the metropolis. The plague was a special hazard, since its recurrence was unpredictable and playing was automatically suspended when the deaths per week rose above a certain number (variable in the reign of Elizabeth, but fixed at thirty in the reign of James). A company would then seek to maintain an income by touring in the provinces, though this might not work out; so Henslowe, writing to Alleyn, then on tour, from London in September 1593, reported that Lord Pembroke's Men had returned to London because they could not make enough to cover their costs, and were forced to pawn their wardrobe.[79] A major outbreak of plague, such as occurred in 1593, 1603, 1610, 1625, 1630, and 1636–7, could cause the theatres to be closed for months on end – thirteen in 1603–4, eight in 1625, seven months in 1630, and well over a year between May 1636 and October 1637. The effect on a company could be shattering, as in the case of Pembroke's Men, who, like the Queen's Men, disappear after 1593.[80]

A third factor that could interrupt the activities of a company was a restraint on playing brought about by a play that for some reason gave

[76] Foakes and Rickert, *Henslowe's Diary*, p. xxviii; Bentley, *Jacobean and Caroline Stage*, I.44.
[77] Chambers, *Elizabethan Stage*, II.105–7.
[78] Foakes and Rickert, *Henslowe's Diary*, p. 7.
[79] *Ibid.*, p. 280.
[80] Chambers, *Elizabethan Stage*, II.130–1.

offence, such as occurred with the production of Nashe's lost play *The Isle of Dogs* at the Swan Theatre in 1597 (see above, p. 7); the company concerned, a newly formed Pembroke's Men, left the Swan and regrouped with the Admiral's Men at the Rose when the owner's licence to stage plays at the Swan was revoked. Yet another hazard that could affect the fortunes of a company was fire. The Globe burned down in 1613, when the discharge of guns during a production of *Henry VIII* set fire to the thatched roof. It seems that on this occasion the players were able to save their playbooks and other belongings. The fire at the Fortune in 1621 was more disastrous for the Palsgrave's Men, who lost all their apparel and playbooks.[81] The company never fully recovered, and was ruined when plague halted playing for months in 1625.

The death of a leading actor like Richard Tarlton, or departure of a celebrity like Edward Alleyn, who retired from playing in 1597, could also be a major blow to a company. But if the record of most of the companies is one of instability, playing was also both glamorous and profitable, and puritan and other critics of the stage never ceased to complain that the theatres were crowded while the churches remained empty. During the later years of Queen Elizabeth's reign the companies relied on aristocratic patronage for support, and it was a considerable enhancement of their status when James I took the leading groups under royal patronage after 1603. Two companies, the Lord Admiral's and the Lord Chamberlain's Men, were exceptional in enjoying relative stability and success over a long period. The Admiral's Men became Prince Henry's Men on the accession of James I, and the Palsgrave's or King of Bohemia's company on the death of Prince Henry in 1612. The leading actor of the Admiral's Men, Edward Alleyn, married the stepdaughter of the owner of the Rose, Philip Henslowe; Alleyn himself owned the Fortune,[82] and after he retired from playing (he returned to the stage in 1600, it is said at the request of the Queen), he retained an interest in the company of his friends and former colleagues almost until his death in 1626. It took the burning of their theatre, the loss of their stock, and a bad plague year to cause the company eventually to fail in 1625.

The ties of family and friendship between theatre owner and company were also vitally important in the even longer and more successful career of the Chamberlain's Men, who became the King's Men under James I. James Burbage, who built the Theatre, was the father of Richard, the leading actor of the company. James probably overreached himself financially in 1596, when he bought part of the Blackfriars complex of buildings intending to

---

[81] Bentley, *Jacobean and Caroline Stage*, I.141.
[82] Foakes and Rickert, *Henslowe's Diary*, p. 302.

convert rooms there to a theatre, only to have the Privy Council prevent him from doing so on the petition of local inhabitants (see above, p. 7). James died in 1597, and his two sons, Cuthbert, who took over as administrator, and Richard, did not have the capital to build the Globe in 1599. They therefore set up a unique arrangement, by which they held one half of the property, with five senior actors in the company each holding an equal share in the other half. In this way sharers in the company became also sharers in the theatre they used. As years passed the personnel of the company changed; Richard Burbage died in 1619, and shares changed hands, but the effect was to consolidate the ownership of the Globe and Blackfriars among the sharers of the King's Men, who controlled the leading company, and the principal public and private theatres, through the later years of James I and the reign of Charles I.

The most famous Elizabethan actors were of two kinds. One kind were clowns, like Tarlton, Wilson, and Will Kemp. Tarlton and Wilson were noted for their ability to improvise; and Tarlton and Kemp were expert at jigs, the farcical afterpieces with songs and dances popular in the public theatres. A drawing of Tarlton shows him playing on a tabor and pipe (see p. 40), and Kemp is represented dancing on the title-page of *Kemp's Nine Days Wonder* (1600), celebrating the occasion when he danced from London to Norwich.[83] The other kind were heroic actors like Alleyn, famous for creating majestic leading roles, among them the original Tamburlaine, Barabas, and Faustus; and Richard Burbage, who made his reputation in roles like Richard III. Alleyn had ceased to act by 1604 or 1605, but Burbage went on to develop a wide range of roles, including, for instance, Hamlet, Malevole in Marston's *Malcontent*, Othello, and Ferdinand in Webster's *The Duchess of Malfi*. After small indoor playhouses became established with the revival of the children's theatres about 1600, some boy actors began to achieve fame with a different range of characterizations, reflecting changing taste and increasing sophistication.

Their rise to fame is significant because virtually nothing is known of the boys who played all the female roles in plays before 1600. In 1561 Queen Elizabeth had given the Master of the Children of the Chapel Royal power to 'take' children from anywhere in the realm in order to maintain the choir,[84] and the Master in 1600, Nathaniel Giles, abused his prerogative by impressing boys from various grammar schools in London to play in his company as actors. One boy, impressed from St Paul's Grammar School at about the age of thirteen was Nathan Field, whose education was continued under Ben

---

[83] Foakes, *Illustrations*, pp. 44–5, 150.
[84] Chambers, *Elizabethan Stage*, II.33.

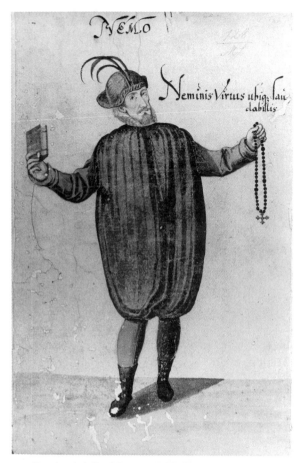

10   Drawing (1608) of the actor John Green as Nobody in the
play *Nobody and Somebody*

Jonson, and who became a playwright and an actor of distinction. Alleyn and
Burbage probably picked up an education, so far as they had one, on the stage,
but Field had been trained in the classics, and was highly literate; he was a
leading actor with the Children of the Chapel, which became the Queen's
Revels company, and then joined the Lady Elizabeth's Men in 1613, finally
becoming a sharer in the King's Men about 1616. By this time he was as
famous as Burbage, and a collaborator in playwriting with Fletcher, in whose
plays he was a noted performer.[85] The evidence suggests he practised a more
refined acting style appropriate to the indoor theatres; so in commendatory
verses, Field praised Fletcher's *The Faithful Shepherdess* (?1608) as possessing

[85] Bentley, *Jacobean and Caroline Stage*, III.301.

Such art, it should me better satisfy,
Than if the monster clapped his thousand hands
And drowned the scene with his confused cry.

The two plays Field wrote on his own, *A Woman is a Weathercock* (Queen's Revels, 1609; printed 1612) and *Amends for Ladies* (1611; printed 1618), are comedies the titles of which emphasize the new importance given to women in Jacobean and Caroline drama; the later play turns on the question of which is the best condition for a woman – to be a maid, a wife, or a widow. Other actors who began as boys playing female roles matured into adult players, like Richard Sharpe, who was the first to play the Duchess of Malfi (1613), or Stephen Hammerton, who 'was at first a most noted and beautiful Woman Actor, but afterwards he acted with equal Grace and Applause, a Young Lover's Part', according to James Wright in *Historia Histrionica*, 1699.[86] He created the part of Oriana in the 1632 revival of Fletcher's *The Wild Goose Chase* (1621). Other distinguished adult actors were noted not for a particular strength so much as for ability to play a variety of roles; an example is Richard Perkins (Queen Henrietta's Men), whose name appears on a number of cast lists, and who was praised by Webster in a note appended to *The White Devil* (1612) as an actor whose 'action did crown both the beginning and the end' – here probably in the part of Flamineo.

This same company at the Cockpit/Phoenix had a noted comic actor in William Robbins, who played the changeling, Antonio, in Middleton and Rowley's play of this name (1622). His playing of this role, and that of 'Rawbone, a thin citizen' in Shirley's *The Wedding* (1626), suggests that he was a very different kind of actor from Tarlton or Kemp, a comedian rather than a clown, one whose talents did not lie in singing, dancing, or improvisation, that is, in fooling about and being himself, so much as in performing a variety of character parts. There may be an analogy here with Robert Armin, the leading comedian of the Chamberlain's/King's Men between the departure of Kemp in 1600 and 1610 or so. However, Armin seems to have been skilled as a clown in Tarlton's vein as well as being a comic character actor, and he was succeeded by John Shank, who was more of a clown in the old style. Perhaps the taste for revivals of old plays, and also of new ones on Elizabethan themes in the 1620s and 1630s,[87] was accompanied by a revival of enthusiasm for clowning and jigs. After a complaint about disturbances at the Fortune, an order was issued for suppressing jigs in 1612,[88] but, like so

[86] *Ibid.*, II.693.
[87] Butler, *Theatre and Crisis*, pp. 185, 198–203.
[88] Bentley, *Jacobean and Caroline Stage*, VI.146.

many other orders, it was probably not enforced for long. The fame of Shank, 'John Shank for a jig', was marked in 1632 in William Heminges's *Elegy on Randolph's Finger*, line 106,[89] a mock elegy on the loss of his little finger in a fight by the dramatist Thomas Randolph; and since the author was the son of John Heminges of the King's Men, and sold his share in the company to Shank, he knew what he was saying. Other notable comedians of this period were Andrew Cane of Prince Charles's Men, and Timothy Read of the King's Revels and Queen Henrietta's Men, who was gifted as a dancer.[90] It is of some interest that the citizen Thrift in the Praeludium to Goffe's *The Careless Shepherdess* (see above, p. 37), remarks

> I never saw Read peeping through the curtain
> But ravishing joy enter'd into my heart.

It seems that Read was still working a trick for which Tarlton had been noted, not only by Henry Peacham (see above, pp. 39–40), but by Thomas Nashe, who recorded in *Piers Penniless* in 1592 how 'the people began exceedingly to laugh, when Tarlton first peeped out his head'.[91]

The business affairs of a company were complex. At first the Admiral's Men relied on Henslowe for help, and the Chamberlain's Men had James Burbage, and after him Cuthbert, to manage matters for them. Later on, actors began to take on administrative roles, as Edward Alleyn did for the Admiral's/Prince Henry's Men at the Fortune, while John Heminges, an actor until 1611 or so, and leading sharer, became full-time manager for the King's Men until his death in 1630. He negotiated performances at court, and dealt with the Master of the Revels in the matter of licensing plays for the stage. Thomas Greene (died 1612) was succeeded as manager of Queen Anne's company at the Red Bull by Christopher Beeston, actor turned manager and entrepreneur; Beeston built the Cockpit in 1616–17, and had a long career successfully manipulating companies to his own advantage at the two theatres in which he had an interest. Another important managerial figure was Richard Gunnell, an actor with Prince Henry's Men, who became a sharer in the new Fortune in 1621, and later at the Salisbury Court theatre, of which he was part-owner.

Little is known about the day-to-day affairs of the companies, but someone had to authorize and organize

the purchase of new costumes and costume materials; paying for new plays by freelance dramatists; getting scripts approved by the Master of the Revels, paying

[89] *Ibid.*, II.563.
[90] Foakes, *Illustrations*, p. 158.
[91] Chambers, *Elizabethan Stage*, II.344.

him for licenses for the theater and for occasional privileges, like playing during parts of Lent; paying the company's regular contributions to the poor of the parish, assessing fines against sharers or hired men for infringement of company regulations; calling rehearsals; collecting fees for court and private performances; supervising the preparation and distribution of playbills; and perhaps for paying the hired men.[92]

It seems to have been customary for sharers to gather to hear a new play read, and decide perhaps on casting; Henslowe laid out 5s. 'for good cheer' at the Sun Inn in New Fish Street when the company met to listen to a new script in 1598.[93] Boy actors were recruited by being apprenticed to sharers, and some, perhaps many, of these boys stayed on after their voices broke to become adult actors or hired men, and were paid a weekly wage to work for a company. The size of the companies has been much debated. Very few cast lists remain, about fifteen printed in the hundreds of published plays, and four in manuscript plays, all dating from 1619 or later;[94] most of these are incomplete. In addition, it is possible to work out much of the casting from the seven surviving dramatic 'plots', or scene-by-scene outlines listing entrances, properties, etc., made for use by the stagekeeper and actors, and presumably posted in the tiring-house during a performance (see p. 48). These outlines date from between 1590 and 1602, and are among the Henslowe–Alleyn documents relating mainly to the Admiral's Men and the Rose theatre.

The matter of the size of the companies has been confused by two considerations. One is the indication, on the title-pages of a number of early play texts printed between 1559 and 1585, of the minimum number of actors necessary to perform the play, usually between four and six.[95] Two later printed plays also have casting indications. The anonymous, and probably old, play *Mucedorus*, first printed 1598, shows how thirteen parts may be played by eight actors (in an enlarged version of 1610 the parts are arranged for ten actors). *The Fair Maid of the Exchange* (printed 1602) shows how 'Eleven may easily act this comedy', which has twenty parts in all. The casting directions in early printed plays probably relate to performances by small touring companies. After the professional London theatres became established, the main London companies toured the provinces in times of plague, and although the number in a travelling company is rarely specified in contemporary documents, there could be as many as twenty, as at Plymouth in 1618–19 and at Norwich in 1634, or as few as fourteen.[96]

[92] Bentley, *Profession of Player*, pp. 147–8.
[93] Foakes and Rickert, *Henslowe's Diary*, p. 88. Another play was read at an unnamed tavern in May 1602; see p. 201.
[94] Bentley, *Profession of Player*, pp. 218–19.
[95] Chambers, *Elizabethan Stage*, III.179.
[96] Bentley, *Profession of Player*, pp. 184–6.

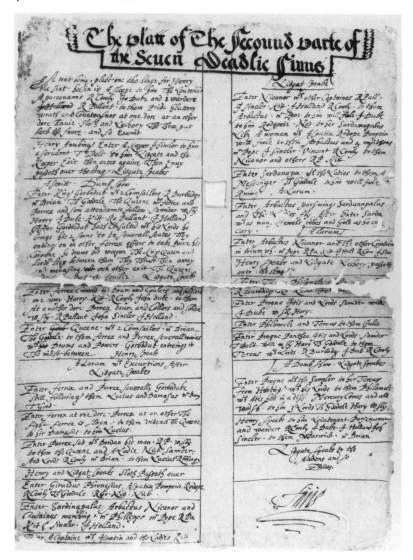

11   The 'plot' of Part 2 of *The Seven Deadly Sins* by Richard Tarlton, as played probably by Lord Strange's Men about 1590; see p. 47

These figures presumably included hired men and boys. A second consideration is the question of the doubling of parts. It is evident from early printed texts that plays were constructed with the doubling of parts in mind. As a consequence, there has been a good deal of speculation about doubling, in plays by Shakespeare especially, and much ingenuity has been exercised in determining how few actors were absolutely necessary to play a large-cast work like *King Lear*. It has usually been argued that Shakespeare wrote for between thirteen and sixteen actors throughout his career.

The fact is that there is no necessary connection between the practice of doubling, or the minimum number of actors necessary, and the size of the company. The professional companies after 1576 staged a number of plays with up to fifty speaking parts. For some of these, the company may have had to rope in everyone available. The 'plot' of *The Battle of Alcazar* (?1597) names twenty-four actors, and that of *Tamar Cham, Part 1* (1602) names twenty-nine, while Peele's *Edward I* (1591; in production at the Rose 1595–6) has one scene requiring twenty-three players to be on stage. A manuscript play, *The Two Noble Ladies* (Red Bull, 1622), has prompt notes calling for a stagekeeper to come on in non-speaking roles as a guard and a soldier. I suspect it was not often necessary to resort to such expedients, for most of the extant repertory of plays in the period have casts normally of around twelve to fifteen speaking roles, with a few other walk-on parts. In the cast lists in plays published in the 1620s, the King's Men seem to have used between six and eight sharers, about four hired men, and four boys.[97] In playing a daily repertory, the companies needed to protect their leading actors, and the extant cast lists suggest that in the 1620s only half to two-thirds of the sharers, and by no means all the hired men, would perform in any one play. The company at this time was quite large: in 1624, the Master of the Revels listed twenty-one names of hired men, 'musicians and other necessary attendants', as attached to the King's Men, in addition to the eleven principal actors or sharers.[98] The companies had to maintain musicians, keepers of the wardrobe (two were employed at Salisbury Court in 1634), stagekeepers, prompters, and gatherers to collect money at the doors. It is not known whether Herbert's list included all of these, or any of the boys, but if we set the thirty-three names he gives against the twenty-nine actors recorded for the Admiral's Men in *Tamar Cham, Part 1* twenty years earlier, it looks as though the major London companies each had more than thirty people on the payroll.

The only late cast list for a play with a huge number of parts, at least forty-

---

[97] *Ibid.*, p. 251.
[98] Bentley, *Profession of Player*, pp. 65–6.

four, is that in the manuscript of Massinger's *Believe as You List* (1631), in which seventeen members (seven sharers, ten hired men) of the King's Men are named to assigned roles, but a number of roles, including all female parts, have no names attached to them. The doubling for this play was very intricate, and divided some small roles, as well as two sizable speaking parts, between two, or in one case, that of the character Demetrius, three actors. Such doubling shows little regard for individuality in all but the main roles in plays of this kind. However, this was an exception, and it would have been practicable for a company of about thirty to thirty-five comfortably to maintain a repertory consisting of plays with, as a norm, eight to twelve significant speaking parts. Even so, an actor's life must have been hectic, especially in the 1590s, when the Admiral's and Chamberlain's Men were competing in bringing out a stream of new plays. For instance, in April 1597 the Admiral's Men, playing on twenty-five days out of thirty, performed thirteen different plays; three were new, and two of them were played several times, but five plays were each staged only once.[99] We have no records of the daily repertories later in the period to show whether the custom of presenting a different play almost every day persisted.

There was a temporary explosion in the number of playhouses after 1600, when the children's theatres began to vie with the public stages, and one visitor to London in 1611 said that seven were playing daily.[100] By 1617 the number of companies working regularly stabilized at four (Globe/Blackfriars, Cockpit/Phoenix, Fortune, Red Bull), and the Salisbury Court was added in 1629 to make five. In these later years the companies still competed for the services of the better playwrights, but also used an accumulated repertory of old plays which had stood the test of time, and suited their particular audience. An actor's life may therefore have been less strenuous than in the 1590s. For all their sweat, there was, of course, plenty of glamour and excitement, and we can catch a glimpse of this in Middleton and Dekker's *The Roaring Girl*, played at the Fortune about 1610: in a speech that, as so often in plays of this period, has a double application, Sir Alexander, showing his own mansion to other characters, in fact describes the theatre as if he were playing to a full house:

> Nay, when you look into my galleries,
> How bravely they are trimmed up, you all shall swear
> You're highly pleased to see what's set down there:
> Stories of men and women, mixed together,
> Fair ones with foul, like sunshine in wet weather –

[99] Foakes and Rickert, *Henslowe's Diary*, pp. 57–8.
[100] Chambers, *Elizabethan Stage*, II.369.

Within one square a thousand heads are laid
So close that all of heads the room seems made;
As many faces there, filled with blithe looks
Show like the promising titles of new books
Writ merrily, the readers being their own eyes,
Which seem to move and to give plaudities;
And here and there, whilst with obsequious ears
Thronged heaps do listen, a cut-purse thrusts and leers
With hawk's eyes for his prey – I need not show him:
By a hanging villainous look yourselves may know him,
The face is drawn so rarely. Then, sir, below,
The very floor, as 'twere, waves to and fro,
And, like a floating island, seems to move
Upon a sea bound in with shores above. (1.2.14–32)

Bibliography

THE THEATRES

For an immense range of information, E. K. Chambers, *The Elizabethan Stage*, 4 vols. (1923) is still indispensable, as is G. E. Bentley, *The Jacobean and Caroline Stage*, 7 vols. (1941–68). These need to be supplemented by Glynne Wickham, *Early English Stages*, Vol. II, Parts 1 and 2 (1963, 1972), and by G. E. Bentley, *The Profession of Player in Shakespeare's Time, 1590–1642* (1984). Andrew Gurr's *The Shakespearean Stage, 1574–1642* (2nd edn, 1980) provides a good general account; for the sixteenth-century stage, Robert Weimann's *Shakespeare and the Popular Tradition in the Theatre* (1978) and Michael Hattaway's *Elizabethan Popular Theatre* (1982) are helpful, and the later private playhouses and companies are surveyed in Keith Sturgess's *Jacobean Private Theatre* (1987). More specialized studies include the essays by Alexander Leggatt on companies and actors, and by Richard Hosley on the playhouses, in *The Revels History of Drama in English, Vol. III 1576–1613* (1975); the essay by G. E. Bentley on 'The theatres and the actors' in *The Revels History of Drama in English, Vol. IV 1613–60* (1981) is also relevant. The most important studies of individual theatres include G. F. Reynolds, *The Staging of Elizabethan Plays at the Red Bull Theater 1605–1625* (1940); John Orrell, *The Quest for Shakespeare's Globe* (1983) and *The Theatres of Inigo Jones and John Webb* (1985); Herbert Berry's two books, on *The First Public Playhouse: The Theatre in Shoreditch, 1576–1598* (1979) and *The Boar's Head Playhouse* (1986), as well as his essay 'The stage and boxes at Blackfriars', *SP* 63 (1966; this essay is reprinted in his book *Shakespeare's Playhouses*, 1987); William Ingram, *A London Life in the Brazen Age Francis Langley 1548–1602* (1978), on the Swan; *Documents of the Rose Playhouse*, ed. Carol Chillington Rutter (1984); and Janet Loengard's discovery of information concerning the Red Lion, 'An Elizabethan lawsuit: John Brayne, his carpenter, and the building of the Red Lion theatre', *SQ* 34 (1983), 298–310. There is useful information in Irwin Smith's *Shakespeare's Globe Playhouse* (1956) and *Shakespeare's Blackfriars Playhouse* (1964), but his drawings and reconstructions are misleading. *Shakespeare's Second Globe* (1973) by C. Walter Hodges deserves attention. E. L. Rhodes's study of *Henslowe's Rose* (1976) is not very reliable. An important general study is John Orrell's *The Human Stage. English Theatre*

Design, 1567–1640 (1988), which examines the theatres in the light of Renaissance architectural theories. The significance of the documents relating to the Red Lion is explored by Herbert Berry in 'The first public playhouses, especially the Red Lion', *SQ* 40 (1989), 134–48. John Orrell and Andrew Gurr have provided the fullest report yet on the remains of the Rose theatre in 'What the Rose can tell us', *Antiquity* 63 (1989), 421–9.

PLAYING AND PLAYGOING

The central documents providing evidence about the working of the Rose and Fortune theatres are gathered in *Henslowe's Diary*, ed. R. A. Foakes and R. T. Rickert (1961), and in W. W. Greg, *Dramatic Documents from the Elizabethan Playhouses*, 2 vols. (1931), which includes facsimiles of the extant dramatic 'plots'. The best discussion of Henslowe as a theatre manager is Bernard Beckerman's essay 'Philip Henslowe' in *The Theatrical Manager in England and America*, ed. Joseph W. Donohue, Jr (1971). There are specialized studies of *The Children of Paul's* by Reavley Gair (1982), and *Children of the Revels* by Michael Shapiro (1977). Contemporary representations of stages and actors are gathered in R. A. Foakes, *Illustrations of the English Stage 1580–1642* (1985). On acting and staging, Bernard Beckerman's *Shakespeare at the Globe 1599–1609* (1962) is full of good sense. Bertram Joseph's claim that acting was formal and stylized in his *Elizabethan Acting* (1951, revised 1964) was countered by Marvin Rosenberg in 'Elizabethan actors: men or marionettes?', *PMLA* (1954). The use of make-up is discussed by Annette Drew-Bear, 'Face-painting in Renaissance tragedy', *RenD* n.s. 12 (1981), 71–93. Ann Jennalie Cook's image of *The Privileged Playgoers of Shakespeare's London 1576–1642* (1981) has been convincingly qualified by Martin Butler in his important *Theatre and Crisis 1632–1642* (1984), and by Andrew Gurr in *Playgoing in Shakespeare's London* (1987). Doubling of parts is discussed by David Bevington in *From 'Mankind' to Marlowe* (1962), and in an influential article by W. A. Ringler Jr, 'The number of actors in Shakespeare's early plays', in G. E. Bentley, ed., *The Seventeenth-Century Stage* (1968); the most recent follow-up is by Richard Fotheringham in 'The doubling of parts on the Jacobean stage', *Theatre Research International* 10 (1985), 18–32. Valuable specialist studies are Dieter Mehl's *The Elizabethan Dumb Show* (1965), C. R. Baskervill's *The Elizabethan Jig and Related Song Drama* (1929), and M. C. Linthicum's *Costume in the Drama of Shakespeare and his Contemporaries* (1936, reissued 1963).

TEXTS

Quotations from plays are cited either from the editions listed in the 'Note on dates, references, and quotations' or from original printings except for the following: Thomas Middleton and Thomas Dekker, *The Roaring Girl*, ed. Paul A. Mulholland (The Revels Plays, 1987); *The Revenger's Tragedy*, ed. R. A. Foakes (The Revels Plays, 1966); *A Warning for Fair Women*, ed. Charles Dale Curran (The Hague, 1975); John Marston, *What You Will*, *The Plays of John Marston*, ed. H. Harvey Wood, 3 vols. (Edinburgh, 1934); John Marston, *Antonio and Mellida* and *Antonio's Revenge*, *The Selected Plays of John Marston*, ed. MacDonald P. Jackson and Michael Neill (Cambridge, 1986); Thomas Heywood, *The Four Prentices of London*, *Dramatic Works*, 6 vols. (1874). In all quotations spellings have been modernized.

2   The arts of the dramatist

Music and poetry were first approv'd
By common sense; and that which pleased most
Held most allowed pass; no, rules of art
Were shaped to pleasure, not pleasure to your rules.

(John Marston, *What You Will*, Induction)

THEATRES, like universities, are among society's most conservative institutions. When they admit or achieve innovation it is often spasmodic rather than prolonged, intense rather than gradual, and the old long lingers beside the new. In the theatre, any balance struck between this *obbligato* to tradition and the *ad libitum* of change requires collaboration: audiences and playwrights and theatre managements must to some extent agree or the institution will collapse economically. When Elizabethan entrepreneurs risked the capital required to erect permanent theatres in the 1560s and 1570s and actors joined into formally organized companies, they created a staggering, and continuing, demand for new material.[1] Seeking to attract and hold an audience, dramatists and theatre companies supplied jigs, folk tales, jingoistic war-plays, courtly pastoral, and much else. Gradually, audiences and companies found one another, and in the later reign of Elizabeth I and in the reigns of her first two Stuart successors, the London theatre world stratified according to a match of styles and taste.[2] Of all the companies, only the King's Men, formerly the Lord Chamberlain's Men, the company of Shakespeare,

---

[1] By the 1590s, the repertory was very large: Philip Henslowe records that the Lord Admiral's Men performed twenty-eight times, 15 September through 15 October 1595, in eighteen different plays. Three plays were performed on three occasions each; three more, including a lost two-part play, twice each; eleven plays performed once each. See R. A. Foakes and R. T. Rickert, eds., *Henslowe's Diary* (Cambridge, 1961), pp. 31–2. For an estimate of the number of new plays produced each half-decade from 1595 to 1639, see table 10 of L. G. Salingar, Gerald Harrison and Bruce Cochrane, 'Les Comédiens et leur public en Angleterre de 1520 à 1640' in Jacquot *et al.*, comp., *Dramaturgie et société*, II.525–76.

[2] See Gurr, *Playgoing*, pp. 155–6 and 183, and above, pp. 37–9 for qualification.

John Fletcher, and Philip Massinger, offered a broadly appealing repertory that mixed innovative plays with old ones, or new ones in the old styles.

In the 1580s and 1590s, a talented but for the most part short-lived generation – the 'University Wits' (Christopher Marlowe, George Peele, Robert Greene, John Lyly, Thomas Nashe, and Thomas Lodge), Shakespeare, Thomas Kyd – supplied plays for the newly professionalized adult and semi-professional boys' companies.[3] Achieving a theatrical sophistication unprecedented in English secular drama, many of these plays had decades-long lives in repertory. To set themselves apart from and above this group, the next dramatic generation – self-consciously innovative playwrights like John Marston and Ben Jonson, for example – parody and ridicule their predecessors, scramble the audiences' expectations and violate recently agreed conventions. As Marston and Jonson did, so do the dramatists who follow them, creating the crescendo of fashions common in artistically inventive and politically volatile eras like late Elizabethan London or, more recently, Weimar Germany. Shakespeare might declare a stock figure old-fashioned – 'Pat! he comes like the catastrophe of the old comedy' (*King Lear*, 1.2.128) – and Jonson might deride Shakespeare's staging of battles 'with three rusty swords, / And help of some few foot-and-half-foot words' (*Every Man in his Humour*, Prologue, 9–10), but their views most assuredly do not mean that either the stock figure or the dramatic technique were out of favour with the, or *a*, London audience. That 'old-fashioned' dramatic strategies continued to please means there were successful, popular dramatists (Thomas Heywood, for instance, or Thomas Dekker) who did not need to adopt current fashion. A chronological account of dramaturgy, of the dramatist's arts, from the 1580s onward would therefore either falsify the story or present a chaos in which every aesthetic choice was virtually co-present with every other, even if the account avoided the trap of claiming a teleological, 'progressive' development.

My approach here assumes that in early modern English drama (and for that matter, in contemporary Continental drama) there exists a group of technical issues and solutions clustered around impersonation and the representing of action. These topics shape my argument. Some of the issues and solutions now appear quaint or puzzling, some have not changed since Aristotle.[4] Throughout, I try to remember that audiences, not rules, come

---

[3] Of this group, Greene, Kyd, Marlowe, and Peele were all dead, and only Shakespeare was active as a dramatist, by 1600; see my *George Peele*, pp. 126–8 and 131–2.

[4] See Peter Brook, *The Empty Space* (1968; New York, 1978), p. 16: 'A living theatre that thinks it can stand aloof from anything so trivial as fashion will wilt. In the theatre, every form once born is mortal; every form must be reconceived, and its new conception will bear the marks of all the influences that surround it. In this sense, the theatre is relativity. Yet a great theatre is not a fashion house; perpetual elements do recur and certain

first. Marston's remarks in *What You Will* (the epigraph above) are far less familiar than Dr Johnson's 'The drama's laws the drama's patrons give / For we that live to please, must please to live', but both writers address the same brute case, at once economic and as mysterious as our delight in mimicry. Yet the ways of pleasing may be analysed and formulated, even if they never occurred to a single playwright as a recipe nor to a single playgoer as a requirement. A principal danger of this approach is that it implies that drama is all, or only, technique – which is false. Making a play and its meanings, conscious and unconscious, aural and literary, personal and social, are communal and interdependent activities, and no discursive narrative can ever fully represent those conditions. As an apologetic substitute, I begin by attempting to undermine the dramatist's supposed priority and authority. I begin with the difficulty of specifying the dramatist's arts.

Drama and performance

Dramaturgy, which at first glance seems so much a textual phenomenon, and performance, most evanescent of experiences, are deeply allied, a transient moment arising from, perhaps preserved in, a residual code. Consider the induction to John Marston's *Antonio and Mellida* (1602). The first stage direction lists six characters who enter *with parts in their hands, having cloaks cast over their apparel*. That is, each actor carries the manuscript of his speeches and cues; their cloaks conventionally indicate travel – the boy actors have just arrived at the theatre. Overlaying their *apparel*, the costumes appropriate to their fictional characters, *cloaks* also identify this episode as half-theatrical, a semi-staged moment.[5]

Galeatzo asks, 'Are ye ready, are ye perfect?'

> PIERO
> Faith, we can say our parts; but we are ignorant in what mould we must cast our actors.
>
> ALBERTO
> Whom do you personate?
>
> PIERO
> Piero, Duke of Venice.
>
> ALBERTO
> O, ho; then thus frame your exterior shape

---

fundamental issues underlie all dramatic activity. The deadly trap is to divide the eternal truths from the superficial variations.'

[5] On costumes and make-up, see Hattaway, *Elizabethan Popular Theatre*, pp. 85–8; on props, see Dessen, *Elizabethan Stage Conventions*, pp. 33–5, 51, 91–8.

To haughty form of elate majesty
As if you held the palsy-shaking head
Of reeling chance under your fortune's belt
In strictest vassalage; grow big in thought
As swoll'n with glory of successful arms.   (Induction, 2–12)

Each of the six is in turn 'cast' into the appropriate, stereotyped 'mould', sometimes giving a sketch of the stock characterization, sometimes speaking the language of the part:

ALBERTO ... one [the fool, Balurdo] whose foppish nature might seem create[d] only for wise men's recreation, and like a juiceless bark, to preserve the sap of more strenuous spirits. A servile hound that loves the scent of forerunning fashion ....
FOROBOSCO Ha, ha, ha; tolerably good; good, faith, sweet wag.
ALBERTO Umph; why 'tolerably good; good, faith, sweet wag'? Go, go; you flatter me.
FOROBOSCO Right; I but dispose my speech to the habit of my part.   (33–6, 40–3)

Metaphors of costume ('fashion', 'habit', 'suit') describe the actors' donning of their off-the-peg roles:

FELICHE Rampum scrampum, mount tufty Tamburlaine! What rattling thunderclap breaks from his lips?
ALBERTO O, 'tis native to his part. For acting a modern Bragadoch under the person of Matzagente, the Duke of Milan's son, it may seem to suit with good fashion of coherence.   (86–90)

Confronted with his 'part' and nothing else, the actor personating Feliche complains that he doesn't know how his character fits into the play: 'I have a part allotted me which I have neither able apprehension to conceit nor what I conceit gracious ability to utter' (89–90).

The induction suits Marston's play, where constricting routines of character are 'part' of the point, and life is theatricalized to an acme of affectation. When Antonio complains about having to play 'two parts in one', Alberto, who will himself double 'Alberto' and Andrugio (21–3), rebukes him:

Not play two parts in one? away, away; 'tis common fashion. Nay, if you cannot bear two subtle fronts under one hood, idiot go by, go by, off this world's stage. O time's impurity!   (73–6)

Recalling a catch-phrase ('go by, go by') from *The Spanish Tragedy* (*c.*1587) or ridiculing *Tamburlaine* (*c.*1587) makes new theatre of these older theatrical moments. As the actors suspect, idiosyncratic behaviour fills the play, and Marston leaves narrative coherence to chance and the audience; Feliche worries that 'it is not possible to limn so many persons in so small a tablet as the compass of our plays afford' (132–3). Bedevilled by folly, the same actor–character later exclaims,

More fools, more rare fools! O, for time and place long enough and large enough to

act these fools! Here might be made a rare scene of folly, if the plat [plot] could bear
it. (3.2.117–19)

Marston's stage world restages another, earlier one, mocks it, and seeks to
displace it. Despite what will prove an anarchic play, a subversive attack on
dramatic conventions, the induction also mimics a common theatrical situation – actors rushing, and rushed, to learn their parts, but leaving both
'character' and coherence to their professional experience and the spectators' familiarity with previous plays.[6]

Given the theatre's insistent demand for new material and a repertory
system that often saw three or more different plays performed in a single
week, rehearsals and performances must often have been chaotic: a mad
hurry simply to memorize or recall parts; actors drunk, absent, forgetful, on
stage too soon or off too late; improvised lines and gestures to restore the
play's general direction or to take advantage of some topical application or of
some spectator in the audience. Playwrights often complained about how far
a performance departed from the texts they had set down; Lord Letoy cor-
rects his acting company:

> But you, sir, are incorrigible, and
> Take licence to yourself to add unto
> Your parts your own free fancy, and sometimes
> To alter or diminish what the writer
> With care and skill compos'd; and when you are
> To speak to your coactors in the scene,
> You hold interlocutions with the audients [sic] –
> (Richard Brome, *The Antipodes* [1638], 2.2.39–45)

The actors' willingness to make *ad lib.* satirical remarks could sometimes
serve as a welcome defence against censorship; on one such occasion,
George Chapman plaintively wrote, 'I see not mine own plays, nor carry the
actors' tongues in my mouth'.[7]

Professional theatre only recently became the decorous, largely bourgeois
event it now usually is. Renaissance public theatre performances, and many
private ones also, must often have been a blend of fairly formal public decla-

---

[6] For studies of how theatre practices may have responded to rapidly changing repertories
and ill-prepared actors, see Bernard Beckerman, 'Theatrical plots and Elizabethan stage
practice' and William B. Long, '*John a Kent and John a Cumber*: an Elizabethan playbook
and its implications' in W. R. Elton and William B. Long, eds., *Shakespeare and Dramatic
Tradition: Essays in Honor of S. F. Johnson* (Newark, Delaware, 1989), pp. 109–24 and 125–
43, respectively.

[7] Chapman's letter of mid-1608, probably to Sir George Buc, modernized from my transcription in *A Seventeenth-Century Letter-Book* (Newark, Delaware, 1983); see pp. 246 and
435–7. On actors' *ad hoc* contributions, see Margot Heinemann's chapter, below, pp.
173–4.

mation, exaggerated gesture (of the silent film sort), and vaudeville or stand-up comedy. Some members of the public theatre audience were physically separate from the open-air stage and hence required lavish and loud acting styles; others pressed close about the stage, or even sat upon it, and they might sometimes arrive uninvited to participate in the spectacle.[8] Remembering the public theatres of the 1630s, Edmund Gayton recalled 'holidays when sailors, watermen, shoemakers, butchers and apprentices are at leisure':

> then it is good policy to amaze those violent spirits with some tearing tragedy full of fights and skirmishes, as the *Guelphs* and *Ghibellines*, *Greeks* and *Trojans*, or the three *London Apprentices*, which commonly ends in six acts, the spectators frequently mounting the stage and making a more bloody catastrophe among themselves than the players.

Gayton describes an audience dissatisfied with the actors' offering:

> I have known upon one of these festivals, but especially at Shrovetide, where the players have been appointed, notwithstanding their bills to the contrary, to act what the major part of the company [audience] had a mind to; sometimes *Tamerlane*, sometimes *Jurgurth*, sometimes the *Jew of Malta*, and sometimes parts of all these, and at last, none of the three taking, they were forced to undress and put off their tragic habits and conclude the day with *The Merry Milkmaids*. And unless this were done and the popular humour satisfied, as sometimes it fortuned that the players were refractory, the benches, the tiles, the laths, the stones, oranges, apples, nuts flew about most liberally, and as there were mechanics [workingmen] of all professions, who fell every one to his own trade and dissolved a house in an instant, and made a ruin of a stately fabric. It was not then the most mimical nor fighting man, [Richard] Fowler, nor Andrew Cane, could pacify; prologues nor epilogues would prevail; the devil and the fool were quite out of favour. Nothing but noise and tumult fills the house.[9]

Such rambunctious theatrical conditions had a large and probably now an incalculable impact on dramaturgy.

Other complicating influences are more obvious: the careers of Lyly, Shakespeare, and others show that a single individual might write a play, participate in its rehearsal, attend its performance or even join the cast.[10] To

---

[8] See, for instance, 'A Prologue at the Globe to his Comedy call'd *The Doubtful Heir* which should have been presented at the Blackfriars': 'But you that can contract yourselves, and sit / As you were now in Blackfriars' pit, / And will not deaf us with lewd noise, or tongues, / Because we have no heart to break our lungs …' (James Shirley, *Poems, etc.* [1646], D4v–5).

[9] Edmund Gayton, *Pleasant Notes upon Don Quixot* (1654), p. 271.

[10] See David Klein, 'Did Shakespeare produce his own plays?', *MLR* 57 (1962), 356–60; Bernard Beckerman, 'Philip Henslowe' in Joseph W. Donohue, Jr, ed., *The Theatrical Manager in England and America* (Princeton, New Jersey, 1971), pp. 19–62, esp. pp. 53–9. For playwrights who attended their own plays, see Gurr, *Playgoing*, pp. 193, 194, 199.

regard the dramatist's arts as those visible in the surviving manuscript or printed playtexts proves more expedient than defensible. The documents, usually small paper-bound quartos, much less often manuscripts, have themselves diverse histories, and many printed texts probably bear the undecipherable signs of actors' and book-holders' contributions as well as the dramatists'. When an individual playwright's script 'entered the theatrical O' and consequently entered the communal process of rehearsal and enactment, it 'lost its singleness yet fulfilled its destiny'.[11] Moreover, printed texts may significantly *mis*represent the dramatist's contribution, for everyone connected with the production and performance of a play would have regarded a printed text as irrelevant to their specifically theatrical activity.

Dramatists and printers frequently claim the printed text differs from the staged version. Published plays might contain less, or more, or simply different material:

I have purposely omitted and left out some fond and frivolous jestures [*sic*], digressing and, in my poor opinion, far unmeet for the matter, which I thought might seem more tedious unto the wise than any way else to be regarded – though, haply, they have been of some vain conceited fondlings [fools] greatly gaped at, what times they showed upon the stage in their graced [i.e., enacted?] deformities.

(Richard Jones's preface to Marlowe's *Tamburlaine* [printed 1590])

I would inform you that this book, in all numbers, is not the same with that which was acted on the public stage, wherein a second pen had good share; in place of which I have rather chosen to put weaker (and no doubt less pleasing) of mine own, than to defraud so happy a genius of his right by my loathed usurpation.

(Jonson's preface to *Sejanus* [printed 1605])

Courteous Reader: You shall find in this book more than was presented upon the stage, and left out of the presentation, for superfluous length (as some of the players pretended). I thought good all should be inserted according to the allowed [i.e., licensed] original.

(Richard Brome's note appended to *The Antipodes* [printed 1640])

Playwrights sold their plays to an acting company, and it was a rare author – Ben Jonson is the most notorious example – who sought fame or money by printing his plays. Except for those who hoped to profit by performing a published text of another company's play (apparently a rare circumstance), the theatrical world regarded the printed text as something that followed, sometimes by decades, rather than preceded or accompanied their activities. (Printed texts did, however, serve as promptbooks, at least for touring per-

---

[11] Stanley Wells, *Re-Editing Shakespeare for the Modern Reader* (Oxford, 1984), p. 111; see also Stephen Orgel, 'Authentic Shakespeare', *Representations* 21 (Winter, 1988), 1–25.

formances and for revivals long after or far distant from the original production.)[12]

Authors' and printers' prefaces to plays clearly distinguish the experience of *reading* a play from that of *seeing* or *hearing* (the two standard words) it performed, and almost unanimously prefer performance:

I shall entreat ... that the unhandsome shape which this trifle in reading presents may be pardoned for the pleasure it once afforded you when it was presented with the lively soul of action.   (Marston, preface to *The Malcontent* [printed 1604])

If any should wonder why I print a comedy, whose life rests much in the actors' voice, let such know that it cannot avoid publishing; let it therefore stand with good excuse that I have been my own setter out. (Marston, preface to *The Fawn* [printed 1606])

A great part of the grace of this (I confess) lay in action; yet can no action ever be gracious, where the decency of the language, and ingenious structure of the scene, arrive not to make up a perfect harmony.

          (Webster, preface to *The Devil's Law-Case* [printed 1623])

... scenical representation is so far from giving just cause of any least diminution, that the personal and exact life it gives to any history, or other such delineation of human actions, adds to them lustre, spirit, and apprehension ...

          (Chapman, dedication to *Caesar and Pompey* [printed 1631])

... though it [the published play] appear not in that natural dress of the scene, nor so powerful, as when it had the soul of action.

          (Shirley, dedication to *The Brothers* [printed 1652])

When a play failed in performance, printing could appeal to a different jury. Webster in the preface to *The White Devil* (1612) and Walter Burre, the printer of Beaumont's *The Knight of the Burning Pestle* (1607), both make this appeal, but no one more vividly than Dekker in his preface to *The Whore of Babylon* (1607):

But of this my knowledge cannot fail, that in such consorts [i.e., casts], many of the instruments are for the most part out of tune, and no marvel; for let the poet set the note of his numbers even to Apollo's own lyre, the player will have his own crochets, and sing false notes, in despite of all the rules of music... if this of mine be made a cripple by such means, yet despise him [the play] not for that deformity which struck not upon him at his birth, but fell upon him by misfortune, and in recompense of such favour, you shall (if your patience can suffer so long) hear now how himself can speak.

Further, every dramatist worked within an embracing set of performance conventions, so an apparently individual touch may prove to be X's variation on a long-lived conventional substratum. That conventional base might orig-

---

[12] See C. J. Sisson, 'Shakespeare Quartos as prompt-copies', *RES* 18 (1942), 129–43.

inate with the actors, or the physical structure of the playhouse, or any number of other performance conditions quite distinct from the human playwright and his theatrical co-workers. So diverse were late-Tudor and Stuart dramatic conditions – large 'public' amphitheatres, smaller and more expensive 'private' theatres, royal palaces, aristocratic houses and city streets or civic halls, theatre companies enduring for decades or existing for a few plague-filled months – that it is futile to dogmatize about the playwright's contribution to the theatrical experience. Even within the putatively well-defined conditions of London's professional theatre, patchy surviving testimony means any single retrospective pattern is probably an historical fiction.

Another central qualification arises from the function of language, that is, represented speech by and among the characters. Speech has a more predominant role in the non-illusionistic Renaissance theatre than in later, increasingly illusionistic theatres. Spoken text prompts the audience's imaginative participation and conveys many of the *circumstances* of speech which an illusionistic theatre communicates in other, often technological ways.[13] Thus, dramatic speech establishes the time of day:

What though we have lost our way in the woods, yet never hang thy head ... for ... I will warrant thy life tonight for twenty in the hundred... What? to lose our way in the wood without either fire or candle...
(Peele, The Old Wives Tale [1590–4], 2–6, 8–10)

> See how the Hours, the guardant of heaven's gate,
> Have by their toil removed the darksome clouds,
> That Sol may well discern the trampled pace
> Wherein he wont to guide his golden car.
> (Arden of Faversham [1591], 10.1–4)

or identifies part of the theatre structure:

> Let us assault this kingly tower,
> Where all their conduits and fountains are;
> Then we may easily take the city too.
> (Peele, David and Bethsabe [c.1587], 180–2)

> Now hang our bloody colours by Damascus,
> Reflexing hues of blood upon their heads
> While they walk quivering on their city walls,
> Half dead for fear before they feel my wrath.
> (Marlowe, Tamburlaine, Part 2 [c.1588], 4.4.1–4)

or identifies persons and places:

---

[13] See Ellis-Fermor, *Jacobean Drama* and Williams, *Drama in Performance*.

The sun doth beat upon the plain [open] fields, wherefore let us sit down, Gallathea, under this fair oak, by whose broad leaves being defended from the warm beams we may enjoy the fresh air which softly breathes from Humber floods.

(Lyly, *Gallathea* [*c.*1584], 1.1.1ff.)

> Now, masters of our academic state,
> That rule in Oxford, viceroys in your place,
>
> .   .   .
>
> Why flock you thus to Bacon's secret cell,
> A friar newly stalled in Brazen-nose?
>
> (Greene, *Friar Bacon and Friar Bungay* [*c.*1591], 2.6–7, 10–11)

When romantic-pastoral comedy and the English history play – genres mainly of the 1590s – fade, innovative drama moves indoors to throne rooms, back corridors, and bedchambers, to battlefield command posts, to country houses and counting houses, and exterior scenes tend to be urban rather than rural.[14] Many of Shakespeare's later plays – *Macbeth, Antony and Cleopatra, Coriolanus, Cymbeline*, for instance – are in this respect belated. While fashionable non-Shakespearian Jacobean plays do include outdoor scenes – for example, Beaumont and Fletcher's *Philaster* (*c.*1609), or Fletcher's *Bonduca* (*c.*1613), or Middleton and Rowley's *The Changeling* (*c.*1622) – the proportion of interior to exterior scenes increases. Intimate, Chekhovian 'reaction' scenes become more common, and stage directions such as *Enter battle* much less so.[15] Setting a Jacobean scene becomes a matter of using dialogue to define relationships among characters rather than using verbal 'scene painting' to allegorize those relations. Middleton's *The Witch* (*c.*1613), for example, opens with the following duologue:

> – My three years spent in war has now undone my peace forever.
> – Good, be patient, sir.
> – She is my wife by contract before heaven
>   And all the angels, sir.
> – I do believe you, but where's the remedy now?
>   You see she's gone; another has possession.
> – There's the torment.

[14] Leonard Tennenhouse, *Power on Display: The Politics of Shakespeare's Genres* (1986), chapters 1 and 2, speculates on why the writing of romantic comedy and chronicle history plays declines after 1600. For the later history play, see Judith Doolan Spikes, 'The Jacobean history play and the myth of the elect nation', *RenD* n.s. 8 (1977), 177–94.

[15] Lawrence Stone has described the roughly contemporaneous ('After about 1620') change in 'standards of values … codes of behaviour … [and] fashions of competition, which affected both "Court" and "Country" alike. From living publicly in the hall and state-rooms, they ["Caroline noblemen"] withdrew into dining rooms, bedchambers, and closets… At bottom, the cause of the change was the rise of individualism, privacy, puritanism, and the cult of the virtuoso' (*The Crisis of the Aristocracy 1558–1641*, abridged edn [Oxford, 1967], pp. 87–8, revised from the original edition [Oxford, 1965], pp. 187–8).

– This day, being the first of your return,
Unluckily proves the first too of her fast'ning,
Her uncle, sir, the Governor of Ravenna,
Holding a good opinion of the bridegroom
As he's fair-spoken, sir, and wondrous mild.

With the evolution of malcontent commentators, dramatized characters whose comments and attitudes frame and distance the action, the dialogue becomes layered; in one layer, a speaker or speakers describe and evaluate other characters as if they were human specimens and literary types. As Delio and Antonio watch the other major characters gather, Webster motivates their *sotto voce* commentary thus:

> DELIO
> The presence[-chamber] 'gins to fill – you promised me
> To make me the partaker of the natures
> Of some of your great courtiers.
>
> ANTONIO
>   The Lord Cardinal's
> And other stranger's, that are now in court?
> I shall ...   (*The Duchess of Malfi* [1614], 1.1.83–7)

And Antonio responds to Delio's later requests – 'Now, sir, your promise: what's that Cardinal?' and 'what's his brother?' – with lengthy verbal portraits similar to the 'character', a popular Jacobean literary genre describing social stereotypes. After Antonio has described the Duchess at admiring length, he alludes to Webster's tactic: 'I'll case the picture up' (1.1.207). With the late nostalgia for things Elizabethan and the return of romantic plots and exotic locales in Cavalier drama, new plays once again moved outdoors, and the older, 'exterior' Elizabethan dramas continued to be revived in the theatres and at court.

Language and rhetoric

The heavily patterned verbal rhetoric of English drama in the 1590s was in many respects word-play writ large. It was 'auricular', appealing first and powerfully to the listener–spectator's rhythmic and auditory sensibilities. Fear energizes successful word-play. A similarity of sound, or spelling, or shape among words or phrases overrides the semantic, conventional, unthinkingly assumed difference between them.[16] Momentarily, the abyss of

---

[16] See Sigurd Burckhardt, *Shakespearean Meanings* (Princeton, New Jersey, 1968), pp. 24–33 and George Puttenham (?), *The Art of English Poesy* (1589): '*auricular* figures be those which work alteration in th'ear by sound, accent, time, and slipper volubility in utterance

a linguistic discourse ordered by sound, not sense, stares back. Tidy semantic demarcations – *bare* from *bear*, *know* from *no*, and (for an Elizabethan ear) *room* from *Rome*, and *word* from *world* – collapse, and we glimpse a different order. That glimpse defies 'logical' order, or at least challenges the claim that one order, semantic difference, is naturally or obviously superior to another, phonic identity. Beyond the increasingly popular and increasingly efficient iambic pentameter cadence, there were the almost incantatory effects – alliteration, repetition, echo, reversal – of the rhetorical figures:

> By wasting all, I conquer all the world,
> And now to end our difference at last,
> In this last act, note but the deeds of death.
> Where is Erastus now but in my triumph?
> Where are the murderers but in my triumph?
> Where the judge and witnesses but in my triumph?
> Where false Lucina but in my triumph?
> Where's Basilisco but in my triumph?
> Where's faithful Piston but in my triumph?
> Where's valiant Brusor but in my triumph?
> And where's great Soliman but in my triumph?
>
> (Kyd, *Soliman and Perseda* [*c.*1590], 5.5.14–24)

> When disobedience reigneth in the child,
> And princes' ears by flattery be beguiled;
> When laws do pass by favor, not by truth;
> When falsehoods swarmeth both in old and youth;
> When gold is made a god to wrong the poor,
> And charity exiled from rich men's door;
> When men by wit do labour to disprove
> The plagues for sin sent down by God above;
> When great men's ears are stopped to good advice
> And apt to hear those tales that feed their vice;
> Woe to the land ...
>
> (Greene and Lodge, *A Looking Glass for London and England* [1590], 3.2.205–15)

> I am weary of these weeds,
> Weary to wield this weapon that I bear,
> Weary of love from whom my woe proceeds,
> Weary of toil, since I have lost my dear.
> O weary life, where wanteth no distress,
> But every thought is paid with heaviness.
>
> (Greene, *James IV* [*c.*1591], 4.4.1–6)

> My late ambition hath distain'd my faith,

... this quality extendeth but to the outward tuning of the speech, reaching no higher than th'ear and forcing the mind little or nothing' (III.134).

> My breach of faith occasion'd bloody wars,
> Those bloody wars have spent my treasure,
> And with my treasure my people's blood,
> And with their blood, my joy and best belov'd,
> My best belov'd, my sweet and only son.
>
> (Kyd, *The Spanish Tragedy*, 1.3.33–8)[17]

Here we hear the fundamental sound patterns as more immediately appealing, more accessible than the words' and phrases' struggle to discriminate, define, divide, and categorize.

A discourse that does not separate *nothing* from *noting* or *heir* from *hair* from *here*, a discourse that almost rhymes *blood* with *belov'd*, is a Wonderland language and a disturbing one, but it is also an oral, overtly rhetorical, and theatrical one. It is the discourse of high-Elizabethan drama. While 'advanced' fashion and tastes changed, the changes were more superficial than critics sometimes allow; Fletcher uses rhetorical repetition throughout his influential Jacobean career (*c.*1607–25), although he rarely binds the repetition to line units so rigidly as did Kyd and his contemporaries.[18] The older style, too, retained broad appeal: the vitality of *The Spanish Tragedy* (still in the Fortune theatre's repertory in the late 1630s), of 'rampum scrampum' *Tamburlaine* (similarly long-lived at the Red Bull theatre), and of *Mucedorus* (*c.*1590) demonstrates so much. Court and private theatre audiences who enjoyed Fletcherian 'refinement' or, later, the love-and-honour exercises of Cavalier gentleman-playwrights also welcomed revivals of Marlowe's *The Jew of Malta* (*c.*1588; performed at court not long before its first printing in 1633), Chapman's *Bussy D'Ambois* (*c.*1603; performed at court in 1634 and 1638), Jonson's comedies and tragedies, and many of Shakespeare's plays through the Stuart period. Old-fashioned and probably simply old when it was first printed in 1598, *Mucedorus* eventually became extraordinarily popular in print and possibly on stage, perhaps because a live bear participated in the court performance, Shrove Sunday, 1610.[19]

Dramatic – *spoken*, oratorical – rhetoric was manifestly successful in the

---

[17] These passages exemplify the rhetorical figures called 'anaphora' and 'epistrophe' (respectively, words repeated at the beginning and end of successive clauses), 'isocolon' (a series of parallel phrases), 'antimetabole' (words repeated in reverse order), and 'anadiplosis' (words ending one clause repeated at the beginning of the next). For further details and examples, see Sister Miriam Joseph, C.S.C., *Shakespeare's Use of the Arts of Language* (New York, 1947).

[18] See Cyrus Hoy, 'The language of Fletcherian tragicomedy' in J. C. Gray, ed., *Mirror Up to Shakespeare: Essays in Honour of G. R. Hibbard* (Toronto, 1984), pp. 99–113.

[19] For the play's numerous reprintings and evidence of its stage popularity, see George F. Reynolds, '*Mucedorus*, most popular Elizabethan play?' in J. W. Bennett *et al.*, eds., *Studies in the English Renaissance Drama* (New York, 1959), pp. 248–68.

Renaissance theatre, but the fashion was not solely theatrical. Patterned speech could also be heard in church, in Parliament, from scaffold and block; indeed, there are powerful arguments for the claim that the Elizabethan auricular rhetoric known to us as a written or printed phenomenon derives historically from centuries-old oral habits.[20] In a Paul's Cross sermon of 1579, Richard Dylos discusses, even as he employs, various ornaments in sermons, and he ends with a Shakespearian comic deflation:

Some would have long texts, some short texts. Some would have Doctors, Fathers, and Councils; some call that man's doctrine. Some would have it ordered by logic; some term that man's wisdom. Some would have it polished by rhetoric; some call it persuasibleness of words. And again in rhetoric some would have it holy eloquence, liable to the Hebrew and Greek phrase; some would have it proper and fitting to the English capacity. Some love study and learning in sermons; some allow only a sudden motion of the spirit. Some would have all said by heart; some would have oft recourse to the book. Some love gesture, some no gestures. Some love long sermons, some short sermons. Some are coy, and can brook no sermons at all.[21]

Or consider the House of Commons, petitioning Elizabeth and feigning that she has considered the dangers of an undecided succession. They

cannot ... but acknowledge how your Majesty hath most graciously considered the great dangers and the unspeakable miseries of civil wars; the perilous intermeddlings of foreign princes with seditious, ambitious, and factious subjects at home; the waste of noble houses; the slaughter of people, the subversion of towns, intermission of all things pertaining to the maintenance of the realm, unsurity of all men's possessions, lives, and estates; daily interchanging of attainders and treasons.[22]

The relentless parallel clauses – the 'dangers' and 'miseries' – overwhelm, in memory and ear, the single verb, 'considered', they all depend on grammatically.

Political or homiletic uses of auricular rhetoric, however, are deeply different from dramatic uses. The preachers' and the parliamentarians' manifest purpose reassures their hearers that design will sooner or later limit rhetoric. For preachers and politicians, circumstance frames and demystifies rhetoric's power to unsettle. In drama, the end is not known. To learn that end we watch and hear the fiction. Rhetoric's local effect (persuasion, hortation, lament) may become known, but the play's teleology, the plot's outcome, is unknown. Allied with the plot, the temporal change of the characters' fortunes, dramatic rhetoric unsettles semantic certainty and thus

---

[20] See Walter J. Ong, S.J., 'Oral residue in Tudor prose style', *PMLA* 80 (1965), 145–54.

[21] Modernized from the text quoted in Millar MacLure, *The Paul's Cross Sermons 1534–1642* (Toronto, 1958), p. 146.

[22] Quoted from Mortimer Levine, *The Early Elizabethan Succession Question 1558–1568* (Stanford, California, 1966), p. 48.

contributes to a larger arc of suspense rather than using a frame of certitude as a fulcrum. Drama harnesses a continuous rhetorical anxiety – the fear that language might regain its primordial union with other sounds – to its own theatrical purposes of suspense and pleasure, the pleasure of a mystery, the pleasure of straining to see and hear something both puzzling and possibly terrifying.

Language and character

Playwrights attribute this rhetoric to their characters, and one form of dramaturgical evolution is the dramatists' increasing skill at distinguishing among the characters by discriminating among their ways of speaking. In most plays of the mid-sixteenth century, the characters all sound alike, or at best sort themselves through speaking a limited number of conventional (and therefore tedious) stock vocabularies.[23] Marlowe, Kyd, and Peele use action(s) as a way of differentiating among dramatic characters whose other features come largely from the pattern book of classical and native literary traditions. In the next theatrical generation – Shakespeare, Jonson, Chapman – the playwrights, especially in comedy, begin to discriminate their characters through tricks of style or vocabulary, but also display, especially in tragedy, the more complicated skills needed to give a single character several levels of speech (intimate and public, for example, or equal-to-equal and superior-to-inferior).

The scene in Middleton and Rowley's *The Changeling* (1622) where Beatrice-Joanna offers money and De Flores demands her virginity as the reward for murdering her fiancé Alonzo de Piraquo is a magnificently orchestrated negotiation over levels of diction. The scene is consequently also filled with invitations to infer 'character'. Beatrice begins with a mincing alliteration and a calculated balance between the formal 'you, sir' and the more intimate 'thy': 'Look you, sir, here's three thousand florins; / I have not meanly thought upon thy merit' (3.4.62–3). When De Flores rejects the three thousand florins – 'What, salary? Now you move me' – and, incredible to Beatrice-Joanna, then rejects six thousand – 'You take a course / To double my vexation; that's the good you do', all she can suppose is that De Flores is as embarrassed to name a sum as she is embarrassed and puzzled by his anger. Ethically jejune, she imagines him financially fastidious:

---

[23] We infer the imaginary construct 'character' from the dramatic personage's speech and acts, so stock vocabularies and stock or type characterizations are reciprocal. See my 'Characterization through language in the early plays of Shakespeare and his contemporaries' in K. Muir, J. L. Halio, and D. J. Palmer, eds., *Shakespeare, Man of the Theater* (Newark, Delaware, 1983), pp. 128–47.

I prithee make away with all speed possible.
And if thou be'st so modest not to name
The sum that will content thee, paper blushes not;
Send thy demand in writing, it shall follow thee,
But prithee take thy flight.   (78–82)

'Prithee' and, earlier, 'Bless me!' – language Hotspur would consider suitable for a comfit-maker's wife – begin to sound strange alongside the now exclusive use of *thee* and *thou*. Soon, De Flores impatiently tries to kiss Beatrice; when she resists, he threatens, 'I will not stand so long to beg 'em shortly'. Her pronoun marks the first sign of conscious alliance between instigator, a sonnet-mistress, and the villain, a market-economist: 'Take heed, De Flores, of forgetfulness; / 'Twill soon betray us' (95–6). De Flores claims equality in sin stipulates equality in sexual desire: 'Justice invites your blood to understand me', and Beatrice struggles to re-establish a barrier of politeness, of verbal decorum. For her, the deed spoken is worse than the deed done:

Speak it yet further off that I may lose
What has been spoken and no sound remain on't.
I would not hear so much offense again
For such another deed.   (103–6)

Throughout the scene, diction is character, and action is debate over socially typed language. De Flores soon delivers the play's most famous line, 'Y'are the deed's creature' (138): Beatrice-Joanna is 'what the act has made you' (136). Commanding Alonzo's death has (re)created Beatrice. Action, verbal action, is character; it makes the dramatic 'creature'. Yet De Flores is only half right, for they are both also creatures of their chosen languages. Proportions vary from scene to scene, even moment to moment, but action and language, 'deed' and 'sound', everywhere construct the play's creatures. As this analysis implies, Renaissance English playwrights apparently composed in scenic units, in short stretches of sequential actions and speech. Characters that manifest a thoroughgoing psychological consistency, the quality so prized in the classical novel and the realistic theatre, are consequently quite uncommon, or at least an accidental or subordinate feature, in Renaissance drama.[24]

---

[24] The theatrical practice of doubling or trebling roles and of dividing roles among two or more actors (see above, pp. 49–50) might further diminish psychological verisimilitude while emphasizing the cast's virtuosity. For a concise account of how conventions, especially of character, represent 'the experience of self in the Elizabethan social context', see Robert

Retrospectively, we may infer that a continuing technical ambition for later Elizabethan dramatists was anchoring purpose within a play's represented agents. Older methods of propelling an action and manipulating the change of the agents' fortunes in time located purpose and *telos* outside human interaction and employed frame structures involving divine or legendary beings or introduced hypostatized emotions and values as allegorical participants. Changing dramatic techniques in the 1580s and 1590s are part of complex cultural phenomena – the 'interiorization' of experience, the creation of models for human individuality – that appear everywhere from ethical argument (over usury, for example) and economic behaviour (joint-stock companies, for instance) to religious controversy and parliamentary debate.[25] The over-full sixth chapter of Aristotle's *Poetics* suggests that audiences deduce character (*ethos*) from judging the agent's *action*, specifically the imaginary personage's (ethical) acts of choice. Aristotle's claim hovers on the edge of type-characterization, precisely the effect English dramatists apparently wanted to avoid. Or rather, they seem to have sought to obscure that effect, for *any* represented agent is to some degree necessarily 'typed', a reductive product of past dramatic characters and conventional aesthetic and cultural expectations.

Seeking dramatic individuation, seeking to make the three or four or five universal plots and the one or two or three 'types' or agent-functions those plots require into varied entertainment, playwrights elaborately developed their characters' verbal analysis of their own actions. Characters talk about motive and purpose because the playwright hopes we will imagine them independent agents. One method, perhaps the oldest, is simple declaration:

> A woeful man, O Lord, am I, to see him in this case.
> My days I deem desires their end; this deed will help me hence,
> To have the blossoms of my field destroyed by violence.
>
> (Preston, *Cambises* [*c.*1565], 5. 570–3)

> Thus have I with an envious forged tale
> Deceiv'd the king, betray'd mine enemy,
> And hope for guerdon of my villainy.
>
> (Kyd, *The Spanish Tragedy*, 1.3.93–5)

R. Hellinga, 'Elizabethan dramatic conventions and Elizabethan reality', *RenD* n.s. 12 (1981), 27–49; see also next note.

25 The second part of Jacob Burckhardt's classic *The Civilization of the Renaissance in Italy* (1860; trans. S. G. C. Middlemore, 1878) is called 'The Development of the Individual', but Burckhardt describes a form of socio-political individualism rather than of interiority or the 'subject'. On the latter, see, for instance, Ernst Cassirer, *The Individual and the Cosmos in Renaissance Philosophy*, trans. M. Domandi (Oxford, 1963), chapter 4; Dollimore, *Radical Tragedy*, pp. 249–71; and Belsey, *The Subject of Tragedy*, chapter 2.

Related to simple declaration are speeches in which a character describes emotions from the outside:

> He's gone, and for his absence thus I mourn.
> Did never sorrow go so near my heart
> As doth the want of my sweet Gaveston;
> And could my crown's revenue bring him back,
> I would freely give it to his enemies,
> And think I gain'd, having bought so dear a friend.
>
> . . .
>
> My heart is as an anvil unto sorrow,
> Which beats upon it like the Cyclops' hammers,
> And with the noise turns up my giddy brain,
> And makes me frantic for my Gaveston.
>
> (Marlowe, *Edward II* [1592], 1.4.304–9, 311–14)

Here, the script does not allow the actor playing Edward to *be* 'frantic' at Gaveston's banishment, or to enact that frenzy. Rather, the actor *says* Edward is frantic.

Humanist rhetorical education stressed adversarial combat, finding or creating 'the' two sides and arguing each against the other. As an educational phenomenon, this binary bias probably derives from legal practice and from humanism's claim to educate counsellors who see and analyse all (but in practice two) sides of a question. As a dramatic phenomenon, the bias produces a bifurcated speaker, two voices in one:

> Yet might she love me for my valiancy,
> Ay, but that's slander'd by my captivity.
> Yet might she love me to content her sire,
> Ay, but her reason masters his desire.
> Yet might she love me as her brother's friend,
> Ay, but her hopes aim at some other end.
> Yet might she love me to uprear her state,
> Ay, but perhaps she hopes some nobler mate.
> Yet might she love me as her beauty's thrall,
> Ay, but I fear she cannot love at all.   (*The Spanish Tragedy*, 2.1.19–28)

Keeping the rhetorical figure (a form of epanorthosis) and letting the sense go produces parody:

> O, she is wilder and more hard, withall,
> Than beast, or bird, or tree, or stony wall.
> Yet might she love me to uprear her state,
> Ay, but perhaps she hopes some nobler mate.
> Yet might she love me to content her sire,
> Ay, but her reason masters her desire.
> Yet might she love me as her beauty's thrall,
> Ay, but I fear, she cannot love at all.
>
> (Jonson, *Poetaster* [1601], 3.4.189–96)

Numerous variations were rung on this two-speakers-in-one device. A character might ask, then answer, a question: 'What is beauty saith my sufferings, then?' (*Tamburlaine, Part 1*, 5.1.160); 'To be, or not to be, that is the question'. Or the character could address an abstraction or a personified self:

> Ah, life and soul still hover in his breast
> And leave my body senseless as the earth,
> Or else unite you to his life and soul,
> That I may live and die with Tamburlaine!
>
> (*Tamburlaine, Part 1*, 3.2.21–4)

> Now, Bajazeth, abridge thy baneful days
> And beat thy brains out of thy conquered head,
> Since other means are all forbidden me
> That may be ministers of my decay. (*Ibid.*, 5.1.286–9)

The printed text of Jonson's *Every Man out of his Humour* (1599) opens with a series of short prose sketches entitled 'The Characters of the Persons'. Fastidius Brisk, for example, is described as

A neat, spruce, affecting courtier, one that wears clothes well and in fashion; practiseth by his glass how to salute; speaks good remnants (notwithstanding the base viol and tobacco) swears tersely, and with variety; cares not what lady's favour he belies, or great man's familiarity: a good property to perfume the boot of a coach...

As this excerpt indicates, by 'character' Jonson does not quite mean the imaginary, imitated human traits attributed to and distinguishing among the play's personae. The word has a more technical meaning: a description of a type of human behaviour, an abstract form of something we might call a 'vignette'. Yet the precisely dramatic sense of *character* is not far away since, among other things, these 'characters' do discriminate among the persons of the play, and many are so precise they almost lose the generalizing quality typical of the literary character. (When the literary character became a popular Jacobean genre, many appear to have been based on identifiable individuals.) The dramaturgical relevance of these 'characters' becomes clear when Jonson concludes the list: 'Mitis, is a person of no action, and therefore we afford him no character'. We do not need a profile of, nor can we infer psychological attributes for, an agent who does not act. A prefatory description of Mitis is irrelevant, perhaps even impossible, since his attributes will not be exhibited in or confirmed by the play's action. 'Character', then, in the common if complicated dramatic sense, is interdependent with action, with the personage's acts of choice, behaviour, and relation with other personages. This interdependence means that character and the effective arrangement of the characters' actions cannot be plausibly separated in our experience of a play, although Aristotle thought the practising playwright could separate them, and needed to, as he composed.

The arrangement of action

Classical or neo-classical plays arrange their plots differently from most Elizabethan plays, and the main contrasts outline English practice. Instead of entering the action near or at the crisis, English plays embrace a long temporal period, prodigally representing action mimetically rather than through retrospective narrative, messenger speeches, dialogues with confidants, and the like. (Stephen Gosson's attack, *Plays Confuted in Five Actions* [1582], indicates the Elizabethan association of a dramatic *act* with the neo-classical unity of *action*. Temporal leaps in English Renaissance plays never occur within a scene, and the largest ones tend to occur between the acts, when a play is so organized.) Instead of concentrating on a small cast closely linked by family ties or social function, spatially confined, and engaged in a single action, English popular drama ranges far in space as well as time, employs diverse, sometimes almost discrete, sets of characters, and places them in varied actions whose formal relation often proves vague or uncertain.

Even when they observe the age-old preference for historical or legendary sources in tragic (or 'serious') drama, Elizabethan playwrights and their successors often adopt the biographical, 'whole life' plot anathematized by Aristotle but familiar from morality drama. Thus, for example, *Tamburlaine*'s success spawned numerous rags-to-realms conqueror plays down through Chapman's *Bussy D'Ambois* and beyond. This expansive biographical formula easily assimilated – in *Cambises* or *Edward II* – another medieval formula, the *de casibus* ('of falls') pattern that represents the rise and especially the fall (*casus*) of its characters.

Comedy, particularly urban and domestic comedy, proved more amenable than tragedy to spatial and temporal compression, even in the Jacobean and Caroline periods when such restrictions appear more frequently in both genres. Beaumont's *The Woman Hater* (1606), which has two rather elaborate main plots but seems to occur between morning and night, *The Revenger's Tragedy* (1607), which employs 'comic' duping intrigues and has a near-affinity with *Volpone*, Jonson's *The Alchemist* (1610), and Massinger's *The City Madam* (1632) indicate some of the possible plot-arrangements. Despite the drift toward neo-classical 'regularity' that later plays show, minor or tangential episodes continue to threaten multiple actions in every genre; they break free in such plays as Marston's *The Dutch Courtesan* (1604), where Cocledemoy's plots develop their own comic momentum, and Fletcher's *The Scornful Lady* (1613), where demonstrating Young Loveless's prodigality becomes a dramatic end in itself. *Nouvelle-* and romance-based plots, now often Spanish rather than French or Italian in origin, reappear in the later Stuart period and continue (in Massinger's *Maid of Honour*, for example) the high-Elizabethan luxuriance of temporal extension, geographical variety, and, sometimes, the near-incoherence of plot with plot. After the legal prohibition of non-dramatic satire (1599) and the revival of the boys' companies in the early 1600s, generic mixture – satiric tragedy, tragicomedy – becomes the norm for avant-garde plays, but as early as *The Spanish Tragedy*, Kyd had effectively invented ironic tragedy through adapting comic intrigue.[26]

One Elizabethan method of arranging a play's action probably derives from medieval allegorical drama: separate, often simultaneous lines of action hardly ever intersect, or do so in realistically improbable ways, but achieve intellectual coherence and a powerful dramatic interreflection through illustrating a single issue or topic. The alternation among these strands of plot has been called 'fugal' narrative, and we do experience them temporally much as we experience varied but repeating musical motifs.[27] When strand eventually coheres with strand, the effect recalls Spenser's 'interlacement' in *The Faerie Queene*, where realistically incoherent plots eventually construct an intellectually perceived treatment of a given virtue and its opposite.

This technique appears very widely in John Lyly's drama, most of it written for boy actors. In his *Gallathea* (*c.*1584), for instance, three distinct sets of characters appear, each group participates in its own narrative, and the groups and plots rarely intersect. *Gallathea*'s cast is stratified socially and ontologically: Olympian deities (Neptune, Venus, Diana, and Cupid); shepherd fathers (Tityrus, Melebeus) and their beautiful daughters (Gallathea, Phyllida, respectively); three under-age sons of a miller (Rafe, Robin, and Dick). In a series of expository speeches, Tityrus plays Prospero to Gallathea's Miranda – 'To hear these sweet marvels I would mine eyes were turned also into ears' (1.1.35–6) – and explains that invading Danes long ago destroyed a temple sacred to Neptune. Enraged, the god first flooded the Lincolnshire countryside and then relented slightly on the condition

that at every five years' day the fairest and chastest virgin in all the country should be brought unto this tree, and here being bound ... is left for a peace offering unto

[26] See Douglas Cole, 'The comic accomplice in Elizabethan revenge tragedy', *RenD* 9 (1966), 125–39.

[27] See Hunter, *John Lyly*, pp. 198–9. For the related structure of early romance plays, see Brian Gibbons's chapter, below, pp. 211–12.

Neptune... [who sends] a monster called the Agar [i.e., 'eagre', a tidal bore].

(1.1.42–4, 48–9)

This 'monster' devours the virgin or conveys her to Neptune or drowns her – the shepherd does not know which. 'To avoid, therefore, destiny, for wisdom ruleth the stars' (1.1.62), Tityrus has disguised his daughter as a boy. So has Melebeus, who fears Phyllida will be sacrificed, and shortly the two boy-actor girl–boys wander the forest, meet, and fall in love. Gallathea and Phyllida quickly suspect the true state of affairs – 'I fear me he is as I am, a maiden'; 'I fear the boy to be as I am, a maiden' (3.2.29, 32) – but each resolves to love as best she/he may (4.4.37–45). Gallathea and Phyllida evidently share a love that does not require, though it might welcome, physical expression; remarkably, they share a 'constant faith where there can be no cause of affection' (5.3.132–3). The fires, melancholy, wild gazes, and broken sleeps of 'unbridled passions' (3.1.56) soon invade the play, however, for truant Cupid has appeared in Lincolnshire to 'play ... pranks' (1.2.32–3) among Diana's nymphs 'under the shape of a silly girl' (2.2.1). His temporary success angers Diana, who seizes the godling: 'thou shalt see that Diana's power shall revenge thy policy and tame this pride' (3.4.79–81). Venus, innocent of her son's pranks, demands that Diana be punished for capturing Cupid, 'Neptune, I entreat thee, by no other god than the god of love, that thou evil entreat this goddess of hate' (5.3.36–7). So far, the play (with the exception of the Rafe–Robin–Dick plot) might seem organized as a review of the 'varieties of love' or as a 'chastity–friendship–sensual love' *débat* – the subjects were popular in contemporary prose romances and, apparently, court conversation.

Submerged in these episodes, however, are conflicts in the relations between gods and men, individuals and groups, freedom and destiny. The strands of plot considered so far all turn upon an abuse or violation of power: the Danes committed an original sacrilege from which flow Neptune's abuse of his divinity and the fathers' abuse of their vows and powers of deceit. Neptune sees these human abuses as equivalent to Cupid run amok amongst the virgins and at the same time implicates himself in what he condemns:

Do silly shepherds go about to deceive great Neptune, in putting on man's attire upon women, and Cupid, to make sport, deceive them all by using women's apparel upon a god? Then, Neptune, that hast taken sundry shapes to obtain love, stick not to practice some deceit to show thy deity, and having often thrust thyself into the shape of beasts to deceive men, be not coy to use the shape of a shepherd to show thyself a god.

(2.2.17–24)

Neptune's brief reminiscence puts in question his present appetite for virgin sacrifice and his authority as a judge of Cupid: the human fathers and the godling adopt the same methods – deceit, disguise – Neptune has himself employed to passionate, illicit advantage and will now employ to show himself a god. This past and this present Neptune must acknowledge and repudiate when he serves as umpire in the divine wrangle. Asking for Cupid's release and Diana's punishment, Venus reminds him: 'show thyself the same Neptune that I knew thee to be when thou wast a shepherd [as, of course, he is now], and let not Venus' words be vain in thy ears, since thine were imprinted in my heart' (5.3.63–6). Neptune compromises:

It were unfit that goddesses should strive, and it were unreasonable that I should not yield, and therefore, to please both, both attend. Diana I must honor, her virtue deserveth no less, but Venus I must love, I must confess so much. Diana, restore Cupid to Venus, and I will forever release the sacrifice of virgins. If therefore you love your nymphs as she doth her son, or prefer not a private grudge before a common grief, answer what you will do. (5.3.67–74)

Giving up the sacrifice of virgins, Neptune restores order to the relation between man and god, forgiving the Danes' ancient crime and the fathers' modern one and therefore evaporating the need for human deceit to avert destiny. Abandoning a practice analogous to Cupid's pranks, Neptune restores the order of heaven as well as earth when he reconciles Diana with Venus even as he accepts both chastity and ('proper') love in himself. Phrased as a conflict between 'private grudge' and 'common grief', the goddesses' dispute has analogies in the human community where Tityrus' and Melebeus' deceit puts the entire country at risk:

consult with yourselves, not as fathers of children, but as favorers of your country. Let Neptune have his right if you will have your quiet... whoso hath the fairest daughter hath the greatest fortune, in losing one to save all ... (4.1.13–18)

Since 'destiny' has so frequently been represented as amorous destiny (Cupid, Neptune, Venus), it is no surprise when one father is accused of incest (4.1.37ff.), but the most mysterious destiny belongs to Gallathea and Phyllida. Venus reverses Neptune's earlier persecution. Where he destroyed, she will create: 'Then shall it be seen that I can turn one of them to be a man, and that I will' (5.3.142–3). Lyly refuses to name which boy–girl–boy will be transformed so we do not forget the significance of a love that does not need a commonplace 'cause of affection'; Gallathea and Phyllida accept their amorous destiny and their love whether homosexual or heterosexual.

As the happy couple and their human and divine entourage head for the church door, Rafe, Robin, and Dick – the miller's sons – 'malpertly thrust themselves' (5.3.180) into the company and are amusingly welcomed as tellers of their fortunes 'these twelve months in the woods' (185–6) and singers at the wedding celebration. We have watched them pursue their fortunes from a scene where they fail to learn the rudiments of seamanship and then decide: 'Come, let us to the woods and see what fortune we may have before they be made ships' (1.4.69–71). Rafe meets an Alchemist – 'If he can do this [make gold], he shall be a god altogether' (2.3.42) – but, disillusioned, leaves him for an Astronomer, who promises 'Thy thoughts shall be metamorphosed, and made hail-fellows with the gods' (3.3.79–80). This career, too, having fallen in, Rafe meets Robin, who has been equally disappointed as an apprentice fortuneteller, although he has learned 'I should live to see my father hang'd and both my brothers beg. So the mill shall be mine, and I live by imagination still' (5.1.33–5). They depart together, seeking Dick who, it is reported, 'hath gotten a master that will teach him to make you both his younger brothers' (5.1.65–6), and the three next appear at the wedding of Gallathea and Phyllida. Despite the humorous satire on professed human learning, these episodes appear nearly incidental until we notice that they all involve various deceitful or deluded attempts to control destiny. The alchemist, astrologer, and fortuneteller fit this description more clearly for an Elizabethan audience than for a modern one; the Mariner tries to subdue the most violent destiny in the play, Neptune, the sea, who may speak for himself: 'destiny cannot be prevented by craft' (5.3.13–14). Dick's unseen master is even more interesting, for he is the human analogue of Venus and her proposed metamorphic powers. He offers (so we are told) a magical escape from every Elizabethan male's genetic and economic destiny: primogeniture.

Such an arrangement has been called 'analogous action'; to resolve the play's meaning, to perceive the relation of plot with plot or situation with situation, we are required to see them as analogies illustrating some overarching situation or argument: 'Gallathea ... is built ... upon diverse situations employing a common formula, the attempt to defy divinity'.[28] Analysing allegory risks paraphrasing a universal into truism, but the 'formula' includes Lyly's emphasis on the movement from disorder to order through the sacrifice of selfish concerns and his differentiation between destructive, human or humanly inspired self-transformation and divine metamorphosis. So stated, the dramatic analogies make a claim that suits an ambitious and hence conservative court-playwright. Queen Elizabeth, before whom the play was performed, would endorse such politically pacific counsels, and she is unlikely to have missed, or disliked, her allegorical association with a variety of Olympian deities. (In George Peele's The Arraignment of Paris, also presented at court and also dating from the two-year period in which Gal-

---

[28] Saccio, The Court Comedies of John Lyly, pp. 97 and 101; my interpretation is indebted to Saccio's.

lathea must have been composed, Elizabeth is said to transcend Venus, Juno, Minerva and Diana.)

Most multiple-plot plays depend upon analogy or analogy's twin, contrast. Lyly's dramaturgy refers the analogies to an allegorical, unstated and static situation (in *Campaspe*) or, in *Gallathea*, to an allegorical, unstated, and dynamic argument. Less allegorical and less mythological plays (that is, most other and later Renaissance drama) represent the focus for their analogies or contrasts mimetically, and we are invited to make psychological or social or political inferences rather than to formulate statements or arguments about abstract categories in the Lylyean manner. Among other things, this difference means that non-allegorical multiple-plot plays tend to be more immediately subversive – 'rebellion is like common theft, but so is rule' (*Henry IV, Part 1*); 'sexual passion is like mental illness, but so are patriarchal social structures' (*The Changeling*) – than Lyly's.

While Lyly's plots at first sight seem out of step with the popular drama of the 1590s, later plays use similar plot structures. A common device explores varied examples within a single category of experience. Marston's *The Dutch Courtesan* (1604), for instance, follows a series of paired lovers – the pattern Shakespeare used in *As You Like It* (1599) and *Much Ado about Nothing* (*c.*1600) – and traces the heterosexual dance by displaying the lovers' relations with themselves and others: Franceschina (the title character) and her now bored lover, Freevill; Franceschina and Freevill's naïvely moralistic friend, Malheureux; Freevill and his 'betrothed dearest', Beatrice; Beatrice's trenchantly witty sister, Crispinella, and her 'blunt' Benedick-like lover, Tysefew. The pairs are related thematically – they exemplify 'varieties of love' – but their dramatic interaction gradually reveals both a value hierarchy and a satiric or moral criticism. The playwright's 'argument' and the audience's pleasure lie in the plot, the characters' relationships through time, rather than (as in *Gallathea*) at the more abstract level of an argument the play illustrates and refines. To show, among other things, the 'difference betwixt the love of a courtesan and a wife', Marston offers paired characters in unstable and changing relations rather than in a fixed (but only gradually revealed) equilibrium.[29] We are thus led to believe that each pair of lovers, and each lover within each pair, learns from his or her experience and from the experiences of the other lovers. As its appearance in Shakespeare's and Greene's romantic comedy suggests, this arrangement of thematically linked and distinguished characters probably derives historically from the

---

[29] Marston's slightly misleading *Fabulae argumentum* ('argument of the play') reads: 'The difference betwixt the love of a courtesan and a wife is the full scope of the play, which, intermixed with the deceits of a witty city jester, fills up the comedy.'

numerous contrasting pairs of lovers who populate Renaissance pastoral poetry and pastoral drama. As he did with other bits and pieces of dramatic tradition and convention, Marston places the derivative comic structure into a decidedly tragicomic context by expanding the range of characters he examines and, again, does so by making that examination dynamic rather than static.[30]

At a slightly greater distance from Lyly's practice than Marston's variation lies the plot where paired characters function not thematically but narratively, and hence discursively in a different way. In *The Conspiracy of Charles, Duke of Byron* (1608), George Chapman distributes common experience among several characters, almost 'doubles' the characters, and thus clarifies the play's intellectual dialectic and incorporates it into the dramatic architecture. Given the facts that Byron is a great soldier and a great traitor, Chapman develops La Fin and the Duc D'Aumale as, respectively, a soldier and a traitor. So much the playwright had from his historical sources. He enriches these doubling characters through Byron's responses to them, or more exactly, to the facts of their careers. In La Fin, Byron's heroic anger is reduced to petty resentment; in Aumale, Byron's future appears, though he mistakes its significance.

Aumale is the simpler, more poignant example. He first appears, an exile at the Archduke Albert's court, listening to a painful but sympathetic recounting of his treachery. Bellievre, one of King Henry's ambassadors, expresses his sorrow that Aumale's 'obstinacy ... [in] ... mortal enmity against the King'

> Should force his wrath to use the rites of treason
> Upon the members of your senseless statue,
> Your name and house, when he had lost your person,
> Your love and duty.   (1.2.57–60)

Aumale's dignified response, 'I use not much impatience nor complaint', seems to end the matter, and Byron chooses Aumale to illustrate his aphorism, 'The bounds of loyalty are made of glass, / Soon broke, but can in no date be repair'd' (145–6). Chapman rarely manages to unite exposition with reflection so neatly, but in character-doubling he finds a method which yields 'binocular' vision of an event. The hero's puzzlement at one of the 'rites of treason' used against Aumale – 'And (for a strange reproach of his foul treason) / His trees about it [Aumale's razed house] cut off by their waists' (152–3) – illustrates his spiritual insensitivity. We need not know the customary sanctions of felling a noble family's trees to see Henry's gesture as

---

[30] For Marston's inventive appropriation of previous drama, see Lee Bliss's chapter in the present volume, pp. 239–42.

a symbol of Aumale's dishonour, his plunge from a tradition of fidelity, his separation and exile from his native soil, and the extirpation of any vestige of his family's long life in France. It is, after all, not a very difficult symbol, and hardly a 'strange reproach'. Pairing Aumale with Byron serves several important purposes: the dialogue with the man himself and Byron's reference to past events give the play the temporal depth; we learn that traitors exist in France and that they are punished; Byron, it appears, does not entirely understand the significance of treason or its punishment.

La Fin, too, partly echoes Byron's situation: both are old soldiers, now unneeded. Berowne's remark, '''tis some policy / To have one show worse than the King's and his company' (*Love's Labour's Lost*, 5.2.510–11), provides a model for La Fin's function. William Empson describes 'pseudo-parody to disarm criticism': two similar characters or characters sharing similar ideals are distributed between an heroic and a pastoral plot.[31] One character draws the audience's criticism, or disbelief, or laughter, while leaving the other unscathed. It is 'pseudo'-parody because the heroic half of the pair is not in fact meant to be qualified by the pastoral *alter ego*. That *alter ego* satisfies certain psychological needs in the audience and makes the naturalistic concession that, for example, cowards exist as well as heroes.

As a method of satisfying incredulous or hostile reactions, pseudo-parody suits a tragedy whose hero strains the common definition of humankind. Instead of flattening Byron's high aspirations to the trivia of La Fin's own goals and personality, his characterization accentuates Byron's unique qualities and makes us more sympathetic to the grand traitor. In part, Chapman distinguishes them through dramatizing La Fin's fear of Byron. The two men have radically different aims, and that difference, we assume, corresponds to an equal difference in their respective characters and virtues. We see, too, the antipodal difference in King Henry's treatment of the two men.

La Fin's role also recalls a traditional use of the foil: he represents aspects of Byron's character – anger, quick resentment at injury, a sense of discarded or ignored merit – in debased form. Consequently, we transfer our horror at Byron's decay from the traitor himself to the tool of treason, a character very similar to Byron in some skewed fashion. Unlike other Renaissance playwrights, Chapman does not pile up parallel, simultaneous examples of the hero's situation. When they are first introduced, neither La Fin nor Aumale mirrors Byron's situation in the way that Laertes or Fortinbras does Hamlet's, or Gloucester Lear's, or Bajazeth Tamburlaine's. The

---

[31] See *Some Versions of Pastoral* (London, 1935), chapter 2.

essential difference is that La Fin and Aumale are not what Byron is, but what he may be.

Initially, Byron and La Fin appear similar because both are veteran warriors; their doubling implies they may become similar in other ways as well. In particular, Byron fears that what has happened to La Fin – exclusion from court despite a good war record – may also happen to him. La Fin says of Byron:

> since he came from Flanders
> He heard how I was threaten'd with the King,
> And hath been much inquisitive to know
> The truth of all, and seeks to speak with me.   (2.1.27–30)

The doubling device in both La Fin and Aumale provides proleptic versions of some future Byron. The play's opening thrusts us into the swirl of plot and counter-plot; Byron's interest in Aumale and La Fin and his ignorance of their full significance are clear. The trans-temporality of Byron's doubles – we have in effect a sequence of time-lapse photographs of days in the life of Byron – distinguishes Chapman's technique from the foil characters of Shakespearian or Marlovian drama.

Right from the start, then, with Aumale and Byron at the Archduke's court and the conspirators' first moves against the hero, character-doubling accentuates the most important subjects in the play: Byron's past in war, his present in peace, and their dual link in time and memory, as embodied in King Henry's favour. The technique achieves complex meaning through trans-temporality, through the powerful presentation of possible events and futures, and, more simply, through explicit reference to past traitors and former men of war. Chapman goes beyond Marston by using a form of Lyly's dramaturgy as a narrative and discursive means to engage the audience in the plot rather than in a significant disposition of the characters.

An alternative method of organizing an action and emphasizing its intellectual coherences associates certain characters and certain values with specific dramatic locales. Romantic comedies use the pastoral dichotomy of country and court or city, and later city comedies, even when they are confined to a single London street, frequently import a carefully defined group of characters, often landed gentry, from elsewhere. Tragedies by writers other than Shakespeare are less likely to employ such geographical pointers because multiple locales almost always require multiple plots, and multiple plots – perhaps in deference to classical practice and precept – are rarer in tragedy than in comedy. Yet, Middleton and Rowley's tragedy, *The Changeling*, vigorously exploits a two-place, two-plot structure, one of its several disconcerting similarities to *A Midsummer Night's Dream*. The play's scenes largely alternate between a madhouse in Alicante and the famous and mighty fortress–palace that dominates the town. In both locales, female beauty and male lust lead both men and women into 'madness', either (feigned) insanity or moral aberration; it gradually becomes clear that society needs protection from its putative protectors, asylum-keepers and castle-dwellers.

Self-conscious dramaturgy and dramatic illusion

In the late 1580s and 1590s, playwrights increasingly employ various narrative, 'framing', or 'distancing' devices: prologues and epilogues, inductions, dumbshows, choruses, presenter or commentator figures, and frame narratives. These devices may serve quite prosaic craftsmanly purposes. They describe action that cannot be represented mimetically; they fill in details (of character relationships or past events, for example) the playwright could not or did not wish to convey in other ways; they condense action. Thus, Skelton in Anthony Munday's *The Downfall of Robert, Earl of Huntingdon* (*Robin Hood, Part 1*) (1598) speaks for many contemporary playwrights: 'there are a many other things / That ask long time to tell them lineally, / But ten times longer will the action be' (2805–7). The devices themselves existed for a 'long time': some imitate classical drama (chorus, prologue), some extend back to the early Tudor period within the English secular dramatic tradition. Thomas Sackville and Thomas Norton's *Gorboduc* (1561), canonized as the first 'regular' English tragedy (five acts, iambic pentameter), elaborately frames its action: each act begins with an allegorical dumbshow, and the chorus appears at the end of each of the first four acts to interpret the dumbshow and draw connections between it and the matters we have just seen and heard.

Extra-dramatic personages – intermediaries between fiction and audience – could be used more complexly than *Gorboduc*'s chorus and dumbshows. At the English secular drama's very start, Henry Medwall's *Fulgens and Lucrece* (1497) opens with two memorable characters, 'A' and 'B', who emerge from a crowd of spectators. B explains to A the 'process', the plot, we are about to see performed. Eventually, A and B enter the fiction, respectively serving as pages to Lucrece's two suitors, and they close the play by arguing the merit of her choice of humble-but-virtuous Flaminus rather than the patrician Cornelius. Robert Greene employs virtually the same device almost one hundred years later in *James IV* (*c.*1591), where two characters from the frame play also enter a fiction (the principal drama) designed to demonstrate an abstract and satiric point. George Peele's *Old Wives Tale* (?1590–4) takes a step towards Pirandello by showing us Madge, the old wife of the title, narrating a romantic story (a wizard, a kidnapped damsel, knights on quest) that very soon comes to life before the eyes of her stage and theatre audiences: 'Soft, Gammer, here some come to tell your tale for you' (129–30). Narration becomes enactment for the length of her story, and the drama ends with a return to the original setting and group of characters.

Technically sophisticated as Medwall's, Greene's, and especially Peele's dramaturgy appears, other playwrights used simpler devices to frame and introduce their plays. The apologetic Prologue to Dekker's *Old Fortunatus* (1599), for example, speaks for 'our muse'. She asks

> That I may serve as chorus to her scenes;
> She begs your pardon, for she'll send me forth,
> Not when the laws of Poesy do call,
> But as the story needs.   (20–3)

Dekker's Muse had reason to be concerned. Instead of appearing regularly, as the 'laws of Poesy' require, the chorus returns only twice (before Acts 2 and 4 in modern editions), each time instructing the audience to imagine major shifts of place and the passage of much time. Marlovian prologues are typically less ingratiating and less overtly informative. *Tamburlaine*'s Prologue spurns ordinary theatrical fare:

> From jigging veins of rhyming mother wits,
> And such conceits as clownage keeps in pay,
> We'll lead you to the stately tent of war,
> Where you shall hear the Scythian Tamburlaine
>   .   .   .
> View but his picture in this tragic glass,
> And then applaud his fortunes as you please.   (1–4, 7–8)

Even when a Marlovian Prologue–chorus does later return to comment upon the action, its initial appearance can be equivocal and challenging:

> Not marching in the fields of Trasimene
> Where Mars did mate the warlike Carthagens,
> Nor sporting in the dalliance of love
> In courts of kings where state is overturned,
> Nor in the pomp of proud audacious deeds
> Intends our muse to vaunt his heavenly verse.
> Only this, gentles: we must now perform
> The form of Faustus' fortunes, good or bad. (*Dr Faustus*, Prologue, 1–8)

Prologue and chorus could merge more consistently into a 'presenter', an actor who set the scene at a play's opening and then returned, at moments roughly corresponding with points a classically inclined audience might regard as act divisions, to comment on the action, predict the future, and generally to serve as the audience's intermediary between theatre and fictional locale. Peele uses the device frequently in the 1590s and, as we have seen, John Skelton helps prepare the drama in Munday's two plays on Robert, Earl of Huntingdon (i.e., Robin Hood). Gower, the consciously anachronistic figure in *Pericles* (1608), is probably the best known such presenter.

At least from the 1560s, playwrights adapt the morality play Vice-figure to manipulate motivation and redirect action, and they consequently create a character who seems, like the presenter, half in and half outside the dramatic action.[32] Such later-Tudor Vices as Ambidexter (*Cambises*) or Revenge (*Horestes*) continue the medieval drama's easy familiarity with the audience. Directly addressing the spectators or commenting 'aside' to them, these characters elide or obscure the differences between play and spectator. Dramatic convention and conventional morality kept the audience from a whole-hearted emotional or intellectual alliance with the Vice, however conspiratorial or confiding.[33] Under changed circumstances of both convention and morality, the same techniques could be employed to ally our sympathies with a tragic hero, or comic rogue, or some still more complex combination of qualities. Marlowe's Machiavelli (Italian devil and outsider) and Tamburlaine (Scythian rebel and outsider) are kindred to the peculiar species of commentator–malcontent hero or heroic criminal that swarms through later plays, especially Jacobean tragedy and tragicomedy. Violent malcontents like Bussy (*Bussy D'Ambois*) and violent and clever ones like Malevole (*The Malcontent*), Vindice (*The Revenger's Tragedy*), and Bosola (*The Duchess of Malfi*) prowl the peripheries of their plays condemning, spurning and, too, gradually joining the characters and action from which they originally divorced themselves.

These characters mediate their represented worlds for the audience, and the increased psychological and dramatic self-consciousness of their plays is part of a wider phenomenon. When children's companies and the more intimate metropolitan indoor playing spaces are revived around 1600, the boys' acting strengths and the plays chosen to exploit those skills give an additional and sometimes strident fillip to dramatic performance as a self-conscious event. Ordinary audiences might now have a theatrical experience hitherto available only in plays prepared or specially adapted for court per-

---

[32] See my 'Early Shakespearian tragedy and its contemporary context: cause and emotion in *Titus Andronicus*, *Richard III* and *The Rape of Lucrece*' in Malcolm Bradbury and David Palmer, eds., *Shakespearian Tragedy*, Stratford-upon Avon Studies 20 (London, 1984), pp. 97–128.

[33] For the Vice's relation with the audience and his importance to dramatic construction, see Peter Happé, '"The Vice" and the popular theatre, 1547–80' in A. Coleman and A. Hammond, eds., *Poetry and Drama 1570–1700* (London and New York, 1981), pp. 13–31.

formance.[34] Typically, plays performed at court self-consciously acknowledge the unrepeatable occasion and unique, royal spectator; away from court and at first especially among the children's companies, a related sense of theatrical occasion generates a knowing (for Marston, smirking; for Jonson, pugnacious) embrace of the dramatic performance as performance. At court, monarch-as-spectacle equalled or exceeded the play-as-theatre; in the private and public theatres, fashionable or would-be fashionable audiences also gathered to be seen as well as to see.[35] Exploiting this interaction, playwrights begin to construct plays that openly and complexly represent themselves as things performed. Techniques of self-analysis, of characters withdrawing to comment upon their own represented behaviour as something itself enacted, are now integrated thematically.

Flamineo, in Webster's *The White Devil* (1612), is a good example of how the commentator or tool villain interacts with an increasingly self-conscious, 'rhetoricalized' dramatic representation.[36] The brilliant second scene displays Flamineo pandaring his sister, Vittoria, to his master, Duke of Bracciano. As he dupes Vittoria's vain, suspicious husband, Flamineo literalizes his status as go-between: he moves back and forth (or speaks louder and softer) between husband and wife in such a way that Camillo believes his brother-in-law heals their marital 'flaw' even as he argues Bracciano's case for adultery:

FLAMINEO ... sister (my lord attends you in the banqueting-house), your husband is wondrous discontented.
VITTORIA I did nothing to displease him, I carved to him at supper-time –
FLAMINEO (You need not have carved him in faith, they say he is a capon already, – I must now seemingly fall out with you.) Shall a gentleman so well descended as Camillo (a lousy slave that within this twenty years rode with the black guard in the duke's carriage 'mongst spits and dripping-pans) –
CAMILLO Now he begins to tickle her.
FLAMINEO An excellent scholar (one that hath a head fill'd with calves' brains without any sage in them), come crouching in the hams to you for a night's lodging?

· · ·

CAMILLO He will make her know what is in me.
FLAMINEO (*aside to Vittoria*) Come, my lord attends you, thou shalt go to bed to my lord.   (1.2.123ff.)

---

[34] Dekker's *Old Fortunatus* and Jonson's *Every Man out of his Humour*, for example, were printed with the extra text adapting them for court performance.

[35] See Orgel, *Illusion of Power, passim*; Goldberg, *King James I*, chapter 3; and Martin Butler's chapter, below, pp. 127–58.

[36] As it happens, *The White Devil* was originally and unsuccessfully produced at a public theatre; dramatic self-consciousness was not limited to the children's companies and their plays, although Flamineo has many cousins in the drama of Marston or Chapman, whose plays were performed by the children's companies.

Rejecting his mother's angry moral intervention, 'What? because we are poor, / Shall we be vicious?' (314–15), Flamineo claims court service has so far made him 'More courteous, more lecherous by far, / But not a suit the richer' and that only pandaring leads to 'preferment'. He concludes the scene with a smug and knowing soliloquy reminiscent of Mosca's praise of the 'parasite' (*Volpone*, 3.1):

> We are engag'd to mischief and must on:
> As rivers to find out the ocean
> Flow with crook bendings beneath forced banks,
> Or as we, to aspire some mountain's top,
> The way ascends not straight, but imitates
> The subtle foldings of a winter's snake,
> So who knows policy and her true aspect,
> Shall find her ways winding and indirect. (347–54)

Soliloquy and scene typify the dramaturgy of Webster's play, a play where numerous self-confident and self-complimenting 'politicians' – first, Flamineo and Bracciano; later, Monticelso and Francisco – spin murderous webs for guilty and innocent alike, and themselves later fall victim to some more competent villain. Each episode, each scene, seems to be framed and viewed in a variety, often a sequence, of political, moral, emotional perspectives. Those perspectives are embodied in a figure or figures who have a fluctuating involvement in the immediate action, sometimes watching and overhearing, at other times participating actively. It is hard to resist seeing such scenes as the 'conscious' product of the characters' scene-making skills, their ability as dramatists within the drama. This italicization of experience has several consequences. Experience in *The White Devil* is self-conscious experience; forms of self-awareness are a subject of the play, and one handled with high intellectual ambition. Theatrical metaphors are never far away, and the master of paradoxically over-confident criminality proves to be the master-manipulator, the manipulator of manipulators, the playwright himself. Further, when we see the play performed we are made self-consciously aware of the experience of experiencing the play. The degree of dramatic 'illusion' may vary, but it is never, and never finally, absolute. We observe, overhear, contemplate our own experience just as the characters do theirs.

Dramatic self-consciousness need not be only metaphorical or inferential. Numerous plays include dramatized preparations for, and often performances of dumbshows, masques, and plays: *Hamlet*, of course, but also such diverse examples as Brome's *The Antipodes* (already quoted), Chapman's *The Widow's Tears*, Tourneur's (or Middleton's) *The Revenger's Tragedy*,

Beaumont and Fletcher's *The Maid's Tragedy*, Webster's *The White Devil*, Middleton and Rowley's *The Changeling*, Middleton's *Women Beware Women*, Massinger's *The Roman Actor* (which contains no fewer than three inset plays), and the numerical winner, Fletcher and Co.'s *Four Plays, or Moral Representations in One* (*c.*1612), which presents four separate 'triumphs' or mini-dramas celebrating a dramatized royal wedding.[37] The local effects of inset dramas are naturally varied: always they provide additional spectacle, and they may have become more common after the Middlesex General Sessions prohibited crowd-pleasing jigs in 1612.[38] (Hamlet indirectly labels 'The Mousetrap', the most famous play-within-a-play, a 'jig' by naming himself 'your only jig-maker', and 'jig' seems to mean 'play' in the second chorus of Greene's *James IV*.) 'A masque is treason's licence' (*The Revenger's Tragedy*, 5.1.181), and inset dramas frequently advance, or murderously conclude, the action; they fulfil in miniature many functions served more expansively by sub-plots. Commonly, when the audience witnesses the preparations for a masque or playlet, the subsequent dramaticule (Samuel Beckett's term) appears bracketed or in quotation marks, emphasizing its own theatricality, duplicity, insubstantiality, and – by extension – that of the larger play, and – by further extension – that of the audience's own extra-theatrical existence, which might indeed be a theatre of the world or a theatre of God's judgements.

Even when plays lack a commenting malcontent or self-conscious villain, or when they lack inset dramatic or quasi-dramatic episodes, they often refer, directly and figuratively, to plays, players, and playing. Shakespeare's lines are, as always, the most familiar: Jaques brusquely dismisses Rosalind and Orlando, 'God buy you, and [if] you talk in blank verse' (*As You Like It*, 4.1.28–9); Fabian objects to the trick on Malvolio, 'If this were played upon a stage now, I could condemn it as an improbable fiction' (*Twelfth Night*, 3.4.121–3); Polonius recalls his role as Caesar; Hermione complains that her unhappiness 'is more / Than history can pattern, though devis'd / And play'd to take spectators' (*The Winter's Tale*, 3.2.33–5), and a Gentleman proclaims the romance-reunion of Perdita and Leontes 'like an old tale still' (5.2.59), and so forth. But such remarks are everywhere, and from an early

---

[37] *Five Plays in One* is known by its title only, although it may have been the same as the lost first part of *The Seven Deadly Sins*, where 'triumphs' or pageant-like shows of each sin could be expected. On this aspect of *The Roman Actor*, see Jonas Barish, 'Three Caroline "Defenses" of the stage' in A. R. Braunmuller and J. C. Bulman, *Comedy from Shakespeare to Sheridan*, pp. 194–212.

[38] See Gurr, *Playgoing*, p. 181, where he interprets some lines in James Shirley's *The Changes* to this effect, and pp. 45–6 above.

period. We have already heard Marston's Feliche claim 'Here might be made a rare scene of folly, if the plot could bear it', and about ten years before, Kyd's Revenge advises the ghost of Don Andrea, 'Here sit we down to see the mystery, / And serve for chorus in this tragedy' (*The Spanish Tragedy*, 1.1.89–90). When the eponymous hero of *Mucedorus* needs a disguise, Anselmo recostumes him as an actor in another play: he offers 'a cassock; / Though base the weed is, 'twas a shepherd's / Which I presented in Lord Julio's masque' (Scene 1), and Mouse makes a good joke in the next scene about the play's actor–bear: 'A bear? nay, sure it cannot be a bear, but some devil in a bear's doublet'.

Later than *The Spanish Tragedy* and *Mucedorus*, Henry Chettle's (or Anthony Munday's?) *The Tragedy of Hoffman* (c.1602; probably revived in the late 1620s), produces a revenger who has rigged up a mini-theatre near his cave. What seems to be a small, curtained alcove initially contains the skeleton of his executed father, hung up in chains, but Hoffman soon adds the corpse of Otho:

> Come, image of bare death, join side to side
> With my long injured father's naked bones.
> He was the prologue to a Tragedy
> That, if my destinies deny me not,
> Shall pass those of Thyestes, Tereus,
> Jocasta or Duke Jason's jealous wife.
> So shut our stage up: there is one act done
> Ended in Otho's death. 'Twas somewhat single;
> I'll fill the other fuller ...   (1.3. 405–13)

Later, Hoffman orders a henchman, 'now or never play thy part; / This act [another murderous trick] is even our tragedy's best heart' (3.2. 1341–2), a line anticipating Vindice's too quickly satisfied remark at an enemy's death, 'When the bad bleeds, then is the tragedy good' (*The Revenger's Tragedy*, 3.5.205).

While these and many other examples seem to anticipate the literary self-consciousness familiar in modern and post-modern works, the earlier references resonate in a different metaphorical system. Princes, preachers, and poets found themselves and all humanity playing roles in *theatrum mundi*, the theatre of the world, a faint but morally pregnant anticipation of eternal life where we will see face to face, not through the dark glass – the mirror, reflection, or play – of what St Paul calls 'imperfect knowledge' (1 Corinthians 13.9–12). Samuel Beckett's references to 'underplot', 'soliloquy', 'a multitude in transports of joy' (i.e., the audience) in *Endgame* operate within the closed system of his play, all earlier plays, and our percep-

tion; superficially similar references in Renaissance drama are both metaphorical and, for the Christian believer, compellingly literal.

The Elizabethan and Stuart professional theatre was hardly ever a theatre of
illusion, hardly ever a theatre manifesting the verisimilar reality of represented beings and events. Instead, it created an intellectual and emotional para-
reality, a quick forge and working-house of thought, where disbelief was not
suspended because verisimilar belief was not invoked.[39] The numerous
examples of 'self-conscious dramaturgy', moments when the play acknowledges its status as play or fiction, are not breakings of an illusion, but blunter
statements of a continuously evident state of affairs and are, usually, ways the
play draws attention not to itself but to the issues and sensations of self-
consciousness or of playmaking. As we have seen, Tudor and Stuart plays
treat dramatic illusion and self-conscious dramaturgy variously, and the
most sophisticated examples exist alongside simple or tangential ones. Yet
the two are always interconnected, and almost always quite distinct from
dramatic illusion as propounded on the realistic or naturalistic stage of the
nineteenth and twentieth centuries, unless the illusion lies in the (imagined)
dramatic feats of a conjuror, a wizard, or some divine or supernatural being,
or perhaps in certain stage effects such as blazing stars, comets, and the
like.[40] Instead, the audience is explicitly invited to collaborate in its dramatic
experience, to create an illusion for itself.[41] This condition naturally means

[39] See R. A. Foakes, 'Forms to his conceit: Shakespeare and the uses of stage-illusion',
Proceedings of the British Academy 66 (1982 for 1980), 103–19.

[40] See R. B. Graves, 'Elizabethan lighting effects and the conventions of indoor and outdoor
theatrical illumination', *RenD* n.s. 12 (1981), 51–69. Graves's very different interest cor-
roborates the argument I make against 'illusionistic' staging: Renaissance dramatists
brought real or real-appearing lighting instruments on stage not to increase illumination,
although they had that effect, but to indicate darkness: 'Light paradoxically represented
darkness, and as such must be accounted not illusionistic' (p. 56). While the Renaissance
theatre was generally unillusionistic, canons of verisimilitude were much less rigid than
neo-classical or naturalistic ones: in Middleton's *Game at Chess* (1624), the Black Bishop
represents the Conde Gondomar, until recently the Spanish ambassador, and the actor
appeared on stage in the very litter Gondomar had used as he travelled about London.
The title-page of Thomas Scott's *The Second Part of Vox Populi* (1624) illustrates
Gondomar's 'chair of ease' and the litter.

[41] Prologues and commendatory verses often emphasize the 'as if' quality of the audience's
emotional involvement: they should 'Think ye see / The very persons of our noble story /
As they were living' (Prologue, *Henry VIII*); they should feel 'A real passion by a counterfeit' (Thomas Stanley's prefatory poem to the Beaumont and Fletcher first folio, 1647).
Pursuing almost the opposite point to mine, Richard Levin collects numerous such passages in 'The relation of external evidence to the allegorical and thematic interpretation of
Shakespeare', *ShakS* 13 (1980), 1–29, esp. pp. 11–21.

that the degree of imaginative involvement, the degree to which the audience 'really believes', will vary throughout the play; self-conscious remarks or episodes are obvious ways in which the dramatist may control, or at least influence, the audience's experience. Furthermore, it seems likely that some of the audience all the time and all of the audience some of the time will be at Dr Johnson's extreme, 'always in their senses', always aware of the 'wooden O', the rain on the neck, the smell of tallow or latrine. Only romantic and post-romantic prejudice makes such a condition seem anti- or un-dramatic, and only neo-classical prejudice (Dr Johnson's own, in fact) sees such a condition as detrimental to dramatic pleasure, or indeed relevant to one's pleasure in plays at all.

Thomas Kyd's influential *Spanish Tragedy* shows how collaborative illusion and un-illusioning and renewed illusion might coexist in a stable and satisfying tension. Surrounded by his numerous victims, Hieronimo concludes his fatal playlet thus:

> Haply you think, but bootless are your thoughts,
> That this is fabulously counterfeit,
> And that we do as all tragedians do:
> To die today, for fashioning our scene,
> The death of Ajax, or some Roman peer,
> And in a minute starting up again,
> Revive to please tomorrow's audience.
>
> (*The Spanish Tragedy*, 4.4.76–82)

Examples are best precepts.

Bibliography

DRAMATURGY
Early studies of Renaissance dramaturgy often approach the plays with an Ibsen-induced bias, tracing various techniques, plot devices, and conventional characters: Mabel Buland, *The Presentation of Time in the Elizabethan Drama* (1912); Harriott Ely Fansler, *The Evolution of Technic in Elizabethan Tragedy* (1914); V. O. Freeberg, *Disguise Plots in Elizabethan Drama* (1915); Clarence V. Boyer, *The Villain as Hero in Elizabethan Tragedy* (1916); Doris Fenton, *The Extra-Dramatic Moment in Elizabethan Plays before 1616* (1930); Paul V. Kreider, *Elizabethan Comic Character Conventions* (1935; reprinted 1975). Robert S. Forsythe, *The Relations of Shirley's Plays to the Elizabethan Drama* (1914; reprinted 1965) tabulates the earlier Elizabethan and Stuart dramatic appearances of plot devices and some character types in James Shirley's plays, and David Klein, *Literary Criticism from the Elizabethan Dramatists* (1910; reprinted 1963) collects many self-referential passages. Less teleological but often still formalist works include: M. C. Bradbrook, *Themes and Conventions of Elizabethan Tragedy* (1935); Howard Baker, *Induction to Tragedy: A Study in the Development of Form in 'Gorboduc', 'The Spanish Tragedy', and 'Titus Andronicus'*

(1939); Mary C. Hyde, *Play-writing for Elizabethans 1600–1605* (1949); Wolfgang Clemen, *English Tragedy before Shakespeare: The Development of the Set Speech*, trans. T. S. Dorsch (1961); Madeleine Doran, *Endeavors of Art: Development of Form in Elizabethan Drama* (1954); M. C. Bradbrook, *The Growth and Structure of Elizabethan Comedy* (1955); David Bevington, *From 'Mankind' to Marlowe: Growth of Structure in the Popular Drama of Tudor England* (1962); Thelma N. Greenfield, *The Induction in Elizabethan Drama* (1969); Richard Levin, *The Multiple Plot in English Renaissance Drama* (1971). Thomas G. Pavel, *The Poetics of Plot: The Case of English Renaissance Drama*, Theory and History of Literature 18 (1985) examines plot structure through a poetics based on transformational grammar. Relevant chapters or sections also appear in books on wider topics; see, for example: Una Ellis-Fermor, *The Jacobean Drama: An Interpretation*, 4th edn (1958); Raymond Williams, *Drama in Performance* (1968; rev. edn 1972); Arthur C. Kirsch, *Jacobean Dramatic Perspectives* (1972); Peter Ure, *Elizabethan and Jacobean Drama* (1974); G. K. Hunter, *Dramatic Identities and Cultural Tradition* (1978); Lee Bliss, *The World's Perspective: John Webster and the Jacobean Drama* (1983); E. M. Waith, *Patterns and Perspectives in English Renaissance Drama* (1988).

TEXTS

I cite original printings and the following editions, modernizing the spelling where necessary: from the Revels series, *Arden of Faversham*, ed. M. L. Wine (1973); Robert Greene, *James IV*, ed. Norman Sanders (1970); Thomas Kyd, *The Spanish Tragedy*, ed. Philip Edwards (1959); Christopher Marlowe, *Tamburlaine, Parts 1 and 2*, ed. J. S. Cunningham (1981); John Marston, *The Malcontent*, ed. G. K. Hunter (1975); Cyril Tourneur, *The Revenger's Tragedy*, ed. R. A. Foakes (1966); John Webster, *The White Devil* (1960) and *The Duchess of Malfi* (1964), ed. J. R. Brown; from the Regents' Renaissance Drama series (Lincoln, Nebraska), Richard Brome, *The Antipodes*, ed. Ann Haaker (1966); Robert Greene, *Friar Bacon and Friar Bungay*, ed. Daniel Seltzer (1963); John Lyly, *Gallathea*, ed. Anne Lancashire (1969); John Marston, *Antonio and Mellida*, ed. G. K. Hunter (1965); Thomas Middleton and William Rowley, *The Changeling* (1966), ed. G. W. Williams; from the Malone Society Reprints (Oxford), Henry Chettle, *The Tragedy of Hoffman*, ed. Harold Jenkins (1951); Thomas Middleton, *The Witch*, eds. W. W. Greg and F. P. Wilson (1950); Anthony Munday, *The Downfall of Robert, Earl of Huntingdon* (1965) and *The Death of Robert, Earl of Huntingdon* (1967), ed. J. C. Meagher; Thomas Kyd, *Works*, ed. F. S. Boas (1901); and Thomas Preston, *Cambises*, ed. R. C. Johnson (1975).

3 Drama and society

The purpose of playing, whose end, both at the first and now, was and is to hold as 'twere the mirror up to nature, to show virtue her own feature, scorn her own image, and the very age and body of the time his form and pressure.   (*Hamlet*, 3.1.20–4)

Literature and history

These familiar lines contain familiar metaphors. Hamlet, of course, was talking about acting, and it is not too difficult to appreciate the aptness of the conceit when considering a play in performance. Some acting *is* based on mimicry or 'mirroring' – indeed the lines could be used to describe either the plain glass of theatrical 'realism' or the distorted glass of a satire. Unfortunately, however, to understand theatre fully we have to understand not only performance but what helps to generate performance, the dramatic text. Mirror metaphors and the metaphors that derive from painting – dramatic 'portraits' etc. – can, it turns out, often be mystificatory when we attempt to describe the workings of a text, made not of images but of words. Even more unfortunately, these 'reflection' metaphors have been prevalent in the *criticism* of poetry and drama from early in its history. This has had the effect of making the writing of an essay like this on 'drama' and 'society' exceedingly difficult.

It is obvious from these opening sentences that some discussion of theory must stand as a prologue to a consideration of our topic. My purpose in what follows, however, is not to threaten the reader with high, astounding abstractions but to generate a sense of method – a necessity because of the wide variety of evidence to be considered.

One avenue of approach for an essay of this kind might be through a study of the relationship between *theatre* and society, paying attention to audiences, the economics of playing, etc.; another leads to examination of the relationship between dramatic literature and *ideas*.[1] (An approach to *King Lear*

---

[1] See, for example, W. R. Elton, 'Shakespeare and the thought of his age' in Wells, *The Cambridge Companion to Shakespeare Studies*, pp. 17–34.

through 'ideas' might lead us to see Edmund as an incarnation of a malignant 'nature': an alternative, *ideological*, approach to the play would take into account its cultural forms and the social processes of its time, and demonstrate how, for example, it could be held to be right for a 'natural son' to be dispossessed of a share in his father's land [see 1.2.16].)

Our task is to sift through certain primary and most complex evidence, dramatic texts, considered as far as is possible as designed for performance, and to test what is now emerging as a consensus view: that in the theatres of the period could be played out contests between, on the one hand, the hegemonic interests of the state and the city, and, on the other, oppositional, and sometimes subversive, readings of state affairs or the proclamation of city vice. There is, in other words, evidence not only of cultural unity but of cultural division. The fact that players operated under the patronage of courtiers may not mean that the drama they presented embodied court values, although it is seldom that the institution of *monarchy* itself is criticized. (Specifically, as Martin Butler has shown [*Theatre and Crisis 1632–1642*], there was no continuous evolution from Elizabethan and Jacobean theatre to a 'Cavalier' theatre serving an élite audience and the royalist cause.) Indeed from about the 1580s theatres took forward the cause of 'reform' at about the very moment that church reformers ceased to deploy godly plays, ballads, and images, and turned from iconoclasm to iconophobia.[2] Theatre is *re*presentation: kings become 'subjects' in the sense that the monarchy and many other institutions become the subjects of the playwrights' analytic endeavours.[3] In an age where literacy was limited, the dramatists served some of the roles of modern journalists: *Swetnam the Woman Hater* (1617–18?), *The Witch of Edmonton* (1621), and *A Game at Chess* (1624) are theatrical essays on contemporary issues (the last a sharp attack on royal policy), and *The Jew of Malta* (*c.*1589) and *Richard II* (1595) were revived in response to particular events.

Perhaps, moreover, as a complement to the claim of Aristotle in the *Poetics* that literature is more universal than history, it is time to stress the *specificity* of the action of the plays of the English Renaissance. Their detail of reference and intricacy of plot generate scepticism or reveal the *lack of correspondence*[4] between theological and moral ideals and political and social

---

[2] See Patrick Collinson's 1985 Stenton Lecture, *From Iconoclasm to Iconophobia: The Cultural Impact of the Second English Reformation* (Reading, 1986).

[3] See David Scott Kastan, 'Proud majesty made a subject: Shakespeare and the spectacle of rule', *SQ* 37 (1986), 459–75.

[4] This is a key term in the writings of E. M. W. Tillyard – see, for example, *Shakespeare's History Plays* (London, 1944), pp. 12ff.

realities. As Brecht showed, dramatic literature can be a reflection *on* experience and not just a reflection *of* it.

What Shakespeare fails to mention in these lines from *Hamlet*, and what has been so much neglected, at least in the British tradition, is language. Historically language has been 'overlooked', regarded as unproblematic. If earlier writers of criticism had a theory it was based on a 'realistic' model. 'Common sense' led to the assumption that the world exists in an unproblematic way and that language serves to reflect or mirror its reality. Meaning is a function of intentional reference to that world, whether this is held to be constituted of objects or states represented by 'facts'. Accordingly – and misleadingly – texts have been held to be simply transparent: we could 'look through' them, it was assumed, to 'realities' or to the author. Early attempts at Marxist critiques of the drama, based on a deterministic relationship between material realities and authorial points of view were equally oblivious to the functioning of language. I will argue that we must concentrate on the texts, their kinds of opacity, and the ways they themselves function as historical evidence.

The work of the current generation of critics has demonstrated the way in which language is not just a function of reality but a factor that itself serves to constitute that reality. Some writers have claimed that meaning may derive not only from reference to the world but from differential relationships in a language system; their arguments have made it almost impossible for us to use the word 'realist' or its derivatives again. We have also, as a consequence, become self-conscious about a second critical metaphor, that of art as 'expression'. Texts were long held to 'express' the point of view of the author who individually and uniquely created them, to be a simple function of the author's intention. But now it is hard to believe that the author is the source of *all* meaning. Dramatic discourse is composed out of language that comes to the author deeply imprinted with ideology, or we may prefer to think of the author composing his text out of a *number* of languages that work in dialogue with one another.[5] Even if we do not fully accept this and do not believe that we are trapped in the prison house of language, we are aware that a *dramatist's* representation of the world is shaped not only by the cultural forms of, say, genre and characterization that he uses, but by the collective endeavours and material realities of the companies and theatres in which he worked, factors that derive as much from his social milieu as from

---

[5] See Mikhail Bakhtin, *The Dialogic Imagination*, trans. C. Emerson and M. Holquist (Austin, Texas, 1981); cf. Michel Foucault, 'What is an author?' in Paul Rabinow, ed., *The Foucault Reader* (Harmondsworth, 1984), pp. 101–20.

any point of view which he may wish to 'express'. Instead of looking, therefore, at the 'signified' of the text and the 'historical realities' to which it may
relate, we must look at the *processes* of signification within the text. It is for
this kind of reason that I have not worked my way in this essay through a
series of chosen authors.

The critical revolution which has led us to abandon the realist–expressive
theory of language has affected not only our notions of art and literature but
of history and society. 'History', as we must now realize, is not 'truth' but
'fiction': no value-free, literal, or scientific historical narrative or account is
possible. Many historians perforce arrange their accounts of events into narratives that can be analysed with the same tools we apply to what are
obviously prose fictions, and historical personages become stylized characters not only in Renaissance chronicles but in Marx. (This is not to deny that
there is a real material history with which these fictions might engage.) The
so-called 'history plays' of the period ought, as we have implied in this
volume, to be redesignated 'political plays'. They are no mere chronicles or
reports upon the events of the reigns they portray but are dramatic essays on
the institution of kingship and on the origins, nature, and transfer of power.
So too 'society', what Hamlet calls 'the body of the time', is not, as he
somewhat misleadingly implies, a material reality but another species of fiction. What we claim to be the truth about an age is not 'there' simply to be
measured, but is something we make. Moreover, like Jonson's Justice
Overdo, 'we hear with other men's ears; we see with other men's eyes'
(*Bartholomew Fair*, 2.1.29–30). When we try to describe the totality of a
community, therefore, or to anatomize (an Elizabethan metaphor) Hamlet's
body politic, we must remind ourselves that we are working not with 'reality'
but with a model, a mental construct – what Hamlet calls a 'form'. The
nature of the model, as anthropologists have had to remind themselves
recently, will depend not only on ascertainable or measurable facts but on
the premises, ideological premises, upon which we build it, the questions
that we ask, the categories we construct.

When we turn again to the other side of our investigation, dramatic texts
(without a time machine we can't investigate performances), we have to
remind ourselves that there are many ways of seeing. All we have are texts
and texts are often structured around debates, sometimes unresolved. The
act of translation from text to performance, moreover, could well have been
an act of transformation. (It may well be paradigmatic of the act of reading,
for all reading is 'reading into'.) That said, I would want to resist the claim of
a recent social historian that literature belongs in a secondary category of the
'imaginative' as opposed to the documentary evidence with which he is

familiar.[6] Dramatic texts *do* offer a record, highly mediated, of the period's perceptions of itself, sometimes of an event or series of events – even if this is only a performance or series of performances. We must have the confidence, therefore, to regard literature as 'in history', although we must be aware of the mediation. Conversely history (as an ideological determinant of *criticism*) is 'in literature': we must remember not only possible differences between text and realization but seek to examine and make explicit our own assumptions or premises, assumptions about the purpose of playing and the composition of the societies in little, the audiences that saw early performances, that affect not only our perception of society but our perceptions of the artistic genres constructed and deployed at any historical moment. As Stephen Orgel put it succinctly in a recent edition of the play: '*The Tempest* is a text that looks different in different contexts'.[7]

This essay attempts not only to relate drama to a complex period but to survey a span of almost a hundred years that concluded in the run-up to a civil war. There is no space for narrative, but what follows is predicated on the assumption that this was an age of radical change that ran roughly from what has been termed the 'Mid-Tudor Crisis' through to the Civil War. This said, we are ready to dislodge another misleading metaphor, again derived from the visual arts, the notion of historical 'background', not only unchanging but inert. Moreover we must confront anew the problem, every time that we deal with a particular text, of whether to start from the 'history' or from the 'text'. 'History' is no mere 'background' and a 'text' is no mere reflector. Instead, we must learn to distinguish cultural forms and perhaps take our cue from Sir Philip Sidney, who spoke of literature as predominantly metaphorical, a 'figuring forth'[8] – or from modern anthropologists. Stephen Greenblatt, whose work shows the influence of anthropology, argues that 'anthropological interpretation must address itself less to the mechanics of customs and institutions than to the *interpretive constructions* [emphasis added] the members of a society apply to their experiences'.[9] Literary texts, in other words, provide evidence not necessarily of the realities of the period nor of the opinions of their authors but rather of the imaginative and ideological constructions, the *mentalités* of a period. This essay will therefore concentrate where possible on language or discourse. Its premise is that the theatres often served the populace as instruments of

---

[6] Sharpe, *Early Modern England*, pp. 56–7.
[7] Shakespeare, *The Tempest*, ed. S. Orgel (Oxford, 1987), p. 11.
[8] *An Apology for Poetry*, ed. G. Shepherd (Manchester, 1973), p. 101.
[9] Greenblatt, *Renaissance Self-Fashioning*, p. 4.

demystification, probing, for example, the processes of signification that served to legitimate power as authority.[10]

But first, we should examine how historians are mapping the early modern period at the moment, and consider how, under the influence of recently developed theories of language and culture, critics are able to play their part in this revisionary endeavour.

The condition of England

From a modern point of view, England in our period was, compared with other European countries at the time, an orderly and well-governed society. To contemporaries, however, it did not feel like that. 'All coherence is gone', said Donne; Jonson used the transforming power of alchemy as the informing symbol of one of his comic masterpieces; and many other of his contemporaries felt that their world was changing fast:

Is change strange? 'Tis not the fashion unless it alter: monarchs turn to beggars, beggars creep into the nests of princes, masters serve their prentices, ladies their serving-men, men turn to women.   (*Honest Whore, Part 1*, 4.3.130–3)

Here is a statement about social mobility which resonates out from a story of intrigue. 'Fashion', indeed, is a key word in this and many other plays of the age, and, conversely, certain dramatists resist the demands of comedy which require that characters be reaccommodated into an ideal order by the time the play ends.

Earlier cultural historians were not good at incorporating this dynamic into their accounts. The myth of Merry England, ruled not by a mortal woman but by Gloriana, dates from the period itself and is celebrated notably, for example, by Dekker in his *Old Fortunatus* (1599). Dekker himself took his theatrical iconography from courtly dramatic entertainments, and this myth has informed not only introductions to Renaissance drama for school children but far too many scholarly works. Working from 'the Elizabethan World Picture' – which is not a picture but a diagram derived from the desires of the Renaissance élite to legitimate inequality by calling it 'order' – a neat model of a static, stratified, hierarchical society was created, and it was assumed that most women and men were happy about their place in it.

The reality was different. 'Corresponding to nothing in the experience or speculative thought of the age, this creed of absolutism served chiefly to bolster up a precarious monarchy which lacked a standing army or an effi-

---

[10] Jonathan Dollimore, 'Shakespeare, cultural materialism, and the new historicism' in Dollimore and Sinfield, *Political Shakespeare*, p. 6; see also Richard Tuck, '*Power* and *Authority* in seventeenth-century England', *The Historical Journal* 17 (1974), 43–61.

cient police force'.[11] Shakespeare's bumbling constables Dogberry and Elbow are no mere comic figures but indices of the limits of rule. In England, moreover, there was no tradition of building up a 'middle class' to provide a stabilizing bureaucracy – offices were held through court patronage – and the interests of citizens and merchants were by no means supportive of the court. Overall, rank and status were giving way to wealth and property. We may not wish to talk of a crisis of the aristocracy, but social change *had* diminished the prominence of the nobility while religious passions might well demolish hierarchy. The uneasy relationships between old nobility and hereditary titles on the one hand, and the newly enriched on the other, a subject Massinger made his own, was contributing to the crisis. Particular effects of this, the sale of titles instituted by King James and the indebtedness of unthrifty noblemen and gentlemen to moneylenders, professionals, and merchants, are commonplaces in the drama. In *The Devil is an Ass* (1616) Jonson offered lines that are doubtless based on the figure of metempsychosis and which were to appear in Webster's *The Devil's Law-Case* (1616–19):

> why look you,
> Those lands that were the clients' are now become
> The lawyers'; and those tenements that were
> The country gentleman's, are now grown
> To be his tailor's.
> (*The Devil's Law-Case*, 2.1.163–7; compare *The Devil is an Ass*, 2.4.33–7)

The interpretive construction from 'nature', 'grown', is ironic, given that Webster is responding to cultural change and not natural evolution.

Political plays and comedies alike suggest, moreover, that rule and order might not extend into the 'alternative societies' of the tavern or the brothel-infested 'suburbs' of the capital, or, more indirectly, the festive or 'green' worlds that lie at the heart of the carnivalesque experience. Princes might propose but the clowns disposed: Falstaff demonstrates that England will never be totally governable, as we can see from the way in which life continues in Gloucestershire (in *Henry IV, Part 2*) untroubled by affairs of state. The sumptuary laws which laid down regulations compelling individuals to dress according to their degree suggest an unsuccessful attempt to conserve a fast-changing social structure, and are generally referred to in the theatre with considerable irony.[12] One of the most famous lines of the age, Tam-

---

[11] Lever, *The Tragedy of State*, p. 5.

[12] See, for example, *The Two Angry Women of Abington*, 2.1.848; see also Jardine, *Still Harping on Daughters*, pp. 146 and 154; see N. B. Harte, 'State control of dress and social change in pre-industrial England' in D. C. Coleman and A. H. John, eds. *Trade, Government and Economy in Pre-Industrial England* (London, 1976), pp. 132–65.

burlaine's 'Lie here, ye weeds that I disdain to wear' (*Tamburlaine, Part 1*, 1.2.41), proclaims the hero's contempt for a world that would keep a man like him as a shepherd. (Any play that used disguise could, in this context, be taken as subversive.) Plays like *The Shoemaker's Holiday* (1599) that construct particular communities reveal during the course of their representation the fissures in their social fabric, even if they end with an assertion of a harmonious order.

The Life and Death of Jack Straw (*c.*1591) opens with the killing of the collector of the king's 'task' or tax. Although the text seems to be revealing thereby the limits of a state which lacked an accepted means of raising revenue, the political significance of the riot – the age's customary mode of self-expression for the poor – is here dissolved by mingling clowns with the rioters. Modern historians of the period also stress the limitations of the state, the way that the reach of government exceeded its grasp, or offer titles that contain 'crisis'. A representative author, Derek Hirst, offers, in *Authority and Conflict*, an opening chapter which concentrates on inflation and unemployment as well as the problems of plague and famine, the latter disingenuously presented by a patrician as a 'natural' phenomenon in *Coriolanus* (1.1.96ff.)

Other factors led to instability of social formations. We could note first certain effects of the 'educational revolution'. There was a massive increase in the number of university-educated males for whom neither honour nor office was obviously available. (The difficulties of the younger or dispossessed sons of the wealthy appear in plays as different as *As You Like It* [1599–1600] and *The City Madam* [1632].) I mention this first because this factor created a tribe of social critics who used the theatre as their pulpit – and the pulpit as their theatre. The 'university wits' and later John Marston, who was a member of the Middle Temple, provided the South Bank playhouses (situated across the river from the Inns of Court) and, later, the private houses with a diet of sardonic dramatic fare which reveals a deep scepticism about political and social forms (as well as about female virtue), and which seems to have been prepared for an audience of alienated male intellectuals. In *The Duchess of Malfi* (1614), Webster's 'malcontent' scholar Bosola has been described as 'neither villain nor hero, [a typification of] the plight of the intellectual in the world of state, at once its agent and victim'.[13]

Another of the most notable features of the English population in the period was its geographical mobility – and this in a society that liked to think

---

[13] Lever, *The Tragedy of State*, p. 10.

of itself as static. The stories of young people leaving home which figure so often in the drama derive not just from folk tale and romance. The court and law drew country gentry to the capital as did the market for labour: two per cent of the population migrated to London in each decade. The Jacobean city of night, that vision of an unstable metropolitan underworld that appears in the comedies of Middleton and others as a threat to the mercantile and industrious values of the capital, attracted the descriptive talents of pamphleteers and engaged dramatists like Jonson, who represented the phenomenon in texts as different as *Bartholomew Fair* (1614) and *The New Inn* (1629). Moreover, the violence of English public life, noted by diplomats and travellers, was recorded in the playhouses, and should not be written off as the natural content of drama, a fictional form which depends upon conflict, or as mere pandaring to popular desires for sensationalism.

The increase in the population was accompanied by a rapid development of capitalist enterprise, which was not matched by much change in the forms of organization of trade and industry. The rampant economic individualism of monopolizing merchants and grandee 'projectors' (like Jonson's Volpone) shouldered aside the collegiate ethos of producers and craftsmen, enshrined in the regulations of craft guilds and trade companies, and the feudal order and custom of the country were threatened by the energies of speculators like Sir Giles Mompesson, who appeared thinly disguised on the stage as Massinger's Overreach (*A New Way to Pay Old Debts* [1625]).

The late age at which people married in England (compared with continental Europe) also had its effects, creating a distinctive youth culture – witness the plays with prentice heroes. Women may often have attained more maturity than Shakespeare's fourteen-year-old Juliet manifests, although their work or the varieties of self-expression available to them are, as in any age, seldom represented. Overall, the dramatic texts may be taken to be as sceptical as they are supportive of the assumption that the virtue of a woman depended wholly on her chastity or fidelity, and of the double standard ('`Tis a greater shame / For women to consent than men to ask')[14] which condoned male promiscuity.

Divisions between rich and poor were increasing:

> England is grown to such a pass of late,
> That rich men triumph to see the poor beg at their gate.
>
> (*The Life and Death of Jack Straw*, 1.1.78–9)

Crime seemed to be rising, provoking an alliance of ministry and magistracy

---

[14] *Swetnam the Woman Hater* (London, 1618), sig. D3v; see Keith Thomas, 'The double standard', *Journal of the History of Ideas* 20 (1959), 195–216.

which called for draconian punishments.[15] It could even be that a minor character in *Measure for Measure* (1603), the Provost, is in fact a provost-marshal (compare Jonson's *The Alchemist*, 1.1.170), indicating that 'Vienna' is being subject to a regime invoked only in time of war. It was under the Tudors that executions were turned into theatrical set-pieces – and so they appear in plays like *The Spanish Tragedy* (c.1587) and *The Atheist's Tragedy* (1611). A play like *Measure for Measure*, on the other hand, seems very sceptical of any attempt to criminalize sin, as is, more indirectly, *A Woman Killed with Kindness*, a play of the same year.

Yet it is often claimed that the eventual political upheaval of the Civil War did not result from social–economic upheaval but from politics and religion. Although the conditions of the poor deteriorated, social tensions did not become critical, perhaps because of the achievement of the Elizabethan Poor Law. In a significant aside, Andrew Gurr refers to the period as being inhabited by 'such a tame society'.[16] If this was so, theatres must have been all the more provocative in the hard ideological questions they asked even if they did not foster popular *revolution*:[17] the poor generally appear as comic rather than deserving figures, and it is seldom that insurrectionary episodes are portrayed sympathetically.

It is indeed difficult to talk of class consciousness in this pre-industrial age, although the popular drama may provide historians with evidence which they have tended to overlook.[18] Certainly it is wrong to construct a model of political practice in which *parties* based on class or status interests appear. Early modern England was fought over by religious and political factions (often based on patronage groups) rather than parties. However, what Beaumont called 'the ordinary and over-worn trade of jesting at lords and courtiers and citizens' (Prologue to *The Woman Hater*, 1606) does suggest that the theatres of the time were important instruments in fomenting populist sentiments.

The ideology that sustained authority, both in the state and in the family, was based on patriarchalism. The influential puritan Richard Sibbes surely had society as well as theology in mind when he wrote, 'The word "Father" is an epitome of the whole gospel.' The fifth commandment, 'Honour thy father and thy mother', was, despite its reference to both parents, the most

---

[15] Collinson, *The Religion of Protestants*, pp. 159ff.

[16] *Playgoing*, p. 58.

[17] See Margot Heinemann's chapter in this volume, and Anat Feinberg, 'The representation of the poor in Elizabethan and Stuart drama', *Literature and History* 12 (1986), 152–63.

[18] Compare Fletcher and Stevenson, *Order and Disorder*. They argue against the notion of a polarized society (pp. 1–15).

frequently cited justification of obedience to political authority in the seventeenth century.[19] This meant that political authority could be legitimated by
reference to the authority of the father and vice versa. Many plays are concerned with the problem of patriarchal authority in household and state alike
– tragedies like *The Duchess of Malfi*, 'histories' like *Henry IV*, and comedies
like *The Shoemaker's Holiday* – and others with the related phenomenon of
masterless men (see, for example, *Bartholomew Fair*).

The court

Bearing in mind Greenblatt's admonition that we consider not just the structure and workings of institutions but 'the interpretive constructions members
of a society apply to their experiences', let us consider three institutions, the
court, the city, and the family. Dramatists acted as intelligencers to the
nation, not only seeing through the cult of monarchical magnificence and the
veneers created for the purposes of performance and patronage to the realities of the private behaviour of courtiers – especially their sexual behaviour –
but also subjecting the whole institution of the court to a more radical
critique. If the 'political nation' by and large accepted royal authority,
dramatists in plays like, for example, Beaumont and Fletcher's *The Woman
Hater*, seem to have wanted to expose the conspicuous consumption and
conspicuous display of courtiers, their 'ten pound suppers' and their rich
attire costing a 'lord's revenue', and to anatomize the ambivalence of the
court, the problems that derived from its functioning as a dual fountainhead,
of rule and of justice. Jonson, Marston, and Chapman were all prosecuted in
various ways for their 'seditious and slanderous' presentations of court life.
(The vision of court corruption that informs the plays of Tourneur and
Webster was turned to a kind of documentary: when the Earl and Countess
of Somerset were tried for the murder of Sir Thomas Overbury in 1615,
contemporary reports of the affair made it seem as though life was imitating
art.)

St Paul had written 'Let every soul be subject unto the higher powers: for
there is no power but of God, and the powers that be are ordained of God'
(Romans 13.1 [Geneva version]). This premise informs early notions of the
'state'. In the later Middle Ages the word can mean the condition of things, a
divinely sanctioned order. In social terms – the word is related to 'estate' – it
can mean high rank: 'Can you not be content with state and rule, / But you
must come to take away my crown', says the king to some dissident nobles in
a play of 1618, *Swetnam the Woman Hater* (1.1.39–40). By the early seven-

---

[19] Hirst, *Authority and Conflict*, p. 50.

teenth century the word had also achieved one of its modern meanings, a particular political structure open to analysis and change. 'States [are] great engines [that] move slowly', wrote Bacon in *The Advancement of Learning* (II.xxiii.1): the mechanistic metaphor will supplant the older metaphors like 'body politic' or 'commonweal[th]' that figure, say, in the discourse of the lower orders in Shakespeare. Hamlet's metaphor 'something is rotten in the state of Denmark' (1.4.90) shows the word poised precariously between the first and third of these meanings. There are similar ideological resonances in the opening soliloquy of Bussy D'Ambois, written a couple of years later:

> Fortune, not Reason, rules the state of things,
> Reward goes backward, Honour on his head;
> Who is not poor, is monstrous; only Need
> Gives form and worth to every human seed.
>
> (Chapman, *Bussy D'Ambois*, 1.1.1–4)

In England, the state, power, and the administrative machine were, as Hamlet implies, centred around the court, and dramatists took as much care in establishing the nature of the political milieux within which their protagonists operated as they did in creating personalities for them. Revenge tragedies – *The Spanish Tragedy* or *Hamlet* – implicitly demonstrate that political realities do not match theological ideals. The opening lines of Webster's *The White Devil* (1612) reveal the contradiction:

> LODOVICO
> Banished?
>
> ANTONIO
>   It grieved me much to hear the sentence.
>
> LODOVICO
> Ha, ha, O Democritus thy gods
> That govern the whole world! Courtly reward,
> And punishment.   (1.1.1–4)

As Lodovico implies, courts have in fact two functions which are irreconcilable: in so far as they are centres of patronage the courts of princes offer reward, in so far as they are courts of law they must administer punishment. The popularity of revenge plays probably derived not only from their exciting stories and the opportunities they offered for the construction of psychologically interesting characters, but from the political charge they delivered: how was an individual to find justice if the fountainhead of justice was itself polluted?[20]

---

[20] See Michael Hattaway, *Hamlet: The Critics Debate* (London, 1987), pp. 81ff.

Courts of princes provided a metaphor for the relationships between those in love. Male lovers professed themselves 'servants' to their 'mistresses', particularly in the plays and masques of the Caroline period that celebrated Platonic love (which could be a figure for political allegiance). These interpretive metaphors drew attention to themselves by their tendentiousness, but may derive from a changing perception of the roles of husbands and wives – or simply be an inversion of realities.

In *Tamburlaine*, Marlowe had begun an anatomy of a world where the hero's 'complete armour and curtle-axe' are emblems of the reality of his power. In *The Jew of Malta* he sets the action on an island, which serves as a demonstration of the way that the 'state' is coterminous with the court. The play contains an outsize hero, a theatrical descendant of the Vices of medieval drama, who dies amidst a stage emblem that recalls medieval illustrations of the torments of the damned. The play is, therefore, a tragedy; but T. S. Eliot's categorization of it as a farce[21] may serve to alert us to the fact that it is concerned not simply with the fate of an individual but with the world in which he works. Like the Vices in earlier plays, Barabas is brought into being by the Christians who surround him. The play is overtly theatrical: it is full of asides, and the players are called upon to convey the delight that derives from the energy of their roles to the audience. This very theatricality, however, serves to offer an insight into the nature of power in Malta.

Much of the action involves political transactions, and not just intrigue and revenge. Ferneze, Governor of Malta, holds his title from the Turk, to whom he should pay tribute. That has not been collected for many years, giving Ferneze the semblance of absolute power, although the appearance of Calymath's Bashaws makes it apparent to the audience that power derives not from God but from a mightier man. As in England, there was no agreed method of raising taxes; the finance of the state was not separate from the finance of the prince. Moreover, power depends upon commodity, the wealth of the Jews which can be seized and used to buy off the Turks, and profit derives not from industry but from colonial adventuring and policy. The Jews may have no place in the political life of the island, but the island depends upon the trade they generate.

Barabas's energy and wit, his 'bravest policy' (3.3.12), please an audience. It has been conventional to label the hero a stage Machiavel, a bogey figure of evil who casts aside all the moral imperatives of his age. That figure is conjured by the sequence in which Barabas and Ithamore vie with one another in their accounts of the evil deeds they have perpetrated (2.3), but

[21] *Selected Essays*, p. 123.

the audience is aware not simply that Barabas may be essentially evil but also that he is an opportunist (see 5.2.44–5). He is a true Machiavellian: his power, it seems, derives from improvisation, analysing the moment, and energetically seizing the occasion. As Barabas himself says, policy begets authority (see 5.2.27–8). Moreover, there is little to distinguish Barabas in this respect from the Christians or Turks in the play. The isle is full of 'Jews', a point made economically in the Royal Shakespeare production (Swan Theatre, 1987), where one actor doubled Machiavel with Ferneze. And it is only by a supreme act of 'policy', betraying both Calymath and Barabas, that Ferneze acquires the power he had desired from the beginning of the action.

The city

The rapid increase in the population – from 120,000 in 1550 to 375,000 by 1650 – and in the wealth of London provoked a strenuous re-examination of the ambivalent metaphor of the city, site of both man's magnificence and his depravity. Volpone's opening speech, which begins 'Good morning to the day; and next my gold', heralds the brave new world of the city plutocrat. The speech is a kind of black mass, a blasphemous violation of a 'natural' order, demonstrating that money is not only the root of all evil but of all power. It begins a play which celebrates the opportunism, wit, energy, and sexiness associated with the reign of Mammon, but also a world where the ubiquitous pursuit of wealth means that characters are reduced to two kinds, knaves and fools, predators and prey. As a consequence the traditional assertions of comedy, love and justice, are transmuted to lust and revenge. However, the anti-acquisitive ethos adopted from older morality plays by Jonson and those who followed his lead in writing city comedies in the early years of the seventeenth century was not the only reaction to the expanding wealth of the metropolis. (This was indeed a fiction, given that Jonson's own patrons were maintaining their courtly life-style by monopolies, patents, and trading in offices.) Playhouses frequented by citizens had commissioned chronicle plays celebrating the brave new world of the city, its guilds, and the magnificence and bounty of its heroes like Sir Thomas Gresham; these plays are satirized in Beaumont's *The Knight of the Burning Pestle* (1607). Merchants became romantic heroes, metaphorically 'venturers', their argosies sailing home richly freighted with commodities from the Mediterranean and the Americas – these risk-takers have parasites as their anti-types. Once merchants could be knighted, the city developed its own gradations of rank: as Luke remarks in *The City Madam*:

> It [is] for the city's honour that
> There should be a distinction between
> The wife of a patrician, and plebeian.   (4.4.79–81)

Wealth-producing industry, however, is – as is usual in most periods – not represented: we seldom if ever see workers labouring at their vocation. Dramatists who, like Jonson, associated themselves with the court, produced a string of anti-bourgeois comedies, in which clever aristocrats outwit citizens, a reflection of the way 'the gentry scorn the city'.[22] (In *The Life and Death of Jack Straw* the rebellion ends when the Lord Mayor acts as champion of the king and slays the arch-rebel Jack Straw – an idealization of the loyalty of the city. It may be for this reason too that the city employed rival dramatists like Dekker to write legend-enacting pageants for the civic rituals which were so important in establishing London's sense of identity.) Accordingly we must not look for a modern radical anti-capitalist ethos in plays of this kind: the action is seen from the point of view not of the labouring poor but of the court. Although the consequences for the poor of the rapacity of the engrossing farmer Sordido are exposed in the first act of *Every Man out of his Humour* (1599), Jonson suggests that such a type is generally pilloried not because he 'is a villain, a wolf i'the commonwealth, but as he is rich and fortunate' (1.3.163–4). Aristocrat and citizen, however, did unite in exalting producers and craftsmen over merchants, monopolists, 'projectors', and speculators. Simon Eyre, hero of *The Shoemaker's Holiday*, is both maker and seller, craftsman and shopkeeper, whereas Jonson's Volpone and Subtle the Alchemist are speculators attempting to make wealth out of nothing. (Eyre amasses enough capital to rebuild the Leadenhall Market [21.130–4]: that fact is suppressed in favour of a celebration of his benefaction.)

The newness of the metropolitan phenomenon seems to have provoked the dramatists to invoke old-fashioned dramatic terms. From about the end of the sixteenth century devils appear not, as in *Doctor Faustus* (1588–92), as tempters of a great man's soul, but as metaphors for the uncontrollable forces of the city economy. Jonson registers the resort to archaism by having Pug, the hero of *The Devil is an Ass* (1616), conjure Vices who speak in fourteeners, a metre not used on the English stage for decades. The language of moral theology is widely applied to social transactions and social types, as in Middleton's *A Trick to Catch the Old One* (1605), where the usurer Dampit (i.e. 'Hell') occupies the moral centre of the play's portrayal of covetousness. As Jonson's Pug remarks:

---

[22] *The Devil is an Ass*, 3.1.31. It is not the case, however, that the nobility lacked economic acumen – see Sharpe, *Early Modern England*, pp. 156ff. In *Westward Ho!* and *Northward Ho!*, however, the citizens dupe the gallants.

> Can any fiend
> Boast of a better Vice than here, by nature
> And art, they're owners of.   (2.2.7–9)

The old vice of covetousness seemed so obviously manifest and focused in city activity that Massinger, some fifteen or twenty years after the appearance of Middleton's *A Trick to Catch the Old One*, sharpened up his satire by adapting its plot and moral schema in *A New Way to Pay Old Debts* to expose the machinations of a *country* land owner, Sir Giles Overreach, who was as successful in amassing land as his dramatic predecessors were in amassing gold. However, no matter how wealthy Sir Giles became, status eluded him. Only by marrying his daughter into the landed class could he make a show at court: the plot of the play, of course, denies him this satisfaction.

The continuing political and economic dominance of the court and the city, therefore, may explain why the country is seldom if ever represented directly. (This may be equally due to the fact that for the most part the players catered to metropolitan audiences.) It is generally a fictive place of resort, a festive, green, or comic world to which characters migrate while in some confusion from which they return to the city having achieved a degree of recognition. Alternatively it is allegorized: pastoral plays and the pastoralized gypsies who appear in dramatic entertainments of the Caroline period have all to do with court life and nothing with true rusticity.

Women and families

What can we say about the condition of women in Renaissance England? Rather than starting from 'history' or text, we might start from an 'interpretive construction', the proverb 'England is the paradise of women, the hell of horses, and the purgatory of servants'.[23] This would seem to imply that England was basically a patriarchal society, in which the popular view was that too many women were on top. However, while citing proverbs, we might remind ourselves of another: 'It is better to be a shrew than a sheep' (Tilley, S412), which reminds us of the manner in which similar social phenomena might be read in different ways. The proverbs taken together point to a problematic relationship between power and sex, in which female 'liberty' was seen as a threat to the whole social order. Local court records between

---

[23] This is the form in M. P. Tilley, *A Dictionary of the Proverbs in England in the Sixteenth and Seventeenth Centuries* (1950), E147 – it is cited in *Honest Whore, Part 2*, 4.1.168–9, and discussed by Jardine, *Still Harping on Daughters*, p. 134n.

about 1560 and 1640 'disclose an intense preoccupation with women who are a visible threat to the patriarchal system'.[24] The productive work that women might do (like that done by men) tended not to be portrayed in the drama, and the only available indices of female virtue were modesty, sexual chastity, and wifely constancy. Conversely any admission of the extent of patriarchal power must be censored. After publishing an anti-feminist tract, Misogynos (the title figure from *Swetnam the Woman Hater*) proclaims:

> How my books took effect! How greedily
> The credulous people swallowed down my hooks;
> How rife debate sprang betwixt man and wife!
> The little infant that could hardly speak
> Would call his mother whore. O, it was rare!   (sig. A4v)

Woman-haters in fact provided a comic type. They duly received their comeuppance – perhaps in deference to the women in the audience – after revealing how, in some instances at least, their misogyny stemmed from fear of feminine sexuality:

> Let not your furious rod that must afflict me
> Be that imperfect piece of nature
> That art makes up, woman, unsatiate woman.
>   (Beaumont and Fletcher, *The Woman Hater*, 3.1.6–8)[25]

The perception encoded in the first proverb quoted above may have been generated by economic realities. The military origins of land laws and the derivation of titles from chivalric orders certainly combined to disadvantage women, although laws governing dowries allowed married women a degree of economic control. All women, however, and their rights, were legally defined in terms of their marital status; that is, their participation in the common law was mediated through men. Women of the middling sort and above did, of course, play a central role in the control of a domestic *economy* which involved, unlike today's, many elements of production as well as consumption. This notwithstanding, 'the subordination of women was intensive, and did not only stem from the landed concerns of the gentry. "Skimmington rides", popular charivaris or shaming rituals directed at households where the wife ruled the roost, occurred over a wide area of England [see

---

[24] D. E. Underdown, 'The taming of the scold' in Fletcher and Stevenson, *Order and Disorder*, pp. 116–36.

[25] For what is virtually a dramatic monologue on woman ('an unfinished creature, delivered hastily to the world before Nature had set that seal which should have made them perfect') delivered by a page boy, see Chapman's *All Fools* (1601), 3.1.159ff.

12   A skimmington (from *Halfe a Dozen Good Wives: All for a Penny*
[London, 1635?])

Plate 12]. Still more harsh was the lot of poor and ugly women: eccentric behaviour could earn for these an accusation of witchcraft.'[26]

The fact that the political nation was not overtly divided until late in our period should not encourage us to overlook stress and division within communities and families. Recent historical demography has exploded two myths which probably derive from literature: first, that marriage took place at an early age (the early marriage of Shakespeare's Juliet was quite abnormal), and, second, that the normal pattern of living in England was based on the 'extended' rather than the nuclear family. This meant that there was a comparatively long period between puberty and marriage, and that bonds between parents and children who had become adults were likely to come under strain, as they do in most of Shakespeare's comedies. There is, in addition, a series of plays with titles which proclaim their investigation into the unaccommodated members of untypical or unhappy households or communities: *The Gentleman Usher* (1602), *The Miseries of Enforced Marriage* (1606), *The Roaring Girl* (1611), *The Widow* (1615–17), *The Changeling* (1622), *The Elder Brother* (1625?), *The Guardian* (1633).

It is not sufficient, however, to examine questions of family history without

[26] Hirst, *Authority and Conflict*, pp. 17–18.

relating them to particular social milieux. Plays about women and the family have all too often been relegated to a sub-genre of 'domestic drama'. The category is unfortunate, as it seems to place emphasis on personality rather than society, whereas plays like the anonymous *Arden of Faversham* (before 1592), Henry Porter's *The Two Angry Women of Abington* (before 1599), and Dekker, Ford, and Rowley's *The Witch of Edmonton* (1621) are, as their titles hint, as much concerned with community stresses as with individual happiness. Faversham, Abington, and Edmonton are scarcely static and idyllic villages out of a pre-industrial Merry England. Indeed, the protagonists in these first two plays are not simply members of the poor, deserving or undeserving, but are pillars of their societies. The action portrays the ways in which marriage and what is called 'neighbour amity' (*Abington*, 1.1.5) are threatened by sexual desire, and the ways in which patriarchal plans for the disposal of property are subverted by feminine will. This is not just the stuff of comic theatre:[27] examination of the records of church courts reveals a large and rising number of defamation and slander cases which reveal the tensions that afflicted real places in 'merry England' – one in seven of the population was denounced for various kinds of sexual deviance.[28] Merry England indeed! From this perspective these plays become not prurient or sensationalist but crusading documentaries. (*Measure for Measure* and *The Duchess of Malfi* may be read as questioning the right of state authority to concern itself with matters of private sexual conduct, *Bartholomew Fair* as a demonstration of the inability of justice to put down 'enormity'.)

The language of *The Two Angry Women* is riddled with bawdy, suggesting a breakdown not only of linguistic but of social decorum. The collapse of neighbourliness in Abington is attributed to wayward women – as always, articulate and angry females are demonized as 'curst' – and the play is resolved, unsatisfactorily, by the good offices of the local gentry and a wise son, but not before the flyting matches, ignited by sexual suspicion, between Mistress Barnes and Mistress Goursey have revealed the tensions that can beset bourgeois marriage, and not before the former's daughter, Mall, has

[27] The Red Bull comedy *Swetnam the Woman Hater* (1618), the title of which would seem to suggest that it addresses itself to social issues, turns out simply to run through variations on stereotypical images of women.

[28] Hirst, *Authority and Conflict*, p. 49; see also J. A. Sharpe, *Defamation and Sexual Slander in Early Modern England: The Church Courts at York*, Borthwick Papers No. 58, n.d.; M. Ingram, 'The reform of popular culture? Sex and marriage in early modern England' in Reay, *Popular Culture*, pp. 129–65. Other areas offer even more sensational figures: concerning F. G. Emmison's researches in Essex, Stone, *The Family*, p. 324, comments 'in an adult life-span of thirty years, an Elizabethan inhabitant of Essex ... had more than a one-in-four chance of being accused of fornication, adultery, buggery, incest, bestiality, or bigamy'.

spoken up loud and clear for her right to dispose of her maidenhead when and to whom she pleases.

Social tensions overlie sexual tensions in most of these plays: Arden of Faversham opens the play that bears his name by complaining not only that his wife seems to be betraying him, 'a gentleman of blood' (1.1.36), but that her lover is a mere steward, a social upstart who has risen from a 'botcher' (a tailor who does repairs). Although Arden is ruthlessly murdered by his wife and her lover, he loses some of our sympathy as it is revealed how he is prepared to evict tenants who held land that has recently come into his hands: the play is as much concerned with property as with passion, and it is impossible to deduce from the text whether Arden is murdered for his rapacity under the eye of a benign providence or whether the audience is expected to attend to the cold-blooded resolution of his adulterous wife. Much of the action is filled with the comic incompetences of the villains hired to do the murder, a device that suggests the unpredictability of a comic world rent by contrarieties. The would-be murderers speak in heroic Senecan while inhabiting a world of farce. Similarly the sub-plot of *A Woman Killed with Kindness* seems to suggest a choleric society in which friendships as well as marriages are easily disturbed by passion.

As for the making of marriages and patterns of betrothal, it is difficult to know whether the predominant endorsement of romantic love in the drama is a reflection *of* a society in which parents – at least those below the rank of gentry – were gradually coming to allow their children more independence in their choice of marriage partners, or a reflection *on* a society in which parents arranged their children's marriages for them primarily for economic reasons. For most families, as in most plays, it was doubtless a problem never simply resolved.

As one way into this mass of material, I intend to examine three so-called deviant figures: a shrew, a witch, and a whore.

The assertion that women were little better than chattels, to be bestowed or acquired by men, is to be found in the drama, although seldom with such directness as we hear when Petruchio describes the status of his wife in *The Taming of the Shrew* (1591?).

> I will be master of what is mine own.
> She is my goods, my chattels, she is my house,
> My household stuff, my field, my barn,
> My horse, my ox, my ass, my anything.   (3.2.229–32)

The lines are in fact an adaptation of the tenth commandment (Exodus, 20.17): a modern audience is likely to find them outrageous, but there is no reason to doubt that certain contemporaries may have reacted in the same way on hearing them spoken on the stage, wrenched out from their familiar context so that the interpretive metaphors are exposed for what they imply. How, then, might we relate a play like *The Taming of the Shrew* to the forms and pressures of its time?

Various readings present themselves: one would write the play off as insignificant farce derived from folklore; another would start from Kate's final speech which recommends wifely submission and conclude that the heroine has finally accepted her role and that of the majority of women in the period; a third would suggest that this conclusion turns the direction of the play with a simple and bold ironic statement – the text is open to subversion in performance; a fourth would see it as a play about the condition of women, and seek to relate the action to economic realities and institutions.

In fact there can be *no* authoritative reading, and certainly we cannot identify an authoritative reading by invoking an original. There is simply no evidence outside the play (save possibly *The Taming of A Shrew*, now known to be a bad quarto, that is one which derives from a memorial reconstruction by actors) to indicate how it was perceived in the theatre by its Renaissance audiences. Nor is there any internal evidence: we do not know when or whether parts of the text, notably Kate's final speech, were realized ironically in performance. As Lisa Jardine says, there is 'no locating tone'.[29]

Although the play is the only one by Shakespeare to have an induction – a device which serves to establish the mode of play – the dramatic narrative is embedded in a frame which is only half complete. *A Shrew*, on the other hand, gives us a final scene in which Sly is borne in wearing his own apparel again and protesting, in the manner of Bottom, that he has had 'the bravest dream', in which he learned how to 'tame a shrew'. From what it contains we can conclude only that the induction to *The Shrew* serves to problematize the mode of the play.

We can approach this another way, through structure. The content of the play employs inversion: Petruchio's therapy (3.1.170–80) seems to reproduce elements of ritual misrule, and the 'shrewishness' of the fair-seeming Bianca stands as an anti-type of acceptable female behaviour. Petruchio could have had recourse to 'cucking-stool' or scold's bridle to tame his unruly partner. Instead he deploys a shaming ritual. His behaviour is like that of a 'skimmington', those curious combinations of festivity and punishment provoked by deviant behaviour. In the account of one in Calne in Wiltshire in 1618 we read of

a man riding upon a horse, having a white night cap upon his head, two shoeing horns

---

[29] Jardine, *Still Harping on Daughters*, p. 59.

hanging by his ears, a counterfeit beard upon his chin made of a deer's tail, a smock upon the top of his garments; and he rode upon a red horse with a pair of pots under him, and in them some quantity of brewing grains, which he used to cast upon the press of people.[30]

This is very like the description of Petruchio's arrival at his wedding day (3.2.40ff.). Agnes Mills, who made the deposition that contains this description, was 'dragged out of the house, thrown into a wet hole, trampled, beaten, and covered with mud and filth'. It's all redolent of the misery to which we are told in 4.1.55ff. Kate was subjected. This would suggest that Petruchio espouses the dominant ideology of his society and uses a typically male form of shaming Kate into submission.

What this implies is that Kate is represented as the inverse of qualities respected in women. (It has been also argued that witches are figures from an upside-down world.)[31] Misrule necessarily invokes the rule it parodies. But Natalie Zemon Davis has suggested 'that charivaris sometimes involved an element of rejoicing at, even encouragement of, female insurrection... It is probably true that these demonstrations reflected an awareness that women could never be dominated to the degree implied in the patriarchal ideal'.[32] Petruchio's behaviour seems outrageous and the text generates sympathy if not approval for Kate. These suggestive analogues to this one episode still do not, however, locate a tone in the text as a whole.

The induction not only says something about the mode of the text but announces *themes* which establish a social context and a critique of social order. These include hunting, conspicuous display, social displacement by Ovidian metamorphosis which ironically materializes the Petrarchan commonplaces, and transvestism. We cannot tell 'who is speaking' when the boy player takes the role of the *belle dame de merci*:

SLY
                    Where is my wife?

BARTHOLOMEW
          Here, noble lord, what is thy will with *her*.

---

[30] Quoted by Martin Ingram, 'Ridings, rough music, and the "reform of popular culture" in early modern England', *Past and Present* 105 (1984), 79–113.

[31] Clark, 'Inversion'.

[32] Ingram, 'Ridings', summarizing N. Z. Davis, *Society and Culture in Early Modern France* (1975), p. 140. Other feminist approaches could be noted here: Coppélia Kahn's *Man's Estate: Masculine Identity in Shakespeare* (Berkeley, California, 1981) offers a psychoanalytical approach. Marilyn French's *Shakespeare's Division of Experience* (London, 1982) speaks of polarized essentialist cultural values: creating and killing associated with women and men respectively. These are reviewed by Kate McLuskie, 'The patriarchal bard' in Dollimore and Sinfield, pp. 88–106. A deconstructionist reading is to be found in Joel Fineman, 'The turn of the shrew' in Patricia Parker and Geoffrey Hartman, *Shakespeare and the Question of Theory* (London, 1985).

The themes are made problematic by this linguistic device of defamiliariza-
tion: the player refers to his fictive self as 'her' not 'me'. All of these elements
invoke, by opposites, a 'puritan' ideal of marriage which, it has been argued,
served to alleviate the lot of wives at the time. Although 'Puritanism was
scarcely an ideology of women's liberation, and in the long run its
mainstream varieties reinforced rather than weakened patriarchal authority
... puritan teaching always stressed the partnership aspect of marriage, and
gave the wife a responsible role in the moral ordering of the household'.[33]
Against this Lisa Jardine, whose account of the position of women rejects a
simple explanation in favour of an investigation of wider economic realities,
demonstrates that if companionate marriage was coming more into its own,
little sign is visible of real dialogue between partners. Virtue in woman was
still associated with silence, vice with articulateness,[34] although
Shakespeare's articulate heroines would seem to be exceptions to the social
rule.

Throughout our analysis, of course, we must inspect the kinds of discourse used to construct the characters. Bianca is just as significant a construct as Katherine. Lucentio signals this with his Petrarchan hyperboles
(1.1.157ff.). He is allowed to describe exactly how Bianca is rendered in the
text: 'Sacred and sweet was all I saw in her' (1.1.176). One important interpretive construction put upon women like Kate in the time was the label
'curst' (see 1.2.85 and 3.2.144ff.). The word then customarily meant
'shrewish' (*OED*, 4). The text's repetition of the word causes it to revert to its
second meaning, 'deserving of a curse, therefore wicked'. In men's eyes
women like Kate appeared as monsters, and in reality scolds and cursers
were likely to bring charges of witchcraft upon themselves. Petruchio's distortion and parody of Kate's behaviour is held to be an accurate reflection of
what is taken by the community to be 'unnatural'.

His punishment of her (or is it therapy?) is to 'kill her in her own humour'
(4.1.180). Perhaps it *is* therapy. Because Kate is articulate there is a danger
of seeing her as a champion of female emancipation. We must remember her
violence – she brings Bianca on stage at a rope's end (2.1.1). Petruchio in his
soliloquy of 4.1 sees Kate in this way. In his production of 1972, Jonathan
Miller presented Petruchio as a father of a godly family of the early seventeenth century, 'a puritan squire'.[35] His BBC television production of 1980
offered a close-up on John Cleese, an actor known for his comic virtuosity:

---

[33] Underdown, 'The taming of the scold', p. 136; the influence of 'puritanism' on marriage is
   questioned by Kathleen Davies, 'Continuity and change in literary advice on marriage' in
   Outhwaite, *Marriage and Society*, pp. 58–80.
[34] Jardine, *Still Harping on Daughters*, pp. 46–7.
[35] *Subsequent Performances* (London, 1986), p. 121.

13   Paola Dionisotti as a lobotomized Shrew in the Michael Bogdanov production for the Royal Shakespeare Company at Stratford-upon-Avon in 1978

> Ay, and amid this hurly I intend
> That all is done in reverend care of her...
> This is a way to kill a wife with kindness
> And thus I'll curb her mad and headstrong humour.
> He that knows better how to tame a shrew,
> Now let him speak – 'tis charity to show. (4.1.174–82)

Is this moral by virtue of being pragmatic, or is it to be delivered as Howard Keel did in *Kiss Me Kate*? (He laughed sarcastically at the sentiments of the lines he had just spoken.) It is just possible that Petruchio is a reconstructed man after all – significantly *A Shrew* suppresses Petruchio's compassion (see 9.48–52). We might feel more confident of this, however, had Kate too been given a soliloquy in which to express her views on this therapy.

What of the final speech? Is its context that of game, with the implication that no statement is being made here? If there is irony, one way of bringing that out would be for the player to stress the word 'honest' in the lines:

> And when she is froward, peevish, sullen, sour,
> And not obedient to his *honest* will... (5.2.157–8)

'Honest' can mean not only worthy of honour but virtuous (*OED*, 2a and 13), the implication being that a woman might rebel against a patriarchal husband as a revenger might take up arms against a tyrannical prince. (Does *A Shrew*, which legitimizes Kate's submission by invoking in this speech the commonplace of a hierarchialized cosmos, record a male player's subversion of tolerance?)

From a shrew we turn to a witch. Although England witnessed some outbreaks of persecution of female (and male) 'witches' led by religious zealots, voices were raised in the period to suggest that the driving forces behind the accusations derived from social stress and prejudice.[36] Elizabethan witchcraft prosecutions generally derived from accusations of evil practices (malefice) and in England, unlike Scotland and continental Europe, there were few if any accusations of diabolism such as we see in *Doctor Faustus*. This in itself suggests that witchcraft accusations were desperate remedies for communities with neither the science to explain accident, illness, and disease nor a constabulary able to investigate crime properly.

The problem was investigated by dramatists, notably by Dekker, Rowley, and Ford, who, in 1621, collaborated on *The Witch of Edmonton*, basing their play on a pamphlet of the same year which reported on the discovery and

---

[36] See, for example, George Gifford's *Discourse of the Subtill Practices of Devils by Witches and Sorcerers* (London, 1587) and *Dialogue Concerning Witches and Witchcraft* (London, 1593). Alan Macfarlane offers the rise of individualism and decline of 'neighbourly' community as an explanation for witchcraft – see his *Witchcraft in Tudor and Stuart England*.

execution of a 'real witch', Elizabeth Sawyer. By this time, in fact, the peak number of witchcraft convictions had passed and the number of acquittals was rising. The play, unlike the pamphlet, places as much stress on the poverty of the heroine and the way in which she is harassed by wealthy neighbours as it does on her 'malice' and consequent dealings with the Devil. Her first and strong-lined speech seems designed to create a reservoir of sympathy that will not be drained by her subsequent actions:

> And why on me? Why should the envious world
> Throw all their scandalous malice upon me?
> 'Cause I am poor, deformed and ignorant,
> And like a bow buckled and bent together
> By some more strong in mischiefs than myself,
> Must I for that be made a common sink
> For all the filth and rubbish of men's tongues
> To fall and run into? Some call me witch,
> And being ignorant of myself, they go
> About to teach me how to be one.   (2.1.1–10)

A sub-plot tells the story of Frank Thornley, a young man who is drawn into a bigamous but profitable marriage by a father whose estates are mortgaged. Dogged by the devil, he tries to escape his predicament by killing his second wife. Neither character is responsible for the predicament that leads to the fatal acts, and the isolation and social marginality of both is established by a comic inset in which morris men create a mythical world of idealized neighbourliness.

Our third example of a female deviant is provided by Bellafront, the central figure in Dekker's two-part play *The Honest Whore*. Like *The Shoemaker's Holiday*, *The Honest Whore, Part 1* (1604–5) is resolved by the intervention of a prince, but the audience may very well feel that the social divisions that have been exposed during the course of the play have scarcely been overcome. The Duke's function is in fact dictated by the author's need to close the play by concluding the comic intrigue, but the ending suggests that, although a prince may propose a solution, character and event combine to dispose: the Duke, after all, has to accept the marriage of his daughter with a man he had attempted to have poisoned. A resolute woman, the whore Bellafront, turns the tables on Matheo who had debauched her (3.3). This is an unusual feature, as generally it is the woman who is punished for a vice which must by its nature be mutually committed. The Duke cheers himself up thus:

> Since Fate hath conquered, I must rest content,
> To strive now, would but add new punishment.   (5.2.389–90)

The theme of the play is constancy, constancy that is required to withstand a whirling world of social change, mortal decay, and moral corruption. In a significant piece of word-play on the words 'cousin' and 'cozen' (3.1.140–8) the bonds of family are set against new kinds of cash nexus. The virtue of constancy is incarnate in Candido the linen-draper, who refuses to lose his temper but calmly takes steps to have punished those who afflict him. It is notable not only that he is a citizen of honesty and integrity, standing against a gang of roaring boys, cheating gallants, and gulls representative of the unindustrious gentry, but that he is a full member of the Senate, a role he values. The city is no longer simply a 'unified' *locus*, as in classical comedy, but a moralized focus of wealth as well as virtue, for we hear of a gentleman borrowing money from a citizen (2.1.113–4).

Bellafront, the whore whose role provides the title, is also constant, having been converted from her vocation by her love for Hippolito, successful suitor to the Duke's daughter. She, however, is the object of his tirades against her vocation. These passages seem to provide another example of a text that demonizes women. However, we can argue – and there is further pertinent material in the second part of the play (3.1) – that the misogynistic tirades (see *Part 1*, 2.1.319ff. and *Part 2*, 3.1.157ff.) are the consequence of obsession or guilt, and that the play is ironical, suggesting that the duty of chastity might be binding on men as well as women, a case strongly put to her husband by Bellafront in 4.1 of *Part 2*. Once converted, Bellafront stands as an emblem of chastity and constancy, a role she maintains through the second part of the play, although poverty almost compels her to revert to her trade (4.1). Overall the patient honest citizen and chaste and supportive wife serve as moral foils to the roaring boys, erring husbands, and domineering wives found elsewhere in the play.

The first part of the play ends at the monastery of Bethlehem where all are fools. Madness, we learn, has been caused by poverty and marital jealousy (5.2.173ff., 5.2.253) and by division between the professions (5.2.145ff.). *Part 2* assembles characters at the prison of Bridewell as a result of the Duke's desire to purge the city of whores, a ritual enactment of which was performed by London's apprentices every Shrove Tuesday. There the sternest punishment is meted out to Bots, the pandar, and Matheo is saved from the penalty for his roistering by the intervention of his wife, Bellafront the reformed whore.

In one area of the study of family life, the study of affective relationships between parents and pre-pubertal children, dramatic texts may have something to offer the historian. The pioneering modern historian of the family, Lawrence Stone, offered a picture of husbands and wives whose marriages had been arranged for dynastic reasons, beset by high mortality, and foolish if they invested 'too much emotional capital'[37] in children. Stone's conclusions are now discounted. Working from diaries and letters – and 'literature' – historians have found evidence of marriages, at least among the middling and lower orders, that derive from the mutual love and affection of the partners. (Ben Jonson's poem 'On My First Son' describes the boy's death as the repayment of a loan divinely bestowed, implying that the child generated the emotional capital rather than the parent.) Although it begs a lot of questions, a play like *The Winter's Tale* depends upon a situation where children are much valued and loved, and where there is strong endorsement of the need for mutual respect between the partners in a marriage. Elsewhere in Shakespeare it is implied that only those who have had children can know the bonds that bind parents to them.[38]

Other cultures

As well as anatomizing their own nation, dramatists offered their contemporaries some understanding of other cultures. Popular plays at the Red Bull may have been unashamedly chauvinist – after the publication of Foxe's *Book of Martyrs* there is no doubt that England had a pride in herself as an elect nation – but the King's Men themselves brought to the Jacobean court reflections on real worlds elsewhere. In the 1590s, Roman plays had offered a comparative study of different kinds of constitution where there seemed to be few checks on rampant ambition, as in *Titus Andronicus*, or where the ideals of republicanism might be set against nascent imperialism, as in *Julius Caesar*. After his deeply complex meditation on the benefits of empire in *Cymbeline*, Shakespeare offered his countrymen a complementary and thoroughgoing anatomy of colonialism in *The Tempest*, a text which stands in ideological opposition to, say, Spenser's *View of the Present State of Ireland*. The play is one of those that has spoken most loudly – but with two voices – to the twentieth century. To some, Prospero has appeared the perturbed philosopher–king restoring his lands to order by an experiment in testing and Christian forgiveness. He is the all-powerful magus, possessed of a quasi-divine power and, like a poet, able to transmute an iron age to gold. Tempest, however, is a metaphor for rebellion in the Virginia Company's pamphlet, *A True Declaration of Virginia*, one of the principal sources for Shakespeare's play: 'the broken remainder ... made a greater shipwreck in the continent of Virginia by the tempest of dissension; every man over-

---

[37] *The Family*, p. 82.
[38] *King John* 3.4; *Macbeth* 4.3.216; *Henry VI, Part 3*, 5.5.63–4.

valuing his own worth would be a commander, every man under-prizing another's value denied to be commanded'.[39] Having read that, we realize that the very title of the play becomes problematic: does it designate natural or cultural process? The tempest is not only a transcendent symbol but a cultural problem. It is, we are told, conjured by a magician: that Prospero can control the elements is concordant with the discourse of magic, the world of Ariel, discordant with discourse of *realpolitik*, the world of Antonio. If we emphasize the cultural–political dimension of the play, Prospero becomes the arch-imperialist whose rule imposes a mortal wound upon the culture of Caliban, whose name indicates his affinities with the noble savages exalted by Montaigne in his essay 'Of the Cannibals'. The play is set vaguely in the Mediterranean, a Virgilian world, in fact, in that, like Aeneas, Alonso was voyaging from Carthage to Naples. But Shakespeare seems to be inscribing the culture of the New World upon the Old, importing slavery from the Americas to anatomize relationships nearer home.[40] According to this kind of reading, moreover, Prospero seeks compulsively to impose his authority not only on his political enemies and colonized natives but on his daughter. Moreover, he had previously wrested the island from a woman, the witch Sycorax. The connection between these two kinds of rule is brought out in a well-known passage from *Civilization and its Discontents* where Freud wrote: 'It is impossible to overlook the extent to which civilization is built up upon a renunciation of instinct, how much it presupposes precisely the non-satisfaction (by suppression, repression, or some other means?) of powerful instincts... Civilization behaves toward sexuality as a people or a stratum of its population does which has subjected another one to its exploitation'.[41] Instead of accepting Prospero's omnipotence, therefore, we might stress how, in what is essentially a comic moment, the wedding masque is interrupted because Prospero has forgotten the foul conspiracy. As a ruler he must abandon his role and resort to improvisation; as a poet he learns about the intractability of his material.

Shakespeare's anatomy of power is focused in a famous theatrical 'gest':[42]

[39] Orgel, *The Tempest*, p. 219.

[40] It is significant, however, that it is only since about 1945 that critics and directors have thought in this way – 'Caliban's politicized image did not penetrate the theatre until the late 1960's'. Virginia Mason Vaughan, '"Something rich and strange": Caliban's theatrical metamorphoses', *SQ* 36 (1985), 390–405.

[41] Freud, *Civilization and its Discontents*, trans. J. Strachey in *Civilization, Society, and Religion* (Harmondsworth, 1985), pp. 286, 294.

[42] Hattaway, *Elizabethan Popular Theatre*, p. 3.

PROSPERO

                    Lend thy hand
And pluck my magic garment from me.
[*Miranda helps him to disrobe*]
Lie there, my art.   (1.2.24–6)

This is the obverse of the famous moment in *Tamburlaine, Part 1*,

Lie here, ye weeds that I disdain to wear:
This complete armour and this curtle-axe
Are adjuncts more beseeming Tamburlaine.   (1.2.41–3)

Orgel usefully gives us in a footnote the famous story of Lord Burghley: 'At night when he put off his gown, he used to say, lie there, *Lord Treasurer.*'

What does all this signify? Might not the separation of man from mantle signify the separation of authority from power? I am defining my use of these words from the moment in *King Lear* when Kent claims that the powerless abdicated king has 'authority' (1.4.30). It is a moment of demystification: power is associated with material reality, the cloak or the curtle axe (cutlass); it is instrumental and not the mystical adjunct of authority celebrated in the tournaments and shows of Elizabeth.

Power is related to sexuality and both are related to language. Prospero has usurped the rule of Caliban. Miranda taught him speech. Note how she is given, *pace* Dryden and a tradition of male editors, the line 'I endowed thy purposes/With words that made them known' (1.2.356–7). Do we hear the accents of Miranda in Caliban's 'poetical' speeches? Does Prospero wish to suppress woman's language?

As well as emphasizing closure, the traditional end of comedy with its desired restoration of harmony and justice, we might note the unregeneracy of Antonio, and that Miranda's marriage has cost her her patrimony. (Perhaps, however, in this respect we could point out Prospero's political skill: by the reduction of Milan to a Neapolitan fiefdom Antonio becomes completely dispossessed.) Our views about Caliban's rights and Prospero's authority will be constructed partly out of our own ideological preconceptions, just as our ideological positions will be partly determined by our reading of the text. (Prospero's aphorism about Caliban

A devil, a born devil, on whose nature
Nurture can never stick   (4.1.188–9)

probably awakened for many generations everything that is now summed up by the phrase 'the problematizing of culture'.)

Even though the play may have had more to do with Stuart ideals than New World realities, we cannot escape from colonialist discourse, just as we cannot escape from feminist discourse in *The Taming of the Shrew*. To suppress either is as political as foregrounding either, nor is there any evidence which allows the cultural historian to adjudicate between these competing readings. Instead I think we must locate these readings in history, in a post-colonial age, and realize that Shakespeare is giving us an account of the *effects* of colonialism. Shakespeare is for all time by virtue of being of an age.

So is Jonson. One of the commonplaces of literary history is that the Renaissance produced a comedy of humours, plays about a constant human nature, whereas the Restoration gave us a comedy of manners, in which the characters are types of the society of their time. Jonson's own masterpiece in this earlier genre, however, gives the lie to this opposition. For, in *Every Man in his Humour*, we learn that psychology depends upon society, nature upon nurture:

COB Nay, I have my rheum, and I can be angry as well as another, sir.
CASH Thy rheum, Cob? Thy humour, thy humour! Thou mistak'st.
COB Humour? Mack, I think it be so indeed: what is that humour? Some rare thing, I warrant.
CASH Marry, I'll tell thee, Cob: it is a gentleman-like monster, bred, in the special gallantry of our time, by affectation; and fed by folly.

(1616 version, 3.4.14–22)[43]

Reading Elizabethan and Jacobean drama

What, in conclusion, does someone working on the relation between literature and society do these days? We must read not only the new social history but dramatic texts in the light of the new theories, all that has served to 'problematize culture', expose the ideological contests for cultural hegemony. We must consider not just individual characters but types and institutions: the family, guild, magistracy, court, state. We must not merely seek to set out the 'thought' of the time: cultural history has, I would argue, come to complement and, in some instances, supplant the old 'history of ideas'. We are often interested in 'ideas' only as they are imprinted and produced in language, frequently in significant interpretive metaphors – court, curst, tempest, etc. – of the kind I have investigated. We are involved in a kind of archaeology on the text. We must remember that *texts are history* and *history is text*.

In critical texts too we will note how descriptive metaphors turn out to be

---

[43] The induction to the later *Every Man out of his Humour*, however, offers a metaphorical model of explanation that tends to the psychological.

evaluative metaphors, revealing the ideological position of their authors. We shall attend to harmony, consistency, resolution but also note discontinuities, divisions, dislocations, fracture, stylistic shifts, all those constructivist strategies (what T. S. Eliot called artistic 'impurities')[44] which 'make strange' for audiences and readers the presented realities.

We might try to isolate particular discourses within texts, concentrating not only on the moment of their production, but attending to successive inscriptions on them during the course of their history. And the contextual 'background', which previously had served merely to highlight the profile of the individual text, may give way to the notion of *intertextuality*, according to which, in keeping with the Saussurean model of language, no text is intelligible except in its relations with other texts.

Let us end with two examples, to see how this kind of reading may go. At the end of *The Tempest*, Prospero says to Caliban:

> Go, sirrah, to my cell;
> Take with you your companions. As you look
> To have my pardon, trim it handsomely.
>
> CALIBAN
> Ay, that I will; and I'll be wise hereafter,
> And *seek for grace* [emphasis added].   (5.1.291–5)

'Seek for grace' means sue for pardon – the phrase was used thus by Spenser. Orgel offers also 'favour' for grace. But is it not also apparent that the discourse of religion has been inscribed on the discourse of power, that signification serves legitimation? Caliban has been taught to perceive the ruler, dressed in a little brief authority, as omnipotent, sole dispenser of what is necessary for salvation.

As a prelude to our second example, let us recall T. S. Eliot on Middleton: 'Middleton is solicitous to please his audience with what they expect; but there is underneath the same steady impersonal passionless observation of human nature... He has no message; he is merely a great recorder ... Middleton is the greatest "realist" in Jacobean comedy'.[45] Here, to test the assertion, is the opening (abbreviated) of *A Trick to Catch the Old One* (1605):

Enter WITGOOD, *a Gentleman, solus.*
WITGOOD (*1) All's gone! Still thou'rt a **gentleman**, that's all; but a **poor one**, that's **nothing**. (*2) What **milk** brings thy meadows forth now? Where are thy goodly **uplands**, and thy **downlands**? All sunk into that **little pit, lechery**. (*3) Why should a gallant pay but two shillings for his ordinary that nourishes him, and twenty times

---

[44] *Selected Essays*, pp. 114ff.
[45] *Selected Essays*, pp. 167–9.

two for his brothel that **consumes** him... (*4) I dare not visit the city: there I should be too soon visited by **that horrible plague, my debts**; (*5) and by that means **I lose a virgin's love, her portion, and her virtues.** Well, how should a man **live** that has no **living**? Hum. Why, are there not a million of men in the world that only sojourn upon their brain, and (*6) **make their wits their mercers**; and I am but one amongst that million, and cannot thrive upon't? (*7) Any trick, **out of the compass** of law, now would come happily to me.
Enter COURTESAN.
COURTESAN (*8) My **love!**
WITGOOD My **loathing!** Has thou been the secret consumption of my purse, and now comest to undo my last means, my wits? (*9) Wilt thou **leave no virtue in me**, and yet thou ne'er the better?

> Hence courtesan, round webbed-tarantula,
> That **dry'st the roses** in the cheeks of youth.
> (Middleton, *A Trick to Catch the Old One*, 1.1.1ff.)

In this passage I have inserted asterisked numbers to define what Roland Barthes termed 'lexias', blocks of signification,[46] although I have not followed the codes he employs to anatomize Balzac's tale of *Sarrasine*. Instead I have emboldened the metaphors, the interpretive constructions Middleton uses to build up his comic world. I leave it to the reader to determine whether he is 'passionless'.

(*1) The first two sentences succinctly sum up all that has been termed the crisis of the aristocracy. They construct a society in transition. A gentleman had originally been born to a rank as well as to wealth: the class had been defined by William Harrison as one who 'can live without manual labour'.[47] In the predatory London of the first years of King James money was supplanting rank as the source of all status. (*2) Wealth had derived from land, according to a 'natural order': accordingly, Middleton 'feminizes' the landscape of Witgood's estate. The uplands and downlands represent the breasts of fertility and the womb, source of new life but also the source of male pleasure. A second metaphor is superscribed, generating thereby a contradictory idea of woman: the fall of the gentleman in rank is analogous to Lucifer's fall into 'hell' – a bawdy designation for the vagina. What is thereby notable here, moreover, is the way that the relationship between work and wealth is completely suppressed in this discourse. (*3) By a suppressed synecdoche (the part for the whole) Witgood demonizes the brothel, the abode of the possessors of vaginas. There a man is apt not only to be stripped of his wealth but to be infected with the fires of venereal disease (consumed).

---

[46] Roland Barthes, *S/Z*, trans. R. Miller (New York, 1974), p. 13.
[47] In Raphael Holinshed, *Chronicles* (London, 1577), vol. 1, bk 2, chapter v.

The audience is by now aware of Witgood's egregious bad faith. It was not involuntarily that he went to the brothel, just as it was not (*4) a natural calamity that threw him into debt. (*5) Women he values not as sources of life but only as sources of living (wealth). (*6) In order to attain wealth he will do anything, including depriving the retailers of fine cloths of *their* legitimate living, the selling of means of concealment. (*7) 'Out of the compass of' seems ambiguous to the point of being contradictory: it means both illegal or devised according to the letter rather than the spirit of the law. (*8) Onto the nameless courtesan Witgood projects a hatred (like that of Dekker's Hippolito, born of guilt?). (*9) Women had for him existed only as Petrarchan virgins: once deflowered, however, their insatiable sexual appetites suck, like a tarantula, the 'virtue' or power from a man, destroying the bloom of his youth.

This passage of prose is the work of a master. History is text and text is history: the balanced sentences are generated by a rhetoric in the service of a mind that will take no contemporary value for granted, no reality as unchanging. It *is* the work of a great entertainer, but one who deserves close attention. Middleton was a recorder who deployed language not only, as Eliot claimed, to record reality but to interrogate reality, not only to enable his contemporaries to recognize themselves, but to serve what Ben Jonson always claimed to be the prime function of theatre, understanding.

Bibliography

SOCIAL HISTORY
Recent social histories of the period are provided by Keith Wrightson, *English Society, 1580–1680* (1982), J. A. Sharpe, *Early Modern England: A Social History, 1550–1760* (1987), and, particularly recommended, Derek Hirst, *Authority and Conflict: England 1603–1658* (1986). Christopher Hill's many books and essays on the period supply pioneering syntheses generated by the author's Marxist approach. Lawrence Stone, *The Crisis of the Aristocracy* (1965), is an essential account of the period based on an examination of social history. These works could be supplemented by political histories like Conrad Russell's *The Crisis of Parliaments: English History 1509–1660* (1971), Penry Williams's *The Tudor Regime* (1979), which gives a clear account of institutions, particularly the court, as well as D. M. Palliser's *The Age of Elizabeth: England under the Later Tudors, 1547–1603* (1983) and Charles Wilson's *England's Apprenticeship, 1603–1763* (1971), both of which offer an account of developments in the economic life of the country. Patrick Collinson's *The Religion of Protestants: The Church in English Society 1559–1625* (1982) is a magisterial survey of the subject.

More specialized studies of social history include Margaret Spufford, *Contrasting Communities: English Villagers in the Sixteenth and Seventeenth Centuries* (1974); Peter Burke, *Popular Culture in Early Modern Europe* (1978); B. Reay, ed., *Popular Culture in Seventeenth-Century England* (1985); Paul Slack's collection of articles from *Past and*

Present: Rebellion, Popular Protest and the Social Order in Early Modern England (1984); Anthony Fletcher and John Stevenson, eds., *Order and Disorder in Early Modern England* (1985); J. A. Sharpe, *Crime in Early Modern England 1550–1750* (1984); Harvey J. Graff, ed., *Literacy and Social Development in the West* (1981); Michael MacDonald, *Mystical Bedlam: Madness, Anxiety and Healing in Seventeenth Century England* (1981). Keith Thomas's *Religion and the Decline of Magic* (1971) was one of the first works of modern history to show the influence of anthropology and offers an encyclopaedic account of witchcraft and much else. It can be supplemented by Alan Macfarlane, *Witchcraft in Tudor and Stuart England* (1970); Christina Larner, *Enemies of God: The Witch-hunt in Scotland* (1981); Stuart Clark, 'Inversion, misrule and the meaning of witchcraft', *Past and Present* 87 (1980), 98–127; Michael Hattaway, 'Women and witchcraft: the case of *The Witch of Edmonton*', *Trivium* 20 (1985), 49–68; and Peter Stallybrass, '*Macbeth* and witchcraft' in J. R. Brown, ed., *Focus on Macbeth* (1982).

Questions concerning family history were challengingly posed by Lawrence Stone, *The Family, Sex, and Marriage 1500–1800* (1977) although most of Stone's conclusions are now disputed. A survey of the debate can be found in Wrightson (see above). Useful statistical material will be found in Peter Laslett, *Family Life and Illicit Love in Earlier Generations* (1977); this can be complemented by the rollicking essay by G. R. Quaife, *Wanton Wenches and Wayward Wives: Peasants and Illicit Sex in Early Seventeenth Century England* (1969). More recent studies include R. B. Outhwaite, ed., *Marriage and Society* (1981); Ralph A. Houlbrooke, *The English Family 1450–1700* (1984); Alan Macfarlane, *Marriage and Love in England 1300–1840* (1986); and Martin Ingram, *Church Courts, Sex and Marriage in England 1570–1640* (1987). Studies of the drama that discuss debates about marriage and the place of women in social and ideological contexts include Lisa Jardine, *Still Harping on Daughters: Women and Drama in the Age of Shakespeare* (1983); Linda Woodbridge, *Women and the English Renaissance*, 1984; and Catherine Belsey, *The Subject of Tragedy: Identity and Difference in Renaissance Drama* (1985). Two essays by Kathleen McLuskie, 'The patriarchal bard', in Jonathan Dollimore and Alan Sinfield, eds., *Political Shakespeare: New Essays in Cultural Materialism* (1985) and '"'Tis but a woman's jar": family and kinship in Elizabethan domestic drama', *Literature and History* 9 (1983), 228–39, as well as Lynda Boose, 'The family in Shakespeare studies; or – studies in the family of Shakespeareans; or – the politics of politics', *RenQ* 40 (1987), 707–42 offer useful surveys and critiques of recent feminist writings.

OTHER CULTURES

Studies of dramatic texts that portray other cultures: G. K. Hunter, *Dramatic Identities and Cultural Tradition* (1978) and Philip Edwards, *Threshold of a Nation* (1979).

THEATRE AND SOCIETY

Studies of the drama that relate texts to the role of theatre in society: David Bevington, *Tudor Drama and Politics* (1968); Jonas Barish, *The Anti-Theatrical Prejudice* (1981); David Aers, Bob Hodge, and Gunther Kress, *Literature, Language and Society in England 1580–1680* (1981); Dollimore and Sinfield (see above); Andrew Gurr, *Playgoing in Shakespeare's London* (1987). Jean-Christophe Agnew's *World's Apart: The Market and the Theater in Anglo-American Thought, 1550–1750* (1986) is a brilliant account of the similarity between interpretive constructions of the theatre and the market. There is also material written by a historian in Robert Ashton, *The English Civil War* (1978).

Modern 'politicized' readings of the drama really began with L. C. Knights, *Drama and Society in the Age of Jonson* (1937), a book which helped generate studies like Alexander Leggatt, *Citizen Comedy in the Age of Shakespeare* (1973) and Brian Gibbons, *Jacobean City Comedy*, rev. edn (1980) and Gail Paster, *The Idea of the City in the Age of Shakespeare* (1985). In another context J. W. Lever's *The Tragedy of State* (1971) helped critics realize that the view of the period offered by E. M. W. Tillyard in *The Elizabethan World Picture* (1943) imposed an unacceptably simple and ideologically biased schema on the period. It was an important influence on Jonathan Dollimore's *Radical Tragedy* (rev. edn, 1989). Margot Heinemann's *Puritanism and Theatre: Thomas Middleton and Opposition Drama under the Early Stuarts* (1980) and Martin Butler's *Theatre and Crisis 1632–1642* (1984) offer essential revisionist readings of the texts that lie within their purview. In the United States brilliant work was published by Stephen Greenblatt, *Renaissance Self-Fashioning* (1980) and Greenblatt, ed., *The Power of Forms in the English Renaissance* (1982), where the methods of the 'new historicism' were set out. Other works of this school include Jonathan Goldberg, *James I and the Politics of Literature: Jonson, Shakespeare, Donne and their Contemporaries* (1983); Leonard Tennenhouse, *Power on Display: The Politics of Shakespeare's Genres* (1986). The nature of the new historicism and of cultural materialism is usefully surveyed by Walter Cohen, 'Political criticism of Shakespeare' and Don E. Wayne, 'Power, politics, and the Shakespearean text: recent criticism in England and the United States', both in Jean E. Howard and Marion F. O'Connor, eds., *Shakespeare Reproduced* (1987). Michael D. Bristol, *Carnival and Theater: Plebeian Culture and the Structure of Authority in Renaissance England* (1985) makes use of the writings of Mikhail Bakhtin. Another wide-ranging study in this field is François Laroque, *Shakespeare et la fête* (1988).

CRITICAL THEORY

Collections of essays that address themselves to reading dramatic (especially Shakespearian) texts in the light of recent critical theory include Dollimore and Sinfield (see above); Patricia Parker and Geoffrey Hartman, eds., *Shakespeare and the Question of Theory* (1985); and John Drakakis, ed., *Alternative Shakespeares* (1985).

TEXTS

In this essay quotations are taken from *Three Jacobean Witchcraft Plays*, ed. Peter Corbin and Douglas Sedge (1986: *The Witch of Edmonton*); *Three Elizabethan Domestic Tragedies*, ed. Keith Sturgess (1969: *Arden of Faversham, A Woman Killed with Kindness*); Henry Porter, *The Two Angry Women of Abington*, ed. Michael Jardine and John Simons (1987); Thomas Middleton, *A Trick to Catch the Old One*, ed. Charles Barber (1968); and the Malone Society Reprints of *Swetnam the Woman Hater* and *The Life and Death of Jack Straw*.

4   Private and occasional drama

This chapter will be discussing four traditions of occasional performance current during the Renaissance: the plays, masques, and miscellaneous entertainments written for the court, the Inns of Court, the universities, and the great provincial aristocratic houses. This drama comprises a small fraction of the period's output, and mostly it was performed only once and before tiny audiences. Yet because these audiences were drawn from the social and political élites, and because the staging was lavish and the rewards substantial, these four traditions had a high public profile, and virtually every major playwright contributed to one or other. Though Shakespeare wrote no court masques, he was probably involved in their performance and he devised at least one heraldic emblem for an Elizabethan tilt.

It is only a slight exaggeration to claim that almost all Elizabethan and early Stuart theatre was occasional. Since the playhouses changed their repertory from day to day, rarely did any play achieve a 'run' of multiple performances; and, as the companies toured the provinces or migrated between theatres, so any play would reach audiences that diverged widely in character and composition. Hence even in the commercial playhouses performances were occasional in spirit, profoundly conditioned by the contingencies of time and place; they could not be insulated against the pressures of the moment as in today's theatre they tend to be. For the rural villager or London citizen a theatre visit was a kind of holiday in miniature. From the player, the ever-changing repertory and audiences demanded a quickness of response and a willingness to permit the play to speak to the fitness of its occasion. (Edmund Gayton recounts the extreme case of a Shrove Tuesday audience that forced the players to abandon the tragedy they were performing in favour of *The Two Merry Milkmaids*.)[1] The insistent dialogue between text and occasion would be almost as continually present in the commercial playhouse as it inevitably was on the private stages.

---

[1] See Edmund Gayton, *Pleasant Notes upon Don Quixote*, quoted above, p. 58.

When Thomas Nashe wrote a pageant of the seasons for performance before Archbishop Whitgift at rural Croydon, *Summer's Last Will and Testament* (1592 or 93), he framed it with a 'real-life' presenter, Will Summers, who constantly interrupted the performance, joking, criticizing, applauding, even joining in. As the pageant proceeded with its celebration of the seasonal wheel and its lament for the brevity of the year and of life, so Summers was insensibly won over and eventually he confessed himself deeply moved by it. Of course Will Summers was himself part of the illusion, but he inhabited the same space as the play's audience and he projected Nashe's sense of the way that, in private theatricals, occasion was transformed into art. In such drama, Nashe reveals, it was the occasion that shaped the play, not vice versa, and the show was not as much a performance as an event. Its fulfilment depended on a fully social, and not merely theatrical enactment. So too Nashe's audience was not so much a public as a community, and the conventions that operated were less literary than festive ones. The occasion was itself the subject, and the play was a vehicle to affirm the social bondings dictated by the occasion.

Given these conditions, there were radical differences between private and public drama, in spite of the latter's occasional dimension. For example, in private theatre there could be no 'willing suspension of disbelief', for the element of compliment or masquerade could never wholly be effaced. Even at the court masques, which used spectacularly illusionist scenery, no spectator ever supposed that Britannocles was anyone other than King Charles. Similarly, at private performances dialogue in the usual sense could not take place; often characters would not talk together but address their remarks to the silent (but dominant) chief spectator. Furthermore, as Stephen Orgel has rightly emphasized,[2] a feature that crucially set private drama apart was the instability of the division between 'spectator' and 'participant'. The court masque in particular was unlike all other drama in that its formal culmination came when the masquers took dancing partners out of the audience and the line between player and spectator was abrogated. Even if other forms of private drama did not suspend that line, they still rendered it less visible – when Elizabeth saw Plautus' *Aulularia* at Cambridge in 1564, the university built her a seat on the stage and watched her watching the play; at Oxford in 1605, James's seat had to be moved so that he could be seen, and as a result he himself could hear nothing. The private performance was always a play-within-a-play, and the outer, framing play was a game which the audience played amongst themselves.

[2] See Orgel, *Illusion of Power, passim.*

It was of course in the nature of the sovereign's presence to turn any court performance into a dialogue, or to attract political applications, even to the most innocent of plays. For example, Lodowick Carlell's *The Deserving Favourite* (1629) has negligible political content (let alone aesthetic content), but after the assassination of the Duke of Buckingham any play with a title like this at Whitehall would have been charged with excitement. A similar kind of double vision clings to plays such as *Measure for Measure* or *The Tempest*, whose autocratic Dukes could at court be measured against King James (and not necessarily to James's advantage), while Jonson's *Bartholomew Fair*, with its induction for the public playhouse and separate prologue and epilogue for the court, is frankly two-faced – the court performance, where the Fair's anarchy was overlooked by the presence of the King, would have been quite different from the public ones. Even in a piece like *A Midsummer Night's Dream* the allusion to the 'fair vestal throned by the West' who alone is beyond Cupid's power (2.1.158) would gain a special resonance from the presence of the Virgin Queen: the compliment to Elizabeth's chastity supplies the play's one missing term while reaffirming her authority outside the play in terms of her iconography of sexual transcendence.

The play which more than any other crystallized the genre of the 'offering to the prince' was George Peele's *The Arraignment of Paris* (*c.*1581–4), which deploys a charming but sophisticated scheme of royal flattery. This play, though probably staged at court, resembles the entertainments mounted for royal progresses in the country in its combination of pastoral setting, mythological fable, and ethico-political debate. Peele dramatized the myth of Paris' choice between Venus, Juno, and Pallas, moralizing it conventionally as an allegory of the claims of love, power, and 'chivalry'. Accused by the gods of 'partiality', Paris eloquently defends his decision to give the golden apple to Venus, but the debate cannot be resolved at this level and he is dismissed to Troy and his tragic destiny. The play seems to be over, but at this point Peele innovates by eliding the ethical impasse and the boundaries of the play simultaneously: Diana is nominated to readjudicate the choice and she reaches out beyond the fiction to offer the apple to Elizabeth. Elizabeth's new Troy reverses the tragic doom of the old because her chastity embodies that national inviolability against which it had been Paris' crime to transgress.

The resonance of *The Arraignment of Paris* derives from the manifold ways it figures the games of Elizabethan courtship.[3] As a shepherd who is wooed

---

[3] This paragraph draws heavily on Montrose, 'Gifts and reasons'. See also von Hendy, 'The triumph of chastity', and Braunmuller, *George Peele*, chapter 3.

by two goddesses and patronized by a third, Paris replicates all those courtier–poets who advertised their part in the competition for honours in the language of pastoral or Petrarchan romance. His plea that he would rather have poverty with contentment than wealth or fame without it (926–42) is disingenuous in view of numerous comparable claims by ambitious courtiers. Similarly, the golden apple which is given to Elizabeth at the end resembles those rich gifts that passed between Queen and courtiers every New Year's Day and which are meticulously listed in the court accounts. Such symbolic exchanges affirmed the bonds between patron and client, celebrating the Queen's power but also signalling her dependence on her (unpaid) servants. The play is in itself one such offering; culminating in an essentially social ritual of deference, it advances Peele's own claims to be considered for preferment. And the form which Peele devises expresses his dependence in the most startling way possible: the dilemmas enacted within the fiction can only be resolved by shattering it in the acknowledgment of a redeeming presence outside the world of the play. The sudden recognition of the Queen saves the drift towards tragedy, but only at the expense of the abdication of the playwright in the face of a superior authority who guarantees such resolutions in fiction and in fact.

The form defined by Peele was clearly to be important for the Jacobean masque, and it is the actual or implied norm for much Elizabethan court drama. Plays such as Marston's *Histriomastix* (1598) and Dekker's *Old Fortunatus* (1599) culminate with similar moments of recognition which abrogate the fictional worlds of the plays. Elizabeth is the transcendental signified of which the moral personifications in the plays (Astraea, Virtue, Fame, etc.) are the mere signs:

> VIRTUE
> All these that thus do kneel before your eyes,
> Are shadows like myself: dread Nymph, it lies
> In you to make us substances.   (*Old Fortunatus*, 5.2.337–9)

In Jonson's *Every Man out of his Humour* (1599) and *Cynthia's Revels* (1600), the Queen's presence is invoked rather more conditionally, as an exploration of the debt royal fame owes to the creative powers of the artist. In *Cynthia's Revels* in particular, Cynthia has little more to do than to authorize the court reformation which Crites, the courtier, scholar, and poet, has already set in motion. But the dramatist who most fully exploited this form was John Lyly, whose *Sapho and Phao* (?1584), *Gallathea* (*c.*1583–5), and *Endymion* (1588) use mythological fictions to conduct a sustained exploration of the same iconography and social practices with which *The Arraignment of Paris* was engaged.

Older commentators used to read Lyly's plays as allusive and specific allegories of court life; they are, rather, prismatic refractions of the serious game played continually between courtier and royal mistress. Their actions turn on fables of frustrated courtship of a mistress who is at one and the same time enticing and chaste, proud, remote, inscrutable, desirable, and dangerous. In *Sapho and Phao*, Venus confers unsurpassable beauty on Phao, the common ferryman, and Cupid strikes the great lady Sapho in love with him. Sapho comes close to declaring her love but gains control of Cupid and starts redirecting his arrows. Her power is proved by her resistance to love, but it is counterpointed with the plight of Phao, whose worth can be pitied but never requited. In *Endymion*, the plight of the courtier who falls in love with Cynthia, the moon, is avowedly a metaphor for the frustrated client. Bewitched by a former mistress, Tellus, into an age-long sleep from which he will awake an old man, Endymion resembles those real-life courtiers who enacted their lack of favour or reward on the tiltyard in the roles of disconsolate knights, shepherds, or hermits. Lyly's drama is saved from preciosity by its underlying humanist concerns and its recurrent suggestions of criticism of Cynthia. In *Endymion*, there is more than a hint that Tellus projects the dark side of Cynthia's radiance; it takes Cynthia's chaste kiss of favour to wake Endimion from his enchanted sleep. In *Gallathea*, the fable (in which two young girls, disguised as boys to evade a local custom of virgin sacrifice, fall innocently in love with each other) is a vehicle for a debate between Venus and Diana which is resolved in favour of Venus: if Diana wants her nymphs not to suffer for their chastity, she must give place to the claims of love.[4]

Behind such plays one readily senses the influence of entertainments devised to welcome Elizabeth during her summer progresses. Except for the 1580s, Elizabeth toured the south and east of England extensively throughout her reign, and wherever she went fictions were staged to express the delight of the locality at her arrival. It is in these entertainments that some of the most characteristic tropes of Elizabethan courtship first became current. Elizabeth was repeatedly welcomed as a goddess whose presence brings summer to the locality and turns everyday into holiday. At Kenilworth in 1575 the castle clock was stopped while she was there; at Bedington in 1599, Sir Francis Carew artificially delayed the ripening of his cherry trees so that her arrival seemed to produce spring out of season. Greetings would

---

[4] *Endimion* is studied in relation to mid-century court entertainments by Marie Axton in 'The Tudor masque and Elizabethan court drama' in M. Axton and R. Williams, eds., *English Drama: Forms and Development* (Cambridge, 1977), pp. 24–47. For *Gallathea*, see A. R. Braunmuller's chapter, above, pp. 73–7.

14   The *impresa* portrait of the Earl of Cumberland by Nicholas Hilliard. George Clifford, as Queen's champion, is dressed for the tilt (see p. 135).

be spoken by gruff porters and elegant country deities. At Kenilworth (which is the first entertainment to appropriate Arthurian legendary material for compliment of the Queen), Elizabeth was welcomed by the Lady of the Lake and by a salvage man; at Elvetham in 1591, the deities included Sylvanus, Neptune, Oceanus, and Neaera. The Fairy Queen herself first turned up at Woodstock in 1575, and she was joined at Elvetham by the Fairy King, Oberon. Elizabeth's part was to receive costly gifts, partake of alfresco banquets and rise to the roles that were offered her; she also liked to shoot at deer from standing butts. It is only a short step from these semi-dramatic welcomes to such fully achieved dramas as *A Midsummer Night's Dream* and *Love's Labour's Lost*.

Considerable ironies attach themselves to these occasions, as later to the Stuart masques; their assurances of unfeigned devotion sit uneasily with private letters expressing anxiety about the fitness or the cost. The climate of the welcomes is carefree, but the £700 that Sir Julius Caesar spent in two days at Mitcham in 1598 included the charges of five earlier reports of Elizabeth's imminent arrival that proved to be false alarms; Sir Henry Lee wrote to Cecil in 1600 urging him to prevent a visit from the Queen which he could ill afford.[5] Not merely the Queen but the whole royal entourage had to be lodged and rewarded; the Earl of Hertford built an entire temporary palace at Elvetham in 1591, as well as excavating a lake. The gifts that Elizabeth expected were stupendously expensive, but had to be given under a pretence of being worthless trifles. The decorum of the occasion demanded that staggering sums be seen to be casually squandered on a single day's entertainment.

On the other hand, the value of such progresses was the opportunity they provided for the establishing of 'points of contact' between monarch and people. John Strype wrote that 'by these means shewing herself so freely and condescendingly unto her people, she made herself dear and acceptable unto them', so creating 'mutual love and affection'.[6] Even in the worst weather, Elizabeth was careful to display herself to her subjects; the welcomes that were presented to royalty were also an occasion for the theatrical presenting *of* royalty. On entry to a city the keys would be delivered to the Queen and returned to the aldermen, a symbolic exchange that resembled the acknowledgment of reciprocal obligations in *The Arraignment of Paris*. The recorder would then use his oration to proffer advice or solicit goodwill (as at

---

[5] J. Lyly, *Queen Elizabeth's Entertainment at Mitcham*, ed. L. Hotson (New Haven, Connecticut, 1953), p. 11; E. K. Chambers, *Sir Henry Lee* (Oxford, 1936), p. 180.

[6] Nichols, *The Progresses and Public Processions*, I. 67, 70. Strype is discussing entertainments presented to Elizabeth in the first year of her reign.

Worcester in 1575, for example). Entertainments on country estates typically represented Elizabeth as the presiding genius of a rural festival. At Kenilworth, a morris, a May Lady, and the annual Shrove Tuesday pageant from Coventry were brought in; at Sudeley in 1592 only the weather prevented a sheep-shearing feast; and at Bisham in the same progress she was met by Ceres and the harvest-cart, the harbinger of a domestic golden age of which she was crowned the May Queen. On these occasions Queen and people played out a myth of holiday solidarity that underpinned a political ideology of national unity. It is a commonplace to note that the lesser public visibility of James and Charles and the decline of the royal progress in the early seventeenth century may have helped weaken those symbolic bonds which Elizabeth was careful to assert. Morris dances, mummings, and seasonal feasts reappear in Stuart masques but as rituals which affirm the royal sense of difference from the people. The one Stuart provincial entertainment of any real stature, Ben Jonson's rollicking *Masque of Metamorphosed Gipsies* (1621), subverts the Elizabethan form by presenting James as fleeced rather than welcomed by aristocratic subjects disguised as gypsies. Jonson's country masque exposes the pretence at the heart of the show of deference: the 'unfeigned' welcome is suspiciously close to a strategy by which mendacious courtiers pick honours and offices from the royal pocket.[7]

Elizabethan progresses were no less opportunities for courtship, but the agreed language was controlled by a greater tact: Sir Edward Dyer's response to disgrace at court was a song of Despair that was sung to the Queen by a musician hidden in an oak tree at Woodstock. The humanist principle of debate that put intellectual flesh on the bones of the spectacle meant that welcomes were often veiled criticism of policy or attempts at political persuasion. Often Elizabeth found herself invited to resolve a dispute between two characters in which serious issues were at stake beneath the game. In Sir Philip Sidney's *The Lady of May*, performed at Wanstead in 1578 under the sponsorship of the Earl of Leicester, the title character warned her that in the debate she was to adjudicate lurked a coded bid for the royal hand by Elizabeth's most eligible English suitor: 'in judging me you judge more than me in it'.

In the context of anxieties over the succession, much court drama before the establishment of the myth of virginity celebrated by Lyly and Peele addressed questions of marriage. 'This is all against me', Elizabeth said to the Spanish ambassador during a play of 1565 in which Juno debated with

---

[7] See D. B. J. Randall, *Jonson's Gypsies Unmasked* (Durham, North Carolina, 1975).

Diana; at a court marriage in 1566 the choice of Paris was again staged, but this time the apple went to the bride.[8] In particular, Leicester used festivity to advance his claim to Elizabeth's affections, beginning in 1561 when, as Robert Dudley, he took the part of Prince Pallaphilos, suitor of Pallas, at the Inner Temple Christmas revels; the role of Olympian champion closely shadowed his militant and anti-Catholic political position. Fifteen years on, the courtship culminated at Kenilworth in a series of interwoven narratives that praised marriage and long-suffering faith, and disparaged virginity. The fictions at Kenilworth were singularly transparent. Leicester's poet, George Gascoigne, admitted that the gifts which had been feigned to be sent by the gods were actually paid for by his patron, and Elizabeth was regaled by presentations involving the Lady of the Lake who is assailed by Sir Bruce Sans Pity, and the cruel nymph Zabeta whose repulses to her suitors have turned them into monsters. But the hazard of occasional drama is that events may not turn out as anticipated: Elizabeth obligingly freed the Lady from Sir Bruce's attentions and failed to be impressed by the song of Deep Desire, transformed into a quaking holly bush. Three years later at Wanstead, which was very much Leicester's final throw, invited by Sidney's May Lady to choose between an active forester and a submissive shepherd – with strong hints that the forester was to be preferred – she chose the shepherd. Sidney's bitter epilogue presented the Queen with the 'rosary' on which Leicester used to pray to St Elizabeth with the plea 'love me much better than you were wont'.[9]

In the following decades the iconography changed: Sidney's last major appearance was as one of the *Four Foster Children of Desire*, in a spectacular tilt of 1581 (during Elizabeth's courtship by the Duke of Alençon) at which the knights jousting in the name of Desire finally acknowledged defeat at the hands of the champions of Perfect Beauty. The knights of Desire were warned not to 'destroy a common blessing for a private benefit: Will you subdue the sun, who shall rest in the shadow where the weary take breath, the disquiet rest, and all comfort, will ye bereave all men of those glistering and gladsome beams'.[10] The later Elizabethan welcomes elaborated themes common to European state festivals (such as the enchanted knights and hermits at Ditchley in 1592), but the roles scripted for the Queen were those of remote and idealized goddesses – Gloriana, Cynthia, Astraea. *Summer's Last Will and Testament* glances sideways at such royal revelry with a promise

[8] Axton, *The Queen's Two Bodies*, pp. 49 and 1.
[9] R. Kimbrough and P. Murphy, 'The Helmingham Hall manuscript of Sidney's *The Lady of May*: a commentary and transcription', *RenD* n.s. 1 (1968), 119.
[10] Wilson, *Entertainments*, p. 75.

that Summer will not expire until Elizabeth has finished her progress, and he bequeathes her what remains of his warm days to keep her unvexed (133–6, 1841). However, at the Archbishop's Croydon, where the Queen was *not* present, such an allusion only served to intensify the awareness of this audience, hedged about by plague and fading summer, that for mere mortals such mythologization was not a real possibility.

Under Elizabeth's successor, the court masque quickly emerged as the leading state entertainment. The form of the Jacobean masque, in which scenery, song, and speech were brought together within a single, integral fable that accommodated flattery of the monarch with an opportunity for social dancing between masquers and audience, was first completely achieved in a late-Elizabethan entertainment, Francis Davison's *Proteus and the Adamantine Rock* (1595). However, it would be misleading to represent the Stuart masque as the culmination of a continuous, quasi-evolutionary process. There was no steady flowering as the form of festival was dictated by the changing social, economic, and political requirements of the court. Royal revelry was first systematically promoted by Henry VIII, who desired to compete publicly with the powerful and high-profile monarchies of Francis I and Charles V. The typical Henrician revel was a neo-medieval tilt or an entry into the court by disguised dancers on a spectacular pageant-wagon such as a castle or a rock, displaying the self-confidence and charm of an ambitious prince and mimicking the glamorous chivalry of Burgundian court festivals. Elizabethan revels seem diffuse and heterogeneous by comparison, largely because Elizabeth herself withdrew to the role of principal spectator and failed to sponsor large-scale festivity: entertainments were presented to the Queen rather than by her, and their forms were improvised to suit the occasion. James and Charles on the other hand were prepared to lavish substantial sums on festivity and to exploit its potential for political statement. The masque developed as their preferred form primarily because of its ritual and almost mystical dimensions: it celebrated the dignity of the prince and choreographed the court into an act of homage to his magical centrality. Furthermore, the masques' emphasis on ceremony, royal glory, and courtly elegance suited the purposes of two monarchs whose attitude towards the dynastic and religious conflicts of Europe was unpopularly pro-Spanish or at best neutral, pacific, and non-interventionist. In striking contrast with the often militantly Protestant and nationalist tone of Elizabethan tilts, the lauding in many Stuart masques of England's peace and separateness from a war-torn Europe marks a significant political as well as artistic

15 Detail of the private wedding masque from the portrait of Sir Henry Unton

departure. The masques ushered the Stuarts into an international community by cultivating the visual and political language of pan-European absolutism.

There has been a tendency to speak of 'the Jonsonian masque' as if Jonson's masques were somehow paradigmatic for the Jacobean form. It is certainly true that Jacobean masquing was dominated by Ben Jonson, whose thirty or so masques, tilts, and welcomes constitute the single most sustained and elaborate exploration of the potentialities of court revel. Yet the *Masque* of Queens (1609), which from many points of view appears the quintessential Jonsonian masque, was achieved only after several years of formal experiment, and embodies a norm which was no sooner realized than it began to be modified. Moreover, though Jonson invented the 'double masque' with separate entries for male and female masquers (*Hymenaei*, 1606) and in *Queens* turned the 'antemasque' (a prefatory show) into the 'antimasque' (a structural foil to the main masque), other crucial innovations occurred in non-Jonsonian contexts. It was Samuel Daniel who first used more than one change of scene and a song for the masquers' departure (*Tethys' Festival*, 1610), and Thomas Campion who first introduced an antimasque subsequent to the main masque and a scene that depicted a setting familiar to the audience (*The Somerset Masque*, 1613) – all of these were to become commonplace features. It is tempting to argue that the single most important event for the development of the form must have been the journey to Italy in 1613 by the principal masque designer, Inigo Jones, and the technological possibilities that Jones's experience of Italian court revel opened up, and yet from another angle no less important must have been the musical trend at about the same time towards the declamatory ayre associated with the vocal writing of Nicholas Lanier and, later, Henry Lawes. As a masque was a multi-media event involving song, dance, architecture, painting, and some poetry, it was difficult for any one contributor completely to dominate it. Equally crucial in the determining of a masque must have been who was paying, who was dancing, and what the social and/or political significances of the occasion were. The masque writer had not only to accommodate his ideas to the scenic and musical skills at his disposal, he had tactfully to negotiate the complex statements and counter-statements passing in the event between King, Queen, Prince, and lords. Little wonder that we often sense that the author was embarrassed, or read contemporary reports that 'the masque did not please'.

Jonson's achievement in the masque was to construct forms which held these competing imperatives in a unity while leaving him free to advance his own elevated notions of the educational potential of recreation, the ability of the masques' 'high and hearty inventions' insensibly to refine their participants by laying hold 'on more removed mysteries' (*Hymenaei*, Preface). His major early performances, *The Masque of Blackness* (1605), *Hymenaei* (1606) and *The Masque of Beauty* (1608), attempted to achieve this by distilling into the ephemeral occasion an unprecedented density of classical learning and symbolic meaning. The performers were participating in no mere courtly masquerade but a ceremony weighty with political and intellectual signifi-

16 Inigo Jones, scene for *Oberon*, 1611

cance. Each masque was, loosely, a quest, and the event was made performative of the King's authority because the fictions cast him as the object of the masquers' search; their political dimensions derived from the way that each celebrated or enacted James's none-too-popular intention of imposing political unity onto his two kingdoms, turning England and Scotland magically into Great Britain. In *Blackness*, the word 'Britannia' resolves a riddle the answer to which the masquers, daughters of Niger, are seeking out; in *Beauty* the same masquers reappear, their black skins transformed by the miraculous power of royal Albion. In *Hymenaei*, Jonson turned a court marriage into a bravura affirmation of the concept of Union: James was greeted as the embodiment of a principle which, in ways both obvious and mystical, sustains the entire universe. And yet structurally these masques remain Elizabethan in feel. The speaking characters were essentially presenters rather than participants, and they inducted masquers who (in *Blackness* and *Beauty*) arrived on what underneath were old-fashioned pageant cars. Nor was the staging fully integral to the action, but basically still a static setting; in

Hymenaei and *Beauty*, the staging was dispersed, not focused on a single point as would later become the norm. It was Inigo Jones rather than Jonson who made the King symbolically central to the masque by placing him opposite the meeting-point of the lines of perspective, privileging him as the only member of the audience with an undistorted view of the spectacle.

Jonson's structural innovations in *The Masque of Queens* (1609) were no less dependent on Jones's technological developments. Earlier masques made use of the *machina versatilis* or 'turning machine', a scenic unit which revolved to discover hidden masquers. *Queens*, however, opened with 'an ugly hell' before which twelve witches danced in an attempt to curse the glory of the court; but suddenly 'the whole face of the scene altered, scarce suffering the memory of any such thing', in place of which were revealed the masquers seated in the House of Fame. Jonson appears to be describing the *scena ductilis*, or system of sliding flats which enabled the entire setting, and not only one unit, to be changed at a stroke. This arrangement turned the masque from a static presentation or discovery into a dynamic action. Queen Anne and her eleven accompanying 'queens' entered the action in a blaze of light before which the witches vanished as if insubstantial; their triumphant discovery mimed the victory of truth over falsehood and fame over envy under the approving and controlling gaze of the royal spectator. The witches were dynamically situated as 'antimasquers', characters who not only introduce but oppose the main masquers, and the masque turned on a principle of contestation in which the enemies of kingship were subordinated by kingly power. Of course, this is not conventional dramatic conflict, as Stephen Orgel has emphasized: unlike opposing characters on the public stages, the masquers and antimasquers cannot occupy the same space, and the queens have only to appear for the witches to vanish.[11] But that is part of the masque's political point: the victory of royal authority was represented as instantaneous and effortless.

The form established in *Queens* was to become standard for Jonson's subsequent masques. Indeed, in comparison with the multiple scene-changes of later Caroline masques, Jonson showed little desire to move any further in the direction of complexity, and the principles of contestation and single magical transformation remained germane in his practice to the end. However, this form was to come under pressure through changing political circumstances and through Jonson's personal ambivalence about a court which, notwithstanding, he chose to celebrate. The worry about the extravagance of court masques which contemporaries sometimes voiced occasion-

---

[11] Orgel, *The Jonsonian Masque*, p. 139.

ally surfaced in Jonson's writings: in *Love Restored* (1612), one antimasquer was a puritan complaining about the expense of court revelry. More personal to the masque writer was the anxiety that the idealization he was compelled to perform might not be the 'teaching through praise' which theoretically it was – leading men into virtue by writing roles which depicted what they should be, rather than what they were – but an inducing of self-congratulation or a papering-over of cracks (Jonson confronted this issue directly in his 'Epistle to Selden' and 'To my Muse'). Such anxieties can only have intensified in the wake of scandal following the discovery that the courtier Sir Thomas Overbury had been poisoned at the instigation of the wife of the Earl of Somerset, the favourite for whom Jonson's *Irish Masque* and *Challenge at Tilt* (1613–14) had been written, and the meteoric rise at court of the glamorous George Villiers, future Duke of Buckingham. To write a masque called *The Golden Age Restored* in 1616 required either an excess of complacency or an excess of faith in the admonitory and persuasive power of art.

The changing political climate affected Jonson's masques in two ways. Firstly, in the masques following *Queens*, there is a tendency for the central transformations to become more provisional, a matter of gradual refinement rather than a switching between absolutes.[12] One sign of this was a willingness to accommodate the antimasquers into the main masque instead of banishing them outright. In *Oberon* (1611), the antimasquers were playful satyrs who had to be instructed not to disturb the solemn celebration but who remained on stage during the triumph of the Fairy King; in *The Vision of Delight* (1617), they were fantastic rather than threatening, and were openly part of the evening's amusements. Such accommodations were underlined by the masques' increasing concessions to comedy: in entertainments such as *Christmas his Masque* (1617) and *Pan's Anniversary* (1621), the comic world of the antimasquers was invoked in such density as to make it difficult to dismiss them out of hand. Further, Jonson's middle masques tended to dwell self-reflexively and critically on the nature of revelling itself, and to treat the miraculous transformations as something problematic rather than to be taken for granted. The outstanding instance here is *Pleasure Reconciled to Virtue* (1618), in which the masquers appear only after the conditions of their idealization have been carefully defined. The antimasque mounts a dramatic fable around the archetype of heroic virtue, Hercules. Hercules rests from the laborious life of virtue, but only when it is established that

---

[12] These developments are considered at greater length by Stephen Orgel in '"To make boards speak": Inigo Jones's stage and the Jonsonian masque', *RenD* n.s. 1 (1968), 121–52.

relaxation does not mean concession to vice: he first has to defeat Bacchus, symbol of riotous indulgence, and the pigmies, symbols of human littleness, who would kill him if he slept too deeply. The masquers themselves descend from the Hill of Knowledge, but they return to it at the end: their sojourn with pleasure is represented as only temporary, and they are led by 'Daedalus the wise' who sings that dancing involves its own discipline:

> For dancing is an exercise
>   Not only shows the movers wit,
> But maketh the beholder wise
>   As he hath power to rise to it   (269–72)

Jonson flatters the masquers as 'born to know' (225) but still insists that their virtue has to be acquired. If other masques made courtly grace look inherent and effortless, *Pleasure Reconciled to Virtue* disclosed virtue as something constructed and sustained, exposing the social engineering beneath the court's miraculous power.

Secondly, Jonson's late masques responded to the political anxieties of the 1620s by increasingly insisting on the social dimensions of the form: the antimasquers excluded from the celebration were represented as common people, vulgar, inquisitive, impertinent, or foreign. Particularly, in the context of James's initiative for wedding Prince Charles to the Spanish Infanta, Jonson found himself using the antimasques to censure would-be political commentators, newsmongers, and satirical poets.[13] Several of these late masques fall frankly into two halves. In *News from the New World* (1620), *The Masque of Augurs* (1622), *Time Vindicated* (1623), and *Neptune's Triumph for the Return of Albion* (1624), the antimasque and masque comprise two opposed worlds, and there is barely any fable or action which connects them: the banishing of antimasque by masque was not a process of education or confutation but simply a *fait accompli* (see p. 144). It is difficult not to feel that the situation of the late-Jacobean court was putting Jonson's form under considerable strain. In *Neptune's Triumph*, a masque written for the Infanta-less return of Prince Charles from Spain, Jonson, unhappy with the country-wide rejoicing at the collapse of royal policy, astonishingly represented the real enemy not as Spain but as the politically minded common people.

Jonson was well suited for the role of principal masque-poet because of his respect for James's pacific and internationalist policies and his distaste for what he saw as popular religious and political fanaticism. However, other masque-poets registered varying degrees of unease about the court and

---

[13] There is an important account of Jonson's late masques by Sara Pearl, '"Sounding to present occasions": Jonson's masques of 1620–5' in Lindley, *The Court Masque*, pp. 60–77.

practised the form in ways that rendered it more problematic. Many outside the court saw masques as inherently suspect; it is no accident that several plays of the period use them as symbols of courtly waste, secrecy or duplicity. Others – most famously Francis Bacon, who said 'these things are but toys'[14] – dismissed the educational or political pretensions which Jonson pursued in the form. Yet Bacon himself wrote tilt speeches for the Earl of Essex and spent £2,000 on presenting *The Masque of Flowers* (1614) to the Earl of Somerset: clearly he knew that revels could be useful vehicles for mediation and insinuation, criticism and compliment.

The debate over the value of revels was thrashed out in prefaces to masques published by Jonson and his rival Samuel Daniel, who won the commission for the very first Stuart masque, *The Vision of the Twelve Goddesses* (1604). Daniel implicitly took up cudgels with Jonson by disclaiming any 'mystical interpretations' (35) and disparaging the seriousness of his masque's mythology: 'whosoever strives to show most wit about these punctilios of dreams and shows are sure sick of a disease they cannot hide' (200–2).[15] In *Tethys' Festival* (1610), he further contradicted Jonson's belief that words were the 'soul' of the masque that survived after the 'body' (the performance) had been forgotten (*Hymenaei*, Preface) by insisting that 'in these things ... the only life consists in show'.[16] A client of Queen Anne, Daniel was none the less deeply sceptical about the forms of panegyric he was expected to write. *The Vision of the Twelve Goddesses* memorialized the union of the kingdoms by depicting the masquers descending from a remote mountain, but the chosen form – a procession by threes alternating with torchbearers – was stiffly old-fashioned, and his verses repeatedly insisted that this was only a masquerade (in contrast to Jonson, who was inclined to efface the distinction between masquer and role). Daniel was careful not to idealize, even while he celebrated; his court play, *The Queen's Arcadia* (1605), significantly depicted an imaginary kingdom undergoing reformation.[17]

Few authors can have felt as uncomfortable about their masques as Daniel, but there were times when conditions at court enabled masques to be receptive to sentiments or attitudes which ordinarily were beyond their scope. In particular, during the period in which Prince Henry (d. 1612) was politically active, and during the diplomacy that culminated in the marriage of Princess Elizabeth to the Calvinist Prince Frederick of the Rhine, court

---

[14] F. Bacon, *The Essays or Counsels*, ed. M. Kiernan (Oxford, 1985), p. 117.

[15] Quoted from the edition by Joan Rees in Spencer and Wells, *A Book of Masques*.

[16] Daniel, *Dramatic Works*, p. 307.

[17] On Daniel, see John Pitcher, '"In those figures which they seeme": Samuel Daniel's *Tethys' Festival*', in Lindley, *The Court Masque*, pp. 33–46.

17 Inigo Jones, designs for an antimasque, probably the contents of the cooking pot in Jonson's *Neptune's Triumph*, 1624–5: (a) a turkey and an unknown animal, (b) a fish and an unknown bird (see p. 142)

festival was several times used to promote policies that cut across James's non-interventionist stance. Henry died at the early age of nineteen, but there had already begun to develop – or to be developed for him – a mythology that cast him in the role of warrior-prince, a militant Calvinist hero who was destined to be a political champion of Protestantism and under whom England would again become a significant European power. James had other ideas for Henry: he intended to wed him to a Catholic princess, a plan complementary to his wedding of his daughter to a Calvinist and part of his studiedly non-confessional position on Europe's religious divisions. What Henry's private views were we cannot tell, but he allowed himself to be seen in festival roles that had a significantly aggressive edge, and he enthusiastically resuscitated the court tilt, with all its nostalgic overtones of the (supposedly) interventionist days of Queen Elizabeth.[18]

Henry's festivals demonstrate how problematic is the interpretation of these deceptively simple masques: it is by no means clear whether the masques were advice *to* Henry or policy statements *by* him, and if the latter whether they were directed to the King or a wider public or both. Jonson, who in *Prince Henry's Barriers* (1610) and *Oberon* (1611) used Arthurian material positively for the only time in his career, was plainly embarrassed by the commissions. Obliged to write in praise of an uncongenial militarism, he paused in the *Barriers* to defend the arts of peace and used *Oberon* to urge Henry to be dutiful to his father: the two entertainments endeavoured to work out common ground between King and Prince (see p. 147). Daniel also praised trade and industry in Henry's investiture masque, *Tethys' Festival* (1610), but he was more respectful of the sub-Arthurian iconography which made Jonson so uncomfortable. His masque dwelt on England's naval strength and located Henry firmly in the Tudor tradition. Presented with Astraea's sacred sword, Henry was provocatively identified as Elizabeth's heir; the chivalric and Spenserian dimensions of this masque were in implicit tension with the classical and imperial iconography that Jonson devised for James.

Henry did not live to see his sister's wildly popular marriage (1613), but his influence can still be felt behind the revels that celebrated it. The official festival (as it were) was Thomas Campion's *The Lords' Masque*. Campion, a client of James's favourite the Earl of Somerset, was not without a heightened sense of the difficulties of panegyric.[19] However, *The Lords' Masque* (possibly the most elaborate Jacobean masque) attempted to contain the Calvinist marriage within a perspective acceptable to the King by dis-

---

[18] See Strong, *Henry, Prince of Wales*.

[19] Campion's masques are fully considered by David Lindley in *Thomas Campion* (Leiden, 1986).

paraging prophetic enthusiasm in the antimasque and emphasizing that the celebrations were controlled by the peace of Jove. Rather different were two masques brought to court by gentlemen of the Inns of Court. Francis Beaumont's *Masque of the Inner Temple and Gray's Inn* was on the Spenserian theme of the wedding of the Rhine and the Thames and included a country morris dance; Beaumont's masquers danced in the roles of priestly knights, consecrated to ideals of ancient and pious heroism. George Chapman's *Memorable Masque* made fun of a frivolous courtier and featured Virginian Indians converted to true religion after the British example; the golden age Chapman had in mind would have come about through respect for honour and law, and through industrious colonial enterprise. It has recently been discovered that some people even had plans for an apocalyptic *Masque of Truth* that openly depicted England leading the Protestant nations in the struggle against Spain and Rome.[20] Not surprisingly, this never left the drawing-board, but it suggests how misleading it is to think of the masque as merely a vehicle for the royal ideology; masques *could* be used to talk back to the king in his own language.

The last major flourishing of the masque came in the 1630s, during the long Caroline peace. These were the most spectacular masques of all, distinguished by their multiple scene-changes, musical virtuosity, settings that ranged from heaven to hell, and by their consistently elevated tone of royal apotheosis. Charles's masque writers were rather second-order poets – Aurelian Townshend, William Davenant, and Thomas Carew – but the interest of the form was sustained by Inigo Jones's technological wizardry: Jones more than fulfilled Charles's wish to project royal power as a force that could transform stormy landscapes to serene gardens under the approving gaze of clouds of deities. Many of Jones's Caroline masques drew directly on Parisian or Florentine festivals, but the alliance between monarch and architect which they proclaimed was entirely characteristic of Jones's Augustan mentality: increasingly, his designs came to dwell on idealized panoramas of London or stupendous classical cityscapes which testify to the civilizing powers of monarchy. The 1634 masque, Carew's *Coelum Britannicum*, which moved from ruined buildings to a distant prospect of Windsor Castle presided over by Eternity, typifies this confident assertion of imperial renewal: so compelling is Charles's example that the gods are supposed to be reforming the heavens after the English model.

In view of the court's inglorious future, it is tempting to interpret these masques as Charles's wish-fulfilling exorcism of intractable political diffi-

---

[20] D. Norbrook, '"The Masque of Truth": court entertainments and international Protestant politics in the early Stuart period', *The Seventeenth Century* 1 (1986), 81–110.

18   Inigo Jones, Prince Henry as Oberon, from Jonson's *Oberon,
the Fairy Prince*, 1611 (see p. 145)

culties, a fantasy world into which he could retreat from reality. But this is to prejudge the issue; it is truer to see these masques as the necessary cultural counterpart to Charles's programme of government without parliamentary subsidy. Charles was seeking to survive by retrenching his finances, tightening up provincial discipline, and suspending military commitments, and his masques argued the case for peace, order, and withdrawal from a Europe torn by religious warfare. Of course Charles's masques encouraged him to take too sanguine a view of his political and financial resources, but for as long as his people continued to co-operate with his needs in government the masques were not so much escapism as images of what he thought he was capable of achieving. Moreover, the Caroline masque was no more monolithic than the Jacobean: King and Queen did not always see eye to eye on policy, and Henrietta Maria seems sometimes to have used her own court theatricals to promote French alliances against Spain.[21] When the crisis finally loomed, Charles made one determined attempt to negotiate his position through revelry, and Davenant's *Salmacida Spolia* (1640) cast him as Philogenes, the Lover of his People who wished to conciliate his subjects, not to fight them. However, three of the masquers dancing with him *were* to fight him and four more were in opposition in the early months of the Long Parliament: the loss of the possibilities for conciliation also marks the point at which the masques ceased to come altogether.[22]

Outside the court, the major traditions of private and occasional playing took place at the Inns of Court and the universities. Both of these were revelling traditions, and almost all of the plays and masques performed in these environments were part of Christmas feasting. The importance of these environments goes beyond the rather mediocre plays that survive from them, as they were the formative milieux of the 'University Wits' on the one hand, and termer-dramatists such as Marston, Webster, Beaumont, and Ford on the other. Moreover, before the establishment of the commercial London playhouses, significant theatrical innovation took place under their auspices: the first English blank-verse tragedy (*Gorboduc*, 1562) was an Inns of Court play, while the Cambridge melodrama *Richardus Tertius* (1579–80) is the earliest surviving English history play. After the coming of the commercial

---

[21] See my 'Entertaining the Palatine prince: plays on foreign affairs 1635–37', *ELR* 13 (1983), 319–44; and my *Theatre and Crisis*, pp. 25–54.

[22] See my 'Politics and the masque: *Salmacida Spolia*' in T. Healy and J. Sawday, *Literature and the English Civil War* (Cambridge, 1990), pp. 59–74.

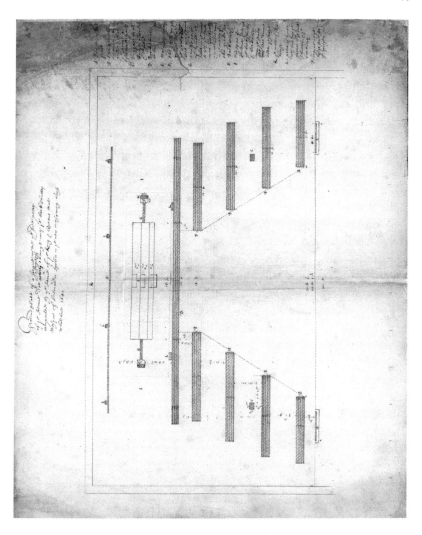

19   John Webb, groundplan for Davenant's *Salmacida Spolia*, 1640

stages, the university and termer traditions ceased to be innovative, and even defined themselves in opposition to the professionals: a band of incompetent common players is ridiculed in Marston's Middle Temple play *Histriomastix* (1598), and Burbage and Kemp among others are 'glorious vagabonds' who are earning undeserved fortunes by 'mouthing words that better wits have framed' in the Cambridge play *The Return from Parnassus, Part 2* (1603?). Unlike the court, which saw too many plays to retain an especially powerful consciousness of the uniqueness of the season,[23] these environments preserved a sense of seasonal revel which had continuity with medieval kinds of communal festivity. At Gray's Inn in 1594, a Christmas champion even entered the hall on horseback and rode around the hearth, which was placed in the middle of the room.[24]

At the universities the custom of electing Christmas princes to preside over the collegiate revels, though provided for in some college statutes, had largely died out by the early seventeenth century. The last such prince of any importance reigned at St John's College, Oxford, during the 1607–8 Christmas, and five shows and two plays in Latin and three shows and three plays in English were mounted for his benefit.[25] Other opportunities for drama were provided by royal visits, for which entertainments had to be prepared to dispel the tedium of academic disputations. As James and Charles visited their universities more frequently than Elizabeth had done, this sort of stimulus was on the increase. James may have seen his first stage set in single-point perspective at Oxford in 1605, and he made a special trip to Cambridge in 1615 merely to see a repeat of George Ruggle's wildly successful Latin comedy *Ignoramus* (with its satire on a puritanical lawyer). Archbishop Laud used the royal visit to Oxford in 1636 as a showpiece for the reforms and patronage he had been lavishing on the university; one play, William Cartwright's *The Royal Slave*, was so admired that its scenes were carried down to Hampton Court for a second performance and Cartwright achieved a brief but interesting career as a semi-professional playwright. The members of Queens' College, Cambridge, were sufficiently committed to the theatre to build their own private playhouse in the 1630s.

However, the impact of college drama on the wider world was limited by the specialized nature of that drama. Much of it was in Latin (when Elizabeth threatened a visit to Oxford in 1592, the Vice-Chancellor

---

[23] But see R. C. Hassel, *Renaissance Drama and the English Church Year* (Lincoln, Nebraska, 1979).

[24] See Bland, *Gesta Grayorum*, p. 14.

[25] The manuscript is edited by F. S. Boas and W. W. Greg as *The Christmas Prince* (Malone Society, Oxford, 1923).

panicked because he had no English plays to show her),[26] and much was entrenched in fighting the obscure battles of civic and college politics. College plays tended to be poor imitations of Italian neo-classical comedy – all sundered families and intriguing pandars, what Milton witheringly described as young divines 'writhing and unboning their clergy limbs to all the antic and dishonest gestures of Trinculoes, buffoons and bawds'[27] (he was thinking of Thomas Tomkis's comedy *Albumazar* [1615]) – or they were staid moralities, of which Tomkis's *Lingua* (1607), an allegory of the five senses, is easily the best. To pass muster with the college authorities, such plays had to be educational or chaste, and the prologue to *Lingua* emphasizes the play's modest innocence; indeed, Oliver Cromwell himself is supposed to have acted in it (though the evidence is thin). Even when popular in style, their academic preoccupations prevented them from being populist.

Much the most interesting college dramas are the three 'Parnassus' plays, the third of which may be by the satirist Joseph Hall, and the plays of Thomas Randolph. *The Pilgrimage to Parnassus* was performed at St John's College, Cambridge, at Christmas 1598–9, and is a formulaic if amusing enough morality in the academic manner: Philomusus and Studioso are journeying to Parnassus (= Cambridge) and have to learn to avoid the twin temptations of Madido (poetic fury) and Stupido (puritanism). But between this and the two *Return from Parnassus* plays (*Part 1*, 1599–1600; *Part 2*, 1603?), the St John's men caught up with the London vogue for snarling satire and humours comedy. The two *Returns* chronicle the future careers of the Cambridge students and reflect farcically but bitterly on graduate unemployment and the world's neglect of merit. The students attempt to live, variously, as tutors, clerks, ministers, writers, balladeers, and hangers-on to rich patrons, but each comes to grief and is reduced to keeping sheep or writing satire. This scheme allows a panorama of scenes from the world of patronage, as well as coney-catching plots and extensive discussions and pastiche of contemporary poets (including Shakespeare). With their bitter perspective on a shiftless and hostile world, the *Returns* are very like two city comedies turned inside-out, with students rather than witty young gentlemen as the heroes, and simonists, undeserving patrons, and exploitative lawyers as the villains. There is a real conflict of attitudes here, as the students demand rewards from a world which they also despise; a combination of anxiety and wounded pride prevents their criticism from being (as it were) merely academic.

---

[26] Boas, *University Drama*, p. 323.
[27] From *An Apology for Smectymnuus* (1642). For the link with *Albumazar*, see Dick, *Albumazar*, pp. 54–5.

By far the most impressive academic playwright is Thomas Randolph (d. 1635), who was the one dramatist successfully to make the transition between college and professional stages. Randolph's handful of comedies take neo-classical forms but use them with theatrical competence and marry them to lively poetry, topical concerns, anti-Laudian jokes, and a healthy intellectual scepticism. His college career began with freshman's 'saltings' (parodies of academic disputations for performance at undergraduate initiations – a form which Randolph's Cambridge contemporary John Milton also attempted)[28] and culminated with *The Jealous Lovers*, staged before the court at Trinity College in 1632. Meanwhile in London Randolph had attached himself to the circle around Ben Jonson and become the first house playwright for the new boys' company at Salisbury Court: his *The Muses' Looking-Glass* (1630) celebrates the opening of the playhouse by conducting a defence of playgoing which amusingly convinces two puritans in the (stage) audience. Had Randolph lived beyond thirty, through him the academic drama might have again significantly influenced the professional stage.

The Inns of Court had a more immediate impact on the London playhouses, not least because the termers (or students) formed a considerable section of the regular audiences (Edward Heath, an Inner Templar of the 1620s, saw forty-nine plays in eighteen months alone).[29] The Inns brought together a unique constituency of gentlemen and aristocrats, many of whom were in residence as much for the acquirement of the social graces as for a proficiency in the law. Some were men who hoped to hold important government posts later in life, and the revels of the Inns have a quality of self-advertisement as well as political rehearsal. Others developed political interests through their legal studies: many future MPs worried about the expansion of the royal prerogative were here. Equally notable were the literary and intellectual interests of the termers, who seem to have developed an insatiable taste for satire, elegy, 'humours', and pastiche: a quality of avant-gardism attaches itself to their sports, which finds an echo in the parodic, sceptical, and sophisticatedly self-reflexive writing of the professional dramatists who emerged from the Inns (such as Webster and Marston). Finally, the Inns were also academies of manners and arenas for intense personal rivalries and competition that sometimes broke out into real violence. As the great contemporary lawyer John Fortescue described them, they were 'a sort of *Academy*, or *Gymnasium*, fit for persons of their station; where they learn singing, and all kinds of music, dancing, and such other

---

[28] See R. Richek, 'Thomas Randolph's *Salting* (1627), its text, and John Milton's sixth prolusion as another salting', *ELR* 12 (1982), 102–31.

[29] Prest, *The Inns of Court*, p. 155.

accomplishments and diversions (which are called *Revels*) as are suitable to their quality, and such as are usually practised at Court'.[30]

Revelling was an intrinsic part of the Inns' life. At the annual reader's Moot, a feast was held, after which stately traditional dances, called the 'measures', were danced by the whole Inn, from judges downwards, to be followed by livelier dances by the students. But the termers also held Christmas 'commons' (feasting and dicing) which, when prosecuted with sufficient enthusiasm, might turn into an elaborate and semi-serious public game. Several of these expensive revels were sustained under Elizabeth, James and Charles, of which the most famous were the *Gesta Grayorum* of 1594–5; always they attracted crowds of genteel sightseers and involved processions through the city, even pageants on the Thames. In such revels, a Christmas prince would be elected who would take a title, appoint officers, and hold court very much as if he had real authority. At Gray's Inn in 1594–5, the Prince of Purpoole nominated an extensive household and processed pompously to the hall. Privy seals were sent out for the raising of finance, parliaments proclaimed, homage taken, and statutes promulgated. An ambassador was received from the Temple and solemn masques performed for him. When events went awry, a trial was held and the Privy Council reformed; an order of knighthood was instituted, and a progress to Russia performed. Such revels would involve the entire community in their enactment (Marston's Middle Temple play *Histriomastix* (1598) calls for a cast of more than 120), though in post-Elizabethan Inns of Court masques, such as William Browne's *Ulysses and Circe* (1615) and Middleton's *The Masque of Heroes* (1619), professional players would be employed for the speaking parts, as happened at Whitehall.

The fascination of the termers' revels lies in their covert dialogue between jest and earnest. These were very much the pastimes of witty and precocious students on holiday from dry studies. In the Gray's Inn *Masque of Mountebanks* (1618), youthful knights magically imprisoned in the closet of Obscurity were rescued and brought out to dance; other revels repeatedly made fun of legal forms and jargon and involved the reading of interminable mock legal documents. They also specialized in rough and scatological humour about social behaviour, the courting of mistresses, the visiting of bawdy-houses and the like, and in a vein of cruel and sceptical parody. It has been plausibly suggested that Shakespeare's *Troilus and Cressida*, which was never 'clapper-clawed with the palms of the vulgar' (1607 preface) was designed for performance at the Inns of Court, and Jonson regarded *Every*

---

[30] Quoted in Green, *The Inns of Court and Early English Drama*, p. 33.

Man out of his Humour as a play fitted to the termers and so dedicated it to them. But, as is suggested by Jonson's dedication to 'the noblest nurseries of liberty and humanity in the kingdom', the termers' revels, for all their mocking of decorum, were understood to be essentially educational. The violent jokes work through an exploration of etiquette at once public and personal, while the elaborate parody of public political institutions was an opportunity for practising roles which one day some might aspire to play in earnest. The Prince of Purpoole presided over a council which debated in all seriousness the question of whether a prince were better to make war, pursue learning, build, get money, follow virtue, or revel; the author of these remarkable set-piece orations was none other than Francis Bacon. The late-contemporary historian of the profession, William Dugdale, claimed that termers did 'not only study the Laws, but [used] such other exercises as might make them the more serviceable to the King's court ... so that these hostels [were] seminaries of the court'.[31] One ambiguous aspect of this interaction between game and earnest was the homage that was done by 'real' political figures to the supposed authority of the Christmas king. Commonly noblemen would send him gifts in tribute, and the Lord Mayor would feast him; on such occasions the procession through the streets became a genuine part of London pageantry. When the Prince of Purpoole passed Greenwich by water, the Queen herself commanded a volley from the Tower for him; at Shrovetide, he took a masque to court and so truly became part of the revels of the real monarch. By 1598, the former Christmas prince was himself a Gentleman Pensioner to the Queen.

Inevitably, there was always a possibility that parody of royal forms might turn into genuine criticism. As periods of misrule, such games skirted collisions with the established authorities, and several times in the 1620s and 30s Christmas princes ran into trouble with the city and even with the King.[32] But the political interests of the lawyers meant that the games could easily be made to carry advice, conciliation, or argument. I have already mentioned Dudley's use of the 1561 revels to bid for power: his games were safer than those of Serjeant Roo (1526–7), who was thrown in the Tower after a play that was taken as a lampoon on Cardinal Wolsey. In the Elizabethan period, plays associated with the Inns of Court tended to feature fictional kingdoms suffering from political division, or from an absence of heirs. *Gorboduc* (1562), *Jocasta* (1566), *Gismond of Salerne* (1567: written in part by the future Lord Chancellor, Christopher Hatton) and *The Misfortunes of Arthur* (1588: with contributions by Bacon) are interesting neo-classical experiments but

---

[31] *Ibid.*, p. 30.
[32] See my 'Entertaining the Palatine prince', p. 327.

can all be read on one level as contributions to the debates on the succession. Some of the shows from the *Gesta Grayorum* have been convincingly related to discussion of James's claim to the English throne: the masque of *Proteus and the Adamantine Rock*, which the termers took to court, reassured the Queen that, however powerful was the magnetic rock situated in the north, the hearts of loyal subjects were still drawn by the influence of Cynthia. Rather more foolhardy was the Middle Templar who in 1597–8 revelled under the name of Exophilus, 'in sawcy imitation of the great Earl' (that is, the court favourite Essex).[33]

Under the early Stuarts, the divisions hinted at in Inns of Court revels were over matters of policy rather than succession. I have already described the implications of the lawyers' shows for the wedding of Princess Elizabeth; the following year, it was only with the utmost difficulty that Bacon got the Grayans to present *The Masque of Flowers* to the court favourite.[34] But the lawyers did not resume large-scale revelling until the 1630s, when there was considerable anxiety over the respect for law of Charles's administration. In James Shirley's *The Triumph of Peace* (1634), a prodigiously expensive masque presented to the court by all four Inns ostensibly as an apology for an affront done to the Queen by William Prynne of Lincoln's Inn, the lawyers used the antimasques to censure the monopolies on which Charles's finances depended and staged in the main masque a fable of the proper relations between Peace, Law, and Justice. Charles was warned that Peace cannot survive if Law is not upheld, and the parade through the streets that opened the evening underlined the political power of the lawyers. The following year, an entertainment at the Middle Temple for the exiled son of Princess Elizabeth advertised the lawyers' concern about England's European obligations; in *The Triumphs of the Prince D'Amour*, Davenant depicted them as enthusiastic for battle. The lawyers may have used courtly forms, but were by no means slaves to courtly attitudes. Charles would have done well to listen to their entertainments.[35]

While James and Charles withdrew from national visibility by restricting the number and range of their progresses, occasional drama in the provinces continued to be sustained in the great aristocratic palaces down to the Civil

---

[33] Axton, *The Queen's Two Bodies*, p. 3. Most of this paragraph is heavily dependent on Axton's study.

[34] Spencer and Wells, *A Book of Masques*, pp. 152–3.

[35] See my 'Entertaining the Palatine prince'; and 'Politics and the masque: *The Triumph of Peace*', *The Seventeenth Century* 2 (1987), 117–41.

War. Indeed, it might be argued that this was the heyday of aristocratic theatricals: documentation or texts survive for well over a dozen early Stuart provincial masques, yet they have never been properly studied as a genre. In all conscience, they are not terribly exciting: most were little family shows written by amateur poets such as Sir Thomas Salusbury or Mildmay Fane, the second Earl of Westmorland, and they tended to involve seasonal fables that welcome a member of the family to the house or celebrate the new year by providing an excuse for the entry of dancers. Unlike Elizabeth's progress entertainments, they were not staged publicly, and the speaking characters usually voiced a sense of local dignity and authority. The speaker was often the Lars Familiaris or the Household God or the Buttery Spirit.

And yet, like other private theatricals, the provincial drama provided a space for experimentation that was not available in the commercial theatre. Here we find not merely women dancers but women *actors* (as in *The Concealed Fancies*, 1644, by girls of the Cavendish family) – unknown on the professional stage before 1660 – and here too were small-scale experiments with scenery. These stages were also politically more adventurous, as they were patently beyond the reach of royal censorship. Mildmay Fane's *Candy Restored* (1640) included some hard talking about Ship Money and the absence of parliament, and it is remarkable that plays and masques were sponsored in the provinces by the family of the Earl of Essex, who was *persona non grata* at court and who has gone down historically as a puritanical nobleman (he fought for Parliament in the 1640s as General of Horse). There is more than a tinge of aristocratic radicalism about *The Masque at Coleoverton* which Essex danced in 1617, with its Spenserian fable and praise of the Earl for his noble piety:[36]

> What thou art, continue still…
> Live with heaven to make thy peace,
> By thy virtues friends increase;
> No faint hopes, nor fears at all:
> If the world crack: Let it fall!

The masque censured swearing Cavaliers, lamented the decline of provincial hospitality, and celebrated local rural industry with an antimasque of dancing coalminers. The amateur plays of Essex's secretary, Arthur Wilson, also

[36] The masque is printed in R. Brotanek, *Die Englischen Maskenspiele* (Vienna, 1902), pp. 328–37 and is to be re-edited in a forthcoming volume of masques by David Lindley. For commentary, see D. Norbrook, 'The reformation of the masque' in Lindley, *The Court Masque*, pp. 102–3. Margot Heinemann discusses Arthur Wilson in *Puritanism and Theatre*, pp. 221–4. On *Candy Restored*, see my *Theatre and Crisis*, p. 123. I attempt to clear some ground for the study of the provincial drama in 'A provincial masque of *Comus*, 1636', *RenD* n.s. 17 (1986), 149–73.

have a puritanical note and may well have been performed in the country. It is easy to see how, for a discourted and disillusioned aristocrat, provincial theatricals might be a way of establishing one's alternative, superior court in the country.

The one provincial masque which no one would willingly let die is, of course, Milton's *Masque at Ludlow* (1634), misleadingly known as *Comus*. This was, in truth, a state occasion, as it was performed for the installation of the Earl of Bridgewater as President of the Council of the Marches and hence was part of Charles's campaign for tighter local discipline, yet, as we might expect, Milton's only masque constituted itself in important and telling ways in opposition to the norms of court drama. Milton's entertainment was less a masque than a cross between a masque and a provincial play: it concluded with general revels but began with a long acted fable in which the main masquers, the sons and daughter of the Earl of Bridgewater, took speaking parts, as they never could have done at court. If at court the silent masquers effortlessly displaced by their dancing the threats constituted by the antimasques, in Milton's revision of the form the masquers were denied precisely that privilege. They had to confront evil on its own ground, in the shape of the tempter Comus who assailed the children as they were lost in the genuinely dangerous woods around Ludlow. What for masquers at court was an easily assumed superiority was for Bridgewater's children a victory won by the skin of their teeth. They had heavenly aid in the shape of a Guardian Spirit (played by the great composer Henry Lawes), but his presence only underlined how remote heaven was, not promptly brought down, as in Charles's masques: the brothers called on the stars to unmuffle but the necessary scene-changes refused to happen. Indeed, the virtue that finally triumphs in this masque is something which was resistant to being projected in spectacular embodiment as it was at Whitehall: the Lady spoke of the Hope and Faith which sustained her by their presence within, but only she could see them, and they remained invisible to the audience. Charmed by Comus into immobility, she told him her mind was still free – but *physically* she was unable to rescue herself.

Comus, the villain, is in some senses a renegade from the world of court masquing, a figure who sums up the long tradition of royal revelry: his animal-headed dancers entered 'glistering' like court masquers (93 s.d.), and his description of the brothers as if they were godlike heroes, 'their port ... more than human' (296), was patently insinuating flattery. The temptation he proposed was intemperance: he spoke for a world of pleasure, ease, revel, and indulgence which was uncomfortably close to the perception of Whitehall by those outside it. The Lady's crushing retort voiced an idea of social justice which repudiated the festival tradition very nearly in its entirety:

> If every just man that now pines with want
> Had but a moderate and beseeming share
> Of that which lewdly-pampered Luxury
> Now heaps upon some few with vast excess,
> Nature's full blessings would be well-dispensed
> In unsuperfluous even proportion,
> And she no whit encumbered with her store,
> And then the Giver would be better thanked,
> His praise due paid, for swinish gluttony
> Ne'er looks to heaven amidst his gorgeous feast,
> But with besotted base ingratitude
> Crams, and blasphemes his Feeder.   (768–79)

Milton may have been writing the finest single aristocratic masque, but his heroine spoke for an attitude that within a decade would have swept court revel aside for ever.

Bibliography

COURT ENTERTAINMENTS

The European background to court festival is outlined by Roy Strong in *Splendour at Court* (1973), second edition called *Art and Power* (1984), and by Enid Welsford in her still-useful study, *The Court Masque* (1927). The early Tudor period is covered by Sidney Anglo, *Spectacle, Pageantry and Early Tudor Policy* (1969) and by Gordon Kipling, *The Triumph of Honour* (1977). The Elizabethan court entertainments are studied by Roy Strong in *The Cult of Elizabeth* (1977) and by Marie Axton in *The Queen's Two Bodies: Drama and the Elizabethan Succession* (1977). The Stuart court has recently been the focus of a glut of research: see Graham Parry, *The Golden Age Restor'd: The Culture of the Stuart Court* (1981); Roy Strong, *Henry, Prince of Wales, and England's Lost Renaissance* (1986); Leah Sinogolou Marcus, *The Politics of Mirth* (1986); R. Malcolm Smuts, *Court Culture and the Origins of a Royalist Tradition in Early Stuart England* (1987); and Kevin Sharpe, *Criticism and Compliment: The Politics of Literature in the England of Charles I* (1987). The tilts have recently been discussed by Alan Young, *Tudor and Jacobean Tournaments* (1987).

ROYAL PROGRESSES AND PAGEANTS

For royal progresses, there are two great treasure troves edited by the antiquary John Nichols: *The Progresses and Public Processions of Queen Elizabeth* (2nd, expanded edn, 3 vols., 1823) and *The Progresses, Processions and Magnificent Festivities of James I* (4 vols., 1828). Some of these are described by David Bergeron in *English Civic Pageantry 1558–1642* (1971), and several are edited, with a substantial introduction, by Jean Wilson in *Entertainments for Elizabeth I* (1980). *Summer's Last Will and Testament* is in *The Works of Thomas Nashe*, ed. R. B. McKerrow, rev. F. P. Wilson (5 vols., 1958), and *The Arraignment of Paris* is in *The Works of George Peele*, gen. ed. C. T. Prouty (3 vols., 1952–70). The standard edition of Lyly is still R. Warwick Bond's (3 vols., 1902), and the best study is by G. K. Hunter, *John Lyly: The Humanist as Courtier* (1962).

THE STUART MASQUE

Modern thinking about the Stuart masque begins with Stephen Orgel's *The Jonsonian Masque* (1965) and continues in his *The Illusion of Power* (1975). Orgel has also edited D. J. Gordon's seminal essays on masque iconography as *The Renaissance Imagination* (1975). There are intelligent treatments of the subject in Philip Edwards, *Threshold of a Nation* (1977); David Norbrook, *Poetry and Politics in the English Renaissance* (1984); and David Lindley, ed., *The Court Masque* (1984). Inigo Jones's designs for the masque are sumptuously edited by Stephen Orgel and Roy Strong in *Inigo Jones: The Theatre of the Stuart Court* (2 vols., 1973). Jonson's masques are definitively edited as volume 7 of *Ben Jonson*, eds. C. H. Herford, P. and E. Simpson (1941). Stephen Orgel's modernized edition (1969) has a rather narrow introduction and inexplicably omits the miscellaneous entertainments. There is a good selection of other masques in *A Book of Masques*, eds. T. J. B. Spencer and S. W. Wells (1968). *Songs and Dances from the Stuart Masque* have been edited by Andrew Sabol (1959; expanded, 1978). Currently the leading study of masque music is Mary Chan's *Music in the Theatre of Ben Jonson* (1980).

UNIVERSITY AND INNS OF COURT DRAMA

On the universities, F. S. Boas's *University Drama in the Tudor Age* (1914), a remarkable scholarly achievement, is still standard. There is nothing comparable for the Stuart period. *The Three Parnassus Plays* are edited by J. B. Leishman (1949). The Inns of Court revels are studied by Marie Axton in *The Queen's Two Bodies* (above), and by P. J. Finkelpearl in *John Marston of the Middle Temple* (1969). The *Gesta Grayorum* are edited by D. S. Bland (1968).

5   Political drama

I

The idea of the developments of the closing years of Elizabeth's reign as providing an appropriate background of national confidence, strength and unity to [the] stupendous cultural achievements no longer finds much favour with historians, most of whom now see this as a time of economic crisis, dislocation and hardship, financial bankruptcy, political disintegration, declining political morality and burgeoning corruption: an age in which things turned terribly sour.[1]

THE political drama of the years 1580–1640 is essentially drama of a changing, troubled, and divided society. This does not mean we should think of it in terms of Roundheads and Cavaliers all the way, for the conflicts, tensions, and contradictions were far more complex than that. Upheavals of the kind seen in Britain and the Netherlands in the sixteenth and seventeenth century

may be conceived not as a simple substitution of one dominant class or economic system for another, but more broadly as a whole social organism outgrowing its skin. Any true revolution must be the response of an entire society, though not of all its members, to a novel situation pressing on it.[2]

Different social groups then developed very different political ideas, and responded to the 'novel situation' in quite different ways. Conrad Russell has formulated this in terms of a *double* revolution:

The English Civil War ... was two revolutions ... The first was ... a rebellion rather than a revolution; it was not a social revolution, but a split in the governing class: a movement by a large number of peers and gentlemen to force a change of policy and a change of ministers on Charles I. The second revolution was a revolution in the full sense of the term: it was an assault on the existing social structure, and particularly on the position of the gentry ... But, alas for simplicity ... the two movements, though socially and ideologically quite distinct, always remained politically confused ... We

---

[1] Robert Ashton, *Reformation and Revolution, 1558–1660* (1985), p. 180.
[2] Victor Kiernan, 'Revolution' in Peter Burke, ed., *The New Cambridge Modern History, Companion Volume* (1979), p. 226.

have then a political rebellion which was to a limited extent successful, and a social revolution which was almost totally unsuccessful.[3]

This can be a helpful way of thinking about the political conflicts articulated in the drama of the pre-revolutionary decades, which connect with the radical revolution that failed as well as the propertied one that succeeded. The plays embody Utopias as well as practical political tactics, people's dreams of a more fulfilling life on earth and in heaven as well as immediate conflicts over taxation, foreign policy, or royal prerogative.

Fundamental changes in accepted ways of seeing the world and one's place in it take a long time to mature and to spread widely through society. Yet without such slow changes in mentalities over a long period the rapid transformations of the revolutionary years would have been unthinkable. Indeed the greatest political drama – *Richard II*, *King Lear* – often seems strangely to prefigure what was to become real material history a generation later.

Every new civilisation as such (however held back, attacked and fettered in every possible way) has always expressed itself in literary form before expressing itself in the life of the state. Indeed, its literary expression has been the means with which it has created the intellectual and moral conditions for its expression in the legislature and the state.[4]

If we understand this as a period 'between two worlds', we shall be less concerned to see all the plays as coherent embodiments of dominant attitudes in the society, or alternatively of subversive ones. We shall rather note the 'doubleness', the irreducible contradictions within outlooks and codes, which fascinated dramatists and audiences the more because they were problematic, newsworthy, and not easily resolved.

II

Political power rested with the monarch, who ruled as well as reigned. The king (or queen), governing with and through his Privy Council, not only controlled the distribution of office and favour, but also determined policy. The monarch's personal character and the company he kept were thus truly matters of deep concern to the people and not merely of curiosity. The naming of so many historical/political plays after the reigns of kings therefore makes more sense than might appear if we think of a monarch in modern terms, as a ceremonial figure or a tourist attraction.

It was nevertheless regarded as a mixed monarchy: the sovereign was

---

[3] Conrad Russell, ed., *The Origins of the English Civil War* (1973), p. 2.
[4] Gramsci, *Selections from Cultural Writings* (1985), p. 117.

King-in-Parliament rather than an absolute ruler. His royal prerogative gave him sole control over foreign policy and emergency action to preserve the state, and considerable authority over religion: but it was assumed that he would use his powers in accordance with ancient law and custom. However, the division between the king's prerogative and the common law was not clearly defined by any written constitution – it was a 'grey area' open to tension and political dispute,[5] as we often see in the plays, from *Gorboduc* (1562) and *Richard II* (1595) to Davenport's *King John and Matilda* (1628).

Parliament too was a very different institution from what it is now, though (as plays like *Woodstock* suggest) it claimed the right from medieval times to be consulted whenever the king thought it necessary to raise extra money or to make war. The House of Commons was an elected assembly, where the wealthier gentry representing the counties sat alongside MPs from the boroughs, but it met only when summoned by the monarch and had limited powers. It was not a public forum either – reporting of its proceedings was forbidden (even though MPs did consult on issues with their constituents and contested elections were on the increase). Moreover there was no right of free speech in Parliament itself – indeed MPs might sometimes be arrested for what they said there.

The state machine was small as compared, say, with France; there were few full-time officers paid by the crown. Administration of law and order was carried on largely on a voluntary, amateur basis by the ruling élites, as part of their status and dignity – by the wealthier gentry appointed as JPs and Lords Lieutenant in the country, by elected corporations in the towns. At the centre, courtiers in high office were paid largely by what they could make out of their posts. Offices were bought as investments and regarded as property to be held for life: the profits came in as fees, fines, and bribes. What we would call corruption was not exceptional but normal; enormous fortunes were made out of the top posts, and courtiers were often rewarded with wardships or with monopolies and patents, all unpopular as burdens on trade.

Unlike contemporary monarchs in Europe the king had no standing army, and the private armies of great peers were becoming obsolete (though in Elizabethan times the very richest still retained their own cannon and forti-fied castles, and went to war partly at their own expense). The militia raised by the crown and the trained bands under the civic authorities were the main basis of defence. Sea war was partly run as private enterprise. Campaigns in Europe – increasingly expensive and underfunded because of the new

---

[5] See Hirst, *Authority and Conflict*, chapter 2, 'The body politic'.

weapons needed – were fought by a mixture of volunteers, mercenaries, and ill-trained, ill-fed, often irregularly paid levies pressed to make up the numbers. The wars looked less glorious to such men, and the stealing of their pay by their officers was a notorious political scandal (dramatically stressed in plays like *A Larum for London* (1599), *Edmund Ironside* (1595 or earlier), Dekker's *If it be not Good* (1611) and *Wonder of a Kingdom* (1631) and Heywood's *Royal King and Loyal Subject* (1602)).

Traditionally the monarch had been expected to 'live of his own', on the income from his lands and traditional feudal dues like customs, except in time of war. But inflation and sales of royal land made this more and more impossible, and the monarchy became (to its disgust) increasingly dependent on extra taxation which had to be voted by Parliament, and assessed and collected by local gentry, who systematically under-assessed themselves and placed the burden on lower ranks. Hence the many bitter disputes, from Elizabethan times on, about taxes, just and unjust, which so often figure in the drama, from *Edward IV* (1599) and *Woodstock* (1592?), through attacks on monopolies in city comedy, to Massinger's *Emperor of the East* (1631) and *King and the Subject* (1638) in the 1630s.

The consent and approval of the 'political nation' was thus of decisive importance in maintaining hierarchy and stability, given the limited powers of coercion possessed by the central state. Hence too the crucial role of the opinion-forming and sustaining aspects of the culture. Foremost of these was still the church, of which the monarchy, not the Pope, was now the head. Printed books, including the English Bible, played a growing part, especially in London, where a higher proportion of the people could read. Finally the drama, no longer controlled by the church or directly by the aristocracy, was a formative and potentially subversive influence.

Political drama in this period is not a distinctive genre, like tragicomedy or pastoral. Political plays are found in every form, though very different according to the theatre and the audience aimed at. Central are history plays, English or classical. But there are also topical news plays and political morality plays, reviving an older form for popular polemical effect (Robert Wilson, Thomas Dekker, much later Richard Brome). There are tragedies like *Massacre at Paris*, *King Lear*, *Sejanus*, where the mainspring of the action is clearly political; satirical comedies like Jonson's *The Devil is an Ass* or Massinger's *New Way to Pay Old Debts*; tragicomedies like *The Bondman* (1623), *The Swisser* (1631), *The Emperor of the East* (1631); or religious and political allegories spiced with contemporary mimicry of public personalities (*A Game at Chess*). Despite the censorship the theatre was shot through with politics at every level, from political court masques at one end to parody-bishops fighting with croziers at the other, from select coterie performances for the court to the political street-pageants of the Lord Mayor's shows. I shall concentrate here on plays which seem to raise fundamental questions of political attitudes and ideas, and within that field on the political plays of the commercial theatres, whether fashionable or popular, indoor or outdoor.

How far should we think of the dramatists and companies as deliberately intervening in contemporary politics? At one end of the spectrum, *Gorboduc* or the royal masques of Charles I's court, at the other *A Game of Chess* or the antiprelatical amphitheatre plays of the 1630s were clearly designed to influence current ideas and political action by the crown, in parliament, or even in the streets. Plays like *A Larum for London* (before 1600) and *The Cobbler's Prophecy* (1590?) represent directly the dangers of peace and the need for military preparedness, in line with the policy of the 'war party' of Leicester, Walsingham, and later of the Essex circle. Dekker's *Whore of Babylon* (1606) and Barnabe Barnes's *The Devil's Charter* (1606) are fierce, even bigoted reactions to Gunpowder Plot – with angels on one side, devils on the other, and a clear (if today unacceptable) immediate political conclusion to be drawn by the audience. Again, since there were no newspapers or documentaries, the companies sometimes filled the slot with representations of topical events.

However, 'political drama' has to be understood as a much wider thing than that. It is difficult to define because there is so much of it. Psychological interest is indeed a later development. The major drama grew out of forms concerned primarily with public, communal events and actions – pageants, civic and village festivities, royal offerings, Lords of Misrule with their ritual reversals of order. Drama of domestic or personal life does exist, but as yet on a more limited scale.

Unlike earlier Tudor drama, based at court or in the private houses of great lords or city magnates, the new Elizabethan and Jacobean companies were financially dependent primarily on a paying audience. In terms of authority, they were still in transition between the old and the new, between the patron whose name and livery they bore and whose protection was legally necessary for them to act at all, and the purely commercial, profit-making set-up in the new public theatres. The occasional performance at court or in city pageants gave them necessary status as well as money. In return, court and patron provided a measure of protection against interference by the civic authorities, or against political and religious censorship and suppression. In this sense the companies still needed the patron.

Nevertheless, the commercial base allowed this 'artisanal theatre' a good deal of independence, contrasted with the situation in Europe, where the players, when they were not directly part of religious organizations, were still largely the direct salaried employees of courts and princes. Because of the popular interest in politics which had few other chances of expression, there was always a financial temptation to deal with 'dangerous matter'. The economic position of the political dramatist was in some ways comparable to that of the 'lecturer' in churches, a salaried preacher paid by the subscription of laymen or town corporations who wished to hear his kind of doctrine, even if his bishop might disapprove it. The character-writer John Cocke commented on the common player: 'howsoever he pretends to have a royal master or mistress, his wages and dependence prove him to be the servant of the people'.[6] Lecturers, said Laud in 1629, 'by reason of their pay are the people's creatures'.[7] In both cases new market forces were breaking down the monopoly of opinion-forming by church and state.

A powerful influence on the political dramatist, therefore, was the nature of the audience – or audiences. The traditions of Lollardy, popular anti-clericalism and religious radicalism went back long before the Reformation, especially in London and the south-east, and the highly profitable audiences there were probably more strongly nationalist, anti-Popery, anti-Spanish and anticlerical than either the monarchy or the government, as was shown in public opposition to the Alençon marriage for Elizabeth at one end of the great period of the drama, or the tumults over a Spanish marriage for Prince Charles at the other.[8]

However, the most important thing about the audience was its broad social and political mix. No doubt the leisured and well-to-do had the opportunity to go to the theatre more often than the craftsman or the labourer. But it does not follow that London playgoers as a whole were the 'privileged' in society.[9] Careful study of the evidence (by Andrew Gurr and Martin Butler in particular)[10] confirms what the plays themselves always suggested, that the audiences for the various kinds of public theatres included more or less everyone except the very poorest. Neither were they all 'anti-puritan' in their opinions, as used to be assumed – unless indeed opposition to the theatre is taken to be the sole definition of puritanism (which would make many orthodox bishops into puritans). Indeed, much city opposition to the theatres was due to fear of disorderly crowds, or infection

---

[6] J. Stephens, *Essays and Characters* (1615). Cited Chambers, *Elizabethan Stage*, IV. 225.

[7] Christopher Hill, *Society and Puritanism in Pre-Revolutionary England* (1986), p. 83.

[8] For popular anti-Catholic feeling, see Robin Clifton, 'Fear of Popery' in Russell, *The Origins of the English Civil War*, pp. 144–67.

[9] This was argued by Ann Jennalie Cook, *The Privileged Playgoers of Shakespeare's London, 1576–1642* (1981).

[10] Gurr, *Playgoing*; Butler, *Theatre and Crisis*, appendix II.

by plague, or absenteeism from work, rather than a principled religious objection to acting as such.[11]

From the 1580s the commercial theatres, together with the pulpits of the popular preachers and the other great innovation of cheap printing, provided the nearest equivalent to the modern mass media, helping to create and form something like a secular public opinion far beyond the limits of the recognized 'political nation', the natural rulers as represented at court, in parliament, and in central and local government. The opening up of secular political discussion and debate to anyone who could put a penny in the box was something quite new, and helped to transform the nature of politics. This novel situation greatly alarmed successive governments, which maintained the authority of the ruling élites in an unstable social order with the help of a comprehensive censorship.[12] What people preached, printed, or staged was not therefore simply what they thought, or what their audience would have liked to hear, but what they were allowed to say. There would have been little point in Queen and Archbishop 'tuning' the pulpits, licensing and limiting the preachers and requiring them to read the official religious–political homilies on Sundays if the players were to enjoy complete freedom to undermine them for the rest of the week.

The playwrights did, indeed, have far more scope than in many European countries at the time; and plays in the London theatres of the 1580s or 1590s show a good deal of relative freedom if we compare them with those of slightly later times when control was tightened up. All the same, we shall misread the drama unless we recognize that it was produced under a general censorship which, unlike our own, was almost exclusively political and religious. (Questions of morality or taste scarcely arose except for the banning of oaths in 1606; rape, incest, mutilation, and brothel realism seem not to have troubled the censors at all.) Ignoring the censorship has indeed led many critics to overstress the role of the drama in upholding the existing political order, rather than at the same time helping to question it and to form critical attitudes.

Imposed by royal proclamation as part of the royal prerogative, censorship and control were exercised through the Master of the Revels, a court official who arranged court entertainments, licensed companies and playhouses, and had to read and approve all plays before they were staged, sometimes refusing to pass them unless changes were made, and taking a handsome fee for his trouble. Printed plays came under the separate censorship of printed

---

[11] See Heinemann, *Puritanism and Theatre*, esp. pp. 18–47, 258–83 and *passim*.

[12] This has recently been admirably discussed in Hill, *Collected Essays I*, pp. 32–71 and (more controversially) by Annabel Patterson, *Censorship and Interpretation* (1984).

books, controlled by the Archbishop of Canterbury and the ecclesiastical authorities, which was often stricter in demanding cuts and changes, and was enforced through the Stationers' Company, a state-licensed monopoly, which wielded the power in the last resort to destroy presses or deprive offending printers of their livelihood. Even after a play had been properly licensed the Privy Council might still intervene to suppress it, and to question, punish, or imprison the dramatist or the company.[13] Since to obtain the right to act at all the companies were required to have a noble patron whose servants they nominally were, a serious clash with the censorship could also lead to loss of patronage and of livelihood.

Suppression was erratic and unpredictable. In quiet times the censor might let a good deal pass (and was probably paid extra fees to do so). But in times of political tension, such as the late 1590s, the first years of James's reign, the early 1620s and the 1630s, government and censors would turn much more touchy and severe. And there is no doubt that they tended to become more repressive over the fifty years before the Civil War, as Sir Henry Herbert recognized when he decided that all old plays must be re-licensed, since 'they may be full of offensive matter against Church and State, the rather that in past times the poets took greater liberty than is allowed them by me'.[14]

In an administration where offices were run for the profit of the office-holder, fees and gifts must often have determined whether a production was allowed or not: and the Master of the Revels might also be influenced by the family or faction to which he belonged. Persecuting archbishops like Whitgift and Bancroft ran a tougher censorship, at least against puritanism and nonconformity, than the puritan-sympathizing Abbot who succeeded in 1610. When Abbot was sequestered from his office and finally replaced by Laud, another persecutor of the radicals, political censorship became heavier and the penalties for offenders much more brutal and violent. This helps to explain how so much critical political theatre got through despite the limits placed on it by the state, while other plays, apparently no more extreme in their attitudes, were suppressed. Staging an obviously political play must always have been a calculated risk.

We know of a number of cases where the companies and writers collided directly with the censorship. Almost every dramatist of importance was involved at some time or other – Marlowe, Shakespeare, Jonson, Daniel,

---

[13] The Privy Council thus intervened to interrogate Shakespeare's company over *Richard II*, Jonson over *Eastward Ho!*, *Sejanus*, and *The Magnetic Lady*, Daniel over *Philotas* and Day's *Isle of Gulls*, and Middleton and his company over *A Game at Chess*.

[14] J. Quincy Adams, ed., *Dramatic Records of Sir Henry Herbert* (1917), p. 21.

Day, Chapman, Middleton, Massinger, Brome, for a start. But the effects went far beyond such specific cases. As G. E. Bentley has shown, while only a small number of the 2,000 or more plays produced in the fifty years before the Civil War directly offended, all managers and dramatists knew that severe punishments and loss of livelihood were within the censor's power.

The inhibitions which such knowledge provided are not difficult to imagine. They affected what the professional dramatist wrote for the companies; they affected what the managers and the sharing members were willing to accept; and they affected what the book-keeper did to the MS as he worked on the prompt-copy and the players' sides.[15]

Thus we cannot simply read off the political and religious 'mentalities', the 'climate of opinion', from the text alone. For example, scholars disagree about how much irreligion and agnosticism there was in the society, though scepticism was clearly one possible response to the frequent changes in official religion. What is certain is that atheistic, Catholic, or even openly puritan plays would have been simply impossible. Elizabeth was indignant because some ministers preached that there was no hell but a torment of conscience, and demanded that they be brought to order. Marlowe prudently put such views only into the mouth of a devil: and after *Doctor Faustus* (1593) no playwright risked touching such dangerous issues at all.

The 1590s, the period of the most energetic development of the national theatre, was also a time of repression of puritanism and religious radicalism under Archbishop Whitgift, whose proceedings against nonconforming ministers were likened by Burghley to those of the Spanish Inquisition. The secretly printed and popular Marprelate tracts, satirizing the bishops, were suppressed, and those suspected of writing or publishing them tortured. Even anti-Martinist plays were banned. The church hierarchy was held by Elizabeth and James I alike to be essential to the stability of the monarchy and civil society: 'no bishop, no king'. MPs who supported puritan reform in the church were warned by Whitgift that they were following the same path as the rebel Jack Straw, who would have no clergy except preaching friars. Religious dissent connoted Anabaptism, 'the craftsman's religion of social protest',[16] Munster, and communism. For the dramatist, the safest way with religion was to leave it alone.

Again, the 1590s was a decade of extreme hardship for the poor, with bad harvests and famine years, and an outcry against corn-hoarders and price-raisers. In the south-east, notably in Essex and Oxfordshire, there were grain riots, and in London itself riots for cheaper bread and against aliens, who

---

[15] Bentley, *The Profession of Dramatist in Shakespeare's Time*, p. 196.
[16] H. G. Koenigsberger, *Estates and Revolutions* (Cornell, New York, 1971), p. 162.

were thought to be taking trade away from local people. These were issues too dangerous for popular literature and theatre to be allowed to treat freely at this moment. Accordingly, the manuscript play of *Sir Thomas More* (by Munday, Chettle, and others, to which Shakespeare probably contributed the scene where More persuades the rioters to return to order) was marked by the censor 'leave out the insurrection wholly and the cause thereof'. So gutted, the play perished and was probably never staged. However orthodox the moral drawn by the playwrights from such turbulent protests (and there is no suggestion that any of them *support* rioting), merely to show this kind of mass action with any sympathy or detachment, or to suggest that the aggrieved people should be leniently treated, could be asking for trouble.

Our own view of political theatre is also skewed because unorthodox or dangerous plays, even if they reached the stage, often remained unprinted. Some of the most controversial political plays we know of have survived only in manuscript, for example *Woodstock, Sir Thomas More, Edmund Ironside, Sir John Van Olden Barnavelt, Believe As You List*. Many others which were probably radical have not survived at all except as titles – including many 1590s history plays; much of the propaganda urging English support of the Protestant cause in the 1620s and 1630s; and the popular anti-bishop and anti-monopolist farces of the 1630s, whose existence is known to us only from the records of their suppression.

Recent work such as that of Martin Butler and Annabel Patterson[17] has shown how some meaningful political drama could be produced in the interstices of state control and repression even in the 1630s, often by using theatrical metaphors to translate political conflicts into sexual terms, or by 'ambiguity' about topical references, or by providing reassuringly happy endings to conflicts which in life were proving insoluble. However, the 'hermeneutics of censorship', as Patterson calls it, had its price. In many cases only an informed in-group could understand and interpret the 'code'. Wide political appeal to a popular audience was largely excluded (which was of course the object). The *emotional* impact of the political action was often altered or blunted, and many central issues could not be treated at all. 'Consensus' was thus largely, much more than has been realized, a product of censorship and self-censorship (though it is always possible that what writers are not allowed to say they may in time cease to think). And this must have helped to alienate many people from the theatres and their playwrights as merely 'royal slaves'.

Without the patrons' continued protection the players could not have

---

[17] Butler, *Theatre and Crisis*; Patterson, *Censorship and Interpretation*.

risked investing in the permanent playhouses that made them financially independent and allowed them to develop as companies, making fortunes not only for the player–sharers but for business entrepreneurs like Henslowe. How close, after that, were their personal links with their patrons? In the early days, when the players were still nominally and sometimes really household servants protected by their lord's livery, they may well have been very close. Later, especially after 1603 when the main London companies were taken under royal (rather than noble) patronage, the name may often have been little more than a flag of convenience. More informal links can be traced through the dedications in playbooks, which usually implied a desire for aid or protection of some kind. The drama's official patrons were by definition high nobility, many of them great officers of state or members of the Privy Council. They were not, however, all completely of one mind politically, and some might well protect or encourage plays which accorded with their own political line and at times diverged from the dominant policy of the crown.

One direct consequence of the Reformation had been the transfer of much of the land, wealth, power, and patronage of the church to the monarchy and its supporting aristocracy and gentry (and often through them by resale to city grandees). Among those whose families were thus enriched were several of the greatest patrons of poets and players, the Dudleys, Earls of Leicester and Warwick (patrons of radical Protestantism from the 1540s); the Walsinghams; the Sidneys; the Herberts, Earls of Pembroke; the Devereux, Earls of Essex; the Rich family; the Russells, Earls of Bedford. Under Elizabeth their wealth and influence helped to patronize and protect a spectacular secular culture. To offer entertainment to the Queen was indeed a necessary investment in their world, and this they did at first through their own troupes of players. Many later became patrons of the new theatrical companies, as well as of preachers whom they appointed to livings in their gift or as private chaplains.

In political and religious terms many of these patrons inclined to a militant Protestantism which on a broad definition could be called puritan, supporting, for example, a strongly anti-Spanish, anti-Catholic foreign policy (about which the Queen had reservations), in opposition to the more conservative and largely Catholic Howard family; limitation of the power and wealth of the English church and hence support of those who wanted to carry reformation further; aid for the Netherlands revolt and for the Huguenots against sovereigns who they considered had become tyrants in religion, but without countenancing rebellion independently by the lower orders. Here again they diverged from the ruling attitudes of both Elizabeth and James I, who saw the Dutch as rebels against their lawful sovereign and dangerous republicans, and were unwilling to commit themselves to consistent support of the Netherlands against Spain.

Certainly there was a clear economic and power basis for these aristocratic attitudes – the huge vested interest in retaining former church lands; business links with the advancing merchant and commercial groups (notably in mining and in overseas trade, piracy, and colonization); fear of a centralization and absolutist control which threatened the remnants of the nobility's feudal-style authority and independent power. But ideas and faith came into it too. For many – notably Philip Sidney and Fulke Greville – there was a strong ideological and intellectual commitment as well as a factional one, reinforced by personal links with Huguenot thinkers like Sidney's friends Languet and Mornay, with advanced heretical philosophers like Giordano Bruno, and with organizers of nonconformist and presbyterian groups in England like Leicester's protégé John Field. Such religious and political ideas gave rise to heroic dreams of a new world worth living and dying for.[18] In England, as in the Netherlands, an important if paradoxical contribution to the political and religious revolution was made by 'blue blood, more inflammable and readier to run risks, to gamble with life and fortune rather than to lose face, drawing on the more cautious money-men', as Victor Kiernan puts it.

We should not, however, think of the patrons as directly suggesting and commissioning all the political plays (though this may sometimes have happened with topical ones), nor of the dramatists as submissively reproducing the political ideas of the noble leader or faction to whom they looked for protection in an emergency. Above all they had to shape their drama for a known audience, whose tastes and prejudices they were in a better position to understand than their 'good lords' were. They had ideas and initiatives of their own. Moreover, while the author is (rightly) no longer regarded as a completely free spirit transcending the pressures of his time, it is equally misleading to type Shakespeare, Jonson, and Middleton as 'busy men of the theatre', too preoccupied with their craft to be deeply concerned with politics or historical ideas except in box-office terms – professional playwrights who 'constructed plays to take advantage of existing public opinion, not to mould it', as one recent critic says about Middleton.[19] It seems more likely, from the evidence we have, that there was some dialectical interaction between the dramatists' thinking and that of both patrons and audiences.

---

[18] For this trend within the aristocratic élite see Norbrook, *Poetry and Politics*.

[19] T. H. Howard-Hill, 'The origins of Middleton's *A Game at Chess*', *RORD* 28 (1985), p. 11.

III

The plays of the first permanent commercial theatres in the 1580s represent both controversial political issues and the common people's grievances in a way that seems extraordinarily bold and direct compared with what came later. Raw nationalism, warlike monarchism, anticlericalism, fear of Catholic invasion and plotting, already present in the popular audience, are appealed to and emotionally reinforced in early chronicle plays like Peele's *Edward I* (1591) or the anonymous *Edmund Ironside*, each with a warrior-king as hero, threatened by the treachery of demonic Spanish queen or Pope-serving archbishop. The same sense of national pride and foreign menace permeates the 'medleys', a mixture of older forms, part pageant, part morality play, part clowning and political cabaret, starring the famous comics Richard Tarlton and William Kemp and scripted for them by Robert Wilson. This, as David Bevington says, was 'the milieu from which the Shakespearean history plays evolved'.[20]

The early professional companies were closely associated with Leicester and Walsingham, leaders of the puritan group on the Privy Council, who first established the Queen's Men as an élite troupe. The tone of their plays may well reflect not only audience taste but also the bid of these statesmen to rouse popular feeling through their patronage for a militant Protestant policy. Tarlton, Kemp, and Wilson were all members of Leicester's Men, and went with him on his Netherlands military expedition in 1585 to take part in the magnificent pageants and entertainments designed to raise his status there (near-royal displays, aimed partly to win radical support, which gave great offence to the Queen).[21] Marlowe, too, had been employed by Walsingham in anti-Catholic espionage and counter-espionage in Europe.

Tarlton, a favourite with all social classes and privileged because he could always make the great laugh, seems to have been very much a *political* comic, using his protective fooling on occasion to parody the corruption of power in church and state, and sometimes in trouble with courtiers for doing so.[22] More than anyone else he kept up the tradition of direct address to the audience (as in later music-hall) and of 'clowns thrust in to play a part in

---

[20] Bevington, *Tudor Drama*, p. 191.
[21] Sidney stood godfather to Tarlton's son, and after he was killed Tarlton appealed to Walsingham on his own deathbed to protect this child. See also R. C. Strong and J. A. Van Dorsten, *Leicester's Triumph* (London and Oxford, 1964).
[22] The 'Play of the Cards' which Sir John Harington says caused offence to certain courtiers may well have been one of those scripted by Wilson for Tarlton. Walsingham apparently defended it on the grounds that 'they that do that they should not, shall hear that they would not'.

majestical matters' criticized by Sidney – the unclassical, alienating style which gives late-Elizabethan political drama its two-eyed, cross-class, stereoscopic quality. In his russet countryman's jacket and baggy trousers, drumming, dancing, and singing popular songs, he was an outsize plebeian stage personality quite apart from any particular plays he appeared in, often stepping out of the play to improvise direct to the audience. His line was not that of the quick-witted devil–Vice of the morality plays, but rather the simple but shrewd 'little man', pushed around by authority yet always bouncing back – a sympathetic persona not unlike that of Charlie Chaplin, another much-loved baggy-trousered entertainer likewise inclined to political radicalism.

The few texts that have survived give only a faint idea of what made Tarlton's and Wilson's pieces effective. In performance they must have been adapted to different audiences and the topical talk of the moment, depending on recognizable caricatures of unpopular individuals and on circus-style slapstick. The general political thrust, however, is clear enough.

Thus in Wilson's *Three Ladies of London* (early 1580s), Tarlton as the comic countryman Simplicity shrewdly detects the four 'knaves of the pack', Fraud, Dissimulation, Usury, and Simony, who operate in the mercenary city ruled by Lady Lucre; but he can never get the better of them. Usury, whom he exposes as a swindler of the poor, continues to trade respectably at the Royal Exchange, while Simony, the corrupt churchman, is placed by rich Lady Lucre in charge of 'such matters as are ecclesiastical', on the grounds that he is a 'sly fellow' with a 'liberal tongue'. He is last heard of at St Paul's, 'very familiar with some of the clergy'. Simplicity's exposure of Simony boldly sets out all the grievances of the Elizabethan puritan movement against the church establishment and its dumb-dog clergy, though for good measure there are also attacks elsewhere on 'precise' kill-joy enemies of the stage:

SIMPLICITY

And Simony ... he is a knave for the nonce;
He loves to have twenty livings at once.
And if he let an honest man, as I am, to have one,
He'll let it so dear that he shall be undone.
And he seeks to get parsons' livings into his hand,
And puts in some odd dunce that to his payment will stand.
So if the parsonage be worth forty or fifty pound a year,
He will give one twenty nobles to mumble service once a month there.

(*Dodsley's Old Plays*, p. 260)

Finally Simplicity himself, caught trying to survive by a bit of petty thieving, is sentenced to be whipped by Diligence the beadle, while the big criminals get away with it. The style and tone of Martin Marprelate's scandalous illicit tracts against the bishops were, as was well known at the time, directly borrowed from such stage satires.[23] As 'Mar-Martin' complains:

> These tinkers' terms and barbers' jests, first Tarlton on the stage,
> Then Martin in his book of lies hath put on every page.[24]

Considered as a patriotic entertainment to honour the Armada victory and the national unity that won it, Robert Wilson's play *The Cobbler's Prophecy* (*c.*1590, printed 1594) is remarkable for the emotional power with which it represents a national *disunity* that almost allows foreign invasion to succeed. The action takes place on two levels – the gods in heaven, where Mercury and Mars finally triumph over Lust and Contempt, and the earthly kingdom of Boeotia, where grasping, traitorous Courtier and greedy, enclosing Landlord gleefully describe (in the manner of earlier estates satire) how ruthlessly they exploit the people, whom Scholar (absorbed in decadent courtly arts) and powerless Soldier have failed to protect. The country is saved only thanks to Ralph the Cobbler, a poor man given the gift of prophecy by the gods, who takes over what ought to be Scholar's function and warns the nation of its danger and the coming Day of Judgement. His bitter outburst on behalf of the poor is directly in the tradition of John Ball or of earlier Reformation 'gospelling' poets like Robert Crowley, and looks forward to the visions of Abiezer Coppe:

> The high hill and the deep ditch
> Which ye digged to make yourselves rich,
> The chimneys so many, and alms not any,
> The widow's woeful cries,
> And babes in street that lies,
> The bitter sweat and pain
> That tenants poor sustain,
> Will turn to your bane I tell ye plain,
> When burning fire shall rain,
> And fill with botch and blain
> The sinew and each vein.
> Then these poor that cry,
> Being lifted up on high,
> When you are all forlorn
> Shall laugh you all to scorn.   (p. 321)

---

[23] Indeed Martin himself directly quotes *Three Ladies*: 'I think Simony be the bishops' lackey. Tarlton caught him in Dumb John [Bishop] of London's cellar' (*Martin Marprelate* (Menston, 1967), p. 19).

[24] Cited Bradbrook, *The Rise of the Common Player*, p. 167.

At the eleventh hour the reigning Duke rallies an army to drive off the invaders. Soldier and Scholar enthusiastically join the colours (Landlord predictably dodges the call-up), and the Cobbler's wife, driven mad by the gods, kills the traitor Courtier. A glorious victory is won, with unity of all loyal subjects achieved under the throne. But the Cobbler's final comment is sceptical rather than triumphant, as he returns grumbling to his lowly trade:

> Ay, ay, and great folk do amiss,
> Poor folk must hold their peace.

Politically, the piece is sophisticated as well as spectacular. By bringing in the heathen classical gods it avoids the charge of direct religious controversy and hence the censorship. But the classical gods were also symbols of the new humanist, educated culture: plays like this brought even the illiterate in touch with what the intellectuals had learned in the universities.

These plays, then, deliberately rough and populist and sometimes bigoted as they are, show how the survivals of folk-comedy, with their images of 'misrule' and the world upside-down, often seen only as a 'carnivalesque' outburst of anarchic feeling against *all* restraining powers, could also be used for more specific political purposes.[25] But the particular balance between popular monarchism and powerful patronage that made such performances possible around the Armada period came to an end, as the rulers' fear of popular disorder and religious radicalism intensified in the economic crisis of the 1590s. Leicester, Walsingham, and Warwick died, and Whitgift's censorship and thought-control extended to puritan as well as Catholic deviance. Moreover we know that Marprelate scandalized mainstream puritans like Cartwright, even though the avant-garde courtier Essex might boast of reading him; and so may the related plays have done. These dramatic forms were in any case going out of fashion. The history plays of the 1590s marked a new, more complex kind of political drama, but the older feelings re-emerge in their nationalism, their military heroes and what Bevington calls the 'staple anticlericalism' of Shakespeare's history plays.

IV

The main form of political drama in the 1590s was the English history play, making the past accessible for thousands who would never read the bulky

---

[25] Wilson was himself not a naïve traditional showman but an educated and sophisticated writer, who later collaborated with Drayton and Munday in Protestant history plays like *Sir John Oldcastle*.

chronicles of Holinshed, Halle, Stow, or Foxe. It appealed to the audience's intense interest in history as such, but also to their anxieties, resentments, and grievances about current politics. Fusing the popular dramatic tradition with new humanist or 'politique' history and argument, it helped both to create a consensus of support for a powerful monarchy and, paradoxically, to undermine it.

History provided a mass of exciting and stageable stories, and the popular battle scenes, sieges, military heroes, and pageantry that helped to sustain patriotic feeling and loyalty to the monarch in time of war. But it also showed the precedents and customs by which the powers of royal government were set and limited – precedents to which common lawyers and Members of Parliament continually referred to define the 'ancient liberties' and traditional rights of aristocrats, freemen, and citizens, which might be threatened by growing royal absolutism.[26] The past could offer political lessons to the present, and dangers and disasters from earlier times could be seen as analogous to contemporary troubles which, given the censorship, could not have been presented directly. Indeed even plays not intended to suggest topical analogies might acquire them through some new turn of events.

The selection and adaptation the dramatists made from the often shapeless chronicle material aimed both to give an impression of the past and its conflicts as they actually happened (including the best-known stories and legends familiar from ballads and folk-plays, which, as Brecht said, would have been missed if they had been left out) and, inevitably, to place the audience in the position of weighing and judging the action. The resulting 'demystification' of the mystery of state, rather than the suggestion of alternative solutions to largely insoluble problems, was the truly instructive and potentially subversive aspect of these plays. Thus at the climax of *Richard II*, when the King is about to be deposed, the Bishop of Carlisle, a divine-right absolutist, appeals to Parliament (4.1.121):

> What subject can give sentence on his King?
> And who sits here that is not Richard's subject?

The dramatic question is posed not only to the stage audience but at the same time to the 3,000 spectators in the theatre, subjects asked to judge the deposing of a king. Right or wrong, the audience is forced to *think* about the political ideas involved as it watches the crown held between two rivals. It is not the answer but the question that subverts. The drama gives people images to think with, and thus reinforces confidence in their own ability to understand and discuss conflicts of state.

[26] See Edna Zwick Boris, *Shakespeare's English Kings, the People and the Law* (1978).

Magnificent royal display and ceremony was an important means of maintaining the monarch's ascendancy and hegemony in the eyes of the people.
Expenditure on the royal household, on pageantry, tilts, the revival of
chivalry, was relatively enormous, at a time when less was spent on a professional state bureaucracy in England than in a single province of France.
One great attraction of the historical–political theatre was spectacle and
pageantry, restaging the colour and brilliance of the court for the benefit of
middle-class and plebeian spectators, often employing the same musicians
and comedians who worked there, and using second-hand the gorgeous
costumes recently worn by real courtiers.

However, it is too easy to assume, as some critics have done, that staging
these royal rituals necessarily helped to reinforce acceptance and deference
for the existing hierarchic order,[27] for the theatrical spectacles, at least in
the earlier years, were seldom uncritical representations serving the
mythology of the monarch's semi-divine status. More often than not, in the
popular theatres, the splendour is distanced, shown as threatened, hypocritical, or hollow. Unlike coronations and royal weddings presented live on TV,
these shows usually have a built-in alienating commentary. The stately
rhetoric of court scenes (say, the openings of *King John* (1596), *Richard II*,
King Lear (1605), even *The Maid's Tragedy* (1610)) is continually undercut by
cynical colloquial asides and soliloquies or by contrasting naturalistic scenes,
revealing the grim realities of the power-game and the competition in flattery.[28] *Richard III* (1593) makes clear how royal spectacles are deliberately
constructed, when Richard appears before the London crowd on a balcony
'betwixt two clergymen', to be greeted with prearranged cheers from the
terrorized citizens.

Only a very inattentive audience could receive all this as confirming the
majesty of power. Stephen Orgel has indeed argued, more convincingly, that
by the last two decades of Elizabeth's reign 'a strong sense of impatience and
disillusion in the royal mythology was being felt ... and its rhetoric was
adopted only by those who had a vested interest in mirroring her self-image'.
To mime the monarch was, he thought, 'a potentially revolutionary act'.[29]

The 'creaturely' aspect of the history plays – the use of colloquial language
for political affairs, the humanization of kings and public figures – is not
simply a delight in the new technique of realistic 'personation' or a failure in

---

[27] On this point my emphasis differs from that of Stephen Greenblatt (*Renaissance Self-
Fashioning*, p. 253).

[28] See *King John* 1.1 and 2.1; *Richard II* 1.1 and 1.2; *King Lear* 1.1; *Maid's Tragedy* 1.2.

[29] 'Making greatness familiar' in *The Forms of Power and the Power of Forms in the Renaissance*,
pp. 41–8.

artistic decorum: it images directly the contradiction between the sacred royal office and the fallible human individual who holds it, making historical actions intelligible as everyday transactions, and bridging the gap between the 'political nation' and those in the theatre yard born 'only to be ruled'. Thus King Lear asks an attendant to 'undo this button', and Constance protests when old Queen Eleanor robs young Arthur of his right to succeed:

> Go to it grandam, child,
> Give grandam kingdom, and it grandam will
> Give it a plum, a cherry and a fig,
> There's a good grandam.   (*King John* 2.1.160–3)

The indecorum is itself a political comment. Sir Henry Wotton thought the spectacular *Henry VIII* (1613) 'sufficient in truth within a while to make greatness very familiar, if not ridiculous'.[30] He had a point.

Insofar as the political drama of the 1590s brings out the value of a strong monarchy, the case is based primarily on the secular pragmatic need for unity between king, nobility, city and commons to maintain order against popular rebellion and defend England against invasion or change in religion. The providential pattern of sacred dynastic succession and divinely ordered hierarchy, which E. M. W. Tillyard[31] saw as a universally accepted belief common to the playwrights and their audience, is much more evident in the older chronicle sources and the official homilies than it is in the plays themselves, where the cause and effect of historical events is increasingly firmly centred in human choices and human actions. The argument for supporting the king – even an unsatisfactory king, or one whose title to the throne is spurious – is the fear of civil war as the alternative, and even that is not automatically ruled out as unthinkable wickedness. Prophecies, dreams, and ghosts may influence the audience's moral attitude to the action (in *Richard III* or *Woodstock* for example), but do not determine its course. Comments on political events are usually those of various human characters, not of the author, and the audience retains the right to judge between them.

Indeed the same chronicles could and did serve as raw material either for 'providential' drama such as the 'Elect Nation' plays (see below) or for frankly 'politique' writers like Sir John Hayward or Sir Henry Wotton, who treated history as a guide to practical statecraft and political wisdom.[32] Both of these last, as it happens, were members of the Essex circle, which included the recent Oxford translators of Tacitus, and the main proponents

---

[30] Quoted in Chambers, *Elizabethan Stage*, II.14.

[31] *The Elizabethan World Picture* (1943); *Shakespeare's History Plays* (1944).

[32] See F. J. Levy, 'Hayward, Daniel and the beginnings of politic history in England', *HLQ* 50 (1987), 1–34.

of a more scientific, accurate, less moralistic history in the manner of
Tacitus, Guicciardini, and Machiavelli – men like Wotton, Fulke Greville,
Francis Bacon, and the ill-starred Henry Cuffe, Oxford professor of Greek,
later secretary to Essex, who taught political theory to Shakespeare's patron
the Earl of Southampton. Shakespeare too can be seen as a politic historian
working in the field of drama, showing providence as acting only through
secondary causes: that is, through human behaviour.[33]

Rather than simply restaging the doctrine of the official *Homily Against
Disobedience* (1570), that rebellion even against a tyrant is always the greatest
of sins against God, the plays openly represent the dilemma of subjects
under a bad or inadequate king. Shakespeare's King John, for example, is
not even a legitimate king but a usurper, as we learn in the first scene
(1.1.40–3). He is presented as neither a good, nor a just, nor a strong
monarch. He is not to be personally relied on to defend England, whether
against the French or the Papal legate (to whom he shamefully kneels); he is
shown as an irresponsible gambler and an ineffective and capricious war
leader, and gives orders for the murder of the child Arthur, who seems to
have the strongest dynastic claim to the throne. It is John's nephew, bastard
son of Richard Coeur de Lion, with no legitimate claim to the throne at all,
who exposes the unscrupulous double-dealing of the kings and stands out as
the brave, iconoclastic, sceptical royal leader with whom the audience is
likely to identify. Yet when some of John's nobility in despair revolt against
him and join the French enemy, the Bastard in the end condemns the rebellion and remains loyal to John – not because he is bound to obey a divinely
appointed ruler, but for the sake of patriotism and national unity. For the
same reasons he swears loyalty to John's son after his death. The rebel peers
are reconciled (apparently without a stain on their characters); and the play
ends with the Bastard's famous appeal to the audience:

> This England never did, nor never shall
> Lie at the proud foot of a conqueror,
> Save when it first did help to wound itself.
> Now these her princes are come home again,
> Come the three corners of the world in arms,
> And we shall shock them. Nought shall make us rue,
> If England to itself do rest but true.   (5.7.110–16)

The non-Shakespearian chronicle plays too are monarchist and Erastian
in feeling; they assume that a strong king, prepared to take sensible advice
and stand up to factious nobles or bishops, offers the best hope of justice and
prosperity for the commons. But the sacredness and divine right of

---

[33] See F. J. Levy, *Tudor Historical Thought* (1967), chapter 7.

monarchy and hierarchy is again less to the point than its practical useful-ness. Thus in Heywood's *Edward IV, Part 1*, Hobs the tanner, a plebeian speaking freely to the disguised King Edward, frankly refuses to judge who is the rightful king.[34]

> I am just akin to Sutton Windmill, I can grind which way the wind blows. If it be Harry, I can say, well fare Lancaster. If it be Edward, I can sing, York, York, for my money.
>
> (*Dramatic Works*, vol. I, p. 45)

He loves the king, he says,

> as poor folks love holidays, glad to have them now and then; but to have them come too often will undo them. So, to see the King now and then 'tis comfort; but every day would beggar us; and I may say to thee, we fear we shall be troubled to lend him money; for we doubt he's but needy.

What concerns him is that taxes should not be too heavy; that the king, whoever he is, should temper justice with mercy; and that he should not corruptly burden the people to enrich the few:

> Those that have [patents] do as the priests did in old time, buy and sell the sins of the people. So they make the King believe they mend what's amiss, and for money they make the thing worse than it is ... Faith, 'tis pity that one subject should have in his hand that might do good to many through the land. (p. 46)

In the same play London is defended against a rebel army led by the dissident aristocrat Faulconbridge (who believes the imprisoned Henry VI is the true king), not by King Edward or the nobility, but by the city authorities who fear disorder and looting of their shops. The Lord Mayor appeals to respectable city youth on behalf of the propertied masters and merchants:

> And prentices stick to your officers,
> For you may come to be as we are now. (p. 17)

And the dutiful apprentices assert their valour against Faulconbridge's rab-ble of soldiers out for spoil, who they say are ale-house brawlers rather than true fighters:

> Nay, scorn us not that we are prentices,
> The Chronicles of England can report
> What memorable actions we have done. (p. 18)

The divine right of kings has little to do with the matter – order, security,

---

[34] On this scene, and the wider use of the folk-motif of the commoner speaking directly to the king, see Anne Barton, 'The king disguised: Shakespeare's *Henry V* and the comical history' in Joseph Price, ed., *The Triple Bond* (1975).

and civic dignity are the issues. All, incidentally, are betrayed by King Edward when he goes on to annex Jane Shore, wife of a city leader. Sometimes the commons in these plays try to appeal to the king over the head of aristocracy, city authorities, or church (as in *Jack Straw* (1597), *Sir Thomas More* (1595), or *Thomas Lord Cromwell* (1600)), but not always with happy results: kings often prove to be unreliable allies.[35]

Concern over the rights and limits of royal power and the danger of absolutism is most sharply dramatized in the reigns of kings who got deposed by their subjects, the traditionally bad and weak monarchs Edward II and Richard II. A right of resistance to tyrants had long been argued in principle by Huguenot, Dutch, and Marian exile writers, who held that rebellion and even tyrannicide might sometimes be justified, especially in case of religious oppression, provided the revolt was led by 'inferior magistrates' (the nobility) and not by the multitude on its own. Although books setting out such views were suppressed and burned by the hangman,[36] the ideas were well known, if not necessarily accepted, among the 'natural rulers'. Nevertheless, in Elizabethan times the *right* of resistance was generally regarded as a Popish doctrine, put forward by the Jesuits to justify plotting against the Queen, and it is seldom articulated in the plays, while republicanism as an alternative to a bad king is never an issue. The orthodox doctrine that even a bad monarch must be obeyed is not questioned in words so much as in the action; for clearly there is a point beyond which in practice subjects do not obey but revolt, often with great damage to the commonwealth. Marlowe, Shakespeare, and the anonymous author of *Woodstock* all dramatize this situation.

Marlowe's *Edward II* is political in an iconoclastic sense, showing the reign and deposition as a naked power struggle between the king and the barons. The country is torn apart and its armies defeated by the Scots. Yet it is deliberately made difficult for the audience to identify morally or humanly with either side. Sympathy and antipathy for the King and his enemies are continually shifted about. This murderous detachment and rejection of easy moralistic patterns was partly what attracted Brecht to the play not long after the First World War.

Edward is shown as a disastrous king because he is given up to self-indulgence and manipulated by his favourites, and therefore unable to con-

---

[35] Compare Maurice Keen, *The Outlaws of Mediaeval England* (1961), p. 56, cited by Barton, 'The king disguised'.

[36] They included *Vindiciae Contra Tyrannos*, signed S. Junius Brutus, probably by Sidney's friend Philippe Du Plessis Mornay; Christopher Goodman's *How Superior Powers Ought to be Obeyed*; George Buchanan's *De Jure Regni Apud Scotos*; John Knox's *First Blast of the Trumpet*; John Ponet's *A Short Treatise of Politic Power*.

trol his feuding barons or make war effectively. The decisive issue is not his homosexuality (though that antagonizes the barons, and probably the audience, they admit that 'the greatest kings have had their minions'), but that it leads him to favour social upstarts and squander wealth on them. The play never sentimentalizes his homosexual love-affairs. On his side there is real infatuation and love for Gaveston, but the very first scene shows Gaveston himself as an ambitious social climber, using his charm to 'draw the pliant king which way I please', refusing to employ honest men, but instead devising an expensive, elegant court culture – 'Italian masques by night,/Sweet speeches, comedies and pleasing shows' – anachronistically resembling the masking and opulence of the Elizabethan court. Spencer and Baldock, who succeed him, are equally unscrupulous.

Yet sympathy with Edward's opponents is deliberately undercut. Take the scene of hysterical violence where Edward and Gaveston physically attack and degrade the old Bishop of Coventry and strip him of his wealth:

> Throw off his golden mitre, rend his stole,
> And in the channel christen him anew! (1.1.187–8)

The brutality cannot but alienate the audience (and will be recalled when a similar retributive humiliation falls on Edward at the end of the play). Yet when the Archbishop of Canterbury, to save the church's property, joins with the peers, the effect is profoundly ambivalent. Though he asks the barons not directly to 'raise their swords against the king', he encourages their resistance, and threatens that unless Edward obeys his Council and banishes Gaveston, he as Papal legate will absolve them of their allegiance. The image of the Papal legate dictating to the King of England would deeply antagonize an audience recalling the Pope's excommunication of Elizabeth, and must affect their response to Edward's next tirade against the church (1.4.97).

Later the church is shown as the most ruthless force for deposing the King. And the barons appear in no very heroic light themselves, the honourable men among them overruled by the savage and sadistic, and their leader Mortimer developing from an apparent patriot to an ambitious Machiavellian schemer. King, favourites, church, and barons are all shown as responsible for the civil war that follows and the brutality with which it is fought. The impasse for the audience is emblematized in Edward's brother Kent, who first tries to restrain the King, then joins the barons to bring him to reason, then remorsefully returns to Edward's side, and is finally executed by Mortimer for his pains.

Only after he has lost power can Edward's hideous sufferings as a man engage much sympathy. Dramatically it is a powerful climax when his young son takes over as a strong ruler and sends usurping Protector and alienated Queen to their doom, not in the name of divine right (to which no one but the anti-patriotic Roman church appeals in this play) but in revenge for his father (5.6.99 ff.).

The conclusion shows the advantage the dramatists had over other writers in not having to pronounce a final judgement. Michael Drayton, Samuel Daniel, and Sir Francis Hubert, all dealing with the story later as poets, seem terrified of suggesting – or even allowing their characters to suggest – that it was oppression of the commons that brought Edward down; hence their many revisions. Marlowe avoids that issue. He shows the deposition not as justified, but as the inevitable result of Edward's actions. Retribution is not divine, but human and historical.

Richard II was an even more disturbing figure. He had, after all, been publicly deposed in Parliament, and succeeded not by his son but by a new usurping dynasty: and yet the sky had not fallen, the usurper had died in his bed. Richard's reign was indeed proverbial for misgovernment long before the dramatists used it, and was often cited as a precedent in political argument right up to the Civil War.[37]

The anonymous *Woodstock*, covering the early part of Richard's reign though drastically altering the history, is in some ways the boldest and most subversive of all Elizabethan historical plays. The young King is seen as seduced by greedy, frivolous courtiers to dismiss his noble Council, ride roughshod over Parliament, and extort taxes from the people to feed the luxury of his court. The dispute is imaged (more consistently than in *Edward II*) in terms of luxurious courtly fashion against country plainness.

Unlike *Edward II*, the play highlights the grievances of the common people, especially the burdens of increased taxation and tax-farming (which was also much resented in the 1590s). This is rendered less risky politically by making the popular spokesman not himself a commoner (like the hero of *Jack Straw*, or Shakespeare's Jack Cade in *Henry VI, Part 2*), but the King's uncle, Thomas of Woodstock Duke of Gloucester, a heroic nobleman with old-fashioned values expressed in simple dress and plainness of speech, whose desire is only to calm and head off a revolt of the angry commons – a

---

[37] For example Sir Francis Knollys, puritan privy councillor and Leicester's father-in-law, described those who favoured the Anjou Catholic marriage for Elizabeth in 1578 as 'King Richard the Second's men'. Among later parliamentarians, Oliver St John in 1615, Henry Parker in 1642, Colonel Rainborough in 1647, and Milton in 1649 all referred to Richard's tyranny and his overthrow as a precedent. (See M. Heinemann, 'Shakespeare und die Zensur' in *Shakespeare Jahrbuch* (Weimar, 1985), pp. 81–2.)

figure wholly unhistorical (the Woodstock of the chronicles was a turbulent war-lord), but dramatically effective. The conflict of loyalty and conscience is thus symbolized not in a minor character like Marlowe's Kent, but at the centre of the drama. Under great provocation Woodstock remains loyal to the orthodox doctrine that a tyrant must be endured as a divine visitation, and dies a martyr to it: but the play finds so much justification for the rebellion led by the Council after his death that it is 'rather a challenge to orthodoxy than a confirmation of it'.[38]

Much of the play is *comic* history in the popular tradition. In a memorable stage image the Duke at home in the country, wearing his frieze jerkin, confronts an effeminate courtly messenger hobbled by ridiculous fashionable shoes, who mistakes him for a groom and tips Woodstock sixpence to hold his horse (probably, in the open-air theatre, a real horse), with which the great man carries on a sympathetic political discussion. This prepares the way for a grimmer confrontation, where the court favourites smuggle themselves into Woodstock's house disguised as maskers (led by Richard himself dressed as Cynthia, the usual symbol for Elizabeth in court entertainment), and abduct plain Thomas to be imprisoned and murdered.

Extortion and oppression are not merely reported, but shown in detail as an outrage against traditional rights and liberties – notably taxation by 'blank charters'; rack-renting and eviction of peasants; tax-farming on a grand scale for the profit of greedy courtiers and corrupt justices (their very profit-and-loss accounts are read out at length, the financial details working to rhetorical effect). Parliament is dismissed and law overruled. Sheriffs lobbying for their towns' ancient privileges and deputations presenting mass petitions against the taxes are arrested and locked up. Clearly the tradition of 'no taxation without representation', and of parliament as the citizens' defence against unjust royal exactions, was already well known and could be appealed to long before the national crisis of the mid-seventeenth century.

The impact on the common people is staged in scenes of farcical satirical comedy, with the villainous Chief Justice and his stooge clerk acting as tax-collectors, bullying and terrorizing the semi-literate townsfolk of Dunstable. In grotesque clowning form these episodes dramatize the total corruption of state. And the censorship itself is parodied when the town schoolmaster composes a comic song against the Justice, and a farmer who whistles the tune to his calves is imprisoned for 'whistling treason'.

After Woodstock's death his brother nobles, no longer restrained by religious loyalty, rise in arms to defeat the King and his flatterers and demand

---

[38] William A. Armstrong, *Elizabethan History Plays* (1965), p. xi.

the hanging of the Chief Justice. The last sheet of the MS is missing, and it is not clear how the play ended, though it was surely not with Richard's deposition, which was still some way off. The old nobility, and especially Woodstock himself, are represented as trying desperately till the very end to defend the commons' rights and so keep them from popular rebellion, with all the connotations of anarchy and communism so feared by the 'political nation'. The play's latest editors dismiss all this as 'sentimental feudalism',[39] but this is perhaps to take an over-simplistic view of historical mentalities. In the sixteenth century real popular movements of discontent often looked either to the monarch (whom they hopefully believed they might separate from the evil counsellors) or to some of the gentry and nobility as allies and patrons. This was in line with the theory of justified resistance to tyrants led by 'inferior magistrates' current in the Sidney and Essex circles, and was probably one of the roles Essex saw for himself (it may be no coincidence that the original Thomas of Woodstock was his remote ancestor).

Shakespeare's *Richard II* has sometimes been regarded as a more politically orthodox remake of *Woodstock*.[40] But although it attends less to the hardships of the commons, the play does not in fact present royal absolutism in a more favourable light. Here Richard is made directly responsible and his flatterers are reduced to mere 'feed' roles. Shakespeare undoubtedly knew *Woodstock*, and would not have chosen to cover the same ground. Attempts to read *Richard II* as a simple vindication of divine right and the wickedness of all resistance do not square with the dramatic effect of the play, nor with the way Shakespeare used and modified the chronicle sources to produce a painful, agonizing conflict in the mind of the audience. What happens when kingly power rests in the hands of a corrupt or lawless ruler? *Is* there ever a right of resistance? Or is that always the greater evil because of the lasting divisions it causes?

In the first part of the play Shakespeare makes Richard wholly unsympathetic, devious, and unscrupulous, and to emphasize this invents a highly sympathetic John of Gaunt (again largely unhistorical), a patriotic elder statesman who, though outraged by his brother Woodstock's murder and by the farming of the realm to favourites, nevertheless 'may never lift/An angry arm against [God's] minister'. When Richard abuses and insults Gaunt on his deathbed, and then seizes his property and disinherits his heir Bolingbroke to finance his Irish wars, he undermines his own hereditary

[39] Introduction to *Woodstock*, ed. G. Parfitt and S. Shepherd (Renaissance Dramatexts, Nottingham, 1979).

[40] See Giorgio Melchiori, 'The corridors of history: Shakespeare the remaker'. British Academy Lecture, 1986.

right and prepares the way for his own fall. The play concentrates on the *property* issues (which J. H. Hexter thinks would appeal not only to the hereditary aristocracy, but to contemporary citizen resentments in the 1590s about the infringement of their craft and trading rights by royal monopolies and patents).[41] Richard has made himself landlord of England rather than king,[42] and alienated his people:

> The commons hath he pilled with grievous taxes
> And quite lost their hearts: the nobles hath he fined
> For ancient quarrels and quite lost their hearts.   (2.1.246–8)

One formerly influential but sentimental reading tried to make Richard a sacred and even Christ-like figure in the latter part of the play. There is, how ever, no warrant for this in the text. Sympathy is aroused for the impossible dilemma facing Richard's subjects and for the personal sufferings of the man after deposition, not for a royal martyr (even if that is how he sees himself).

Indeed it cannot have been clear to an Elizabethan audience that Richard's overthrow was necessarily the worst outcome for England (though understandably the censors were alarmed by the deposition scene and it does not appear in the first printed edition in 1597). On this point the chroniclers disagreed. In Shakespeare the audience is prevented from finding an easy solution. But on balance the play inclines no more to Holinshed, who thought the people very ungrateful for rebelling against a king under whom they had prospered, than to Foxe, who concluded that it was because Richard had deserted true religion and turned to persecuting the Wycliffites (whose patron was John of Gaunt) that God turned against him.[43]

This alternative tradition helps to explain how Essex's followers might have seen this 'old play' as worth restaging on the eve of their adventurist revolt. Having attended many performances, they were perhaps in a better position than we are to judge whether on balance it would encourage the popular audience to approve or disapprove of rebellion: though Shakespeare's company, when questioned by the Privy Council, were able to convince them that they had had no topical or seditious intent.

As we know, Essex wildly miscalculated the support for his 'last honour revolt'.[44] The city and commons' grievances over monopolies, taxes, and

---

[41] J. H. Hexter, 'Property, monopoly and Shakespeare's Richard II' in P. Zagorin, ed., *Culture and Politics from Puritanism to the Enlightenment* (Berkeley, 1980).

[42] For the significance of this phrase, and of Richard's failure to rule according to the law, see Donna B. Hamilton, 'The state of law in *Richard II*', *SQ* 34 (1983).

[43] John Foxe, *Acts and Monuments* (1583), p. 513.

[44] The phrase is from Mervyn James, *Society, Politics and Culture* (1986), chapter 9: 'At a cross-roads of the political culture: the Essex Revolt, 1601'. For support of Essex by puritan preachers, see Patrick Collinson, *The Elizabethan Puritan Movement* (1967), pp. 444–7.

religion were not felt primarily against the crown: the old Queen remained more popular than her nobility and was still widely seen as guardian of the nation's independence. Moreover Essex did not command either the wealth and military power or the degree of court influence which had enabled his stepfather Leicester to take within limits an independent line. Essex was personally popular as a military hero, but that was not enough to rally to him the money-men of the city whose support he expected. The anticipated 'historical bloc' of dissident aristocracy, discontented officers, disappointed office-seekers, city magnates, puritan preachers and their congregations fell ingloriously apart, and Essex and many of his followers went to execution.

Yet the divisions underlying the revolt were serious enough. A generation later Essex's son, the third Earl, who also considered himself marginalized and badly treated by the crown, *did* inherit Essex's popular reputation, and *did* for a time ally with city leaders and alienated aristocrats against increasingly absolutist rule under Charles I. In this alliance religion (represented by the London puritan preachers who had already supported the second Earl) played an important part, along with grievances over law, taxation, poverty, and property rights.

For the time being, the Essex disaster brought history plays of the existing type to a halt. No English history at all could be published without special authority from the Privy Council; and the King's Men made prudent cuts in their *Henry IV, Part 2* before publication in 1600. Celebratory national history, as in *Henry V* (1599), gives place to a *tragic* sense of history in *Hamlet* (1601), *Sejanus*, or *King Lear*. Nevertheless Richard II (and Shakespeare's version of his story) continued important in later political discussion. The argument of some modern historians that the Civil War and the English Revolution were not the result of long-term ideological and political divisions seems less than convincing if one studies the drama in the 1590s, when the regime was still stable enough to allow a degree of frankness that later became impossible.[45]

V

The death of Essex marked the end of an ideological epoch; and the tragic political implications of his fall resonate through much early-Jacobean drama, partly because the case was felt as much more than an individual one. The proud favourite and war leader, in conflict with an increasingly

---

[45] On this aspect of *Richard II*, see R. L. Smallwood, 'Shakespeare's use of history' in Wells, *The Cambridge Companion to Shakespeare Studies*, esp. pp. 147–51.

centralized absolutist state, and finally crushed as a traitor, was very much a figure for the times, and could suggest Ralegh as readily as his rival Essex. A deepening rift between the crown and sections of dissatisfied aristocrats and gentry, excluded from a central power increasingly controlled by a single faction (at this time Cecil's), opened terrifying prospects of instability whichever side one inclined to. But for many people Essex was still unequivocally a Protestant hero and a protector of puritan clergy, 'framed' for his opposition to a Catholic-inspired succession.[46] His memory was appealed to in many writings over the next thirty years.

Thus Samuel Daniel (a protégé of Greville and Lady Pembroke) was summoned before the Privy Council in 1605 because his tragedy *Philotas* (1604), dealing with a general of Alexander the Great tortured and executed for treason, was held to refer too directly to the Essex affair (though the playwright denied writing it for that purpose). On the other side of the case, William Barlow's official funeral sermon for Essex, preached by Cecil's order at Paul's Cross to justify to the people the execution of their hero, drew an extended parallel between Essex and Coriolanus, a comparison which both Shakespeare and his audience would have known about. The most striking dramatic analogy is in Chapman's two-part play from modern French history about Charles Duke of Byron (executed in 1602), where analogies are specifically drawn between Byron and Essex by the doomed protagonist himself.[47] These plays too attracted censorship, and many passages appear to be missing from the published text.

The real-life Byron had been a friend of the Earl of Southampton and an associate of Essex, who like him fought in the French wars of religion on the side of Henri of Navarre, the Huguenot leader who became Henri IV. Chapman shows Byron in peacetime growing personally arrogant and ambitious and hence easily manipulated by the King's enemies. While on an embassy to England he is warned by Queen Elizabeth of the dangers of subjects aspiring to compete with kings, but pays no heed and rushes headlong to his destruction. The protracted struggle between the cool, skilful monarch and his enraged and passionate aristocrat-general is rendered in powerful Marlovian verse. Although Henri IV (despite his politic conversion to Catholicism) was still regarded as a great hero and ally, both by Chapman's particular patron Prince Henry and by the English Protestant public, the regret and pain aroused on Byron's behalf creates an intense effect of tragedy and waste. The Machiavellianism of the King's counsellors, and his

---

[46] Compare Lucy Hutchinson, *Memoirs of the Life of Colonel Hutchinson* (reprinted 1968), p. 61.

[47] *The Tragedy of Charles Duke of Byron*, Act 4, scene 1; Act 5, scene 1.

inevitable use of informers and *agents-provocateurs*, attract a degree of sympathy to Byron even in his blindness and folly. The figure of the individual bastard-feudal war-lord frustrated by dependence on the new absolutist state – a Tamburlaine without the space to dominate the world – is applicable both to this play and to *Bussy D'Ambois*, and perhaps also to Alcibiades in *Timon* and to *Coriolanus*.

More generally, the characteristic images of Jacobean historical plays are no longer of brave Talbot or Henry V, battles and sieges (less suited anyway to staging after war with Spain had ended and in the indoor theatres), but rather the state, the machine, the 'set-up' caging in the heroes. Spies and informers, driven by poverty and lack of political preferment, serve in dissolute courts under rulers shown as corrupt or even mad, aided by unscrupulous churchmen. The Italian, French, Spanish, or Roman settings distance all this and make it acceptable for the censor.

More serious was a growing sense that the new reign, from which so much had been hoped, was proving not less but more autocratic than the old. The acute crisis in royal finances sharpened conflict between King James and the Commons, and explicit assertions of his divine right to rule by prerogative alarmed his subjects with the danger of absolutist power. John Chamberlain, writing in 1610, feared that

if the practice should follow the positions, we are not like to leave our successors that freedom we received from our forefathers.[48]

Much of what is usually called Jacobean 'revenge tragedy' or 'tragedy of blood' can equally be seen as political drama. The opening of *The Duchess of Malfi*, for example, sets the horrors to come not in a universal darkness where *all* men are 'merely the stars' tennis balls', but in the specific conditions of a tyrannic Italian city-state: conditions deliberately contrasted by the virtuous Antonio, in the opening scene of the play, with the enlightened monarchy of France, where the king rules wisely in agreement with honest outspoken councillors:

> In seeking to reduce both state and people
> To a fixed order, their judicious King
> Begins at home: quits first his royal palace
> Of flattering sycophants, of dissolute
> And infamous persons – which he sweetly terms
> His master's masterpiece, the work of Heaven;
> . . . .

[48] N. McClure, ed., *Chamberlain Letters* (1939), I.301.
[49] Bacon on Machiavelli in *De Augmentis*, chapter 2 (Spedding, ed., *Works* 1857–74, V. 17).

And what is't makes this blessed government
But a most provident council, who dare freely
Inform him the corruption of the times?
Though some o' th' court hold it presumption
To instruct princes what they ought to do,
It is a noble duty to inform them
What they ought to foresee.   (1.1.5–10, 16–22)

The 'shadow or deep pit of darkness' where 'womanish and fearful mankind live' is thus not timeless but historical, man-made. To establish this seems the only reason for Webster's opening the play with such a speech. A similar point is made in *White Devil*, *Revenger's Tragedy*, and with especial force in Middleton's *Women Beware Women* (4.1).

Fears of unlimited power are often articulated in classical history plays, based mainly on Tacitus (which were not subject to the general ban imposed on writing English history after the Essex revolt). Since the earlier, heroic Rome of Plutarch's *Lives* had been a republic, tyrannous emperors could not claim a divine right to rule sanctioned by the Christian God, but only the right of conquest and power. Hence the indictment of arbitrary rule arose naturally from the historical narrative and became symbolic. Sejanus was indeed used as an example in later political discussion as often as Richard II – in a famous instance, by Sir John Eliot denouncing Buckingham in the Commons in 1627.

Jonson's *Sejanus* (1603) is the story of a power struggle in which the emperor Tiberius, apparently manipulated by his unscrupulous upstart favourite, secretly leads him on to his own destruction. It is Jonson's contribution to the new 'politique' view of history, which aims to help political understanding and teach statesmen by showing 'what men do, and not what they ought to do'.[49] The play is frightening because – unlike *Woodstock*, *Henry V*, or even *Richard II* – it offers no way a good man can act or survive in such a state. Good characters do exist in this Rome, but as passive onlookers, incapable of action, their highest virtue shown in stoical endurance of injustice (stoicism, as J. W. Lever has stressed, representing the moral value appropriate to a despotic reign of terror). The climax is a brilliant and wholly negative staging of the Senate in session, showing the assembled senators shifting along the benches to get close to Sejanus while he is still believed to be the favourite, then, as Tiberius' agent reads out the speech which dooms him, shifting hastily away. Jonson himself had no faith in parliaments as a check on tyranny and folly in rulers. A plea for the value of history – scientific, unflattering history as a guide to future times – is written into the action through the historian Cordus, who before his execution defends the right of the chronicler to show the Caesar-killers Brutus and Cassius as heroes. James, we recall, disliked the vogue for Tacitus as a historian, thinking he defended tyrannicide and was far too critical of rulers.[50]

The play is very close to the sources Jonson was dramatizing in Tacitus and Suetonius, but this did not prevent his being questioned by the Privy Council and threatened about it when it was printed. Although he denied that any modern political 'application' was intended, he must have known that it would be so interpreted by some of the audience, and that this was indeed part of the interest. The 'application' the audience was likely (or intended) to make could not, however, have been (as some critics suggest) to Essex, whom the analogy in no way fits. Sejanus in Jonson is a dissimulator who skilfully (on Machiavellian principles) conceals his real motives, Tiberius a ruler who tricks, manipulates, and is morbidly afraid of the people; whereas Essex was a popular figure notoriously unable to hide his feelings, and Queen Elizabeth could not possibly have been identified by the audience with the evil Tiberius – indeed the nostalgic harking-back to her reign as a golden age for the people was already beginning.

The really damaging analogy was more general, with a court where scheming flatterers could be promoted over better men who had proved themselves in the wars and service to the state. Significantly, the prosecution of Jonson was initiated by the clever and ambitious Henry Howard, Earl of Northampton, out of favour under Elizabeth but becoming rich and power-ful through the spoils of office under James. He disliked not only this play, but the whole movement towards spreading education and instruction of which such learned drama was a part.

For my own part, I think that so many schools as there is, is a great decay unto learning, for the number of raw scholars makes such a division and is a cause to broach so many new opinions ... when the scum are sent out of the university.[51]

Sejanus was a failure with the audience when first performed at the open-air Globe, probably not so much because of the long speeches (*Tamburlaine* had plenty of those) as because of its total blackness, with no active heroic characters (as in Shakespeare's adaptations of Plutarch) and no comic low-life contrasts. Indeed there *are* no common people, except for the off-stage mob who mindlessly tear Sejanus to pieces at the end. The element of folk-

---

[50] For the influence of Tacitus in the period, see Peter Burke, 'Tacitism' in T. A. Dorey, ed., *Tacitus* (1969), and Blair Worden, 'Classical republicanism in the puritan revolution' in H. Lloyd-Jones, V. Pearl, and B. Worden, eds., *History and Imagination* (1981). For his dra-matic influence, see Alan T. Bradford, 'Stuart absolutism and the utility of Tacitus', *HLQ* 46 (1983) and Martin Butler, 'The Roman actor and the early Stuart classical play' in Howard, *Massinger*.

[51] Forster, Proceedings in Parliament, 1610, I. 79, cited Linda L. Peck, *Northampton* (1982).

wisdom or colloquial commentary on tragic wickedness is absent. After this play and the trouble it brought him Jonson seems to have changed tactics, making his political comment (city comedy apart) through court masques honouring godlike rulers and their servants and so persuading them to goodness. Criticized for flattering such men too much, he argued that "Twas of purpose to have made them such'.

The parody of serious matters by the wise clown or sceptical commoner indeed tends to disappear in a later drama increasingly directed towards a gentle audience. The common soldiers and rebels in Beaumont and Fletcher (*Philaster, Bonduca*) or Ford (*Perkin Warbeck*) are merely contemptible or ridiculous. In early-Jacobean times, however, political plays in the open-air theatres still make great use of intelligent plebeian characters, and the counterpointing of clown and king reaches a new sharpness in *King Lear* (1605), one of the latest plays Shakespeare wrote for the Globe as distinct from the Blackfriars. Whatever other topical allusions may be found in *Lear* (to the controversy over the union of the kingdoms of England and Scotland for instance), centrally the play deals with a decaying social order based on links of loyalty, fealty, and patriarchal kinship, breaking down in conflict between the arbitrary old King and the predatory royalty and ambitious upstarts who surround him – all at the expense of the helpless suffering poor, who are ever-present in the poetic imagery though not in the cast list.

Recent studies of the alternative texts[52] have confirmed that the play was indeed thought to be dangerously political. The obvious reading is also the most likely – that the flattering, cadging courtiers and upstarts were seen at the time as flattering, cadging courtiers and upstarts, like James's expensive and much-resented Scottish favourites (or, prophetically, like the Duke of Buckingham – the analogies are not personal but historical). The Fool's references to Lear's having given away his land and his independence with it, and to lords and ladies snatching at monopolies (1.4), ring of the Jacobean court and state – patent-holders, tax-farmers and all. And these are precisely the references which the new textual analysts most strongly believe were censored or self-censored in a second version of the play. More broadly, *King Lear* dramatizes for a mass Globe audience the contradiction between absolute arbitrary power and the 'foolish, fond old man, fourscore and upwards' who wields it. The common people, whose wisdom underlies the Fool's proverbial gibing wit, know that justice is a matter of rank and money, and Lear comes to echo this insight.

The mock-trial scene, where Fool, King, and (pretended) madman sit in

[52] Gary Taylor and Michael Warren, eds., *The Division of the Kingdoms: Shakespeare's Two Versions of King Lear* (Oxford, 1983). See esp. p. 103.

parody-justice on the political villains, is one of the most prophetic in Renaissance drama, and it is hard to agree with those critics who think that in cutting it out (because the same point can be made more economically in the verse and it is difficult to act) Shakespeare made a better play.[53] For the visual image *reinforces* what is said, embodying in a single memorable icon the whole tradition of the Fool as prophet and the idea that the world upside-down may truly be the right way up. The scene foreshadows visions that were to appear again in the 'second revolution' – that unsuccessful popular revolution without which the first, the gentry or bourgeois revolution, could never have succeeded. In so doing it gives more insight into the complex, contradictory pattern of Jacobean politics than could be conveyed in the verse alone.[54]

Certainly this play is not as wholly alienated and despairing as *Sejanus*, and may therefore have been more likely to please a Globe audience. But the political conflict is still inescapably a *tragic* one, to which no solution is (quite deliberately) made possible. Cordelia's death is Shakespeare's addition to his sources. No one can now put the old system back as it was, and Edgar's final speech rejects any strong reassuring conclusion. Absolute loyalty to this King demanded forms of resistance to this King: and look how it ended. So, as Henry Parker argued in 1642, Richard II ought to have known that his real friends were not his flatterers but those who took up arms against them,[55] but it was impossible that he should see this until it was too late.

VI

Meanwhile a quite different kind of political drama – optimistic, confident, monarchist, and patriotic – was growing up in the popular theatres. Sometimes seen as orthodox and non-controversial, in fact these plays on Tudor history, sometimes called 'Elect Nation' plays, centred on one of the main political controversies of the age: was England to be Protestant or Catholic, how far was the Protestant Reformation to go, and what right if any did godly subjects have to resist an ungodly prince? Uncertainty about the succession had made all this a burning question in Elizabeth's last years, giving the impetus for a new line of militant Protestant history plays based largely on John Foxe's *Acts and Monuments*. Both *Sir John Oldcastle* (1600)

---

[53] For an opposite view, see Roger Warren's article in *The Division of the Kingdoms*.

[54] We do not know that the amended version, if that is what it is, was ever performed: and indeed there is no record of any revival for *King Lear*, as there is for *Othello, Hamlet,* and *Macbeth*.

[55] Henry Parker, *Observations Upon Some of His Majesty's Late Observations and Expresses*, 1642, ed. W. Haller, p. 195.

and *Thomas Lord Cromwell* (1600) were built round idealized heroes who stood out for religious reform in the name of conscience and were martyred for it.

The peaceful accession of the Protestant James I, rather than the Spanish Infanta, did not end the fear of growing Catholic influence. His arrival with an ostentatiously Catholic queen was soon followed by an unpopular peace treaty with Spain and the first suggestion of the detested Spanish marriage for the heir to the throne. The hopes of the godly were dashed and Protestant fears confirmed by James's refusal to grant any increased toleration of puritan ministers in the church (1604), and above all by Gunpowder Plot (1605).

This context gave a political edge to a drama directly based on Foxe's narrative, and embodying his vision of history as the working out of God's purpose for England, an 'elect' or chosen people in the cosmic struggle against Antichrist, with the English monarchy as leader and future ruler over God's kingdom on earth. The reigns of Henry VIII and Queen Elizabeth, tricky or impossible to dramatize while she lived, and with them the events of the English Reformation, now became available matter for the stage. And Elizabeth, in whose time Foxe's book had been placed by order in all churches, was here cast as the outstanding heroine of Protestantism – a role that in her lifetime she had not always been so willing to accept, useful though she found it on occasion. The plays emphasize not the complexities, moral dilemmas, and contradictions of political action, as the 1590s histories so often do, but rather a clash between good and evil, right and wrong. In this sense 'they may profitably be viewed as post-Reformation versions of the religious drama which the early Reformation had suppressed in England'.[56] Equally they can be seen in their context as political plays, where the black-and-white moral scheme helps to make the story exciting, as it does still in the popular genres of spy-thriller and science fiction. And nostalgic praise of Elizabeth becomes an implied critical comment on James's reign.

In drama like this political issues, as so often in the seventeenth century, take a religious form; or rather politics and religion are inseparable, as they were in life. For what is felt to be at stake, at the popular level, is the survival of England as an independent and prosperous nation, the freedom of individual conscience, and hostility to the Pope. (Religion in the sixteenth century, as Namier put it, is often another word for nationalism.)

Almost all the Foxeian plays were originally staged in the amphitheatres,

---

[56] Judith Doolin Spikes, 'The Jacobean history play and the myth of the Elect Nation', *RenD* n.s. 8 (1977), 117–48.

and their appeal, in both politics and dramatic style, is clearly to the citizen audience. Several of the playwrights also devised pageants and Lord Mayor's shows for the city – Munday, Heywood, Dekker, Webster, later Middleton – and some city pageants are directly reproduced in the plays, several of which were repeatedly revived at the Red Bull and the Fortune and many times reprinted over the next thirty years.[57] Their detailed application varied with the political situation. They helped to rouse enthusiasm for Prince Henry, widely looked to as a more warlike, militant Protestant figure than his father (the parallel with the young Edward VI stands out in Samuel Rowley's play on Henry VIII, *When You See Me You Know Me*); after his death, to celebrate the marriage of Princess Elizabeth to the Protestant Elector Palatine in 1613 (several were reprinted at that time); and later, in the 1620s and 1630s, to reinforce feeling against a Spanish marriage and for recovery of the Palatinate. *The Duchess of Suffolk* (1624), directly taken by Thomas Drue from Foxe's account, and Middleton's *Game at Chess* and *Hengist, King of Kent* (1618–21?) make use of similar traditions.

Although the doctrine, like that of Foxe's book itself, is wholly orthodox, the effect, especially at the time when Archbishop Bancroft was 'harrying the Puritans' with James's leave, may have been less so.[58] The central stage confrontation is between heroic Protestant individuals, victimized for conscience's sake, and rich, self-seeking, persecuting bishops (led by Cardinal Wolsey or by Gardiner, Bishop of Winchester, a scheming villain in play after play), who seek to persuade the monarch that his most loyal subjects are traitors. These are of course *Catholic* bishops, appearing in rich vestments, and acting openly as agents of Papal and Spanish rule. But in the early 1600s, when clergy who refused vestments and ceremonies as Popish survivals were being deprived, the stage bishops Gardiner and Bonner were likely also to recall those conforming bishops in the contemporary Church of England who sought to live in much the same pomp and wealth as their pre-Reformation predecessors had done.[59]

The dramatists probably avoided trouble with the censor because, like Foxe himself, they exalted the monarchy and royal supremacy over the

---

[57] Heywood's *If You Know Not Me, Part 1*, achieved nine quarto editions; Samuel Rowley's *When You See Me You Know Me* reached four.

[58] Puritans who petitioned the King on the issue in 1604, led by the moderate puritan MP Sir Francis Hastings, were told that to combine thus 'in a cause to which the King had shown mislike … was little less than treason … and tended to sedition', and when they refused to sign a submission they were deprived of their local offices (Russell, *The Crisis of Parliaments*, pp. 210, 263).

[59] See Joel Berlatsky, 'The Elizabethan episcopate: patterns of life and expenditure' in R. O'Day and F. Heal, *Princes and Paupers in the English Church* (1981).

church as the alternative to the Papacy, and made no attack on bishops and church hierarchy as such. Moreover, Gunpowder Plot frightened the King as well as his subjects. With strong apocalyptic and millennial overtones, the plays also highlighted the call for solidarity with the Protestant cause abroad: thus Dekker's allegory *The Whore of Babylon* shows the Fairy Queen promising aid to the oppressed Netherlanders, as the closest neighbours in both trade and religion, who by commerce 'are grown so like us/That half of them are Fairies: the other half/Are hurtful spirits'.

The common people, rather than the gentry, are represented as the strongest sympathizers with Protestantism and its martyrs. In Heywood's *If You Know Not Me, You Know Nobody* (1604), Princess Elizabeth on her way from the Tower to house arrest at Hatfield is greeted by demonstrations of loyal townspeople and children offering bunches of flowers, and comments: 'The poor are loving, but the rich despise'. In the sequel (*If You Know Not Me, Part 2*, 1605), the growing political influence and confidence of the city magnates is imaged in the great merchant Gresham, builder of the Royal Exchange, and the rich plain-spoken haberdasher Hobson, founder of civic charities, who offer a more-than-princely contribution (idyllically free of interest) to the Queen for the defeat of the Armada.

A new heroic model emerges, not always a warrior (though the Protestant rebel Wyatt in *Sir Thomas Wyatt* (1604) is deliberately paralleled with Essex) but a type of civic courage. Religion based on individual Bible reading and rational argument, rather than reverent submission, is imaged in figures like the Wycliffite Oldcastle in the play of that name, defending his right in the name of conscience to reject Papal domination, though not to organize 'conventicles' or rebel against the king. Often these figures are women. Thus Queen Catherine Parr, a strong-minded Protestant, sucessfully upholds her loyalty against the bishops who accuse her of heresy and treason to the King, in the presence of the confused but still terrifying old Henry VIII. The Duchess of Suffolk is another powerful personality, going into exile rather than submit to the Catholic restoration, and shown defending her husband sword in hand. Elizabeth herself, in *If You Know Not Me* and *The Whore of Babylon*, provides the supreme example.

The wicked bishops are shown not only as agents of Rome, but also as greedy schemers seeking their own wealth and power. Reformers like Oldcastle and the low-born Thomas Cromwell attack the church's right to abbey lands, proposing (not altogether historically) to use them for the poor rather than to maintain idle monks. Within the stylized providential framework the playwrights humanize their subjects, using clowns and comics for satirical parody and comment, and providing naturalistic colloquial scenes for citizens and working people, represented as the true religion's strongest supporters.

The Bible in English, symbol of the reformed religion, is a key recurrent image. In *If You Know Not Me, You Know Nobody, Part 1* it becomes literally the magic talisman that Elizabeth carries to protect her life, and frightens off the friars sent to murder her in prison. It is also the visible symbol of unity with her godly people. At the end of the play, when she enters London in triumph as Queen, it is the Bible that the Lord Mayor offers in his civic welcome (as he did in life), and she gracefully receives it:

> An English Bible: thanks, my good Lord Mayor,
> You of our body and our soul have care
> 　　　　·　·　·
> This book that hath so long concealed itself,
> So long shut up, so long hid, now lords, see
> We here unclasp: for ever it is free.　　　　(1580–1, 1584–6)

Again this is not as uncontroversial as it looks; it had political and democratic connotations. In Henry VIII's time the reading of the English Bible had been restricted by law to the upper classes. And there were still those who thought a religion based on reading the Scriptures dangerous to the social order. The political conclusions were drawn much later by William Cavendish, Duke of Newcastle, writing in the 1650s to his former pupil, the exiled Charles II. 'The Bible in English under every weaver and chambermaid's arm hath done us much hurt.'

VII

In the last years of James's reign the theatres were openly involved in the intense political controversy over the Spanish marriage project. Whether England was to follow the King's policy and enter an alliance with Spain, cemented by a royal marriage between Prince Charles and the Infanta, was a momentous political and social decision as well as a religious one, as was indeed recognized at the time:

The Catholic issue may well be a red herring, for the political significance of the Spanish alliance is far more revealing [than the religious]. The House of Hapsburg represented social order and stability in a world threatened by Dutch and presbyterian republicanism. The 'instructions additional' given to Sir John Digby on his embassy to Spain in 1617 expressed the hope that an Anglo-Spanish alliance would halt 'a creeping disposition to make popular states and alliances to the disadvantage of the monarchy'.[60]

---

[60] Simon Adams, 'Foreign policy and the Parliaments of 1621 and 1624' in Kevin Sharpe, ed., *Faction and Parliament* (Oxford, 1978), p. 140.

After the long-expected war broke out in Europe, and the King's daughter Elizabeth and her husband, the refugee Queen and King of Bohemia, became the focus of the Protestant cause, demands for effective English intervention increased. The debates on the issue in Parliament were conducted, says Simon Adams,

> between men who saw events as part of a pattern of Protestant apocalypticism and men who, fearing the revolutionary implications of such an ideology, sought a policy more conducive to the stability of the political and social status quo.[61]

There were deep divisions about both policy and strategy, impossible to summarize here. But there seems no doubt about the keen interest of Londoners in the European events, or the general hostility at a popular level to the Spanish alliance.[62]

At the outset of the Thirty Years' War, Fletcher and Massinger's *Sir John Van Olden Barnevelt* (1619), directly political and topical, dealt with the downfall and execution of the famous Dutch Arminian statesman, accused of conspiring with Spain against the Calvinist Stadholder Prince Maurice of Nassau, leader of the Netherlands revolt against Spanish rule (which was to break out into open war once more in 1621). The play was at first banned by the Bishop of London, but a little later the players 'found means to go through with it' (presumably with the help of influential patrons). Heavy censorial intervention in the surviving MS, which included rewriting the ending, confuses the final political effect of the play. It was evidently intended, however, to show the great advocate as ambitious and disloyal, rather than a victim of judicial murder like Ralegh, and would have appealed strongly to the intense interest of London audiences in the European conflict.

In the following years censorship clamped down, with a royal proclamation against public talk of affairs of state and especially the Spanish marriage. Preachers were forbidden to touch on it, and several who did were gaoled, as were MPs who insisted on their right to discuss the issue. Poets such as Drayton were silenced, and George Wither sent to prison for *Wither's Motto* in 1621.[63] However, the climate changed when in 1623 Buckingham and Prince Charles returned from their abortive romantic expedition to Spain *without* the Infanta. Bells and bonfires greeted their arrival in London, and

---

[61] *Ibid.*

[62] For a brief account of the political and strategic issues involved, see Simon Adams, 'Foreign policy'. The general context is set out in Hirst, *Authority and Conflict*, esp. pp. 126–59. See also Norbrook, *Poetry and Politics*, pp. 215–34 and S. R. Gardiner, *History of England 1603–1642* (London, 1883) IV.118–19.

[63] For sermons and pamphlets against the marriage, see Jerzy Limon, *Dangerous Matter* (Cambridge, 1986).

Charles temporarily became more popular than he was ever to be again. As Prince and opportunist favourite placed themselves for a time at the head of a 'war party' to recover the Palatinate, the edge of the censorship was blunted by divisions between them and the King, and the way was cleared for renewed political drama hostile to the Spanish alliance, and favouring solidarity with the Protestant cause.[64] Plays with this general message were put on in all types of theatre, appealing to a variety of political interests and anxieties in their different audiences. Thus Jonson (who had earlier been writing on King James's side of the case) produced *Neptune's Triumph for the Return of Albion*, a celebratory court masque in which Charles and Buckingham themselves intended to appear.[65] Massinger's *The Bondman*, performed first at Whitehall and then for the mainly élite audience at the Cockpit in 1623–4, embodied through classical history the desire of the puritan gentry for chivalrous leadership in war abroad and aristocratic order at home. *The Duchess of Suffolk*, played at the down-market Fortune after being heavily censored for 'dangerous matter', was a typical popular Foxeian play, adjusting history to parallel the sufferings of the dethroned Queen of Bohemia more closely with those of the royal Duchess exiled under Queen Mary. The most famous of all, Middleton's *A Game at Chess*, put on at the open-air Globe in August 1624, played for a record run of nine days to packed houses before it was suppressed by the King's order, and was

> frequented by all sorts of people old and young, rich and poor, masters and servants, papists and puritans, wise men, etc., churchmen and statesmen.[66]

There were probably more plays with a similar political slant, now lost and known only by their titles – *The Hungarian Lion*, *A Match and No Match*, *The Spanish Viceroy*, *The Spanish Contract*.

Massinger's tragicomedy *The Bondman*, an outstanding example, represents a nostalgic ideal of aristocratic, patrician leadership to resolve the national political crisis. Set in ancient Syracuse, and coupling two separate classical histories from Plutarch and Herodotus to make a political point, it uses the rhetoric of Roman virtue in Plutarch and Seneca to expose state corruption, luxury, and softness among the élite. If the nation is to prosper, natural rulers must not neglect defence, give state power to upstart favourites, or allow injustice by the rich at home. Although the play is not a

---

[64] On the differences in politics and strategy between Buckingham's war policy and that favoured by the House of Commons, see Hirst, *Authority and Conflict*, pp. 129–30.

[65] It was cancelled at the last minute, apparently because of objections by the Spanish ambassador.

[66] John Chamberlain to Sir Dudley Carleton, 12 August 1624. *Chamberlain Letters*, II.578.

consistent allegory, it certainly allows strong contemporary analogies to be drawn.

The role of civic hero and pattern of political virtue is divided here between two leaders, Timoleon and Marullo. Timoleon, arriving as general from campaigning abroad (rather like Sir Horace Vere in 1623), rouses the effete Syracusans to defend their country against invasion by Carthage, calls on the young aristocrats to follow him rather than leave the fighting to conscripts or mercenaries, and demands that the rich pay for the war. But after the army leaves for the front, the ill-treated slaves at home, led by the second hero Marullo, rise in revolt, take over the palaces, and force the rich and noblewomen to serve them. Once the army returns victorious, however, the social upheaval is quickly set to rights. The fighting slaves are instantly cowed by the sight of whips in their masters' hands, which remind them of their servile status – though they are treated (unhistorically) with leniency, because the rich were proud and cruel and needed to be taught a lesson. Finally Marullo emerges as a hero and a gentleman (disguised as a slave for love of the princess), who by turning the social order briefly on its head has led the way to a juster and more secure state.

The grotesque 'world-upside-down' scenes are powerful dramatically, resonating with the acute economic distress among farmers and clothworkers in the 1620s; and the slaves are allowed some shrewd (and topically Jacobean) comments on the greed and incompetence of their masters. But the low, whatever sympathy they attract by the way, must be firmly kicked back into their places at the end. Marullo's orations to them indeed sound strikingly democratic and egalitarian, but in the context this dangerous effect is largely cancelled out, and social criticism is kept safely within bounds. The political outlook and moral (as S. R. Gardiner noted a century ago of Massinger's work in general) corresponds closely to that of the 'puritan' aristocratic war faction, lineal and ideological descendants of the puritan faction on Elizabeth's council, among them Lord Chamberlain Pembroke and his brother the Earl of Montgomery, to whom the printed play was dedicated because he had liked it on its first performance at court.[67]

A Game at Chess was unique not only in its boldness, but because it appealed far beyond the 'political nation' (who themselves attended in the best seats) to an audience that straddled the social divide, the kind of appeal that noble patrons would in normal times have been most unwilling to make.

---

[67] See S. R. Gardiner, 'The political element in Massinger', *Contemporary Review* 28 (August 1876), 495–507. For Massinger's connection with the Herberts and their general patronage of political and puritan writings, see my *Puritanism and Theatre*, chapters 10 and 12 and appendix A.

Referred to in contemporary records as 'our famous play of Gondomar', its main attraction was the caricature of the widely hated Spanish ambassador as a smooth, witty dissembler, popularly believed to have the ageing King in his toils. It is closely based on the famous illegal but widely circulated pamphlets of the puritan divine Thomas Scot, particularly his *Vox Populi*, first published in 1620 at a time when Buckingham and Charles (as well as King James) were all for the Spanish match. This was truly a subversive source, for Scot was a radical in politics as well as religion, continuing as a political refugee in Holland to issue pamphlets full of polemical praise for Parliament as the greatest hindrance to Spanish plots, and the Dutch republicans as the model of democracy and prosperity.[68]

In style the play is a mixture of forms, in part a chess-game allegory (where the sexual moves of the black pieces represent the Jesuits' attempt to entrap the individual white Protestant soul), in part direct impersonation of public 'pro-Spanish' personalities such as Gondomar, Bishop Antonio de Dominis, and Lord Treasurer Cranfield. King, Prince, and Duke are also staged, though more respectfully. The satire on the Fat Bishop (as distinct from fat cardinals) would normally have been banned entirely by the censor. The fact that the real De Dominis (incidentally a propagandist for royal absolutism) was only a Catholic turncoat *pretending* to be an Anglican bishop for his own profit, and had changed back before the date of the play, gave the opportunity for a kind of anticlerical clowning which had been impossible because of censorship since the 1580s.

In this bid to rouse and reinforce public opinion, doctrinal controversy (whether between Protestantism and Catholicism or between Calvinism and Arminianism) does not figure much. Catholicism is presented rather as a political and military threat to England, plotting to enlarge the 'universal monarchy' of Spain and the Pope. The Jesuit black pieces are its military and diplomatic spies, as are the Catholic laity under their control. The appeal is national as much as religious, recalling earlier plays about the Armada and Gunpowder Plot; and the Fat Bishop is mocked not for his beliefs but (as in Marprelate) for living luxuriously and immorally at the people's expense. Since the doctrine is held to be only a smoke-screen for greed and aggression anyway, it is secondary and at the popular level can be largely ignored. Archbishop Abbot, out of favour with James because of his pro-puritan and anti-Spanish stance, appears briefly as the good White Bishop, who (with only seven lines to speak) saves the White Queen from rape and prostitution

---

[68] Scot had escaped arrest only by fleeing to the Netherlands, where he was closely associated with the Queen of Bohemia's circle.

by the Black House, and earns commendation from the White King whom he has undeceived – not a heroic role, but enough to distinguish between *good* Anglican bishops and tools of Rome.

A Game at Chess was indeed a challenging polemical play, despite suggestions by recent critics that it was merely part of Buckingham's and Charles's propaganda campaign, and that by the time it was staged the issues it dramatized were no longer controversial. The original scenario might well have seemed acceptable to Buckingham (if he ever saw it), since it somewhat ironically supported the romanticized account he gave to Parliament justifying his journey to Spain, which was widely and deliberately 'leaked'. But the play is much more than an attack on the marriage: it also involves Catholicism generally and its growing political influence at court (which was to increase further in Charles's reign).[69] Buckingham can scarcely have been its direct sponsor, if only because of his own and his family's connections; his wife was a crypto-Catholic, his mother a well-known recent convert, and his sister and Buckingham himself on the edge of conversion in 1622 (much to the King's alarm) and persuaded against it with difficulty. Moreover, by the time the play was staged in August 1624, Buckingham already knew that the *French* Catholic marriage for Prince Charles, currently being negotiated in Paris, would entail concessions to the Catholic religion in England similar to those the Spaniards had demanded, and which James had promised Parliament he would never grant – though this fact was successfully concealed from Parliament until Charles was safely married to Henrietta Maria.[70]

All this suggests that the support which encouraged such a risky performance came from other patrons – perhaps from puritan city magnates, from the Pembroke connection, or from the Queen of Bohemia's circle at the Hague, all of them much more politically committed than Buckingham to the anti-Habsburg cause.[71] The punishment visited on the King's Men was certainly lighter than it would have been in normal times ('A year since they would all have been hanged for it', as one letter-writer commented), but it was still sharp enough to prevent the players repeating the offence. The company was forbidden to play for a time, till a letter from their patron Lord Chamberlain Pembroke released them on a promise of good behaviour, while Middleton himself had to go into hiding and may even have been

---

[69] See the detailed study by Caroline Hibbard, *Charles I and the Popish Plot* (Chapel Hill, North Carolina, 1983), *passim*.

[70] A potential 'leak' was forestalled by arresting the danger-man John Reynolds, puritan tutor to Buckingham's nephew, then in Paris, and keeping him in prison for two years on a minor censorship charge for writing *Vox Coeli*.

[71] See Heinemann, *Puritanism and Theatre*, chapter 10.

imprisoned. The brief 'censorship holiday' came to an end, and nothing quite like this play, appealing so directly to so wide a public, appeared again.

But the varied political opinions and feelings that preceded and made possible the 1624 plays – nationalist and chivalric, religious and iconoclastic, patrician and artisan – could not so easily be abolished, but persisted long after policy at the top had again changed. Indeed the feelings then released and reinforced by the drama were to contribute to the unpopularity and impeachment of Buckingham, and much later to the downfall of Charles himself.

The great age of the drama was perhaps the worst in English history for impoverishment and suffering among the poor and dispossessed.[72] Yet this can find relatively little direct expression in the political drama, though the pressure of discontent and the danger of disorder is never far away. Those plays that do show economic distress with some sympathy also voice the fear that any revolt will lead to anarchy and plunder.[73] Given the censorship and the real fear of rioting by desperate people, it could hardly have been presented otherwise. The aspirations and mentalities of the radical and democratic 'second revolution' are articulated, if at all, in Utopian fables and wishful fantasies of a poor man's heaven, divine revenge on the rich, a world magically turned upside-down.[74]

A new mood of insubordination can, however, be sensed in some popular plays of the 1630s and early 1640s, satirizing wine monopolists, proctors, and bowing at altars, or in dramatic pamphlets such as 'Canterbury's Change of Diet' (1641) where Archbishop Laud and his chaplain, having martyred Prynne, Burton, and Bastwick, are put in a cage to be mocked by the jester with the refrain 'Who's the Fool Now?'[75] Something very like the comic-political tradition of Tarlton and Wilson surfaces again in the dramatized tracts published over the pseudonym 'Margery Marprelate' (and probably written by the Leveller Richard Overton) around the time when the theatres closed.

Bibliography

GENERAL HISTORY

To understand the political drama requires some knowledge of the sequence of historical and political events. All the following general histories provide a readable

[72] See Michael Hattaway's chapter on 'Drama and society' in this volume.
[73] See *The Life and Death of the Horrible Rebel Jack Straw* (1593).
[74] e.g. Dekker, *If It Be Not a Good Play the Devil is in It* (1612) and *The Wonder of a Kingdom* (1631); Heywood, *Fortune by Land and Sea* (1607–9) and *The Royal King and the Loyal Subject* (1602, printed 1637).
[75] See my *Puritanism and Theatre*, chapter 12, and Butler, *Theatre and Crisis*, chapter 8.

narrative and enough detail to be useful for reference. Conrad Russell, *The Crisis of Parliaments. English History 1509–1660* (1971); Christopher Hill, *The Century of Revolution* (1980); Derek Hirst, *Authority and Conflict: England 1603–1658* (1986). For the European political context it would be useful to consult Victor Kiernan, *State and Society in Europe, 1550–1650* (1980). R. Cust and A. Hughes (eds.), *Conflict in Early Stuart England* (1989), which appeared too recently for me to make use of it in this chapter, provides an invaluable analysis of religious and political divisions.

POLITICAL IDEAS

J. P. Sommerville, *Politics and Ideology in England, 1603–1640* (1986); David Wootton, ed., *Divine Right and Democracy, an Anthology of Political Writing in Stuart England* (1986).

LITERARY HISTORY, CRITICISM, AND INTERPRETATION

Space allows for listing only a very small selection of relevant books (the notes will suggest many more). Marie Axton, *The Queen's Two Bodies* (1977); David Bevington, *Tudor Drama and Politics* (1968); M. C. Bradbrook, *The Rise of the Common Player* (1979); Martin Butler, *Theatre and Crisis, 1632–1642* (1984); Walter Cohen, *Drama of a Nation: Public Theater in Renaissance England and Spain* (1985); Jonathan Dollimore, *Radical Tragedy: Religion, Ideology, and Power in the Drama of Shakespeare and his Contemporaries* (1984); Jonathan Dollimore and Alan Sinfield, eds., *Political Shakespeare* (1985); Stephen Greenblatt, *Renaissance Self-Fashioning: From More to Shakespeare* (1980); Stephen Greenblatt, ed., *The Forms of Power and the Power of Forms in the Renaissance* (1982); Margot Heinemann, *Puritanism and Theatre: Thomas Middleton and Opposition Drama under the Early Stuarts* (1980); Christopher Hill, *Collected Essays, Vol. I: Writing and Revolution in Seventeenth Century England* (1985); J. N. King, *English Reformation Literature: The Tudor Origins of the Protestant Tradition* (1982); J. W. Lever, *The Tragedy of State* (1971); David Norbrook, *Poetry and Politics in the English Renaissance* (1984); Stephen Orgel, *The Illusion of Power: Political Theatre in the English Renaissance* (1975); Albert Tricomi, *Anti-Court Drama in England, 1603–1642* (1989); Robert Weimann, *Shakespeare and the Traditions of Popular Theatre* (1978).

TEXTS

For individual texts see the following: Robert Wilson, *Three Ladies of London* and *Three Lords and Three Ladies of London* in *Dodsley's Old Plays*, ed. W. Carew Hazlitt (selection reissued 1964); *Woodstock*, ed. G. Parfitt and S. Shepherd (1979); George Chapman, *Conspiracy and Tragedy of Charles, Duke of Byron*, ed. J. Margeson (1988); Thomas Middleton, *A Game at Chess*, ed. J. W. Harper (1966); Thomas Heywood, *Edward IV* in *Dramatic Works of Thomas Heywood*, ed. Collier, vol. I (1874). Malone Society Reprints include the following: Thomas Heywood, *If You Know Not Me, You Know Nobody, Parts 1 and 2*, ed. M. Doran (1934–5); P. Massinger and J. Fletcher, *Sir John Van Olden Barnavelt*, ed. T. Howard-Hill (1980); Samuel Rowley, *When You See Me You Know Me*, ed. F. P. Wilson (1952); Robert Wilson, *The Cobbler's Prophecy* (1914); Anon., *Edmund Ironside*, ed. W. W. Greg (1911), *Sir Thomas More*, ed. W. W. Greg (1911), *Sir John Oldcastle* (1908), *The Life and Death of Jack Straw*, ed. K. Muir (1957).

6   Romance and the heroic play

T HE terms 'romance' and the 'heroic play' are useful as broad categories applied to Elizabethan drama, but they cannot be clear cut or definitive; rather, we find a proliferation of hybrid kinds of play, with certain exceptionally impressive works imposing an influence on their successors. Elizabethan dramatists were very ready to innovate, to combine different literary traditions and dramatic kinds in risky ways; at the same time they had to be practical, writing for fairly small acting companies and particular playhouses and, above all, striving to please audiences whose approval was vital: Elizabethan theatre was a commercial venture.

The main features of the early Elizabethan romance, part folk tale, part chivalric, are traceable right through the period, down to the later Jacobean masterpieces *Cymbeline* and *The Winter's Tale*, both of which, indeed, deliberately recall the early kind. *Sir Clyomon and Sir Clamydes* is an early play, and though it is not often read it is discussed here because it shows clearly many key features of Elizabethan romance. As for heroic drama, the impact of Marlowe's *Tamburlaine* is so great that some attention to it is essential. Having looked at one romance and at one heroic play, this chapter goes on to explore the increasingly diverse kinds of play, and diverse forms of attention, devoted to the heroic life (whether martial, political, or amorous) and to romance (whether fantastic or historical, exotic or familiar, sublime or travesty). It is impossible to be properly systematic, since this would be to falsify the contexts in which these plays were devised and performed; and while there is a line of chronological sequence to be traced, it does not imply any quasi-Darwinian process of overall formal or stylistic evolution. The crudest and earliest kinds of romance and heroic play persist throughout this period, at certain amphitheatre playhouses, although it is a feature of other theatres that styles change rapidly in certain phases, for instance at about the time of *Tamburlaine*, then later at the time of *Hamlet*. This subject of 'romance and the heroic play' cannot be confined in a nutshell; but then tidiness is not one of the heroic virtues, whereas magnificence and extravagance certainly are.

I

Here is a stage direction from *Sir Clyomon and Sir Clamydes*, a heroic romance of *c.*1570:

Enter King Alexander the Great as valiantly set forth as may be, and as many Lords and Soldiers as can.

We are reminded of the daring of the Elizabethan dramatists in presenting the grandest imaginable heroes: Agamemnon, Orlando, Julius Caesar, Helen of Troy, Cleopatra, Robin Hood, Joan of Arc – the list is long. The ambition of the playwrights and the challenge of staging such material are evident. As the above-quoted stage direction shows, the players are required to make this Alexander's processional entry as impressive as the size of their company permits; traditions of pageantry and street processions being splendid at the time, one may suppose the audience was not disappointed. Still, it is hard for the modern reader to feel impressed when this Alexander speaks, for later Elizabethan drama's blank verse has made his style sound very clumsy and old-fashioned.

> After many invincible victories and conquests great achiv'd,
> I, Alexander, with sound of fame, in safety am arriv'd
> Upon my borders long wish'd-for of Macedonia soil,
> And all the world subject have through force of warlike toil...
> In field who hath not felt my force where battering blows abound?
> King or keysar, who hath not fix'd his knees to me on ground?[1]

This sounds like the tyrant in a mystery play or some warrior hero in a pageant or St George folk-play,[2] where the two-dimensional figures stand for something essentially too remote and extraordinary to be conceived of in terms of mere human personality: the whole point is the superhuman scale, the remoteness in time and space, the essential strangeness. On the other hand this playwright generally reveals a quite literate understanding of the romance mode.

---

[1] *Sir Clyomon and Sir Clamydes*, thought by Dyce to be by Peele, is now usually supposed to be anonymous. Quotations from Dyce's edition of *The Dramatic and Poetic Works of Greene and Peele* (1861), pp. 497–8.

[2] On folk-plays see E. C. Cawte *et al.*, *English Ritual Drama* (1967) and Alan Brody, *The English Mummers and Their Plays* (1969). An excellent recent essay with a good bibliography is Thomas Pettitt, 'English folk drama', *RenD* n.s. 13 (1982), 1–34. The best study of dramatic romance is Leo Salingar, *Shakespeare and the Traditions of Comedy* (Cambridge, 1974).

Although its clumsy dialogue is a barrier, in fact *Sir Clyomon* gives dramatic form to virtually all the key elements of romance and seriously attempts to create and manipulate audience response in the special terms associated with the genre, where intuition of some higher power shaping human lives is implied in complex plots, which the reader or spectator knows more fully than individual characters in the fiction do, but where surprises and revelations to the reader or spectator also occur, the more vivid for their shattering the illusion of superior knowledge. The rhythmic alternation between idyllic episodes of pleasure, of robust comedy, danger, physical and emotional deprivation, and ecstatic reunion, means that romance narrative has as its primary function the sustaining and developing of an emotional trajectory: and the episodes are significant in this respect before any other.

In *Sir Clyomon* the dramatist aims at a full-blooded representation of the familiar material to please a paying audience, so he begins with a hero entering alone and clearing the air with a big speech developing an epic simile, in which he compares his state to that of a wandering voyager at last returning home from the sea:

> So likewise I Clamydes, Prince of Suavia, noble soil,
> Bringing my bark to Denmark here, to bide the bitter broil
> And beating blows of billows high, while raging storms did last,
> My griefs were greater than might be, but, tempests overpast,
> Such gentle calms ensued have ...
> So that I have through long travail at last possess'd the place
> Whereas my bark in harbour safe doth pleasures great embrace. (p. 491)

The metaphors here are given no personal psychological resonance, though they have potential: when Clamydes says (completing the figure comparing his lovesuit to a tempestuous voyage) that his beloved lady Juliana

> Did me permit with full consent to land upon her shore   (p. 491)

there is no personal shaping of the metaphor. Marlowe in *Dido* (1587? 1591?), by contrast, uses such images for their erotic and psychological implications:

> DIDO
> Speaks not Aeneas like a conqueror?
> Oh blessed tempests that did drive him in!
> Oh happy sand that made him run aground!...
> Oh that I had a charm to keep the winds
> Within the closure of a golden ball;
> Or that the Terrene sea were in mine arms

> That he might suffer shipwrack on my breast,
> As oft as he attempts to hoist up sail![3]

In early-Elizabethan popular dramatic romance, characters directly announce their identity to the audience; exits and entrances are undisguised acts of theatre, motives are openly asserted, expository speeches are delivered in a choric manner, the audience is frankly acknowledged. These surviving representational conventions of medieval drama are often consciously retained in romantic plays throughout the period, as if the dramatist felt their naïve quality essential to the mode. This is something easily recognized in Shakespeare's most mature and original work in the mode, where he retains among other more subtle and profound styles the naïvely presentational, as in Charles the wrestler in *As You Like It*, Gower in *Pericles*, Cloten or Pisanio in *Cymbeline*, Camillo or Autolycus, for instance, in *The Winter's Tale*.

In *Sir Clyomon* Juliana abruptly presents Clamydes with a heroic task, to bring her from the Forest of Strange Marvels the head of a flying serpent that has an insatiable desire for women, but she seems very matter-of-fact about this, and Clamydes makes no comment. He simply departs, pausing only to get a knighthood from his royal father in Suavia. He resolves to

> address myself, in hope of honour's crown,
> Both tiger fell and monster fierce by dint for to drive down.   (p. 493)

Flying serpents, tigers, minotaurs, they will all serve equally well in a romance, the choice is arbitrary; but the structural code by contrast is very precise: the hero must be chivalrous and a virgin to overcome his exact opposite, a sexually depraved monster roaming in a wilderness.

The structural patterning is prominent in other areas, too: this mode is at once naïve and elaborately artificial. For example, immediately juxtaposed to this scene presenting Clamydes we have the first entrance of Clyomon, the other wandering knight. He enters alone, then calls back off stage to some 'fellow'. It turns out to be Subtle Shift the trickster–Vice who suddenly makes an entrance '*backwards, as though he had pulled his leg out of a mire, one boot off*'. The stage image offers a perfect parodic inversion of the lofty or bombastic heroic entrances we have just witnessed. Shift establishes an informal relationship with the audience, using humour, jokes, and asides to develop an ironic stance to his roles within the romance fiction. His place in the symmetrical pattern is equidistant to all the other characters, reflecting yet also questioning and subverting what they stand for: Shift as a shape-

---

[3] Christopher Marlowe, *The Tragedy of Dido Queen of Carthage*, ed. Roma Gill (Oxford, 1971), p. 38.

changer is at once part of the fiction and superior to it, like a mortal and yet not one (even at one point assuming an allegorical name). No mere wizard is a match for him. In him we recognize the seeds of familiar Shakespearian characters as diverse as Autolycus and Falstaff, the Fool in *Lear*, and Ariel in *The Tempest*.

In subsequent interwoven adventures, although the surface impression may be of naïve shapelessness, there is in fact a consistent design arranging narrative motifs in parallel. There are two knightly combats fought on stage: the first shows Clyomon killing the traitor king of Norway, the second shows villainous Sans Foy run away from Clamydes. These symmetrically related combats are balanced against two intervening occasions when Clyomon and Clamydes face one another but Alexander prevents them fighting. Such prominent symmetry is a permanent feature of romance drama.

A reader's impression of crowded, wide-ranging, and exotic action is not likely to correspond with an audience's experience of the play in performance. The knights' sea-journeys are referred to but not depicted on stage (at one point there is an off-stage noise of mariners and a single boatswain does appear on stage, but he is not even wet). There is a monster, but only its severed head is shown and a description of the battle with it has to suffice. There is a rustic and his dog (a traditional comic turn); he refers to neighbours, Madge, Joan, Hodge, Nicholl, Gillian, Jack, Jenkin, but we do not see any of them. Properties are simple and emblematic: knights have shields, one white, one golden; heroic persons bear swords, kings have royal maces, shepherds sheephooks, wizards wands. Clyomon acquires a monster's head, Shift a bag of gold. A god descends to a tomb-property. Different locations could have been marked by painted backcloths, the courts by a chair of state, the prison by a grille in wall or stage floor. In the writing we note equally simple demands for acting and interpretation. At the same time what is narrated but not shown has potential for a much more extravagant and spectacular kind of treatment: there are divine and infernal episodes, sea voyages to 'ferne strondes', and divers exotic foreign races. Clamydes speaks of the Hydra and the Minotaur, kills a monster, is enchanted, and meets one of the Nine Worthies.

What all this does show is the dramatist's awareness of the kind of theatrical experience heroic romance should offer: a narrative in which submerged patterns, cross-linked, are slowly made to emerge, and then with wonder welling up through the surface effect of surprise. It offers dramatic rather than simply literary prototypes of scene building and stagecraft for romance; and the all-important control and manipulation of audience response and involvement is attempted.

The final reconciliation in the play, between Clyomon and his long-lost beloved, is prepared for by taking the audience through a rapid sequence of surprises and contrasting emotions: mystery, farce, joyful revelation. A beautiful mysterious lady is brought to Clyomon, and bemuses him with a series of riddling questions; these allow the audience to guess at her identity moments before Clyomon at last realizes with astonished joy that she is indeed his beloved. The structure of this episode is a clear prototype for those richly emotional endings Shakespeare contrives in his romantic plays, most obviously perhaps *All's Well, Twelfth Night, The Winter's Tale,* and *Cymbeline*; what is achieved there, and only implied here, is a sense of personal reintegration, or spiritual union, which poetic and visual stage metaphors can suggest.

Such early plays as *Sir Clyomon and Sir Clamydes* are clearly designed with certain practical constraints in mind (limited staging resources, a small company of actors): these are features of the professional stage at the time in London, where the Red Lion opened in 1567, Burbage's Theatre in 1576, and the Curtain in 1577. Most of the plays listed by Alfred Harbage in his *Annals of the English Drama* for the years 1570 to 1585 are lost, although heroic romances are listed regularly (there are twelve, plus a number of other 'romances' which may have been 'heroical'). A number of the titles suggest similarity to *Sir Clyomon: Herpetulus the Blue Knight* (1574), *The Irish Knight* (1577), *The Solitary Knight* (1577), *The Knight in the Burning Rock* (1579). Of the plays actually extant from the time, *Cambises* (1561), *Patient Grissel* (1559), *Horestes* (1567), *Common Conditions* (1576), we can note that they are different enough from one another to prevent firm classification. Reading *Sir Clyomon*, with no other English heroical romances of the time to compare it with, is therefore likely to remind us of non-dramatic romances translated from Spanish or French: indeed the play's source has been found in one of the six folio volumes, in French, of the romance *Perceforest* (1528). Sir Philip Sidney's mocking description of heroical romance plays confirms that *Sir Clyomon* typifies the early kind. Andrew Gurr argues[4] that romantic narratives like *Sir Clyomon* were 'evidently the staple of the amphitheatre playhouses at first, and their popularity evoked enough protests from the more educated end of the audience range to give early notice of a social division in tastes. George Whetstone in 1578, and in the 1580s Stephen Gosson, Philip Sidney, and John Lyly all poured scorn on the medleys of romantic fantasy staged with cardboard monsters and knockabout clowns. The vigour of the protests might be taken as an acknowledgement of the popular hold such

[4] Gurr, *Playgoing*, p. 116.

plays had, and also of the players' aim to attract a mass rather than a select audience.'

At the same time, the great magnates Leicester and Sussex, who played a part in sponsoring the new playhouses, did so partly because it fitted in with their ambitious schemes for self-advancement: to be granted the honour of presenting plays at court was a conspicuous sign of power and influence. The chivalric romance play might support such a drive for court prestige in its highly stylized and idealized representation of the aristocratic life, while its endearing rustics and witty servants provided regional English local colour to set off the international culture, alliances, and fame of the hero. The vagueness about time, place, and political issues might be very welcome, and tactful, at court; so too, perhaps, might be the fact that the noble characters tend to be little more than ciphers and likely to pass the censorious eye of the Master of the Revels, who selected plays for court performance, editing and amending them as he saw fit.

Elizabeth followed her predecessors Henry VIII, Edward VI, and Mary in imposing censorship on the drama. The Proclamation of May 1559 forbade performance of all plays without prior licence; magistrates were charged not to license plays 'wherein either matters of religion or of the governance of the estate of the commonweal shall be handled or treated', because these are only to be treated by 'menne of aucthoritie learning and wisedome, nor to be handled before any audience, but of grave and discreete persons'.[5] We may note of the romance and heroic play like *Sir Clyomon*, the earlier, naïve kind, that conservatism is implicit in the dominance of conventional values through the agency of a token providence. The deliberately distanced presentation of the heroic reinforces not simply the prevailing English social system of ranks and estates but a whole official *Weltanschauung*. The polarization of high and low characters means that non-heroic characters express themselves with familiar directness and physical crudity. This also licenses the expression of rebellious attitudes, but in plays of this type this scarcely constitutes a threat to topple the state.

By contrast the non-dramatic heroic romances of Sidney and Spenser persistently explore the complexities, moral, political, and psychological, of the role of hero and the nature of courts and government, including treacherous servants and rebellious rustics – though always under the veil of pastoral convention. It is these two great non-dramatic writers who gave powerful precedent to later Elizabethan dramatists in the presentation of aristocratic life at court – seen with deep perception and a forthright, even bleak, recognition of the ways of power and the nature of princes. *The Faerie*

---

[5] Cited by Wickham, *Early English Stages*, II.1.75.

Queene and *The Arcadia* furnish sources for various kinds of play: pastoral love-romance, grand tragedy, satire, tragicomedy: they also offer models for the structure of narrative, which dramatists took over for their own use.

The bizarrely contradictory potential of Elizabethan romance, for idealism and for mere ambitious self-assertion, is nowhere better illustrated than in the Earl of Leicester's extraordinarily lavish and spectacular display of entertainments for Queen Elizabeth at his castle of Kenilworth in 1575. Time, space, and money were virtually unlimited (a striking contrast to the staging of formal plays whether in public or at court), and the programme included simple traditional rustic events involving local people, as well as Arthurian and classical shows. The whole affair, however much credit it might throw on the earl, derived its essential energy from a sense of communal, local, and regional pride, from a spirited celebration of popular and learned modes of festivity in which extreme contrasts and diversity were accepted, indeed savoured, each having its own integrity. The earl's castle of Kenilworth and its surrounding park was the setting: at the Queen's arrival she was welcomed by the classical hero Hercules and ten sibyls; there were chivalric jousts later, and a great water pageant took as its theme chivalric romance, with floating islands for Merlin's prison and the Lady of the Lake, dolphins to carry Proteus and Tryton, and dragons with fireworks. Mingled with these Arthurian and classical shows were rustic events, such as a Brideale (a mock wedding of two ugly rustics), and a Hock Tuesday play performed out of doors by the citizen guildsmen of Coventry, representing the battle of the English and the Danes in 1042, and including foot and mounted soldiers, with words as well as drums and much physical action. It is characteristic of the occasion that the play was performed twice because the first time the Queen was distracted by dancing being performed in the room from which she was watching. Another entertainment, the courtly work of Gascoigne, was, it seems, not performed because the Queen's humour[6] changed, though Gascoigne did succeed in another role, as Green Man, clad in moss and ivy, appearing from a wood and addressing a eulogy to the Queen as she passed by. It is remarkable that although some events took place out of doors – even on a real lake – both theme and spectacle were emblematic. Rather than striving for illusionistic realism, the aim was to assimilate the actual castle and estate into pageantry, to give them fuller meaning. The Green Man's surprise appearance is an irruption of folk-tale supernaturalism into ordinary life which accords with episodes in popular romantic plays.

[6] See Helen Cooper, 'Location and meaning in masque, morality, and royal entertainment' in Lindley, *The Court Masque*, pp. 135–48.

The lavishness as well as the variousness and extremely extended duration of the Kenilworth entertainments show how strong the ambition of the earl was to display his princely magnanimity and his regional authority as part of his courtship of the Queen. The court at its Christmas revels or at a great wedding would customarily mount entertainments along similar lines. In the Tudor court, compliment to the monarch would very often be combined with self-advertisement in masques and entertainments. When Montmorency came as suitor to Queen Elizabeth in 1582 entertainments included a tournament in which a castle on wheels (a wooden frame hung with painted canvas) and manned by the four Foster Children of Desire (Sidney, Fulke Greville, Lord Windsor, and the Earl of Arundel) besieged the Castle or Fortresse of Perfect Beautie, which was simply the Queen's gallery over the tiltyard, but graced by Elizabeth's presence in it. Similar entertainments would be staged by students of the Inns of Court, as we can see from the descriptions of the Gray's Inn Revels;[7] but the range of events would be less wide, and less various.

Chivalric romance, which is so prominent an element in the Kenilworth entertainments, was widely circulated in various forms and was extremely popular among non-aristocratic classes. A Coventry citizen, Captain Cox, the chief actor in the Kenilworth Hock Tuesday play, had a collection of chivalric romances,[8] and though his owning so many books might have been exceptional, it is clear that the spirit of the Coventry players accords with the similar type of entertainment offered on the professional stages in London in the 1570s and 1580s.

Popular romance in the early phase concerns heroes who are remote in every way; meanwhile court romance characteristically invites oblique application to real persons of the time while sustaining the fictional nature of the material. In the 1590s and later, forms of romance are evolved by the playwrights in which identifiable real persons of the past and of the present

---

[7] See D. S. Bland, ed., *Gesta Grayorum* (Liverpool, 1968). A brief selection is printed in G. Blakemore Evans, ed., *The Riverside Shakespeare*, pp. 1838–9. For further discussion, see Martin Butler's chapter, above.

[8] Cox, by trade a mason, owned copies of 'King Arthurz book, Huon of Burdeaus, The foour sons of Aymon, Beuys of Hampton, The sqyre of lo degree, the knight of courtesy and the Lady Faguell, Frederik of Gene, Syr Eglamour, Sir Tryamour, Sir Lamwell, Syr Isenbras, Syr Gawyn, Clyuer of the Castl, Lucres and Eurialus, Virgils life, The castle of Ladiez, The wido Edyth, The King & the Tanner, Frier Rous, Howleglas, Gargantua, Robinhood, Adambel, Clim of the Clough & William of cloudesley …' and many more, listed by Robert Laneham in his letter describing the Kenilworth entertainments. A discussion of the books is given by F. J. Furnivall in his edition, *Robert Laneham's Letter … 1575* (1871, reprinted 1907), pp. xii–cxxxvii. Quotation above from pp. 29–30.

are represented, their stories given romantic form; there are ballad heroes who are adopted as subjects for drama, plays freely based on legendary or regional folk heroes, and major figures of recent British history endowed with heroic stature in chronicle histories, formed in romance terms, to assert a providential destiny guiding the nation. Such dramatic forms are hybrid, and include varying combinations of elements, as will be shown in the following sections of this chapter. It should be remembered nevertheless that, though some kinds of drama evolve formally and stylistically and intellectually, others do not. Heywood's mythological romances at the Red Bull show scarcely a trace of conceptual development from plays two generations earlier. This lack of evolution in certain kinds is partly to be explained by the specialization in naïve and spectacular sorts of play in certain amphitheatre playhouses, with their appeal to a less demanding audience; and the fact is that certain very popular plays were revived regularly. The Fortune and the Red Bull amphitheatre playhouses 'sustained the repertoire of the 1590's right through to the closure in 1642, with Marlowe at its core throughout'.[9] Chamberlain's (later the King's Men) at the Globe, and at their indoor house at the Blackfriars after 1609, attracted not only citizens and artisans but the upper ranks of the population, Inns of Court students, gentlemen, and nobility, and performed most of the important plays of the period. That new kinds of play, and rapid evolution in established kinds, are a feature of the King's Men's repertoire, must have some connection with the appetites and responsiveness of the audience they played to as well as the resourcefulness of the players.

Folk-tale and mythic elements have an imaginative power, when expressed in naïve form, appealing to simple and sophisticated taste alike; it is this which explains the ambivalent style of *The Old Wife's Tale*,[10] perhaps. Sections of the play present folk tales, The Grateful Dead, The Three Heads of the Well, and motifs from others, Childe Roland, Red Ettin, Jack the Giant-killer; at the same time intervening episodes involving the on-stage audience of Madge the old wife, and the Pages, induce the audience to reflect self-consciously on the inset actions: thus both naïve popular comedy and sophisticated critical comedy alternate, without either seeming to inhibit the other. That so completely naïve a heroic romance as *Mucedorus* was revived in 1610 may be partly due to the fashion for medieval romance and chivalry

---

[9] Gurr, *Playgoing*, p. 151. For an excellent recent discussion of spectacular plays in the period see Lomax, *Stage Images*, chapters 1, 2, and 4.

[10] There are admirable editions of *The Old Wife's Tale* by Charles W. Whitworth Jr (The New Mermaids, 1984); Patricia Binnie (Revels Plays, 1980) and the fullest, by F. S. Hook (Vol. III of the Yale Peele, 1970).

led by the Jacobean court. Shakespeare's first response to plays of this kind had been mocking, in the pageant of the Nine Worthies in *Love's Labour's Lost* and the tragical mirth of Pyramus and Thisbe in *A Midsummer Night's Dream*.[11] *Mucedorus* features a prince disguised as a shepherd. He rescues a princess who enters and exits pursued by a bear. The prince gives chase and makes a heroic entrance with the severed head of the bear, much to the 'content' of the princess. The prince also outwits and brains the wild man Bremo with his own club. The episode in *Cymbeline* in which the would-be rapist Cloten is challenged and beheaded by a prince disguised seems to recall *Mucedorus*. In *The Winter's Tale* old Antigonus exits pursued by a bear so that the life of the infant princess Perdita is saved. In both cases the mixture of elements, gravely serious but partly ludicrous, corresponds to the early-Elizabethan heroical romance of Shakespeare's youth, but here wonderfully transformed in a new kind of dramatic experience, which enriches it. Both the strength of the folk-tale tradition and its playfulness are captured, while at the same time the ironic and allusive qualities recalling court drama give recognition to political and cultural pressures of the early-Jacobean period: both extremes of romance are accommodated, with a degree of real tension.

II

As the 1580s drew to a close several events, historical and theatrical, occurred of great significance for romance and the heroic play. In 1586 Sidney died of wounds at the battle of Zutphen. In the same year was performed *The Famous Victories of Henry V*. In 1587 appeared *The Spanish Tragedy*, *Tamburlaine*, and *Alphonsus, King of Aragon*; and the Rose theatre was built. In 1588 the Armada was defeated. Militarism became extremely popular, in the theatre and the nation. Between them Kyd and Marlowe expanded the possibilities of the unrhymed pentameter, blank verse, for dramatic speech, and the expressive possibilities of dramatic stagecraft in the Elizabethan theatre.

Marlowe's *Tamburlaine, Part 1* has a prologue which mocks 'the jigging veins of rhyming mother wits', thereby insultingly lumping together formal drama's rhymed verse with the farcical song-and-dance acts, or 'jigs', performed as end-pieces by clowns such as Tarlton.[12] In place of such doggerel

---

[11] See Patricia Russell, 'Romantic narrative plays' in Brown and Harris, *Elizabethan Theatre*.

[12] See J. S. Cunningham's note on this line in his edition of *Tamburlaine* in The Revels Plays, 1981, p. 113. See in the same edition pp. 21–2 for an outline of the problem of whether comic passages were cut from the text before printing, and if so, who wrote them.

Marlowe presents stateliness and 'high astounding terms', a hero who scourges kingdoms. The romance elements in *Tamburlaine*, its vast territorial scope, its wandering hero, the great exploits in war and love, the generation of emotions of sublime awe, wonder, horror, its gratification of wish-fulfilling fantasy, its providential design (however qualified), are in tension with its chronicle-history basis. More important, perhaps, is the Bible,[13] as a source for the treatment of the central ideas and for the scale of the conception.

And his eyes were as a flame of fire and on his head were many crowns: and he had a name written, that no man knew but himself.

And he was clothed with a garment dipped in blood, and his name is called, THE WORD OF GOD.

And the warriors which were in heaven followed him upon white horses, clothed with fine linen white and pure.

And out of his mouth went out a sharp sword, that with it he should smite the heathen: and he shall rule them with a rod of iron: for he it is that treadeth the wine press of the fierceness and wrath of the almighty God.

(Revelation 19.12–15, Geneva version)

Eighteen years separate the last performance of the York mystery cycle of miracle plays and the first performance of *Tamburlaine*. Marlowe's is an extraordinary reorientation of the signs and conventions of religious drama and pageant, but it remains a drama presenting world history by means of episodic scenic narrative, and in fact *Tamburlaine* does have debts[14] to those mid-century plays its Prologue mocks. What is new, and extremely important, in *Tamburlaine*, however, is the attention to political and strategic issues, and to the detailing of many real geographical locations and nations. This gives an air of authentic worldliness that counters the impression usual in allegorical drama or romance that ordinary time, place, and causality are suspended or reordered. This may partly be due to Marlowe's source, George Whetstone. It was he who presented Tamburlaine's career plainly as that of a 'poore labourer, or in the best degree a meane souldiour, descended from the Partians: notwithstanding the povertyie of his parents: even from his infancy he had a reaching & an imaginative minde', and a 'ruling desire'.[15] In taking this as his central concern Marlowe revolutionized thinking about the heroic. It is its sheer intelligence, its radical drive, which makes

---

[13] See Weil, *Christopher Marlowe*, p. 201 n.35.

[14] Pickering's *Horestes*, 1567, offers the example of an episodic chronicle making the transition from allegorical morality; some allegorical characters are retained but they are now part of a sequential action. A more direct structural model for *Tamburlaine* is *Cambises* (1561), which presents a sequence of episodes of chronicle history but structured to illustrate the hero's progressively iniquitous career until its end in retribution.

[15] Cited by Cunningham, p. 11, who makes the point that Whetstone ignores the ancestry of the historical Timur the Lame in the line of Tartar Khans.

Tamburlaine so alarming, and meant that its early imitators fell so short when they recognized only its more superficial features.

Thomas Kyd in *The Spanish Tragedy*, performed in the same year, presents a complex personal drama interwoven with political intrigue and focused on social issues, in recognizable contemporary terms – and for that very reason, perhaps, distanced by being set in Iberia. Full recognition is given to the force of human will in conflict with cultural sanctions and princely power; but this intently human drama is introduced, surveyed, and set in perspective, by supernatural characters positioned above the stage, one the ghost of Andrea, the other Revenge. At the end we learn that the human characters descend from the stage to infernal regions. Whatever our sense of their human pain, there they will play an endless tragedy. Kyd exploits the traditional triple division of the medieval drama, the stage-heavens, the world-stage or main acting area, and understage hell.

Marlowe's *Tamburlaine* has no scenes utilizing stage-heavens or hell, there are no supernatural characters, nor are there presenters to guide the audience in interpreting the events or to provide moral guidance. The audience instead must draw its own conclusions from the speech and action and visual spectacle. The hero, moreover, is himself an active and self-conscious deviser of pageants illustrating his role, and Marlowe places great importance on Tamburlaine's will to create his own role. Thus where in earlier romance or heroic plays a character simply presents his fictional self to an audience, in *Tamburlaine* the audience is required to give critical attention to the art: it is a question of persuasiveness: in this play the analogy between theatrical and actual role-play is raised in the opening scenes, and its profound implications lead to the very centre of the dramatic conflict, on the one hand serving to display the operation of power in terms recalling Machiavelli, on the other hand showing how powerful imagination can wield the systems of rhetoric, the art of persuasion and expression, to dissolve limits hitherto supposed fixed. Tamburlaine is endowed with a great range of cultural reference. Western classical mythology is at his command, and is disconcertingly defamiliarized in the mouth of this 'Scythian shepherd', especially when the audience finds itself irresistibly drawn by his astonishing language and exciting presence:

> Ye petty kings of Turkey, I am come
> As Hector did into the Grecian camp
> To overdare the pride of Graecia,
> And set his warlike person to the view
> Of fierce Achilles, rival of his fame –
> I do you honour in the simile: (*Part 2*, 3.5.64ff.)[16]

---

[16] Quotations from the Revels edition, 1981.

Tamburlaine's vast conquests would persuade the audience that there are other views of the world than that which the Christian West promotes. In place of absent divinities Tamburlaine presents himself as a scourge of God, and towards the end of *Part 2* an audience may be reminded of apocalyptic images from the Book of Revelation; at the same time Marlowe withholds the Scriptural corollary of wrath, the dispensation of subsequent grace, so that Tamburlaine cannot be accommodated to this scheme. Perhaps the idea is, precisely, too conventional, as Marlowe would have found it in Richard Knollys, who explained the victories of the Turks as 'the just and secret judgement of the Almightie'.[17] Montaigne notes in his essay 'Of Prognostications' that in public disorders men stunned by their fate will throw themselves back, as on any superstition, on seeking in the heavens the ancient causes and threats of their misfortune.[18] Marlowe's way of involving an audience in a process of critical thinking by frustrating stock responses can be illustrated in his shaping of the episodes in *Part 2* concerning the Christians under Sigismond. Having made a pact, sworn on oath, with the Turk Orcanes, Sigismond reluctantly gives way to his Christian comrades' argument that a treacherous attack on the Turk would be 'necessary policy'; in addition they argue that oaths sworn with unbelievers are not binding. But Sigismond is defeated and interprets his defeat as God's vengeance. The Turk, musing on his own survival, remarks 'Now Christ or Mahomet hath been my friend'. Was the outcome a sign of the Christian god's justice? His comrade Gazellus drily answers

> 'Tis but the fortunes of the wars, my lord,
> Whose power is often proved a miracle.   (*Part 2*, 2.4.31–2)

In the final act of *Part 2* Tamburlaine commits three deeds of great cruelty and impious pride: he razes Babylon, breaks his oath to the governor whom he shoots in cold blood, and burns copies of the Koran. Tamburlaine's fatal illness follows and may be seen as the climax of this sequence, as retribution. Yet, as David Bevington[19] remarks, Marlowe insists on a medical explanation by the hero's doctor: Tamburlaine's long life, his exertions, his temperament, naturally lead to death:

> I viewed your urine, and the hypostasis,
> Thick and obscure, doth make your danger great;
> Your veins are full of accidental heat
> Whereby the moisture of your blood is dried:

[17] *Ibid.*, p. 80.
[18] Weil, *Christopher Marlowe*, p. 200 n.15.
[19] Bevington, *From 'Mankind'*, p. 215. Bevington has a chart setting out the structure of the two Parts, on pp. 204 and 207.

. . .

> Besides, my lord, this day is critical,
> Dangerous to those whose crisis is as yours: (*Part 2*, 5.3.82–5, 90–1)

Yet if we will we may ascribe this sickness to yet another cause, Soria's curse (4.1.178). This is then a more complex pattern than the case of Sigismond, where the first explanation is the Christian one, with scepticism having the last word; yet still here in the final act the issue of retribution is left provocatively unresolved. Both episodes take up the theme of 'policy', of the art of gaining and maintaining secular power, an issue clearly voiced in the very first moments of the play and set in abrupt relation to the sheer will demonstrated by Tamburlaine.

The invocation of a specifically Machiavellian perspective so early in the play exposes the audience to issues of Ragion del Stato, rule as art, not inherited mystery: a thing separate from religion, morality, or national custom; instead secular, international, impersonal. Machiavelli, who had himself meditated on the career of Tamburlaine, concedes in *The Prince* that fortune is of great importance to princes; but he ascribes equal importance to the possession of free will, and notes that fortune favours impetuosity, especially in young men, who are more ardent and audacious. It is Tamburlaine's unhesitating certainty which marks his first appearance, discarding his shepherd's clothes and assuming armour before the eyes of the captured princess Zenocrate and his own men, with the loads of treasure serving as a portable display of triumph. Tamburlaine accepts the adulation of his men, who amplify his impressive show with epic similes:

> As princely lions when they rouse themselves,
> Stretching their paws and threat'ning herds of beasts,
> So in his armour looketh Tamburlaine:
> Methinks I see kings kneeling at his feet,
> And he with frowning brows and fiery looks
> Spurning their crowns from off their captive heads.   (*Part 1*, 1.2.52–7)

This is hyperbole, the figure appropriate for the extreme: later in the play this fantastic spectacle will become actual, as Tamburlaine strives to realize his wildest imagining; but when the audience does see it, then, the effect is less controlled. The expression of princely wrath on a princely scale has already been heard when Mycetes gloats with sick cruelty on the martial triumph he expects:

> I may view these milk-white steeds of mine
> All loaden with the heads of killed men,
> And from their knees even to their hoofs below
> Besmeared with blood, that makes a dainty show.   (*Part 1*, 1.1.77–80)

Ironically, the colour scheme so obscene and insanely visualized ('dainty') by this weakling, will be set before the audience's eyes in Act 4 when a white-robed Tamburlaine uses a captured king, Bajazeth, as a footstool to his throne, from where he declares:

> So shall our swords, our lances and our shot
> Fill all the air with fiery meteors;
> Then, when the sky shall wax as red as blood,
> It shall be said I made it red myself,
> To make me think of naught but blood and war.   (*Part 1*, 4.2.51–5)

To turn the sky itself red to suit a mood (as the stage was hung with black when a tragedy was acted) becomes actual in Tamburlaine's mind even as his imagination creates the metaphor. Expanding from his poetic conceit in which the flashing blades and glinting lances suggest lightning, the cannon shot become actual meteors, supernatural omens: these disorders become apocalyptic, seemingly instantaneously, 'then' – as in Revelation (6.12):

And I beheld when he had opened the sixth seal, and, lo, there was a great earthquake; and the sun became as black as sackcloth of hair, and the moon became as blood.

Tamburlaine's changes of costume and of his tents, all white, then red, then black, mark the sealing of the fate of Damascus. This is more than military pageantry, too. No doubt Marlowe had in mind the colour sequence white–red–black of the horsemen of the apocalypse in Revelation. The Elizabethan audience are confronted with the existential immediacy, before their eyes, of something only just tolerable when read from a book. It is a serious and deliberate, not a sensationalistic, dramatic decision, like that of Shakespeare in *Titus* when he brings on stage the ravished and mutilated, tongueless daughter of the hero, exacting a response from her horrified brothers and father on stage. It requires the audience to measure the adequacy of words, but also confronts them with the spectacular potential of theatre, where those used to listening must also look. The story of Philomel, in Ovid, was familiar: translated to the stage, it is almost unbearable.

Tamburlaine is full of injunctions to look, to admire, or to be horrified by the expressions of the human face, the posture, costume, and gesture of its characters; Marlowe certainly seeks to exploit the differences between language and show, and he makes Tamburlaine's refusal or inability to distinguish between what can be imagined and what can be actualized a central issue in the play's exploration of the heroic. Tales about the hero, writes Eugene M. Waith,[20] do not so much excuse his moral defects as point to a

---

[20] Waith, *The Herculean Hero*, p. 16.

special morality. 'What matters most is something difficult to define, which pushes the hero to the outermost reaches of the human and even beyond.' It is a greatness that has less to do with goodness than 'with the transforming energy of the divine spark'. Marlowe's Tamburlaine pursues a career of sustained expansion, enlarging our sense of what it means to be without limits; it is not only that he makes actual what he imagines, but that he dares to imagine on so grand a scale.

Marlowe multiplies associations, historical and mythological, in expanding the significance and scale of *Tamburlaine*. Timur the Lame was the last great nomad Mongol Khan.[21] His predecessor Chingis (Ghengis) Khan had used his swift and devastating cavalry to win an empire embracing China and nearly all of Asia. The Ottoman Turks themselves had been horsemen from the steppes before converting to Islam and mounting a holy war against Christendom. The actual military campaigns dramatized in *Tamburlaine* concern Timur the Lame's defeat of the two Muslim states which menaced Christian Byzantium. Though in the short term this brought relief to the Christians, in the long run it led to their defeat. Though sixteenth-century European knowledge of Asia was imperfect in substance and muddled in method, the colossal scale and importance of this subject was obvious. That Marlowe takes with utmost seriousness the secular significance of this background may be seen in his focus on the nature of imperialism, both as a cultural phenomenon and in its individual human embodiment in the hero. *Tamburlaine*, in short, is not a play concerned with the past; indeed its hero asserts that he will make all the maps of the world obsolete by discovering new regions, and his new map of the world will have his conquest Damascus at its meridian. In the historical Tamburlaine's lifetime America had yet to be discovered. Elizabethan spectators, understanding this, might well be prompted to compare the activities of European conquerors in their own time in that new fourth region.[22] Nor were there lacking men prepared to believe the fantastic tales of riches and wonders profusely abundant in that region. Ralegh remembered his Mandeville (though not gullibly) when exploring Guiana.[23] Tamburlaine is neither European nor Christian, but

---

[21] This material derives from J. H. Parry, *The Age of Reconnaissance* (1963; new edn 1981), pp. 22–4.

[22] A useful anthology is Louis B. Wright, *The Elizabethans' America* (1965). See also Richard Marienstras, *New Perspectives on the Shakespearean World* (Cambridge, 1985), chapters 5, 6, and 7.

[23] For Ralegh's reactions see Hakluyt, *Voyages*, in the Everyman edition (Dent, 1907), VII. 328–9. Hunter's discussion of Mandeville's *Travels* in his *Dramatic Identities*, p. 7, implies that Ralegh was gullible, which is misleading. Ralegh cites Mandeville, but also seeks objective evidence to confirm his account of strange creatures in Guiana.

stands above mere national significance: what is focused in him is a question as applicable to Asia as to the Mediterranean, located in the historical past but illustrative of the avant-garde thought of Machiavelli, immediately applicable, moreover, to dangerously near events in the Netherlands or Ireland as well as to Peru or the colony of Virginia. It is to be emphasized that only one of Marlowe's works is set in England, and that play of *Edward II* is memorable for the extreme wilfulness and idiosyncrasy of the King and for his suffering perhaps the most terrible of all deaths in Elizabethan drama. In other plays Marlowe focuses on the great issues of the European Renaissance: on the conflict of values in Aeneas just before he founds Rome (*Dido*); on the interplay of commercial, political, and cultural rivalries between Christian, Turk, and Jew (*The Jew of Malta*); on state politics and religious persecution in recent history (*The Massacre at Paris*); on the agonizing implications of Calvinism, and the terrors of spiritual struggle for the Christian (*Doctor Faustus*). After Marlowe and Kyd, Shakespeare and Chapman create heroic dimensions in drama for the treatment of political and religious crisis, but, as Peter Berek[24] shows, the challenge to orthodox social and moral thinking presented by *Tamburlaine* is not confronted in the heroic plays which followed, *Alphonsus King of Aragon*, *The Battle of Alcazar*, *Locrine*, *Orlando Furioso*, *The Wars of Cyrus*, *The Wounds of Civil War*, *A Looking Glass for London and England*, or *Selimus*. Lodge's *Wounds of Civil War*, set in ancient Rome, offers stage spectacle reminiscent of *Tamburlaine* but neither of its heroes, Marius or Scilla, is driven by boundless ambition or imagination. By contrast in Shakespeare's first Roman play, *Titus Andronicus*, the hero breaks all bounds as he becomes mad, and challenges the gods in wreaking his sublime and atrocious revenge.

III

Although in the wake of the Armada patriotic mass emotion was strong enough to prompt the appearance of many plays about war and English history, there were also plays devoted to local heroes celebrated in popular ballads or in such narratives as those of Thomas Deloney. It is important to grasp the significant social divisions in Elizabethan society, to which the plays frequently refer and in terms of which they are often to be understood. Harrison, in his *Description* of the nation published in Holinshed's *Chronicles* in 1577, defines the realm's four estates. The first estate included royalty, nobility, and gentlemen, all those entitled to a heraldic coat of arms. The

---

[24] See Peter Berek, 'Tamburlaine's weak sons', *RenD* n.s. 13 (1982), 55–82.

second estate consisted of citizens, those 'free' (that is, members of a guild who are employers not employees) within the cities. Yeomen were the country equivalent of citizens, free men born English, worth six pounds a year, and owning their own land. They were the third estate. The fourth and lowest estate comprised poor farmers, labourers, artisans, 'tinkers, shoemakers, carpenters, brickmakers, masons &c'. The rest, the unhoused, the unemployed, vagrants, beggars, and thieves, are given no estate at all by Harrison. Education and/or wealth might make the sons of the citizens or yeomen into gentlemen, and poverty might force them downwards in the social scale. There was an eightfold increase in vagrancy in London between 1560 and 1601.

In *George a Greene the Pinner of Wakefield* (1590) the yeoman hero's love defiantly sings a ballad commemorating his sturdiness and her contentment with a yeoman as a future mate:

> I care not for earl, nor yet for knight,
> Nor baron that is so bold:
> For George a Greene, the merry Pinner,
> He hath my heart in hold.   (p. 256)

At the end of the play this positive view of the national hierarchy is reinforced when George refuses a knighthood: he expresses solidarity with authority:

> Then let me live and die a yeoman still:
> So was my father, so must be his son.   (p. 269)

A popular hero's fame also depends on his being of the people, as he shrewdly notes:

> For 'tis more credit to men of base degree
> To do great deeds, than men of dignity.   (p. 269)

George's achievement of folk-hero status is shown to irritate the greatest of all English folk-heroes, Robin Hood himself, who has a part in this play. On his first appearance he is being harassed by Maid Marian about his falling ratings:

> whensoever I do walk abroad
> I hear no songs but all of George a Greene
> And this, my Robin, galls my very soul.   (p. 264)

What the play offers is a warm-hearted domestication of the mingled romance, using historical, legendary, and ballad material. It has an outer frame consisting of the internal and external threats to the rule of King

Edward of England. A group of discontented nobles led by Kendall start the play with martial display and speeches of heroic ambition. Kendall makes direct allusions to Tamburlaine:

> Lest I like martial Tamburlaine lay waste
> Their bordering countries, leaving none
> Alive that contradicts my commission.   (p. 253)

The difference is that these are English rebels threatening English 'country swains' to support treason against an English king. These traitors collude with the King of Scotland, who is first seen menacing a fair young English mother who refuses his adulterous proposals even when he prepares to kill her plucky young son. The crude emotionalism the dramatist is aiming at involves confronting the purest innocence with the blackest villainy. That once achieved, actual death is avoided, for it will be necessary to gloss over the brutal and treacherous character of the King of Scots for the sake of the play's overall tone. Furthermore, in a chronicle romance like this the writer needs the King of Scots later on where he can serve as the object of the English king's magnanimous clemency, be firmly subordinated to England, and penalized:

> Then let king James make good
> Those towns which he hath burnt upon the borders;
> Give a small pension to the fatherless,
> Whose fathers he caus'd murthered in those wars.   (p. 269)

It is interesting indeed that the English king raises this question about the king's responsibility for the victims of war, and it is characteristic that the issue is seriously explored in Shakespeare's English history plays, and glossed over – except for its sentimental patriotic value – here.

   This story of a double military threat to King Edward is no sooner introduced in stagecraft recalling *Tamburlaine* or *Henry VI* (1590) than it gives way to a quite different kind of drama, where the ballad hero speaks with the accent of Clyomon:

> Why I am George a Greene,
> True liegeman to my king,
> Who scorns that men of such esteem as these
> Should brook the braves of any traitorous squire.   (p. 254)

George makes one of Kendall's knights actually eat the seals on his commission. This broad comic mode is designed to prompt a crude response from the audience, playing on their normal feelings of discontent at the privileged and proud but channelling these feelings towards stereotypes as vague as any morality might offer: they can hiss a typical earl leading an insurrection, a typical invading Scots king, but this is old news when all dates are erased and nothing very specific is said. What is interesting is the fact that the focus is shifted to view state affairs from below. George is told that the earl has put his horses in the town's cornfields, so that we see how this feels to ordinary people. The messenger, moreover, tells the whole story in an absurd mode. First he appealed to the horses: 'One of them hearing me ask what he made there held up his head and neighed, and after his manner laughed'.

This satiric equation of horses with lords (which is still current in English images of their aristocracy) is quickly improved on when the nobles actually appear and he introduces them as 'three geldings'. This nonsensical mode is the trickster's or fool's weapon against authority. For a popular hero the corresponding mode is simple physical courage and a bit of native cunning. George strikes the traitor earl, but talks his way out of being beaten up; he goes on to entice the traitors to visit a local magician who can prophesy (this will be him in disguise). So develops a romance fantasy in which yeoman virtue and rural cunning overcome the perfidy of the great, a victory against huge odds achieved with much comedy and complete success.

The King of England decides to go to Wakefield in disguise and see George a Greene for himself. What is dramatized here is the negotiation of a cultural barrier between the common people and their ruler, but it goes further than that. As various strangers seek entrance to the town they are challenged and refused entry unless they fight a bout at longstaff. True to his trickster role, Jenkin jokes his way round this challenge. Robin Hood and his Merry Men are challenged by George, who fights bouts against Will and Much, beating both of them: an honourable way is thus clear to a truce with Robin, avoiding the awkwardness of a combat in which neither folk-hero could be imagined as loser. The king, disguised, is challenged and avoids combat. This failure to fight earns him George's contempt, but we may note that both king and clown evade the rules. Once he has seen George, the king reappears in royal guise, congratulating George as one chief to another; they reaffirm the treaty between monarch and people, an act which the play goes on to associate with the treaty between the states of England and Scotland. Beneath the crude populist manner the play expresses some important cultural values which align the people's hero with royal dynastic rule and the law; it draws parallels between folk tale and chivalric romance, according each rights and dignity.

In contrast Shakespeare's *Henry VI* presents two studies of a popular hero springing from obscurity to shake the state when the confusion of national crisis shows the weakness of dynastic rulers. *Part 1* of *Henry VI* centres upon the war between England and France. A simple pageant style is used to present Talbot, 'brave Talbot, the terror of the French' in Nashe's phrase,[25] an earl but loved by his loyal men. Joan of Arc, his opponent, is associated by many echoes with Tamburlaine, from her origins as a shepherd's daughter inspired by prophecies that she is to be 'the English scourge' to her victorious leadership and personal magnetism. She is a woman, but in armour (from the English patriot's viewpoint a terrible parody of Boadicea or Spenser's Britomart), she meets the Dauphin's challenge to personal combat and masters him. She is witty and ironic, and scorns aristocratic honours: when Talbot is dead and an English knight gives a roll-call of his titles (all thirteen of them) Joan replies in a true Tamburlaine style:

> The Turk, that two and fifty kingdoms hath
> Writes not so tedious a style as this.
> Him that thou magnifi'st with all these titles
> Stinking and fly-blown lies here at our feet.   (4.7.73–6)

Joan ascribes her power partly to destiny, partly to her virgin state. The French nobles treat this ironically, and there is Marlovian music and Marlovian irony in the Dauphin's praise of her victorious leadership of his armies:

> A statelier pyramis to her I'll rear
> Than Rhodope's of Memphis ever was.   (1.6.21–2)

Rhodope had been a courtesan, but these unconscious and conscious French allusions to Joan's sexuality remain unproved, while Joan's martial valour is unquestionable. She takes Rouen with witty tactics; the bluff Talbot, defeated, ascribes her success to witchcraft, thus exposing him (to the discomfort of patriotic English audiences) as mean-minded. Shakespeare provokes his audience in these ways to take an unfamiliarly French view of Joan, something reinforced by showing the close similarities between English and French court impotence and irresponsibility. But Shakespeare cannot, perhaps, go all the way and anticipate Shaw; the English patriotic fervour is gratified by two crude episodes[26] in which Joan is seen exactly as English propaganda presented her. This ending is abrupt and theatrically reactionary: her evil spirits '*walk and speak not*', '*They hang their heads*', '*They shake their heads*', '*They depart*' (5.3.12–23). Joan has some characteristics of the clown, her sexual ambiguity gives her magic power, her will (until fortune deserts her) is boundless.

Talbot was a patriotic hero, which inhibited Shakespeare's treatment of him as a political figure; but in *Part 2* Shakespeare is free to explore a much

---

[25] *Pierce Peniless* 1592 (edition of 1966 at Edinburgh University Press, p. 87).
[26] 5.3.1–44; 5.4.1–92.

more dangerously ambivalent folk hero, Jack Cade, a brutal man of the people, claiming to embody their desires, asserting their right to power. Though dispensing atrocity Cade does not act arbitrarily, he precisely inverts the civilized codes. The theories of Bakhtin[27] about carnival serve to illuminate his nature and function. Cade roots his leadership in a mock genealogy.[28] His comrades treat it ironically, not only as a parody of noble politics but in response to the whole spirit of inversion, mockery, and blasphemy customary at a feast of misrule. Their punning genealogy of Cade satisfies the criteria for a carnival king: a thief, the son of a bricklayer doing time in prison and of a midwife (proverbial for drunkenness) who gave birth to him under a hedge; his wife is a pedlar's daughter. A criminal vagrant of this kind does not even belong to the fourth estate of Elizabeth's commonwealth; no wonder the citizens flee when he enters London at the head of his rabble. Cade twists official discourse to serve his lawless appetites, but he would claim that this is what authority uses its language for anyway. His comrades make reductive puns, saying Cade is only linked to the noble Mortimers in the sense that his father worked with bricks and mortar. Cade's argument against written law is insistently, reductively material:

Is not this a lamentable thing, that the skin of an innocent lamb should be made parchment? that parchment, being scribbled o'er, should undo a man?

Cade mocks the honourable art of war, too, acclaiming Dick the Butcher of Ashford for behaving in battle as if he were in his own slaughterhouse,[29] and rewarding him with a limited trade monopoly, parodying state tradition. Cade commands his inauguration to be celebrated by causing 'the pissing conduit' to run with claret for a year. The London landmark yields an anatomical pun (coarsely anticipating the fable of the belly in *Coriolanus* [1608]). Anatomical too is Cade's command to burn all the records of the realm: 'my mouth shall be the Parliament of England'. This Rabelaisian assertion is edged by a comrade who fears Cade's gargantuan appetite: 'we are like to have biting statutes, unless his teeth be pull'd out',[30] which illustrates the equivocal mode in which a carnival king is served. Cade's culminating pageant has a true spirit of Tamburlaine in it, too: severed heads of royal officials are stuck on poles and made to kiss; the now speechless voices of

---

[27] Bakhtin focuses on non-dramatic written narrative, in Rabelais, Dostoevsky, and others. The first of his studies to appear in English was *Rabelais and his World* in 1968. Bakhtin earned the disapproval of Stalinist authorities for his theories about the place of carnival and the comic as revolutionary expressions of the common people.

[28] *Henry VI, Part 2*, 4.2.31–71.

[29] *Henry VI, Part 2*, 4.3.1–8.

[30] *Henry VI, Part 2*, 4.7.16–17.

authority are mocked for their part in the defeat in France. Since Elizabethan traitors' heads were actually displayed on poles on London Bridge,
Cade's pageant can be seen precisely to appropriate the official legal code in
such a way as to make it seem itself atrocious; at the same time, Cade would
claim that they usually stick the wrong heads on the bridge. This attempt to
uproot the official discourse of law and hierarchy obeys some of the laws of
proletarian revolution, but its barbarous excess conforms to the rites of
festival rather than anything tolerably populist: it does resemble insane
tyrannies of modern history.

IV

London doubled in population between 1580 and 1600 as its importance
and wealth grew. The subject of the city of London became popular in the
1590s and 1600s in plays of many kinds.[31] Performed for audiences of
Londoners, such plays naturally included allusions to local landmarks,
streets and districts, and famous and legendary characters such as Dick
Whittington. Local colour was interwoven with romance to produce encour-
aging images of the city as a benign paternal structure, its guilds preserving
traditional values and guaranteeing patriotic sentiment in return for royal
endorsement of its self-government. The city had its own kind of folk-hero,
and playwrights invented freely to fill out the genealogy (much as heralds did
for the citizens who bought coats of arms). Near the beginning of *The Famous
Victories of Henry V* (1586), a play climaxing in the heroic national victory
under the great hero, there is a scene in which representatives of the fourth
estate, John Cobler, Robin Pewterer, Lawrence Costermonger, assemble to
keep the watch in Billingsgate ward, and gossip about the (as yet unre-
formed) future king Henry V. Cobler says 'I dare not call him theefe, but
sure he is one of these taking fellowes';[32] the vintner's boy gives them some
gossip from the Counter prison, where Prince Hal has been taken with his
ruffian companions after a drunken brawl in the streets. The boy is concerned because his master's wine pots were smashed. This episode makes
very clear social distinctions and a strong emphasis on property – indeed it is
in just these terms that the depth of the Prince's outrageous conduct is to be
judged. In later plays these matters of fact in the daily lives of real Londoners
are interwoven with romance and heroic elements to create a distinct kind of

---

[31] After Jonson's comedy *Every Man in his Humour*, 1598, ostensibly set in Italy but with
vividly contemporary city life and dialogue, a stream of satiric comedies, mainly from the
children's companies, rivalled the amphitheatres' output of plays featuring citizens. See
the discussion in Gibbons, *Jacobean City Comedy* and Leggatt, *Citizen Comedy*.

[32] Quotation from the edition in *Chief Pre-Shakespearean Dramas*, ed. J. Q. Adams (1924), p. 669.

late-Elizabethan popular hero, the citizen and the apprentice. At its most vivid in Dekker's play *The Shoemaker's Holiday* (1599), the celebration of the city as a land of romance and the citizen as a hero is seen more clearly by contrast with a heroic romance performed at a rival playhouse, Shakespeare's *Henry V* (1599).

The audience is persuaded to respond to intense emotions of awe, exultation, and wonder at the climactic victory of the hero–king, though the persistence of his low companions might be felt to imply that in the long run chivalric attitudes and heroic life are impossible.[33] The sublime, aesthetically speaking, needs protection from other modes, especially satire and farce, which are the stock-in-trade of popular comedy. *Henry V* is too intelligent a play, too dialectical in style as well as politics, simply to endorse sublime heroism, and its hero ascribes his victory to God. *The Shoemaker's Holiday* is also partly concerned with war in France, and a victorious English king appears in the concluding scenes, but this play is set entirely in London, focusing on the secular and civic institutional sphere of the city. Yet the hero, Simon Eyre the citizen, guildsman, and employer of shoemakers, does achieve a kind of heroic destiny, rising to be Lord Mayor and Sheriff, to build a market hall and establish a leather market there, which he duly opens with a Shrove Tuesday feast for the apprentices. The king himself attends, conferring market privileges on the building, which he names Leadenhall.

Eyre is Lord of the Feast at the conclusion, yet throughout he behaves as a kind of image of bounty, dispensing good cheer, energy, and a continual stream of catch-phrases that exalt both himself and the community to the status of popular legend. This glorification of citizen life is simple but vivid, as when Eyre enters wearing a new gold chain about his neck, to address his wife:

See here, my Madgy, a chain, a gold chain for Simon Eyre! I shall make thee a lady. Here's a French hood for thee. On with it, on with it. Dress thy brows with this flap of a shoulder of mutton, to make thee look lovely. Where be my fine men? Roger, I'll make over my shop and tools to thee. Firk, thou shalt be the foreman. Hans, thou shalt have an hundred for twenty. Be as mad knaves as your master Sim Eyre hath been, and you shall live to be sheriffs of London. How dost thou like me, Margery? Prince am I none, yet am I princely born! (10.149–58)[34]

Such sheer energy and conviction in the theatre masters an audience's emotions. The painful, potentially bitter, realistic story of Ralph, impressed for

---

[33] For a recent intelligent discussion of the ambiguities of interpretation possible in *Henry V*, see Ralph Berry, *Changing Styles in Shakespeare* (1981).

[34] Quotations from the Revels Plays edition by R. L. Smallwood and S. Wells (1979), which has some useful material in the Introduction on the play's sources and its relation to other plays featuring shoemakers.

the French war at the beginning, to return destitute and crippled towards the end, is given a romantic colour. He is rescued by an army of shoemakers, '*all with cudgels, or such weapons*', who drive off the bluecoat servants of his upper-class rival. This is also an instance of the dramatist's substitution of civilian uniforms and urban set-piece displays for the war spectacle of *Henry V*; the city has its own heraldic costumes and banners, rivalling chivalric pageantry. Yet the social issue of the returned soldiers bereft of livelihood is dissolved in the play's mass emotion of community dressed in festival guise.

In Beaumont's comedy *The Knight of the Burning Pestle* (1608) a citizen grocer in the audience interrupts the Prologue to object to the proposed play, titled 'The London Merchant', when he suspects it to be satiric. Instead he demands a play about a grocer doing 'admirable things'; his wife suggests 'let him kill a lion with a pestle', possibly directly alluding to[35] *The Four Prentices of London* (1594), in any case a satire of typical romance motifs (such as we see in the tragical mirth of *Pyramus and Thisbe*). Once thrust into the play, Beaumont's Rafe the grocer's apprentice sounds very like one of the Four Prentices of London: they dutifully serve their masters, mercer, goldsmith, haberdasher, and grocer, but no sooner do they hear a drum and a proclamation calling volunteers to the holy wars in Jerusalem, than they are off. *The Four Prentices of London* begins in what could be the London of the audience in 1594, but recedes at once into the vague past of romance, where a limited and predictable series of adventures involving trials of physical strength, skill in fighting, loyalty, and sexual honour are played out with increasingly exotic foreigners, from the Spanish and French in Boulogne to Italian *banditti* and ultimately to the Turks. There is nostalgia from Eustace:

> Oh that I had with me
> As many good lads, honest prentices,
> From Eastcheap, Canwick-street and London-stone,
> To end this battle[36]

and Charles exclaims 'O, for some Cheapside boys for Charles to lead!' These are sentiments which echo on in Kipling and in the literature of the British Empire. They may be naïve and familiar, but they express a strong ideology for all that: his back to the wall, and far from home, the British soldier responds first to an ideal which is rather local than patriotic in the full sense: his mates, his regiment, his family at home, these are the kinship bonds that hold in the field, and persist after demobilization. Nor have

---

[35] This is discussed by Michael Hattaway in his edition of the play for The New Mermaid Series (1969), p. xvii.

[36] Quotation from the edition titled *Dodsley's Old Plays*, with additional notes and corrections by Reed, Gilchrist, and the editor (1825), vol. VI, p. 427.

Charles and Eustace been wasting their time among the savages; they have done their best to reform them according to English custom:

> Taught them manners and civility:
> All rape and murder we repay with death;   (p. 428)

A motif straight from naïve folk romance, such as *Mucedorus* (?1590) recurs in a later episode when a wild man of the woods, bearing a pole-axe in each hand, appears to drive off the Turks; it is characteristic of the one-dimensional mode of the play that this should turn out to be only Guy in disguise. The Turks are modelled on Marlovian examples, but the values of the play are propagandist in their glamorization of the English. The wish-fulfilling fantasy is not made stronger by some cheap sentiment when the arms of city livery companies are placed in the Temple in Jerusalem.

V

Plays like the *Four Prentices of London* domesticate the romance hero, making him reflect the loyalties and values of a citizen audience of a specific kind; the burlesque of such plays offered by *Eastward Ho!* is designed to appeal to a different group, an audience with different interests as well as taste for more complex and ironic observation of the times. Ben Jonson, in his great comedy *Bartholomew Fair*, set in Smithfield on a particular day in August 1614, presents a puppet-master through whom are caricatured the hack dramatists of the period. He defends his commercialism and crude workmanship, his little imagination, by claiming that audiences will respond only to the simplest stuff and that it is no good giving them classical masterpieces: Musaeus and even Marlowe are 'too learned and poetical' for them, so *Hero and Leander* must be reduced in every sense, Leander becoming a dyer's son about Puddle Wharf and Hero a wench from Bankside, the god of love a drawer in a tavern.[37] This attack on hack dramatists is not at any rate fair to Heywood, who at the Red Bull presented spectacularly wild extravaganzas dramatizing classical mythology which, for all their crude construction, do genuinely express something of the strangeness and grandeur of those heroic fables. In scorning romance in dramatic form Jonson was consistent to his principles, that only classically decorous conformity to the unities was approvable: romance thus 'made nature afraid'.[38] Perversely, Jonson used

---

[37] Jonson, *Bartholomew Fair*, 5.3.
[38] In the Induction to *Bartholomew Fair* the author is asserted to be 'loth to make Nature afraid in his plays, like those that beget Tales, Tempests and such-like drolleries'. Elsewhere, in 'An Ode, to Himself' Jonson refers, in stanza 3, to *Pericles* as a 'mouldy tale'. These views are not given prominence in his commendatory poem 'To the Memory of my beloved, the Author, Mr William Shakespeare, and what he hath left us'.

strict comic form and observed the unities to reveal the fantastic and the monstrous right under the citizens' noses in London's Blackfriars and Smithfield, for *The Alchemist* and *Bartholomew Fair* (ironically enough) have, both of them, more concern with the strange and the marvellous, with human aspiration and the reckless endeavour it inspires, than many ostensibly romantic plays, such as *The Travels of the Three English Brothers* which is based on adventures of sons of Sir Robert Sherley (died 1612), but never rises above the prosaic, despite the potential of the material.

Jonson's attack upon the travesty of heroic values by hack writers, too, is an attempt to insist on the importance of preserving understanding of the real thing: he feared for the trivialization of the whole heroic mode. It is therefore disappointing that he was unable to recognize that in *Pericles* it is precisely through the revival of old-fashioned, naïve Tudor convention of heroical romance that the audience is conditioned to experience a journey which is not simply an external adventure but a drama of the spirit, where stage events are metaphors for inner exploration as well as narrating a geographical journey.

The essence of romance is an encounter with events so strange that the hero is challenged to the limits, yielding an experience so radical that it produces a transformation. Although erotic love is an important element in heroic romance, and the chivalric ideal personifies virtue as woman, the central concern of heroic romance goes beyond: even when a woman is the hero, as in *Comus* (the work of Milton which exalts the court masque form by infusing it with folklore and miracle and expanding its scale to epic), even in *Comus* it is the energy of heroic aspiration, the transcendence of limits, which is the centre. Beaumont and Fletcher followed Shakespearian tragicomedy, especially *The Winter's Tale* and *Cymbeline*, but turned the action decisively inwards; further, they decisively narrowed the drama to sensationalistic confrontations of chivalric and courtly values; heroic romance serves as occasion for effects of horror and astonishment too often contrived by meretricious turns of plot; formulae of situation and attitude are evolved for courtly and would-be courtly taste. *The Two Noble Kinsmen*, in which Fletcher collaborated with Shakespeare, displays the older Tudor idea of heroical romance, but is curiously lacking in vital energy, as if too careful a reconstruction.

To compare *The Two Noble Kinsmen* with Heywood's *Ages* plays, or *Mucedorus* with *Cymbeline*,[39] or either of them with the later *Comus* (1634) is

[39] For further discussion of the use, in *Cymbeline*, of earlier dramatic traditions see Lomax, *Stage Images*, chapter 5. For an account of *Cymbeline* as a play concerned with old and new dramatic styles as part of its treatment of the cultural history of Britain, see Brian Gibbons, 'Fabled *Cymbeline*', *ShJ(West)* (1987).

to recognize the kaleidoscopic variousness of this tradition. As in a kaleido-
scope, each viewer is free to enjoy many patterns; and in romances, as in
kaleidoscopes, random and arbitrary elements contribute much to the
pleasure of the beholder – as critics need to remember.

Bibliography

PLAYS AND TEXTS

Quotations in this chapter are taken from *George a Greene* and *Sir Clyomon and Sir
Clamydes, The Dramatic and Poetic Works of Peele and Greene*, ed. Dyce (1861) (the
latter is also available in Tudor Facsimile Texts and the Malone Society). Other early
romances, *The Rare Triumphs of Love and Fortune* and *Mucedorus*, are in vols. 6 and 7
respectively of R. Dodsley, *Old Plays*, 4th edn, ed. W. C. Hazlitt, 1874–6. George
Gascoigne, *The Princely Pleasures of Kenilworth*, ed. J. W. Cunliffe, in *The Works of
George Gascoigne* (1907–10), goes with *Robert Laneham's Letter ... 1575*, ed. F. J.
Furnivall (1871). I quote from J. S. Cunningham's edition of *Tamburlaine* in the
Revels Plays, and the edition of *The Shoemaker's Holiday* in the same series, ed. R. L.
Smallwood and Stanley Wells. *The Travels of the Three English Brothers* is in Bullen's
edition of Day (1881); *The Knight of the Burning Pestle* in the New Mermaid edition of
Michael Hattaway (1969).

THE STAGE

Many plays were written collaboratively and under pressure: see Neil Carson, *A
Companion to Henslowe's Diary* (1988), for illustration of this in the period 1592–1604.
On different types of audience and their tastes see Andrew Gurr, *Playgoing in
Shakespeare's London* (1987). On staging see Richard Southern, *The Staging of Plays
before Shakespeare* (1973) and Michael Hattaway, *Elizabethan Popular Theatre* (1982).
The interrelation of dramatic and theatrical questions concerns T. W. Craik, *The
Tudor Interlude* (1958) for the early period, while for the later period there is Marion
Lomax, *Stage Images and Traditions, Shakespeare to Ford* (1987), with an excellent
account of the somewhat neglected Thomas Heywood.

ROMANCE

Romance in Elizabethan drama is discussed in Madeleine Doran, *Endeavors of Art*
(1954); M. C. Bradbrook, *The Growth and Structure of Elizabethan Comedy* (1955, rev.
edn 1973); and Leo Salingar, *Shakespeare and the Traditions of Comedy* (1974), in
many ways the fullest and most valuable account to date. C. L. Barber, *Shakespeare's
Festive Comedy* (1958) remains important reading, now supplemented by François
Laroque, *Shakespeare et la fête* (1987), soon to appear in English. On romance see also
Walter Davis, *Idea and Act in Elizabethan Fiction* (1969); Max Bluestone, *From Story to
Stage* (1974); Paul Salzman, *English Prose Fiction 1558–1700* (1985). On theatrical
elements in Spenser, C. S. Lewis, *Spenser's Images of Life* (1972), is interesting. A
short excellent discussion is Patricia Russell, 'Romantic narrative plays', *Elizabethan
Theatre*, Stratford-on-Avon Studies 9 (1966). On folk-plays see E. C. Cawte *et al.*,
English Ritual Drama (1967); Alan Brody, *The English Mummers and their Plays* (1969);

Thomas Pettitt, 'English folk drama', *RenD* (1982). Richard Marienstras, *New Perspectives on the Shakespearean World* (1985), uses structural anthropology in an original study of popular romance dramas.

THE HEROIC PLAY AND MARLOWE
On the transition from Tudor to Elizabethan drama see David Bevington, *From 'Mankind' to Marlowe* (1962), and on Marlowe himself an excellent bibliography is in Judith Weil, *Christopher Marlowe, Merlin's Prophet* (1977). See also Eugene M. Waith, *The Herculean Hero* (1962). Simon Shepherd, *Marlowe and the Politics of Elizabethan Theatre* (1986), is a recent lively study.

COURT DRAMA
On court drama E. K. Chambers, *The Elizabethan Stage* (1923), remains essential; there is a good bibliography of secondary literature in David Lindley, ed., *The Court Masque* (1984).

CLASSICAL AND ITALIAN INFLUENCES
David Orr discusses *Italian Renaissance Drama in England before 1625* (1970); see also David Wiles, 'Taking Plautus seriously: recent critical approaches to Plautus' in *Themes in Drama* 10 (1988), and Louise George Clubb, 'Shakespeare's comedy and late cinquecento mixed genres' in M. Charney, ed., *Shakespearean Comedy* (1980); also Eugene M. Waith, *The Pattern of Tragi-comedy in Beaumont and Fletcher* (1952); G. K. Hunter, 'Italian tragi-comedy on the English stage', *RenD* (1973); and Arthur Kirsch, *Jacobean Dramatic Perspectives* (1972).

7   Pastiche, burlesque, tragicomedy

THE roots of Jacobean drama lie in a late sixteenth- and early seventeenth-century rebellion against the inherited literary forms and assumptions of high-Elizabethan culture. Wittily erotic epyllia claimed a place beside idealizing sonnet sequences and epic; satires that adapted Juvenal and Persius to attack contemporary vices provided one answer to the fabulous world of romance adventure. The vogue for Ovidian epyllia faded, while an official ban in 1599 ended the career of formal verse satire, but the restless, critical spirit such innovations embodied was an aspect of, and response to, the changing times, not limited to a particular genre or literary fad. In the theatre, pastiche and burlesque mockingly dissected earlier plays, styles, even whole genres, while, in the hands of the most inventive dramatists, coercing something fresh out of the fragments of a ridiculed past. More comprehensive revision of traditional genres produced new variants of comedy and tragedy and legitimated new kinds of subject matter. Partly out of such skirmishes with their predecessors, these dramatists created tragicomedy, a hybrid form that straightforwardly challenged the whole idea of a hierarchical separation of genres.

The initiators of the fashion for erotic epyllia were dramatists – Thomas Lodge, Christopher Marlowe, William Shakespeare; some later contributors, like John Marston and Francis Beaumont, became dramatists. The late 1590s verse satire was more wholly a product of this younger generation, and the provenance of its authors and readers predicts the close interrelation between playwrights and one segment of their public at the beginning of the next century. The verse experiments addressed a classically educated, literarily sophisticated audience; their most enthusiastic readers were university-trained young men, often gentlemen by birth, who came down from Oxford and Cambridge to pursue legal studies at the Inns of Court, or at least to enter one of the Inns as a base from which to enjoy worldly London, dabble in literature, or seek preferment at court.

Inns of Court men both produced and consumed the latest in literary fashion: poems for private circulation in manuscript, printed collections of epigrams and satires that mixed classical and topical allusion, satiric 'characters' of social types that often veiled personal attacks on contemporaries, and plays. Dramatic interest extended beyond the Inns' own efforts: from the young John Donne of Lincoln's Inn, in the 1590s 'a great visiter of Ladyes, a great frequenter of Playes,' to Edward Heath of the Inner Temple, who in the late 1620s attended forty-nine plays, theatre-going was a favoured pastime.[1] Closer involvement came with the reopening of London's two private theatres, closed during the 1590s: the Children of Paul's started playing again in 1599; the Children of the Revels, at Blackfriars, in 1600.

The private theatres were not the sole source of theatrical change, but for the short period in which they flourished they attracted some of the most innovative playwrights and proved powerfully influential, both in their own offerings and in the challenge they posed for the established, adult companies.[2] The satirist John Marston (Middle Temple) began writing for the revived children's troupes immediately; other members, like Edward Sharpham, wrote a few plays for them. Francis Beaumont (Inner Temple) started writing plays for Paul's, then Blackfriars; John Fletcher, not a templar but son of a bishop of London, began with the children's companies. Older poet–playwrights like George Chapman and Ben Jonson, who had initiated the fashion in 'humours' comedy with the adults, soon allied themselves with the more socially prestigious private theatres – as, briefly, did Samuel Daniel, John Webster, and Thomas Dekker – and with the overlapping theatrical and poetic circles that linked the private theatres with the Inns of Court and its avant-garde intellectual life.

Economic pressures favoured the young dramatists' rebellious predilections. The reopened private theatres needed to establish an identity, a commercially attractive difference beyond the novelty of child actors. They needed new repertories since, as Marston joked in *Jack Drum's Entertainment*, plays left from the first Paul's company, like John Lyly's court comedies, seemed by 1600 'mustie fopperies of antiquitie'. Thus, despite the fact that numerous authors – Jonson, Dekker, Webster – wrote for both stages, and that private-theatre playwrights – Beaumont, Fletcher, Middleton – moved easily into later careers with the adults, the initial emphasis was on difference. Through the so-called War of the Theatres, the *Ho*-play rivalry

---

[1] For the Inns' own dramatic tradition, see Finkelpearl, *John Marston*, pp. 23–31. On Donne, see Sir Richard Baker, *A Chronicle of the Kings of England* (London, 1653), p. 617; Heath's self-tally is cited in Prest, *The Inns of Court*, p. 155.

[2] Foakes, 'Tragedy at the children's theatres', p. 39. On both private and public theatres and their audiences, see Gurr, *Playgoing*.

between Paul's and Blackfriars, and some daring political tragedies, the private theatres rapidly established a distinctive reputation. In trouble with the authorities in virtually every year of their existence, the private theatres were exciting. And to the promise of up-to-date social or political satire, they added the allure of dramatic novelty.

An exhilarating combination of iconoclasm, eclecticism and originality marks these early years, and nowhere is this mixture more apparent than in the plays with which John Marston helped inaugurate the second Paul's, probably in the winter of 1599/1600, first with the bizarre romantic comedy *Antonio and Mellida* and then with its tragic companion play, *Antonio's Revenge*. Clearly fascinated with his new medium, Marston reveals an acute awareness of its traditions – classical as well as Elizabethan – and, equally important, its fresh potential. He mocks theatrical stereotypes and audience expectations, forcing characters, scenes, and speeches from different kinds of plays into unsettling conjunctions; he also uses the elements of the traditions he has fractured to fashion something new. The Antonio plays are paradoxically blatantly derivative and yet wholly unlike their models or competitors.

From the beginning, Marston focuses on play-making and the creation of dramatic illusion as one of his subjects. The Prologue to *Antonio and Mellida* with ostentatious modesty presents the play as the product of 'slight idleness', and the tongue-in-cheek dedication of the printed text to 'Nobody' crystallizes this attitude and offers an aptly paradoxical apology for having affected '(a little too much) to be seriously fantastical'. Marston's method is a difficult one to bring off: a juggling act requiring a sophisticated audience very like himself. Even before the promised drama begins, Marston prepares us for a witty farrago of theatrically familiar bits and pieces from revenge melodrama, satire, and romantic comedy. The conventional dramatic Induction, an apparently spontaneous pre-play discussion among the actors, becomes the means to ensure our complicity. The potential liability of boys in adult roles is turned into an asset, made part of a self-conscious dramaturgy that offers us the pleasure of recognizing and sharing the theatrical jokes and allusions.[3]

The boy players enter, parts in hand, worried about their adequacy to the dramatist's assignment, and we are introduced to the type characters and rhetoric the play will both parody and adapt. The tyrant conqueror – in Tamburlaine's vein – is immediately recognizable to players and audience

---

[3] For a fuller account of the play's use of child actors to enhance its parody of theatrical convention, see Foakes, 'John Marston's fantastical plays' and, in the present volume, pp. 55–7.

alike. If the answer to the question 'Whom do you personate?' is 'Piero, Duke of Venice', the automatic observation follows: 'O, ho; then thus frame your exterior shape / To haughty form of elate majesty / As if you held the palsy-shaking head / Of reeling chance under your fortune's belt' (7–10). Confidence is bred of familiarity, but also contempt, for 'Such rank custom is grown popular' (15).

Marston has great fun mocking what had become rhetorical and situational clichés, but in what follows he does more than stitch together a simple dramatic pastiche. Verbal parody extends the play's pervasive attention to speech: language becomes an index of moral attitudes, yet is itself scrutinized as an instrument for expressing and controlling human experience. Marston marks off his fools and fops by their misuse of language, but we also hear the accents of Senecan stoicism and, in Antonio, both Petrarchan idealism and suicidal despair. A wide range of dissonant linguistic registers (including a twenty-line duet in Italian) draws our attention to dramatic style and the way it shapes both our understanding of character and our expectations for action. The Babel of languages and the abruptness with which characters like Antonio shift between different, though equally stylized, responses, reflect the characters' helplessness in the face of events over which they seem to have no control. They are puppets of the available roles, in speech and action, and those roles prove inadequate; the play is rescued for comedy by Marston's imposition of another dramatic convention, the tyrant Piero's sudden moral conversion. The characters remain distanced from us – sharply etched, two-dimensional dramatic types that also represent social, philosophical, and moral categories. They are doubly estranged by a dramatic technique that continually punctures the illusion to remind us of our complicity in the process of play-making.

With *Antonio's Revenge, Part 2* of *Antonio and Mellida*, Marston creates a generic diptych. *Part 1*'s happy ending is reversed; its earnestly moral protagonists are now forced to seek justice within a surrealistically corrupt political world.[4] Many of *Part 1*'s characters remain, but the satirized frivolity of Piero's court shades into lethal farce when Balurdo's inanity coexists with Strotzo's and Piero's gloating villainy. Although the self-conscious Induction is not repeated, dramatic technique also links these plays, and sharp contrasts within as well as between scenes again complement discontinuous characterization. If *Antonio and Mellida* played fast and loose with dramatic coherence, as well as theatrical illusion and convention, however, *Antonio's Revenge* yokes its borrowings to a shapelier purpose. *Part 1* had no dramatic

---

[4] On the relationship between the two parts, see G. K. Hunter's introduction to *Antonio's Revenge* (Lincoln, Nebraska, 1965), pp. ix–xii, xix–xx.

precedent for its kind of comedy; *Part 2* takes clearer generic aim: *Antonio's Revenge* reconstructs a whole popular native form, revenge tragedy.[5]

Characteristically, Marston's approach is academic, eclectic, and theatrically sensational; rather than naturalize convention, he heightens our sense of artificiality. In verbal and visual allusions, Kyd's *Spanish Tragedy* appears throughout, as does, we assume, the now lost *Ur-Hamlet*. Although the idea for the ghastly paternal banquet – or for adding it to an already full canvas of revenge incident – may have come from Shakespeare's *Titus Andronicus*, to which he also alludes, Marston returns to Seneca's *Thyestes* (as well as, to a lesser extent, *Medea* and *Octavia*) and borrows or inventively transposes, sometimes in Latin, phrases and speeches from throughout this archetypal revenge drama. Also in the background lies Christopher Marlowe's *Jew of Malta*, both its unorthodox fusion of vitriolic satire and knock-about comedy and, as a model for Marston's tyrant Piero, Marlowe's Barabas, at once ruthless Machiavellian egoist and vaudeville clown.

Every parodic aspect of *Antonio and Mellida*, not just the external allusion, is heightened in *Antonio's Revenge*. The dramatic poles of violent action and stoic passivity, impassioned rhetoric and prosaic comedy, are more extreme yet also more tightly yoked in *Part 2*'s firmer structure, and their unpredictable confrontations produce even more unsettlng self-commentary. Before Piero murders him in a trick reminiscent of *The Spanish Tragedy*, the tool-villain Strotzo repeatedly mocks his master's exaggerated tyrant's rant. Balurdo as comic foil becomes more prominent, his deflating juxtaposition with the 'tragic' declamations of both Piero and Antonio more devastating. As in *Part 1*, Marston does not simply strain his theatrical illusion, he rends it. Antonio's hyperbolic despair at his father's death is met by Pandulpho's stoic invitation to sit and 'talk as chorus to this tragedy', and Piero later tells us that 'now *Tragoedia Cothurnata* mounts' (1.5.63; 2.5.45). In Act 2, scene 1 Balurdo enters complaining about his make-up, since his beard is only half glued on; when Pandulpho finally joins the revengers he reassesses his former philosophic equanimity as a theatrical role 'Like to some boy that acts a tragedy' (4.5.48).

Marston's dramaturgy ensures a certain aloofness from the passions that sweep his characters first one way, then another. The disengagement that allows us to appreciate witty allusion and downright pilfering also prepares us for the philosophic as well as generic challenge in Marston's final twist: instead of dying in the confused mêlée of their torture and execution of Piero, Marston's revengers survive. More surprising still, despite the ghost's

---

[5] On Marston's use of contemporary revenge plays, especially Kyd's, see Bowers, *Elizabethan Revenge Tragedy*, pp. 118–19, and Foakes, 'John Marston's fantastical plays'.

blessing and the Venetian senators' approval, these disillusioned justicers find their own deed insupportable, for it has shown them their entanglement in the whole mad, depraved world exposed by the play's events. *Antonio's Revenge* ends not with the expected coda celebrating the defeat of evil and restoration of order, but with the revengers' choice of monastic seclusion and a lifetime of atonement.

Out of a pastiche of classical and contemporary plays Marston creates a compendium of revenge tragedy, one that calls attention to its constructed nature. Such a procedure exaggerates the distance between stage and reality; we are forced to recognize how much an unreflective use of convention excludes. The emphasis on artificiality, underscored by repeated reference to its theatrical enactment by boys, enables Marston to present a double critique – both of the genre he has placed before us and of his own play – and to offer a version that incorporates the conventions of its models while it also, in breaking them, becomes something new.

With such sophisticated parody Marston established himself theatrically as a distinctive critical voice and advertised the repertoire of his troupe as avant-garde and fresh. An even bolder adapter of conventional materials to new ends, Francis Beaumont in *The Knight of the Burning Pestle* (c. 1607) fashioned for the Blackfriars boys a burlesque of the kind of citizen-adventure play popularized by Thomas Heywood at theatres like the Curtain and Red Bull. In this case, the dramatist's interest in probing and extending his medium exploded the borrowed form: Beaumont created something very different and modern, but also a baffled first audience and a commercial failure.

Initially, the topical social and literary satire seems rather straightforward, private-theatre ridicule of the inept, socially offensive glorification of citizen achievements by hack dramatists, as well as the ill-educated audience to which they pandered. Dissatisfied with the Blackfriars offering of the day, a city comedy called 'The London Merchant' that they rightly suspect will mock their class and values, a grocer and his wife climb onto the stage to sit among the gallants and demand a play more to their taste. Compromising with the boy-Prologue, the citizens allow the official play to go on if it will accommodate their impromptu, self-aggrandizing creation, 'The Grocer's Honour' (maliciously renamed by the boy 'The Knight of the Burning Pestle'), starring their own apprentice Rafe. The grocer's list of the plays he would prefer and willingness to pay for the flattery he wants ('I will have a grocer and he shall do admirable things' – Induction, 33–4), as well as Rafe's audition with Hotspur's speech on honour from *Henry IV, Part 1* (and later use of *The Spanish Tragedy*), suggest the corruption of art by commerce and a debasement both of heroic ideals and the dramatic forms associated with them. The citizens' continued interruptions, their demand to see Rafe whenever they want and even that he intervene in 'The London Merchant', their imperviousness to the boy's pleas for dramatic decorum or plot coherence, and their delight in a mish-mash of typical romance episodes further indict their aesthetic and moral sensibility.

Yet Beaumont's play does not continue as it began. His interest, like Marston's, is also metadramatic, and expanding the Induction's on-stage 'audience' allows him scope to explore other facets of the theatrical experience. Particular satire is largely left behind as *The Knight of the Burning Pestle* turns to investigating how the theatre and its conventions try to capture and direct the audience's eager but unruly imagination. The citizens' naïve misapprehensions, not just their interruptions, defeat the smooth progress of the professional play: real-world judgements about runaway apprentices and daughters who refuse their fathers' choice of husbands negate the values conventionally assigned these characters and situations. The wife stops the play to comment on the child actors or offer homely remedies for fictional chilblains; when she does pay attention, she wrongly admires the vapid 'aristocratic' rhetoric of the doltish suitor, cannot foresee the lovers' final union, and wants to call the London Watch when the story threatens violence.

The citizens' untutored reactions and attempt to create their own play make them comic butts but also heighten our consciousness of plays as artistic mechanisms, contrived structures that rely on learned conventions and a whole set of social assumptions about the nature of the theatre itself. Beaumont has fun with the wife's censure of Merrythought, the prodigal father in 'The London Merchant', for she knows the value of 'a penny i' th' purse while I live' (376); she can no more see this apostle of good fellowship and philosophic 'mirth' as the play's comic ideal than she can tell good suitor from bad. She is also right. Merrythought's value is a literary and dramatic one. As festive spirit of misrule, his singing humour fills the play with snatches of contemporary ballads, and he is structurally necessary to the comic conclusion. At the same time, his total refusal of responsibility would be intolerable outside his conventionally defined role.

Beaumont's play appears to be all conflict – art vs. life, satire vs. carnivalesque celebration, structured drama vs. chaos, gentlemen-spectators and actors vs. citizens, the playhouse comedy vs. the 'story' of Rafe's adventures that ends in his death. In fact, Beaumont's discordant elements do cohere. Despite their shortcomings as audience, his citizens are no puritan censors, demanding an end to playing. They are Beaumont's lords of misrule, who liberate other examples of spontaneous playmaking in the players and, especially, Rafe; they are also Beaumont's agents of unity. Apparent contradictions repeatedly collapse or assume a wholly new perspective. In the last episodes, city comedy and Rafe's romance establish a surprising *rapprochement* of spirit. Moreover, although the citizens seem untouched by Merrythought's life-enhancing ethic, the comic pattern is fulfilled in the epilogue when the wife invites the gentlemen-spectators to her house for wine and the tobacco she earlier denounced. Beaumont has found an encompassing tone, but his own work certainly lacks the conventionality of its two interior playlets. Clashing types and plot lines constantly redefine our response, and the citizens burst in unpredictably with their own insistent reality. Any single authorial stance evaporates under the play's shifting point of view.

The Knight of the Burning Pestle's failure in its own time is less significant than its existence, one index of the range of experimentation that distinguished the early seventeenth century – on the public stage, for a Shakespeare or a Jonson, as well as in the private houses. Marston and Beaumont borrow common generic materials for their early plays, but through exaggeration and the sharp juxtaposition of different sets of conventions, they fracture a conventional response and demolish the hold a single genre usually exercises. Distinctions collapse while dissonance increases; the audience cannot remain passive, for the initially familiar materials are put to unexpected uses. Given their taste for creating new plays by subverting established ones, it is not surprising that Marston and Beaumont should challenge the traditional separation and hierarchy of genres. With very different plays, each helped establish what was to become the century's most popular dramatic form, tragicomedy.

The appearance of tragicomedy in the early seventeenth century was not solely the work of these two playwrights, of course, nor was mixing comic and tragic elements new. What A. P. Rossiter called 'the play in two tones', characteristic of England's peculiarly 'gothic' drama from its beginnings, in the 1560s and 1570s produced a number of plays advertising themselves as 'A Lamentable Tragedie mixed full of plesant mirth' (*Cambises*) or, in the term invented by Richard Edwards for the prologue to *Damon and Pithias*, 'tragical comedy'.[6] Dramatically crude, these early plays earned Sir Philip Sidney's condemnation in *The Defence of Poesie* as 'neither right Tragedies, nor right Comedies' but merely basely conceived 'mungrell Tragycomedie.' In the late 1580s and 1590s, Sidney's ideal was not rigorously pursued, but distinctions were by and large preserved. Despite a tendency to mix generic

[6] Rossiter, *English Drama*, chapter 10 and epilogue.

elements in practice, even as boldly as Robert Greene in *James IV* or Marlowe in *The Jew of Malta*, English playwrights and critics seem not to have recognized tragicomedy as a distinct dramatic species.

At the century's turn, the iconoclastic use of old plays and rhetorical styles coexists with other ventures in creating new dramatic 'kinds'. In the private theatre, 'comical satyre' and then city comedy offered one reaction to the Petrarchan idealization of Elizabethan romantic comedy; generic revision and emphasis on the lower end of the social scale opened excluded areas of contemporary experience – and tension – to theatrical representation. In formal terms, tragicomedy's structure is comic, and it is most fruitfully seen as a transformation that would free romantic comedy itself to include the kinds of experience, personal relationships and philosophic questioning formerly associated with its generic opposite.[7]

Continental developments spurred interest in tragicomedy as a distinct form with English possibilities. Giambattista Guarini's controversial pastoral tragicomedy, *Il Pastor Fido*, had been available in London since 1591, but in 1602 its final revised form appeared in English translation, bound now with the *Compendio della poesia tragicomica*, in which Guarini defends his apparent violation of artistic decorum as a respectable genre in its own right. Guarini's play found few English imitators; its challenge to accepted categories, however, prompted some inventive native responses. In early experiments by Marston, Shakespeare, Beaumont and Fletcher, the English 'mixed mode' is more self-consciously extended; practice is raised to the theoretical level and claims recognition as genre.

The main line of English tragicomedy appears so unlike the Italian because it discards Guarini's apolitical shepherds and rethinks the form's emphasis. Italian pastoral tragicomedy defended itself as a re-creation of the Greek satyr play, thus claiming as respectable a genealogy as comedy and tragedy. That the English understood tragicomedy's protagonists to be as legitimately satyrs as shepherds is illustrated by the engraved title-page to Ben Jonson's 1616 *Workes*, where *Tragicomoedia* is supported equally by *Pastor* and *Satyr* (Plate 20). The common, erroneous derivation of *satire* from *satyr* – a being distinguished by rough style as well as skin, associated with rude jokes and personal attacks – suggests just how far from Arcadia tragicomedy might wander. Emphasizing *Satyr* rather than *Pastor* for English writers allied tragicomedy with the 1590s world of topical, urban, social, and moral verse satire.[8] To varying degrees, English tragicomic authors locate

---

[7] Cf. Foakes, 'Tragicomedy and comic form', pp. 74–6.

[8] Hunter, 'Italian tragicomedy', pp. 141–5, and for a more general account of Renaissance tragicomedy, Waith, *The Pattern of Tragicomedy*, pp. 43–70.

the new form's focus on love and private relations within satirically anatomized social and political worlds.

The Malcontent (1603–4) emphatically seizes on the *Satyr* implications. Marston's tragicomedy in one sense grows naturally out of his early verse satire and fondness for radical dramatic experiment, already suggestively linked in the thematic issues and generic juxtapositions of the Antonio plays. *The Malcontent*'s numerous quotations from the 1602 translation also establish Marston's familiarity with *Il Pastor Fido*; that he may have been self-consciously recasting the new form to English taste appears in Marston's own hesitant designation of his play. In the epistle to the printed text he calls it 'this Comedy' and asks that it 'pass with the freedom of a satire'; in the Stationers' Register the play is entered as 'An Enterlude called the Malecontent Tragicomoedia'. Guarini is superficially acknowledged in quotation, but absorbed at the fundamental level of form; Marston freely pursues his own interests.

In *The Malcontent*, Marston uses pastoral tragicomedy's principal concern, faithful and unfaithful love, to refashion revenge tragedy more positively than in *Antonio's Revenge*. Political restoration for the deposed Altofront, disguised as a malcontent tool-villain, depends in part on benevolent chance; it also springs from the witty manœvrings by which Malevole finally converts the original usurper, Pietro, and outwits his successor, Mendoza. Families as well as dukedoms are restored and, regaining his political identity, Altofront is reunited with his duchess Maria, imprisoned under Mendoza's tyranny. Although the play appears dominated by political plots and Malevole's satiric commentary, Maria is in fact central to the final sense of stability. In refusing Mendoza's proxy courtship, her sexual as well as political fidelity provides a hopeful counter to Pietro's lascivious Duchess Aurelia (unfaithful mistress to Mendoza). Maria breaks the pattern by which each new political aspirant establishes his position through seducing his rival's wife. Mendoza can be expelled rather than executed because his intended murders have misfired, but also because a whole moral as well as political order has been restored with the rule of Altofront and Maria.

Early on Malevole tells us his desired revenge is not death but the 'heart's disquiet' (1.3.158). Psychological torment more than punishes Pietro; by the end of Act 4 it convinces him to renounce power and enact in deed his holy hermit disguise. But these cues for a non-tragic ending are strained by what goes on between them, and *The Malcontent* severely tests its tragicomic structure. Mendoza's intentions are murderous, and this Senecan villain seems a natural product of the world Marston anatomizes. Almost everywhere he turns, Malevole finds vice as well as folly – from a fickle populace, through

20   Title-page to Ben Jonson's 1616 *Workes*

court fops and toadies eagerly seeking the usurper's favour, to the insidious union of sex and politics in the shifting power relations among princes. The speech that completes Pietro's conversion is both calculated, part of Altofront's political strategy to regain his dukedom, and a horrified epitome of what he has learned as Malevole: the earth is a graveyard in which all transient things rot, man no more than 'the slime of this dung-pit', and rulers merely 'jailers' charged with keeping naturally vicious men 'in bonds' (4.5.110–21). The play has provided a good deal of support for this climactic set-speech on human depravity, and Pietro's stoic renunciation seems appropriate. Unlike Antonio or Pietro, however, Altofront–Malevole is disillusioned but not unhinged by this knowledge, and he has yet to discover Maria's fidelity, the captain's loyalty, and the 'whirl of fate' by which the people now support him and events conspire to restore him to office. The world of *The Malcontent* finally proves not so dark as the *contemptus mundi* vision at its heart, but the power of that vision lingers to qualify our response to the final restorations.

The successful introduction into one genre of subject matter and techniques from its theoretical opposite is easier hypothesized than accomplished. In practice, the necessary balancing act proved easily upset by local emphases, a unifying tone for such disparate material hard to establish. However effectively *The Malcontent* controls its hybrid elements, that success rests on the more bewildering juxtapositions of the Antonio plays, just as Shakespeare's late tragicomedies follow such diverse experiments as *Troilus and Cressida* and *Measure for Measure*. The distinctive 'Beaumont and Fletcher' tragicomedy that proved an influential model for the rest of the century reveals another such chequered past. After the failure of *The Knight of the Burning Pestle*, clearly comedy but beyond that unique, Beaumont next collaborated with John Fletcher on a tragedy drawn from aristocratic pastoral romance. To the two stories lifted from Sidney's *Arcadia* and a death-count rivalling *Hamlet*'s, however, *Cupid's Revenge* (1608) adds scenes and techniques of characterization derived from satiric city comedy that undermine the play's focus and inhibit any sense of tragic inevitability. *Cupid's Revenge* strives, against genre, to be something else; though apparently commercially successful with this play, Beaumont and Fletcher do not repeat its form.[9]

What they found truly congenial in Sidney lay at a more fundamental level than plot, and some features of his romance lingered to help shape the

---

[9] John H. Astington, in 'The popularity of *Cupid's Revenge*', argues for this success and suggests it as the reason the King's Men engaged Beaumont and Fletcher immediately, despite individual failures, in 1608–9 (*SEL* 19 [1979], esp. 218–19).

pattern of later collaborations and explain why their 'Englishing' of the tragicomic form should prove so different from Marston's. They develop their
own version of Sidney's partly pastoral, partly aristocratic milieu, and they
learn what Sidney himself discovered in revising his own work: a 'timeless'
thematic structure, allowing for sharp contrast between kinds of scenes,
replaces plot as the primary organizing principle. Finally, Beaumont and
Fletcher continued to seek dramatic expression for Sidney's witty, sophisticated, self-mocking narrative tone.

The aesthetic advance that marks *Philaster* (1609) derives from a bolder
reshaping of this material, but also from Fletcher's pastoral tragicomedy *The
Faithful Shepherdess*, probably written the same year as *Cupid's Revenge*.[10]
Fletcher models his title on Guarini's and chooses the same dramatic mode,
but his play is strikingly different and its other debts are English. Working
within a unifying pastoralism, Fletcher transmutes material that had proved
disruptive in *Cupid's Revenge* into a more clearly articulated and controlled
generic blend. Some of the main character-types reappear, arranged now in
a hierarchy that measures its lovers' moral stature against the spiritual devotion of Clorin, the title-character whose chastity is a living memorial to her
dead shepherd. Fletcher's slender plot is his own, designed to provide a
shifting configuration of lovers rather than a true narrative sequence. Each
shepherd's nature is established early, as he or she arrives in the wood;
Fletcher then moves them through all possible permutations, confrontations,
and misunderstandings until each has found the proper mate or been
deemed unfit for marriage, and the forest Satyr is left to serve the solitary
Clorin.

Fletcher's thematic patterning may have been inspired by Sidney and
Book III of Spenser's *Faerie Queene*; the structural advance over *Cupid's
Revenge* begins with a narrowed scope (temporally, and in the smaller cast's
integration into a single plot) and the adoption of a dramatic model, the
'magical woods' scenes of *A Midsummer Night's Dream*. In tone, too,
Shakespeare here reinforces Sidney. The final effect of Fletcher's delicate
combination of gods and shepherds, lyricism and earthy humour, threatened
loss and (in the middle section) farce, is a sophisticated double view of love.
We are made to see and respond to love's unique importance, its power to
make every obstacle tragically significant; we are asked also to share the
dramatist's appreciation – acknowledged over the heads of his characters –
of humankind's mortal folly in love. Exaggeration and poetic stylization make

---

[10] On the links among these three plays, see Bliss, *Francis Beaumont*, chapter 4; on *The
Faithful Shepherdess*, the same author's 'Defending Fletcher's shepherds'.

the characters' purposefully heightened emotions simultaneously both real and remote.

In *The Faithful Shepherdess* Fletcher learns to introduce tragic potential while subordinating it to comedy's final reconciliations. He discovers in practice what the printed text's 'To the Reader' (*c.*1610) defends in theory: tragicomedy is seen as a sophisticated marriage of genres that results not in the awkward yoking that Sidney scorned but in a new genre with its own distinctive style and effect. The commercial failure of his play may have stemmed from Fletcher's uncompromising pastoralism; despite some stageworthy surprises (the River God's rising from a well with the supposed-dead Amoret in his arms; the confused young lover Perigot's twice stabbing his beloved), perhaps the emphasis on love debate and lack of a fully developed plot were more than even a Blackfriars audience could take to its heart. Fletcher blamed his audience's ignorance of the play's form, and his anger produced the first theoretical defence of tragicomedy in English. Adapting Guarini's *Compendio*, Fletcher defines the new genre's latitude in subject matter, character, and style:

A tragi-comedy is not so called in respect of mirth and killing, but in respect it wants deaths, which is enough to make it no tragedy, yet brings some near it, which is enough to make it no comedy, which must be a representation of familiar people, with such kind of trouble as no life be questioned, so that a god is as lawful in this as in tragedy, and mean people as in comedy.

Fletcher helped both to establish the term as part of the English critical vocabulary and to legitimize tragicomedy as a valid theatrical form.

Philaster demonstrates the lessons learned. Fletcher's pastoralism finds its place – the lyric despair of the lovers, a hunting scene that now juxtaposes earthy rustics with exquisitely refined aristocrats – but within a larger scheme of political usurpation and restoration. Various developments, however tonally different from each other, all retard or advance one overarching plot line. The characteristic tragicomic vision may derive largely from prose romance, but the successful and influential form discovered with *Philaster* results from re-examining and reworking theatrical practice. Marston's tragicomedy is certainly in the background, as is the distraught Antonio. In their first play for the King's Men, however, the young dramatists find their own way and, in the process, elect Shakespearian exemplars – *Hamlet, Othello, Twelfth Night* – for the kinds of plays out of which their own mixed mode will be built.

Philaster is neither pastiche nor parody. A thorough transmutation of Shakespeare guides the play's general shape; within this structure, Beaumont and Fletcher discover the local balance of discordant tones and perspectives that gives their tragicomedy its self-reflexive quality and curious power to elicit almost simultaneous engagement and detachment. The satiric comedy so destructive to *Cupid's Revenge* returns, aptly, to help define the corrupt world within which the prince and his beloved Arethusa seek to establish a private haven. More surprisingly, it also qualifies our response to the exquisitely sensitive young lovers themselves. Lord Dion and his friends open the play as political and moral commentators; they establish a cynical, 'realistic' voice – about politics, love, the vulgar populace – that, in various characters and scenes, forms one of *Philaster*'s competing views of its own action.

Against this background Philaster, Arethusa, and the maligned page Bellario must maintain the signal importance of their love for and fidelity to each other. For most of Acts 3 and 4 the play suspends its forward movement to explore the psychological havoc wrought by Philaster's doubt of both mistress and page; adopting the structure of Fletcher's tragicomedy, the dramatists move their despairing principals through every possible emotionally charged confrontation. Yet even in the carefully orchestrated sequence leading to Philaster's stabbing both Arethusa and Bellario, the playwrights do not allow the heightened language and emotion wholly to control our response. Interspersed scenes force upon us the courtiers' and Woodmen's bawdy comic prose, or Dion's sudden political confrontation with the king; they disturb our sense of developing tragedy. Arethusa, Philaster, and Bellario may here seem to have stepped out of *The Faithful Shepherdess* (even the stabbing is borrowed), but they are not granted the supporting generic backdrop. In the play's boldest juxtaposition, Beaumont and Fletcher allow that outer world to invade and challenge the lovers' apparently separate realm of pastoral romance. As Philaster stabs the willing Arethusa, they are interrupted not by a lovelorn shepherd but by the Country Fellow's comic turn. Berated for his 'ill-bred' intrusion on their 'private sports', this stolid rustic provides a common-sense perspective outside the conventions of language, emotion, and action that created the scene he has stumbled into: 'I know not your rhetoric, but I can lay it on if you touch the woman' (4.5.97–8).

The passionate heart of *Philaster* lies in the lovers' response to an apparent betrayal of love, their entry into a private nightmare of such extreme despair and self-alienation that each seeks death. That emotional pitch is also 'placed', by the treatment of the lovers themselves and by the principle of alternation and contrast that refuses them, or their private drama, the isolation they seek. The competing perspectives do not cancel each other out; we participate in both. The Country Fellow releases us from Philaster's claustrophobic hysteria and, for a moment, turns us back into amused spec-

tators. No longer asked wholly to adopt the lovers' valuation of their predicament, we find the distance appropriate to a play that will reverse its
apparently fatal trajectory and, through a citizen uprising and the discovery
of Bellario's true identity, restore harmony to both public and private worlds.

This self-reflexive juxtaposition of perspectives and unsettling combination of conventions and characters from different kinds of plays also appear
in Beaumont and Fletcher's last joint tragicomedy, *A King and No King*
(1611), although the delicate generic balance that marked *Philaster* tips now
toward the comic emphasis Fletcher seemed to find more congenial. In
spirit, *A King and No King* approaches the kind of tragicomedy Fletcher was
later to purvey, alone and with other collaborators, and it looks more
squarely toward later English practice in both tragicomedy and heroic
drama.

Instead of creating a multifaceted view of character and event, satiric and
romantic perspectives clash in ways that more nearly cancel each other out.
So, too, the romance discoveries are fundamentally different. When Bellario
reveals she is a woman, she allows *Philaster* to end happily instead of doubling back on itself to repeat Arethusa's persecution; the revelation does not
negate the problem of distinguishing appearance from reality or cancel
Philaster's inability to believe Arethusa's innocence. In *A King and No King*'s
tale of King Arbaces' apparently incestuous love for his sister Panthea,
resolution comes when Arbaces finds he is really son to Gobrius, not the
princess's brother. The terror occasioned by an experience of uncontrollable
passion that threatens civilized institutions seems erased when that passion is
redefined as the normal love-at-first-sight attraction of a legitimate romantic
couple. The new range of intellectual and emotional possibilities to which
tragicomedy had seemed to open the comic form is here almost wholly
closed off again in the reassuring denouement.

A King and No King has not quite completed this passage. The violence of
Arbaces' passion still disturbs, since he feels that if he cannot marry Panthea
he must rape her. Such love may be legitimated, but it cannot be retroactively idealized as ennobling devotion. The play repeatedly undercuts its
protagonist, even while it asks us to pity and, in part, admire him. Good
counsellor and spokesman for Arbaces' virtues, Mardonius also mocks his
king's hubristic speeches. A more dramatically conceived foil is Bessus, the
cowardly, amoral captain who would seem the warrior-monarch's opposite
but is at times tellingly made his double. Bessus is largely relegated to the
farcical sub-plot, but his efforts to redefine his cowardice as 'honour' link
him with Arbaces' more disturbing attempt to deny, by royal fiat, that Panthea is his sister. The darker implications of Bessus' amorality penetrate the

main plot when he cheerfully offers to procure his monarch's sister – indeed, his mother, if Arbaces wants her also. Here the laughter Bessus provokes is not normative; his effect is unlike the Country Fellow's in *Philaster*. Though concerned with reputation and appearances, Bessus stands outside the moral order, and his buffoonery brackets major scenes of strained interaction or passionate self-denunciation. Elsewhere, too, the heightened rhetoric of the main plot's confrontation with issues of human bestiality and the betrayal of honour is cross-cut with voices that assert more mundane concerns and public indifference. In the tiny, wholly extraneous Act 2, scene 2, for instance, several rowdy citizens hilariously misinterpret Arbaces' triumphal home-coming speech.

Other elements of *A King and No King* contribute to its distancing of characters as well as issues. Although Arbaces obviously extends the line of young men tormented by life's contradictions, he lacks Philaster's comparative centrality and complexity, and he must share his stage with Tigranes and Spaconia, who constitute another strand of the main plot's investigation of aristocratic love and honour. All Beaumont and Fletcher's plays employ external characterization, but with Arbaces it remains the dominant mode; even after the opening evaluations, Mardonius continues to define and interpret his king. An extraordinarily heavy use of the 'aside' further checks our involvement in any single individual's plight. Dramatic focus blurs when, in a crowded public scene such as Act 3, scene 1, our attention is repeatedly shifted from the ongoing action to one or another character's private response to it. Finally, although both Arbaces and Tigranes demonstrate passion's arbitrary power over even the best human intentions, the more sensational form of this threat self-destructs when Arbaces finds that the answer to his demand to 'tell me who I am' need only be genealogical.

The play's challenge to traditional ideas about man's nature, its hints of a wild, Hobbesian universe, are muffled. Our attention is directed to the brilliant artifice of *A King and No King*'s construction and, at the end, we even discover the dramatists have playfully included their own surrogate. With Gobrius' revelations we retroactively see both problem and solution as largely the product of his manipulations; like any tragicomic playwright, he knows that timing is all: 'Now it is ripe … Now is the time' (5.4.65, 108). Only when passion and confusion have reached an unendurable level will full disclosure have its greatest theatrical impact.

The sophisticated self-consciousness that asks us to share, finally, the artist's urbane distance rather than his characters' amorous involvement met an appreciative reception. Beaumont and Fletcher's skill in fashioning the turns and counterturns of a continually exciting plot, as well as their characters' amorous dilemmas and impassioned rhetoric, were consistently praised and imitated. Contemporary taste is suggested by *Philaster*'s subtitle, 'Love lies ableeding' (used as sole reference as early as 1610), and by the title-page woodcut of the 1620 quarto depicting the climactic scene's mixture of erotic violence and rustic incomprehension (Plate 21).

The celebration of theatrical artifice, as well as an attraction to romance materials, link Beaumont and Fletcher with the colleague from whose earlier work they borrowed so much. Through the 'Calumniated Woman' motif, both *Philaster* and Shakespeare's *Cymbeline* (*c.*1609) also dramatize the experience of love threatened by ungovernable jealousy, of self-betrayal and suicidal despair, and of a final recovery of self and place that can be reinscribed within a political world no longer inimical to human desire. Shakespeare widens the scope of his investigation, however: beyond the personal significance of romantic love, he is concerned with families as the social structures that mediate between private and public worlds and give the individual an identity rooted in time. The Posthumus–Imogen plot closely resembles *Philaster*, but the story of kidnapped princes introduces a sudden sense of family history, and the dreaming Posthumus discovers the parents and brothers he never knew when their spirits arrive to defend him. This widened scope extends from the fairy-tale extremes of good and evil characters to the geographical sprawl of the action and generic variety of the sources from which that action is constructed. The welter of significant characters engaged in proliferating plots further disperses the dramatic focus. In a technique shared with Beaumont and Fletcher, sudden alterations in perspective enhance a sense of mounting tension and confusion while also regulating our involvement with individual characters. When Imogen awakes next to the headless body she identifies as her husband's, *Cymbeline* insists on both the tragic intensity of her despair and the grotesque comedy of her mistake, since she in fact mourns over the corpse of the dead villain, Cloten.

In reminding us of our privileged view and drawing attention to the frankly theatrical coincidences by which they avert tragedy, these dramatists admit their artifice and ask our recognition of it as part of the plays' appeal. Yet where Beaumont and Fletcher point us to the world of art and the men who shape and enjoy such fictions, Shakespeare is finally more self-effacing. *Cymbeline*'s competing perspectives dissolve as the characters converge on Cymbeline's court to find themselves and their place among loved ones thought lost. Jarring shifts among scenes from Italian intrigue comedy, chronicle history, and pastoral tragedy culminate in the surprise descent of the god Jupiter. The comically drawn-out final scene of revelations and

PHYLASTER.

Or, Loue lyes a Bleeding.

Aĉted at the Globe by his Maiefties Seruants.

Written by { *Francis Baymont* and *Iohn Fletcher*. } Gent.

21   Title-page to 1620 edition of Beaumont and Fletcher's *Philaster*

restorations then subsumes all characters, events, and genres under romance's banner. Individual voices blend to become partial narrators of the
larger, intricately interwoven story we have seen, and the characters' wonder
at the apparent miracle by which they have fulfilled Jupiter's riddling prophecy is matched by ours, as we watch Shakespeare disappear behind the
cosmic playwright whose art he mirrors.[11] In *Philaster* and *A King and No
King* the gods and miraculous landscape of earlier plays disappear; in *Cymbeline* the gods are immanent and guarantee a final stability and harmony
more sweeping than that offered by Beaumont and Fletcher.[12]

Beaumont and Fletcher provide no final, comprehensive transformation.
The dissonant note of minor characters who resist the call to love, honour,
and forgiveness remains, even at the end, and reminds us of the dramatists'
early alliance with the children's companies and the influence of satiric comedy as well as Shakespeare. They belong to, and write to entertain, a generation experiencing the breakdown of a whole system of integrated beliefs and
practices. If Shakespearian tragicomedy accepts the premises of romance
and reasserts that order in idealized form, Beaumont and Fletcher's finds
disjunction. While conventions of plot, incident, and characterization provide a romance patina, they function as literary and theatrical counters stripped of metonymic weight. This darker side, a hinted fragmentation rather
than consensus of values beneath the formal solutions, suggests at least sub-
terranean links between their work and John Webster's *The Devil's Law-
Case*, a play that at first glance seems to reject developments by Beaumont,
Fletcher, and Shakespeare in order to return to Marston and Marlowe.[13]

Like Marston, Webster emphasizes the *Satyr* genealogy for a play the
1623 quarto calls 'Tragecomoedy', although the biting wit and aphoristic
commentary appropriate to Malevole's malcontent role belong, in *The Devil's
Law-Case*, not just to the cynical merchant–protagonist Romelio but to
nearly everyone. Repeatedly, censure of a particular crime dilates to include
a whole class or profession; even idealistic *sententiae* often function satirically, condemning the speakers who use them to mask self-interested
manœuvring. Such gnomic generalization distances us from the immediate
action, but also darkens it by translating individual folly or vice into permanent, 'natural' human characteristics; it exalts not the innocent victims, but
those who outwit their opponents. In *The Malcontent*, the Altofront–Malevole
frame mitigates the impact of a foolish, knavish court: the moralist stands

---

[11] See also Kirsch, *Jacobean Dramatic Perspectives*, pp. 73–4.

[12] For a fuller comparison, see Bliss, 'Tragicomic romance'.

[13] Despite the usual assumption of 1617, *The Devil's Law-Case* may have been composed a
good deal earlier; Bentley argues for *c.* 1610 in *The Jacobean and Caroline Stage*, IV. 1250–1.

between us and the action, verbally controlling the viciousness he denounces, while the tragicomic plot frustrates murderous intentions until power and morality can be reunited. Romelio is less central to his play, and he provides no moral centre. Webster chooses as his model Marlowe's Machiavellian Jew: Romelio is dedicated to using everyone, including his sister Jolenta, for his own advantage.

In *The Devil's Law-Case* situations and characters change – or reveal new facets – with lightning rapidity, and the pace of plot and counter-plot becomes vertiginous. No one controls the action or our perspective on it, and the smooth social surface of the play's opening soon disintegrates under the anarchic amatory and economic passions that fuel individual schemes. Characters remain flat but intense, as they channel their violent energies to the narrow roles dictated by the evolving plots. The tendency to turn serious matters, even their own suffering, into material for sardonic jests – as Jolenta does when in Act 3, scene 3 she agrees to aid Romelio, despite his role in the apparent death of her lover – helps push the play toward grotesque farce.

Dissonance among the play's constituent elements enhances the impression of extreme dislocation. Nodding, perhaps, toward the popularity of romantic tragicomedy, Webster introduces two high-minded noble suitors, but their Petrarchan wooing and honourable duel over Jolenta must coexist with Julio's bawdy commentary, the surrounding manœuvres of self-made entrepreneurs of law and business, and a world in which mothers declare their sons illegitimate and pregnant nuns seek to avoid disgrace. In their stiff rhetoric, rigid code of honour, and blindness to others' motives, Ercole and Contarino might have stepped out of a Beaumont–Fletcher play, but they lack the prominence or context that would give them weight as representatives of idealism and nobility of feeling.

Webster presents an unstable compound of clashing character types and generic signals: the play's focus is as scattered as that of the lawyer Crispiano, sent by the king to investigate Romelio's economic crimes but also 'What mad tricks has been played of late by ladies' (3.1.9). Whenever the play seems to have taken a decisive turn toward disaster or concord, a new scene and another stratagem reverse our expectation. The means by which this madly spinning top is brought under control are as improbable as its characters' schemes. Romelio's sudden moral conversion and the final pairing of some very unlikely couples abruptly halt the frantic rush of events. One of the few upright characters, Ariosto, in the last lines dispenses wise judgements and advice, but he has not created this happy resolution. If events demonstrate heaven's power to 'invert man's firmest purpose' (5.5.14), as the Capuchin claims, heaven is shown to have little but human self-destructiveness to work with. Pitting plot against counter-plot temporarily frustrates bad intentions, but the aggressive, egoistic energy behind them can be tamed only by a bare-faced imposition of comic convention. Webster's denouement stresses the genre's inadequacy, not its elegance or the way a controlled balancing of elements can give the engineered ending its own sense of dramatic rightness.

Pursuing a different formal tack, Middleton and Rowley's *A Fair Quarrel* (1615–17) reveals the strong influence of Beaumont and Fletcher's tragicomic dramaturgy, particularly as Fletcher developed it after Beaumont's early retirement. In tragicomedies and comedies like *The Honest Man's Fortune* (1613) and *Monsieur Thomas* (1615), Fletcher drops the political component of earlier plays and extends *A King and No King*'s tendency to stratify its plots by social class and genre. Middleton and Rowley accept this taming of tragicomedy's disruptive potential, though between the 'high' plot's exquisite moral dilemmas and investigation of the meaning of honour, and Chough's and Trimtram's efforts to learn the language and behaviour of roaring boys, the dramatists introduce a third term: the middle-class world in which Jane seeks approval for her love-marriage from Russell, a father whose wholly economic values require that she marry wealth.

A Fair Quarrel shapes material from disparate sources into a thematically unified whole whose alternating plot lines comment on each other without bringing their value systems into open confrontation.[14] Jane's citizen sense of honour – her decision to remain true to her secret marriage even at the cost of her reputation – balances the satiric treatment of her father's mercantile ethic. Her decision exemplifies, in domestic form, what the main plot's hot-headed Colonel and Captain Ager discover through the apparent death of the Colonel in their duel. Friendship and respect among equals are more important than public reputation; duelling is finally understood as a form of 'vengeance' that at best brings only a Pyrrhic victory, 'A miserable triumph, though a just one' (3.1.78). Chough's low-comedy antics ridicule false ideas of honour in the other two plots. Uniting this high–middle–low triple structure is the fact that, despite the threat of death, two of the three actions are recognizably comic from their inception, and the late addition of a main-plot sister, who will bind the Colonel and Ager not only as friends but as brothers-in-law, enhances our sense of a general convergence toward comedy's festive vision.

---

[14] R. V. Holdsworth discusses the dramatists' skilled transformation of their sources in his New Mermaids edition of *A Fair Quarrel*, pp. xv–xviii; on the play's sophisticated triadic plotting, see also Levin, *The Multiple Plot*, pp. 66–75, 153–4.

Middleton's other romantic tragicomedies fail to establish a harmonious balance among varied stories and conventions. Here, incorporating a main plot fashionably preoccupied with duelling and hence with definitions of honour, he avoids a total schism between its extreme passions and rhetoric and either the intrigue city comedy of Jane's final triumph or the farcical scenes of the would-be roaring boys. *A Fair Quarrel*'s social concerns centre on manners, not on competing economic, political or class codes, though it may use such conflicts to build suspense. It dissolves contradictions in a new sense of honour and dramatizes a real, albeit gradual, seventeenth-century shift from a primarily feudal, aristocratic code to a concept that stressed inner worth and respect rather than competition among 'honourable' men.[15] Here we find neither the unassimilable 'loose ends' of early Beaumont and Fletcher, those reminders of a world resistant to artistic convention or generic order, nor a self-conscious flaunting of the dramatist's arbitrary control. Yet while *A Fair Quarrel* works to establish communal values, it does so very differently from *Cymbeline*. Middleton and Rowley suggest no metaphysical implications for their action – beyond asserting that right behaviour is also Christian behaviour – and they repeatedly smudge the hard edges that might have defined a real confrontation of philosophies embodied in the juxtaposed genres.

Unlike *The Devil's Law-Case*, which with the exception of Ercole and Contarino could have been written in the early years of James's reign, *A Fair Quarrel* is of its time and Janus-faced in both content and technique. The triple plotting looks back to Middleton's city comedy and, in the emphasis on romantic idealism, to the aristocratic love comedies of the 1590s. Translated into a tragicomic structure that widens the main-plot issues to include honour as well as love, while narrowing the social disparity among its plots' characters, *A Fair Quarrel* follows Fletcher's own development.

More than any early tragicomedy here considered, with the exception of *A King and No King*, *A Fair Quarrel* thus looks forward to later Caroline and Restoration practice. In part because the tragicomic situation is so extreme, characters become flatter – almost abstract spokesmen for their dilemmas – and more wholly a product of their rhetoric. Although city types familiar from earlier satiric comedies remain in the 'low' plot, any consistently satiric perspective has gone the way of the early plays' political concerns. This emphasis on good-natured comedy insulates us from the threat of tragedy and makes it more titillating than frightening; the comic plot slides into

---

[15] C. L. Barber, *The Idea of Honour in the English Drama, 1591–1700* (Gothenburg, 1957), pp. 330–6.

'comic relief' and assures us nothing really serious is at stake. Like *The Honest Man's Fortune*, *A Fair Quarrel* leans toward a mixture of the sensational and the sentimental that earlier tragicomedies did not allow to go unexamined. When no obstreperous, farcical perspective is allowed to 'contaminate' the rhetoric and assumed values of the heroic plot, the self-reflexive potential of even juxtaposed scenes shrinks to the less-demanding pleasures of variety offered by a simple alternation of moods. Violations of decorum are corrected, and while in plot terms suspense may remain a goal, the handling of the dramatic materials no longer generates its own internal tensions.

Failures as well as successes dot the dramatic landscape of the early seventeenth century, but the principle of rebellion and reinvention is central. Since theatres were commercial ventures, individual assertion had to find a public voice that would satisfy changing taste and earn an audience. Formal experiments express a generation of writers seeking to define its own voice; these authors were also part of a generation of Englishmen becoming restive, in a larger sense, under the 'forms' – intellectual, social, religious, economic – of its inheritance. The challenge to the idea of literary hierarchies and distinctions among genres had social, political and philosophical implications, and these innovative dramatists by and large found an enthusiastic public. In plays that indirectly explored the breakdown of the absolute authority of the aristocracy (for which heroic conventions and the high rhetorical style had been accepted as a natural expression), they called in question a traditional symbolic ordering of the world that supported rigid social as well as artistic categories.

Bibliography

TEXTS

For the sake of consistency, modern-spelling editions have been used throughout. G. K. Hunter has edited *Antonio and Mellida* (1965) for the Regents Renaissance Drama series and *The Malcontent* (1975) for the Revels Plays; W. Reavley Gair has edited *Antonio's Revenge* (1978) for the Revels. *The Knight of the Burning Pestle* appears in the Revels series, edited by Sheldon P. Zitner (1984); *The Faithful Shepherdess* can be found in C. R. Baskervill's *Elizabethan and Stuart Plays* (1934) and, more recently, edited by Cyrus Hoy (1976), in vol. 3 of the old-spelling standard edition of Beaumont and Fletcher appearing under the general editorship of Fredson Bowers, *The Dramatic Works in the Beaumont and Fletcher Canon* (6 vols. to date). Andrew Gurr has edited *Philaster* (1969) for the Revels series, and Robert K. Turner, Jr, *A King and No King* (1963) for the Regents Renaissance series. *Cymbeline* appears in the Arden Shakespeare series, edited by J. M. Nosworthy (1955). For the New Mermaids, Elizabeth M. Brennan has edited *The Devil's Law-Case* (1975) and R. V. Holdsworth *A Fair Quarrel* (1974).

CRITICISM

Further discussion of the influence of the Inns of Court and the private theatres can be found in Philip J. Finkelpearl, *John Marston of the Middle Temple* (1969); R. A. Foakes, 'Tragedy at the children's theatres after 1600: a challenge to the adult stage', in *Elizabethan Theatre II*, ed. David Galloway (1970); Michael Shapiro, *Children of the Revels* (1977). The New Mermaids, Regents Renaissance, and Revels series all provide extensive discussion of individual plays. In addition to Finkelpearl's book on Marston, other studies of this dramatist include: Anthony Caputi, *John Marston, Satirist* (1961); R. A. Foakes, 'John Marston's fantastical plays: *Antonio and Mellida* and *Antonio's Revenge*', *PQ* 41 (1962); T. F. Wharton, '*The Malcontent* and "dreams, visions, fantasies"', *EIC* 24 (1974); William Babula, 'The avenger and the satirist: John Marston's Malevole', and R. A. Foakes, 'On Marston, *The Malcontent*, and *The Revenger's Tragedy*', both in G. R. Hibbard, ed., *Elizabethan Theatre VI* (1978). Two general surveys of the development of tragicomedy are Frank Humphrey Ristine, *English Tragicomedy* (1910; reprinted, 1963) and David L. Hirst, *Tragicomedy* (1984); other studies, which include discussion of individual plays, can be found in: Eugene M. Waith, *The Pattern of Tragicomedy in Beaumont and Fletcher* (1952); Richard Proudfoot, 'Shakespeare and the new dramatists of the King's Men, 1606–1613', in J. R. Brown and B. Harris, eds., *Later Shakespeare* (1966); Arthur C. Kirsch, *Jacobean Dramatic Perspectives* (1972); G. K. Hunter, 'Italian tragicomedy on the English stage', reprinted in *Dramatic Identities and Cultural Tradition* (1978); R. A. Foakes, 'Tragicomedy and comic form', and Lee Bliss, 'Tragicomic romance for the King's Men, 1609–1611: Shakespeare, Beaumont, and Fletcher', both in A. R. Braunmuller and J. C. Bulman, eds., *Comedy from Shakespeare to Sheridan* (1986). For further discussion of Beaumont and Fletcher, see: Una Ellis-Fermor, *The Jacobean Drama* (1935); John F. Danby, *Poets on Fortune's Hill* (1952); Philip Edwards, 'The danger not the death: the art of John Fletcher', in *Jacobean Theatre*, J. R. Brown and B. Harris, eds. (rev. edn, 1965); Philip J. Finkelpearl, 'Beaumont, Fletcher and "Beaumont & Fletcher": some distinctions', *ELR* 1 (1971); Michael Neill, 'The defense of contraries: skeptical paradox in *A King and No King*', *SEL* 21 (1981); Lee Bliss, 'Defending Fletcher's shepherds', *SEL* 23 (1983), and *Francis Beaumont* (1987). Three books on John Webster that discuss the development of tragicomedy and include chapters on *The Devil's Law-Case* are Jacqueline Pearson's *Tragedy and Tragicomedy in the Plays of John Webster* (1980), Lee Bliss's *The World's Perspective* (1983), and Charles R. Forker's *Skull Beneath the Skin* (1986). Studies of *A Fair Quarrel* can be found in: Samuel Schoenbaum, 'Middleton's tragicomedies', *MP* 54 (1956); Richard Levin, *The Multiple Plot in English Renaissance Drama* (1971); Dorothy M. Farr, *Thomas Middleton and the Drama of Realism* (1973).

8 Comedy

FLOTE'S VOICE Oh, but, oh, a world ruled by seriousness alone is an old world, a grave, a graveyard world. Mirth makes the green sap rise and the wildebeest run mad.

Peter Barnes, *Red Noses* (1985)

Boundaries

AT the start of a lecture on Shakespearian comedy and romance, Northrop Frye finds himself in a minority of critics, 'a somewhat furtive and anonymous group who have not much of a theory, implicit or explicit, to hold them together'.[1] This group has barely changed through the course of literary history. If reticence distinguishes current members, discontinuity has remained an invariable. Specifically, theories about comedy fail to connect not only with one another but with dramatic practice. As a result, no lexicon exists to define comedy in general or the Tudor and Stuart version in particular.

From humanists and puritans to the playwrights themselves, English Renaissance critics sporadically devised generic norms for comedy according to structure, content, and moral import. Most dramatists regularly ignored those norms, as they ignored the norms for tragedy, producing a genre irrepressible in its creative innovation and variety. Four centuries later modern scholarship has attempted to study this unfettered comedy by catching and fixing the plays in an assortment of matrices, paradigms, and systems. Often it categorizes Shakespearian and Jonsonian types, or romantic and satiric comedy. Yet these divisions break down almost at once for the critics who use them, as Madeleine Doran admits immediately after setting up the guide-lines: 'these clear differences in emphasis are seldom maintained in English comedy with any purity'.[2] More promisingly, recent criticism has introduced the image of a spectrum in delineating Renaissance

---

[1] *A Natural Perspective: The Development of Shakespearean Comedy and Romance* (1965), p. 2.

[2] *Endeavors of Art*, p. 150.

comedy as well as other genres. So G. K. Hunter views sixteenth- and seventeenth-century English comedy as 'a spectrum of comic forms running from the dynamic at one end to the static at the other', from farce to romance.[3]

Hunter's flexible concept and vocabulary define comedy in terms of the interaction between plot and character: plot dominates in farce, character in romance. While this terminology allows Renaissance comedy its range and consistencies, it does not fully explain the miscellaneousness of individual plays or the genre as a whole. For that crucial feature modern genre theory supplies helpful descriptive terms: Alastair Fowler describes a genre or 'kind' as 'a type of literary work of a definite size, marked by a complex of substantive and formal features that always include a distinctive (though not usually unique) external structure'. Since the Middle Ages, new genres have been composed from older ones: 'Either the new kind is a transformation of an existing one, or else it is assembled. Assembly, too, uses existing generic materials'. From the post-medieval kinds, Fowler singles out Renaissance comedy for the large repertoire of genres on which it drew:

> It would require a separate book even to outline the assembly of the complex comic repertoire. But it should be plain already that Renaissance dramatists did not lack generic materials. Renaissance comedy was certainly a new kind. But it was not one created out of nothing by Lyly or Shakespeare or Jonson.[4]

The 'external structure' of English Renaissance comedy – the consecutive arrangement of its parts – derived from Roman models as the later age perceived them. In the 1530s humanist commentaries began to influence the way students understood the design of texts by Plautus and Terence; from the middle decades onwards, performances of Italian versions strengthened the impression of a distinct comic form. According to these renderings, comedy is a representation that progresses through time in two orderly sequences at once, a narrative and a rhetorical argument. The narrative moves forward in three phases whose proportions may vary: exposition and beginning of the action, complication of incidents, anastrophe or resolution. Typically this sequence commences with an error which leads to confusion finally dispelled in a happy ending. Meantime a series of debates argues a central question as well as subordinate issues. Renaissance comedy's structure therefore appears coherent from two points of view, however miscellaneous its other features may seem. Both viewpoints give events an ironic

---

[3] 'Comedy, farce, romance', in Braunmuller and Bulman, eds., *Comedy from Shakespeare to Sheridan*, p. 31.

[4] *Kinds of Literature: An Introduction to the Theory of Genres and Modes* (Cambridge, Massachusetts, 1982), pp. 74, 156.

cast, as the audience observes characters whose behaviour indicates misunderstanding of their situations or the matters in question.[5]

This duplex construction could accommodate elements from a wide range of forms literary and non-literary, small and middle-sized. Of course it admitted other components of Latin or Italian-Latin comedies with their type characters and complicated intrigues. During its heyday in the late sixteenth and early seventeenth centuries, it took in whole genres, from romance and satire to sonnet and epigram; it borrowed subgenres or modes; it incorporated theatrical conventions like the court masque; and it continued to admit the traditions of carnival or popular culture. When playwrights like Shakespeare or Jonson used it, Renaissance comedy even made space for native and contemporary dramatic kinds. But its artistic self-consciousness, part of its Roman legacy, remained incidental rather than structural. Comedy of this era thus kept a distance from extensive burlesque. In its inclusiveness and plasticity, it more closely resembled the protean novels of Rabelais and Cervantes.[6] Many generic elements mingled within the host form, the myriad configurations producing a remarkable variety of individual comedies.

Early developments

During the Middle Ages and first half of the sixteenth century in England, most components of Renaissance comedy – even parts of its structure – floated free.[7] Now and then a number of them clustered, as they did in some of the interludes written by members of Sir Thomas More's circle. John

---

[5] In this paragraph on comedic structure and the chapter generally, I have attempted to condense vast quantities of scholarship into lucid explanations. Notes indicate the materials which proved most significant, helpful, or provocative in coming to terms with such a complex genre. Accordingly, Fowler, pp. 60–1, should be cited here for his definition of 'external structure'. Ruth Nevo, *Comic Transformations in Shakespeare* (1980), refers to the tripartite narrative format and concisely documents relevant criticism; Altman, *The Tudor Play of Mind*, offers a thorough discussion of rhetoric's place in Renaissance comedy and other dramatic genres. 'Anastrophe' is Frye's term, pp. 72–3, instead of 'catastrophe', for the conclusion of a comedy.

[6] The similarities become clear in M. M. Bakhtin's analyses of the novel as a genre and the work of Rabelais and Cervantes. See *The Dialogic Imagination: Four Essays*, trans. Caryl Emerson and Michael Holquist, ed. Michael Holquist (Austin, Texas, 1981), and *Rabelais and His World*, trans. Hélène Iswolsky (Bloomington, Indiana, 1984).

[7] Michael Hattaway stresses the variety of these components in Part 1 of *Elizabethan Popular Theatre*, and François Laroque gives an exhaustive account of those deriving from festivals in *Shakespeare et la fête: Essai d'archéologie du spectacle dans l'Angleterre élisabethaine* (Paris, 1988). Both point out how the Elizabethan clown – purveyor of jests and jigs – could produce his comic routine from folk materials. See also Hattaway's chapter on 'Drama and society' in this volume.

Heywood, the best-known playwright in that group of Catholic humanists, produced a small corpus of dramatic works between 1519 and 1533 which together converted debate into comic theatre.

Of the six interludes and late fragment usually attributed to Heywood, probably *The Four P.P.* contains the most diversified mixture of comic ingredients. Characteristically, disputation governs the other elements in this play, its models antique and medieval. Two debates occupy the Palmer, Pardoner, 'Pothecary, and Pedlar; both arise to establish 'mastery' or the relative superiority of the men. In the first debate, each argues his importance by claiming to offer the most expedient means of salvation. In the much longer second, the 'Pothecary and Pardoner engage in a lying match, opposing a fabliau against a short tale. But the Palmer, not an official participant in this contest, wins it unintentionally with a twenty-three-line speech where he insists: 'Of all the women that I have seen,/ I never saw nor knew in my conscience/ Any one woman out of patience' (p. 57).

Richly ironic, these characters contradict themselves in debate: their behaviour fails to accord with their vocations, and mastery has no place in saving human souls. Like the fabliau and tale in the lying match, other forms or genres – flyting, satire, farce – contribute to the irony. Word-play and modulations in the verse enhance these effects, pointing speciousness in the dialogue.

Irony yields to religious faith, however, at the very end of the interlude. After the Palmer gives up his unexpected advantage, the Pedlar declares a stalemate. Yet he proceeds to resolve 'the debate wherewith ye began' (p. 61) through a sermon, which first exposes the debate's inconsistencies and finally leaves judgement of the disputants and issues to the church. The text closes with the Palmer's prayer in rhyme royal, possibly addressed to both court and populace, 'Beseeching our Lord to prosper you all/ In the faith of his Church Universal' (p. 64). At a time of political and religious uncertainty, *The Four P.P.* thus endorses humanist reform and the ideal church as an agent of social harmony.[8]

Between that time and the early 1550s, meagre theatrical records provide almost no substantive evidence of assembly or the influence of Heywood's dramaturgy. Meanwhile comic structure took shape within the academy: grammar schools and both universities performed the comedies of Plautus and Terence; students at every level analysed the structures of these Latin texts. Finally two original plays amplified the Roman models and reintroduced the miscellaneousness that would distinguish Renaissance comedy.

---

[8] Bevington discusses the auspices of *The Four P.P.* in *From 'Mankind'*, pp. 38–9; and he analyses the interlude's political implications in *Tudor Drama*, pp. 70–3.

Their precise dates still undetermined, *Gammer Gurton's Needle* by 'Mr. S., Master of Art' and *Ralph Roister Doister* by Nicholas Udall share first place as English comedies built on Latin frames.

Both plays distribute the tripartite narrative sequence over five acts as Renaissance commentators advised: protasis occupies the first two acts; epitasis the second two; and anastrophe the last. In each case the structure appears sharply outlined, because the unities are observed and every act takes its appointed place in the total format. *Gammer Gurton's Needle*, produced at Christ's College, Cambridge, makes the Terentian format an object of wit; it co-ordinates the plot with a developing scatological motif and with a series of obscene puns drawing upon the original all-male performance. At the same time it renders the debate component absurdly concrete, circling the question of who took a needle with characters who act out their confusion through brawling in literal darkness.[9] Like the composition of *Ralph Roister Doister*, this well-organized structure contains a variety of forms ranging from proverb and flyting to mock-heroic combat. Similarly the dramatis personae incorporate features from a number of classical and native types.

Ralph Roister Doister shows even greater heterogeneity. Written by a schoolmaster for performance by boys, it directs its wit with a difference. Udall borrows a simple action from the sub-plot of Terence's *Eunuchus*, expanding it with all manner of rhetorical, literary, and popular conventions to mock folly from divers angles. For instance, he fills out the narrative with bits and pieces of other Latin plays such as Terence's *Andria* and *Adelphi*, and probably Plautus' *Miles Gloriosus* and *Pseudolus*. In addition he deconstructs an old medieval debate over the ideal lover – soldier or scholar – using the first term as a character and the second as a plot device (i.e., the construing of a mispunctuated letter).

Through a protagonist who combines braggart soldier and wooing knight, Udall burlesques the whole chivalric tradition. With the mispunctuated letter that protests devotion to a lady, he parodies not only conceited ignorance but also a ritual of courtly love. When the lady rejects both missive and protagonist, a battle results which turns chivalric standards upside-down: the knight attacks his mistress's house; he has been armed with a kitchen pail on his head and furnished with other devices linked to the festivities Breughel painted in 'The Battle of Carnival and Lent'. Earlier Roister Doister had enacted his despair by pretending to die and participating in his own funeral,

---

[9] For discussions of the play's artfulness, see R. W. Ingram, '*Gammer Gurton's Needle*: comedy not quite of the lowest order?', *SEL* 7 (1967), 257–68; and J. W. Robinson, 'The art and meaning of *Gammer Gurton's Needle*', *RenD* n.s. 14 (1983), 45–77.

an accurate imitation of Roman Catholic rites.[10] Setting up each bizarre exposure of the protagonist, the character Matthew Merrygreek – like Diccon in *Gammer Gurton's Needle* – functions as classical parasite, medieval Vice, and Renaissance fool.

Udall's comic repertoire includes Chaucer and popular romance; songs, proverbs, and folk-plays; topical references to the middle class and his own life. From this collage a blatantly ironic portrait emerges, a title-character who misunderstands the abstract code on which he acts and the events which his actions generate. Through Merrygreek's comments Udall invites his audience to enjoy the irony and appreciate its moral implications.

Little evidence of such deliberate comic fusion survives the period from mid-sixteenth century until 1583, although Italian comedies imported for academic and court circles show a degree of hybridization. Among these, George Gascoigne's *Supposes* (Gray's Inn, 1566) translates Ariosto's *I Suppositi* (*The Substitutes*). Classically formulated, Ariosto's skilfully wrought intrigue plot – from Plautus' *Captivi* and Terence's *Eunuchus* – arranges its three-part narrative in five acts. When Gascoigne conflated the original texts in his version, he further refined the continuity of the sequence.

As a result, *Supposes* elegantly portrays a love-relationship obstructed by troublesome fathers. A young man gains secret access to his mistress by changing places with his servant, *'The first suppose and ground of all the supposes'* (1.1.111). With three fathers on the scene in the fourth and fifth acts, parents of the lovers and servants, complications intensify until 'a man might make a comedy of it' (5.7.55–6). At last the dénouement reveals true identities, unites the lovers, and reconciles their fathers.

Gascoigne emphasizes the dialectic of this plot in the 1575 edition, where he first defines and then annotates the 'supposes' which propel the action. According to 'The Prologue or Argument', 'our Suppose is nothing else but a mistaking or imagination of one thing for another' (14–16). The notes identify twenty-five supposes, which grow more and more concentrated with the intricate tangle of the epitasis. In their context, the play becomes an enactment of *dianoia*: 'that ongoing process of reasoning and problem-solving which the commentators suggest is the action of comedy'.[11]

Ariosto had set this double-edged intrigue in contemporary Ferrara,

---

[10] On the parodic components of *Ralph Roister Doister*, see especially Plumstead, 'Satirical parody in *Roister Doister*'. Michael D. Bristol describes images of carnival and Breughel's painting in a way that throws light on the two comedies (*Carnival and Theater*, p. 67).

[11] See Altman, *The Tudor Play of Mind*, p. 139, n. 16 and pp. 157–61. Shakespeare would make use of both action and dialectic from *Supposes* in the sub-plot of *The Taming of the Shrew*.

where its first performance took place in 1509. If the Italian playwright brought Roman comedy up to date, Gascoigne Anglicized its tone with standard jokes, word-play, and balanced prose anticipating Lyly's. The characters in *Supposes* quibble on hanging, cuckoldry, and related topics:

CLEANDER I perceive you are no very good Bibler, Pasiphilo.
PASIPHILO Yes, sir, an excellent good bibbler, specially in a bottle. (1.2.37–40)

Throughout the dialogue, conspicuously rhetorical passages sound euphuistic. So the disguised lover, Erostrato, laments his situation early in the comedy:

But, alas, I find that only love is unsatiable: for, as the fly playeth with the flame till at last she is cause of her own decay, so the lover that thinketh with kissing and colling to content his unbridled appetite, is commonly seen the only cause of his own consumption. (1.3.81–6)

Appropriation

The annals of English drama between Udall and Lyly disclose little about genres; many titles of lost plays – and the probability of lost titles – frustrate attempts to classify or estimate the number of comedies in different venues. While these uneven records imply that three to four dozen comedies may have appeared at court, the universities, and the Inns of Court, published attacks on the theatre after 1576 indicate the genre's popularity elsewhere. In his pamphlet *Plays Confuted in Five Actions* (1582), for example, Stephen Gosson declares: 'I may boldly say it, because I have seen it, that … bawdy comedies in Latin, French, Italian, and Spanish, have been thoroughly ransacked to furnish the playhouses in London'.[12] Together this evidence gives the impression of a genre gaining favour with all social classes. By the mid-1580s comedy poised before its giddy ascent in the Elizabethan/Jacobean theatre, where it would finally surpass tragedy by a ratio of three to one.

John Lyly heralds this change in his occasional theory and his practice, exemplifying the kind of paradox which has become the hallmark of his work. Sometimes his prologues acknowledge a new audience of mixed character and taste demanding the extension of generic limits: 'what heretofore hath been served in several dishes for a feast, is now minced in a charger for a gallimaufry' (Prologue to *Midas*, 17–19). More than once Lyly claims politely to exceed the bounds himself: 'If we present a mingle-mangle, our fault is to be excused, because the whole world is become an hodgepodge'

---

[12] Modernized from the quotation in F. P. Wilson, *The English Drama: 1485–1585*, pp. 118–19.

(Prologue to *Midas*, 19–20).[13] Yet his eight plays, written for boys to act at court and in private theatres, clearly belong to the province of comedy distinguished by wit.

Endymion, performed at court on Candlemas night, *c.*1587/88, remains Lyly's most elaborate and well-known comedy. Modelling external structure to new effect, the dramatist assembles within it an intricate comic repertoire for his aristocratic audience. Here the Prologue rejects dramatic kinds in favour of unrestrained fancy: 'We present neither comedy, nor tragedy, nor story, nor anything, but that whosoever heareth may say this: Why, here is a tale of the Man in the Moon' (9–11). But the text which follows brilliantly reworks the neo-classical sequence to emphasize contradictions in theme, character, and reality at large. Although exposition follows the rules and occupies the first two acts, it presents Endymion's love-conflict in oblique allegorical terms which the audience must decipher. Moreover, the protagonist does not enact the complications which ensue in Acts 3 and 4: he sleeps while other characters deal with the consequences. During the fifth-act dénouement, a restored Endymion stands alone and silent for more than eighty lines among a group of odd couples.

Lyly has forced a gap between the inherent logic of comic format and the events of his play. As the dramatic narrative advances the gap widens, because the main action is reflected in a number of other plots and episodes. Endymion's unrequited love for Cynthia appears in four other versions, including a burlesque: Eumenides' for Semele; Corsites' for Tellus; Tellus' for Endymion; and Sir Tophas', 'a foolish braggart's', for Dipsas, 'an old enchantress' (Dramatis Personae, p. 19). Under the stress of passion, both Corsites and Sir Tophas fall asleep; Sir Tophas' dream corresponds with Endymion's.[14]

Complicating his art-form through dissonance, multiplication, and symmetry, Lyly makes it represent a basic paradox of human experience: the coexistence of order with arbitrariness, reason with illogic. It also represents more specifically the contradictions of court life and values. A court entertainment, *Endymion* was presented before Queen Elizabeth on a religious feast-day which celebrated aspiration to purity and wisdom. In three distinct phases of debate which accompany the three phases of action, this theatrical piece argues coterie issues in what was originally a spiritual con-

---

[13] Robert Weimann has recently studied the implications of these lines from the Prologue to *Midas* in 'History and the issue of authority in representation: the Elizabethan theater and the Reformation', *NLH* 17 (1986), 449–76.

[14] On Lyly's 'analogous action' and its use in later plays, see A. R. Braunmuller's 'The arts of the dramatist' in this volume.

text: 'What kind of relationship must the Courtier have with his sovereign? Should love or friendship bear the greater sway in determining men's actions? What constitutes royal justice?'[15] Like the narrative, this debate ends on a note of ambivalence.

In order to build his frame, Lyly used three accounts of the *Endymion* myth: the handsome shepherd loved by the moon (related by poets and fabulists); the sleeper (analysed by philosophers); and the astronomer rumoured to love the moon (described by Pliny). He consulted Ovid's *Metamorphoses* and *Heroides*, Cicero's *Tusculan Disputations*, Castiglione's *Courtier*, and Marc Antonio Epicuro's *Mirzia* (an Italian pastoral drama published in 1582). Among its furnishings, this complicated structure displays elements from many other literary and dramatic kinds: romance in Eumenides' adventures and Dipsas' evil enchantment; psychomachia, or allegorized conflict of the soul, in Eumenides' encounter with Geron at the fountain; masque in its spectacle, music, and complimentary vision of Queen Elizabeth; Petrarchan sonnets throughout the lovers' speeches. Moreover, four types of allegory – physical, court, Neoplatonic, and Christian – permeate the whole work. For Sir Tophas alone Lyly borrowed Chaucer's knight from *The Canterbury Tales*, the *miles gloriosus* from Latin comedy, the *capitano millantatore* and *pedante* of Renaissance Italian comic drama.[16]

Patterns of correspondence and antithesis link characters, scenes, and ideas; and these devices allow Lyly's prose – in fiction as well as drama – to analyse complex subjects clearly and logically.[17] In *Endymion* a key matter for debate is the experience of love, and dialogue breaks it down most strikingly by echoing the hero's discourse in the key of burlesque. This strategy begins with the first two acts, when Endymion expresses his feelings at length in a highly wrought style. Through one soliloquy, for instance, he projects the self-image of Petrarchan lover with traditional conceits and rhetoric:

Sweet Cynthia, how wouldst thou be pleased, how possessed? ... Desirest thou the passions of love, the sad and melancholy moods of perplexed minds, the not-to-be expressed torments of racked thoughts? Behold my sad tears, my deep sighs, my hollow eyes, my broken sleeps, my heavy countenance. (2.1.4–12)

A few moments later the pages anatomize these symptoms, reducing them through literalism and word-play:

DARES Come, Samias, diddest thou ever hear such a sighing ... for moonshine in the

---

15 Altman, *The Tudor Play of Mind*, p. 216.
16 For helpful studies about the background and meaning of *Endymion*, see Hunter, *John Lyly*, pp. 184–94; Saccio, *The Court Comedies of John Lyly*, pp. 169–86; and Susan D. Thomas, '*Endimion* and its sources', *CL* 30 (1978), 35–52.
17 A seminal analysis of Lyly's technique is Barish's article 'The prose style of John Lyly'.

water? ... How say you, Favilla, is not love a lurcher, that taketh men's stomachs away that they cannot eat, their spleen that they cannot laugh, their hearts that they cannot fight, their eyes that they cannot sleep, and leaveth nothing but livers to make nothing but lovers?   (2.2.1–13)

Verbally deflated at once, Endymion's aspiring love both sounds and looks farcical later in Sir Tophas' rendition:

love hath, as it were, milked my thoughts and drained from my heart the very substance of my accustomed courage; it worketh in my head like new wine, so as I must hoop my sconce with iron, lest my head break, and so I bewray my brains. But I pray thee, first discover me in all parts, that I may be like a lover, and then will I sigh and die. Take my gun and give me a gown: *Cedant arma togæ*.   (3.3.23–9)

As the echoes make an abstract concept progressively more concrete, they expose its potential absurdity. At the same time they direct that absurdity away from the central character, leaving him with most of his dignity intact.

Innovations like these in style, content, and-form mark Lyly's influence on dramatic comedy until the end of the English Renaissance. With other plays in the comic mode – Peele's *Arraignment of Paris*, Greene's *Friar Bacon and Friar Bungay*, the anonymous *Fair Em* – his theatrical work established love between the sexes as a theme for the stage. When Shakespeare explored the subject during the 1590s in comedies from *Love's Labour's Lost* to *Twelfth Night*, he made Lyly's techniques part of his comic repertoire. Jacobean playwrights would examine romantic love with blunter instruments.

Meantime comedy engaged in other experiments. Between 1590 and 1604, for instance, a small group of plays adopted whole plots from Plautus and Terence. They include Shakespeare's *Comedy of Errors* (c. 1590–3) and Chapman's *All Fools* (c. 1599–1601), comedies which manipulate their originals to heighten romance and satire.

Apparently *The Comedy of Errors* was performed first at Gray's Inn and ten years later at court, both times as part of Christmas festivities. The dramatist's awareness of audience and occasion may have inspired his sophisticated assembly of classical sources. Like some late-Renaissance Italian comedies, Shakespeare's early work practises multiple *contaminatio*: it merges two plots (a method advocated by Terence in *Andria*), complicating them and still maintaining the unities.[18] The young playwright drew his intrigue from Plautus' *Menaechmi*, a text well under twelve hundred lines. Filling it out for Elizabethan performance, he elaborated the Roman plot and

---

[18] On the influence of audience and occasion, see Catherine M. Shaw, 'The conscious art of *The Comedy of Errors*', in Maurice Charney, *Shakespearean Comedy*, pp. 17–28; on this Italian connection and the technique, see Louise George Clubb, 'Shakespeare's comedy and late cinquecento mixed genres', in Charney, *Shakespearean Comedy*, pp. 129–39.

characters. Plautus based his action on the mistaken identities of a pair of twins, one accompanied by an unnamed wife; Shakespeare doubles the twins by adding a pair of identical servants, makes the wife prominent in the action, and gives her an unmarried sister as confidante. Moreover Shakespeare's version incorporates material from Plautus' *Amphitruo* for Act 3, scene 1, the pivotal scene where the wife, Adriana, feasts the twin she mistakes for her husband.

By doubling the twins, Shakespeare adds not only symmetry but scope for confusion. Plautus depended on errors of cognition or identity to advance his plot; Shakespeare introduces numerous errors of association – wrongly attributed actions to rightly identified characters – with the set of twin Dromios.[19] The servants also contribute an element of burlesque, re-enacting their masters' bewilderment at a farcical level and commenting on the play's serious issues in parodic terms. Since *The Comedy of Errors* represents identity as both appearance and selfhood, it raises many questions about the ways individuals define themselves through social bonds. The entire play discourses on this theme as characters struggle with bizarre situations.[20] At points the questions actually become subjects for debate: Adriana and her sister, Luciana, argue the appropriate roles of husband and wife in marriage (2.1); Antipholus of Ephesus and Balthasar, a merchant, different aspects of hospitality (3.1); Antipholus of Syracuse and Dromio of Syracuse, the importance of timeliness in social behaviour (2.2). When the latter match ends, Antipholus of Syracuse indicates that Dromio's argument mocks the whole process of disputation: 'You would all this time have proved, there is no time for all things' (99–100).

As Shakespeare adapted Plautus' comic drama, he intensified its romance as well as its intrigue. In Latin comedy the long separations, adventures, and reunions of families had come ultimately from Hellenic romance. Elizabethan audiences were familiar with such events from countless Greek, medieval, and Renaissance romances and their offshoots. Exploiting romance's sentiment and fortuitousness, Shakespeare framed the separation–adventure–reunion sequence from Plautus with the story of Egeon and Emilia. The tribulations of this couple probably come from John Gower's narrative about Apollonius of Tyre in the *Confessio Amantis*. While this action

---

[19] Timothy Long differentiates these two kinds of errors in 'The calculus of confusion: cognitive and associative errors in Plautus's *Menaechmi* and Shakespeare's *Comedy of Errors*', *Classical Bulletin* 53 (1976), 20–3.

[20] See R. A. Foakes's Introduction to his Arden edition, pp. xliii–xlix; Alexander Leggatt, *Shakespeare's Comedy of Love* (1974), chapter 1; and Altman, *The Tudor Play of Mind*, pp. 165–74.

resolves the plot's discords through the agency of Emilia as Abbess, it also demonstrates an alternative set of social values. An idealized marriage contrasts the materialistic views central to the main plot; moral and ethical concerns displace legalistic and commercial preoccupations; and a gossips' feast transforms the chaos of Adriana's banquet to harmony.

Analysing the total comedy, Harold Brooks concludes that about 750 of its approximately 1,750 lines promote the intrigue; about 300 serve comic rhetoric; the remainder develop romance features. *The Comedy of Errors* thus contains the genre of romance within that of comedy, the whole organized by wit, informed by irony, and tailored to meet theatrical expectations. Different types of verse counterpointed with prose simultaneously emphasize the characters' failure to communicate with one another and distinguish various strata of the intrigue. Yet audiences rarely see the 'Shakespearean palimpsest' which results, because production since the eighteenth century has tended to stress broad humour at the expense of subtler qualities.[21]

George Chapman's *All Fools* suffers from neglect rather than high spirits, a fate it shares with his seven other comedies. During the late-Elizabethan age, however, it seems to have enjoyed success in three kinds of theatrical settings: the Rose, the Blackfriars, and court. Evidently the polish of its form attracted spectators with different backgrounds and tastes. A result of *contaminatio*, the highly finished dramatic narrative meshes three short plays by Terence. The main intrigue and a variety of situations come from the *Heautontimoroumenos*, along with a basic premise: a deceiver can use truth as a means to his end. From *Adelphi* Chapman selected character traits for his principal figures, and from *Eunuchus* he took a few incidents and passages. Primarily he owes Terence the traditional comic paradigm of father and son in conflict over love, a model which appears twice in *Heautontimoroumenos*.

While the central plot edges forward in a series of convoluted intrigues, Chapman's invented sub-plot follows a slightly less intricate course and broadens the play's satire. In the principal action deceits converge on the covetous Sir Gostanzo, a 'rustic machiavel', through the machinations of Rinaldo, a 'university wit'.[22] Gostanzo's rakish son, Valerio, has married against the old man's wishes, and through Rinaldo contrives to keep both his bride and his inheritance. Meanwhile Rinaldo's brother, Fortunio, pursues Gostanzo's daughter with similar objectives and devices. As Rinaldo

[21] Harold Brooks, 'Themes and structure in "The Comedy of Errors"', in John Russell Brown and Bernard Harris, eds., *Early Shakespeare*, Stratford-upon-Avon Studies 3 (1961), p. 69. Shaw, 'The conscious art', p. 26, describes the play as 'a Shakespearean palimpsest'.

[22] Altman's epithets, *The Tudor Play of Mind*, p. 175.

manipulates Gostanzo into absurd schemes for which the victim takes credit, Gostanzo eagerly participates in his own gulling. With the secondary action this process goes into reverse and emphasizes the ubiquity of fools. Rinaldo arranges stratagems to trick Cornelio, a jealous humour-figure obsessed with fear of cuckoldry. Just as his plans culminate and both plots meet in the fifth act, Cornelio outwits Rinaldo in front of all the other characters. Each of the major ruses (in 4.1 and 5.2) turns on the revelation of truth.

Earning its title from the holiday, *All Fools* exposes folly at large in a society growing commercial, opportunistic, and self-centred. It makes its point not only through complex plotting but also through debate, set speeches, and occasional parodies. In both verse and prose it regularly criticizes women (1.1, 3.1, 5.2). Some passages mock literary styles, imitations of Lyly (3.1.195–9), and the vogue for 'comical satire' (2.1.336–49, 5.2.46–7). Just before the dénouement, corresponding soliloquies by Rinaldo and Cornelio sum up the follies which constitute the play. Emblematically the scene itself occurs in a tavern, a place of revelry where (as Valerio says) 'there are no degrees/ Of order' (5.2.61–2). At its conclusion, Valerio caps the play's running mock-argument – the characters' rationalizations for their mad behaviour – with the ultimate irrationality: a panegyric on 'this present age, which we term the horned age' (227–8). Chapman's Prologue and Epilogue make the cuckolded age include the audience. Finally, that is, he presents Terence from a Horatian point of view.[23]

Chapman exemplifies not only the handful of dramatists who imitated Plautus and Terence, but also the larger group who offered the gallimaufry that Lyly had defended. Over several decades bridging the two centuries, many writers produced eclectic comedies from various literary and non-literary conventions. Creating their own models, they built the tripartite frame out of divers materials.

Chapman's *Gentleman Usher* illustrates this type of comedy, in this instance exploiting the resources and catering to the audience at the Black-friars. Its main action stems from the rivalry between Duke Alphonso and Prince Vincentio, his son, over the lovely young Margaret. Although its source is unknown, this plot has familiar antecedents in classical and Renaissance drama. The sub-plot relates the story of Strozza, Vincentio's loyal friend, whose adventures lead him through an epiphany. Giving the play its philosophic implications, this narrative comes from a medical treatise that

---

[23] On the satire in *All Fools*, see Frank Manley's Introduction to his Regents Renaissance Drama edition (Lincoln, Nebraska, 1968) and David C. McPherson, 'Chapman's adaptations of New Comedy', *EM* 19 (1968), 51–64.

shades into Christian Platonism.[24] As the plots unfold side by side, Chapman dramatizes a Platonic hierarchy of love with Alphonso's unnatural desire at the bottom and Strozza's heavenly vision at the top. Often the action pauses for rituals that comment symbolically on this theme. Devised for a children's company to perform, *The Gentleman Usher* embellishes both action and rituals with music, dance, and visual displays. The pattern of exposition, complication, anastrophe barely contains these elaborate components.

Within that pattern an unusual design takes form. A series of shows, or stylized performances within the play, begins in the opening scene. After a brief but formal reading of terrible poetry and the ridiculous enactment of three lines from Plautus' *Curculio*, numerous characters prepare to rehearse a pageant. The pageant with its music and spectacle occupies the second scene, enacting Alphonso's amorous suit to Margaret. When this scene ends, another readies the stage for the show that fills Act 2, scene 2. Now the performers deliver Alphonso's message in rough but explicit verse: 'Thus Lady and Duchess we conclude,/ Fair virgins must not be too rude:/ ... / Yet take you in your ivory clutches/ This noble Duke, and be his Duchess' (2.2.112–17).

Both longer shows misrepresent rituals: the first distorts features from medieval spring fertility games; the second, May-game tradition.[25] With other elements of mimesis in the first two acts, they invite the audience to recognize and interpret allegorical representations later in the comedy. As a result the third-act gulling of Bassiolo, the foolish gentleman usher, shows its connections with misrule or topsy-turvydom. In the fourth and fifth acts, rituals attending the marriage of Vincentio and Margaret, the visionary experience of Strozza, and the curing of Margaret's deformity all carry symbolic weight. These ceremonies emphasize miraculous recovery and renewal in the pattern of events, implying that the harmony restored at last to Alphonso's court emanates from a higher order. Like Lyly, Chapman has led his audience to decipher a complex allegorical narrative.

Obviously *The Gentleman Usher* gives ample space to other genres and modes within its comic structure. Folk-drama coexists with masque, allegory with medical tract. For details of characterization Chapman borrowed from classical, Italian, and English Renaissance comedy (including his own). Like significant episodes in the sub-plot and the heroine's marvellous restoration,

---

[24] For an account of this source, see John Hazel Smith's Regents Renaissance Drama edition of *The Gentleman Usher* (Lincoln, Nebraska, 1970), Introduction, pp. xvii–xx and appendix A.

[25] See Henry M. Weidner, 'The dramatic uses of Homeric idealism: the significance of theme and design in Chapman's *The Gentleman Usher*', *ELH* 28 (1961), 121–36.

some of the dramatis personae originate in romance. Towards the end dangers and injuries threaten the comic form, straining it with the contradictions of tragicomedy. Finally the play settles into its genre, its eclecticism conveying the contraries of Chapman's own nature: idealist/cynic, classicist/romantic, conformist/iconoclast.[26]

Not all comic medleys are so serious or complicated. Between 1595 and 1605, for example, about half a dozen plays set lively intrigues in the English countryside. Like *Gammer Gurton's Needle*, these 'nocturnal' comedies grow more and more perplexed in literal darkness. Their broad ironies result from violations of middle-class domestic or community norms, and from their assembling of popular elements within the comic structure.

Among these plays, Henry Porter's *Two Angry Women of Abington* (Admiral's Men, *c.*1598) won public success and commissions for two sequels. The intrigue seems an original variation on the classical formula: obstreperous mothers interfere with the courtship of their children. But the play begins with the community rather than the lovers. Centring on a visit between neighbours, the exposition shows how the women's anger disrupts what had been two perfectly balanced family groups: Master Goursey and his wife; Master Barnes and his wife; their sons Frank Goursey and Phillip Barnes; their servants Dick Coomes and Nicholas Proverbs. In order to restore peace, Master Barnes plans the marriage of his daughter, Mall, to Frank, inadvertently launching the complications. Half-way through the action the lovers agree to marry, and the rest of the plot develops from the machinations to unite them by deceiving their mothers. At the turning-point characters start to enter the wood, which becomes increasingly dark as a metaphor of their confusion. Finally the sun rises on the anastrophe, a scene of betrothal and reconciliation. Porter has observed the unity of time, sometimes neglecting consistencies of place and action.

Throughout the play characters argue the meaning of authority and the value of social ties, defining key issues through comic intrigue. Meanwhile the two family servants reflect the absurdity of events in their behaviour, idiosyncrasies which Porter devised from popular tradition and drama. Coomes represents a theatrical fashion, the one-dimensional or humour-figure whose readiness to quarrel motivates everything he says and does. A more novel creation, Proverbs can express himself only through maxims – ninety-eight of the approximately 150 in the play – which generally come from oral tradition. His speeches parody the remaining aphorisms in the text

---

[26] Kreider surveys the background of Chapman's characters in *Elizabethan Comic Character Conventions* and Samuel Schoenbaum defines the contraries in '*The Widow's Tears* and the other Chapman', *HLQ* 23 (1960), 338.

which sum up a moral code, and at the same time they burlesque the wide-spread use of proverbs in contemporary literature and drama. In similar ways Porter gently deflates other literary conventions: romance with the realism of local places and customs, satire with the boisterousness of farce. His prose and blank verse, imitating the accents of ordinary discourse, check any potential lyricism.

Another nocturnal comedy written shortly after Porter's, the anonymous *Merry Devil of Edmonton* also pleased a large audience. According to its 1608 title-page, 'it hath been sundry times acted, by his Majesty's Servants, at the Globe'; Jonson called it 'Your dear delight, "The Devil of Edmonton"' in the Prologue to *The Devil Is an Ass* (1616); and it went through five reprint-ings in the first half of the seventeenth century. On the whole it too derives from popular tradition, literature, and theatre.

The dramatist created part of the intrigue for his main action from a chapter in the prose pamphlet *The Famous History of Friar Bacon* (first extant edition 1627, but apparently known to Greene *c.*1590); his title, Induction, and some details come from the legend of magician Peter Fabel; and the account of harrowing spirits in 4.2 originates in a jest. At the heart of the intrigue he invented the tale of Millicent Clare and Raymond Mounchensey, two young lovers thwarted by her parents for his lack of substantial revenues. Despite its variety, this hodgepodge of materials assumes the familiar comic form. The play immediately establishes the conflict between generations, and Fabel begins to direct the lovers' action by the third scene. Meantime a sub-plot takes shape among four citizens who plan 'to steal some of the king's deer' (2.1.53). Of course one breach of propriety calls attention to the other since covetousness plays a role in both actions. Yet high jinks set the tone as the two plots unwind together, becoming intertwisted during the night and finally resolved by morning. Like Porter, the anonymous playwright observes the unity of time.

Set *c.*1500 in the countryside north of London – Enfield, Waltham, Cheston – *The Merry Devil of Edmonton* incorporates stories connected with its locales and families. But this nocturnal makes romance elements notice-able with a Prologue and Induction that feature magic or sleights. In a burlesque of Marlowe's *Doctor Faustus*, Act 5, Fabel outwits the spirit Coreb and gains seven more years of life. As he embarks on this span, he steps into the action proper to manipulate events through disguises and tricks. At several points he and other characters anticipate or review events not only for one another but for the audience. Their workaday blank verse ensures clarity and, with the prose of the sub-plot, voices the play's argument: ''tis in vain to cross the providence' (5.1.260), or to disregard those values that order and enrich social life.[27] Although its diction frequently echoes contemporary drama, Shakespeare's in particular, *The Merry Devil of Edmonton* parodies theatrical and literary styles less often than *The Two Angry Women of Abington*.

Within a decade or so of *The Merry Devil of Edmonton*, 'his Majesty's Servants' began to act at the Blackfriars theatre (*c.*1609/1610). John Fletcher helped to provide them with comedy polished for a sophisticated audience; he developed a comic eclecticism so refined that it gives the impression of homogeneity. At times he reduces a number of sources to fragments for building new plots; or he converts different models into recognizably parodic versions of themselves. Always he elaborates the comic narrative through other genres and modes. However diverse these materials, he consolidates them by means of a comic structure which subsumes the generic repertoire into an elegant symmetry.

The Wild Goose Chase was performed by the King's Men at court in the Christmas season 1621/22 and probably in public some time earlier. Illustrating Fletcher's mature style, it delighted not only the Jacobean audience but Fletcher himself, as two actors from the original production testify in their Dedication to the published script: 'The play was of so general a received acceptance, that (he himself a spectator) we have known him ..., he as well as the thronged theatre (in despite of his innate modesty), applauding this rare issue of his brain' (p. 242). The rareness of the issue is its form.

Fletcher invented two intrigues for this comedy, both involving sexual pursuits. In the main chase Oriana tries to capture her betrothed Mirabel, 'the wild goose, a travelled *monsieur* and great defier of all ladies in the way of marriage, otherwise their much loose servant' (p. 249). In the sub-plot Belleur and Pinac, Mirabel's travelling companions, attempt to woo Rosalura and Lillia-Bianca, beautiful sisters. Both actions, set in Paris, generate stratagems primarily to trap Mirabel and test his friends' sincerity and perception.

After the exposition has sorted out the three couples, each intrigue evolves as a series of performances within the play. The secondary plot establishes the pattern in Act 2, scene 2, when Lillia-Bianca – ordinarily a serious student – dances and entertains Pinac until she has worn him out. Once Lillia-Bianca has baffled her suitor, in Act 2, scene 3 Rosalura – ordinarily sociable and plain-spoken – delivers a satiric attack on men who travel which dumbfounds Belleur. Mirabel encourages both companions to retaliate for

---

[27] Bristol, *Carnival and Theater*, pp. 167–72, discusses the play's treatment of authority in relation to social values.

his own sport: 'Wooing and wiving, hang it: give me mirth,/ Witty and dainty mirth' (3.1.312–13); and immediately he becomes unwitting spectator to the first of Oriana's shows. For this relatively simple playlet her brother, De Gard, pretends to be a noble suitor threatening offenders of her reputation. Mirabel regrets the loss of Oriana in a speech quickly interrupted by a servant who reveals the trick.

None of these scenarios ends decisively; each results in confusion and disappointment for the players or their audience. During the fourth act three more inconclusive shows counterpoint one another until the finale, which occupies most of the fifth act and involves all of the major characters. Oriana plays the part of a wealthy Italian lady bequeathed by her brother to Mirabel, who is caught this time with the lure of a fortune. As this ruse reaches its climax the other couples agree to marry, and Fletcher completes his portrayal of courtship as an intricate network of love and deceit. From the start his participants in the chase have discussed and enacted this paradoxical view. The symmetry of their pursuits implies a certain grace and continuity in the process of wooing, but constant play-acting qualifies the compliment. The characters' changing faces, their anticlimactic performances, and the persistent sense of opposition suggest the unpredictability of individual hearts and therefore of sexual relationships. Appropriately the closing lines, spoken by the men, express these contradictions – social and psychological – in a promise of union and a *double entendre*:

> MIRABEL
> This wild goose chase is done, we have won o' both sides.
> Brother, your love, and now to church of all hands –
> Let's lose no time.
>
> PINAC
>   Our travelling, lay by.
>
> BELLEUR
> No more for Italy; for the Low Countries, I.   (5.6.105–8)

With characteristic variety Fletcher incorporates other generic elements in this comedy. Performances within the play borrow from ritual, mumming, disguising, masque, and tragicomedy. Through Oriana's name and situation the dramatist adds features of chivalric romance which the context inverts ironically; and he may also refer to an Italian intrigue comedy (Giambattista Della Porta's *Il moro* [1607]), the cult of Oriana/Queen Elizabeth, and earlier Beaumont and Fletcher plays. Characters defend their (im)moral postures with rhetorical devices and satiric thrust. Yet this diversity went unremarked by Fletcher's admirers, whereas his 'comic geometry', accomplished with wit and flexible blank verse, impressed his audience and lasted as a model into the Restoration.[28]

Rule a Wife and Have a Wife, licensed and performed at court late in 1624, also remained popular for similar reasons. In its composition Fletcher seems to have fused two Spanish novels: Cervantes' *El Casamiento engañoso* became the sub-plot, and probably Salas Barbadillo's *El sagaz Estacio* served the main one. The principal action, in which a husband subdues his intemperate wife, shows as well the influence of Shakespeare's *Taming of the Shrew* (which Fletcher had reworked *c.*1610 in *The Woman's Prize*, another comedy).

Hastening through two courtships to two marriages, *Rule a Wife and Have a Wife* focuses on deceptions between wedded couples. In both relationships each partner intends to exploit the other for material gain or, in one case, means to conceal sexual indulgence. In each situation one partner assumes mastery through superior wit. Two sequences of intrigues result from the contests, which counterpoint each other like the actions in *The Wild Goose Chase*. Again Fletcher transforms deceit to art, but he synchronizes the coincidences of plot even more precisely in the later work.

This comedy balances a gentleman husband who outwits his heiress wife against a maidservant wife who outwits her soldier husband. Once it has established the character notes of the heiress, Donna Margarita, and the copper captain, Michael Perez, these two victims discover the real natures of their spouses – a full act later than the audience – in corresponding scenes (3.4 and 3.5). When the play ends, they will surrender consecutively (5.3 and 5.4). As Richard Levin points out, another equation connects the victors, Leon and Estifania: 'they both succeed in duping their prospective mates by misrepresenting themselves, outface them when the deception is revealed, force them to surrender, and then relent somewhat for a harmonious resolution'.[29] In *The Wild Goose Chase* Fletcher's calculations supported his working hypothesis about the paradoxes of courtship; here they corroborate a proposition about the contrarieties of marriage.

Moreover a third and farcical action parallels the other two plots in *Rule a Wife and Have a Wife*, emphasizing that dupes outnumber wits in the domain of this play. Episodes involving Cacafogo, a foolish usurer, heighten the folly and mercenary interests which inform the rest of the action. As a result satire enters this comedy, sustained in passages on lawyers and governors specifi-

---

[28] Rota Herzberg Lister gives the fullest discussion of this comedy's background in the Introduction to her critical edition of *The Wild Goose Chase* (1980); Cyrus Hoy coins the phrase 'comic geometry' as he considers the play in 'Fletcherian romantic comedy', *RORD* 27 (1984), 9.

[29] *The Multiple Plot*, p. 52.

cally, humours and women in general. But satire does not exclude other genres or forms; comedy admits masque, declamation, even the fleeting moment of romance. With supple blank verse and typical éclat, Fletcher again creates the effect of unity from miscellaneousness.

Urban designs

Porter's eclectic *Two Angry Women of Abington* belongs to a group of plays which Alexander Leggatt defines as 'citizen comedy' in his book on this facet of English Renaissance drama. From the 1590s until *c.*1610 these comedies about the middle class dealt with contemporary social issues in contemporary social milieux: 'the action is often stylized, but the settings are prosaic and familiar – streets, shops, private houses'.[30] Sparse during the first decade, citizen comedy proliferated during the second in the form Brian Gibbons describes as 'Jacobean city comedy'. Gibbons distinguishes plays of this type 'by their critical and satiric design, their urban settings, their exclusion of material appropriate to romance, fairy-tale, sentimental legend or patriotic chronicle'.[31]

In effect a new comic style emerged at the turn of the century, satirizing urban life by sharply focusing its preoccupations with finance, power, and (inevitably) sex. Topical discourse became a notable part of the generic repertoire, and the genre became part of the Jacobean dialogue about disturbing cultural changes. As it took shape, city comedy attracted some outstanding playwrights: Ben Jonson, John Marston, Thomas Middleton. Once established between 1604 and 1607, it generated many 'hurried imitations and adaptations' which testify to its popular success.[32] During its prime it appeared in public and private theatres, and at court.

Jonson not only shaped city comedy in its initial phase but continued to experiment with it throughout his career. At the start, *Every Man in his Humour* helped to establish the form and launched his profession as dramatist. Though he had already written other plays, Jonson considered this comedy his début: it stands at the head of his folio or collected *Workes*, and in its dedication there he calls it 'of the fruits, the first' (11). He revised this early play between its first printing in quarto (1601) and its second in folio (1616), the two versions indicating how his view of city comedy matured along with his art. Modifications add coherence to the plot, characters, and argument of

---

[30] *Citizen Comedy*, p. 4.
[31] *Jacobean City Comedy*, p. 11.
[32] Gibbons, *Jacobean City Comedy*, p. 102. For other discussions of city comedy, see Leinwand, *The City Staged* and Paster, *The Idea of the City*, chapters 6 and 7.

Every Man in his Humour. Most important, the experienced dramatist relocates the play in London.

Originally performed by the Lord Chamberlain's Men (with Shakespeare, Burbage, and Kempe in the cast), *Every Man in his Humour* premièred successfully in 1598, became part of the company's repertory, and played at court in 1605. But Jonson did not cater to popular tastes at the Curtain or Globe; instead he presented a new type of comedy assembled from existing generic materials. It seems that he composed this play from a number of models rather than particular sources: Latin comedy, satire, moral interludes, and the idiosyncratic or 'humour' characters in Chapman's *An Humorous Day's Mirth* (1597). He combined elements from each in a format which both reflects and departs from the classical precepts he espoused. In his Prologue to the folio edition, a famous passage states the essential components and purpose of this new comedy:

> deeds, and language, such as men do use:
> And persons, such as Comedy would choose,
> When she would show an image of the times,
> And sport with human follies, not with crimes. (21–4)

Distinguishing the subject of city comedy from Gascoigne's supposes and Shakespeare's errors, the next lines identify follies specifically as 'Our popular errors' (26).

Both versions of *Every Man in his Humour* use Latin comedy as a frame, borrowing the familiar narrative sequence of father–son conflict mediated by a subordinate. Yet this situation immediately connects with several others – the gulling of assorted relatives and acquaintances, the tribulations of a water-bearer, the irrational acts of a jealous merchant – in a convoluted plot that makes up with invention what it lacks in credibility. As a modern critic demonstrates (with the folio edition), the playwright links different groups of characters through coincidence: 'The country gull Stephen is the cousin of Young Knowell, who happens to be the close friend of Wellbred, who for his amusement is "humouring" two city gulls, one of whom, Matthew, is courting Bridget, who happens to be the sister of Kitely, who is married by chance to the sister of Wellbred, ...'[33]

Nevertheless, Jonson maintains order with a number of devices: tripartite comic structure, unity of time, economical staging, symmetrical arrangements of characters, and recurrent situations. In the folio play, the narrow strip of London and its northern suburbs which contains the action also enhances the impression of control. Finally, an argument structures each version. Capped

---

[33] Ralph Alan Cohen, 'The importance of setting in the revision of *Every Man in his Humour*', *ELR* 8 (1978), 192–3.

oratorically by the son, an explicit defence of poetry occurs in the early version. Later the defence becomes implicit, its encomium replaced by the Prologue and its dialectic absorbed into the perfect balance of the medium.[34]

T. S. Eliot perceived this harmony in Jonson's canon as 'poetry of the surface', and he found it in characterization as well as verse: 'Whereas in Shakespeare the effect is due to the way in which the characters *act upon* one another, in Jonson it is given by the way in which the characters *fit in* with each other'.[35] According to this distinction, Jonson's characters are 'constituents' of his dramatic scene. In Eliot's sense they 'fit in with each other', no matter how they do or do not interact. *Every Man in his Humour* frequently illustrates the general point, whether dramatis personae clash (sometimes violently) or indulge their eccentricities alone.

In the late sixteenth century such eccentricities became known as humours, a term defined by Jonson's next play:

> when some one peculiar quality
> Doth so possess a man that it doth draw
> All his affects, his spirits, and his powers,
> In their confluctions, all to run one way;
> This may be truly said to be a humour.
>
> (*Every Man out of his Humour*, Induction, 105–9)

Not all of the characters in *Every Man in his Humour* appear so totally overcome; however most become engrossed in fantasies of themselves – as cavalier or poet or cuckold – which divide them from the others in solipsistic isolation. Moreover each behaves as if he (or she) belongs in another genre – love-lyric, romantic tragedy, prodigal-son fable, cuckolding farce – enacting burlesques of those forms within the sphere of city comedy.[36]

By means of revision Jonson fully realized each 'syndrome of folly' and its parody with matching linguistic distortions.[37] As a result the final version heightens irony of the whole: characters live by illusions of self-importance or centrality while coexisting in a system of other deluded spirits: 'For Jonson is not writing about common agreement on the outside world at all. He is

---

[34] Daniel C. Boughner analyses the tripartite structure in *The Devil's Disciple: Ben Jonson's Debt to Machiavelli* (New York, 1968), chapter 9. I am grateful to William Blissett for permitting me to see in typescript his essay 'The concinnity of *Every Man in his Humour*', where he examines the play's symmetry and points out the change between the two defences.

[35] 'Ben Jonson', from *Selected Essays 1917–1932*, reprinted in Jonas A. Barish, ed., *Ben Jonson: A Collection of Critical Essays*, pp. 14, 18.

[36] Watson, *Ben Jonson's Parodic Strategy* examines *Every Man in his Humour* as 'a system of integrated parodies' (p. 19), chapter 1.

[37] Barish measures Jonson's linguistic achievement in *Ben Jonson and the Language of Prose Comedy*, pp. 98–104.

writing about diverse and unmergeable inner worlds, about the impossibility of common agreement, about the psychological artificiality of a commonly defined outer world, even when it is a moral necessity'.[38]

Between versions of *Every Man in his Humour,* Jonson wrote *The Alchemist,* among various other comedies. In 1610 the King's Men gave this comic masterpiece the first of its successful seventeenth-century performances. Using a method that had by then become his practice, Jonson assembled *The Alchemist* from models rather than sources. The frame derives from Latin comedy and farce, Plautus' *Mostellaria* and the Italian *Candelaio,* as well as late morality plays; it struck Coleridge as one of 'the three most perfect plots ever planned'.[39] Within the frame constant and various references – from classical works and alchemical literature to current events and Jonson's own dramas – add to the play's wealth of details, a source of its intensity.

If the sub-plots of *Every Man in his Humour* seem to miss a link now and then, those in *The Alchemist* never fail to connect. The later work also begins with its framing action: the multifaceted 'venture tripartite' (1.1.135) by means of which three rogues – Subtle, Face, and Dol Common – cheat divers gulls out of their goods and money. In this comedy, however, the frame totally contains the sub-plots. Once Jonson has set it up, he introduces the victims individually: Dapper the clerk, Drugger the tobacconist, Sir Epicure Mammon, Ananias the Anabaptist. The intrigues centring on these characters become entwined with one another and new complications. Drugger introduces Dame Pliant and her brother, Kastril, to the action; Surly, the gamester who arrived with Sir Epicure, makes a fool of himself in pursuit of Dame Pliant; and finally the returning Lovewit, master of the house, participates in a device to resolve the confusion.

This perfect plot moves forward with perfect clarity, regulated by Jonson so that its tempo increases steadily along with its involution. As R. V. Holdsworth points out, the characters appear in larger and larger groups: five in the first act, seven in the second, eight in the third, nine in the fourth, and twenty-one (including neighbours, officers, and parson) in the finale. Similarly phased, the intrigues not only accumulate but grow progressively more convoluted.[40]

Meantime the rogues need to keep most of their gulls from encountering one another. When the action begins, each knock on the door occasions disposing of one victim in preparation for the arrival of the next; and it leads

---

[38] See Gabriele Bernhard Jackson, ed., *Every Man in his Humour* (Yale edition, 1969), p. 20.

[39] *Table Talk* (1835), quoted in R. V. Holdsworth, *'Every Man'*, pp. 148–9. Coleridge ranks *The Alchemist* with the *Oedipus Tyrannus* and *Tom Jones.*

[40] Holdsworth, *'Every Man'*, Introduction, p. 26.

to costume changes by the three partners. As the number of gulls and their visits multiply, separating them becomes more and more difficult. Separation results in surprises, reversals, the ultimate farce rushing at high speed through interruption and counterpointed episodes, reaching maximum velocity in the fourth act.[41]

The achievement of this form calls attention to the playwright's skill: 'one has the sense of watching a juggler add more and more objects to those already in the air, and anticipating with ever greater suspense the inevitable loss of control'.[42] But control never slips. Jonson exercises it through the familiar tripartite structure reinforced here by the introduction–explanation–illustration format of Aristophanic comedy.[43] More importantly, he observes the unities to striking effect. Within its classical format the action takes place (except for one small lapse) in the time required by performance. Jonson sets it not only in London but in the district of Blackfriars, specifically 'Your master's worship's house, here, in the Friars' (1.1.17). By establishing this location he confines the hectic events to a small space, further intensifying the bustle and confusion of the characters; and he identifies setting with playhouse (the Blackfriars theatre, probable site of this play's first production), characters with audience, and issues on stage with events in the city:

> Our scene is London, 'cause we would make known,
>   No country's mirth is better than our own.
> No clime breeds better matter, for your whore,
>   Bawd, squire, impostor, many persons more ...   (Prologue, 5–8)[44]

These issues are realized through the play's central metaphor of alchemy, 'science, philosophy, mystique, and con game'.[45] In its manifestations alchemy represents a number of different processes, from the fantasies by which people gratify their desires to the art which has distilled this comedy.

---

[41] For additional discussion of the play's mechanics, see Barton, *Ben Jonson, Dramatist*, pp. 142–3; Una Ellis-Fermor, *The Jacobean Drama*, pp. 44–9; and Alvin B. Kernan, ed., *The Alchemist* (Yale edition, 1974), p. 243. Gibbons, *Jacobean City Comedy*, pp. 134–6, analyses the technique of the remarkable fourth act.

[42] Holdsworth, *'Every Man'*, Introduction, p. 26.

[43] Boughner examines the tripartite structure in *The Devil's Disciple*, pp. 198–205; C. G. Thayer points out the Aristophanic pattern in 'Theme and structure in *The Alchemist*', *ELH* 26 (1959), 23–35.

[44] Patrick R. Williams studies the play's use of space in 'Ben Jonson's satiric choreography', *RenD* n.s. 9 (1978), 130–9; and a number of critics discuss the implications of setting: for example, Paster, *The Idea of the City*, pp. 164–5; R. L. Smallwood, '"Here, in the Friars": immediacy and theatricality in *The Alchemist*', *RES* n.s. 32 (1981), 142–60; Watson, *Ben Jonson's Parodic Strategy*, pp. 113–14; Womack, *Ben Jonson*, pp. 115–19.

[45] Thayer, 'Theme and structure', p. 28.

Always it stands for change, and so the conservative dramatist presents it with more distrust than tolerance. Throughout the action rogues and gulls dispute its authenticity (with key arguments at 2.1 and 2.3, 4.6 and 4.7); at the ambivalent conclusion Lovewit treats it indulgently, 'though with some small strain/ Of his own candour' (5.5.151–2).

While the comedy's principal metaphor represents change, its characters embody stasis, a contradiction promoting irony. Jonson fixes all of the victims and two of the rogues by social position, humour, distinctive idiom, and enough details to suggest their day-to-day lives. Again characters parody types in other genres, contributing to the play's metatheatricality.[46] At the top of the social hierarchy Sir Epicure Mammon (with his endlessly meaningful name) dominates the procession of gulls in the first two acts. His girth matches the dimensions of his fantasies, which he articulates in brilliant displays of Jonson's prosodic range. Generally he speaks with the kind of specificity that informs the whole comedy: 'The verse is laden with nouns and particularities, arcane terms and lists of various kinds, all miraculously quickened by the energy and aggressiveness of the speakers'.[47] But unusual inventiveness distinguishes Mammon's blank verse – its vigorous syntax, breadth of allusion, plentiful images – and it reveals in imaginative terms different aspects of his heart's desire. At the same time Mammon's idiom demonstrates how brilliantly Jonson transmutes many components from his vast comic repertoire into a unified and satirical comic impression.

As Mammon enters the second act, he introduces Surly to the house of alchemy with hyperbolic language from current lexicons of exploration and commerce: 'Now you set your foot on shore/ In *novo orbe*; here's the rich Peru:/ And there within, sir, are the golden mines' (2.1.1–3). Continuing to express both his wonder and his greed, the knight describes alchemical practices in lines that grow thick with fabulous or mythological allusions:

> Both this, the Hesperian garden, Cadmus' story,
> Jove's shower, the boon of Midas, Argus' eyes,
> Boccace his Demogorgon, thousands more,
> All abstract riddles of our stone.   (2.1.101–4)

Between flights of fancy he states his philanthropic visions in plainer verse: 'I'll undertake, withal, to fright the plague/ Out o' the kingdom, in three months' (2.1.69–70)

[46] See Watson, *Ben Jonson's Parodic Strategy*, chapter 5, for a full account of the characters' interactions.

[47] Barton, *Ben Jonson*, p. 149. There are several fine analyses of language in *The Alchemist*, including Ian Donaldson, 'Language, noise, and nonsense: *The Alchemist*' in Earl Miner, ed., *Seventeenth-Century Imagery: Essays on Uses of Figurative Language from Donne to Farquhar* (1971), pp. 69–82 (reprinted in Holdsworth, *'Every Man'*, pp. 208–19).

These visions seem to have diminished since he related them to Subtle (according to Subtle's account at 1.4.11–29); they no longer spark his imagination. By now sensual dreams have taken their place, filling his speeches as they fill his mind:

> I will have all my beds blown up; not stuffed:
> Down is too hard. And then, mine oval room,
> Filled with such pictures as Tiberius took
> From Elephantis, and dull Aretine
> But coldly imitated. Then, my glasses,
> Cut in more subtle angles, to disperse
> And multiply the figures, as I walk
> Naked between my *succubæ*.   (2.2.41–8)

Exaggeration, antiquity, and fable combine here to produce an obscene image with Mammon at its centre. Elaborating the image he continues to speak in Marlovian accents – the outmoded cadences of Tamburlaine and Faustus – and commercial terms, portraying himself as the indecent version of a romantic hero. Jonson sets off this diction with pragmatic lines of dialogue. By modulations of language and metre, he explodes Mammon's visionary schemes long before the rogues explode his project.

The energy which animates every part of *The Alchemist* slackens in the late plays. Nevertheless in *The Staple of News*, performed in 1626 after his ten-year absence from the public stage, Jonson endeavoured to carry out a more specialized task. When he wrote this comedy during the 1620s, in effect he entered a competition with his own earlier texts published in the 1616 folio – plays like *Volpone* and *The Alchemist* (which were in repertory during 1623 and 1624) – as well as the work of other dramatists. Consequently *The Staple of News* tests both the lasting values of his topical intrigues and the capacity of the Renaissance comic structure. Mislabelled a 'dotage' in Dryden's criticism, it reveals a self-conscious artist still experimenting with his medium.[48]

Typically Jonson composed *The Staple of News* from models, in particular morality play, Latin comedy, and masque. Again the action takes shape in three phases, and it observes the unities of time and place. But this comedy does not assimilate the different elements; instead it displays them conspicuously within the external structure. For instance the main narrative about Peniboy the son and heir, deriving from prodigal-son tradition along with the

---

[48] Douglas M. Lanier discusses Jonson's self-reference in 'The prison-house of the canon: allegorical form and posterity in Ben Jonson's *The Staple of Newes*', *Medieval & Renaissance Drama in England* 2 (1985), 253–67.

morality play, runs through the entire comedy; it depicts the trials of a young man learning to live the golden mean in an immoral world.

Borrowing the diction of courtly love, the hero in his romantic mode woos Pecunia. She and her waiting-women, more abstractions than ladies, originate in allegory. As the plot which contains them all grows increasingly complex, it admits elements of New Comedy, intrigues affecting the prodigal's conflict with his uncle over Pecunia and setting up the dénouement with a ruse against the villain Picklock. In the climactic fourth act, when Peniboy [junior] succumbs to temptation, Jonson mixes features from three kinds of representations: the tavern scene from morality drama, rituals from the pre-Lenten carnival season, and components from masque. Of course satire also occupies large portions of the script. Jonson criticizes the spectators of his blank-verse comedy by framing the acts with an Induction and intermeans: prose exchanges by characters who sit on the stage like members of the audience. In addition, the first three acts ridicule the fledgeling news industry; and the play repeatedly attacks other abuses of language such as jeering and cant.[49]

Although Jonson sets the action in London, he gives it much less of the particularity which distinguished his previous city comedies. The lack of detail and presence of allegory suggest his deliberate attempt to emphasize more universal themes and to create a drama transcending its time. Ultimately *The Staple of News* does make its points about moral virtue in general terms familiar since Aristotle, yet its satire continues to reflect the political, economic, and social realities of contemporary England: developments in popular education, journalism, monopolies, and professional associations, even fashion. Most emphatically, however, the comedy as a whole evaluates current theatrical practices within the context of theatre history. It makes this assessment by juxtaposing modern and ancient forms of representation in a series of shows within the play; it allows their interaction to comment on their integrity.

When [Jonson] says that the Staple of News is a place 'wherin the age may see her owne folly' he means the news office, his own play, and the succession of plays made within it where the spectators take the stage and in affirming their independence are made to display the ignorance of their judgment and their betrayal of true theatre... The several levels of the action ... express with sharpening irony a hierarchy of values

---

[49] The most thorough studies of traditions informing *The Staple of News* appear in the Introductions of two editions: Devra Rowland Kifer's in the Regents Renaissance Drama series (Lincoln, Nebraska, 1975) and Anthony Neil Parr's in the Revels series (Manchester, 1989). Levin focuses on satire and the inter-plot connections, *The Multiple Plot*, pp. 184–91.

according to which the theatrical forms become more sophisticated and their substance more degenerate as we move in towards the masque.[50]

Jonson's contemporary John Marston had less opportunity to take the measure of contemporary drama in general or Renaissance comedy in particular. During a stormy theatrical career which lasted only a decade, Marston wrote one independent city comedy (and one of his last plays) c.1603–1605: *The Dutch Courtesan*, performed first by the Queen's Revels Children at the Blackfriars and revived in 1613 at court to celebrate the marriage of Princess Elizabeth to Frederick, the Elector Palatine. In plot, tone, and setting, this unsettled play must have seemed a strange wedding presentation. The dramatist's emphasis on satire and potential disaster sometimes threatens to distort his comic structure.

Marston constructed his main action and one sub-plot from a variety of sources which he combined in novel ways. For the central plot he recast a French pastoral romance, a story in Nicolas de Montreulx's *Le premier livre des bergeries de Juliette* (1585), to dramatize ideas from two of Montaigne's *Essays* about friendship and love (1603, trans. John Florio; I.xxvii and III.v). So Freevill and Malheureux, young gallants and friends, act out different concepts of love in relationships with virtuous Beatrice and wicked Franceschina. In this new version of a Plautine device – 'a young man's choice between *virgo* and *meretrix*, innocent maiden and wily courtesan' – they choose between moral and immoral options, chastity or marriage and illicit sex.[51] The sub-plot which reduces these serious issues to farce borrows its episodes from William Painter's *Palace of Pleasure* (1566 and 1567) and Elizabethan drama. Contributing to each act, the roguish Cocledemoy gulls the puritan vintner Master Mulligrub and his wife; he reproduces Freevill's stratagem, tricking Malheureux for his own good, at the level of fabliau. Marston also invents another sub-plot about two down-to-earth lovers, Crispinella and Tysefew, whose sensible dialogue exposes pretension and sentimentality in the Malheureux–Freevill action.

During the first two acts stoical Malheureux chooses badly, his self-control giving way before his lust for the Dutch courtesan Franceschina. His bad judgement sets off the intrigues and counter-intrigues which call for a sensational resolution in the fifth act. Moreover his involvement with

---

[50] D. F. McKenzie, '"The Staple of News" and the late plays', in Blissett, Patrick, and Van Fossen, *A Celebration of Ben Jonson*, pp. 102–3. This essay, pp. 83–128, gives a first-rate analysis of the comedy's metatheatrical structure.

[51] Richard Horwich, 'Wives, courtesans, and the economics of love in Jacobean city comedy', *CompD* 7 (1973–74), 293. The two most recent critical editions of *The Dutch Courtesan*, by Peter Davison (in the Fountainwell Drama Text series, Edinburgh, 1968) and M. L. Wine, summarize the sources.

Franceschina makes prostitution a central focus in the play, bringing to life a metaphor introduced by the opening scenes. Through set speeches in Act 1, scenes 1 and 2, both Freevill and Cocledemoy link brothels with other forms of exploitation in the city. Echoing Freevill, Cocledemoy's 'oration' to the bawd Mary Faugh makes this connection and in the process defines the scope of Marston's satire:[52]

List, then: a bawd, first for her profession or vocation, it is most worshipful of all the twelve companies; ... whereas no trade or vocation profiteth but by the loss and displeasure of another – as the merchant thrives not but by the licentiousness of giddy and unsettled youth, the lawyer but by the vexation of his client, the physician but by the maladies of his patient – only my smooth-gumm'd bawd lives by others' pleasure, and only grows rich by others' rising. O merciful gain! O righteous income!

(1.2.29–48)

By locating the main and sub-plots in contemporary London – among its shops, exchanges, and markets, between its districts of crime and punishment – Marston sharpens not only his urban satire but also his analysis of moral and immoral love. Malheureux's passion has dire consequences in a world presented as real; his rationalized moral failings lead him, along with Mulligrub, to the point of execution. Nevertheless Marston places some distance between his philosophical and satiric commentaries by adjusting diction to subject-matter. On the whole his characters address general issues in the generalized language of moral precepts, psychology, and philosophical discourse; and they describe current affairs in earthy, often obscene particulars. With other modulations in verse and prose, diction also reveals the speakers in broad terms as witty or dull, true or false, idealistic or cynical.[53]

Thomas Middleton generates subtler tensions in *A Chaste Maid in Cheapside*. At the mid-point of his career in 1613, he capped half a dozen city comedies with this skilfully crafted play before turning his hand to tragicomedy and tragedy. According to R. B. Parker, the pivotal text shows traces of all three genres (as well as city pageant). Written for a combined company of adult and boy actors – Lady Elizabeth's Men and the Queen's Revels Children – it appeared first at the Swan theatre. Its satire as well as its stage directions show the influence of Middleton's previous experience in the private theatre.[54]

---

[52] Gibbons, *Jacobean City Comedy*, pp. 90–4, thoroughly describes the play's satire.

[53] On language in *The Dutch Courtesan*, see Finkelpearl, *John Marston*, pp. 202–19, and Hamilton, 'Language as theme'.

[54] Samuel Schoenbaum defines the play's context with '*A Chaste Maid in Cheapside* and Middleton's city comedy', in Josephine W. Bennett, Oscar Cargill, and Vernon Hall, Jr, eds., *Studies in the English Renaissance Drama* (1959), pp. 287–309; Parker gives background as well as the most thorough account of date and first performance in the Introduction to his Revels edition; and Gibbons discusses the mix of coterie and popular elements in the play in *Jacobean City Comedy*, pp. 127–30.

Depending on no particular model or source, Middleton built his comic structure with materials ranging from Latin comedy and Spanish novel to pamphlets and folklore. He turned bits and pieces into a unified whole remarkable for its inventiveness. In this play the three-part form contains three major plots, one minor action, and assorted vignettes of Jacobean city life. As Richard Levin originally pointed out, all four intrigues centre on sex triangles involving one woman and two men; they connect through family ties, geographical proximity, and causal relationships. During the first three expository scenes, the main intrigues begin to gather associations with one another. While the action advances this complexity grows, augmented by the fourth plot and digressions. Twice ensemble scenes (at 3.2 and 5.4) bring the plots together, the second finally disconnecting the entire system with a startling marriage.[55]

Like Marston's courtesan, Middleton's sex triangles focus the satire in his comedy: each of these arrangements has an economic base. In the frame narrative, a parodic version of New Comedy, Yellowhammer the goldsmith and his wife, Maudline, frustrate their daughter's love to increase their wealth and status: they thrust Moll (with her dowry) at Sir Walter Whore-hound despite her attachment to Touchwood Junior. Although Sir Walter pursues this match to restore depleted funds, he has already fathered seven children on another man's wife. In the sequence that epitomizes the play, cuckoldry is a business; Sir Walter supports the Allwit family, and Mr Allwit (the wittol) revels in his gain:

> He gets me all my children, and pays the nurse
> Monthly or weekly; puts me to nothing,
> Rent, nor church-duties, not so much as the scavenger:
> The happiest state that ever man was born to!   (1.2.18–21)

Meantime Sir Walter's kinsman Sir Oliver Kix and his wife bargain with Touchwood Senior, a decayed but fertile gentleman, to help them conceive a child. Touchwood Senior complies successfully – and literally – in effect disinheriting Sir Walter. Finally the Yellowhammers' son, Tim, marries a cast-off mistress of Sir Walter's, led to believe her a Welsh gentlewoman, 'Heir to some nineteen mountains' (1.1.128).

Arising from interactions between the gentry and middle class, each tri-angle takes shape within a family disrupted or perverted by economic con-cerns. Financial contracts replace emotional bonds; sex becomes a commodity; and the familial unit turns into an enterprise. Within this play's

---

[55] See Levin, *The Multiple Plot*, pp. 194–202.

geometry the plots come together to figure an age grown materialistic and competitive. Appropriately Middleton localizes this world in the old market-place of London, a wide street in which 'the usual women "chased" … were the prostitutes whipped through it at a cart's tail'.[56]

Since many topographical references have symbolic implications, they not only make the satire immediate but give the naturalism an allegorical edge. At one point, for example, Tim heads for Trig Stairs on the Thames (4.2.5). 'Trig' means not only a narrow passage but also a coxcomb, making the location suit the character. When the Allwits plan to take a house in the Strand (5.1.158), they anticipate their future by naming a street that is both fashionable and infamous for expensive courtesans. In a similar way the seasonal background, Lent to Easter, heightens the dramatist's ambivalent representation of moral and religious standards. It provides the context for interpreting many of the play's images – animals, fish, water – in terms of both death and resurrection, decay and renewal.

Gibbons concludes that Middleton created his art from a quarrel with himself, 'turning over the question "why is this feasible if it is immoral?"' (p. 130). This quarrel or argument sustains the delicate balance of other dramatic elements: characters both offensive and appealing, diction obscene and witty, events fantastic and real. As Middleton scorns this creation with irony looking forward to Swift's, he laughs at it with the tolerance of Rabelais. The play's blank verse, extraordinarily flexible and sensitive to context, provides fluent expression for both points of view. Bringing the action to an end, for instance, it moves easily through an epitaph, a marriage ceremony, exposure of a gulling, and a final business agreement. Finally it stops with two speeches of equal length that juxtapose satire with comedy in the play's characteristic style:

> TIM
> I perceive then a woman may be honest
> According to the English print, when she is
> A whore in the Latin; so much for marriage and logic!
> I'll love her for her wit, I'll pick out my runts there;
> And for my mountains, I'll mount upon –
>
> YELLOWHAMMER
> So fortune seldom deals two marriages
> With one hand, and both lucky; the best is,
> One feast will serve them both! Marry, for room,
> I'll have the dinner kept in Goldsmiths' Hall,
> To which, kind gallants, I invite you all. (5.4.108–17)

---

[56] Parker, *A Chaste Maid*, p. xlvii. My next paragraph summarizes Parker's conclusions about setting.

City comedies after Jonson and Middleton imitate their plays without the plays' intensity. In *The City Madam* (1632), for example, Philip Massinger echoes *Volpone* and *The Alchemist*, picking up general themes like greed and hypocrisy rather than the complex particulars of form, setting, or diction. The later comedy, acted by the King's Men at the Blackfriars, depends less on details of city life to declare its satiric opinions.

Drawing on elements from contemporary drama, Massinger probably invented his comedy's double action, an arrangement that works variations on a single theme. First he introduces the immediate family of a merchant recently knighted, Sir John Frugal. As this sequence begins, a conversation between two of Sir John's apprentices reveals that his wife and daughters suffer from ambition, a seventeenth-century equivalent to pride: 'The want of [a title]/ Swells my young Mistresses, and their madam mother/ With hopes above their birth, and scale' (1.1.15–17). Soon the exposition sketches another relative equally typological: Sir John's prodigal brother, Luke, just returned from a debtors' prison and treated like a servant by the women in Frugal's home.

Until Act 2, scene 2 the women continue to display their follies, at last offending a pair of eligible suitors; by Act 2, scene 1 Luke indicates that his subdued behaviour conceals evil motives. The intrigue that will enlighten the ladies and uncover Luke's villainy begins in Act 2, scene 3: Sir John and his cohort Lord Lacy cause Luke to think that he has become the manager of Sir John's estate. Of course Luke abuses this trust, the ladies, and everyone else who crosses his path. It takes an elaborate pageant in the fifth act to conclude the intrigue successfully.

A handful of scenes in one of the city's dissolute haunts parallels the main action at crucial points to emphasize its moral import: so a bawd and a prostitute in Act 3, scene 1 caricature the behaviour of Frugal's daughters with their suitors in Act 2, scene 2. While these episodes underscore motifs, however, they hardly localize events in the city. They add just a few items from London's topography and customs to the central plot's mention of shops and other buildings. Moreover, the biblical parables which fill this play counteract specific impressions of urban life. As Michael Neill shows, the comedy's argument elaborates well-known scriptural texts, and St Matthew's parable of the unjust debtor (Matthew 18.21–35) informs the entire action.[57]

Massinger does place events chronologically with allusions to contemporary people and happenings. As a result his late city comedy directs its satire

---

[57] See '"The tongues of angels": charity and the social order in *The City Madam*', in Howard, *Philip Massinger*, pp. 193–220.

at broad targets: current manifestations of sin and breaches of decorum in the social hierarchy of Caroline England. In this play old landed wealth and new money get along when both observe traditional proprieties. Conflict arises from the transgression of principles not fixed by place or time, status or possessions. Consequently the dramatist arranges his characters in relation to moral and ethical norms; and his blank verse distinguishes them not merely by social rank but by their expression of spiritual values.

Departures

In plays like Chapman's *Gentleman Usher* and Marston's *Dutch Courtesan*, the prominence of certain generic elements – satire, treatise, even tragedy – now and then disturbs the comic structure. When these elements are especially striking or extensive, they threaten to interfere with comedy's most definitive phase: its anastrophe or happy resolution. Usually this effect seems unintentional and temporary, a result of the dramatist's preoccupation with the content of his work. But Shakespeare's seventeenth-century comedies – *Troilus and Cressida*, *All's Well That Ends Well*, and *Measure for Measure* – purposefully unsettle the genre: 'Shakespeare is transforming the traditions of comedy into something, still called comedy, which challenges all those many traditions'.[58] Each play subverts its folkloric sources, legend or romantic tale, as it undermines both the narrative and dialectic order of the comic form. Relying on different strategies, each proves dramatic comedy and related traditions inadequate representations of human experience.

Measure for Measure, written *c.*1604 and influenced by the accession of King James I, defies generic expectations with unwavering singleness of purpose. At the level of narrative it begins with an exposition that introduces ambiguous characters and events; continues with an unpredictable intrigue that ignites and subdues passion by calculated deceit; ends with a resolution that leaves six characters silently uncommitted to their fates. At the level of dialectic 'the play avoids good arguments and clear theses, and instead proceeds by means of indirections, good arguments badly put, specious arguments and desperate stratagems'.[59] Shakespeare dramatizes the administration of justice in these uneasy terms, perhaps stressing inadequacies in the art form to reflect for the benefit of the new king inadequacies in the legal system.

---

[58] David Daniell, 'Shakespeare and the traditions of comedy', in Wells, *The Cambridge Companion to Shakespeare Studies*, p. 117.
[59] Paul Hammond, 'The argument of *Measure for Measure*', *ELR* 16 (1986), 497.

Often the uncertainties that transform comic structure in *Measure for Measure* do not arise from the play's generic mixture, despite the prevalence of satire and potential for calamity. Rather they originate primarily in language: denotations continually point in one direction, connotations and style in another. When the Duke rationalizes the folk convention of the 'Disguised Ruler' and explains his hurried departure from Vienna in Act 1, scene 3, for instance, he claims that he intends to restore legal order through his deputy Angelo. Yet his words emphasize serious deficiencies in the law and contempt for the people it governs; they describe painful constraints on unruly animals: 'We have strict statutes and most biting laws,/ The needful bits and curbs to headstrong jades,/ Which for this fourteen years we have let slip' (1.3.19–21). A moment later they reduce the immediate gravity of the present situation through personifications, absurd images, and a combination of diction and metre which sounds flippant:

> so our decrees,
> Dead to infliction, to themselves are dead,
> And Liberty plucks Justice by the nose,
> The baby beats the nurse, and quite athwart
> Goes all decorum.   (27–31)

In the end the harsh laws seem a bad alternative to current misbehaviour, an unsatisfying explanation for leaving a deputy in charge. Soon the Duke admits that he has 'Moe reasons for this action' (48), and he concludes the scene by expressing his intention to test Angelo: 'Hence shall we see/ If power change purpose, what our seemers be' (53–4).

Once the Duke appears to have left Vienna the 'Monstrous Ransom' or 'Corrupt Magistrate' plot gets under way, a narrative that Shakespeare borrowed mainly from George Whetstone's comedy *Promos and Cassandra* (1578). Vincentio's substitute demands sexual favours from the novice Isabella in exchange for releasing her brother from the death penalty. Between the second and third acts an intense psychological drama plays itself out, the words and cadences revealing naturalistically the speakers' confusion:

> ANGELO
> What's this? What's this? Is this her fault, or mine?
> The tempter, or the tempted, who sins most, ha?
> Not she; nor doth she tempt; but it is I
> That, lying by the violet in the sun,
> Do as the carrion does, not as the flower,
> Corrupt with virtuous season.   (2.2.163–8)

At the same time language also betrays dark, unconscious impulses. It exposes Isabella's sensuality, for example, as she defines her chastity in sexual language:

> That is, were I under the terms of death,
> Th'impression of keen whips I'd wear as rubies,
> And strip myself to death as to a bed
> That longing have been sick for, ere I'd yield
> My body up to shame.   (2.4.100–4)

When the Duke intervenes at the centre of the action, this medium changes abruptly. Prose displaces verse, initially with old-fashioned euphuism: 'The hand that hath made you fair hath made you good. The goodness that is cheap in beauty makes beauty brief in goodness; but grace, being the soul of your complexion, shall keep the body of it ever fair' (3.1.179–83). Addressed to Isabella just after her most hysterical outburst, these lines clearly announce their hollowness with their artificiality. Again, what the Duke means differs from what he says, and the disjunction facilitates his manipulating of events.

During the course of this play Vincentio never makes an unequivocal statement of his purpose. At best he relates the mechanics of a stratagem, not its object. Yet he fails to communicate even this much to most of the other characters. While he equivocates his subjects frequently express more than they realize, disclosing vagaries of their minds and hearts beyond his control. Shakespeare arranges his materials in a narrative about authority contending with human nature, organizing situations – especially sexual relationships – to mirror one another in ironic ways. Yet decisive causal factors generally remain hidden not only from many characters but also from the audience. If these witnesses can finally comprehend the progression of events, they can hardly apprehend its rationale. *Measure for Measure* flaunts the logic implied by authority and art with the realities of human behaviour. In Frye's words (but not his positive sense), the dramatist writes 'a comedy about comedy' as he turns his attention to tragedy and romance.[60] The familiar comic sequence disintegrates as it advances, unequal to the stresses of Shakespeare's Vienna.

Withstanding such reversals and competition from other genres, English Renaissance comedy flourished until the theatres closed. It had become a strong presence both as a full-scale kind and as a mode or partial kind: 'Modes have always an incomplete repertoire, a selection only of the cor-

---

[60] *The Myth of Deliverance: Reflections on Shakespeare's Problem Comedies* (Toronto and Buffalo, New York, 1983), p. 25.

responding kind's features, and one from which overall external structure is absent'.[61] In the early Tudor period the comic mode was pronounced in certain interludes, and from the mid-sixteenth century on it infiltrated other dramatic genres. By the end of the century, comedy appeared regularly in history plays and tragedies; often it unexpectedly shifted perspective on plot or characters. Clown scenes in Marlowe's *Doctor Faustus* re-enact the protagonist's demonic bargain to emphasize its absurdity; episodes of carnival in the anonymous *Famous Victories of Henry V* and Shakespeare's *Henry IV* plays multiply images of political disorder throughout the kingdom. Comedy becomes 'a possible starting point, or a running accompaniment, or even a constituent element, of Shakespeare's tragic vision'.[62] Of course the mode contributed vitally to the new seventeenth-century genre of tragicomedy.

Considering English Renaissance comedy as a whole or in part, critics have sometimes asked 'Why now? and Why this way?' Why did romantic comedy prosper at the end of the sixteenth century and city comedy at the beginning of the seventeenth? What made the genre so popular through most of the era? So far the general evidence – many and various plays from both public and private theatres – suggests few specific answers. In this case modern genre theory often raises more questions.[63]

Although this brief survey cannot trace the many cultural sources of Tudor or Stuart comedy, it should perhaps take a cue from Lyly towards one or two reasonable conclusions about the genre. According to Lyly's Prologue to *Midas* (*c.*1589), a mixed theatre audience – soldiers, courtiers, countrymen – wanted to see themselves reflected in mixed forms of theatre. The playwrights may have been responding to this demand not only when they mingled dramatic kinds, but also when they exploited the versatile comic genre. For some reason comedy enjoyed unusual freedom of expression: 'of all the dramatic kinds, comedy was the least controlled, and was allowed, even by classical precept, the greatest variety of style'.[64] As Eliot observes in his essay on Massinger, such freedom invites experimentation: 'In comedy, as a matter of fact, a greater variety of methods were discovered

---

[61] Fowler, p. 107.

[62] Susan Snyder, *The Comic Matrix of Shakespeare's Tragedies: 'Romeo and Juliet', 'Hamlet', 'Othello', and 'King Lear'* (Princeton, New Jersey, 1979), p. 55.

[63] Quotation from Leinwand, *The City Staged*, p. 20. For additional questions, see William W. E. Slights, 'Unfashioning the man of mode: comic countergenre in Marston, Jonson, and Middleton', *RenD* n.s. 15 (1984), 69–70. For a theory about the rise and fall of romantic comedy, see Leonard Tennenhouse, *Power on Display: The Politics of Shakespeare's Genres* (1986), chapter 1; on the progress of city comedy, see Gibbons, *Jacobean City Comedy*, chapters 2–4.

[64] M. C. Bradbrook, *Growth and Structure*, p. 43.

and employed than in tragedy... [B]oth individual temperament, and varying epochs, made more play with comedy'.[65]

The best playwrights conducted their experiments on the times, analysing social conditions through art. If their romantic comedy took an outsider's view of court life, their city comedy gave an insider's assessment of urban experience. For several years these two forms overlapped, but finally one supplanted the other to register political change: a patriarchal style of monarchy, increasing economic and social fluctuation. Other types of comedies, diverse and eclectic, filled the space around these two forms, commenting on everything from middle-class courtship and marriage to the gullibility of country gentlemen. Even the second-class imitations of first-class comedies mirrored audiences' concerns in the form whose resolution dispels anxiety. All in all the genre of English Renaissance comedy proved to be in itself a mingle-mangle which represented the hodgepodge of contemporary life, a gallimaufry which satisfied its age.

Bibliography

TEXTS

References in this chapter include the following editions, modernized where necessary: *The Dramatic Writings of John Heywood*, ed. John S. Farmer (1905); George Gascoigne's *'Supposes' and 'Jocasta'*, ed. John W. Cunliffe (1906). *Gammer Gurton's Needle* and *Ralph Roister Doister* have both been frequently anthologized. The chapter refers to critical editions of two other plays which have also been anthologized several times each: Henry Porter, *The Two Angry Women of Abington*, ed. Marianne Brish Evett (1980), and the anonymous *Merry Devil of Edmonton*, ed. William Amos Abrams (1942). I quote John Marston's *Dutch Courtesan*, ed. M. L. Wine (1965) from the Regents Renaissance Drama series, and Thomas Middleton's *A Chaste Maid in Cheapside*, ed. R. B. Parker (1969) from the Revels series.

SCHOLARSHIP AND CRITICISM

General concepts of Renaissance genres in this essay have been shaped in part by Rosalie Colie, *The Resources of Kind* (1973); Heather Dubrow, *Genre* (1982); and Barbara Kiefer Lewalski, ed., *Renaissance Genres: Essays on Theory, History, and Interpretation* (1986).

For helpful studies on English Renaissance comedy, see the works by Bradbrook, Braunmuller and Bulman, Doran, Gibbons, and Leggatt in the Bibliography's section 'General critical studies and collections of criticism'. Two books which deal with city comedy are Theodore B. Leinwand, *The City Staged: Jacobean Comedy, 1603–1613* (1986), and Gail Kern Paster, *The Idea of the City in the Age of Shakespeare* (1985), Chapters 6 and 7. Two volumes about Shakespearian comedy throw light on

---

[65] Reprinted from *Essays on Elizabethan Drama* (1932) in Kaufmann, *Elizabethan Drama*, p. 351.

the Renaissance genre as a whole: Maurice Charney, ed., *Shakespearean Comedy* (1980), and Leo Salingar, *Shakespeare and the Traditions of Comedy* (1974).

On individual comedies, there are two especially pertinent works: David Bevington, *Tudor Drama and Politics: A Critical Approach to Topical Meaning* (1968), and Richard Levin, *The Multiple Plot in English Renaissance Drama* (1971). The chapter also refers to Joel B. Altman, *The Tudor Play of Mind: Rhetorical Inquiry and the Development of Elizabethan Drama* (1978) for the analyses of rhetoric in Elizabethan comedy; and R. V. Holdsworth, ed., *'Every Man in his Humour' and 'The Alchemist': A Casebook* (1978) for essays on those two plays.

9   Tragedy

Tragedy ... openeth the greatest wounds, and showeth forth the ulcers that are covered with tissue [and] teacheth the uncertainty of this world, and upon how weak foundations gilden roofs are builded.

Sir Philip Sidney, 'A Defence of Poetry' (1582)[1]

this majestical roof fretted with golden fire, why, it appeareth to me nothing but a foul and pestilent congregation of vapours. What a piece of work is a man, how noble in reason, how infinite in faculties ... and yet to me what is this quintessence of dust?

William Shakespeare, Hamlet, 2.2.301–8

A theory of Renaissance tragedy

ART exists for a reason; it is not mere decoration, but a necessary worker in the necessary business of a human culture. No system of thought – mythological, religious, scientific – has yet represented reality to its believers so fully, accurately, and coherently that the system never fails,[2] that the gold roofs beneath which we stage our glories never collapse. Most forms of art are used to reconcile apparent contradictions in a culture's consensual view of reality; some radical forms, tragedy in particular, serve to acknowledge those contradictions and reconcile us to the problems and pain they generate. Contemporary criticism has an unfortunate tendency to construct artificial barriers between past and present, to scold modern students for attempting to experience Renaissance tragedies as accessible expressions of precious if painful insights. English Renaissance culture was in many ways different from ours, but not so different as to prevent us from recognizing the kinds of conflicts its tragedies explore, or to deprive those tragedies of any direct impact on the conflicts we ourselves face.

The valid argument that one cannot discuss literature outside its historical

---

[1] Sir Philip Sidney, 'A Defence of Poetry', ed. J. A. Van Dorsten (Oxford, 1966), p. 45.

[2] Cf. the 'Incompleteness Proof' of Kurt Gödel, which indicates that any system of unified explanation inevitably develops internal incoherencies; see his *On Formally Undecidable Principles*, trans. B. Meltzer (London, 1962).

setting is usually made either too narrowly or too broadly. Those who conclude that art is merely a subordinate agent of an essentially economic social
entity forget that societies face cognitive crises as well as political ones
(though they often run in parallel). The commonly cited pressures toward
the realignment of hierarchy and the redistribution of wealth are not the only
ones that threaten the stability of a culture; without art to help us process our
experience coherently, our daily lives would be a chaos as devastating as any
rebellion. Those who claim, more broadly, that human beings perceive
wholly different kinds of reality in different historical periods, that shifting
ideologies and epistemes necessitate a kind of archaeological detachment
from the literary artifacts of the Renaissance, overlook the way drama, as a
communal representation of human experience, itself refutes such exaggerated exclusions. The history of drama shows no direct line of survival
from the great flowering in ancient Greece to Elizabethan England; the very
fact that tragedy and comedy reassert themselves (like stubborn plants) after
long burial, however, indicates that something persistent in Western civilization demands those particular forms of representation. Even two thousand
years before Shakespeare, drama portrayed human traits and situations that
still seem very familiar: fascism and democracy struggling for political power,
with recognizable kinds of schemers and idealists on both sides; married
couples squabbling over money and the perpetual lure of infidelity; sibling
rivalries and (of course) oedipal conflicts; losses that are still agonizing and
(perhaps most remarkable) jokes that are still funny.

Nevertheless, many sophisticated commentators consider it dubious and
even politically pernicious to suppose that there are any fundamental truths
about 'human nature'. They warn that such 'essentialist' thinking ignores
cultural, class, and historical difference. Certainly nothing is quite universal
– West African tribesmen evidently offered some unorthodox interpretations
of the Hamlet story[3] – but Shakespearian drama originally reached an
audience that stretched all the way across the class spectrum, and the same
drama has continued to command fascination (though its focus undergoes
revealing shifts) over several historical periods. The plays have survived
translation into print, into foreign languages, even into cultures as foreign as
that of modern Japan (where the Shakespeare industry thrives). Tragedy
typically reminds its audience of something they share and commonly struggle to forget: the progress from aspiration to death, from moments that
promise glory (even if they are only the infantile fantasies of omnipotence) to
eventual surrender (even if it is only the banal fact of mortality). Tragedy also
attunes itself to the sharings of primal guilt, in the practice of ritual sacrifice

---

[3] Laura Bohannan, 'Shakespeare in the bush', in James P. Spradley and David W.
McCurdy, eds., *Conformity and Conflict* (3rd edn; Boston, 1977), pp. 13–23.

it essentially re-enacts, as well as in durable parables like that of Oedipus. Perhaps great tragedy is that which resists history, and retains humanity.

Several recent studies of Renaissance literature have been concerned with the notion that the unified 'subject', the emotional, volitional, or psychological self was simply not invented until the seventeenth century.[4] It is difficult to understand how anyone who has read even such standard and various works as the Book of Job, the Meditations of Marcus Aurelius, and the Confessions of St Augustine, can accept so extreme an assertion. Can self-consciousness and self-knowledge be such radically new notions if the central admonitory wisdom on the most revered oracle of the ancient world (at Delphi) was 'Know Thyself'? To insist that historical changes have altered only a small percentage of human consciousness and conduct is not to deny that even such fractional changes may be significant, or to deny that some forms of art will be especially concerned with exploring precisely those fractions. Among cultural historians the idea that the Renaissance produced a discernible increase in individualism has been a valuable commonplace for well over a century.[5] But to conjure an historical disjunction so sharp that it excludes all familiarity and all prior commentary (a tactic popular in the French academy and increasingly rewarded in the British and American) unjustifiably reduces the tragedies from immediate visions of life to alienated evidence of change.

The spectacle and imminence of death must surely have reminded people that they had integral individual existences – unitary, or at least binary, with body and soul reciprocally dependent. 'Only we die in earnest – that's no jest', concluded Sir Walter Ralegh; clever fictions cannot impinge very far on biological facts. Even taxes have been with us throughout recorded history, on tablet, papyrus, and paper, with much the same rationalizations on the part of the collectors and much the same complaints and evasions on the part of the taxed; it seems perverse to insist that those other eternal verities, sex and death, are much newer inventions and more completely subject to transient ideologies.[6] Humanists in the Renaissance understandably construed

---

[4] See for example Catherine Belsey, *The Subject of Tragedy* and Joel Fineman, *Shakespeare's Perjured Eye: The Invention of Poetic Subjectivity in Shakespeare's Sonnets* (Berkeley, California, 1985). Most such arguments originate from Michel Foucault, *The Archeology of Knowledge*, trans. A. M. Sheridan Smith (New York, 1972).

[5] The classic work in this regard is Jacob Burckhardt, *The Civilization of the Renaissance* (1860; reprinted New York, 1960).

[6] By the same token, those who claim that human experience and behaviour are historical contingencies shaped by language and have no fundamental reality outside it must consider it a remarkable coincidence that other species, lacking anything accepted as language, engage in so many complex social and sexual behaviour patterns congruent to those of humans.

the classical world as an Other, yet they worked confidently toward a reconciliation. Though significant changes have certainly occurred, four hundred years or twenty-four hundred are a minuscule span in the history of the human creature, and to estrange the community of the past is destructive to the desperate need – in a period of racism, economic injustice, ongoing ecological disaster, and potential nuclear war – to expand our sense of kinship and our faith that communication and co-operation are possible.

English Renaissance tragedy repeatedly portrays the struggle of a remarkable individual against implacable, impersonal forces, a struggle no less impressive for its failure. The protagonists can be heroes even when they are not triumphant or highly virtuous, because the defeat of their aspirations (however tainted with blasphemy or selfishness) reflects a frustration common to the human psyche and heightened by the mixed messages of Renaissance culture. The aspiring mind of Faustus confronts the restraints of conventional Christian morality and the banal facts of the physical universe; Macbeth, one of the most intensely subjective characters ever created, confronts literal prophecy, recorded history, and cyclical nature. Though no single paradigm can accurately describe the range of Elizabethan and Jacobean tragedies, a remarkable number of the memorable heroes are destroyed by some version of this confrontation between the desiring personal imagination and the relentless machinery of power, whether social, natural, or divine. The revenger is denied the satisfactions of true justice by civil law, political privilege, and Christian principles; the malcontent is denied respect and advancement by the perceived stupidity of his society and its hierarchies. Noble soldiers and lovers cannot escape the stubborn canker of envy and connivance in human nature, or the persistent pressures toward dynastic marriage and historical change in human society. And great spirits of all kinds face inevitable extinction by mortality, the ultimate power-broker and person-breaker.

It is hardly surprising that English Renaissance tragedy rehearses obsessively this archetype of betrayal; in all other theatres of life, the liberated self was repeatedly colliding with powerful impersonal machinery. Renewed human innovation and exploration were constantly running up against the stubbornness and mysteriousness of physical nature; thematically, *Doctor Faustus* (1588–92) was overdetermined by its surrounding culture. People displaced from hereditary feudal identities and employments were harshly repressed as they attempted to enter new arenas and arrogate new personal status; *Macbeth* (1606) (along with a variety of other Shakespeare plays in which the natural order punishes ambition)[7] may thus serve as a parable about the destructive tendencies of a society pursuing the contradictory goals of growth and stability. Worldly pleasure and individual identity – both increasingly valued in this period[8] – were never far from destruction by the plagues of the time, bubonic and otherwise. The intense pieties Protestantism instilled in the individual conscience were generally understood to be unavailing against God's inscrutable predestination of damnation.

Agonizing as these contradictions may have been, they none the less generated the kind of dual vision that enabled artists to convert agony into extraordinary beauty. The triumphs of Renaissance art, in a variety of media, depend on the conjunction of an active religious faith, a quest for transcendence, with an evolving science of realistic observation, a quest for empirical truth.[9] Furthermore, the same tension that enabled the greatness of Renaissance art made tragedy – inasmuch as tragedy draws its native energy from cultural schisms – uniquely capable of exploiting that opportunity. The most joyous art finds ideal beauty in real things; tragic art shows ideal beauty in collision with real things.

One traditional theory describes the literary upsurge in Renaissance England as the outgrowth of a new national identity and an upsurge in national confidence – as if literature fluctuated in the same way as the stock market, and for much the same reasons. Certainly England achieved new prosperity during the mid-sixteenth century through the cloth trade and the commercial and colonial uses of navigation. But it would be cruelly untrue to the experience of vast numbers of English men and women to depict this as a time of universal comfort and prosperity. As in most social reorganizations and economic booms, many human lives were squandered or devoured by the system, and certainly the people who tried to make their living as authors were almost always scraping for their meals. A converse theory has therefore developed, suggesting that literature necessarily evolved as an outlet for protest – and for regulating protest – against the emergent horrors of capitalism and centralized power.

Fortunately it is possible to avoid the old-fashioned scholarly élitism of

---

[7] Robert N. Watson, *Shakespeare and the Hazards of Ambition* (Cambridge, Massachusetts, 1984), *passim*.

[8] See the documentation and explication of this intensifying conflict in Phillipe Ariès, *The Hour of Our Death*, trans. Helen Weaver (New York, 1982).

[9] Murray Roston, *The Sixteenth Century* (New York, 1982), makes this argument with eloquent concision.

claiming that Renaissance art succeeded because some bright young men studied the classics, without resorting to the current proletarian chic that makes culture an economic machine in which authors perform only alienated labour. Both assertions are just true enough to mislead. Perhaps the remarkable development of English literature in the later sixteenth century, like the triumphs of the arts in Italy in the preceding centuries, depended on the constant tension between the material changes reshaping daily life and the stable abstract authority of classical art and morality. (The English language itself was perfectly poised in the Renaissance to express this polarity, as an earthy Anglo-Saxon strain mixed with the Latinate diction encouraged by the humanist élite.) When one complete and valued world-view (the native Christian legacy) is actively tested against another (the revered classical example), and when new practical problems (merchandising, manufacturing, navigation, optics, epidemiology) present themselves in a context imbued with established and evolving religious faith, powerful new perceptions are inevitable, and so are the artistic innovations that will seek to assimilate and expand those perceptions.

Medieval English culture – roughly speaking, of course – was unified across different times and nations and topics by a reliance on authority; in both science and religion, received wisdom had priority over empirical observation. In the Renaissance, science and religion are actively transformed, as both nature and God become more accessible to the immediate experience of individuals. Art history reveals an essential difference – corresponding to the tragic conflict – between medieval and Renaissance painting. Flat, iconic portrayals of Jesus and Mary yield to Renaissance *pietàs* and crucifixion scenes with ordinary faces in real pain, and in the background real cities, rocks, and forests. What makes Leonardo da Vinci's religious works so awesome if not their intimate involvement of the spiritual in a world that we recognize as intensely real? It is impossible to say whether discoveries such as perspective are cause or effect of a fresh way of seeing, but clearly they are part of an extremely powerful cycle.

The history of philosophy reveals the same sort of dialectic. On one side are the optimistic spiritual reconceptions emerging from the Italian Renaissance: Ficino's Neoplatonism and Pico's 'Oration' suggest that human beings can exalt themselves, by reason and love, into something like divinity. On the other side are the documents of the Counter-Renaissance,[10] such as Machiavelli's *The Prince*, which studiously avoids transcendent moral

---

[10] Hiram Haydn, *The Counter-Renaissance* (New York, 1950), explicates this dark counter-current to humanist rationality and optimism. The works of Montaigne are especially informative about the development of selfhood and scepticism in this period.

reference in favour of pragmatic political tactics, in much the way painters forsook ideal faces in favour of realistic ones. As the relative values of art and nature become prominently contested,[11] the theory that art enables and records a mystical union between the human soul and divine harmonies collides with a theory that defines art as the skill and practice of holding a mirror up to nature. The debate remains active even today, as a function of the continuing tragic disjunction between our spiritual sense that each individual person is a universe of eternal meaning, and our practical suspicion that each person is instead a transient and largely redundant event in the meaningless functions of nature.

Defining tragedy is impossible, because the word has meant different things at different times.[12] Even a broad ethical definition would involve articulating all the complexities and extremities of human suffering. The footprints of Aristotle, Hegel, and Nietzsche in the dust hardly assuage a critic's sense of rushing in where angels might fear to tread. Nevertheless, the correlations between these theories and Renaissance practice deserve explication, particularly because the Renaissance example reconciles some of their apparent discrepancies.

Aristotle writes in the *Poetics* that tragedies must represent a complete, serious, and important action that rouses and then purges (by *catharsis*) fear and pity in the spectators, with a central character who moves from happiness to misery through some frailty or error (*hamartia*). The precise translations and applications of these terms are still hotly debated, but they certainly seem compatible with Renaissance tragedies that enabled their audiences to examine and exorcise their collective frustrations by watching a hero fail to fulfil his glorious aspirations. If there is any value in the supposed etymology of the word 'tragedy' from the Greek *tragoidia* or goat-play, it lies in the recognition that the tragic hero is essentially another version of the sacrifice offered throughout known human history to appease an angry god – in other words, both to acknowledge and to repress a contradiction in the culture's agreed way of perceiving reality.

The desperate Renaissance struggle to reconcile the beautiful aspirations of the mind with the fierce demands of the body corresponds to the battle – which Nietzsche identified as the essence of tragedy – between Apollo (the god of civilization, rationality, daylight) and Dionysius (the god of frenzy,

---

[11] Edward Tayler, *Nature and Art in Renaissance Literature* (New York, 1964), *passim*.

[12] See for example the discussion of the medieval variations of the term in H. A. Kelly, 'Chaucer and Shakespeare on tragedy', *Leeds Studies in English* 20 (1989), 191–206.

passion, midnight). Renaissance philosophy and theology highlighted the perplexing juxtaposition of the angelic human being, a creature of reason and art under the paternal benevolence of God, with the human being as a beast of appetite, subject to God's terrible anger.

Hegel argues that tragedy is generated when a heroic individual becomes trapped between the conflicting demands of two godheads, between two sets of values that are each imperative and mutually exclusive. Thus, in Sophocles' *Antigone*, the heroine's familial and religious obligation to bury her brother collides with the laws and needs of the state. Similarly, Aeschylus' Orestes (facing a dilemma that has significant echoes in *Hamlet*) is violently torn between two aspects of his filial obligations, each advocated by a supernatural power.[13] These tragic figures cannot do good without doing evil; they are doomed, not by a random predestination of bad luck, but by a situation in which all roads lead to wrong. The tragedy lies not in the final destruction of the hero – indeed, many classical tragedies end with the hero in a state of redemption – but in the impossible conflicts the hero's particular situation serves to reveal. Tragedy thus allows its audience not only to confront its fears of suffering, but also to confront the half-recognized contradictions in its assumptions about truth and justice. The tragic genre voices the shared anxiety of a society enduring earthquakes generated by some ideological equivalent of tectonic plates, moving against each other with immense destructive power, and thereby threatening the stability of every superstructure built upon them.

Hegel distinguishes ancient tragedy from modern – in which category he includes those of the Renaissance – as focusing more on the conflict of values than on the personality of the person enduring them. This contrast between the classical and Renaissance versions of tragedy becomes less troublesome if we recognize that an increase in subjective personal identity is itself at the core of many profound Renaissance cultural conflicts. Protestantism itself can be viewed as a personalizing of salvation, away from group sacramentalism. Around the turn of the seventeenth century, anxieties about self-made men, exalted by new money and fine clothes, manifest themselves not only in sumptuary laws,[14] but also in comedy through the deflation of pretentious foreigners and fops, and in tragedy through the depredations of unprincipled Italianate schemers who (whether called Machiavel as in

---

[13] G. W. F. Hegel, *The Philosophy of Fine Art*, reprinted in Anne and Henry Paolucci, eds., *Hegel on Tragedy* (New York, 1962), pp. 177–8.

[14] Lawrence Stone, *The Crisis of the Aristocracy* (Oxford, 1975), pp. 27–9, 184–8, 547–81, discusses conspicuous consumption and its relation to the class system.

Marlowe's 1589 *The Jew of Malta*, compared to one as in Middleton's 1624 *A Game at Chess*, or merely acting like one as in Shakespeare's 1603 *Othello*) feed on the naïve trust of a traditional social order. Perhaps most important of all, the recognition of unique inward experience made the prospect of its annihilation in death much more terrifying. The fact that Renaissance tragedies end in death thus may not mean that the playwrights mistook personal disaster for the real meaning of tragedy; instead, death itself may have been the culminating instance of the kind of tragic conflict generated by this culture, the destruction of the feeling individual through collision with unfeeling larger orders. Indeed, the chief consolation at the end of many Renaissance tragedies is the recognition that the hero has reasserted his or her personal will and identity in the very face of death.

The seemingly facile formula that defines comedies as plays ending in marriage and tragedies as plays ending in death corresponds significantly to two other theories. One theory describes comedy as cyclical and tragedy as linear.[15] Another describes comedy as focused on types and tragedy on individuals. What underlies all these formulations is the perception that the story of each human life is essentially tragic, a plot of rise and fall, charting the linear path of each unique individual toward mortal annihilation. Comedy escapes this tragic pattern by showing that some basic human qualities survive across generations, whether in the genetic likenesses produced by fertile marriage, or by the recurrence of behavioural patterns that override individuality (Jonson's 'humours', for example). The individual hero of comedy or romance may triumph on behalf of his progeny or his social class (or both, as in Dekker's 1599 *The Shoemaker's Holiday*); in history plays he may triumph on behalf of his country (like the Henry V of the 1586 *Famous Victories* or Shakespeare's 1599 version); but when the individual hero is principally important for inward qualities of love, courage, or imagination, the play becomes a tragedy of extinction.

A history of English Renaissance tragedy

The story of English Renaissance tragedy is usually told diachronically as a literary genealogy, rather than as a synchronic matrix of social pressures. What might be called the authorized version of that story is full of speculations that have petrified into assumptions through frequent repetition, but it is worth telling, provided we understand that stories are not necessarily true, that many different stories can be told about the same historical

---

[15] See for example Northrop Frye, *Anatomy of Criticism* (Princeton, New Jersey, 1957).

phenomenon, and that the leap from facts to explanations is always a hazardous one. Even the most conscientiously 'objective' histories eventually prove more revealing about the culture that made them than about the culture they purport to describe, and the following summary will doubtless prove no exception.

Provoked by the excesses of decadent Roman spectacle, the increasingly powerful Christian church effectively abolished theatre in Western Europe by the sixth century AD. For several hundred years, tragedy survived only in the form of Mass, with Christ as the tragic hero, priests as chorus, and congregations as audience. Both the history of Christ and the Christian story of human history follow a tragic pattern of early greatness, betrayal, a mortal succumbing to human frailty, and a palliating suggestion that the suffering earns transcendence and redemption. Gradually, dormant elements of theatre began to re-emerge around that core. As the church expanded its repertoire of indoctrinating devices, responsive readings (such as the ninth-century *Quem Quaeritis* trope) became elaborated into liturgical drama, moved from the church to outdoor festivals (as with the early Corpus Christi plays), where English replaced Latin, and the scenes were woven together into entire 'cycles' of the biblical story. To the extent that these were affirmations of orthodox beliefs through familiar narratives, they lacked the interrogatory power of tragedy, but suspense and villainy became possible once these performances were liberated from the precise narrative of the Bible and the sanctity of the church-house.

In the fifteenth century, amid growing disputes about the mechanisms of salvation (and growing proto-Reformation resistance to the idolatrous representation of sacred figures), the morality play emerged, an allegorical genre in which a variety of personified abstractions battle for the soul of a figure known as Everyman or Mankind. Morality plays (and the succeeding 'moral interludes') portray the struggle between good and evil in psychological rather than historical terms (though the genre quickly proved congenial to political controversy).[16] By describing the protagonist as a microcosm of universal forces, it may have anticipated the tragic formula in which the hero

---

[16] Skelton's *Magnificence* (1515–23), *Respublica* (1553), and Bale's *King John* (1538/1558–62) were staged equivalents of modern political cartoons; one could warn Henry VIII against the schemes of Wolsey as well as Humanum Genus against the schemes of the Devil. The legacy of the morality play is obvious in Marlowe's *Doctor Faustus* and Dekker's *Old Fortunatus* (1599), and more subtly pervades countless other tragedies of the period. Bernard Spivack, *The Allegory of Evil* (New York, 1958), and Alan Dessen, *Jonson's Moral Comedy* and *Shakespeare and the Late Moral Plays* (Lincoln, Nebraska, 1986), ingeniously explicate this pervasive influence. By the time of Jonson's *The Devil is an Ass* (1616), parody has robbed the genre of its power.

internalizes contradictions dangerously at large in the culture. Furthermore, the conjunction of morality plays with historical and religious re-enactments may have prepared drama for the crucial Renaissance conjunction of abstract moral thought with realistic personal presence.

Rapid economic change and growth – perhaps the emergence of capitalism itself – along with radical expansions in science and world exploration, made Elizabethan England ripe for artistic innovation. Exciting but dangerous notions of individualism seeped in from the Continent. The progress of urbanization and commercialism made the theatre a viable new industry, less constrained by aristocratic conventions than poetry or prose romance (though portrayals of the emergent middle class tended toward chauvinistic propaganda or satiric comedy rather than tragedy). Although English history and classical stories were already providing some tragic material, the catalyst that precipitated the great tragedies of horror and revenge out of this mixture was the drama of Seneca, a Stoic philosopher from the first century AD. Long available to the intellectual élite, these tragedies achieved a renewed impact through their translation into English in the second half of the sixteenth century, as part of the general revival of classical learning that gives the Renaissance its name. Seneca's tragedies, based on Greek mythology, conveniently combined classical stature with sensationalism; revenge-motives took the place of classical polytheistic or fatalistic ideas that might have been harder for the Renaissance to assimilate.

This rediscovery might have meant nothing if the Elizabethans were not already developing dramatic techniques adequate to exploit it. Medieval *de casibus* tragedies – stories of the fall of great ones, on the relentlessly turning wheel of fortune – continued to be told in prose form, particularly as cautionary tales about young prodigals or bad kings. Thomas Sackville, the most important contributor to an important collection of these tales called *A Mirror for Magistrates* (1559), collaborated with Thomas Norton to adapt this admonitory genre for the stage in *Gorboduc* (1562), the earliest surviving tragedy in English. Sir Philip Sidney, condemning English drama in his 'Defence of Poetry', was willing to exempt *Gorboduc* on the grounds of its 'stately speeches' and 'notable morality'. Stiff and schematic as the play may be, it does manage to reconcile its classical–scholarly origins with current concerns about the unsettled Elizabethan succession, a type of combination crucial to the greater works that followed. Humanistic training enabled some workmanlike if static production in academic circles, and the so-called University Wits included many of the great founders of Elizabethan drama: Greene, Lyly, Peele, Lodge, Marlowe. Mere story-telling (as in the naïve chronicle plays) became artistically complex with the introduction of sub-plots that resonate themes from the central story.[17] Contrary to traditional precepts (and much to Sidney's dismay), the sub-plots in tragedies were often farcically comic, even in as grand a classical story as *Horestes* (1567), or as lurid a story of tyrannical violence as Preston's *Cambises* (1558–69). These early Tudor tragedies generally strike modern audiences as dull or crude or both, often labouring along in the verse form known as 'fourteeners' (for the number of syllables per line), with predictable didactic morals and psychologically unbelievable characters. *The Battle of Alcazar* (1589) is chaotic and bombastic; *The Misfortunes of Arthur* (1588) merely stultifying; *Gismond of Salerne* (1566–8) has all the inevitable incongruities of a Boccaccio story told in a Senecan mode.

The breakthrough to greatness may be located in Thomas Kyd's rich and vivid *Spanish Tragedy* (1582–92), and in the several triumphs of Christopher Marlowe, whose tragedies have the kind of naïve power that often characterizes artifacts from young cultures discovering their strength. Marlowe's radical mind and poetic ear made a 'mighty line' out of blank verse and put its full power in the hands of overreaching heroes who conveyed the simultaneous grandeur and cynicism of this brave new Elizabethan world and its unbridled colonial appetites. With astonishing energy, he liberated English drama from the complacencies of both its academic and its popular conventions. As learned and popular drama commingled, the upper and lower classes became jointly invested in theatre. The despised and fugitive trade of player became increasingly respectable; its noble patronage became more than a technical defence against vagabondage laws. Popular theatres, mostly on the outskirts of London, provided an outlet for the new ideas and boisterous energies of the era.

By the turn of the century, however (the story goes), the fires of Elizabethan optimism had burnt out, and tragedy sadly poked the glowing ashes. The genre distinctions deteriorated in new ways, as comedy sagged under the weight of social problems and tragedy savoured gallows humour. Coterie theatres (a haven for the old academic strain of drama) provided an outlet for a third genre, satire, when it was banned in printed form (1599). Their use of child actors helped heighten the functions of social satire and literary parody, since exalted rant and profound lust in the mouths of babes brought pretentiousness and theatrical self-consciousness to the fore. These

---

[17] For example, see William Empson, *Some Versions of Pastoral* (London, 1935), pp. 48–52, on the interplay between the main plot and the sub-plot of Middleton and Rowley's *The Changeling*. Richard Levin, *The Multiple Plot*, discusses the development of this dramatic technique; however, his *New Readings vs. Old Plays* warns that the ingenuity of critics in finding such correlations sometimes borders on fraud. More broadly, current critical theory mistrusts the entire practice of 'thematizing' literature, of mistaking an artwork for a coherent and objectively identifiable argument.

strategic exaggerations affected the competing adult theatres long after the fad for boys' companies had faded.[18] The senescence of Elizabeth may have encouraged an increasingly cynical attitude toward women (complicated by the reliance on all-male casts), and with it a sense of cultural decadence, though the tragedies were generally set in foreign countries to reduce the very real danger of offending the English court. Some dramatists could be justly accused of pandaring to the gender prejudices and social *malaise* of the audience, even to its sadism. Before condemning the famous mayhem of Elizabethan tragedy as pathological, however, one must recall that violence has always been a selling point in commercial entertainments, and that Elizabethans were (necessarily) considerably less squeamish than modern Englishmen about many aspects of the human body, not just its violent abuse.

Broad representations of royal politics and warfare steadily gave way to domestic tragedies, heavily moralized stories about unruly passions destroying ordinary families. This subgenre (which probably derived from popular ballads about actual domestic crimes) began with the anonymous *Arden of Faversham* (1585–92), a grimly realistic play loosely based on a contemporary case of husband-killing, and after a short eclipse reappeared in *A Warning for Fair Women* (*c.* 1599). The prolific Thomas Heywood liberated domestic tragedy from reliance on local events and spousal cruelty with *A Woman Killed with Kindness* (1603), in which Frankford treats his wife Anne so nobly after she betrays him that she dies of remorse. Domestic tragedy was also a favoured string in the equally versatile bow of Thomas Middleton; *Women Beware Women* (1623) demonstrates that playwright's talent for penetrating moral realism, and indicates the way domestic tragedy brought psychological issues and female protagonists to the fore in the Jacobean period.

Various individual dramatists – if indeed it is valid to talk about personal authorship in this period[19] – while all riding the crest of tragedy as a redis-

---

[18] R. A. Foakes, 'Tragedy at the children's theatres after 1600', *Elizabethan Theatre II* (Toronto, 1970), pp. 37–59.

[19] See Michel Foucault, 'What is an author?' in Donald F. Bouchard, ed., *Language, Counter-Memory, Practice*, trans. Donald F. Bouchard and Sherry Simon (Ithaca, New York, 1977); and Roland Barthes, 'The death of the author', in *Image, Music, Text*, trans. Stephen Heath (New York, 1977). Furthermore, the authorial attribution of many major Renaissance tragedies remains uncertain, largely because no one at the time felt it was an important fact. Prior to Ben Jonson's rather presumptuous publication of his *Workes* in 1616, plays were rarely considered proprietary to their authors. The play-texts were often written in collaboration, they were owned (under a weak system of copyright) by the theatre companies, and they existed primarily for the purpose of production, which was necessarily a group endeavour. For a flawed but fascinating view of the complexities of plays as literary property in the period, see Joseph Loewenstein, 'The script in the marketplace', *Representations* 12 (1985), 101–14.

covered genre, moved through the medium with their own characteristic strokes. Even Shakespeare, whose 'infinite variety' of triumphs seem 'not of an age / But for all time', nevertheless followed a cycle of Elizabethan comic optimism about the promise of new life and Jacobean tragic pessimism with its nihilistic overtones, modulating finally into the tragicomic escapism of the romances. In telling the stories of Bussy, Byron, and Chabot, George Chapman applied his classical learning to recent French court history, turning studies of decaying social orders into rhetorically difficult tragedies of ideas. Ben Jonson's more pedantic classicism, mired in historical facts and footnotes, made *Sejanus* (1603) and *Catiline* (1611) emotionally stillborn. Cyril Tourneur's mode was ironic and macabre, though his *Atheist's Tragedy* (1611) contrives an orthodox moral conclusion. In plays such as *Antonio's Revenge* (1600), the up-market satirist John Marston indulged in wild generic mixtures and wild 'fustian' vocabulary.

The various authors worked infinite variations on stock tragic figures such as the revenger (probably an expression of popular nostalgia for the private retribution abrogated by the centralized Elizabethan legal system, and of ambivalence about Christian doctrines demanding passivity to injuries), the malcontent (probably a reaction to the late-Renaissance epidemic of melancholy among frustrated courtiers), and the Machiavel (probably a reflection of the terror of a society changing from a traditional system of class and honour to a hierarchy of money and the rules of commercial competition). It is tempting to correlate the decline of Renaissance tragedy with the ironic conversion of these stock figures into self-conscious stereotypes, but in fact such metadramatic ironies were already common in the time of Elizabeth. Heroic tragedy may have become outdated for a sophisticated audience, and revenge tragedy may have exhausted its conventions through sheer repetition, but there is no clear reason why the emergent tragedy of sexuality could not carry an equivalent power. Something else seems to have happened to sap the strength of tragedy.

As dramatists wrote for increasingly élite audiences (at indoor theatres or court masques), the habit of realism deteriorated. As London became a more cynical city, the idealistic element could no longer keep company with plain observation. The alternative to the destructive *Realpolitik* that had replaced the jingoistic attitudes of chronicle, and to the sexual decadence that had replaced romantic love, was pastoral escapism: the slick professionals Beaumont and Fletcher, though they continued both the domestic and political strains of tragedy with some success in *The Maid's Tragedy* (1608–11) and *A King and No King* (1611), showed little appetite for searching moral questions. They were most important for leading a commercially successful effort to show tragic dilemmas (with the excessively elaborate plot and language now displaced into rustic and courtly tenors) miraculously undone in the genre known as tragicomedy or romance.

The dark alternative is visible in Webster's episodic dramaturgy, which showed a grand brittle world and its no less grand and brittle inhabitants doomed to meaningless suffering and annihilation. He was to Jacobean tragedy what Hardy was to the nineteenth-century novel. His and Middleton's tragedies constitute a magnificent final expression of the cultural explosion that would merely echo in the decadence of Caroline tragedians such as John Ford, who aggrandized twisted passions (as in *'Tis Pity She's a Whore*, 1632, and *The Broken Heart*, 1629), but with a kind of resignation. There remain the chilly, dispirited tragedies of Massinger and the versatile, businesslike work of James Shirley (as in *The Cardinal*, 1641, an unsatisfactory echo of Webster's *The Duchess of Malfi*, 1614), but the prodigious energy and sense of new possibilities that were so clear in Marlowe seem already to have been exhausted. Perhaps the English Civil War demonstrated that some cultural contradictions had proved impossible to negotiate by less violent communal rituals such as tragic theatre. Perhaps the decay of tragedy signalled that such crucial negotiations had moved onto other stages.

This provisional history of tragedy thus ends where the preceding theory began, with the recognition that drama is part of an elaborate and essential mechanism that adjudicates cultural dissonances. The theatres were closed in 1642 by a fanatical puritan Parliament that declared its repugnance toward both the concept and the excesses of drama, then staged a ceremonious public deposition and decapitation of the King,[20] a contradiction less horrible but no less obvious than the accompanying slaughter of sisters and brothers over the true Christian way to save their souls. The tragedy that returned to the stage with the restoration of the monarchy in 1660 was formal even in its passions and violations; the so-called 'heroic drama' celebrated extremes of love and honour in a declamatory style, with a loyalty to literary conventions rather than realistic psychology. For all its pomp and polish, Restoration tragedy thus reverted to some of the characteristics of *Gorboduc*. The novel, which similarly exploits informality, indeterminacy, and interiority,[21] would eventually assume some of the func-

[20] Franco Moretti, '"A huge eclipse": tragic form and the deconsecration of sovereignty', in Stephen Greenblatt, ed., *The Power of Forms in the English Renaissance* (Norman, Oklahoma, 1982), pp. 7–8, suggests that tragedy helped create a receptive audience for these acts.

[21] Mikhail Bakhtin, 'Epic and novel' in his *The Dialogic Imagination*, ed. Michael Holquist, trans. Caryl Emerson and Michael Holquist (Austin, Texas, 1981), attributes the emergence of the novel as the essential modern genre to its ability to encompass 'heteroglossia', an indeterminate juxtaposition of conflicting attitudes and levels of speech.

tions of great Renaissance tragedy, but by the middle of the seventeenth century the remarkable ride in the tragic vehicle had come, full circle, to an end.

Brief readings of six major tragedies follow. Without claiming to be definitive or more than loosely interconnected, these readings may suggest some ways in which the preceding theoretical and historical paradigms help to generate interpretive depth and energy. This selection of canonical works is divided into two sections. The first three tragedies – *The Spanish Tragedy*, *Hamlet*, and *The Revenger's Tragedy* – belong to a distinct subgenre, revenge tragedy, a phenomenon with deep roots in both social and literary history. The other three engage a philosophical theme, theodicy, the enquiry into the nature of evil and the means by which it enters Creation. The fact that Hegelian tragic dilemmas were available at all must have been troubling to a culture committed to the idea that the world had been made by a unitary, infallible, and benevolent God. Superficial discord could be blamed on the Fall, but the classical model of an innocent hero caught in a conflict among gods, or between the state and the gods, would have been profoundly threatening to a monotheistic culture that defended state authority as a natural extension of divine will. In *Doctor Faustus* the diabolical enters the world through the pride of a single man, whose demise exposes the hazards of his aspiring culture. In *Othello* the diabolical villain comes to represent the endlessly contagious evils of envy and self-consciousness that can subvert even an ideal civilization. *The Duchess of Malfi* presents evil as the natural by-product of the decadence, the social entropy, that one heroic woman resists to the limits of her mortality.

   Each section begins with one of the earliest and greatest public-theatre tragedies; they may actually have been composed in the same room, since Kyd, under torture, testified that the atheistic papers found in his possession belonged to his room-mate Marlowe; within a few years of writing these masterpieces, both young men were dead. The second play in each group is by Shakespeare, who characteristically converts the generic conventions into indeterminate parables about the fundamental problems of revenge and evil; if *Hamlet* compels its audience into an uncanny identification with the tragic hero, *Othello* compels an uneasy association with the villain. The third in each group, by men about whom we know very little but their writings, reflects the macabre excess and the satiric self-consciousness typical of mid-Jacobean tragedy. Within each group, the plays are separated by intervals of about a decade, marking something like the youth, maturity, and senescence of Renaissance tragedy; altogether the selection covers the great quarter-century of the genre.

Three tragedies of revenge: The Spanish Tragedy, Hamlet, *and* The Revenger's Tragedy

Revenge tragedy diverges from its master genre in that the protagonist is usually in his miserable quandary from the beginning, so he neither falls from prosperity (the medieval *de casibus* model) nor makes a fatal error (the Aristotelian *hamartia* model).[22] When critics seek out the moral of revenge tragedies (and most do), they must look elsewhere, and the primary question is almost always whether the revenger ought rather to have left it to God to enforce justice, as Christian orthodoxy instructed: vengeance is mine, saith the Lord. English literature thus continues its seemingly life-long task of reconciling Christian heroism with an ancient legacy of tribal codes and instinctive behaviours. The contradiction certainly seems sufficient to generate Hegelian tragic dilemmas for the protagonist. Yet the oxymoronic quality of Christian revenge rarely proves to be the core of such plays; even where ethical debate becomes prominent, as in Shakespeare's *Hamlet* (1599–1601) or Chapman's *The Revenge of Bussy D'Ambois* (1610–12), the morality of revenge receives less consideration than mortality, Stoicism, and epistemology. The vengeful ghost inherited from Seneca is steadily exorcised, and God rarely intervenes to take its place. The world of revenge tragedy is primarily a human world, and the bloody rule is to do unto others as you have been done to.

The reason playwrights neglect the ethical conflict may be quite simple: audiences in Renaissance theatres, like those in modern cinemas, probably enjoyed identifying with a hero whose bitter wrongs are, after a long delay, violently and ingeniously repaid. It seems to be a basic human fantasy, a balm to the helpless indignation most people regularly feel from early childhood onward; and Elizabethan audiences would presumably have been no more grateful than modern ones to be scolded for their cruelty and reminded that the sneering villain is often kind to dogs and children. Nearly every successful action movie of recent decades has wooed its audience primarily with this formula, including (as in the 'Rambo', 'Dirty Harry', and 'Death Wish' series) a portrait of the legal system as merely another infuriating obstacle between the revenger and true justice. Again, given the striking continuities, it seems pointless to defamiliarize the Renaissance experience by attributing

---

[22] Helen Gardner, *The Business of Criticism* (Oxford, 1959), pp. 41–2, observes these divergences.

this formula to the particularities of Elizabethan theatrical convention and government policy.

This is not to deny that such conventions and policies helped to shape the genre. The efficient cause for the prevalence of revenge plots in English tragedy is the example of Seneca, both directly and through the mediation of *The Spanish Tragedy*. Many of the ironies of subsequent plays become illegible unless we recognize the conventions they are exploiting. Furthermore, this Senecan model could hardly have proliferated so rapidly unless there were tensions in Elizabethan society to which it answered. Duels of honour would become a serious problem among the Jacobean aristocracy, but they are probably a secondary manifestation of a more basic shift that was already troubling the Elizabethan populace. Local justice, based in the competing interests of families, was rapidly giving way to a centralized legal bureaucracy in which personal passions and honour counted for little and patronage and rhetorical skill became all-important. Little wonder that the revenger is usually a powerless outsider avenging an inflammatory offence to a lover or close kin; little wonder, too, that such stories still have such overwhelming appeal.

Furthermore, for a society increasingly fearful of death as absolute annihilation, there would have been a supplementary pleasure in the suggestion – implicit throughout the stories of blood-revenge, as in many tribal cultures – that death is a contingent and unnatural event that can somehow be corrected by punishing the fatal agent. Mortality becomes conveniently externalized and localized in a villain, a villain both morally and practically more assailable than nature itself. Revenge tragedy offers a figurative way of saying (with Donne), 'Death, thou shalt die'; isolating the source of mortality in a human villain is a fantasy that cures the passivity and futility of mourning. If René Girard is correct that human societies are perpetually threatened by a potentially endless cycle of blood-revenge, and that theatre (as well as law) exists largely as a ritual circuit-breaker for that dangerous social malfunction,[23] it is also true that this notion of universal murder helps to conceal the inevitability of universal death. Revenge tragedy relocates mortality within the realm of human volition, sometimes even disguises it in the black robes of justice. The nostalgia for personal retribution in an increasingly impersonal legal system may have reflected also a heightened concern about the fate of individual consciousness in what was increasingly recognized as the apathetic, intolerant machinery of biological nature. The individual will, finding itself increasingly excluded from the construction of

[23] René Girard, *Violence and the Sacred*, trans. Patrick Gregory (Baltimore, Maryland, 1977).

an order of justice, finds itself similarly irrelevant to the order of nature. Many crimes are committed in *King Lear* (1605–6), but are any finally more disturbing than the simple biological fact that Cordelia is 'dead as earth' and will 'come no more. Never, never, never, never, never'? Neither the audience nor Lear himself can find any consolation, because they can conceive no revenge, when the true enemy is revealed as indifferent mortal nature: 'Why should a dog, a horse, a rat have life, and thou no breath at all?'

Elizabethan and Jacobean revenge tragedies are probably most memorable for their macabre elements: the vivid sadism of the elaborate killings, and the abuses of severed body parts: Hieronimo's tongue in *The Spanish Tragedy*, Alonzo's finger in Middleton and Rowley's *The Changeling* (1622), the detached hand and leg in *The Duchess of Malfi*, Annabella's heart in Ford's *'Tis Pity She's A Whore*. Even Shakepeare, to whom we tend to attribute the high dignity conferred by the relentless approval of cultural authorities, spices *Titus Andronicus* (1593) with a variety of severed hands as well as a rape-victim's severed tongue, leading to the serving of human bodies as a pasty for their mother. In these plays, and many others, the dance of death becomes the work of autopsy, the ritual theatre of blood enters the scientific anatomy theatre.

The lurid excesses of revenge tragedy are not hard to explain. Some of the causes have already been suggested. If Renaissance playwrights mistook Senecan closet drama for stage drama, they might have felt emboldened to show horrors that were originally intended only to energize the rhetoric.[24] If Renaissance playhouses were analogous to modern cinemas, then we can recognize a common appetite for increasingly explicit gruesomeness in popular entertainments, particularly given the popularity of brutal mutilations as public judicial events in the Renaissance. Playwrights were writing for the immediate commercial needs of their theatres, not for the approval of some future refined academic reader, and competition among companies for spectators (as well as the jading of those spectators) would naturally have led to an escalation of horrors. A glance through the plots of Renaissance tragedy confirms that the genre, competing as it did with adjacent entertainments such as prostitution and bear-baiting, concerned itself as much with the marketing principles of the shock-tabloids as with the artistic principles of Aristotle's *Poetics*.

It would be wrong to dismiss these plays as misguided or trivial works merely because of their sensationalism; there is a necessary genius behind the misprision and exploitation of Senecan violence. Murder and incest are

---

[24] See the reconsideration of this traditional idea in Gordon Braden, *Renaissance Tragedy and the Senecan Tradition* (New Haven, Connecticut, 1985).

sensational precisely because they are important; they are primal violations of human bodies and of the social order established to protect them. If we feel a guilty, voyeuristic pleasure in watching these events, it is partly the Freudian relief of confronting the forbidden, here safely encased within the frame of artistic ritual and convention. Characters such as Oedipus and Macbeth remain the most vivid in the public mind, not because they are the worst or best of people, but on the contrary because they are Everymen whose circumstances provoke them into violating the most basic rules civilization has constructed. Revengers are specialists in the tragic contradiction of shattering the most fundamental rules of civil behaviour on behalf of fundamental justice.

THE SPANISH TRAGEDY

No play in this period is more important historically than Thomas Kyd's *The Spanish Tragedy*, which established many of the themes, plot lines, and atmospheric traits that the great subsequent tragedies have in common. The play was frequently reprinted and revived (once with new passages commissioned by the enterprising producer Philip Henslowe from Ben Jonson), and the numerous contemporary parodies affirm its prominence. The chief characteristics of Renaissance tragedy are all abundantly on display here: the metatheatrical self-consciousness, the extreme ritualized violence, the black humour and the blacker mourning, the variety of stage business, the mixture of elegant and passion-torn speech, the concern with court corruption, and the centrality of furtive and finally excessive revenge to the plot. *The Spanish Tragedy* also shares with many of its great descendants – Shakespeare's *Romeo and Juliet* (1595), Webster's *The Duchess of Malfi*, Marston's *Sophonisba* (1605), Middleton and Rowley's *The Changeling*, and Ford's *'Tis Pity She's a Whore* and *The Broken Heart* – a particular version of the tragic conflict between individual desire and powerful impersonal mechanisms: the disastrous insistence that a woman subordinate her marital preference to the interests of a greedy and tradition-bound patriarchal society. The demands of dynastic marriage override true affection as well as true justice.

The historical importance of *The Spanish Tragedy* is inseparable from the astonishing plenitude of the play in its own right, a richness of plot, character, symbol, spectacle, and rhetoric. Kyd gave his audience its money's worth. The story is framed by the observations of Revenge and the Ghost of Don Andrea, who together oversee the disasters that follow from Andrea's death in battle at the hands of Balthazar, Prince of Portugal. Andrea's friend Horatio vies with the Spanish nobleman Lorenzo for the credit of capturing

Balthazar, a rivalry that becomes more complicated when both Horatio and Balthazar become enamoured of Lorenzo's sister, Bel-imperia. Lorenzo, hoping for social advancement, and the Spanish king, hoping for geopolitical advantage, both favour the match with Balthazar. Bel-imperia, however, loves Horatio, and meets him in secret. Not secret enough, though: Lorenzo and Balthazar interrupt the tryst, imprison Bel-imperia, and stab and hang Horatio. Horatio's father Hieronimo finds the body and goes mad, but recovers enough control to plot revenge. Frustrated in his attempts to reach the king directly with his complaint, Hieronimo (who has been reading Seneca) apparently lets himself be humoured with the privilege of staging a play for the combined royal courts of the two countries. His play, rich in correspondences to the aforementioned events, is acted (like a court masque) by the aristocrats themselves, and under the guise of play-acting, Hieronimo stabs Lorenzo while Bel-imperia stabs Balthazar. Hieronimo's subsequent suicide attempt is foiled, but he bites off his tongue to prevent any confession, and when he is ordered to confess in writing, he uses the knife provided to sharpen his pen to kill Lorenzo's father and finally himself. The play ends with Andrea's Ghost gleefully planning perpetual joys for his dead friends and an 'endless tragedy' for his dead enemies.

In telling this lurid and intricate tale, Kyd rediscovered the potential of tragedy for representing life in its beautiful and destructive complexity, rather than as a vessel for preconceived and predictable moral lessons. The burgeoning cultural conflicts of the Renaissance clamoured to be represented and adjudicated, and from the opening words of the play we find ourselves at contested boundaries:

> When this eternal substance of my soul
> Did live imprison'd in my wanton flesh,
> Each in their function serving other's need,
> I was a courtier in the Spanish court.
> My name was Don Andrea, my descent,
> Though not ignoble, yet inferior far
> To gracious fortunes of my tender youth:
> For there in prime and pride of all my years,
> By duteous service and deserving love,
> In secret I possess'd a worthy dame,
> Which hight sweet Bel-imperia by name.
> But in the harvest of my summer joys
> Death's winter nipp'd the blossoms of my bliss,
> Forcing divorce betwixt my love and me.
> For in the late conflict with Portingale
> My valour drew me into danger's mouth,
> Till life to death made passage through my wounds.

The Ghost of Don Andrea, himself a liminal creature compromising the boundary between life and death, thus ushers us into the play, and ushers in the great age of Elizabethan tragedy. These first seventeen lines, laden with paradoxes and reciprocities, discuss the conflicts between mind and body and between hereditary and achieved nobility (both very lively Renaissance disputes), and sketch a story of secret love against bitter death (a favourite Renaissance polarity which will constantly tangle the kissing of Horatio and Bel-imperia in motives and metaphors of killing).[25] Death itself came at a liminal point, since the battle occurred 'where Spain and Portingale do jointly knit / Their frontiers, leaning on each other's bound' (1.2.22–3). In the remainder of this opening soliloquy, continuing to mix the familiar with the exotic, Kyd draws into his tale of modern Spain (a place of more than casual interest to the Elizabethans) the powerful precedents of classical literature, as Andrea narrates his death in battle (which recalls that of Achilles), his stranding on the banks of the river Styx, and his liberation by Don Horatio, who (like Antigone) performs the neglected burial. Andrea then must walk a spiritual tightrope between a sort of hell and a sort of heaven, overseen by the *discordia concors* of Pluto and Proserpine, who represent the primal oppositions evoked by those seventeen lines: war and love, death and life, winter and summer.

As the play proper begins, the King of Spain attempts three related reconciliations: his country to Portugal, power to justice, and Lorenzo to Horatio. The tragedy will occur precisely because it is impossible to reconcile such oppositions in a fallen world – not only a world of money, politics, and betrayal, but a world of scarcity, where there is only one royal Balthazar to be claimed as prisoner, only one beautiful Bel-imperia to be married, and only one mortal Horatio to carry all of Hieronimo's paternal hopes. The events that follow quickly sketch a test between love and friend-ship, and again between love and war, all presented simultaneously as psychologically realistic stories and as grand mythological confrontations. There is a powerful critique of lawlessness within a no less powerful critique of government, and every attempt to do justice becomes self-contradictory.[26] War becomes a place of amity, peace of treacherous bloodshed. This flood of unresolved oppositions might be dismissed as artistic carelessness rather than artistic genius, but nearly all the great Elizabethan tragedies display a reckless delight in inclusiveness, an appetite for multiplying complexities. The very lack of an authorized tradition in the genre comparable to those

---

[25] See for example 1.4.60–8, 2.2.21–40, and 2.4.32–49.

[26] G. K. Hunter, *Dramatic Identities*, pp. 214–29, identifies 'ironies of justice' as thematically central to *The Spanish Tragedy*.

long established in poetry may have allowed tragedy a freedom that made it adaptable to the new energies of Renaissance culture, itself an overflow of countless divergent influences. *The Spanish Tragedy* can be located at the perfect Nietzschean axis for tragedy,[27] with the chilly Apollonian courtliness in constant tension with the Dionysian passions and horrors – a tension sustained right through the astonishing last scene, in which Hieronimo's brutal revenge takes place within the high-cultural rituals of a theatrical performance at court. Metaphors become grimly literalized, and golden aspirations are perpetually ironized by the physical body, as when Lorenzo cruelly mocks the hanging Horatio with the observation that 'Although his life were still ambitious proud, / Yet is he at the highest now he is dead' (2.4.60–1). No play could articulate more clearly, in its texture and its plot, its genesis from a culture struggling to resolve the many paradoxes in its evolving view of the universe.

The most memorable figure in *The Spanish Tragedy* is Hieronimo, father of the heroic victim Horatio. Though he is not established early as a protagonist – Kyd is too busy weaving the plot – Hieronimo becomes the emotional centre of the story. His nobly unified roles – as a man of love and of justice, of art and of law, as a husband and a father, a servant of family and of king – all become contradictions through his son's murder. Hieronimo thus wanders into a play-world thematically charged with paradox, and we are able to watch its effect on a sentient and eloquent creature. His predominant passion is mourning, and his predominant mode is madness: he is overwhelmed by the utterness, injustice, and irreversibility of his son's annihilation in death. Amid all the whirling of the plot, Hieronimo's speeches keep returning us to the plain truth at the core of the tragedy: the fact of death and the futility of trying to change or transcend it through love, honour, art, progeny, or justice. (The paganistic frame allows Kyd to leave the viability of religious redemption, along with the problem of Christian revenge, tactfully unexamined.) This thematic focus, more deeply than the many shared points of plot and style, is what *The Spanish Tragedy* bequeaths to Shakespeare's *Hamlet*; it is also a distinctive concern of Renaissance culture, as the facts of error and mutability erased each mortal dreamer of glory.

No wonder, then, that revenging well seemed the best revenge. The performance of that revenge by a theatrical ritual in *The Spanish Tragedy* – a motif that recurs in *Hamlet*, *The Revenger's Tragedy*, and *'Tis Pity She's a Whore* – may constitute an acknowledgment that such satisfactions are allowable and feasible only within a frame of fantasy. At an aesthetic distance, the

---

[27] Thomas McAlindon, *English Renaissance Tragedy*, p. 56, remarks on this resemblance, but dismisses it because he finds Kyd too mistrustful of both extremes.

massacre becomes an elaborate sacrifice, a sacrifice which may serve to exorcise the demons of helpless frustration at perceived injustice, demons so common in the human animal, so heightened in the aspiring minds of the Renaissance, so focused in the fierce economies of Elizabethan England and Elizabeth's court. Hieronimo drops his metadramatic role to tell the assembled royalty,

> Haply you think, but bootless are your thoughts,
> That this is fabulously counterfeit,
> And that we do as all tragedians do:
> To die today, for fashioning our scene,
> The death of Ajax, or some Roman peer,
> And in a minute starting up again,
> Revive to please tomorrow's audience.
> No, princes, know I am Hieronimo,
> The hopeless father of a hapless son.   (4.4.76–84)

And here he shows the unreviving body of Horatio, for which he has repaid these fathers in kind. By having Hieronimo negate the fictionality of his show in this way, Kyd removes one crucial level of detachment between his spectators and his play. Drama is not some academic historical exercise, the author-figure here reminds his audience; it is about real and present lives, and therefore about real and imminent deaths. Countless Elizabethans, bereaved by war, poverty, or religious persecution, could have conceived a complaint similar to Hieronimo's against their monarch; *The Spanish Tragedy* allowed them to witness and approve an almost inconceivable treason that follows naturally, by the logic of revenge, from that complaint.[28]

HAMLET

To locate an intrinsic meaning in *Hamlet* is to defy augury, as well as critical fashion. This play has been subjected to the most intensive hermeneutic scrutiny of any work in Western culture, except perhaps those believed to be dictated by God. Yet the critical community still does not concur on whether the motivating ghost is angel or devil, whether Hamlet does or does not, should or should not, act promptly, or what the most famous line of the play ('To be or not to be') really means; nor can editors agree what the central

---

[28] New Historicist criticism might question whether such representations of treason serve to subvert royal sanctity, or instead to contain such subversion safely within a self-consuming artistic exercise. Intriguingly, the story of Christ can be viewed as engaging this same rebellious impulse, authorizing each sinner to execute the son of the ruling and bereaving King of Heaven.

word is in the second most famous soliloquy ('O that this too too sallied/ sullied/solid flesh would melt'), or whether another famous soliloquy ('How all occasions do inform against me') even belongs in the text. This may partly reflect the critical industry's instinct for self-perpetuation, or the inevitable indeterminacy of any text read closely enough, but it certainly ought to make a conscientious coward out of anyone tempted to say what this play means.

Hamlet is therefore an embarrassing play for a scholar to write about, as 'To be or not to be' is an embarrassing line for an actor to speak. It is partly an embarrassment of riches, but partly also a recognition that it has been done so often before, done so well and done so badly. Moreover, this most famous of plays is particularly renowned for its infinite interpretability, for the way it (like the 'Mousetrap' Hamlet himself stages) causes its viewers to project themselves into the play. In this sense, *Hamlet* is less a tragedy than a frame and a stimulus for the creation of tragedies, infinitely various personal refractions of an archetypal story. Shakespeare uses an array of standard Renaissance tragic conflicts – mortality against ambition, Christianity against revenge, love against sexual horror, private truth against political imperatives – to compel a deep, sympathetic recognition of the way cultural contradictions agonize the sensitive individual. Observers in subsequent centuries who perceive the play as fundamentally concerned with their own crises may appear absurdly egoistical, but in a sense they are making good use of this tragedy-making machine.

Shakespeare biographers read *Hamlet* as Shakespeare's metaphorical autobiography, the story of a brilliant young man who liked to stage revealing plays and was doomed to be understood and admired only in the future retelling of his stories; the legend that Shakespeare himself played the Ghost of Hamlet's father corresponds suggestively to the fact that Shakespeare had a son named Hamnet who died young. Theatre historians insist that the play cannot be understood properly without viewing it as an artifact of the historical theatre (as a revenge tragedy largely borrowed from Kyd), and radical modern directors claim that its essential truths are best revealed by radically modernizing its setting. When the great actress Sarah Bernhardt played Hamlet, she told interviewers that Hamlet was, after all, predominantly feminine.[29] The two most famous interpretations of *Hamlet* follow this reflexive pattern: melancholic intellectuals have described the play as a study of intellectual melancholy, and psychoanalytic critics have characterized the play as prescient psychoanalysis. Both interpretations are built around an

---

[29] See for example *Poet Lore* 4, New Series (1900), 149.

interpretive crux as stubborn as that of Iago's motivation: Hamlet's delay in avenging his father.[30] Delays while the protagonist plots his elaborate revenge are quite conventional in Elizabethan tragedy, but that does not preclude interpreting Hamlet's delay as psychological evidence, since Shakespeare characteristically awakens conventions into expressions of deep questions or truths.

Nearly two hundred years ago, several deep thinkers, oppressed by the brutal actions of the French and Industrial Revolutions, described Hamlet as a deep thinker trapped in a world of brutal action. Romantic poet–philosophers in Germany and England – Goethe and Schlegel, Coleridge and Hazlitt[31] – discerned a romantic poet–philosopher named Hamlet, drawing their keynote from the end of the 'To be or not to be' soliloquy:

> Thus conscience does make cowards of us all,
> And thus the native hue of resolution
> Is sicklied o'er with the pale cast of thought,
> And enterprises of great pitch and moment
> With this regard their currents turn awry
> And lose the name of action.   (3.1.82–7)

How can anyone become a decisive executioner, this interpretation asks, in a world so lacking in absolute truth and moral purity that 'There is nothing either good or bad but thinking makes it so ... Use every man after his deserts and who should 'scape whipping? ... I am myself indifferent honest, but yet I could accuse me of such things that it were better my mother had not borne me' (2.2.249–50, 529–30; 3.1.121–3)? Hamlet's intelligence makes him cripplingly aware of the good and bad pertaining to any action, and so he accomplishes nothing until he yields the decisions to a Higher Intelligence: 'There's a divinity that shapes our ends, rough-hew them how we will', he tells Horatio (5.2.10–11), and later, 'There is special providence in the fall of a sparrow' (5.2.219–20).

Contemplation reveals action to be futile as well as unjustified. Hamlet's royal father was effectively forgotten after a few months by his own wife; and, as Hamlet observes in the graveyard, neither the lovely cosmetics of the lady

---

[30] Eleanor Prosser in *Hamlet and Revenge* (Stanford, California, 1967) offers another perspective on this crux; taking seriously the paradox of Christian revenge, she argues provocatively that an Elizabethan audience would have recognized the Ghost as diabolical and that Hamlet's fatal mistake was his failure to delay further.

[31] Though divergent in many of their views, these commentators both recognized themselves in this hero: Coleridge remarked that 'I have a smack of Hamlet myself', and Hazlitt commented, 'It is *we* who are Hamlet'. See the 24 June 1827 entry in T. Ashe, ed., *The Table Talk and Omniana of Samuel Taylor Coleridge* (London, 1905), p. 47; and *The Collected Works of William Hazlitt* (London, 1902), I. 232.

nor the clever ploys of the lawyer have kept them from becoming rotting skulls. Indeed, imagination can 'trace the noble dust of Alexander till 'a find it stopping a bunghole' (5.1.203–4). The head emptied of its brains makes actions difficult to justify, just as the head full of brains did in another way. It is not surprising that Hamlet contemplating the skull of Yorick is this play's best-known image: the entire play may be aptly described as a skull set on stage confronting the audience with the most perplexing facts human beings have to assimilate as we commit ourselves to choices and efforts. Death, the great 'common' equalizer, mocks Hamlet's aspirations (and not only Hamlet's); only at the end does he recognize that the imminence of death can provoke action rather than dissuade from it.

A century after the Romantics, a new movement (again emerging from the Austro-German intellectual community) claimed *Hamlet* for itself. Psychoanalytic critics (beginning with Ernest Jones) interpreted Hamlet's delay as a psychoanalytic symptom. Hamlet cannot kill Claudius because Claudius, having killed Hamlet's father and married Hamlet's mother, is too deeply identified with Hamlet's own Oedipal impulses. This explains Hamlet's obsessive interest in the incestuous aspect of the violation, and explains also the sudden loathing of himself and of women that disturbs everyone around him (the influence of this theory upon Laurence Olivier's film version of the play is unmistakable).[32] Thus, *Hamlet* has been simultaneously puzzling and compelling for so long because it draws on the darkest and most essential secret underlying all human behaviour. Like Oedipus, we all attack the riddle eagerly, and find the answer is ourselves; like him, we have chosen to be blind at the edges of our insight. The play provokes subconscious recognitions; if dramatic characters are not really living people with full psychological histories, audiences still are, and *Hamlet* is an instrument of group psychotherapy, a tragedy designed to exorcise the demons of the nuclear family.

No self-respecting critic can choose simply to submit to Shakespeare's illusionist trick and believe complacently that *Hamlet* is really about the critic's own life and world. If there is to be any hope of nailing this protean spectre down to a few solid interpretive foundations, one must enquire about the things *Hamlet* might have meant, or at least meant differently, to an Elizabethan audience, with its indoctrinated ideas about revenge tragedy, incest, kingship, suicide, and mortality.[33] On the other hand, it seems foolish

---

[32] Dale Silviria, *Laurence Olivier and the Art of Film Making* (London, 1985), pp. 171, 174.

[33] Roland Mushat Frye, *The Renaissance Hamlet* (Princeton, New Jersey, 1984), and Arthur McGee, *The Elizabethan Hamlet* (New Haven, Connecticut, 1987), are good sources for such an enquiry.

and pointless to dispel the peculiar magic of this play by refusing to acknowledge its suggestiveness as commentary on so many lives in so many times, including ours. There are moments of seemingly timeless penetration, when the particular story of this Danish prince gestures toward universality. When Hamlet discovers that the gravedigger began work on the very day of Hamlet's birth and his father's great victory, the play acquires the archetypal power of tragic fate, the uncanny navigation to a predestined place of doom.

Shakespeare draws on another archetype by suggesting that the world has become 'an unweeded garden' of evil and mortality ever since the 'serpent' Claudius poisoned old Hamlet in his 'orchard'. *Hamlet* thus takes place during the awkward extended adolescence of the human world as well as of its hero. Eden has given way to a place that will err and decay until the purifying apocalyptic ending; the radiant world perceived in childhood has become infected with repellent hypocrisy and lust, answerable only with violence. In this sense, the plot of *Hamlet* is an elaborate vindication of cynical adolescence, which is itself a period of painful contradictions requiring tragic explication: the former great father really has been usurped by a weak conniving lascivious figure who turns the sainted mother into a horrifying figure of corrupt sexuality, while stupidity and self-interest really have made love and friendship treacherous. Shakespearian tragedy never merely tells a sad story. The stories are always symbolic systems that allow us to re-experience and re-define the crises in the making of our own identities; the plays do also for the individual what I have suggested tragedy characteristically does for the culture as a whole.

Like Holbein's famous painting of 'The Ambassadors', *Hamlet* is a perfect two-faced Janus for the Renaissance, balanced as the culture was between the aspiring rediscovery of selfhood and the material world, and the cautionary heritage of medieval Christianity. One face of *Hamlet* is 'the mirror up to nature' Hamlet himself recommends for drama, a 'counterfeit presentment' of living families and kings, inspiring renewed awe and affection for the human voice and the human mind. The other face is the anonymous skull Christianity has insistently urged people to contemplate, a *memento mori* that inspired *contemptus mundi*, a reminder of death that would teach people to emphasize spiritual salvation over transient worldly pride and pleasures. The conflict between heroic fantasies and mortal abjection was heightened in the Renaissance, but it was far from new then, and could hardly be called outdated now. Spectators at a production of *Hamlet* are looking simultaneously at a mirror and at a skull, and they are seeing themselves. They recognize in Hamlet versions of their own ideas and their own life-narratives, then must share his graveyard recognitions and his graveyard destiny. When the audience is compelled to reconcile the two images, to see itself as both 'the wonder of the world' and 'this quintessence of dust', the juxtaposition generates the tragic effect in an extraordinarily pure form.

Perhaps, as T. S. Eliot's Prufrock says, we are not Prince Hamlet. Certainly we are not medieval Danish princes commanded by ghosts to murder our royal uncles. But we enter the stage of 'this distracted globe' born to a role and its 'cursed spite' (1.5.97, 188). We can hardly help seeing ancestors in the 'mind's eye', sensing a possessive spirit of heredity that tells us what class status, what mental and physical abilities and abnormalities, what ancient grudges, will shape our ends, rough-hew them how we will. As children of Adam and Eve, we live out the fatal legacy of our parents' crimes; as children of Israelis or Palestinians, as Christians or Moslems, we (like Fortinbras and his troops) kill and die on behalf of fruitless ancestral feuds, meaningless cycles of fear and vengeance. As *The Spanish Tragedy* suggests, such ghosts exact a terrible price from the world of the living: is there any worse poison that could be poured in our ears than these legacies of blame and hatred?

No wonder, then, that so many of us identify with Hamlet; the extraordinary genius of this play is the way it allows us to recognize that we, too, are tragic heroes. The metadramatic elements have as much to do with classical Stoicism as with literary criticism. Hamlet finally offers us nothing more, and nothing less, than a model for performing our painful roles most nobly. Whenever some haunting image from the past (like Hamlet's father) tells us who we must be and what we must die for, whenever friends (like Rosencrantz and Guildenstern) betray us for profit, whenever lovers (like Ophelia) suddenly inexplicably reject or disgust us, whenever all those things make us wonder who ruined the world we once dreamt of ruling, then we become Hamlet, and are glad to have his company as we sit in 'this distracted globe', in these 'goodly' prisons of body and world (2.2.242–4).

THE REVENGER'S TRAGEDY

Traditional literary historians might agree with their theoretical antagonists that *The Revenger's Tragedy* cannot be safely attributed to any single author. Traditionalists have regularly tugged suspiciously at the slender thread by which the attribution to Tourneur hangs, and the play fits easily into the repertoire of Middleton, plausibly even that of Marston. Theoreticians increasingly advocate a new model in which the attribution of any play to any person is misleading, either because plays were not proprietary to their authors in the Renaissance, or because the entire concept of authorship is a sentimental modern fiction disguising the fact that authors (like other individuals) are not really autonomous agents, but products of their cultures. Indeed, Tourneur and Webster both might serve as cautionary instances for traditional practice, since the extremely meagre biographical record of both men has lured critics into absurdly circular arguments in which the plays serve as evidence of the attitudes of the playwrights, and those posited attitudes are then used to explain the plays.

In the case of *The Revenger's Tragedy*, the same evidence supports both the traditional and the theoretical doubts about attribution. Deducing the author from internal evidence is difficult precisely because this tragedy seems so thoroughly a determinate product of its time. Many authors were writing this kind of satiric tragedy of horrors; it is full of devices (of plot, language, and stagecraft) familiar from earlier tragedies; and its fascination with the corruptions of lust and power at court seems to have been an obsession of the age. The device of disguising the body of the Duke for a second killing (5.1) comes from Marlowe's *The Jew of Malta*. The commonplaces uttered to the skull (3.5.84–98) distinctly recall *Hamlet*. There are traces of Chettle's *Hoffman*, and the revenger incorporates, among other stock roles, the pose of the murderous Machiavel (1.1.93–6). The absurdly improbable disaster (5.3) in which two competing sets of killers coincidentally each endeavour to assassinate Lussurioso under the guise of coronation masques suggests an ironic acknowledgment that this Senecan convention had become outworn. The author in effect declares his awareness that *The Spanish Tragedy* has been performed too often (something asserted more explicitly by other Jacobean authors),[34] and that the only viable move remaining is its conversion to black humour through hyperbole.

The mistrust of law that helps to fuel revenge tragedy as a genre is here abundantly endorsed. When Antonio's virtuous wife is raped, the power of the Duchess precludes the execution of justice – that is, the execution of her son the rapist (1.2). Antonio appears to be quoting proverbial wisdom when he remarks, '*Judgement in this age is near kin to favour*' (1.4.55). A few scenes later, when Lussurioso is arrested for supposedly attempting to kill his father the Duke, we see that the law is just as cynical an exercise in its severities as in its mercies (2.3). Finally, after the avengers have at last repaid the wrongs,

---

[34] *The Spanish Tragedy* is regularly parodied from Greene's *Orlando Furioso* (1591) to Beaumont and Fletcher's *Knight of the Burning Pestle* (1607); the Induction to Jonson's *Bartholomew Fair* (1614) mocks spectators who will still 'swear *Jeronimo* and *Andronicus* are the best plays yet'.

the noble Antonio arrests them upon taking power, because 'You that would murder him would murder me' (5.3.105). Perhaps Jacobean censors would have resisted a play endorsing the killing of even such corrupt rulers; perhaps the author was seeking an extra twist in completing the requisite bloodbath; perhaps Antonio has some grounds to fear the precedent. Yet, having seen the play essentially through the eyes of the revengers, the audience is likely to experience this ending as one more proof that law bears very little relation to the felt truths of justice.

Though Vindice's opening soliloquy lacks the richness of contradiction that characterizes Don Andrea's induction to *The Spanish Tragedy*, it none the less establishes the polarity that gives *The Revenger's Tragedy* its fascinating energy. On the one hand, as he contemplates the skull of his murdered mistress, Vindice is the classic brooding revenger. But the alternative to the physical decay represented by the skull is merely the moral decay embodied by the ruling family, not (as in *Hamlet*) the transcendent glory of the human mind. As he narrates the entrance of the court, Vindice offers a dumbshow apt to a satiric comedy rather than a Senecan tragedy. Again the peculiar amalgam of Renaissance literary consciousness is at work: the medieval obsession with mortal decay must find a way to function within a classical satire on Jacobean social decadence. As in the opening lines of Donne's 'The Relique',[35] the rhapsodic description of the beloved's beauty and purity must endure interruption, not only by the acknowledgment of the decaying corpse, but also by cynical observations on sexual corruption. Vindice says of the skull,

> When life and beauty naturally fill'd out
> These ragged imperfections,
> When two heaven-pointed diamonds were set
> In those unsightly rings – then 'twas a face
> So far beyond the artificial shine
> Of any woman's bought complexion,
> That the uprightest man (if such there be
> That sin but seven times a day) broke custom,
> And made up eight with looking after her.　　(1.1.17–25)

The sentence becomes a terrible let-down, and a significant one. If this is the only consequence of such beauty and virtue, then we have fallen very far from the redemptive Neoplatonic model. If Jacobean tragedies do reflect a

---

[35] Donne's lyric tribute to chaste love begins, 'When my grave is broke up againe / Some second ghest to entertaine, / (For graves have learn'd that woman-head / To be to more than one a Bed)'.

bitter disappointment with the results of earlier Renaissance idealisms (a disappointment prophesied in *Doctor Faustus*), then this collapse of a Petrarchan rhapsody engages *The Revenger's Tragedy* with that cultural crisis from the opening scene. One may take sufficient revenge on the corrupt dukes with sword and poison, but the only recourse for a disappointed malcontent in the court of Renaissance culture is to inject cruelty and farce into its noblest undertakings. In this sense, the author of *The Revenger's Tragedy* – whoever he was, to whatever extent he was distinguishable from the culture as a whole – becomes the primary embittered revenger of his own play.

Vindice himself is a self-conscious playwright of poetic justice:

> Now to my tragic business; look you, brother,
> I have not fashion'd this only for show
> And useless property; no, it shall bear a part
> E'en in it own revenge. This very skull,
> Whose mistress the duke poison'd, with this drug,
> The mortal curse of the earth, shall be reveng'd
> In the like strain, and kiss his lips to death.   (3.5.99–105)

Hippolito replies, 'Brother, I do applaud thy constant vengeance, / The quaintness of thy malice, above thought'. As tragedy becomes a more self-conscious ironic exercise in the Jacobean period, the applause is reserved for quaint malice rather than grand virtue. Vindice has the heroic role, but he taints it with the sardonic cruelty of the satirist, a popular figure at the start of the seventeenth century, deflected into drama from other genres by government censorship. The discrepancy between Vindice's heroic and satiric roles may correspond to a tragic schism between hope and experience in Renaissance England. Drama and society both yield to an increasing scepticism about the possibility of meaningful virtuous action – to the extent that John Ford will be obliged to find heroism, by a sheer act of assertion, within Giovanni's incest, blasphemy, and murderous mutilation of his beloved pregnant sister in *'Tis Pity She's a Whore*.

The quaint malice of artful revenge generates only a sterile admiration; the notion of resorting to art when life ceases to make sense is delusive, because without a coherent meaning to sustain or subvert, art becomes merely distraction and decoration. As the final vestigial ideals concerning law, love, and nobility decay around them, the inhabitants of this play-world become puppets of desire and vengeance. The Duke, his heir Lussurioso, and his bastard Spurio, are all destroyed through their jaded mechanical pursuit of lust; the rest fall through vengeful scheming. The anguish anticipated by *Doctor Faustus* of attempting to live without spiritual absolutes, the anguish of the Renaissance gone astray, here manifests itself in the portrayal of a world in which people are nothing more than desperate little bodies consuming each other, indistinguishably in sex and murder. Even when his plot against Lussurioso backfires, Ambitioso can find no reason to change course, because the absolutes have become absurdly self-referential: 'there is nothing sure in mortality, but mortality. Well, no more words, 'shalt be reveng'd i' faith' (3.6.89–91). If human life has no meaningful connection to anything beyond, then revenge becomes the only game in town. The thunder and the comet that accompany the culminating vengeance are theatrical effects that carry no Christian conviction. Vengeance is still referred to as 'Murder's quit-rent', but no one is under the illusion that it really cures anything. The revengers save no one, and no one thanks them; Antonio, the only vindicated victim left alive, does quite the opposite. Furthermore, the essentialist naming of the central characters virtually forbids any redemptive conversions or growth beyond the functions of the plot. In this sense, *The Revenger's Tragedy* harks back toward the earlier allegorical drama, but it is hard to have a morality play without morality; and now there are only negative forces, cynicism earns better success than faith, and Everyman can triumph only by joining the carnage in both body and spirit.

The pull of horror on our sympathetic emotions in *The Revenger's Tragedy* is rarely equal to the pull of excess on our comic intellect, particularly when we are coached by the hard-hearted jeerings of villains and avengers alike. Of the fatally victimized women who might have provided a focal point for sympathy, only one appears on stage – as a grinning skull. In a classic misogynist dichotomy, women in *The Revenger's Tragedy* are either monsters of maternal corruption (the Duchess, who seduces her step-son, and Gratiana, who plays pandar to her daughter) or passive occasions for male idealization and outrage (Antonio's wife, Vindice's dead mistress and living sister). The result is a slashing and haunting portrayal, funny and horrifying at the same moments, of a world propelled eagerly to ruin by blood-lust, sex-lust, and power-lust. Modern critics and audiences seem to enjoy *The Revenger's Tragedy* as a sort of Hallowe'en toy, and indeed it glows in the dark. Events seem so deeply inscribed into the *ethos* and the artistic conventions of the Jacobean period that we feel little guilt in our sadistic and voyeuristic pleasures. Still, the play should not be dismissed as camp. It thrives at second-hand from the motives that first made rape, blood-revenge, and irreligion compelling topics for dramatic exploration, but the satiric detachment may itself be an important signal of cultural crisis. In a world learning to snicker at escalating outrages, perhaps people sought out experiences that might still rouse authentic horror, to test whether the social innovations of the Renaissance – including capitalism, colonialism, and relativism – had completely deadened their former moral sensibilities.

Three tragedies of theodicy: Doctor Faustus, Othello, and The Duchess of Malfi

DOCTOR FAUSTUS

In the later sixteenth century, provoked by the fearsome warnings of the Reformation, morality plays became increasingly likely to feed the protagonist to the stage prop known as the hell-mouth, marking his damnation. That is precisely what happens at the end of Christopher Marlowe's *Doctor Faustus*, which puts the morality formula in the service of a devastating cultural critique. Faustus may be a remarkably brilliant and errant scholar, but he is also an Everyman who compels Renaissance audiences, and modern ones as well, to examine the perplexing choices facing a creature of desire and doubt in a changing world.

The play flirts with traditional moral allegory. The seven deadly sins parade across stage, but Faustus enacts those same vices within common forms of human conduct. He receives conflicting advice from good and bad spirits, but these spirits become increasingly human, embodied in feeling speakers such as the good Old Man and Mephostophilis, who renew the tug-of-war on Faustus's final day. The play may thus serve as a sort of geological record of the old stark moralistic patterns of dramatic conflict metamorphosing into the subtler complexities of human ambivalence; in the process, the play similarly records the seismic collision of medieval and modern segments of Western spiritual history. The schematic battle among allegorical figures is still plainly visible here, but tied into the real temptations of a psychologically plausible human life. The vicious cycle of pride and despair becomes less demonology than psychopathology.

The moral of the story may seem orthodox and simple enough: to borrow a rhetorical question from the Book of Matthew, 'What profits it a man if he should gain the whole world, and lose his own soul?' That moral becomes tragically complex in a culture enthusiastically engaged in gaining the world (through imperialism, commerce, science, and humanistic philosophy) despite the Christian doctrines of humility and *contemptus mundi* to which it nominally still subscribed. From a medieval perspective the chief of sinners, Faustus from another perspective dies for the sins of modern civilization, which was evidently finding the temporal world less contemptible than before. Again, as in the Hegelian model, tragedy shows a hero answerable to the contradictory demands of two ruling deities of his culture, which both nurtured and feared ambition. Faustus may seem Promethean, or at least Icarian, sacrificing himself to liberate human aspiration from physical instrumentalities and constricting superstitions, until the limiting 'heavens conspir'd his overthrow', in the ominous phrase of the opening Chorus. But to project Marlowe's own theological radicalism directly onto Faustus is to overlook the fact that tragedy is finally answerable less to an individual than to a culture, and less to opinion than to conflict. The Renaissance fusion is visible here in its full ambivalence. Magic appeals to Faustus because it allows intellectual activity to control the material world;[36] he is betrayed, as were many Renaissance aspirations, by the impossibility of freeing his intellectual activity from the material sphere and materialist motives.

Faustus opens the play as the perfect Renaissance man, on the brink of great new enterprises. His dilemma looks common and innocuous enough, the choices of a new graduate wondering whether to enter law school (but it is too boring), medical school (but people eventually die anyway), or graduate school in theology (but damnation is predestined – though Faustus here reads only a misleading fragment of the biblical text). Faustus's alternative career is sorcery, a practice that looks very much like an extension of the emergent Renaissance sciences: it involves astronomy, optics, ancient history, foreign languages, and navigation for exotic delicacies that may be exchanged for money and court favour. Faustus is even a Reformer, using his omnipotent book to attack the Pope and refute the power of Catholic rituals.

By a version of the 'Foolish Wish' motif familiar from folklore, Faustus discovers that purchasing the ability to violate the rules of nature is inevitably a bad bargain. The world he now commands is a small and flimsy one, and so the quest for transcendence generates only more claustrophobia. In exchange for his forfeited soul, Faustus receives merely some slapstick revenge, a little money, praise from the ignorant, unfulfilling fulfilments of his sexual fantasies, and a horrible spiritual emptiness. This list will seem unpleasantly familiar to many modern readers; even a relatively good life could easily be thus dismissed, perhaps because materialism in recent centuries has proved a rather limited recompense for losses of personal authenticity and religious faith. The play openly accuses Faustus of being responsible for his own fall through his wickedness and stupidity, but always reminds us on another level, just when we assume a complacent stance of

---

[36] C. L. Barber, *Creating Elizabethan Tragedy*, p. 123, asserts that 'the heroic quality of the magic depends on fusing these divine suggestions with tangible values and resources of the secular world'.

condemnation, that we may be making the same mistakes in less dramatic fashion. As in the Aristotelian model, the tragedy provides the audience with a catharsis of its shared tension by showing the fall of a great man, a fall which (to the extent that it results from his characteristic error) rouses our pity, and (to the extent that it results from a characteristic problem of our culture) rouses our fear as well.

Instead of using the face of the skull to mock worldly ambitions, Marlowe here uses the face of the clown; an old iconographic tactic gives way to a dramatic one. The sub-plot (whether or not it is actually part of Marlowe's original conception)[37] underscores the stupidity of Faustus's bargain. Faustus mocks the petty uses the clown finds for his stolen magical powers, but his own magical works are not so different, and he has paid a far higher price for them. Wagner says the clown 'would give his soul to the devil for a shoulder of mutton', an offer the clown refuses unless the mutton has 'good sauce to it' (1.4.7–11); does Faustus appear any wiser when he uses his dearly bought powers to steal food off the Pope's plate? It is more exalted gravy, but gravy none the less. The clown tries to use magic to pay his bar tab; Faustus uses his to defraud the horse-trader. The clown says he would use magic to shrink himself into a flea so that he could infiltrate women's underwear, and to enchant the kitchen-wench Nan Spit into dancing for him naked. Faustus's first demand of Mephostophilis is a beautiful spouse, and his final magical project is conjuring the legendary beauty of Helen of Troy. Commerce has become a confidence game, the quest for exotic treasures has been reduced to trivial gourmandizing, and the revived appetite for physical pleasures degraded to the most sterile kind of lust (the same trio of failings will occur comically in Ben Jonson's Epicure Mammon and Volpone). In the assault on the Pope, the Reformation has become vandalism.

In other words, Doctor Faustus is a parable about spiritual loss in the modern world, a warning, not only about damnation in the conventional sense, but about the fatal corruption awaiting all Renaissance aspirations. Faustus's early vision of glorifying the human race with a vast benevolent empire quickly fades, and instead he ends trying to please emperors with groceries and holography. He uses his magic, not to turn men into gods, but instead to turn his hecklers into beasts. Any idealistic era must fear that the movement will lose direction, that its spirit will sour. Doctor Faustus confirms that this anxiety lurked in English Renaissance culture from its early days, the fear that the brilliant dreams of converting humanity into a race of angels

---

[37] Neither the 1604 version nor the 1616 version provides a satisfactory text; see the Textual Introduction to *The Complete Works of Christopher Marlowe*, ed. Fredson Bowers (Cambridge, 1973), II. 123–59.

would instead – as in fact happened – fall into the hands of cheaters and tyrants who would use improved science and navigation to crush the spirits and plunder the lands of foreign peoples, and to brutalize their own people through improved weaponry and centralized government; learning would become merely another tool of the class system, used to impress monarchs at court in hope of stray favours; productions of beauty would be consumed in the ostentation of power.

The conversion of the earlier religious and allegorical versions of drama into a prototype of more naturalistic Renaissance tragedy in *Doctor Faustus* hardly involves a forfeiture of spiritual values. Instead, once again, the combination of grand spiritual questions with the detailed observation of real life creates a compelling form of Renaissance art. Tragedy is of course much older than Christianity, and offers its own wonderful inspirations and terrifying warnings for the human soul. Pride and despair, as reciprocal ailments of the human spirit, hardly began or ended with the Christian fervour of Western Europe in the Middle Ages and Renaissance. In his awe-inspiring final soliloquy, a terrified Faustus is unable to stop the flow of mortal time, and unable either to accept Christ's forgiveness or to bear God's wrath. He has nowhere to go, and he is rapidly going there. This is a Christian warning, certainly, but more than that it is a warning to anyone living in a world (like Marlowe's, or ours) that invites short-sighted pride in individual status and the technological achievements of our species, a world haunted by religious uncertainties and irrational denials of mortality. The wicked tempter is certainly a devil, but also plausibly stands for everything that stirs our superficial egotistical appetites, all the choices we will look back on at the hour of our death (as individuals, or perhaps as a species in nuclear war) and wonder what we have so proudly, blindly, spent our souls on.

OTHELLO

Othello (1603–4) is a tragedy disturbingly grafted onto a comic structure, a vision of social harmony undone by the persistent inscrutable agency of conflict and evil. Shakespeare wrote *Othello* at the moment in his career when he was turning from comedy to tragedy, and the first half of the play is a classic comic plot,[38] a pair of true lovers overcoming the usual dramatic obstacles: discrepant origins, a repressive father who uses his access to the laws of the state to forbid the marriage, swordfights with domestic and foreign rivals, and separation by a storm at sea. But love and valour triumph; the Herald

---

[38] Susan Snyder, *The Comic Matrix of Shakespearean Tragedy* (Princeton, New Jersey, 1979) explores the functions of this kind of generic mixture.

announces that the miraculous defeat of the Turks and the joyous reunion of the newlyweds will be celebrated with dancing and revelry, and calls down the blessing of Heaven on this happy little world of Cyprus. All that is missing for the ending of a typical Shakespearian comedy is the hero's closing couplet, and a few lines later we have that too: 'Come my dear love: / The purchase made, the fruits are to ensue. / The profit's yet to come 'twixt me and you' (2.3.8–10). At precisely this instant, however, Iago re-enters. He watches this domestic bliss from the margin like Milton's Satan gazing, first with enchantment, then with bitter envy, at the joy of the loving couple in their Eden. If love is the fulfilling mystery that propels comedy, then jealousy is the hungry mystery that sits in the audience, like Iago on the battlements at Cyprus, feeling inferior or excluded, and needs to poison that happiness. The spectator becomes another voyeur, unwillingly complicit with Iago in the destruction of comic confidence. We meet the enemy of such joys in *Othello*, and it is us.

The destructive agent known as Iago is overdetermined in Renaissance dramatic convention. He is partly the scheming Machiavel common throughout Renaissance tragedy, partly the vengeful malcontent of revenge plays, partly the instigator of jealousy characteristic of domestic tragedy, and partly (as Othello suggests in the final scene) the devil incarnate of morality plays. The seemingly endless critical debate about Iago's motivation (like the projective interpretations of *Hamlet*) reflects a truth, rather than a confusion, about the play. This is a villain who seems to tap the very root of the evil (as Hamlet taps the roots of conflict) that manifests itself in various ways in various other tragedies. Shakespeare invites us to distance ourselves from Iago by alluding to his diabolical attributes. But if it is disturbing to suspect that a devil may be lurking around us in human form, perhaps within our most trusted friend, it is even more disturbing to realize that this devil may be (as anthropology suggests most are) a reflection of our own destructive tendencies. Iago becomes the voice of pointless envy, the perpetual enemy of friendship, love, and trust that we have always rationally but futilely willed out of existence. Desdemona is the ally of those virtues, an ally we unwittingly banish. So the residue of morality drama, the theological allegory that makes Iago 'hellish' and Desdemona 'heavenly' is on one level (as in *Doctor Faustus*) a figurative acknowledgment that we meet evil tempters and good angels in human form every day. Torn between them is Othello, an inclusive kind of Everyman. He is animal and angel, pagan and Christian, black and white, soldier and lover, foreigner and patriot. Iago exploits those schisms, making Othello rant like a beast, renounce Christian belief for pagan magic and blood-sacrifice, feel ashamed of his blackness, turn the bloody honour of the soldier against the gentle heart of the lover, and, in committing suicide, turn the patriot fiercely against the foreigner.

Iago's effectiveness is plausible because he is an insider of social spheres where his victim inevitably feels insecure. He is opaque precisely because he seems so typical, a bawdy, back-slapping, hard-drinking soldier who believes in practical thinking and male loyalty. Furthermore, watching the brilliant, oblique way Iago rouses and focuses Othello's doubts makes it hard for us to feel complacent, to pass the kind of judgement Thomas Rymer did in the seventeenth century against Othello for mere brute stupidity. If any of us were to provoke a passionate secret resentment in a supposed friend who knew how to speak in perfect harmony with our own worst inward voices, offered to prove the truth of our worst fears of humiliation, and to justify all the worst vengeful impulses those fears provoke, we would doubtless fall also, even if we weren't a stranger in a strange land, the only black face in a city of white ones, a romantic innocent in a world of sexual intrigue.

Iago is an insider in another, more metaphysical sense as well: he appears at times to be less an actual person than a demonic possessor of the victims he reads so preternaturally well. He seems to be a catalogue of bad motives: social envy, sexual jealousy, lust and bloodlust, greed and pride. But instead of presenting us with a parade of the sins like that in *Doctor Faustus*, *Othello* hints at an essential spiritual deformity underlying all these forms of evil. Iago has a faculty of envy as insatiable as Faustus's faculty of desire, and thereby as devastating to his society as Faustus is to his own soul. Iago's peculiar encounters with the verb 'to be' are symptoms of the disease: 'Were I the Moor, I would not be Iago', 'I am not what I am', 'And knowing what I am, I know what she shall be', 'He's that he is ... If what he might he is not, / I would to heaven he were' (1.1.57, 65; 4.1.73, 270–2). This version of the villainous Italianate 'New Man' is also a hollow man, a Machiavellian with no self to serve.[39] Iago has a pathological tendency to see other people in his place – his rank, his night-cap, his sheets – as if he were invisible to himself, as if a kind of an ontological lack compelled him constantly to replenish himself from the more authentic selves around him. His revenge against those he suspects of stealing his share of human authenticity is to bankrupt their love, their trust, even their socially constructed identities: Brabantio declares in anguish he no longer has a daughter, Cassio that he has lost his name and rank, Desdemona that she has lost her lord, and Othello that his occupation is gone, that he has no wife, and finally, that he is no longer

---

[39] W. H. Auden, 'The joker in the pack', in his *The Dyer's Hand* (New York, 1962), comments on the difficulty of defending against a villain who seeks no profit but the satisfaction of a perverse spite.

'Othello'. If there is any truth to the notion that subjective selfhood was being (re-)invented at this historical moment, then Iago may be seen as a first symbol – and a first victim – of existential inauthenticity. No jealousy could be more pervasive; like the jealousy of the dead toward the living that sometimes seems to be driving Don Andrea's ghost in *The Spanish Tragedy*, it could drive a man to decimate the world and gloat over the ruins.

At the end of the play Shakespeare taunts us with the riddle of Iago's motivation, by having Iago vow never to explain himself. Again Shakespeare repeats a convention (Hieronimo's refusal to testify in *The Spanish Tragedy*, for example) in a way that infinitely expands its suggestiveness. Why is this refusal so disturbing? Iago has explained that he resents Othello for promoting Cassio over him. But (in soliloquy, where only a profoundly inauthentic person would have reason to lie) he has also attributed his vengefulness to love of Desdemona, and hatred of Othello; he is jealous of Othello and Emilia, or perhaps Cassio and Emilia; he covets Roderigo's money, or Cassio's 'daily beauty'. Psychoanalysts diagnose repressed homosexuality behind all the spite and evasions, as if this were nothing a little therapy could not clear up. Christian-minded critics focus on the allegory of an 'eternal villain', 'demi-devil', and 'viper' attacking the angelic Desdemona and dragging Othello's soul to damnation in the process; nothing, in other words, that could not be cured by a good exorcist. Historical critics link him to the malcontent figures such as Bosola in *The Duchess of Malfi*, embittered beyond reason or morality by lost promotions; so there is nothing here that cannot be explained away by theatrical tradition and Renaissance court politics.

Though each of these arguments has some validity, and Shakespeare provides them all with ample material on which to build, their limitations reveal the impossibility of defining the problems that tragedy poses. Such answers are consoling, and that is precisely why they are wrong. People turn to therapists, exorcists, or even historians, when their changing worlds place them in impossible and even inarticulate conflicts. The role of tragedy is to acknowledge those conflicts, to represent them in their unconquerable complexity, and generally to offer no solution except endurance on the part of the hero and awed sympathy on the part of the audience. Brabantio can blame witchcraft when his world collapses, the Venetian Senate can blame the Turks, Lodovico can diagnose madness, Othello can see a devil. Modern critics can blame the Fall, capitalism, or patriarchy. If we could know who or what or why Iago is, if we could understand why the comic dreams of love fulfilled come unravelled, then we could control that evil. We cannot, and we go to tragedy to reconcile ourselves to that hard truth.

Venetian society is as desperate as modern criticism to analyse Iago's motives: 'Torments will ope thy lips' (5.2.305). Society must explain and isolate the agent of discord which it necessarily calls evil, the corrosive on its necessary lines of trust. But the inexplicable thing at the heart of evil – the evil in our hearts – cannot be so efficiently regulated. The deceptive movements of the Turkish fleet can be successfully analysed in the bright lights of the Senate chamber, but outside in the darkness a more inward enemy will wreak the same kind of destruction to the Christian state and its values. Iago is the continuation of pagan subversion by other means, by the eternal enemy swirling in the storm around the little island of civilization here represented by Cyprus.[40] From the beginning to the end of the play Iago is the voice of street crime, of sexual violation and murder in the dark, the waking embodiment of Brabantio's wicked dream, all the fears that make people lock their doors at night. He allies himself with the 'Turk' – by the play's metaphor, the enemy of Christian civilization – within each Venetian: with Brabantio's racism and sexual possessiveness toward his daughter; with Roderigo's wastrel spending, illicit lust, and cold-blooded violence; and with the vanity, hostility, and lust accessible in Cassio through the devilish 'spirit of wine' (2.3.281–3).

Above all, Iago rouses the residue of pagan violence lurking in Othello. As the play moves geographically to the East, Othello seems to come back under the spiritual gravity of his old world, where handkerchiefs have supernatural force, where people mate like goats and monkeys, where women bear a sinister magic, where murder can be called sacrifice, and where justice is revenge in the dark rather than deliberation in the bright light of the official reason.[41] That is why Othello, unable to kill Iago, settles for killing this revivified pagan self, a suicide by which he reasserts the identity that made him a hero in the Christian society:

> And say besides, that in Aleppo once,
> Where a malignant and a turban'd Turk
> Beat a Venetian and traduc'd the state,
> I took by th' throat the circumcised dog,
> And smote him – thus.
> [*He stabs himself.*]   (5.2.352–6)

This amputation may save the status of the hero, but it cannot again protect his adopted society; the good that dies at the end of this tragedy does not really take the evil with it. Lodovico and the Venetian emissaries do what they can to clean up the mess – closing curtains around the bodies, reassigning Othello's responsibilities and possessions, designating punishments for

---

[40] Alvin Kernan describes this symbolic siege in his superb Introduction to the Signet *Othello* (New York, 1963), pp. xxvii–xxix.
[41] Kernan, pp. xxix–xxxi, traces the effect of this migration on Othello.

the villain, and shutting things up with another couplet that promises a full report to the authorities. But these official formulae cannot assure us that the evil has disappeared, especially not in performance, because we see all too plainly that Iago is still there – still here. Iago has emerged from nowhere, the hero has failed to kill him, and the authorities have failed to explain him. The state can send out armies against the infidels, build prisons and torture-racks for the criminals, but to some extent such efforts are merely symbolic gestures; the scapegoat may be confined, but the destructive principle remains at large. The mere fact that someone cruelly destroys a potentially happy marriage is sad, but not necessarily tragic. What gives *Othello* its magnificence is the immense beauty of its language and its passions; what gives the play its lasting penetration is the warning that there is an enemy lurking in human nature, in each of our human natures, waiting for a chance to rewrite the potential joyful comedy of life into a tragedy.

THE DUCHESS OF MALFI

The Duchess of Malfi (in Webster's version of the story) is a young widow who, despite the fervent warnings of her brothers (Duke Ferdinand and the Cardinal), decides to remarry. She successfully conceals this remarriage until the malcontent Bosola, hired by the brothers to spy on her, discovers that she has borne a son. After two more children appear, Ferdinand furiously confronts the Duchess, but she conceals Antonio's identity (especially necessary because he had been merely her lowly steward) and smuggles him out of Amalfi. Unfortunately, she confides her plans to Bosola, so the couple are separated, and Ferdinand and Bosola torment the imprisoned Duchess with a swarm of madmen, a dead man's hand supposedly belonging to Antonio, and a wax *tableau non vivant* supposedly showing her slaughtered husband and children. Bosola then strangles her, but her noble defiance at the point of death, and the continuing failure of the brothers to reward his service, convince him that he should save Antonio. Ironically, in his first effort to strike down the Cardinal, Bosola accidentally kills the man he had come to save; he does finally kill the Cardinal, only to exchange fatal wounds with Ferdinand, whose guilt concerning the Duchess has driven him into a lycanthropic madness.

This plot, based on events that took place a century earlier in Italy, is clearly less important than its vivid characters and its haunting atmosphere. The action is generated by the jealousy, greed, and pride of the brothers, but the tragedy is less concerned with evil than with corruption, with the struggle of Bosola to maintain his integrity. Bosola is a spiritual kinsman of Vindice: a malcontent revenger whose strong moral instincts have been perverted by the decadent court he inhabits. He leads the moralized parade of characters which (as in *The Revenger's Tragedy*) opens the play, where he is described as the conventional 'railing' satirist; and his first words, a complaint of official neglect, mark him as the conventional malcontent: 'I have done you better service than to be slighted thus' (1.1.24, 33). This might identify Bosola as another Iago, a treacherously 'honest' Italian confidant of the passionate unlikely lovers at the heart of the story. Iago, however, is interesting because his evil is too essential to be changed, whereas Bosola is interesting because the nobility of the Duchess reawakens his bitterly repressed virtues.

If it were not for the Duchess herself, *The Duchess of Malfi* would end this triad of theodicean tragedies in the same ironic vein as the triad of revenge tragedies. Without her steadfastness and tenderness, this would be a play of irony and scorn like *The Revenger's Tragedy*, rather than (as it proves) of passion and sorrow. Like *The Revenger's Tragedy*, *The Duchess of Malfi* toys with the queasy humour of theatrical self-consciousness, as in Delio's remark on the passage of time between the second and third acts. More often, however, Webster uses metadrama for serious interrogations of identity and predestination. The Duchess tells Bosola, 'I account this world a tedious theatre, / For I do play a part in't 'gainst my will' (4.1.99–100). This is partly Stoicism – an essential component of most Renaissance tragic heroism – but it is also (as in *Hamlet*) a commentary on tragic human destiny. For her to carry her archaic virtues successfully to the Jacobean audience, she must redeem the genre of the play she inhabits from the satiric tragedy of decadence and horror envisioned by Bosola.[42]

Unfortunately, as many critics have complained,[43] *The Duchess of Malfi* does not end with the heroine's courageous and redemptive death that closes the fourth act. She may be present in the wistful disembodied echo that subsequently tries to warn Antonio away from his doom, but that prophetic voice proves as futile as Cassandra's (5.3.21–54). She scores heroic victories against many of the villains of Jacobean culture – false pride of rank, greed for inheritances, religious doubt, political corruption, patriarchal tyranny – but her victories endure only within her subjectivity, which may itself be vulnerable to her death. The fact that Bosola inadvertently continues to do the work of evil when he tries to perform virtuous retribution suggests that

[42] Norman Rabkin characterizes this tragedy as predominantly satirical in the Introduction to his edition of *Twentieth Century Interpretations of 'The Duchess of Malfi'* (Englewood Cliffs, New Jersey, 1968), p. 10; the volume contains many valuable essays and excerpts.

[43] See for example William Archer, *The Old Drama and the New* (New York, 1929), p. 60. For a contrary view, see Lee Bliss, *The World's Perspective*, pp. 158–9.

this play-world suffers not from a few evil men or evil choices, but rather from a decadence so pervasive and an entropy so unprovidential that individual assertions count for little. The theodicy of *The Duchess of Malfi* thus becomes virtually the opposite of *Doctor Faustus*, where one person perversely rejected a redemptive universe; now evil is a normative condition of civilization that only a heroic will can defy. As the death of Elizabeth and the growth of astronomy renew anxieties about mutability, and as Reformation theology sinks deeper into popular consciousness, the notion that individual virtue can meaningfully affect destiny becomes ever scarcer. This may help to explain the emergence of women as tragic protagonists: especially after the death of the Virgin Queen, male playwrights increasingly acknowledge this tragic deprivation of control as the normative condition of women. *The Duchess of Malfi* leaves us perplexed as to whether the heroine's long endurance is the redemptive truth of the tragedy, or whether the continuing descent into irony, error, and destruction in the final act proves that even such a magnificent embodiment of the old virtues cannot finally redeem a world – her Italian one or the author's Jacobean one – from a loss of meaning, an epidemic of moral as well as physical decay. She makes a good end and a beautiful corpse, but dying well may not be good enough.

Furthermore, her task as tragic protagonist is to escape precisely the grand scenes of ambition that Elizabethan tragic heroes pursued so avidly. All she seeks is happy domesticity with her accountant husband, and she faces assassination with pious acceptance and a last request that could hardly be more poignantly maternal, or further from questions of politics and revenge: 'I pray thee look thou givest my little boy / Some syrup for his cold, and let the girl / Say her prayers ere she sleep' (4.2.207–9). This subjugation of traditionally heroic values to bourgeois ones[44] may signal a growing Jacobean despair about the prospects for managing with adequate skill or kindness the brave new worlds currently under siege. The captured King Lear certainly seeks a comparably domestic refuge, forswearing all political involvement and begging permission merely to live in playful solitude with his daughter Cordelia.

In tragedy, some envious force on the fringe of the domestic paradise intervenes to subvert this familiar comic solution. *Othello* shifts suddenly and chillingly from the marriage celebration to the perspective of the villain; *The*

---

[44] Rabkin, *Interpretations*, p. 7, perceives a despondent Jacobean inversion of tragic values in this transformation of a great heroine into a 'good bourgeoise'. Bliss, pp. 144–6, 167–8, explicates this idea perceptively. It is worth noting, however, that even Faustus and Macbeth express regret, in their final moments, that they did not settle for pleasant little dinners with their friends.

Duchess of Malfi allows us our first glimpse inside the Duchess's happy household, only to confront us shockingly with its nemesis. As the Duchess banters with her husband and her serving-woman about sex, marriage, and grey hair, her companions sneak playfully out of the room, and she turns to find herself alone with the murderously jealous Ferdinand, who has overheard all this domestic prattle (3.2.1–79). The world of tragedy is Manichaean; Ferdinand is the Duchess's evil twin who will lie in ambush for years, if necessary, to reclaim her from her little world of bliss. The invading serpent merely reflects the contradictions fundamentally present in the civilization.[45] The impulse to use Renaissance arts to build a new Eden always proves a dangerous delusion in drama, whether that paradise is envisioned with tragic grandeur as in *Doctor Faustus*, with satiric excess as in Jonson's *The Alchemist* (1610), or in romantic transformation as in Shakespeare's *The Tempest* (1611). In these three cases one can blame the new Fall on vanity; the forgotten darker side of human nature (embodied by devils, cheaters, and savages respectively) exacts retribution. In the case of the Duchess's domestic retreat, however, the audience confronts the possibility that destruction needs no licence from sin, that a mutable indifferent world consumes each caring mortal creature, that (as Bosola says) 'We are merely the stars' tennis balls, struck and bandied / Which way please them' (5.4.63–4). By sustaining her faith, hope, and charity until her final belated breath, the Duchess of Malfi strives to forestall that recognition, but her end is not the play's end, and her last word – 'Mercy' – hardly characterizes the random carnage of the closing scenes.

In the world of *The Duchess of Malfi*, 'all things have their end' (5.3.18), and no one has control – an impression the abrupt shifts in Webster's dramaturgy serve to reinforce. The magnificent Duchess may conceal and protect her family for a while, but eventual punishment is promised and performed. The tough and crafty Bosola may scheme, but his goals are dictated against his wishes, and even his successes are without reward. Ferdinand makes hyperbolic efforts to forbid and punish his sister's remarriage, but she promptly defies both his warnings and his tortures, and madness soon prevents him from controlling even himself. The Cardinal, the most detached and powerful manipulator, finds events fatally run away from him even among his family and his hirelings, and dies with the saddest, most defeated last words of all: 'And now, I pray, let me / Be laid by, and never thought of' (5.5.112–13). Even the Duchess's surviving young son who (in the manner of a common tragic consolation) righteously assumes power at

---

[45] Rabkin, *Interpretations*, p. 7, defines the evil of this play-world as merely the condition naturally generated by a world in decline.

the end already seems doomed to early violent death by the horoscope made at his birth (2.3.72–80).

Naturally it is facile to schematize cultural shifts by quoting lines out of context, yet it is hard to mistake the profound collapse of optimism signalled by the change from Faustus's youthful exclamation, 'O what a world of profit and delight, / Of power, of honour, and omnipotence, / Is promised to the studious artisan' (1.1.80–2) to Bosola's dying question, 'In what a shadow, or deep pit of darkness, / Doth womanish and fearful mankind live?' (5.5.125–6). Faustus fails, but he leaves us thinking about the human mind; Jacobean tragedy more often reverts to the medieval model by leaving the skull instead, with its mocking grin, as our dominant impression. In Jacobean playwrights, as in the Metaphysical poets of the same era, the spiritual component of human experience struggles perpetually to avoid eclipse by the physical. Bosola associates his own corruption from a moral idealist into a Machiavellian pragmatist with the Renaissance fashion in painting that rejected the grand iconic style in favour of realistic reproduction of the lowliest things: 'Now for this act, I am certain to be rais'd, / And men that paint weeds to the life are prais'd' (3.2.378–9).

At the same time, however, Jacobean tragedy and Metaphysical poetry commonly strive to rescue individual experience and expression from absorption by the conventional. *The Duchess of Malfi* resonates this fundamental Renaissance ambivalence about the relative values of the abstract (which imposes impersonality, but may permit transcendence) and the empirical (which permits individual experience, but imposes the limits of physicality). T. S. Eliot remarks that 'The art of the Elizabethans is an impure art' because they sought 'to attain complete realism without surrendering any of the advantages which as artists they observed in unrealistic conventions'; but contamination can sometimes be enrichment, and so it is in the case of Webster's dramaturgy.[46] Though many of the devices of plot and spectacle in *The Duchess of Malfi* are quite conventional, the powerful impression of doomed personality evoked by the fragments of Webster's poetry is not; once again the tragic hero inhabits a universe that constantly threatens to eradicate her individuality. The Duchess herself gratifyingly combines unrealistic extremes of conventional virtue with realistic bodily frailties, including impetuous appetites for food and sexual love; the plot of the play, concerning her doomed determination to obey her personal desires, is virtually inseparable from the tension inherent in the literary form itself. She is a heroic individual, a tautology in that Renaissance tragedy

---

[46] Inga-Stina Ekeblad, 'The "impure art" of John Webster', in Rabkin, *Interpretations*, pp. 49–64, comments on the potential richness of such mixtures.

made individuality a precondition for heroism, an oxymoron in that conformity to a heroic role necessarily entails some surrender of individual traits, and loyalty to the heroic principles commonly leads to the obliteration of individual existence in death. Even the Duchess, who abjures traditional public heroism for the sake of private experience, must endure this bitter paradox.

No wonder, then, that the Renaissance tragic hero is so often shadowed by a negative image of individualism, the self-fashioned, self-conscious Machiavellian villain who coldly assumes that human identity has neither a stable core nor a meaningful connection to anything beyond itself. The brothers lure Bosola into this condition, and the Duchess retrieves him from it by sustaining her virtues through the worst morbid and satiric tragedies he can cast her in. The fear and pity the malcontent Bosola feels may therefore pass through him to the cynical audience of Jacobean tragedy. In the haunting *pas de deux* of the torture scene – a scene of modern absurdist, more than medieval macabre, terror – the archetypal confrontation between the heroic individual and the implacable, impersonal forces of the physical universe becomes starkly visible. Bosola comes to the Duchess aptly disguised as a tomb-maker and as the old bell-man who visits condemned prisoners; when her personal misery leads her to curse 'the world / To its first chaos', he tauntingly replies, 'Look you, the stars shine still' (4.1.118–20). Yet in the following scene, as Bosola relentlessly attacks her morale with his *memento mori* commonplaces, the Duchess replies defiantly, 'I am Duchess of Malfi still' (4.2.115–39). These counterpoised declarations are each manifestly true. Death (fuelled by the evils of pride, greed, and jealousy that propel the other tragedies of theodicy) does indeed destroy her, and the world goes on. But she also retains her heroic integrity in the very face of death, forbids it to compromise the power of her will and the tenderness of her heart. Compelled to adjudicate this confrontation, the audience must internalize the tragic ambivalence, the choice between absorption in the determinate forces of decay, and futile rebellion on behalf of the human individual and her unfathomable capacity for love.

Conclusion

Ideally, the modern audience of Renaissance tragedy must remain simultaneously aware that the plays were created within a particular historical context and that they may nevertheless bear on the audience's own world. A tragedy is a product of the very specific issues in crisis at the time of its generation; it may also speak to persistent problems of human existence. It is possible to locate English Renaissance tragedies within the conventions and circumstances that helped to generate them without eclipsing the continuities and analogies that enable them to bear on problems of modern life. The currently fashionable New Historicism shares with old-fashioned historical criticism a tendency to isolate the plays as artifacts: their primary value is as evidence of political history, and their secondary aesthetic value can be unlocked only through specific historical keys that tell us which character represents which courtier, which convention dictates a particular speech, or (in the new version) which governmental orthodoxies are being implicitly endorsed or subverted.

Such information is certainly useful, but allowing it to estrange us from the implied psychological experience of the characters is wasteful, because there are at least two important ways of connecting the past with the present. The liberal-humanist viewpoint, which has been fundamental to most teaching of Renaissance tragedy (and may have been fundamental to the writing of that tragedy as well),[47] suggests that canonical literature is the vessel by which eternal human truths and values are conveyed across time. The new alternative method is to find in tragedy the ancestry of modern radicalism,[48] a frequency-channel on which ideas that undermine the status quo and common wisdom of Renaissance cultures (by exposing them as arbitrary) were already audible. The theatre is thus a place of subversion, though (some New Historicists now believe) a strategically isolated one.

Surely art does both things, preserves cultural values and tests their weaknesses. Surely there is validity and virtue in both the liberal-humanist fear of losing the past with its accreted moral wisdom, and the cultural-materialist fear of remaining inscribed in regressive values; in both the liberal-humanist insistence that personal experience must not be obliterated by systematic political thinking, and the cultural-materialist warning that sentimental focus on the tragic individual conduces to quietism concerning the mechanisms of widespread social injustice. Circumventing the severe but literal-minded censorship of the Revels Office, Renaissance tragedy was often an expression of anarchical popular will and a cry of protest against the shared agonies of historical change, but it may not have its ultimate

---

[47] Hardin Craig, 'The shackling of accidents', in Kaufman, *Elizabethan Drama*, p. 24, argues that the Renaissance 'doctrine of imitation ... rests ultimately upon the great doctrine of similitude. The Renaissance looked upon man as a universal being repeating in his life the deeds of all men ... Men's actions are always alike because their natures are always the same ... A modern who absorbed the ancients ... acquired their virtues.'

[48] See for examples the essays in Jonathan Dollimore and Alan Sinfield, eds., *Political Shakespeare* (Manchester, 1985), and John Drakakis, ed., *Alternative Shakespeares* (London, 1985).

reference, or offer practical solutions, to specific political or economic problems, because it cannot isolate or erase the contradictions created by our cognitive failings, by our simultaneous co-operation and competition in the business of survival, by our mixed nature as mental and physical beings, or by our status as creatures aware of our ineluctable and imponderable mortality. These are not crises of an age, but for all time.

Still, the points of contestation in a late twentieth-century intellectual community often diverge from those of Elizabethan culture, so modern students and theatre audiences may feel compelled to highlight and to challenge aspects of the plays that are likely to have been inactive ingredients to Elizabethan consumers. Some criticism discerns tragedians who were prophetic, but necessarily covertly so, in challenging the humanism, the class system, the gender discrimination, even the Christianity of their societies. Other criticism assumes the tragedians were complacent or even propagandistic on these points,[49] and attacks them for that failing. Is *The Changeling* a proto-feminist play, for showing its female protagonist destroyed because (like Gertrude in *Hamlet*) she has no imputed power except as an object of sexual and marital desire? Or a sexist play, for failing to focus our outrage on that aspect of her dilemma? Or an historical artifact to which modern feminist terminology cannot justly or productively be applied? Similar questions can of course be raised about racism in Marston's *Sophonisba*, anti-semitism in Marlowe's *The Jew of Malta*, or the class system in Fletcher's *Bonduca* (1611–14). The questions are impossible to answer, and well worth asking.

In fact, tragedy is a genre of unanswerable questions that are worth asking. Renaissance theatres were, as the authorities often suspected, the breeding-grounds of profoundly seditious conspiracies, not because the heroes advocated destruction of the social order, but because the tragic dilemmas of those heroes performed a kind of deconstruction on the limiting and contradictory aspects of the current vocabulary of belief. Every culture has lines of enquiry it must forbid in self-defence; the Renaissance strained the mechanisms of repression and diversion to their limits, and one result was a variety of great drama. When ideology loses its ability to explain away human suffering and mortality, what remains is a sympathetic recognition of our kinship with the victims. Tragic theatre is not only a precious institution for the negotiation of cultural change, it is also the supreme instrument for

---

[49] E. M. W. Tillyard, *The Elizabethan World Picture* (London, 1943), has been the main target of revisionists seeking to liberate the plays from the hierarchical ideas of their time, or seeking to prove that those ideas were in fact the propaganda of the power élite rather than universal belief.

nurturing such sympathy. For most students and audiences the language of Renaissance tragedy must now be almost opaque, the conventions unfamiliar; yet something survives that makes the modern appreciation of these works more than merely archaeological. Is it really surprising that dramatic confrontations with jealousy, revenge, and mortality should exercise continuing power? One does not need a mystical theory of archetypes to believe that human beings can recognize, learn from, care about the suffering of even their distant kindred. This is not to exclude the diversity of human experience by sentimental appeal to an essentialist idea of human nature, but rather to acknowledge the force of shared recognitions when they are made available – and tragic theatre has long been the most compelling medium for the shared recognition of what many human beings, in their passions and their losses, have in common.

Bibliography

TRAGEDY

The most important philosophical writings on tragedy are contained in Aristotle's *Poetics*, Hegel's *Philosophy of Fine Art*, Nietzsche's *The Birth of Tragedy* and Kierkegaard's *The Ancient Tragical Motif as Reflected in the Modern*. Excerpts from these and other major works (by Jaspers, Santayana, Sewall, Krieger, Lukàcs, Langer, Goldmann, Hyman, Burke, Barthes, etc.) on the theory of tragedy are collected in Robert W. Corrigan, ed., *Tragedy: Vision and Form* (2nd edn, 1981). Northrop Frye explains tragedy by his highly influential theory of natural cycles in *Anatomy of Criticsm* (1957).

ENGLISH RENAISSANCE TRAGEDY

The fundamental document for twentieth-century work on Shakespeare's tragic practice – and therefore the primary target of contemporary revisionists – is A. C. Bradley's *Shakespearean Tragedy* (1904). Certain complacent humanistic assumptions underlying that book have been widely attacked, for example in Catherine Belsey's feminist *The Subject of Tragedy* (1985), and in Jonathan Dollimore's *Radical Tragedy* (1984), which perceives English Renaissance tragedy as crucially subversive toward Christian humanism. G. Wilson Knight's *The Wheel of Fire* (1930) has exercised considerable influence over students of Shakespearian tragedy for the past sixty years, but, perhaps because of its visionary qualities, has proved a less appealing target for the revisionists than Bradley's solid readings of character and plot.

Other classic works from earlier in the century include Theodore Spencer's *Death and Elizabethan Tragedy* (1936) and M. C. Bradbrook's *Themes and Conventions of Elizabethan Tragedy* (1935). Madeleine Doran, *Endeavors of Art* (1954), provides a broadly enlightening survey of the traditions shaping Elizabethan drama. On the native ancestors of English Renaissance tragedy, see Willard Farnham, *The Medieval Heritage of Elizabethan Tragedy* (1936); Howard Baker, *Induction to Tragedy* (1939); and David Bevington, *From 'Mankind' to Marlowe* (1962). On the Senecan factor, see F. L. Lucas, *Seneca and Elizabethan Tragedy* (1922); Gordon Braden, *Renaissance*

Tragedy and the Senecan Tradition (1985); and G. K. Hunter, 'Seneca and the Elizabethans', *Shakespeare Survey* 20 (1967). For a traditional look at the revenge tradition, see Fredson Bowers, *Elizabethan Revenge Tragedy* (1940); for a revisionist view, see Susan Jacoby, *Wild Justice* (1983). On the genesis of the villain figure, Bernard Spivack's *The Allegory of Evil* (1958) has proved influential.

Recent books discussing English Renaissance tragedy in general include Irving Ribner, *Jacobean Tragedy* (1962); Robert Ornstein, *The Moral Vision of Jacobean Tragedy* (1965); T. B. Tomlinson, *Elizabethan and Jacobean Tragedy* (1964); Stephen Booth, *'King Lear,' 'Macbeth,' Indefinition, and Tragedy* (1983); J. M. R. Margeson, *The Origins of English Tragedy* (1967); Roger Stilling, *Love and Death in English Renaissance Tragedy* (1976); Thomas McAlindon, *English Renaissance Tragedy* (1986); Roland Wymer, *Suicide and Despair in the Jacobean Drama* (1986); and on a lighter note of darkness, Nicholas Brooke, *Horrid Laughter in Jacobean Tragedy* (1979).

MODERN CRITICAL APPROACHES

Neither Cultural Materialist criticism (despite the impressive efforts of Terry Eagleton, Peter Stallybrass, and others), nor its American cousin, New Historicism (well represented in *Representing the English Renaissance*, ed. Stephen Greenblatt, 1988), has yet colonized tragedy as successfully as they have several other Renaissance genres. Nor has deconstruction found especially good hunting, perhaps because the tragedies are avowedly multivocal and indeterminate. Some structuralist arguments, based in anthropology, have gained attention, such as René Girard's *Violence and the Sacred*, trans. Patrick Gregory (1977), which locates tragic theatre as an essential social ritual used to forestall potentially endless cycles of blood-revenge; and Susan Cole's *The Absent One* (1985), which describes tragedy as a displaced ritual of mourning. Feminist approaches to the genre are increasingly prominent, focused primarily on the exploitative tendencies of patriarchy; in addition to Belsey, see Coppélia Kahn, *Man's Estate* (1981); Lisa Jardine, *Still Harping on Daughters* (1983); and Dympna Callaghan, *Woman and Gender in Renaissance Tragedy* (1989); for a controversial attack on feminist readings of tragedy, see Richard Levin, 'Feminist thematics and Shakespearean tragedy', *PMLA* 103 (1988), 125–38.

TEXTS

All references to Marlowe and Webster are based on the standard editions cited at the front of this volume. References to Shakespeare are based on the Riverside edition, ed. G. B. Evans *et al.* (1974). *The Spanish Tragedy* is cited from the Revels version, ed. Philip Edwards (1959); *The Revenger's Tragedy* is also cited from the Revels series, ed. R. A. Foakes (1966).

10   Caroline drama

The repertory and the audience

UNTIL recently, it was customary to lump together all plays written during the reign of Charles I as Cavalier drama.[1] These plays were thought to have appealed exclusively to an élite courtly audience that patronized private theatres and to have ignored those alternative ideologies that had animated the more popular drama written during the reigns of James and Elizabeth. And indeed, there were such plays: pastoral and heroic romances promoted royalist ideals by allegorizing the court, and witty comedies celebrated the manners of Cavalier society. Yet Cavalier drama did not figure significantly in the repertory of the theatres, which throughout the Caroline period survived on Elizabethan revivals. The old-style popular playhouses – the Fortune, the Red Bull, and, in the summer, the Globe – were sustained almost exclusively by a nostalgic and nationalistic diet of apprentice plays, pseudo-histories, chivalric adventures, and low-life farces. With their old-fashioned spectacle, festive exuberance, and indecorous mixture of kings and clowns, such plays appealed to a regressive plebeian taste. But the fashionable theatres, too – the Blackfriars, the Phoenix, and the Salisbury Court – indulged this Elizabethan nostalgia by including many old 'popular' plays in their repertories.

These plays, in fact, were frequently revived at the expense of new plays. The state of the theatre was far from healthy during the first years of Charles's reign. Several of the great Jacobean dramatists had died or retired from the stage, and theatre companies, perhaps sensing a waning interest at court, grew chary with commissions: a robust count of thirty-six new plays, masques, and academic dramas in 1624 declined to only nine in 1630.[2] The majority of new plays, furthermore, were still informed by uncourtly (if not

---

[1] Alfred Harbage's account of theatre in the period, for example, is simply called *Cavalier Drama.*

[2] Harbage, *Annals of English Drama.*

anti-royalist) attitudes and borrowed heavily from popular drama of the preceding age – from Shakespeare and Webster, from Jonson and Middleton. It is tempting, therefore, to measure them by the moral fervour of their originals and find them wanting. Such judgement, though, may be unfair, for however much Caroline playwrights were indebted to earlier drama, they adapted it to a new context and dramatized issues of immediate social and political concern. By doing so, they found voices of their own.

Economic concerns were one such issue. Rapid social mobility, and particularly the influx of people from the country into London, had upset the traditional distribution of wealth: commercial interests put money increasingly into the hands of the middle class – merchants, lawyers, tradesmen – and left many gentlemen impoverished.[3] Money supplanted land as the chief source of power and prestige, and the rivalry between commercial enterprise and inherited wealth disrupted the conservative social hierarchy in which old noble families reigned indisputably supreme. Rich merchants were now in a position to buy estates forfeited by the nobility; young nobles, in turn, were forced to marry 'down' in order to keep those estates. James had further cheapened the nobility by selling titles. But more dire than this redistribution of wealth was the lack of it: high unemployment and widespread poverty had become a drain on national resources and a blot on England's pride. In this context, the court's self-indulgence, its ostentatious display, its cultivation of fashion, its abuse of power – in short, its morality – were open to criticism.

Opposition to the Caroline court is often said to have sprung from 'puritanism', and there is some justice in this claim, for puritans felt threatened by Charles's empowerment of the bishops and by his apparent neutrality towards Protestant countries in foreign affairs. Fundamental disagreement over matters of church and state, furthermore, prompted Charles to dissolve Parliament in 1629 and, for the next eleven years, to exercise personal rule – years during which those critical of the court grew ever more vocal. So-called 'puritan' values came to be shared not only by the sectarians so often lampooned in earlier drama, but by a growing body of nobility and gentry who opposed Charles's policies.[4]

The gentry are usually identified with the country, and their determination to preserve traditional liberties placed them squarely in opposition to courtly patronage, to courtly élitism, and, worst of all, to the court's economic exploitation of the country for private ends. The gentry valued a stable social order founded on the rights of place and property, and their provincial

---

[3] Derek Hirst, *Authority and Conflict: England 1603–1658* (London, 1986).

[4] On the relationship of puritanism to the drama, see Heinemann, *Puritanism and Theatre*, pp. 200–57, and Butler, *Theatre and Crisis*, pp. 84–99.

paternalism clashed with Charles's national paternalism. Others, too, joined the chorus of disapproval: city merchants who objected to Charles's granting of monopolies, lords out of favour or fearful of the court's Catholic orientation. Those critical of the court, therefore, were not a homogeneous group, but a loose alliance; yet their geographic demarcations grew less distinct as the gentry flocked to London in search of entertainment and commercial gain, thus creating a fashionable town, as distinct from the city, in which to gather opposition to court policy.

In the town, private theatres were a focal point for entertainment; audiences were drawn from a mixture of privileged classes – from court, town, and city alike. The commonly accepted notion that audiences at these theatres formed an exclusive courtly coterie thus is not entirely accurate.[5] Although more aristocratic than the pluralist crowds at public theatres, Caroline audiences in fact represented diverse social and political views. The dramatist of the previous generation who had best understood the tastes and values of such fashionable audiences was John Fletcher. Although he died in 1625, the same year as King James, he nevertheless exerted considerable influence on later dramatists, and his plays – mostly tragicomedies in which threats to the social and political hierarchy, and often to the court, are introduced only to be swept away in a tide of romantic improbability – were frequently revived on the Caroline stage.

Fletcher's distinctive treatment of social and political issues characterizes the work of certain Caroline dramatists as well, especially those who, like James Shirley, adapted the forms of Jacobean drama for an audience that no longer shared its values. The most prolific writer of Caroline writers, with over thirty plays to his credit, Shirley was a favourite at court. His imitations of plays by Shakespeare, Webster, and Tourneur largely eschew the criticism of courtly society found in the originals: they have topicality without a Jacobean moral thrust. Yet they are not stereotypically Cavalier drama either. Shirley's best plays, especially his comedies, bestride the worlds of court and town – the court, whose members he wished to please, and the town, from whose ranks his audience increasingly came.

Hyde Park (1632) is a case in point. An elegant comedy of manners, it resembles *Much Ado About Nothing* shorn of its Italian locale and set instead in a world of fashion where the gentry rub elbows with the nobility. Far from the commercial London depicted in Jacobean city comedy, Shirley's London resembles the aristocratic milieu of Shakespearian romantic comedy. Hyde Park itself – a new and fashionable place of recreation – is equivalent to

---

[5] Butler, *Theatre and Crisis*, pp. 100–40; also Michael Neill, '"Wits most accomplished Senate": the audience of the Caroline private theatres', *SEL* 18 (1978), 341–60.

22 Barry Kyle's 1987 Royal Shakespeare Company production of Shirley's *Hyde Park*, Swan theatre

those green worlds where characters repair to play love games and to make all odds even. The main characters, too, are Shakespearian. Mistress Carol, fetching her lineage from Beatrice and Kate, mocks her suitors mercilessly and uses wit to hide her affection for the man she truly loves, Fairfield, while he, a contemporary Benedick, wins the game by forcing her to pledge that she will never love him, then making her jealous when he flirts with another woman (actually his sister) in Hyde Park. Carol is a splendid example of a new kind of woman – apparently 'liberated' – who owes her being as much to puritan reform as she does to Shakespeare. The old aristocratic double standard by which arranged marriages led men to commit adultery was gradually being challenged by the ideal of a chaste marriage based on love and mutual respect.[6] As a consequence, women in certain fashionable circles achieved greater social freedom than they had once had, and such freedom is satirically expressed in Carol's sermon to Mrs Bonavent on the virtues of a single, economically independent life:

> What is in your condition makes you weary?
> You are sick of plenty and command; you have
> Too, too much liberty, too many servants;
> Your jewels are your own, and you would see
> How they will shew upon your husband's wagtail.
> You have a coach now, and a christian livery
> To wait on you to church, and are not catechis'd
> When you come home; you have a waiting-woman,
> A monkey, a squirrel, and a brace of islands,
> Which may be thought superfluous in your family,
> When husbands come to rule...
> And will you lose all this, for
> *I, Cicely, take thee, John, to be my husband?*   (1.2, p.475)

However reflective of new bourgeois attitudes, Carol's feminism in fact rejects marital equality for a brand of personal rule that borders on tyranny. Such rule allies her with Charles's court rather than with the town and thus defies the social compromise for which certain 'puritan' elements in society strove.[7]

To demonstrate alternatives, Shirley balances the main plot with two parallel plots, each reflecting a different conception of marriage and woman's place. In one, Mrs Bonavent chooses to ignore Carol's advice and to remarry on the very morning that her husband, presumed dead for seven

---

[6] See Juliet Dusinberre, *Shakespeare and the Nature of Women* (London, 1975), pp. 3–5 and chapter 1, 'The idea of chastity', *passim*. A different view is taken by Kathleen Davies, 'Continuity and change in literary advice on marriage', in R. B. Duthwaite, ed., *Marriage and Society* (London, 1981).

[7] Butler, *Theatre and Crisis*, p. 178.

years, returns home in disguise. Joining the wedding festivities, he reveals his identity late in the game, just in time to save his wife from unwittingly committing adultery with her new 'husband'. This romantic plot, by dramatizing the virtues of chastity and constancy in marriage, tempers the excesses of Carol's more liberal philosophy.

The other plot broaches the responsibilities of class. In it, the chastity of Fairfield's sister Julietta is tested by her jealous suitor Trier, who encourages the rakish Lord Bonvile to seduce her. By virtue of his social position, Bonvile expects women of an inferior class to bow to his will, and Julietta is sensible of her obligations to a man of his rank. His noble blood, fortunes, and titles, she admits, 'are characters/ Which we should read at distance', for 'where the king has seal'd/ His favours, I should shew humility' (5.1, p.529). But as Bonvile presses her to collapse that social 'distance' by giving in to his importunity, she reads him a stern lesson in class obligation, claiming that unless he proves 'a friend to virtue', she will 'in such infinite distance' be 'As much above [him] in [her] innocence' (pp. 529–30). In the tones of puritan homily she proceeds to instruct him in the proper behaviour for a lord, who, as a member of England's ruling class, ought to set an example for those beneath him; and as she shames him by enumerating the 'sins of [his] wild youth' – fornication, adultery, atheism – she reveals how the bourgeoisie may contest the nobility's abuse of power yet at the same time preserve a respect for its authority.

Shirley thus dramatizes a compromise between court and town. Mildly critical of the excesses of both, in Carol's feminism and Bonvile's lechery, he nevertheless demonstrates how, in the pastoral retreat of Hyde Park, discord among classes may yield to harmony. This harmony is achieved in the conventional reconciliations of romantic comedy: the sharp-tongued protagonists forsake wit for plain declarations of love, a husband returns to his wife as if by miracle, a suitor is taught a lesson about jealousy, a lord is converted to honesty by a good woman's virtue, and all is as innocent as maidenhead. By suggesting that London's privileged classes may happily coexist so long as they honour their obligations to one another, Shirley promotes an essentially conservative ideal. Yet his compromise is morally disengaged; for by idealizing social relations, he evades the moral and political questions that gave rise to class divisions in the first place.

To measure its disengagement, we may compare *Hyde Park* with a tragicomedy by Massinger that deals with similar class divisions and violations of social obligation. *The Picture* (1629) concerns the knight Mathias's test of his wife's virtue – a test similar to Trier's test of Julietta, only more fantastical and far removed from fashionable London. Leaving his country estate for the Hungarian wars, Mathias takes with him a magic picture of his wife which will change colour if she is tempted by another man in his absence. In the event, Mathias is more sorely tempted to fall at the Hungarian court – and by the queen, no less – than is his wife Sophia by remaining at home. She easily spurns the advances of two wanton courtiers sent by the queen to debauch her, and, when told of her husband's magic picture, she gives vent to a self-righteous fury that threatens the comic resolution.

Mathias begs her forgiveness, but she will not be easily placated. She denounces him as a miscreant and demands a divorce, challenging the double standard in sexual morality: 'therefore know/ And 'tis my boon unto the King, I do/ Desire a separation from your bed' (5.3.178–80). Massinger here takes womanly indignation much further than Shirley does when Julietta scolds Trier for his suspicion: where Julietta offers Trier 'charity', Sophia insists on justice. She embodies the puritan ideal of equality in marriage, and only when everyone in attendance – led by the queen, on her knees – begs her to take pity on Mathias does she agree to be reconciled.

Massinger juxtaposes this ideal of marriage with the practice at the Hungarian court. There, the royal marriage is not in balance: the king dotes on his wife so much that he ignores the conduct of his own wars, and he vests such power in her that he becomes a mere 'vassal' before her 'absolute tyranny' (1.2.142). More pointedly, Massinger exposes the court as a place of sexual intrigue, humiliation, and, literally, bondage. The queen envies her subjects' chastity and so would ruin it; by threatening violence should Mathias not accede to her demands, she demeans the power vested in her. Massinger thus incriminates the court for failing in its obligations to those classes who look to it for an example. The court corrupts where it should educate. Paradoxically, *The Picture* dramatizes how the gentry can educate the court: Mathias's steadfastness leads the queen to virtue. Yet her conversion does not mitigate the potent moral criticism that pervades the play. Unlike Shirley, Massinger was an uncompromising moralist who recognized in the ideals of puritanism an ethos finer than that of the court. There is an incisive political message in Sophia's victory over the queen.

The ethos of Caroline tragedy

Shirley never treated virtue and vice so seriously as Massinger. Even in his tragedies, where moral questions might have weighed most heavily, he strove for intricacy rather than depth, content, like Fletcher, to manipulate the conventions he had inherited from earlier dramatists but to sidestep their ideological concerns. Indeed, no one else handled the conventions of revenge tragedy so dextrously, as the enduring popularity of *Love's Cruelty* (1631), *The Traitor* (1631), and *The Cardinal* (1641) attests. If these plays seem like inferior reworkings of Kyd or Webster or Tourneur, they none the less adopt a sophisticated courtly ethos that makes them distinctive.

Shirley depicted the court as a place of conventional Italianate corruption. Politics were infected by sexual intrigue, dukes were lechers, their attendants were Machiavels with an eye to the main chance, and women had to die to preserve their chastity. All this was formulaic; it pandared to a taste for lurid tragedy that had changed little from the days of James. Unlike their Jacobean precursors, however, Shirley's tragedies do not indict the court politically. Their moral posturing lacks the conviction, and their satire the moral sting, of the originals. *The Traitor*, for example, broaches the issues of regicide and usurpation which, since Elizabeth's reign, had lodged fearfully in the public imagination;[8] but for Shirley, these issues were only part and parcel of theatrical tradition, devices to heighten suspense but devoid of any special moral significance.

Rather, Shirley lavished attention on what has been called the 'choreography' of intrigue.[9] The main plot of *The Traitor* embellishes the well-known intrigues of *The Revenger's Tragedy*: Lorenzo, kinsman to the Duke of Florence and a Machiavel, plots to supplant the Duke, and his chief strategy for doing so requires him to get the irascible Schiarra to procure his sister, the chaste Amidea, to satisfy the Duke's lust. Like Vindice, Schiarra is a malcontent who, disgusted by courtly corruption, 'rehearses the satiric clichés of Jacobean tragedy';[10] and Lorenzo cunningly ensures Schiarra's complicity in his scheme by promising that they will murder the Duke when he is in Amidea's bed. Schiarra makes love to his employment: playing the role of Vice, he tempts his sister to sin. She, however, resolves to '[S]tand in the ivory register of virgins' unto death (2.1.254); and Schiarra, satisfied that she has passed the chastity test, tells her of Lorenzo's scheme. In the bedroom scene that follows, Shirley ingeniously stands Tourneur's plot on its head, for rather than be an accessory to crime, Amidea prefers to seduce the Duke to virtue by a show of her own nobility. Calling upon 'Lucrece's fair example', she wounds herself in the arm with a poniard and threatens suicide unless the Duke repents. Her success momentarily turns the play into a

---

[8] Alvin Kernan discusses the enactment of regicide on the Elizabethan and Jacobean stage, and its emotional impact on audiences, in J. Leeds Barroll *et al.*, eds., *The Revels History of Drama in English* 3 (London, 1975), p. 251.

[9] Gordon Braden, 'James Shirley', *Dictionary of Literary Biography* 58 (Detroit, Michigan, 1987), p. 257.

[10] Kathleen McLuskie, in Philip Edwards *et al.*, eds., *The Revels History of Drama in English* 4 (London, 1981), p. 250.

tragicomedy: the familiar device of a woman proving her chastity through violence had never been used to such sensational effect.

In the remaining acts, Shirley plays baroque variations on Tourneur and on Beaumont and Fletcher's *The Maid's Tragedy* as well. Schiarra, now identified as a traitor, pleads with his sister – this time in earnest – to save his life by capitulating to the Duke's reawakened lust. (Lust in great ones seldom sleeps.) Schiarra is at once adamant and reluctant, wishing to spare her chastity yet arguing that if she does not sacrifice it in a good cause, she will be raped anyway. For her part, Amidea (like Isabella in *Measure for Measure*) shames her brother for equating the loss of her immortal soul with his own paltry loss of life. But then she reverses her strategy. To force him to recognize the ignominy of what he is entreating her to do, she pretends to give in; but Schiarra, suddenly struck with horror by her capitulation, mortally wounds her. She, however, lives long enough to forgive him and vow to her older brother that she stabbed herself – an echo of Desdemona's dying words that had become *de rigueur* for self-sacrificing Jacobean heroines. In Shirley, then, crises of honour and chastity are titillating rather than morally earnest. They serve only to precipitate the sudden reversals, clever shifts of role, and misunderstood trials that are the glories of his art. By stripping off the layers of moral philosophy that sometimes encrusted earlier revenge plays, Shirley, like Fletcher, drew attention to the artifice of his own construction. The manipulation of plot – the outdoing of earlier practitioners in the genre – was an end in itself; and the behaviour of his characters was determined almost exclusively by the traditions of revenge tragedy to which he subscribed.

The same was not true of John Ford, who may justifiably be called the last of the great Renaissance tragedians. His revenge tragedies – *The Broken Heart, Love's Sacrifice, 'Tis Pity She's A Whore*, all published in 1633 – are certainly as contrived as those of Shirley, but they possess an artistic and a moral daring that Shirley never dreamed of. Not content simply to work within the parameters of tragedy defined by Elizabethan and Jacobean dramatists, Ford set out to discover new heaven, new earth; and though he regularly mined the plays of his forebears, particularly Shakespeare, for plots, he did so with the understanding that only original moral premises – the shock of breaking already permissive social codes – could revitalize the genre.

'Tis Pity illustrates this strategy best. From the outset, Ford consciously advertises his debt to *Romeo and Juliet*: attractive young lovers, Giovanni and Annabella, are advised by their two mentors, a friar and a nurse, to deny their love or to keep it hidden from the eyes of a censorious society, and the

play moves inexorably to Annabella's marriage to Soranzo, a man she does not love, and to her murder and Giovanni's suicide. This much is derivative; but Ford gives it new life by revealing that the lovers are in fact brother and sister. Unlike Romeo and Juliet, this incestuous pair consummate their love early: the dramatic consequences of their doing so – her pregnancy and subsequent marriage of convenience, her husband's discovery of the deception, and his revenge on her – all take the play into territory more corrupt and sexually overheated than any charted by Shakespeare. It has been commonplace, therefore, for critics to regard Ford as a purveyor of Caroline decadence who appealed to his audience's taste for the merely sensational. His dramatic power, however, resides not in sensationalism, but in the iconoclasm of his moral sympathies; for in a world of jaded self-interest such as Ford creates, where adultery flourishes, revenge is commonplace, and even the cardinal makes no pretence to morality, the love of Giovanni and Annabella stands as something finer, nobler, and more passionate than anything those around them are capable of.

In drama of this period, incest served as 'a vehicle for the expression of illicit desire, a challenge to the fundamental conventions of society';[11] but where Webster in *The Duchess of Malfi* (*c.* 1613) had used it as a metaphor for moral decay and Beaumont and Fletcher in *A King and No King* (*c.* 1611) as an excuse for prurience, Ford treated it more imaginatively as the basis for a new morality – for a sublime defiance of social respectability. Arguing the case for incest with the incredulous friar, Giovanni essentially becomes a law unto himself: the sexual taboo is also a religious taboo, and its violation marks him as an atheist as well as a criminal. Yet Ford allows us to admire Giovanni much as we admire the Marlovian overreacher, as one whose assertion of individual will towers heroically above the carping of those petty poseurs who populate his world; and the verse in which he and Annabella express their love and their suffering, by refashioning the language of Romeo and Juliet, breathes new pathos into tired Petrarchanism:

> GIOVANNI
> Kiss me; if ever after-times should hear
> Of our fast-knit affections, though perhaps
> The laws of conscience and of civil use
> May justly blame us, yet when they but know
> Our loves, that love will wipe away that rigour
> Which would in other incests be abhorr'd.
> Give me your hand; how sweetly life doth run

[11] Leggatt, *English Drama*, p. 229. David M. Bergeron, too, discusses the incest of *'Tis Pity* in the light of dramatic precedent in 'Brother–sister relationships in Ford's 1633 plays', in Anderson, *'Concord in Discord'*, pp. 195–219.

In these well-coloured veins! how constantly
These palms do promise health! but I could chide
With Nature for this cunning flattery.
Kiss me again – forgive me.

ANNABELLA
              With my heart.

GIOVANNI
Farewell.

ANNABELLA
    Will you be gone?

GIOVANNI
            Be dark, bright sun,
And make this midday night, that thy gilt rays
May not behold a deed will turn their splendour
More sooty than the poets feign their Styx!
One other kiss, my sister.

ANNABELLA
           What means this?

GIOVANNI
To save thy fame, and kill thee in a kiss.   (5.5.68–84)

Next to such limpid beauty as this, the judgements of those hypocrites who condemn the lovers seem mean-spirited. Ford thus challenges conventional morality where others, like Shirley, pandared to it. His artifice draws attention to the power of theatre to promote alternate systems of value; Shirley, in contrast, merely drew attention to his own cleverness. At his best, as in the climactic scene in which Giovanni enters bearing Annabella's heart on his dagger – a grotesque emblem of the self-sacrificing love he holds as truth – Ford writes with an aesthetic and moral potency unrivalled by any of his contemporaries.

The theatre takes stock of itself

Despite the common assumption that Caroline playwrights were a decadent lot, therefore, many were deeply concerned with questions of morality; and when, in the first years of Charles's reign, commissions for new plays all but dried up, playwrights grew understandably fearful that the theatre was losing its credibility as a cultural force. Thus they began to use plays as forums to debate – and justify – their own roles as social and moral arbiters. Massinger led the way: his concern with the power of theatre to instruct and reform reflects the precarious position of dramatists writing under a monarch who had absolute authority over their profession and for a public often sceptical of theatrical enterprise. Massinger was particularly sensitive to the power of censorship, having felt the lash early in his career, and he attacked both censorship and patronage in *The Roman Actor*, performed in 1626, shortly after Charles came to the throne. Modelled on Jonson's *Sejanus* (1605) – itself the victim of censorship – and tellingly set in the lurid days of imperial Rome, Massinger's tragedy focuses on the relationship of Rome's leading actor, Paris, to those in political power: the emperor Domitian Caesar, his empress Domitia, and the consul Aretinus.

In the first act, Paris and his fellow players stand accused 'of treason, / As libellers against the state and Caesar' (1.3.33–4) and, more generally, of traducing persons of rank – accusations levelled against actors in Massinger's day, and a certain provocation to censorship. Paris' defence against these allegations is usually interpreted as Massinger's apology for the theatre. Briefly, he argues that theatre educates and ennobles; that its representations of virtue and vice inspire spectators to ethical behaviour, never to passion; and that it exposes to ridicule only character types, not individuals.[12]

Massinger subverts these arguments in three plays-within-the-play, however, and thereby betrays some ambivalence about the theatre's claim to be morally instructive. In the first one, Caesar commands Paris to reform the old miser Philargus by performing a play called *The Cure of Avarice*. Paris, alluding to *Hamlet*, claims that Philargus will 'see his own deformity ... as in a mirror ... and loathe it' (2.1.97–9); but he fails to substantiate his claim. Philargus is unmoved by the play and consequently is put to death by the emperor for resisting correction. Tyranny gets results where the theatre cannot. The empress Domitia then commands Paris to perform a second play, based on a sensational Ovidian tale, just so that she may watch him enact the role of a lover. His performance so heightens her lust for him that she loses control of herself and disrupts the play. So much for Paris' claim that the theatre leads spectators to virtue.

Massinger subverts Paris' defence even more devastatingly in the third play, entitled *The False Servant*, which the emperor requests after discovering Paris in the arms of Domitia. Paris of course plays the title role, and Caesar casts himself as the wronged husband. But he forgets his lines in mid-performance and, incited to revenge, murders Paris on stage – an imitation of the famous catastrophe of Kyd's *Spanish Tragedy*. With an irony by which

---

[12] Jonas Barish notes that Paris' arguments are indebted to Elizabethan apologists – Sidney, Nashe, Heywood, and Jonson – in 'Three Caroline "Defenses" of the stage', in Braunmuller and Bulman, *Comedy from Shakespeare to Sheridan*, p. 196.

Massinger underscores the precariousness of his profession in a despotic state, the emperor declares,

> 'twas my study
> To make thy end more glorious to distinguish
> My Paris from all others.
>
> . . .
>
> 'twas my plot that thou
> Shouldst die in action, and to crown it die
> With an applause enduring to all times,
> By our imperial hand. (4.2.290–2, 297–300)

Caesar thus conceives of the court as a private theatre where he can act any role to impose his absolute will. Massinger reinforces the point by having him invoke the spirit of a notorious ancestor who conceived of Rome as one big stage: 'since Nero scorn'd not/ The public theatre, we in private may/ Disport ourselves' (4.2.224–6). At least inferentially, *The Roman Actor* criticizes the Caroline court's tendency to dramatize itself, to use theatrical self-fashioning as an instrument of power and persuasion. According to Annabel Patterson, the histrionic excesses of the King and Queen were becoming a matter of common gossip;[13] and just a few years later William Prynne, in his virulently anti-theatrical tract *Histriomastix* (1633), made the identification of Charles with the play-acting Roman tyrants, especially Nero, explicit.

The Roman Actor ushered in the defensive spirit of Caroline drama. It was the first among several plays to take theatre as its subject; collectively, they provide evidence that the theatre was suffering a crisis of identity in which dramatists asserted their power to influence an audience while in fact fearing their own impotence. Massinger resorted to the artifices of Elizabethan revenge tragedy to make his point. Others addressed the subject by recreating the wishful world of Elizabethan romance – a world of mythic metamorphoses and miraculous conversions. In his tragicomedy *The Lover's Melancholy* (1628), Ford tests the power of theatre to effect psychological cures in a manner reminiscent of Shakespeare's late romances.

In the play's parallel plots, the borrowing from Shakespeare is shameless. Both plots hinge on melancholy. One concerns Prince Palador of Cyprus, an Orsino-figure who has ignored all the duties of a monarch and lapsed into indolence since the disappearance of his beloved Eroclea, a virgin who had been wooed surreptitiously by Palador's licentious and tyrannical father Agenor, now dead. The other concerns Eroclea's aged father Meleander who, like King Lear, has fallen into a violent madness since Agenor robbed him of his daughter, lands, and title. The action focuses on the cure of their

---

[13] *Censorship and Interpretation*, p. 91. See also Goldberg, *James I*, pp. 203–9.

melancholy made possible by Eroclea's return from exile disguised as a boy –
a clear imitation of Viola's cross-dressing as Cesario.

Although Ford was undoubtedly influenced by Burton's *Anatomy of
Melancholy* (1621), he was less interested in the power of medicine than in
the power of theatre to minister to a mind diseased.[14] Corax, the physician at
Palador's court, is in fact a stage manager who speaks of his cures as an art;
they can be achieved only through theatrical revelation. Ford thus focuses on
the process of discovery, on poignant scenes of awakening and reconciliation, to dramatize those cures. To cure Palador, Corax stages a masque of
melancholy with illustrative types drawn from Burton. Only the melancholic
lover is left out: that role is assumed by Palador himself, who is, in a sense,
drawn into the masque, the spectacle moving him to exorcise his own afflic-
tion. Theatrical artifice thus prepares him for a poignant reunion with
Eroclea and for a resumption of his duties as monarch.

The cure of Meleander is theatrically more complex, for Corax must stage
a scene to involve him without his knowing it. The old man is given a potion,
and while asleep, he, like Lear, is dressed in new robes. Upon awakening, he
is approached by three messengers from the prince, who ceremonially
restore his honours, titles, and, in a picture, his daughter. The counterfeit
prepares him for the entrance of Eroclea herself – nature here is hand-
maiden to art – and the scene is replete with echoes of Lear's reconciliation
with Cordelia:

> EROCLEA
> [*Kneeling*] Dear sir, you know me?
>
> MELEANDER
>   Yes, thou art my daughter,
> My eldest blessing. Know thee? Why, Eroclea,
> I never did forget thee in thy absence.
> Poor soul, how dost?
>
> EROCLEA
>   The best of my well-being
> Consists in yours.
>
> MELEANDER
>   Stand up; the gods, who hitherto
> Have kept us both alive, preserve thee ever!   (5.2.108–13)

Later in the scene, when Palador arrives to confirm all that the 'play' has
promised, Meleander again echoes Lear: 'Great, gracious sir, alas, why do
you mock me?/ I am a weak old man...' (ll.233–4). What Ford achieves with

---

[14] For an astute analysis of Burton's limited influence on the play, see Michael Neill, 'The
   moral artifice of "The Lovers Melancholy"', *ELR* 8 (1978), 85–106.

these allusions, however, is not the ethos of *Lear*, but rather a sentimental vision of social harmony controlled by the magic of art.

Ford is sometimes accused of not measuring up to the writers he imitates, but this misses the point. It is a fundamental misunderstanding of his plays to assume that they should explore themes already explored by Shakespeare – the self-discovery that comes with tragic suffering, or the shifts of gender and tests of love that make fifth-act couplings so richly earned. Instead, Ford transfigures Shakespearian material to advance his own ideas. In *The Lover's Melancholy*, he tests the claim that theatre has the power to reform the spectator, just as Massinger does in *The Cure of Avarice*; but where Massinger dramatizes the failure of the claim, Ford triumphantly dramatizes its success. He attributes to theatre an almost mythical power of persuasion. And although his politics are muted by the play's romantic affirmations, they are none the less clear: the theatrical self-fashioning abused by the imperial court in *The Roman Actor* becomes, in Palador's court, a force of political and social regeneration.

The conviction that theatrical illusion may be therapeutic informs Richard Brome's *The Antipodes* as well. Patterned in part on *The Lover's Melancholy*, this comedy was performed nearly a decade later, in 1638, when theatres had been closed by the plague for seventeen lean months and needed an affirmation of their own health. *The Antipodes* attests to the ethical function of theatre in contemporary London – the world of Jonsonian comedy, far from imperial Rome and romantic Cyprus. Brome learned his craft at Jonson's feet: his play is therefore stuffed with exaggerated characters and humorous incidents. It focuses on Peregrine, a melancholic young man from the country who, like Palador, is cured by means of stage magic.

An obsession with Mandeville's travels has prevented Peregrine from consummating his marriage of three years. His distressed father thus seeks out a house in London where a fantastical lord named Letoy, who keeps a troop of actors on hand, will take Peregrine on an imaginary journey to the Antipodes, where, presumably, he will learn to appreciate his own world by witnessing the world turned upside-down. The play's central conceit proclaims 'that upon the southern side of the globe manners and morals are exactly contrary to those upon the northern side';[15] but ironically, what Antipodean scenes most often reveal is not an Anti-London, but a satirical distortion of London as it is. Brome no doubt depended on his audience to recognize in the Antipodes the topoi of city comedy: babbling lawyers, lecherous judges, hypocritical churchmen, corrupt statesmen, and unfaithful

---

[15] Donaldson, *The World Upside-Down*, pp. 81–4.

wives all come in for a drubbing. In fundamental ways, London and Anti-London are indistinguishable.

Like Palador and Meleander, Peregrine is cured by being drawn into the action, unwittingly becoming an actor in a fiction he cannot distinguish from reality. But Brome aims his satire more directly at those who can so distinguish – the aristocratic Londoners gathered at the Salisbury Court theatre. Brome offers *The Antipodes* as a funhouse mirror in which they may view the nature of their society. At the outset he makes clear that the audience for whom he intends his cure encompasses everyone in the theatre: 'my house, which now/ You may be pleas'd to call your own, is large/ Enough to hold you all' (1.1.12–14). To expel the plague that infects them, he recommends a doctor who administers

> medicine of the mind, which he infuses
> So skilfully, yet by familiar ways,
> That it begets both wonder and delight
> In his observers, while the stupid patient
> Finds health at unawares.   (24–8)

Brome here invokes a popular theory of comic catharsis.[16] Comedy may purge an audience of its folly through wonder and delight; the metaphor is medicinal, and Brome the doctor. A more subversive writer than Ford or even Massinger, he affirms that theatre *has* a social function. Through all its absurdities, *The Antipodes* insists that comedy can reform the spectator – morally and politically.

Throughout the Caroline period, therefore, dramatists were intensely preoccupied with the ideological implications of theatre. Threats of court censorship, a shrinking of audiences, and a growing opposition to the theatre among more zealous puritans made dramatists sensible of the precariousness of a livelihood they had once taken for granted; and in their plays, consequently, theatrical self-reference took a decidedly introspective turn. Massinger was sceptical that theatre had *any* salutary power. His *Roman Actor*, written at the juncture of two oppressive reigns, dramatizes a theatre that has become a social liability: actors are sycophantic, their performances rouse spectators to immoral behaviour, and the stage is co-opted by a tyrannical court. Paris' old-fashioned, platitudinous defences lie bleeding on the field.

Subsequent dramatists, Ford and Brome among them, tried to revive those stricken defences by dramatizing the power of theatre to 'cure' spectators – to reform them for ethical ends. But their plays lack the political

---

[16] See, for example, its use in Jonson's comedy of humours. The medicinal idea of comic catharsis is discussed by Donaldson, *The World Upside-Down*, pp. 94–7, and by J. L. Davis, 'Richard Brome's neglected contribution to comic theory', *SP* 11 (1948), 520–8.

urgency of Massinger's and resort either to romantic fantasy or to farce. In fictions that bore no relation to the actual condition of theatre during this period, dramatists strained to affirm their value to a society that was growing increasingly suspicious of them. As witness to this, one marks in their plays nostalgic references to, even recreations of, plays of an earlier generation – *The Spanish Tragedy, Hamlet, Twelfth Night, Lear*, Jonsonian city comedy. Through such nostalgic reference, Caroline dramatists perhaps hoped to stem the tide of dissent: their plays, each in its own way a defence, imagine societies redeemed by theatrical enterprise from the process of political and social disruption. But that process eventually proved unstoppable, hurled England into civil war, and rendered all such defences nugatory.

Jonson and his legacy

In his early comedies of humours, Ben Jonson had been a strong apologist for the theatre, arguing its essentially moral function. Not surprisingly, then, Caroline dramatists turned to the models he had provided: no writer influenced the development of Caroline comedy more strongly than Jonson. Yet there is a paradox here, for Jonson's Caroline plays were themselves unpopular, and his Jacobean comedies dramatized a moral ambiguity and social fragmentation that unsettled Caroline audiences. His theory of humours revealed scepticism that human nature could change as a result of experience, and his satirical depiction of urban folly excluded the harmony, forgiveness, and social unity that characterized Elizabethan comedy. Jonson's obsession with rapacity and his portrayal of London low-life – the bawds and pimps, parasites, and cheats who were the natural offspring of bourgeois commercialism – did not always appeal to a more refined Caroline audience. Nevertheless, his comedies inspired many of the best Caroline dramatists to try their hand at city comedy. If those dramatists preferred to deal with more aristocratic types than Jonson, to blunt the point of his satire, and to soften his moral indictment of urban society, they none the less borrowed liberally from his plots and adapted them to social concerns of their own age.

Shackerley Marmion's fine comedy *Holland's Leaguer* (1631) illustrates how Jonson's muse was modified for an audience as interested in manners as in morals. The plot involves the gulling of two young men – a humorous gallant named Trimalchio, who has recently squandered his father's estate, and his protégé Capritio, who has come from Norfolk to learn the manners of the town. Marmion's focus on newcomers reflects the enormous growth in population London had undergone, and in particular the movement of country gentry to the town. From a decidedly courtly perspective, Marmion ridicules the *naïveté* of these fashion-mongers: Trimalchio is a dissolute precursor of Sir Fopling Flutter, and Capritio a country dolt who would make Margery Pinchwife look sophisticated.

Like Jonson, Marmion satirizes London types (in the impostor Agurtes and his disciple Captain Autolicus, for instance); but unlike him, he draws those types not from the bourgeoisie, but from the privileged classes. With Jonsonian wit, he indicts the materialism of his society, mocks the aspirations of the gentry, and exposes the immorality of cavaliers; but in un-Jonsonian fashion, he balances the satire with an ennobling romantic plot wherein the narcissistic Lord Philautus is converted to virtue by the first woman he cannot seduce. Because this woman is actually his sister Faustina, whom he (preposterously) fails to recognize, his attempt to seduce her is rife with Fletcherian possibilities; but Marmion chooses not to exploit them. Instead, he dramatizes the power of platonic love to transform human nature. 'For how can that be love', Faustina asks her lecherous brother,

> which seeks the ruin
> Of his own object, and the thing beloved?
> No, true love is pure affection,
> That gives the soul transparent, and not that
> That's conversant in beastly appetites.   (3.4,p.59)

That Philautus is a lord is significant, for, as Faustina implies (just as Julietta would suggest to Lord Bonvile in *Hyde Park* a year later), the nobility ought to set a moral tone for the whole society. Philautus's imprisonment by self-love may thus be symptomatic of an entire class that had forsaken its moral responsibility and become the source of vanity in others, such as the aspirant courtiers Trimalchio and Capritio. His conversion at the hands of a chaste woman, furthermore, may pay tribute to Queen Henrietta who, by promoting Neoplatonic idealism (see pp. 376–7), was attempting to educate courtiers to virtue.

Other dramatists, less courtly in orientation, attempted to show the emerging *beau monde* of London its own image 'in parks, squares, taverns and gaming houses, supplying standards against which forms and codes of behavior could be established, scrutinized and adjusted'.[17] Their plays thus served an important social function and may rightly be called 'town' rather than 'city' comedies. *Hyde Park* is one example; Thomas Nabbes's *Covent Garden* is another. Brome, however, was the foremost writer of such plays, and *The Weeding of Covent Garden* (?1632), like his later *Antipodes*, reveals

---

[17] Butler, *Theatre and Crisis*, p. 111.

how successfully he applied Jonson's techniques to an essentially un-Jonsonian world.

Inspired in part by *Bartholomew Fair*, *The Weeding* concerns the settling of country gentry into the newly fashionable Covent Garden district, a place which a local justice (descended from Jonson's Adam Overdo) and a humorous country gentleman named Crosswill fail to weed of those roisterers and whores with whom Crosswill's wilful children fraternize. Brome creates a comic image of the chaos that results when too many arbitrary laws, such as those by which Charles attempted to control England's economic and social life, compete with one another.[18] But whether or not one reads it as a political allegory, *The Weeding* is clearly concerned with social adjustment in London, and in particular with inhabitants of the town and their values: how they govern themselves, how they allow themselves to be governed. Brome portrays a wider social spectrum than Shirley, Marmion, and Davenant do. Where they confine themselves largely to the aristocracy, Brome ranges from the gentry to the bourgeoisie to the underclasses and outlaws, thereby capturing something of the confusion of Ursula's stall at Bartholomew Fair. His encompassing social vision harks back to Jonson and makes this play, in tone and style, a true descendant of Jacobean comedy.

Similar concerns with social adjustment inform Davenant's popular comedy *The Wits* (1634), in which a country gentleman named Pallatine the Elder and a humorous older knight named Thwack, having put their estates in trust, come to London vowing to live off their wits – by which they mean to live off women and thereby prove their mastery of town arts. The main plot involves the gulling of Pallatine the Elder by the witty Lady Ample and by his younger brother, whom necessity has already taught to master such arts; and for this plot, Davenant refashions the central situation of *The Alchemist* to satirize aristocratic manners rather than commercial chicanery. Lady Ample is a wealthy ward of the absent Sir Tyrant Thrift, whose house she uses as a place to humiliate the elder Pallatine into acknowledging the superior wit of women. She schemes with the younger Pallatine to lead his brother naked into a bed where, instead of receiving the expected gratification, he is arrested as a male bawd; later, when he is pressing his suit, she causes him to hide in a chest by telling him that Thrift has unexpectedly returned. He is freed from the chest only after deeding a country manor to his brother – an inheritance younger brothers could never legitimately claim.

The Wits, however cynical, is more benign than *The Alchemist* in its depic-

18 Butler, *Theatre and Crisis*, pp. 151–8.

tion of social relations. Pallatine the Elder recognizes the folly of his plans, acknowledges the superior wit of his brother and Lady Ample, and, in return, is given the lady's hand in marriage. The tones of feminism may be heard distinctly in her refusal to submit to male domination:

> But, sir, if I should marry you, it is
> In confidence, I have the better wit,
> And can subdue you still to quietness,
> Meek sufferings, and patient awe.   (5.3, p.220)

Thrift, as a result of this marriage, is done out of the inheritance he had hoped to gain by marrying his ward; and in an act of splendid generosity, Thwack, who is childless, makes the younger Pallatine his heir. Social harmony is thus assured. As in the best Elizabethan comedy, Jack has Jill and nought goes ill.

The social premises of *The Wits*, however, resemble those of *The Weeding of Covent Garden* more than Elizabethan comedy. Davenant, like Brome, dramatizes the consequences of the movement of country gentry to the town, but, unlike Brome, he implies that life in town may be unsuitable for those who fail to live by their wits. Chastened by the gulling, Thwack decides to write letters 'down to th' country, to dehort [dissuade]/ The gentry from coming hither, letters/ Of strange dire news' (4.2, p.199); the dire news includes satire on puritanism, on drinking and abstention, and on the dissipation at Covent Garden. Thwack's letters comically recall Charles's proclamation of 30 June 1632 'commanding the gentry to keep their residences at their mansions in the country, and forbidding them to make their habitations in London and places adjoining'[19] (a proclamation Crosswill had flouted in *The Weeding*), and the action of the play affirms its validity: the country *is* a more fitting place for old-fashioned gentry like Thwack to live and govern, though for reasons quite different from those Charles set out in his decree.[20] Despite Thwack's satirical attack on the town, however, Davenant suggests that town and country are complementary rather than opposed. The country, portrayed in pastoral terms, is England's backbone, the seat of traditional values, and in it those gentry who have estates to manage – men of substance – rightly belong. In town, on the other hand, good sense can make a living and even thrive: the town is an appropriate place for younger brothers and others without estates to inherit. This view of the proper relationship between country and town is perfectly in keeping with the court's, and it marks Davenant, more than Jonson's other imitators, as a royalist.

---

[19] Kaufmann, *Richard Brome*, p. 69.
[20] Butler, *Theatre and Crisis*, p. 144.

While Jonson's Jacobean comedies were widely imitated, his Caroline plays – *The Staple of News* (1626), *The New Inn* (1629), *The Magnetic Lady* (1632), *The Tale of A Tub* (1633) – were paradoxically unpopular in their own day, dismissed as 'dotages' by Dryden, and even today are regarded as products of a dramatist in decline. True, Jonson had seen better days: he had suffered a paralysing stroke in 1628, he had not found the favour in Charles's court that he had found in James's, and his vigorously English comedy did not appeal to the increasingly Europeanized audience that flocked to revivals of Beaumont and Fletcher. Jonson confronted the situation with characteristic perversity. While more fashionable writers refined his comic muse to accommodate the manners of court and town, Jonson himself turned anomalously to an unfashionable genre, that of Shakespearian romance, for his best Caroline play.

Though a failure when first performed in 1629, *The New Inn* clearly is no dotage. Its nostalgic vision of an Elizabethan social order may not have interested the Caroline audience, but as society under the Stuarts fell (or seemed to fall) further and further away from the ideals of Elizabeth's golden age, Jonson came to feel a kinship with the great writer whose romantic comedies awakened the imagination to the power of love and forgiveness.[21] In *The New Inn*, romance is tamed to a suburban setting. Shakespeare's green world becomes the Inn of the Light Heart in Barnet, to which aristocrats from the city repair to undergo their metamorphoses. Chief among them are Lord Lovel, a melancholic who pines for the love of Lady Frampul, and the lady herself, a professional virgin who arrives for an afternoon of courtly games, involves Lovel in them, and loses her heart to him.

Jonson frames this courtly-love play in a plot so full of coincidences that Shakespeare himself could not have matched its absurdity. Indeed, it is possible to interpret the plot as an irreverent parody of the romantic falsehoods Jonson once had deplored.[22] Goodstock, the well-spoken host of the Light Heart (as out of place there as Duke Senior in the Forest of Arden), is none other than Lord Frampul, the lady's father, who years earlier deserted

---

[21] Anne Barton discusses Caroline nostalgia for things Elizabethan, and accounts for the impact of Shakespeare's First Folio (1623) on Jonson's Caroline plays, in 'Harking back to Elizabeth: Ben Jonson and Caroline nostalgia', *ELH* 48 (1981), 706–31. See also John Lemly's essay on Jonson's use of Shakespearian elements in his late plays, '"Make odde discoveries!" Disguises, masques, and Jonsonian romance', in Braunmuller and Bulman, *Comedy from Shakespeare to Sheridan*, pp. 131–47.

[22] See, for example, Larry S. Champion, *Ben Jonson's 'Dotages': A Reconsideration of the Late Plays* (Lexington, Kentucky, 1967), pp. 76–103, who regards the play as an abortive court satire, and Watson, *Ben Jonson's Parodic Strategy*, pp. 210–25, who argues that Jonson treads a fine line between earnestness and send-up.

23   John Caird's 1987 Royal Shakespeare Company production of Jonson's *The New Inn*, Swan theatre

his wife and two young daughters and now, in penance, has 'coffined' himself in the inn. The boy Frank who works there is, unbeknown to him, his second daughter Laetitia. In a humorous situation beholden to *Twelfth Night*, Lady Frampul dresses 'Frank' in sport as her own lost sister to deceive Lord Beaufort, who promptly falls in love with her. Even more absurdly, the Irish nurse who abducted Laetitia and brought her in disguise to the inn turns out to be her own mother, Lord Frampul's wife. These fifth-act revelations have the effect of 'a poignant wish-dream' in which the main focus, as in Shakespeare's romances, is on family reunion:[23] missing children return as from the dead, spouses are reconciled after years of separation, disguises are shed, each daughter is matched with a suitable husband, and Frampul himself, like a suburban Prospero, ends his revels.

Jonson's adoption of Shakespeare's romantic patterns does not mean he had abandoned moral comedy. On the contrary, he used romance to criticize and to counter those forces that had disrupted the family in Caroline England. 'The transfer of power and wealth from country estate to urban institution had hastened the separation of families', and great households no longer served as centres of familial, economic, and political life as they had done

---

[23] Barton, *Ben Jonson*, p. 281.

during Elizabeth's reign.[24] The Inn of the Light Heart itself is a place for unfulfilled people to congregate without making serious commitments to one another or to life. It is, in a sense, a sterile inversion of Penshurst, the Sidney family estate Jonson had once idealized; but in the 'odde discoveries' made there, Jonson miraculously converts the new inn into a place where old virtues may be reclaimed.

Goodstock and Lovel, who share the perspective of years, lament the passing of a better age. Together they indict the morality of Stuart courtiers, who make a fetish of form but scoff at the ideals that once gave form a purpose. When Lovel, for example, elegiacally extols the virtues of a chivalric education at court, Goodstock replies:

> Aye, that was when the nursery's self was noble,
> And only virtue made it, not the market,
> That titles were not vented at the drum
> Or common outcry; goodness gave the greatness,
> And greatness worship: every house became
> An academy of honour, and those parts –
> We see departed, in the practice, now,
> Quite from the institution. (1.3.52–9)

Among the current practices at court – the 'seven liberal deadly sciences/ Of pagery' (82–3) – Goodstock particularly rails against sexual promiscuity, gambling, and false honour: his invective echoes that of Jonson's earlier malcontents. Furthermore, the satire of court morality finds more comic expression below-stairs, where a motley militia drawn in the style of Jonsonian humours comedy – Colonel Glorious, Bat Burst, Hodge Huffle, a drawer, tapster, chamberlain, ostler, and others – drink, brag, abuse a lady, and ride roughshod over civilized values. By using low comedy to mirror the main plot, Jonson shows himself to be still the master of Jacobean comic form.

The cult of Neoplatonism

The New Inn focuses on a court of love that Lady Frampul holds for an afternoon's entertainment. In it, Lovel is given the chance to win the lady's affection in sport by discoursing on platonic love. His speeches, riveting testimonials to an enduring ideal, pay homage to the Neoplatonic conceits of Donne's great love poetry. Love, he says, stamps the idea of the beloved on oneself; minds, like glasses, reflect the form of the beloved; love is a spiritual

---

[24] See Michael Hattaway's edition of *The New Inn* (Manchester, 1984), Introduction, pp. 5–6.

coupling of souls. And like Donne, Lovel argues his point in legal fashion against those who would defend the superiority of carnal desire:

> The body's love is frail, subject to change,
> And alters still, with it: the mind's is firm,
> One, and the same, proceedeth first from weighing
> And well examining what is fair and good;
> Then, what is like in reason, fit in manners;
> That breeds good will: good will desire of union.   (3.2.157–62)

Such sentiments crop up in later comedies as well, as we have seen in *Holland's Leaguer*; they anticipate the Neoplatonic idealism fostered at court in the 1630s by Henrietta Maria. Her Neoplatonism was a serious attempt to reform the behaviour of courtiers. Indeed, as Stephen Orgel and Roy Strong suggest, it was a political assertion as well, tied to Charles's claim of absolute monarchy: 'About the Queen revolved all passion, controlled and idealized by her Platonic beauty and virtue, as about the King all intellect and will'.[25] Jonson was equally serious about Neoplatonism and, like the Queen, saw it as a way to subdue immorality. Two years after *The New Inn*, he glorified its sublime idealism in two court masques; and although *The New Inn* was written before the Neoplatonic cult had fully blossomed, it none the less demonstrates that in ethical commitment, if not in theatrical taste, Jonson was at one with the court.

From the beginning of her reign, Henrietta Maria had striven to allegorize the court in terms of pastoral romance. Interest in Sidney's *Arcadia* revived, and various plays and masques celebrated the court's Neoplatonism by finding sources in French pastoral romances such as Honoré d'Urfe's *Astrée*, a work to which Jonson alludes in *The New Inn* (3.2.205). A new production of Fletcher's *The Faithful Shepherdess* in 1634 revealed the Queen's determination to promote her own interests through the theatre. At her request, this Jacobean satire on sexual licence was essentially reinvented as a Caroline idyll, a celebration of chastity. That the play had been 'misinterpreted' and thus failed in 1608 but succeeded in 1634 was seen, according to Annabel Patterson, as 'simultaneously an indictment of the earlier age' and 'a proof of the new court's finer morals and esthetics'.[26]

As with any cult, however, the Queen's cult of Neoplatonism was eventually trivialized and travestied. It seemed to its critics both frivolous and immoral, a smokescreen for the behaviour it was attempting to eradicate. The very phrase 'platonic love' became a code for elaborate games of

---

[25] *Inigo Jones: The Theatre of the Stuart Court* (London, 1973), I. 55, and see chapter 4, 'Platonic politics', pp. 49–75, *passim*.
[26] *Censorship and Interpretation*, p. 173.

amorous intrigue and adultery, the kind of illicit love for which the Cavalier court is now remembered.[27] Even courtly writers acknowledged the tension between the ideal and the practice. Davenant, for example, in his masque *The Temple of Love* (1635) and in his tragicomedy *The Platonic Lovers* (1636), celebrated the Neoplatonism of the royal couple while gently parodying its hypocrisy as practised by courtiers. However, in the work of less polished dramatists – those amateurs who hovered about the Queen – the course of the cult can most clearly be traced.

Thomas Killigrew is a case in point. An impecunious courtier who attached himself to the Queen's circle, Killigrew produced between 1635 and 1637 three tragicomedies which catered to the court's taste for chivalric romance, replete with exotic contests of love and honour. All three had a common source in *Ariane*, a heroic romance published at Paris in 1632 and in vogue with the platonic *précieux* at both the French and the English courts. By the end of the decade, however, Killigrew felt free to write a ribald comedy of manners called *The Parson's Wedding* – in part a spoof on the artificial idealism of his earlier plays – without fear of incurring the court's displeasure. In it, two witty and fortune-hunting gallants plot to win an attractive young widow and her friend away from the dull platonic lovers who assiduously woo them. Battle lines are drawn on the field of platonic love: the ladies defend the ideals of such love even though they are bored by their hypocritical wooers' pledges of constant service, and the gallants attack 'the spiritual nonsense the age calls Platonic love', even though, at the end, they submit to the conventions of marriage.[28]

This play is, decidedly, Cavalier drama. Killigrew directs his satire against Parliament and political reform, against dissenting clergy and religious agitators, against the military, against creditors. The gallants themselves, like Cavaliers of the period, are prototypes for the rakes of Restoration comedy, and the heroines differ from Restoration heroines only in so far as they are not yet fully emancipated from the assumptions of Neoplatonism. Although written about 1640, *The Parson's Wedding* was probably not performed until after the Restoration, when, as acted by Killigrew's company, it proved popular with the coterie audience. The audience of that time was far more homogeneous than Caroline audiences had been, and it was symptomatic of such homogeneity that when the theatres reopened in 1660, Davenant and Killigrew – two Cavalier dramatists, both former members of the Queen's circle – were granted exclusive patents to form rival companies. As

---

[27] On the trivialization of the cult of platonic love, see Barton, *Ben Jonson*, pp. 264–5, and Hattaway, *The New Inn*, Introduction, pp. 31–3.

[28] James C. Bulman, 'Thomas Killigrew', *Dictionary of Literary Biography* 58, 123–31.

managers, they helped to shape a repertory more élitist and limited in appeal than England had yet known.

Caroline drama was once regarded as the precursor of Restoration drama, an enervated, immoral body of work appealing to a uniformly Cavalier audience; and in the plays of Davenant and Killigrew we can perhaps find justification for this view. But clearly the situation is more complex. Other, greater dramatists – Massinger, Ford, Shirley, Jonson, Brome – wrote for audiences much more varied, of heterogeneous social and political views, even if alike in privilege. True, these dramatists largely ignored the public theatres and thus may not be considered popular in the way that Shakespeare was, or other Elizabethans whose plays they imitated: Caroline drama was, after all, self-consciously derivative, concerned with artifice, manners, codes of behaviour. But in so far as it anatomized the tensions within an increasingly strained society, it caught the spirit of the Caroline moment; by dramatizing, in copious detail, the pressures arising from social difference, it helped to shape the self-consciousness of a politically diverse audience. Like the better-known drama of preceding generations, Caroline drama was a reflection on, as well as of, its age.

Bibliography

SOCIAL ISSUES IN CAROLINE DRAMA

Recent criticism has demonstrated Caroline drama's lively involvement in social issues of the age. Two books have been particularly influential: Margot Heinemann's *Puritanism and Theatre* (1980) and Martin Butler's indispensable study of *Theatre and Crisis: 1632–1642* (1984). Annabel Patterson's *Censorship and Interpretation* (1984) and portions of Jonathan Goldberg's *James I and the Politics of Literature* (1983) also have focused attention on plays traditionally regarded as the inferior offspring of worthy Elizabethan and Jacobean parents.

FORD AND MASSINGER

Ford and Massinger have particularly benefited from this renewed interest in the Caroline period. In *Philip Massinger: A Critical Reassessment*, ed. Douglas Howard (1985), contributors cover a wide range of topics, from Massinger's use of theatrical language (Colin Gibson) to his treatment of gender (Philip Edwards), from his political tragedies (Martin Butler) to the social order of his comedies (Michael Neill). Massinger's work is the subject, too, of several essays in *Comedy from Shakespeare to Sheridan*, ed. A. R. Braunmuller and J. C. Bulman (1986), of which Gail Paster's exploration of Middleton's influence on Massinger, Philip Edwards's of Massinger's comical histories, and Jonas Barish's of Caroline defences of the theatre are particularly valuable.

Ford, like Massinger, is the subject of an important new anthology – *'Concord in Discord': The Plays of John Ford, 1586–1986*, ed. Donald K. Anderson (1986) – in which Robert Heilman, Eugene M. Waith, Alan Dessen, David Bergeron, and others provide an eclectic summation of the best in traditional approaches to Ford's work. Focusing with particular clarity on aesthetic and moral evaluations, they build on earlier studies such as Mark Stavig's *John Ford and the Traditional Moral Order* (1968) and Ronald Huebert's *John Ford: Baroque English Dramatist* (1977) without essentially challenging them. Dorothy M. Farr's *John Ford and the Caroline Theatre* (1979) has more materialist concerns: Farr considers Ford's plays in the light of the venues (Blackfriars, Phoenix) for which they were written and the audiences for which they were performed.

JONSON AND DAVENANT

In the past decade, Jonson's Caroline plays have been re-evaluated in three important books: Alexander Leggatt's *Ben Jonson: His Vision and His Art* (1981), Anne Barton's *Ben Jonson, Dramatist* (1984), and Robert N. Watson's *Ben Jonson's Parodic Strategy: Literary Imperialism in the Comedies* (1987). Perhaps more surprising than this resurgent interest in Jonson's late plays has been the attention accorded William Davenant, older studies of whom, such as Alfred Harbage's *Sir William Davenant, Poet Venturer 1606–1668* (1935) and Arthur H. Nethercot's *Sir William D'Avenant, Poet Laureate and Playwright–Manager* (1938), have recently been supplanted by Philip Bordinat and Sophia Blaydes's *Sir William Davenant* (1981) and Mary Edmond's *Rare Sir William Davenant* (1987).

Surprisingly little work has been forthcoming on other major Caroline writers – Shirley and Brome in particular – as well as on lesser lights such as Marmion and Killigrew (see the bio-bibliographies).

TEXTS

I have quoted from the following editions of particular texts: the Revels editions of Ford's *The Lover's Melancholy*, ed. R. F. Hill (1985) and *'Tis Pity She's a Whore*, ed. Derek Roper (1975); the Regents Renaissance editions of Brome's *The Antipodes*, ed. Ann Haaker (1966) and Shirley's *The Traitor*, ed. John Stewart Carter (1965); and the Garland Renaissance Drama edition of Brome's *The Weeding of Covent Garden*, ed. Donald S. McClure (1980).

Biographies and selected bibliography

1. Reference works and bibliographies
2. General critical studies and collections of criticism
3. Masques, pageants, academic and folk drama, etc.
4. Selected biographical sources
5. Biographies and bibliographies of individual authors

In the bio-bibliographies of individual authors, we have tried to list at least one modern collected edition of play texts, even if 'modern' means Victorian (and possibly unreliable), along with a short list of critical studies. Essays and books principally devoted to biography, textual bibliography, or source study have not been included, nor have editions of individual plays when a standard collected edition, however inferior, exists. Many of the titles in the 'General critical studies' section devote individual chapters or sections to single plays or playwrights; these titles are not repeated under the entries for individual authors. The bibliographies to individual chapters include relevant titles not mentioned here. Non-dramatic works are generally not listed in the bibliographies. Abbreviated periodical titles are listed at the beginning of this volume.

1. Reference works and bibliographies

Arber, Edward, ed. *A Transcript of the Registers of the Company of Stationers of London: 1554–1640*. 5 vols. London, 1875–7. Reprinted, New York, 1950.

Bentley, Gerald Eades. *The Jacobean and Caroline Stage*. 7 vols. Oxford, 1941–68.

Berger, T. L. and W. C. Bradford. *An Index of Characters in English Printed Drama to the Restoration*. Englewood, Colorado, 1975.

Bibliothèque de l'Humanisme et de la Renaissance. Annual Bibliography of Renaissance Studies (Geneva, 1966–80; Chicago, 1981–).

Bland, D. S. 'A checklist of drama at the Inns of Court'. *RORD* 9 (1966), 47–61; 12 (1969), 57–9; 21 (1978), 49–51.

Chambers, E. K. *The Elizabethan Stage*. 4 vols. Oxford, 1923.

Clark, Andrew. 'An annotated list of sources and related material for Elizabethan domestic tragedy, 1591–1625'. *RORD* 17 (1974), 25–33.

English Literary Renaissance. Amherst, 1971–. Publishes regular bibliographic articles on selected authors.

Foakes, R. A. *Illustrations of the English Stage 1580–1642*. London, 1985.

Fordyce, Rachel. *Caroline Drama: A Bibliographic History of Criticism.* Boston, 1978.
Greg, W. W. *A Bibliography of the English Printed Drama to the Restoration.* 4 vols. London, 1939–59.
Dramatic Documents from the Elizabethan Playhouses. 2 vols. Oxford, 1931.
Harbage, Alfred B. *Annals of English Drama. 975–1700.* Rev. edn S. Schoenbaum and S. Wagonheim. London and New York, 1989.
Henslowe, Philip. *Henslowe's Diary,* ed. R. A. Foakes and R. T. Rickert. Cambridge, 1961.
Kawachi, Yoshiko. *Calendar of English Renaissance Drama, 1558–1642.* Garland Reference Library of the Humanities, vol. 661. New York, 1986.
Kolin, Philip C. 'An annotated bibliography of scholarship on the children's companies and their theaters'. *RORD* 19 (1976), 57–82.
Kolin, Philip C. and R. O. Wyatt II. 'A bibliography of scholarship on the Elizabethan stage since Chambers'. *RORD* 15–16 (1972–3), 33–59.
Lancashire, Ian. *Dramatic Texts and Records of Britain: A Chronological Topography to 1558.* Toronto, 1984.
Leech, Clifford and T. W. Craik, gen. eds. *Revels History of Drama in English,* Vols. 3 (1576–1613) and 4 (1613–1660). London, 1975–81.
Logan, Terence P. and Denzell Smith, eds. *A Survey and Bibliography of Recent Studies in English Renaissance Drama.* 4 vols. Lincoln, Nebraska, 1973–8.
Malone Society. *Collections.* Oxford, 1909–.
PMLA. Annual Bibliography. New York, 1922–.
Pollard, A. W. and G. R. Redgrave. *A Short-Title Catalogue of Books Printed in England … 1475–1640.* London, 1926. Rev. edn W. A. Jackson, F. S. Ferguson, K. F. Pantzer. 2 vols. London, 1976–86.
Records of Early English Drama. Various editors. Toronto, 1979–.
Ribner, Irving and Clifford C. Huffman. *Tudor and Stuart Drama.* Goldentree Bibliographies in Language and Literature. Chicago, 1978.
Shapiro, Michael. 'Annotated bibliography on original staging in Elizabethan plays'. *RORD* 24 (1981), 23–49.
Stevens, David. *English Renaissance Theater History: a Reference Guide.* Boston, 1982.
Stratman, Carl J. *Bibliography of English Printed Drama, 1565–1900.* Carbondale, Illinois, 1967.
Studies in English Literature, 1500–1900. Annual Survey of Studies in Elizabethan and Jacobean Drama. Houston, Texas, 1961–.
Studies in Philology. Annual Bibliography of Renaissance Studies, 1917–69.
Tannenbaum, Samuel and Dorothy R. Tannenbaum, comps. *Elizabethan Bibliographies.* 41 vols. in 39. New York, 1937–50.
Wilson, F. P. and G. K. Hunter. *The English Drama: 1485–1585.* New York, 1969.

2. *General critical studies and collections of criticism*

Adams, Henry Hitch. *English Domestic, or Homiletic Tragedy, 1575–1642.* New York, 1943.
Altman, Joel B. *The Tudor Play of Mind.* Berkeley and Los Angeles, 1978.
Axton, Marie. *The Queen's Two Bodies: Drama and the Elizabethan Succession.* London, 1977.

Barber, C. L. *Creating Elizabethan Tragedy: The Theater of Marlowe and Kyd.* Chicago, 1988.

Barish, Jonas. *The Anti-Theatrical Prejudice.* Berkeley and Los Angeles, 1981.

Belsey, Catherine. *The Subject of Tragedy.* London, 1985.

Bevington, David. *From 'Mankind' to Marlowe.* Cambridge, Massachusetts, 1962.

   Tudor Drama and Politics: A Critical Approach to Topical Meaning. Cambridge, Massachusetts, 1968.

Bluestone, Max and Norman Rabkin, eds. *Shakespeare's Contemporaries.* 2nd edn. Englewood Cliffs, New Jersey, 1970.

Bowers, Fredson. *Elizabethan Revenge Tragedy, 1587–1642.* Princeton, 1940. Reprinted, 1966.

Bradbrook, M. C. *Themes and Conventions of Elizabethan Tragedy.* 2nd edn. New York, 1980.

   The Growth and Structure of Elizabethan Comedy. New edn. London, 1973.

   English Dramatic Form: A History of Its Development. New York, 1965.

Braunmuller, A. R. and J. C. Bulman, eds. *Comedy from Shakespeare to Sheridan: Change and Continuity in the English and European Dramatic Tradition.* Newark, Delaware, 1986.

Bristol, Michael D. *Carnival and Theater: Plebeian Culture and the Structure of Authority in Renaissance England.* New York, 1985.

Brown, John Russell and Bernard Harris, gen. eds. *Jacobean Theatre.* Stratford-upon-Avon Studies 1. London, 1960.

   gen eds. *Elizabethan Theatre.* Stratford-upon-Avon Studies 9. London, 1966.

Butler, Martin. *Theatre and Crisis 1632–1642.* Cambridge, 1984.

Cohen, Walter. *Drama of a Nation: Public Theater in Renaissance England and Spain.* Ithaca and London, 1985.

Cope, Jackson. *The Theatre and the Dream: From Metaphor to Form in Renaissance Drama.* Baltimore, 1973.

Craik, T. W. *The Tudor Interlude.* Leicester, 1958.

Davidson, Clifford, C. J. Gianakaris, and John H. Stroupe, eds. *Drama in the Renaissance: Comparative and Critical Essays.* New York, 1986.

Dessen, Alan C. *Elizabethan Stage Conventions and Modern Interpreters.* Cambridge, 1984.

Dollimore, Jonathan. *Radical Tragedy: Religion, Ideology, and Power in the Drama of Shakespeare and his Contemporaries.* Rev. edn. Brighton, 1989.

Doran, Madeleine. *Endeavors of Art: A Study of Form in Elizabethan Drama.* Madison, Wisconsin, 1954.

Edwards, Philip. *Threshold of a Nation: A Study in English and Irish Drama.* Cambridge, 1979.

The Elizabethan Theatre. Vols. 1–3 ed. D. Galloway; vols. 4–9 ed. G. R. Hibbard; vols. 10– ed. C. E. McGee. Hamden, Connecticut; Toronto, 1969–81; Port Credit, Ontario, 1982–.

Ellis-Fermor, Una M. *The Jacobean Drama: An Interpretation.* 4th edn. London, 1958.

Farley-Hills, David. *Jacobean Drama.* London, 1988.

Farnham, Willard. *The Medieval Heritage of Elizabethan Tragedy.* New York, 1956.

Ford, Boris, ed. *The Age of Shakespeare.* Rev. edn. Harmondsworth, 1982.

Frost, David L. *The School of Shakespeare: The Influence of Shakespeare on English Drama, 1600–42.* Cambridge, 1968.

Gibbons, Brian. *Jacobean City Comedy.* 2nd edn. London, 1980.

Goldberg, Jonathan. *James I and the Politics of Literature.* Baltimore, 1983.

Green, A. W. *The Inns of Court and Early English Drama.* New Haven, 1931.

Greenblatt, Stephen. *Renaissance Self-Fashioning from More to Shakespeare.* Chicago, 1980.

  ed. *Representing the English Renaissance.* Berkeley and Los Angeles, 1988.

Greenfield, Thelma. *The Induction in Elizabethan Drama.* Eugene, Oregon, 1969.

Griswold, Wendy. *Renaissance Revivals: City Comedy and Revenge Tragedy in the London Theatre, 1576–1980.* Chicago, 1986.

Gurr, Andrew. *Playgoing in Shakespeare's London.* Cambridge, 1987.

  The Shakespearean Stage, 1574–1642. 2nd edn. Cambridge, 1980.

Habicht, Werner. *Studien zur Dramen Form vor Shakespeare: Moralität, Interlude, romaneskes Drama.* Heidelberg, 1968.

Harbage, Alfred. *Cavalier Drama.* New York, 1936.

Hattaway, Michael. *Elizabethan Popular Theatre: Plays in Performance.* London, 1982.

Haydn, Hiram. *The Counter Renaissance.* Reprinted, Gloucester, Massachusetts, 1966.

Heinemann, Margot. *Puritanism and Theatre: Thomas Middletōn and Opposition Drama under the Early Stuarts.* Cambridge, 1980.

Herrick, Marvin T. *Tragicomedy: Its Origins and Development in Italy, France, and England.* Urbana, Illinois, 1955.

Honigmann, E. A. J., ed. *Shakespeare and his Contemporaries: Essays in Comparison.* Manchester, 1986.

Hunter, G. K. *Dramatic Identities and Cultural Traditions: Studies in Shakespeare and his Contemporaries.* Liverpool, 1978.

Jacquot, Jean, ed. *Dramaturgie et société ... aux 16e et 17e siècles.* 2 vols. Paris, 1968.

  ed. *Fêtes de la Renaissance.* 2 vols. Paris, 1956.

  ed. *Le Lieu théâtral à la Renaissance.* Paris, 1964.

Kaufmann, R. J., ed. *Elizabethan Drama: Modern Essays in Criticism.* New York, 1961.

Kirsch, Arthur. *Jacobean Dramatic Perspectives.* Charlottesville, Virginia, 1972.

Klein, David. *The Elizabethan Dramatists as Critics.* New York, 1963.

Leggatt, Alexander. *Citizen Comedy in the Age of Shakespeare.* Toronto and Buffalo, New York, 1973.

  English Drama: Shakespeare to the Restoration, 1590–1660. London, 1988.

Leinwand, Theodore B. *The City Staged: Jacobean Comedy 1603–1613.* Madison, Wisconsin, 1986.

Lever, J. W. *The Tragedy of State.* London, 1971; rev. edn, 1987.

Levin, Richard. *The Multiple Plot in English Renaissance Drama.* Chicago, 1971.

  New Readings vs. Old Plays: Recent Trends in the Reinterpretation of Renaissance Drama. Chicago, 1979.

Loftis, John. *Renaissance Drama in England and Spain: Topical Allusion and History Plays.* Princeton, 1987.

Lomax, Marion. *Stage Images and Traditions: Shakespeare to Ford.* Cambridge, 1987.

Long, J. H., ed. *Music in English Renaissance Drama.* Lexington, Kentucky, 1969.

McAlindon, Thomas. *English Renaissance Tragedy.* London, 1986.

McLuskie, Kathleen. *Renaissance Dramatists: Feminist Readings*. London, 1989.

Maguire, Nancy K., ed. *Renaissance Tragicomedy: Explorations in Genre and Politics*. New York, 1987.

Orgel, Stephen. *The Illusion of Power: Political Theater in the English Renaissance*. Berkeley, Los Angeles, and London, 1975.

Ornstein, Robert. *The Moral Vision of Jacobean Tragedy*. Madison, Wisconsin, 1965.

Paster, Gail Kern. *The Idea of the City in the Age of Shakespeare*. Athens, Georgia, 1985.

Prest, W. R. *The Inns of Court under Elizabeth and the Early Stuarts, 1590–1640*. London, 1972.

Prior, Moody E. *The Language of Tragedy*. Bloomington, Indiana, 1966.

Ribner, Irving. *The English History Play in the Age of Shakespeare*. Rev. edn. Princeton, 1965.

Ricks, Christopher, ed. *English Drama to 1710*. Rev. edn. London, 1987.

Ristine, Frank H. *English Tragicomedy*. 1910. Reprinted, New York, 1963.

Rossiter, A. P. *English Drama from Early Times to the Elizabethans*. London, 1950.

Salingar, Leo. *Dramatic Form in Shakespeare and the Jacobeans*. Cambridge, 1986.

Sisson, C. J. *Lost Plays of Shakespeare's Age*. Cambridge, 1936.

Tomlinson, T. B. *A Study of Elizabethan and Jacobean Tragedy*. Cambridge, 1964.

Tricomi, Albert H. *Anticourt Drama in England, 1603–1642*. Charlottesville, Virginia, 1989.

Ure, Peter. *Elizabethan and Jacobean Drama: Critical Essays*. Ed. J. C. Maxwell. Liverpool, 1974.

Waith, Eugene M. *Ideas of Greatness: Heroic Drama in England*. New York, 1971.
Patterns and Perspectives In English Renaissance Drama. New York, Delaware, and London, 1988.

West, Robert Hunter. *The Invisible World: A Study of Pneumatology in Elizabethan Drama*. Athens, Georgia, 1939.

Wickham, Glynne. *Early English Stages 1300–1660*. 3 vols. in 4. New York, 1959–81.

Young, Steven C. *The Frame Structure in Tudor and Stuart Drama*. Elizabethan and Renaissance Studies, 6. Salzburg, 1974.

3. Masques, pageants, academic and folk drama, etc.

COLLECTIONS, SOURCES

Chambers, E. K. *The English Folk-Play*. Oxford, 1933.

Leishman, J. B., ed. *The Three Parnassus Plays (1598–1601)*. London, 1949.

Records of Early English Drama. Various editors. Toronto, 1979–.

Spencer, T. J. B. and Stanley Wells, eds. *A Book of Masques: In Honour of Allardyce Nicoll*. Cambridge, 1964.

Streitburger, W. R., ed. *Jacobean and Caroline Revels Accounts. Malone Society Collections* 13. Oxford, 1986.

STUDIES AND BIBLIOGRAPHIES

Baskervill, Charles R. *The Elizabethan Jig and Related Song Drama*. Chicago, 1929.

Bergeron, David M. *English Civic Pageantry 1558–1642*. Columbia, South Carolina, 1971.

ed. *Twentieth-Century Criticism of English Masques, Pageants and Entertainments 1558–1642. With a supplement on Folk-Play and Related Forms* by H. B. Caldwell. San Antonio, Texas, 1972.

Boas, F. S. *University Drama in the Tudor Age.* Oxford, 1914.

Brody, A. *The English Mummers and their Plays.* London, 1970.

Brotanek, Rudolf. *Die englischen Maskenspiele.* Vienna, 1902.

Dewey, Nicholas. 'The academic drama ...' (1603–1642): a checklist of secondary sources'. *RORD* 12 (1969), 33–42.

Dietrich, Julia C. 'Folk drama scholarship: the state of the art'. *RORD* 19 (1976), 15–32.

Gordon, D. J. 'Poet and architect: the intellectual setting of the quarrel between Ben Jonson and Inigo Jones'. *JWCI* 12 (1949), 152–78.

Helm, A. *The English Mummers' Play.* Woodbridge, Suffolk, 1981.

Lindley, David, ed. *The Court Masque.* Manchester, 1984.

McGee, C. E. and John C. Meagher. 'Preliminary checklist of Tudor and Stuart entertainments: 1558–1603', *RORD* 24 (1981), 51–155.

  'Preliminary checklist ... entertainments: 1485–1558'. *RORD* 25 (1982), 31–114.

  'Preliminary checklist ... entertainments: 1603–1613'. *RORD* 27 (1984), 47–126.

  'Preliminary checklist ... entertainments: 1614–1625'. *RORD* 30 (1988), 17–128.

Nicoll, Allardyce. *Stuart Masques and the Renaissance Stage.* London, 1937.

Orgel, Stephen and Roy Strong. *Inigo Jones: The Theater of the Stuart Court.* 2 vols. Berkeley and Los Angeles, 1973.

Petit, Thomas. 'Early English traditional drama: approaches and perspectives'. *RORD* 25 (1982), 1–30.

Reyher, Paul. *Les Masques anglais.* Paris, 1909.

Sabol, Andrew, ed. *Four Hundred Songs and Dances from the Stuart Masque.* Providence, Rhode Island, 1978.

Welsford, Enid. *The Court Masque.* Cambridge, 1927.

Withington, Robert. *English Pageantry.* 2 vols. Cambridge, Massachusetts, 1918–20.

4. Selected biographical sources

Bowers, Fredson, ed. *Elizabethan Dramatists.* Dictionary of Literary Biography, 62. Detroit, 1987.

  ed. *Jacobean and Caroline Dramatists.* Dictionary of Literary Biography, 58. Detroit, 1987.

Dictionary of National Biography. Leslie Stephen and Sidney Lee, gen. eds. New York, 1908, and supplements.

Drabble, Margaret, ed. *The Oxford Companion to English Literature.* 5th edn. Oxford, 1985.

Eccles, Mark. *Brief Lives: Tudor and Stuart Authors.* Texts and Studies. *SP* 79. Fall, 1982.

Foster, Joseph. *Alumni Oxonienses ... 1500–1714.* 4 vols. Oxford and London, 1891–2.

Hartnoll, Phyllis, ed. *Oxford Companion to the Theatre.* 4th edn. New York, 1983.

Hoffmann, Ann. *Lives of the Tudor Age: 1485–1603.* New York, 1977.

Meres, Francis. *Palladis Tamia or Wit's Treasury.* 1598. Reprinted, New York, 1938.

Nungezer, Edwin. *A Dictionary of Actors.* New Haven, 1929.

Palmer, Alan W. *Who's Who in Shakespeare's England.* Brighton, 1981.

Renaissance Drama. Introduction by Derek Traversi. New York, 1980.

Riddel, Edwin, ed. *Lives of the Stuart Age: 1603–1714.* London, 1976.

Shapiro, Michael. *Children of the Revels.* New York, 1977.

Venn, John and J. A. Venn. *Alumni Cantabrigienses, Part 1 ... to 1751.* 4 vols. Cambridge, 1922–7.

5. Biographies and bibliographies of individual authors

BEAUMONT, FRANCIS (1584/5–1616)

Born 1584/5, Grace-Dieu, Leicestershire, third son of justice Francis Beaumont. Entered Broadgates Hall, now Pembroke College, Oxford, 1597, at age 12. Entered Inner Temple 1600. Friendly with Jonson and Drayton. Wrote *The Woman Hater* for Paul's Boys *c.*1606 and *Knight of the Burning Pestle c.*1607 for Blackfriars. Lived with Fletcher and with him wrote for Blackfriars, then King's Men and Queen's Revels Children 1606–13, producing at least seven joint plays, including *Philaster, The Maid's Tragedy,* and *A King and No King.* Wrote masque for Princess Elizabeth's wedding of 20 February 1613. Ceased writing upon marriage to heiress Ursula Isley 1613. Died 6 March 1616, aged thirty-two. Buried in Westminster Abbey.

Works:

Bowers, Fredson, gen. ed. *The Dramatic Works in the Beaumont and Fletcher Canon.* Cambridge, 1966–.

Glover, Arnold and A. R. Waller, eds. *The Works of Francis Beaumont and John Fletcher.* 10 vols. Cambridge, 1905–12.

Studies:

Bliss, Lee. *Francis Beaumont.* Boston, 1987.

Danby, John F. *Poets on Fortune's Hill: Studies in Sidney, Shakespeare, Beaumont and Fletcher.* London, 1952.

Davison, Peter. 'The serious concerns of *Philaster*'. *ELH* 30 (1963), 1–15.

Finkelpearl, Philip J. 'Beaumont, Fletcher, and "Beaumont & Fletcher": some distinctions'. *ELR* 1 (1971), 144–64.

Mincoff, Marco. 'The social background of Beaumont and Fletcher'. *EM* 1 (1950), 1–30.

Neill, Michael. 'The defence of contraries: skeptical paradox in *A King and No King*'. *SEL* 21 (1981), 319–32.

'"The Simetry, Which Gives a Poem Grace": masque, imagery, and the fancy of *The Maid's Tragedy*'. *RenD*, n.s. 3 (1970), 111–36.

Pennel, C. A. and William P. Williams, eds. *Francis Beaumont and John Fletcher, 1937–1965.* Elizabethan Bibliographies Supplements 8. London, 1968.

Samuelson, David H. 'The order in Beaumont's *Knight of the Burning Pestle*'. *ELR* 9 (1979), 302–18.

See also Fletcher, John.

BROME, RICHARD (*c.*1590–1652/3)

Born *c.*1590, apparently from a poor family. May have attended Eton. Earliest record of him is in 1614 as secretary to Ben Jonson, who later commended him as his 'faithful servant ... and loving friend'. Jonson mentions him by name as the poet's 'man' in *Bartholomew Fair*. Wrote plays steadily throughout the 1620s and 30s for the King's Men at the Globe and Blackfriars and the Queen's at the Cockpit and Salisbury Court. Wrote for provincial companies during mid-1630s. Fifteen plays survive, primarily Jonsonian city comedies and romantic dramas. Friend to many dramatists, including Fletcher, Dekker, and Ford; dedicated plays to the Duke of Newcastle and the Earl of Hertford, who apparently served as patrons. Lived in poverty for ten years after closing of theatres; known dead by 1653, when five of his plays were gathered for publication.

Works:
The Dramatic Works of Richard Brome Containing Fifteen Comedies. 3 vols. London, 1873. Reprinted, New York, 1966.

Studies:
Andrews, Clarence E. *Richard Brome: A Study of His Life and Works.* 1913. Reprinted, Hamden, Connecticut, 1972.
Davis, Joe Lee. *The Sons of Ben: Jonsonian Comedy in Caroline England.* Detroit, 1967.
Haaker, Ann. 'The plague, the theater, and the poet'. *RenD* n.s. 1 (1968), 283–306.
Kaufmann, R. J. *Richard Brome, Caroline Playwright.* New York, 1961.
Shaw, Catherine. *Richard Brome.* Boston, 1980.

CARTWRIGHT, WILLIAM (1611–1643)
Born December 1611, Northway, near Tewkesbury, of a wealthy and educated family. King's Scholar to Westminster. Entered Christ Church, Oxford, as a gentleman commoner in 1628, M.A. in 1635. Took orders, 1638. Author of four plays written as academic exercises for Oxford students, believed to have been performed at Christ Church, 1635–8. His *Royal Slave*, with music by Henry Lawes, was performed at Oxford before Charles I in 1636. Appointed Succentor of the church in Salisbury, October 1642; chosen junior proctor of Oxford the following year. Died at Oxford, November 1643; buried in Christ Church cathedral.

Works:
Evans, G. Blakemore, ed. *Plays and Poems.* Madison, Wisconsin, 1951.

Studies:
Davis, Joe Lee. *The Sons of Ben: Jonsonian Comedy in Caroline England.* Detroit, 1967.

CHAPMAN, GEORGE (c. 1559–1634)
Born c.1559, Hitchin, Hertfordshire. May have studied at Oxford and Cambridge; took no degree. In Europe, 1585–91; military service in Netherlands likely. On Henslowe's payroll as dramatist for Admiral's Men (1596–9) writing the earliest of numerous comedies and perhaps inventing 'the comedy of humours' (*An Humorous Day's Mirth*). Completed Marlowe's *Hero and Leander* (1598). *Bussy D'Ambois*, produced by Paul's Boys c.1604 and later revived by King's Men. Imprisoned with Jonson

for his share in *Eastward Ho!* (Blackfriars, 1605), which offended James I. Soon in trouble again for offending the French ambassador with *The Conspiracy and Tragedy of Charles, Duke of Byron* (1608). Apparently withdrew from active playwriting *c.*1612; concentrated on Homeric translations. Wrote a masque for Princess Elizabeth's wedding (1613). Patronized by Robert Carr, Earl of Somerset, as late as 1624–5. Mentioned by Meres as among the best for comedy, tragedy, and translation, and for having 'mightily enriched' the English tongue. Died 12 May 1634, in London. Buried in St Giles-in-the-Fields, with a monument erected by Inigo Jones.

Works:
Holaday, Allan, gen. ed. *The Plays of George Chapman: The Comedies.* Urbana, Illinois, 1970.
   gen. ed. *The Plays of George Chapman: The Tragedies.* Cambridge, 1987.
Parrott, T. M., ed. *The Plays and Poems of George Chapman.* 2 vols. London, *Comedies,* 1914, *Tragedies,* 1910. Reprinted, New York, 1961.

Studies:
Bergson, Allen. 'The ironic tragedies of Marston and Chapman: notes on Jacobean tragic form'. *JEGP* 69 (1970), 613–30.
Bliss, Lee. 'The boys from Ephesus: farce, freedom, and limit in *The Widow's Tears*'. *RenD* n.s. 10 (1979), 161–83.
Braunmuller, A. R. *Natural Fictions: George Chapman's Major Tragedies.* Newark, Delaware and London, 1990.
Burton, K. M. 'The political tragedies of Chapman and Ben Jonson'. *EIC* 2 (1952), 397–412.
Herring, Thelma. 'Chapman and an aspect of modern criticism'. *RenD* 8 (1965), 153–79.
Hibbard, G. R. 'Goodness and greatness: an essay on the tragedies of Ben Jonson and George Chapman'. *RMS* 11 (1968), 5–54.
Jacquot, Jean. *George Chapman, sa vie, sa poésie, son théâtre, sa pensée.* Paris, 1951.
Kreider, Paul V. *Elizabethan Comic Character Conventions as Revealed in the Comedies of George Chapman.* Ann Arbor, 1935.
MacLure, Millar. *George Chapman: A Critical Study.* Toronto, 1966.
Muir, Edwin. '"Royal man": notes on the tragedies of George Chapman'. *Essays on Literature and Society* (1949), 20–30.
Pagnini, Marcello. *Forme e Motivi nelle Poesie e nelle Tragedie de George Chapman.* Florence, 1958.
Rees, Ennis. *The Tragedies of George Chapman: Renaissance Ethics in Action.* Cambridge, 1954.
Spens, Janet. 'Chapman's ethical thought'. *E&S* 11 (1925), 145–69.
Spivack, Charlotte. *George Chapman.* New York, 1967.
Ure, Peter. 'The main outline of Chapman's Byron'. *SP* 47 (1950), 568–88.
Waddington, Raymond B. 'Prometheus and Hercules: the dialectic of *Bussy D'Ambois*'. *ELH* 34 (1967), 21–48.
Waith, Eugene M. *The Herculean Hero in Marlowe, Chapman, Shakespeare and Dryden.* New York, 1962.

Wieler, John W. *George Chapman – The Effect of Stoicism Upon His Tragedies*. New York, 1949.

CHETTLE, HENRY (1560–*c.*1607)
Son of London dyer Robert Chettle. Apprenticed to stationer Thomas East, becoming a freeman of the Stationers' Company in 1584. Entered partnership in printing business with Danter and Hoskins from 1589 to 1591. Writing plays for Admiral's Men, both alone and in collaboration, by 1598. Collaborated with Dekker and Haughton on *Patient Grissel*. Possibly died in plague of 1603; known dead by 1607. Credited by Henslowe with many plays (possibly more than fifty, alone or in collaboration), of which only *Tragedy of Hoffman* is extant. Also active as satiric pamphleteer. Mentioned by Meres as 'among the best for comedy'.

Works:
Jenkins, Harold, ed. *The Tragedy of Hoffman*. Malone Society Reprints. Oxford, 1951.

Studies:
Jenkins, Harold. *The Life and Work of Chettle*. London, 1934.

DANIEL, SAMUEL (*c.* 1562–1619)
Born *c.*1562, Somerset. Probably son of music-master John Daniel. Entered Magdalen Hall, Oxford, 1581; left without taking degree. By 1585 served as agent to Walsingham in France and, by 1592, entered the circle of Mary (Sidney), Countess of Pembroke; later patrons included Fulke Greville (q.v.), Charles Blount (Lord Mountjoy), and Lady Anne Clifford. Closet tragedy *Cleopatra* published 1594 and twice revised (1599, 1607). Composed *Vision of the Twelve Goddesses*, a masque, for James's new court in 1603, and *Tethys' Festival* for Prince of Wales's investiture (1610). Summoned before the Privy Council in 1605 for his tragedy *Philotas* (Queen's Revels), believed to defend Essex's rebellion; licenser of Queen's Revels (1604). Two pastoral tragicomedies (1605 and 1614), both performed for Queen Anne. Groom (from 1607) and then Gentleman Extraordinary (1613) of the Queen's Privy Chamber. Died October 1619; buried on farm at Beckington, Somerset. Listed by Meres as among best for elegy and for having 'mightily enriched' the English tongue.

Works:
Grosart, Alexander B., ed. *The Complete Works in Verse and Prose of Samuel Daniel*. 5 vols. London, 1885–96.

Studies:
Brettle, R. E. 'Samuel Daniel and the Children of the Queen's Revels, 1604–5'. *RES* 3 (1927), 162–8.
Harner, James L. *Samuel Daniel and Michael Drayton: A Reference Guide*. Boston, 1980.
Rees, Joan. *Samuel Daniel: A Critical and Biographical Study*. Liverpool, 1964.

Seronsy, Cecil. *Samuel Daniel*. New York, 1967.
Spriet, Pierre. *Samuel Daniel (1563–1619): sa vie, son oeuvre*. Paris, 1969.

DAVENANT, SIR WILLIAM (1606–1668)
Born February 1606, Oxford. Educated at Lincoln College, Oxford, from 1620, leaving without degree. Active as dramatist, theatre manager (governor of Beeston's Boys in 1640–1), and producer of masques, at least one with Inigo Jones. Fought for Charles I in Civil War; knighted at siege of Gloucester in 1643. Manager of Drury Lane Theatre after Restoration. Later transferred royal patent from Duke's House to Covent Garden. In 1656 staged *The Siege of Rhodes*, first legitimate public theatre performance since closing of theatres, with first appearance of an actress (Mrs Coleman) on an English public stage, and music by Henry Lawes. Died 7 April 1668; buried in Westminster Abbey.

Works:
Maidment, James and W. H. Logan, eds. *Plays*. 5 vols. Edinburgh, 1872–4.

Studies:
Blaydes, Sophia B. and Philip Bordinat. *Sir William Davenant*. Boston, 1981.
    Sir William Davenant: An Annotated Bibliography 1629–1985. New York and London, 1986.
Collins, Howard S. *The Comedy of Sir William Davenant*. The Hague, 1967.
Edmond, Mary. *Rare Sir William Davenant*. Manchester, 1987.
Harbage, Alfred. *Sir William Davenant: Poet Venturer, 1606–1668*. Philadelphia, 1935.
Nethercot, Arthur H. *Davenant, Poet Laureate and Playwright–Manager*. Chicago, 1938.
Squier, Charles L. 'Davenant's comic assault on *Préciosité: The Platonic Lovers*'. *University of Colorado Studies*. Series in Language and Literature, vol. 10 (1966), 57–72.

DAVENPORT, ROBERT (*fl.* 1624–1640)
No certain information before 1624, when Herbert licensed his first known plays, *The City Night Cap*, a Euphuistic romance with strong borrowings from Greene, and *Henry I and Henry II* (perhaps two plays). Actively writing as late as 1640, including divine and moral verse; some play titles registered in 1650s. May have been alive as late as 1655, when *King John and Matilda* was published with a preface signed by the author.

Works:
Bullen, A. H., ed. *The Works of Robert Davenport*. Vol. 3 of *A Collection of Old English Plays*. London, 1882–5. Reprinted, New York, 1964.

DAY, JOHN (1574–*c*. 1640)
Born at Cawston in 1574. A farmer's son from Norfolk; educated at Ely. Entered

Gonville and Caius College, Cambridge, as sizar in 1592; expelled (1593) for stealing a book. First London mention is August 1598 in Henslowe, listed as collaborator with Chettle. Wrote for Admiral's Men from 1599 to 1603, mostly in collaboration with Dekker, Chettle, and Haughton, specializing in domestic tragedy. Later wrote alone for Children of the Revels. Twenty-two known plays, alone or in collaboration, only one of which saw print. Continued to write plays after 1608, mostly in collaboration with Dekker. Reappears in 1610 as author of *The Mad Pranks of Merry Moll*, genre unknown. Associated with Dekker as dramatist in 1619 and 1623.

Works:

Bullen, A. H., ed. *The Works of John Day*. 2 vols. London, 1881. Reprinted, 1963, ed. Robin Jeffs.

Studies:

Schoenbaum, Samuel. 'John Day and Elizabethan drama'. *Boston Public Library Quarterly* 5 (1953), 140–52.

DEKKER, THOMAS (*c.* 1572–1632)

Born *c.*1572, London. According to Henslowe, who first hired him as dramatist in 1598, Dekker was sole author of eight plays and joint author of at least thirty-eight more with Drayton, Jonson, and others between 1598 and 1602, for the Admiral's and Worcester's Men. Only six plays from this period survive, the best known being the popular city comedy *The Shoemaker's Holiday*. *Satiromastix* (1601) replies to Jonson's caricature of him in *Poetaster*. Already established as a leading dramatist, Dekker turned to prose works, including *The Gull's Hornbook* (1609), a satire with vivid glimpses of theatrical life. Continued to write during the last years of his life in collaboration with Ford, Massinger, and Rowley, primarily for Prince Charles's Men. Listed by Meres as one of the best for tragedy. Died in debt, August 1632.

Works:

Bowers, Fredson, ed. *The Dramatic Works of Thomas Dekker*. 4 vols. Cambridge, 1953–61.

Hoy, Cyrus. *Introductions, Notes and Commentaries to Texts in 'The Dramatic Works of Thomas Dekker'*. 4 vols. Cambridge, 1980.

Studies:

Bergeron, David M. 'Thomas Dekker's Lord Mayor's shows'. *ES* 51 (1970), 2–15.

Clubb, Louise George. '*The Virgin Martyr* and the *Tragedia Sacra*'. *RenD* 7 (1964), 103–26.

Conover, James H. *Thomas Dekker, An Analysis of Dramatic Structure*. The Hague, 1969.

Donovan, Dennis, ed. *Thomas Dekker, 1945–1965; Thomas Heywood, 1938–1965; Cyril Tourneur, 1945–1965*. Elizabethan Bibliographies Supplements 2. London, 1967.

Jones-Davies, M. T. *Un peintre de la vie londonienne: Thomas Dekker*. 2 vols. Paris, 1958.

Kaplan, Joel H. 'Virtue's holiday: Thomas Dekker and Simon Eyre'. *RenD* n.s. 2 (1969), 103–22.
Price, George R. *Thomas Dekker*. New York, 1968.
Thomson, Patricia. 'The Old Way and the New Way in Dekker and Massinger'. *MLR* 51 (1956), 168–78.
Ure, Peter. 'Patient Madman and Honest Whore: the Middleton–Dekker oxymoron'. *E&S 1966*, 18–40.

DRAYTON, MICHAEL (1563–1631)

Born 1563, Hartshill near Atherstone, Warwickshire. Brought up as page and educated in the household of Sir Henry Goodere of Powlesworth, Warwickshire, who was his early patron. Drayton's later patrons included the Princes Henry and Charles and Lucy, Countess of Bedford. Wrote plays for the Admiral's Men between 1597 and 1602. Described as one of best for tragedy by Meres. Shared in approximately nineteen plays according to Henslowe, none of which survives. Sharer in Children of the King's Revels at Whitefriars theatre (1607–8). Died 1631. Buried in Westminster Abbey. Jonson included an epitaph for Drayton in his *Underwoods*.

Works:
Hebel, J. William, ed. *The Works of Michael Drayton*. 5 vols. Oxford, 1931–41. Rev. edn Bent Juel-Jensen, 1961.

Studies:
Hardin, R. F. *Michael Drayton and the Passing of Elizabethan England*. Lawrence, 1973.
Harner, James L. *Samuel Daniel and Michael Drayton: A Reference Guide*. Boston, 1980.
Newdigate, B. H. *Michael Drayton and his Circle*, corr. edn. Oxford, 1961.

EDWARDS [EDWARDES], RICHARD (1524–1566)

Born 1524, Somersetshire. B.A., Corpus Christi College, Oxford, 1544; elected to fellowship the same year. May have taken orders between 1547 and 1550. Upon advancement to M.A. (1547), encouraged acting of plays at Christ Church, previously a rare event. Appointed Gentleman of the Chapel 1560 and Master of the Children of the Chapel Royal, 1561–5; took the Boys to Lincoln's Inn 1565–6 for their first performance away from court. Praised by Meres as among best for comedy and by Hollyband in *The French Schoolmaster* (1573) as a 'great player of plays'. Prologue to *Damon and Pithias* (1564/5; published 1571) contains the first statement of dramatic principles in an English play, including the earliest use of 'tragicomedy'. Died October 1566.

Works:
White, D. Jerry, ed. *Richard Edwards' 'Damon and Piethias': A Critical Old-Spelling Edition*. New York, 1980.

Studies:
Cope, Jackson. *Dramaturgy of the Demonic*, chapter 2. Baltimore, 1984.

Mills, Laurens Joseph. 'Some aspects of Richard Edwards' *Damon and Pithias*'. Indiana University Studies, no. 75 (June, 1927).

FIELD, NATHAN (1587–1619/20)
Baptized at St Giles, Cripplegate, 17 October 1587. Son of preacher John Field, an outspoken opponent of the stage during the 1580s. Two known brothers: Nathaniel, a printer, and Theophilus, eventually Bishop of Hereford. Scholar of St Paul's School; by the age of twelve was pressed into the Children of the Chapel Royal at the second Blackfriars theatre by Nathaniel Giles and may have appeared in *Cynthia's Revels* in 1600 and *The Poetaster* in 1601. Leading actor at the Chapel, performing Bussy in Chapman's *Bussy D'Ambois* (c.1604), his most famous role, and in Jonson's *Epicœne* (1609). His company was absorbed into Lady Elizabeth's Men in 1613, and he became their leader. Joined King's Men in 1615 and remained until at least 1619 (his name appears after that date only in the list of actors in Shakespeare's First Folio, 1623). Wrote *Woman is a Weathercock* and *Amends for Ladies* and collaborated with other playwrights between 1612 and 1619, including Massinger on *The Fatal Dowry*, as well as writing a defence of the stage. Portrait in Dulwich College gallery. Highly praised as an actor, he was ranked with Burbage as 'best actor' by Jonson in *Bartholomew Fair*. Died 1619/20.

Works:
Peery, William, ed. *Plays.* Austin, Texas, 1950.

Studies:
Brinkley, R. F. *Nathan Field, The Actor–Playwright.* New Haven, 1928.

FLETCHER, JOHN (1579–1625)
Born December 1579, Rye, Sussex. From a distinguished family; younger son of Richard Fletcher, vicar of Rye, who later served as chaplain at execution of Mary, Queen of Scots, and was eventually Bishop of Bristol and of London. Nephew to Giles Fletcher the elder; cousin to clerical poets Giles Fletcher the younger and Phineas Fletcher. Probably entered Benet College, now Corpus Christi College, Cambridge, October 1591. Real success begins c.1607 with friendship and collaboration with Beaumont (q.v.). They wrote at least seven plays together, including *Philaster*, *The Maid's Tragedy*, and *A King and No King*. Sole author of at least sixteen plays, including *The Faithful Shepherdess*; collaborator on numerous romantic tragedies and tragicomedies with Massinger, Middleton, Rowley, and possibly Jonson. Collaborated with Shakespeare on *The Two Noble Kinsmen*, *Henry VIII*, and the lost *Cardenio*. Died August, 1625, of plague. Buried at St Saviour's, Southwark.

Works:
Bowers, Fredson, gen. ed. *The Dramatic Works in the Beaumont and Fletcher Canon.* Cambridge, 1966–.
Glover, Arnold and A. R. Waller, eds. *The Works of Francis Beaumont and John Fletcher.* 10 vols. Cambridge, 1905–12.

Studies:

Bliss, Lee. 'Defending Fletcher's shepherds'. *SEL* 23 (1983), 295–310.

Hoy, Cyrus. 'The language of Fletcherian tragicomedy' in J. C. Gray, ed., *Mirror up to Shakespeare* (Toronto, 1984), pp. 99–113.

Leech, Clifford. *The John Fletcher Plays*. London, 1962.

Mincoff, Marco. 'Shakespeare, Fletcher and baroque tragedy'. *ShS* 20 (1967), 1–15.

Pearse, Nancy C. *John Fletcher's Chastity Plays: Mirrors of Modesty*. Lewisburg, Pennsylvania, 1973.

Squier, C. L. *John Fletcher*. Boston, 1986.

Waith, Eugene M. 'Characterization in John Fletcher's tragicomedies'. *RES* 19 (1943), 141–64.

The Pattern of Tragicomedy in Beaumont and Fletcher. New Haven, 1952.

See also Beaumont, Francis.

FORD, JOHN (1586–*c.*1640)

Born at Ilsington, Devon, baptized 17 April 1586. From an established landed family. Second son of a gentleman; probably related through mother to Lord Chief Justice Popham. Matriculated at Exeter College, Oxford, 1601; entered Middle Temple in 1602. Intermittent patronage of Duke of Newcastle, Lord Craven, and Earls of Antrim and Peterborough. May have practised law; by 1613 was writing for the stage, collaborating with Dekker on comedies at first. Last known play published 1639. Believed to have returned to Devonshire before his death, *c.*1640.

Works:

Bang, W. and Henry De Vocht, eds. *John Ford's Dramatic Works*. 2 vols. Louvain, vol. 1, 1908; vol. 2, 1927.

Gifford, William, ed. *The Works of John Ford*. 3 vols. 1827. Rev. edn. A. Dyce. London, 1869.

Studies:

Anderson, D. K. *John Ford*. New York, 1972.

ed. *'Concord in Discord': The Plays of John Ford 1586–1986*. New York, 1986.

Barish, Jonas. '*Perkin Warbeck* as anti-history'. *EIC* 20 (1970), 151–71.

Barton, Anne. 'He that plays the king: Ford's *Perkin Warbeck* and the Stuart history play' in Marie Axton and Raymond Williams, eds., *English Drama: Forms and Development* (Cambridge, 1977), pp. 69–93.

Champion, Larry S. 'Ford's *'Tis Pity She's a Whore* and the Jacobean tragic perspective'. *PMLA* 90 (1975), 78–87.

Davril, Robert. *Le Drame de John Ford*. Bibliothèque des langues modernes, 5. Paris, 1954.

Farr, Dorothy M. *John Ford and the Caroline Theatre*. London and New York, 1979.

Huebert, Ronald. *John Ford Baroque English Dramatist*. Montreal and London, 1979.

Kaufmann, R. J. 'Ford's tragic perspective'. *TSLL* 1 (1960), 522–37.

'Ford's "Waste Land": *The Broken Heart*'. *RenD* n.s. 3 (1970), 167–88.

Leech, Clifford. *John Ford and the Drama of His Time*. London, 1957.

Neill, Michael. '"Anticke Pageantrie": the mannerist art of *Perkin Warbeck*'. *RenD* n.s. 7 (1976), 85–106.
'Ford's unbroken art: the moral design of *The Broken Heart*'. *MLR* 75 (1980), 249–68.
ed. *John Ford: Critical Re-Visions*. Cambridge, 1988.
Oliver, H. J. *The Problem of John Ford*. Melbourne, 1955.
Orbison, Tucker. *The Tragic Vision of John Ford*. Jacobean Drama Studies 21. Salzburg, 1974.
Sargeaunt, M. Joan. *John Ford*. Oxford, 1935.
Sensabaugh, G. F. *The Tragic Muse of John Ford*. Palo Alto, California, 1944.
Stavig, Mark. *John Ford and the Traditional Moral Order*. Madison, Wisconsin, 1968.
Tucker, Kenneth. *A Bibliography of ... John Ford and Cyril Tourneur*. Boston, 1977.
Ure, Peter. 'Marriage and the domestic drama in Heywood and Ford'. *ES* 32 (1951), 200–16.

FRAUNCE, ABRAHAM (1558–1633)

Born 1558, Shrewsbury. Entered Shrewsbury School, where he became acquainted with Sir Philip Sidney. Pensioner at St John's College, Cambridge, in May 1575, Lady Margaret scholar in November 1578, and fellow in 1581. Proceeded B.A. in 1579–80 and M.A. in 1583. Gained notice as an actor and dramatist in Cambridge productions of Latin plays, rendering an Italian play into the Latin comedy *Victoria*, performed at St John's in 1579. Believed to be the author of Latin *Hymenaeus*, the first university play based on a novella, acted at St John's in 1579. Receiving an administrative post with the Council of Wales in the service of the Earl of Bridgewater shortly after 1590, he seems to have abandoned literary pursuits. Died 1633.

GAGER, WILLIAM (1555–1622)

Born 24 July, 1555, Long Melford, Suffolk. Educated at Melford and Westminster School. Entered Christ Church, Oxford, as Queen's Scholar 1574, advancing B.A. 1577, M.A. 1580; incorporated M.A. Cambridge 1581. Senecan tragedy *Meleager*, written shortly after 1580, highly successful and revived for Earls of Leicester and Pembroke 1584/5. Rhetor at Oxford, 1583–4; doctorate in civil law, 1589. His comedy *Rivales* and tragedy *Dido* performed at Christ Church before Polish Count Albert Alasco in June 1583. Hostile to the professional stage (engaging in 1592–3 academic stage quarrel with Rainolds); friend of George Peele, and an outspoken advocate of the educational value of university plays in classical languages. Major dramatic presence throughout the 1580s at Christ Church. Last and best play, *Ulysses Redux*, performed 1592 at Christ Church; *Rivales* revived with great success for Elizabeth same year. Chancellor of the diocese of Ely, 1606. Last major work, a poem on the Gunpowder Plot, presented to James in 1608. Buried in All Saints' Church, Cambridge, September 1622.

Works:

Binns, J. W., ed. *Oedipus* (acted 1577–92) and *Dido* (acted 1583). Renaissance Latin Drama in England, 1st Series, 1. New York, 1981.
ed. *Meleager* (1592), *Ulysses Redux* (1592), *Panniculus Hippolyto* (1591). Renaissance Latin Drama in England, 1st Series, 2. New York, 1981.

Studies:
Binns, J. W. 'William Gager's *Meleager* and *Ulysses Redux*' in Elmer M. Blistein, ed., *The Drama of the Renaissance: Essays for Leicester Bradner* (Providence, Rhode Island, 1970), pp. 27–41.
Brooke, C. F. Tucker. 'The life and times of William Gager'. *Proceedings of the American Philosophical Society* 95(4) (1951), 401–31.

GASCOIGNE, GEORGE (*c.* 1 5 3 4–1 5 7 7)
Born at Cardington, Bedfordshire. Elder son of Sir John Gascoigne of Cardington, Bedfordshire, and Margaret, daughter of Sir Robert Scargill of Scargill, Yorkshire. Educated at Trinity College, Cambridge, left without taking degree. Entered Gray's Inn, 1555; MP for Bedfordshire, 1557–9. Translated *Supposes* (acted Gray's Inn, 1566), which later supplied Shakespeare with the Lucentio sub-plot for *Taming of the Shrew*. Military service in Holland 1572–75. Wrote entertainment for Elizabeth (Kenilworth 1575) and *The Spoil of Antwerp* (1577). His *Jocasta*, from Euripides' *Phoenissae*, was the first Greek tragedy on the English stage. Died 7 October, 1577; buried at St Mary's, Stamford.

Works:
Cunliffe, John W., ed. *The Complete Works of George Gascoigne.* 2 vols. Cambridge, 1907–10.

Studies:
Johnson, Robert C., ed. *Minor Elizabethans. Roger Ascham, 1946–1966; George Gascoigne, 1941–1966; John Heywood, 1944–1966; Thomas Kyd, 1940–1966; Anthony Munday, 1941–1966.* Elizabethan Bibliographies Supplements 9. London, 1968.
Prouty, C. T. *George Gascoigne, Elizabethan Courtier, Soldier and Poet.* New York, 1942.

GLAPTHORNE, HENRY (1 6 1 0–*c.* 1 6 4 3)
Born 28 July 1610, Whittlesey, Cambridgeshire. Educated at Corpus Christi College, Cambridge. Wrote nine known tragedies and comedies performed between *c.*1632 and 1642 at court as well as at the Globe, the Cockpit in Drury Lane, and Salisbury Court theatre. *Argalus and Parthenia*, based on Sidney's *Arcadia*, printed in 1639, as was *Albertus Wallenstein*, an historical tragedy. Publication of *White-Hall: A Poem* (1643) is last known mention.

Works:
Shepherd, R. H., ed. *The Plays and Poems of Henry Glapthorne.* 2 vols. London, 1874.

Studies:
Davis, Joe Lee. *The Sons of Ben: Jonsonian Comedy in Caroline England.* Detroit, 1967.

GOFFE (OR GOUGH), THOMAS (1 5 9 1–1 6 2 9)
Born 1591 in Essex. Son of a clergyman. Queen's scholar at Westminster School;

scholarship at Christ Church, Oxford, November 1609. B.A. 1613; M.A. 1616; B.D. 1623. Also incorporated M.A., Cambridge, 1617. Took orders and received the living of East Clandon, Surrey, 1623. While at Christ Church he wrote three tragedies, acted after 1616 while he was still resident there. *The Careless Shepherdess*, a tragicomedy, was successfully acted before Charles I and at the Salisbury Court theatre.

Works:

Carnegie, David, ed. *The Raging Turke*. Oxford, 1968. Revised, 1974.
   ed. *The Courageous Turk*. Oxford, 1974.

GOSSON, STEPHEN (1554–1624)

Baptized April 1554, Canterbury, Kent, eldest son of craftsman Cornelius Gosson and Agnes Oxenbridge. Entered Queen's School, Canterbury, at age 14. Educated at Corpus Christi College, Oxford, 1572–6; B.A. applied for in 1576 but apparently never granted. Resident in London as dramatist and poet from 1576; according to Lodge, acted during this time. Published anti-theatrical pamphlet, *The School of Abuse* (1579). His *Plays Confuted in Five Actions* (1582) admits authorship of one comedy, one tragedy, and one morality, none extant. Rector of Great Wigborough, Essex, 1591; rector of St Botolph's, Bishopsgate, 1600. Married Elizabeth Acton, 25 April 1587. Died February 1624. Buried in chancel of his church.

GREENE, ROBERT (1558–1592)

Baptized 11 July 1558, Norwich. Son of a sadler of comfortable though not wealthy family. Sizar at St John's College, Cambridge, 1575, taking a B.A. in 1578. Returned to Clare Hall, Cambridge, after European travels, to take M.A. in 1583; incorporated M.A., Oxford, 1588. By 1587 was writing romantic histories and comedies for the Admiral's and Queen's Men, including *James IV* and *Friar Bacon and Friar Bungay*. Achieved literary notoriety by 1588, gaining patronage of the Earls of Arundel and Essex, and friendship of Peele, Nashe, Marlowe, and Lodge. Mentioned by Meres as among best for comedy. Died in squalor 3 September 1592. Buried in New Churchyard, near Bedlam.

Works:

Collins, John Churton, ed. *The Plays and Poems of Robert Greene*. 2 vols. Oxford, 1905.
Grosart, A. B., ed. *The Life and Complete Works in Prose and Verse of Robert Greene*. 15 vols. London, 1881–6. Reprinted, New York, 1964.

Studies:

Braunmuller, A. R. 'The serious comedy of Greene's *James IV*'. *ELR* 3 (1973), 335–50.
Crupi, Charles W. *Robert Greene*. Boston, 1986.
Dean, James Seay. *Robert Greene: A Reference Guide*. Boston, 1984.
Empson, William. *Some Versions of Pastoral*. London, 1935.
Johnson, Robert C., ed. *Robert Greene, 1945–65; Thomas Lodge, 1939–1965; John*

Lyly, 1939–1965; Thomas Nashe, 1941–1965; George Peele, 1939–1965. Elizabethan Bibliographies Supplements 5. London, 1968.

Jordan, J. C. *Robert Greene.* New York, 1915. Reprinted, New York, 1965.

Muir, Kenneth. 'Robert Greene as dramatist' in Richard Hosley, ed., *Essays on Shakespeare and Elizabethan Drama in Honor of Hardin Craig* (Columbia, Missouri, 1962), pp. 45–54.

Senn, Werner. *Studies in the Dramatic Construction of Robert Greene and George Peele.* Bern, 1973.

Weld, John. *Meaning in Comedy: Studies in Elizabethan Romantic Comedy.* Albany, New York, 1975.

Wertheim, Albert. 'The presentation of sin in *Friar Bacon and Friar Bungay*'. *Criticism* 16 (1974), 273–86.

GREVILLE, SIR FULKE (1554–1628)

Born at Beauchamp Court, Warwickshire; educated with Sir Philip Sidney at Shrewsbury, then a fellow-commoner at Jesus College, Cambridge. At court with Sidney, he became a favourite of Elizabeth. Member of Harvey's Areopagus group and entertained Giordano Bruno on his visit to London in 1583. Held various offices of state under Elizabeth and James; Privy Councillor to James. Friend of Bacon, Camden, Coke, Daniel, and Davenant. Granted Warwick Castle by James I and created first Baron Brooke. Two closet political tragedies, *Mustapha* and *Alaham*, survive, with a sonnet sequence (*Caelica*), and a series of learned poems.

Works:
Bullough, Geoffrey, ed. *Poems and Dramas.* 2 vols. London, 1939.

Studies:
Larson, Charles. *Fulke Greville.* Boston, 1980.
Morris, Ivor. 'The tragic vision of Fulke Greville'. *ShS* 14 (1961), 66–75.
Rebholz, R. A. *The Life of Fulke Greville, First Lord Brooke.* Oxford, 1971.
Rees, J. *Fulke Greville, Lord Brooke, 1554–1628: a Critical Biography.* London, 1971.

HATHWAY, RICHARD (*fl.* 1598–1603)

According to Henslowe, wrote for the Admiral's Men (1598–1602) and for Worcester's Men (1602–3). Collaborators included Drayton, Munday, Haughton, and Chettle. Only extant play is *Sir John Oldcastle* (1600), a successful comedy written in collaboration with Drayton and others for the Admiral's Men as an answer to Shakespeare's Falstaff in *Henry IV.*

Work:
The Life of Sir John Oldcastle. 1600. London, 1908.

HAUGHTON, WILLIAM (*c.* 1575–*c.* 1605)

Earliest mention of any certainty is in Henslowe, November 1597, referring to him as 'yonge Horton'. Wrote steadily for Henslowe thereafter, producing a series of comedies and tragedies, usually in collaboration with Chettle, Day, Dekker, and others.

Perhaps best-known collaboration is with Dekker and Chettle on *Patient Grissil* (1600). One play of his sole authorship probably written early in 1598: *Englishmen for my Money: Or, A Woman will have her Will*, the first 'city comedy' of London life and very popular. Supposed author of *Grim the Collier of Croydon* (*c.*1600), also a popular play. Last mention is in September 1602, when he was engaged on 'a playe called "Cartwright"'.

Works:
Baillie, William M., ed. *A Choice Ternary of English Plays*. Binghamton, New York, 1984.

HEYWOOD, THOMAS (1573/4–1641)
Born 1573/4, probably in Lincolnshire. Educated at Cambridge. Mentioned by Henslowe in 1594. Actor with the Admiral's Men 1598–9 and subsequently for Worcester's company (later Queen Anne's) from 1602/3–19. Refers to having 'an entire hand, or at least a main finger' in over two hundred and twenty plays, most of them lost. Wrote an important early defence, *An Apology for Actors* (*c.*1607/8; published 1612). Went into semi-retirement in 1619 but reappears in the 1630s, enjoying revivals of his earlier plays and writing two successful new plays. Buried in St James's, Clerkenwell.

Works:
Shepherd, R. H., ed. *The Dramatic Works of Thomas Heywood*. 6 vols. London, 1874. Reprinted, New York, 1964.

Studies:
Baines, Barbara J. *Thomas Heywood*. Boston, 1984.
Boas, F. S. *Thomas Heywood*. London, 1950.
Brown, Arthur. 'Thomas Heywood's dramatic art' in Richard Hosley, ed., *Essays on Shakespeare and Elizabethan Drama in Honor of Hardin Craig* (Columbia, Missouri, 1962), pp. 327–40.
Clark, Arthur M. *Thomas Heywood, Playwright and Miscellanist* (1931). Reprinted, New York, 1967.
Donovan, Dennis, ed. *Thomas Dekker, 1945–1965; Thomas Heywood, 1938–1965; Cyril Tourneur, 1945–1965*. Elizabethan Bibliographies Supplements 2. London, 1967.
Grivelet, Michel. *Thomas Heywood et le drame domestique élizabethain*. Paris, 1957.
'The simplicity of Thomas Heywood'. *ShS* 14 (1961), 56–65.
Johnson, M. L. *Images of Women in the Works of Thomas Heywood*. Jacobean Drama Studies, 42. Salzburg, 1974.
Rabkin, Norman. 'Dramatic deception in Heywood's *The English Traveller*'. *SEL* 1 (1961), 1–16.
Smith, Hallett. '*A Woman Killed with Kindness*'. *PMLA* 53 (1939), 138–47.
Townsend, F. L. 'The artistry of Thomas Heywood: double plots'. *PQ* 25 (1946), 97–119.
Ure, Peter. 'Marriage and the domestic drama in Heywood and Ford'. *ES* 32 (1951), 200–16.

Velte, F. Mowbray. *The Bourgeois Elements in the Drama of Thomas Heywood* (1924). Reprinted, New York, 1966.

Wentworth, Michael. *Thomas Heywood: A Reference Guide*. Boston, 1986.

JONSON, BENJAMIN (1572/3–1637)

Born at or near London between May 1572 and May 1573. Posthumous son of a clergyman, probably of Scottish border descent. Attended Westminster School under William Camden. Military service in Flanders by 1592. Working for Henslowe as player and dramatist in 1597. Joined Pembroke's Men; imprisoned summer 1597 for his part in authorship of *Isle of Dogs*, allegedly seditious. Wrote for Admiral's and Lord Chamberlain's Men, Children of Queen's Chapel, and Lady Elizabeth's Men, establishing reputation as a leading writer of comedy with *Every Man in his Humour* (1598). Plays performed at court and at the universities. Leading figure in 'War of the Theatres'; regularly suspected of sedition, popery, or *lèse-majesté* in plays such as *Eastward Ho!* and *Sejanus*. Leading figure with Inigo Jones in court masques. Chronologer of London, 1628; lost royal patronage in 1631 on quarrel with Inigo Jones. Died August 1637. Buried in Westminster Abbey with epitaph, 'O rare Ben Jonson'.

Works:

Herford, C. H., Percy and Evelyn Simpson, eds. *Ben Jonson*. 11 vols. Oxford, 1925–52.

Orgel, Stephen, ed. *Ben Jonson: The Complete Masques*. New Haven, 1969.

Redwine, James D., Jr, ed. *Ben Jonson's Literary Criticism*. Lincoln, Nebraska, 1970.

Studies:

Allen, Don Cameron. 'Ben Jonson and the hieroglyphics'. *PQ* 18 (1939), 290–300.

Barish, Jonas. 'The double plot in *Volpone*'. *MP* 51 (1953), 83–92.

    Ben Jonson and the Language of Prose Comedy. Cambridge, 1960.

    ed. *Ben Jonson: A Collection of Critical Essays*. Englewood Cliffs, New Jersey, 1963.

Barton, Anne. *Ben Jonson, Dramatist*. Cambridge, 1984.

Beaurline, L. A. *Jonson and Elizabethan Comedy: Essays in Dramatic Rhetoric*. San Marino, California, 1978.

Blissett, William. 'The venter tripartite in *The Alchemist*'. *SEL* 8 (1968), 323–34.

Blissett, William, Julian Patrick, and R. W. Van Fossen, eds. *A Celebration of Ben Jonson*. Toronto, 1973.

Brock, D. Heyward. *A Ben Jonson Companion*. Bloomington, Indiana, 1983.

Bryant, J. A. Jr. 'The significance of Ben Jonson's first requirement for tragedy: "Truth of Argument".' *SP* 49 (1952), 195–213.

    The Compassionate Satirist: Ben Jonson and his Imperfect World. Athens, Georgia, 1973.

Burton, K. M. 'The political tragedies of Chapman and Ben Jonson'. *EIC* 2 (1952), 397–412.

Chan, Mary. *Music in the Theatre of Ben Jonson*. Oxford, 1980.

Cope, Jackson I. '*Bartholomew Fair* as blasphemy'. *RenD* 8 (1965), 127–52.

Creaser, John. '*Volpone*: the mortifying of the Fox'. *EIC* 25 (1975), 329–56.

Dessen, Alan C. *Jonson's Moral Comedy*. Evanston, Illinois, 1971.

Donaldson, Ian. *The World Upside-Down: Comedy from Jonson to Fielding*. Oxford, 1970.

'*Volpone* – quick and dead'. *EIC* 21 (1971), 121–34.

Dutton, A. Richard. '*Volpone* and *The Alchemist*: a comparison in satiric techniques'. *RMS* 18 (1974), 36–62.

Ben Jonson: To the First Folio. Cambridge, 1983.

Enck, John J. *Jonson and the Comic Truth*. Madison, Wisconsin, 1957.

Guffey, George R., ed. *Robert Herrick, 1949–1965; Ben Jonson, 1947–1965; Thomas Randolph, 1949–1965*. Elizabethan Bibliographies Supplements 3. London, 1968.

Hibbard, G. R. 'Goodness and greatness: an essay on the tragedies of Ben Jonson and George Chapman'. *RMS* 11 (1967), 5–54.

Jackson, G. B. *Vision and Judgment in Ben Jonson's Drama*. New Haven, 1968.

Knoll, Robert E. *Ben Jonson's Plays: An Introduction*. Lincoln, Nebraska, 1964.

Leggatt, Alexander. 'The suicide of *Volpone*'. *UTQ* 39 (1969), 19–32.

Ben Jonson, his Vision and his Art. New York, 1981.

Lehrman, Walter D., Dolores J. Sarafinski, and Elizabeth Savage. *The Plays of Ben Jonson: A Reference Guide*. Boston, 1980.

Levin, Richard. 'The structure of *Bartholomew Fair*'. *PMLA* 80 (1965), 172–9.

Meagher, John C. *Method and Meaning in Jonson's Masques*. Notre Dame, Indiana, 1966.

Orgel, Stephen. *The Jonsonian Masque*. Cambridge, Massachusetts, 1965.

Partridge, Edward B. *The Broken Compass: A Study of the Major Comedies of Ben Jonson*. London, 1958.

Redwine, James D., Jr. 'Beyond psychology: the moral basis of Jonson's theory of humour characterization'. *ELH* 28 (1961), 316–34.

Ricks, Christopher. '*Sejanus* and dismemberment'. *MLN* 76 (1961), 301–8.

Rowe, George E. *Distinguishing Jonson: Imitation, Rivalry, and the Direction of a Dramatic Career*. Lincoln, Nebraska, 1988.

Talbert, Ernest W. 'The interpretation of Jonson's courtly spectacles'. *PMLA* 41 (1946), 454–73.

Thayer, C. G. *Ben Jonson: Studies in the Plays*. Norman, Oklahoma, 1963.

Watson, Robert. *Ben Jonson's Parodic Strategy: Literary Imperialism in the Comedies*. Cambridge, Massachusetts, 1987.

Womack, Peter. *Ben Jonson*. Oxford and New York, 1986.

KILLIGREW, THOMAS (1612–1683)

Born 7 February 1612, Lothbury, London. Page to Charles I at age twenty-one. Plays first performed in London by 1636, at the Phoenix and the Cockpit in Drury Lane. Given grant with Davenant of exclusive patents to open two new theatre companies in 1660. Built playhouse on current site of Drury Lane theatre (1663); opened training school for young actors at the Barbican (1673). Master of the Revels (1679). Died at Whitehall 19 March 1683.

Works:

Reich, William T., ed. *Claricilla*. New York, 1980.

Summers, Montague, ed. *The Parson's Wedding, The London Cuckolds, and Sir Courtly Nice, or, It Cannot Be.* London, 1921.

Studies:
Harbage, Alfred B. *Thomas Killigrew, Cavalier Dramatist, 1612–1683.* Philadelphia, 1930.

KYD, THOMAS (1558–1594)
Baptized at church of St Mary Woolnoth, London, 6 November 1558. Son of scrivener Francis Kyd. Attended Merchant Taylors' School, London, where he was a contemporary of Spenser. Began career as a translator and dramatist, entering the service of a lord (possibly Ferdinando, Lord Strange) in 1590. Lived with Marlowe in 1591; associate of Greene, Nashe, and Lodge. Best-known work, *The Spanish Tragedy* (*c.*1587) gained immense popularity and numerous parodies. Believed to have written early version of *Hamlet*. Arrested 12 May 1593, on suspicion of 'lewd and mutinous libels', specifically heresy and atheism. Died poor in 1594.

Works:
Boas, F. S., ed. *The Works of Thomas Kyd.* Oxford, 1901; rev. edn, 1955.

Studies:
Ardolino, Frank R. *Thomas Kyd's Mystery Play: Myth and Ritual in 'The Spanish Tragedy'.* New York, 1985.
Carrere, Felix. *Le Théâtre de Thomas Kyd: contribution a l'étude du drame élizabethain.* Toulouse, 1951.
Edwards, Philip. *Thomas Kyd and Early Elizabethan Tragedy.* Writers and Their Works. London, 1966.
Freeman, Arthur. *Thomas Kyd: Facts and Problems.* Oxford, 1967.
Hill, Eugene D. 'Senecan and Vergilian perspectives in *The Spanish Tragedy*' in A. F. Kinney and D. S. Collins, eds., *Renaissance Historicism: Selections from 'English Literary Renaissance'* (Amherst, Massachusetts, 1987).
Hunter, G. K. 'Ironies of justice in *The Spanish Tragedy*'. *RenD* 8 (1965), 89–104.
Jensen, Ejner. 'Kyd's *Spanish Tragedy*: the play explains itself'. *JEGP* (1965), 7–16.
Johnson, Robert C., ed. *Minor Elizabethans. Roger Ascham, 1946–1966; George Gascoigne, 1941–1966; John Heywood, 1944–1966; Thomas Kyd, 1940–1966; Anthony Munday, 1941–1966.* Elizabethan Bibliographies Supplements 9. London, 1968.
Murray, Peter B. *Thomas Kyd.* New York, 1970.

LODGE, THOMAS (1558–1625)
Born in West Ham, son of Sir Thomas Lodge, Lord Mayor of London. Attended Merchant Taylors' School and Trinity College, Oxford, 1573–7; entered Lincoln's Inn 1578. M.D. University of Avignon, 1598 and Oxford, 1602. His *Wounds of Civil War* (*c.*1587) is an early classical history play; collaborated with Greene on *A Looking Glass for London and England* (*c.*1588). An acknowledged recusant, Lodge continued

medical career along with translating and writing. Died in London in 1625, probably of plague.

Works:
Gosse, Edmund, ed. *The Complete Works of Thomas Lodge*. 4 vols. Glasgow, 1883.

Studies:
Cuvelier, Eliane. *Thomas Lodge: témoin de son temps*. Paris, 1984.
Johnson, Robert C., ed. *Robert Greene, 1945–65; Thomas Lodge, 1939–1965; John Lyly, 1939–1965; Thomas Nashe, 1941–1965; George Peele, 1939–1965*. Elizabethan Bibliographies Supplements 5. London, 1968.
Paradise, N. B. *Thomas Lodge: The History of an Elizabethan*. New Haven, 1931.
Rae, W. D. *Thomas Lodge*. New York, 1967.
Tenney, Edward A. *Thomas Lodge*. Ithaca, New York, 1935.

LYLY, JOHN (1554?–1606)
Born in Weald of Kent. William Lily, his grandfather, was High Master of St Paul's School; his father, Peter Lyly, a diocesan official in Canterbury. Attended King's School, Canterbury; took B.A. (1573), later M.A. (1575) under Burghley's patronage at Magdalen College, Oxford; incorporated M.A., Cambridge (1579). Admitted to Gray's Inn, Christmas 1594. Best-known work, the prose romance *Euphues, the Anatomy of Wit*, appeared in 1578. Vice-master of Children of St Paul's through Earl of Oxford's patronage in 1580s; leased the Blackfriars theatre, where he wrote and produed numerous plays. Wrote for Paul's Boys and for court performance. With Nashe, wrote retorts to Martin Marprelate pamphlets (1589–90); MP for Hindon, Aylesbury, and Appleby respectively, 1589–1601. Sought and failed to obtain position as Master of Revels. Died November 1606, London.

Works:
Bond, R. Warwick, ed. *The Complete Works of John Lyly*. 3 vols. Oxford, 1902.

Studies:
Barish, Jonas. 'The prose style of John Lyly'. *ELH* 23 (1956), 14–35.
Houppert, Joseph W. *John Lyly*. Boston, 1975.
Hunter, G. K. *John Lyly: The Humanist as Courtier*. London, 1962.
  Lyly and Peele. Writers and Their Works. London, 1968.
Jeffery, Violet M. *John Lyly and the Italian Renaissance*. Paris, 1928.
Johnson, Robert C., ed. *Robert Greene, 1945–65; Thomas Lodge, 1939–1965; John Lyly, 1939–1965; Thomas Nashe, 1941–1965; George Peele, 1939–1965*. Elizabethan Bibliographies Supplements 5. London, 1968.
Knight, G. Wilson. 'Lyly'. *RES* 15 (1939), 146–63.
Saccio, Peter. *The Court Comedies of John Lyly: A Study in Allegorical Dramaturgy*. Princeton, 1969.

MARLOWE, CHRISTOPHER (1564–1593)
Born 6 February 1564, Canterbury. Son of shoemaker John Marlowe and Catherine

Arthur of Dover. Educated at King's School, Canterbury, 1578–80; Queen's Scholar 14 January 1579. Entered Corpus Christi College, Cambridge, 1580, as Parker Scholar. Awarded B.A. (1584) and M.A. (1587). Moved to London 1587–8 to pursue career as dramatist. Immediately successful, most of his plays performed by the Lord Admiral's Men. *Tamburlaine* (*c.*1587) was widely imitated. Knew many in London literary scene; testimonials from Blount, Nashe, Chapman, Jonson, and Drayton. Walsingham's secret agent; probably the 'Marlin' who carried letters from France to Cecil in 1592. Arrested for coining in Low Countries 1591/2. Died 30 May 1593, in drunken quarrel with Ingram Frisar over tavern bill. Meres describes his death as a 'judgment of God' for 'epicurism and atheism'. Buried in parish church of St Nicholas, Deptford.

Works:

Bowers, Fredson, ed. *The Complete Works of Christopher Marlowe.* 2 vols. Cambridge, rev. edn, 1981.
Case, R. H., ed. *The Works and Life of Christopher Marlowe.* 6 vols. London, 1930–3. Reprinted, New York, 1961.

Studies:

Barber, C. L. 'The form of Faustus' fortunes good or bad'. *TDR* 8 (1964), 92–119.
Battenhouse, Roy W. 'Tamburlaine, the scourge of God'. *PMLA* 56 (1941), 337–48.
Bluestone, Max. '*Libido Speculandi*: doctrine and dramaturgy in contemporary interpretations of Marlowe's *Doctor Faustus*' in Norman Rabkin, ed., *Reinterpretations of Elizabethan Drama* (New York, 1969), pp. 33–88.
Brooke, C. F. Tucker. 'Marlowe's versification and style'. *SP* 19 (1922), 186–205.
Cole, Douglas. *Suffering and Evil in the Plays of Christopher Marlowe.* Princeton, 1962.
Cope, Jackson I. *Dramaturgy of the Demonic*, chapter 4. Baltimore, 1984.
Friedenreich, Kenneth, Roma Gill, and Constance B. Kuriyama, eds. *'A Poet & a filthy Play-maker': New Essays on Christopher Marlowe.* New York, 1988.
Giamatti, A. Bartlett. 'Marlowe: the arts of illusion'. *YR* 61 (1972), 530–43.
Hattaway, Michael. 'The theology of Marlowe's Doctor Faustus'. *RenD* n.s. 3 (1976), 51–78.
Hunter, G. K. 'The theology of Marlowe's *The Jew of Malta*'. *JWCI* 27 (1964), 211–40.
Johnson, Robert C., ed. *Christopher Marlowe, 1946–1965.* Elizabethan Bibliographies Supplements 6. London, 1967.
Kernan, Alvin, ed. *Two Renaissance Mythmakers: Christopher Marlowe and Ben Jonson.* Baltimore, 1977.
Kocher, Paul H. *Christopher Marlowe: A Study of His Thought, Learning and Character.* Chapel Hill, North Carolina, 1946.
Kuriyama, Constance Brown. *Hammer or Anvil: Psychological Patterns in Christopher Marlowe's Plays.* New Brunswick, New Jersey, 1980.
Leech, Clifford. 'Marlowe's *Edward II*: power and suffering'. *CritQ* 1 (1959), 181–96.
    ed. *Marlowe: A Collection of Critical Essays.* Englewood Cliffs, New Jersey, 1965.
Levin, Harry. *The Overreacher: A Study of Christopher Marlowe.* Cambridge, Massachusetts, 1952.

Mangan, Michael. *'Doctor Faustus': A Critical Study*. Harmondsworth, 1987.

Morris, Brian, ed. *Christopher Marlowe*. Mermaid Critical Commentaries. New York, 1969.

Powell, Jocelyn. 'Marlowe's spectacle'. *TDR* 8 (1964), 195–210.

Ribner, Irving. 'Marlowe's *Edward II* and the Tudor history play'. *ELH* 22 (1955), 243–53.

Rothstein, Eric. 'Structure as meaning in *The Jew of Malta*'. *JEGP* 65 (1966), 260–73.

Sanders, Wilbur. *The Dramatist and the Received Idea: Studies in the Plays of Marlowe and Shakespeare*. Cambridge, 1968.

Steane, J. B. *Marlowe: A Critical Study*. Cambridge, 1964.

Waith, Eugene M. *The Herculean Hero in Marlowe, Chapman, Shakespeare and Dryden*. New York, 1962.

'*Edward II*: the shadow of action'. *TDR* 8 (1964), 59–76.

'Marlowe and the jades of Asia'. *SEL* 5 (1965), 229–45.

Weill, Judith. *Christopher Marlowe: Merlin's Prophet*. Cambridge, 1977.

Wilson, F. P. *Marlowe and the Early Shakespeare*. Oxford, 1953.

MARMION, SHACKERLEY (1603–1639)

Born January 1603, Brackley, Northamptonshire. Educated at Thame free school under Richard Burcher; commoner of Wadham College, Oxford, 1618; proceeded B.A. 1621/22 and M.A. 1624. Went to Low Countries as soldier in 1625. Gained reputation as a writer of three plays; Charles I is said to have liked his work. Plays acted by Prince Charles's servants and by the Queen's Men at Salisbury Court, the Cockpit, and at court. Included along with eminent writers as contributor of verse to the *Annalia Dubrensia*, honouring the Cotswold Games. Died January 1639; buried in St Bartholomew, Smithfield.

Works:

Maidment, James and W. H. Logan, eds. *The Dramatic Works of Shakerley Marmion*. Edinburgh, 1875.

Studies:

Davis, Joe Lee. *The Sons of Ben: Jonsonian Comedy in Caroline England*. Detroit, 1967.

MARSTON, JOHN (1576–1634)

Baptized 7 October 1576, Wardington, Oxfordshire; of a prominent Shropshire family. Brasenose College, Oxford 1592–4; B.A., 1594. Resident in Middle Temple by 1595. Began writing during early years in Temple, publishing erotic and satirical poems as 'W. Kinsayder'. Start of dramatic career coincides with prohibition of non-dramatic satire (June 1599) and public burning of Marston's poems, among others. Mentioned by Henslowe (1599), but majority of plays written for various children's companies; may have been a sharer in Children of Queen's Revels at Blackfriars, *c.*1604–8. Abandoned the stage after 1608, having been briefly imprisoned in New-gate, apparently for writing or producing a play that offended James. Took orders (1609), eventually becoming incumbent of Christchurch, Hampshire, 1616–31. Died

25 June 1634, Aldermanbury, London. Buried next to his father in Middle Temple, under a stone bearing the now-destroyed epitaph *Oblivioni Sacrum* [sacred to oblivion].

Works:
Wood, H. Harvey, ed. *The Works of John Marston.* 3 vols. Edinburgh, 1934–8.

Studies:
Axelrad, A. José. *Un malcontent élizabethain: John Marston (1576–1634).* Paris, 1955.
Bergson, Allen. 'The ironic tragedies of Marston and Chapman: notes on Jacobean tragic form'. *JEGP* 69 (1970), 613–30.
'Dramatic style as parody in Marston's *Antonio and Mellida'. SEL* 11 (1971), 307–25.
Caputi, Anthony. *John Marston, Satirist.* Ithaca, New York, 1961.
Finkelpearl, Philip J. *John Marston of the Middle Temple.* Cambridge, Massachusetts, 1969.
Foakes, R. A. 'John Marston's fantastical plays: *Antonio and Mellida* and *Antonio's Revenge'. PQ* 41 (1962), 229–39.
Geckle, George L. *John Marston's Drama: Themes, Images, Sources.* Rutherford, New Jersey, 1980.
Hamilton, Donna B. 'Language as theme in *The Dutch Courtesan'. RenD* n.s. 5 (1972), 75–88.
Ingram, R. W. *John Marston.* Boston, 1978.
Kaplan, Joel H. 'John Marston's *Fawn*: a saturnalian satire'. *SEL* 9 (1969), 335–50.
Kernan, Alvin. 'John Marston's play *Histriomastix'. MLQ* 19 (1958), 134–40.
Schoenbaum, S. 'The precarious balance of John Marston'. *PMLA* 67 (1952), 1069–78.
Scott, Michael. *John Marston's Plays: Themes, Structure and Performances.* New York, 1978.
Tucker, Kenneth. *John Marston: A Reference Guide.* Boston, 1985.
Ure, Peter. John Marston's *Sophonisba*: a reconsideration'. *DUJ* 10 (1949), 81–90.

MASSINGER, PHILIP (1583–1640)
Son of Arthur Massinger, who had served as a steward and man of business to Henry Herbert, second Earl of Pembroke; baptized at Salisbury 24 November, 1583. Served as a page at Wilton, and attended Salisbury School. Left St Alban Hall, Oxford, in 1606 without taking a degree. Maintained his links with the Herbert family – Philip, Earl of Montgomery and later (1630) fourth Earl of Pembroke became his chief patron. Although Catholicism is treated sympathetically in his plays, his political allegiances seem to have been more with 'puritans' and parliamentarians. Worked for the King's Men (1616–23); later joint author of plays with Daborne, Field, and Fletcher. After Fletcher's death, the leading playwright of his time. Buried at St Saviour's, 18 March 1640.

Works:
Edwards, Philip and Colin Gibson, eds., *The Plays and Poems of Philip Massinger.* 5 vols. Oxford, 1976.

Studies:
Ball, Robert H. *The Amazing Career of Sir Giles Overreach*. Princeton, 1939.
Butler, Martin. 'Massinger's *City Madam* and the Caroline audience'. *RenD* n.s. 13 (1982), 157–87.
Clubb, Louis George. '*The Virgin Martyr* and the Tragedia Sacra'. *RenD* 7 (1964), 103–26.
Dunn, T. A. *Philip Massinger: The Man and the Playwright*. Edinburgh, 1957.
Eliot, T. S. 'Philip Massinger' (1920) in his *Selected Essays* (London, 1951), pp. 205–20.
Enright, D. J. 'Poetic satire and satire in verse: a consideration of Jonson and Massinger'. *Scrutiny* 18 (1951–52), 211–23.
Howard, Douglas, ed. *Philip Massinger: A Critical Reassessment*. Cambridge, 1985.
Neill, Michael. 'Massinger's patriarchy: the social vision of *A New Way to Pay Old Debts*'. *RenD* n.s. 10 (1979), 185–213.
Thomson, Patricia. 'The Old Way and the New Way in Dekker and Massinger'. *MLR* 51 (1956), 168–78.

MIDDLETON, THOMAS (1580–1627)

Son of a prosperous London bricklayer and builder who had a coat of arms. Attended Queen's College Oxford although he may not have graduated. Wrote *The Wisdom of Solomon Paraphrased* (1597) as well as prose satires. Henslowe's Diary reveals that he was writing for Worcester's Men and for the Admiral's Men in 1602. By that year and until 1607 wrote also for Paul's Boys. Collaborated with Rowley, Munday, Drayton, Webster, and Dekker – and may have collaborated with Shakespeare on *Timon of Athens*. From 1604 to 1611 wrote satirical city comedies; from 1613 to 1618 he concentrated on tragicomedies, and from 1618 on tragedies. From 1607 to 1616 was writing city pageants and masques as well as plays and maintained his allegiance to city interests and parliamentary puritans till his death. 1620 became Chronologer to the city. *A Game at Chess* (1624) caused political furore. Buried at Newington Butts 4 July 1627. For studies of *The Revenger's Tragedy*, see those listed under Tourneur.

Works:
Bullen, A. H., ed. *The Works of Thomas Middleton*. 8 vols. London, 1885–6.

Studies:
Barker, R. H. *Thomas Middleton*. New York, 1958.
Braunmuller, A. R. '"To the Globe I rowed": John Holles sees *A Game at Chess*'. *ELR* 20 (1990), forthcoming.
Chatterji, Ruby. 'Theme, imagery and unity in *A Chaste Maid in Cheapside*'. *RenD* 8 (1965), 105–26.
Covatta, Anthony. *Thomas Middleton's City Comedies*. Lewisburg, Pennsylvania, 1973.
Dessen, Alan C. 'Middleton's *The Phoenix* and the allegorical tradition'. *SEL* 6 (1966), 291–308.
Donovan, Dennis, ed. *Thomas Middleton, 1939–1965; John Webster, 1940–1965*. Elizabethan Bibliographical Supplements 1. London, 1967.

Ewbank, Inga-Stina. 'Realism and morality in *Women Beware Women*'. *E&S* (1969), 57–70.

Farr, Dorothy M. *Thomas Middleton and the Drama of Realism*. Edinburgh, 1973.

Friedenreich, K., ed. *'Accompaninge the Players': Essays Celebrating Thomas Middleton 1580–1980*. New York, 1982.

Heinemann, Margot. *Puritanism and Theatre: Thomas Middleton and Opposition Drama under the Early Stuarts*. Cambridge, 1980.

Holmes, David M. *The Art of Thomas Middleton*. London, 1970.

Jump, J. D. 'Middleton's tragedies' in Boris Ford, ed., *The Age of Shakespeare* (rev. edn, Harmondsworth, 1982), pp. 457–70.

Lake, D. J. *The Canon of Thomas Middleton's Plays*. Cambridge, 1975.

Levin, Richard. 'The Dampit scenes in *A Trick to Catch the Old One*'. *MLQ* 25 (1964), 140–52.

'The three quarrels of *A Fair Quarrel*'. *SP* 61 (1964), 219–31.

The Multiple Plot in English Renaissance Drama. Chicago, 1971.

Rowe, G. E., Jr. *Thomas Middleton and the New Comedy Tradition*. Lincoln, Nebraska, 1979.

Schoenbaum, S. *Middleton's Tragedies: A Critical Study*. New York, 1955.

Steen, S. J. *Thomas Middleton: A Reference Guide*. Boston, 1984.

MUNDAY, ANTHONY (1560–1633)

Son of a London draper. Apprenticed to the stationer John Allde who went out of business in 1582, before the apprenticeship was complete; freeman of Drapers' Company, 1585. In Rome in 1578, seeking information about Roman Catholics at the English College, which furnished him with material for ballads and anti-Catholic prose polemics. Actor with Oxford's company and Pembroke's company (1598). For Henslowe and the Admiral's company wrote some seventeen plays from 1594 to 1602, often in collaboration, most of which are lost. Francis Meres in 1598 called him one of 'the best for comedy' and 'our best plotter'. Probably collaborated on *Sir Thomas More* (*c.*1593) with Shakespeare and others. Satirized as Antonio Balladino in Jonson's *The Case is Altered* (1598) and as Posthaste in the anonymous *Histriomastix* (1599?). Wrote pageants and entertainments for the city from 1605 as well as a collection of romances. Used pseudonym Lazarus Piot. Friend of John Stowe, and brought out posthumous edition of the *Survey of London*. Buried 10 August 1633, at St Stephen's, Coleman Street.

Works:

Hosley, Richard, ed. *Fedele and Fortunio*. New York and London, 1981.

Meagher, John C., ed. *The Huntingdon Plays … The Downfall and the Death of Robert, Earl of Huntingdon*. New York and London, 1980.

Pennell, Arthur E., ed. *John a Kent and John a Cumber*. New York and London, 1980.

Studies:

Johnson, Robert C., ed. *Minor Elizabethans, Roger Ascham 1946–1966 … Anthony Munday, 1941–1966*. Elizabethan Bibliographies Supplements 9. London, 1968.

Turner, Celeste. *Anthony Mundy, an Elizabethan Man of Letters.* Berkeley, 1928.

NABBES, THOMAS (*fl.* 1638 *d.* 1645)
Native of Worcestershire, entered Exeter College, Oxford, thence into service with Worcestershire families. From 1630 in London; friend of Inns of Court men and of Shackerley Marmion. Wrote plays for the Queen's company, generally performed at Salisbury Court. Wrote city comedies, a tragedy, masques (including *Microcosmos* and *Spring's Glory*), which were published from 1637. A collection of poems published in 1639. One of the Tribe of Ben [Jonson].

Works:
Bullen, A. H., ed. *The Works of Thomas Nabbes.* 2 vols. London, 1882–9.

Studies:
Vince, R. W. Thomas Nabbes and the professional drama 1630–1642. Unpublished Ph.D. dissertation, Northwestern University, 1968.

NASHE, THOMAS (1567->1601)
A minister's son, baptized at Lowestoft, Suffolk, in November, 1567. Matriculated St John's College, Cambridge, 1582. B.A. in 1586. Left university in 1588, from which time he produced a succession of books and witty pamphlets, containing criticism of actors and the scholar Gabriel Harvey. Possibly, with Lyly, contributed to the opposition to the anti-episcopalian tracts of Martin Marprelate. Of the circle of 'University Wits', and was patronized by various members of the aristocracy and by Archbishop Whitgift. In 1597 his collaboration with Jonson on the *Isle of Dogs* gave political offence, and he had to flee to Yarmouth to escape apprehension. In his *Lenten Stuff* (1599) he charged that Jonson's part of the play had caused all the trouble. *Summer's Last Will and Testament* (1592), which was probably performed at Archbishop Whitgift's palace at Croydon, is his only extant complete play.

Works:
McKerrow, R. B., ed. *The Works of Thomas Nashe.* Rev. edn, F. P. Wilson. 5 vols. Oxford, 1958.

Studies:
Hibbard, G. R. *Thomas Nashe: A Critical Introduction.* Cambridge, Massachusetts, 1962.
Hilliard, Stephen S. *The Singularity of Thomas Nashe.* Lincoln, Nebraska, 1986.
Hutson, Lorna. *Nashe in Context.* Oxford, 1988.
Johnson, Robert C., ed. *Robert Greene, 1945–1965 ... Thomas Nashe, 1941–65 ... George Peele, 1939–1965.* Elizabethan Bibliographical Supplements 5. London, 1968.
Nicholl, Charles. *A Cup of News: The Life of Thomas Nashe.* London, 1984.

NORTON, THOMAS (1532–1584)
Born in London, the son of a wealthy grocer, educated Cambridge and Inner

Temple. 1571 Remembrancer of City of London and sat in Parliament for London. A Calvinist and opposed to public stage. 1583 accused of treason. *Gorboduc* or *Ferrex and Porrex*, written in collaboration with Thomas Sackville (q.v.), is his only extant play and the first tragedy in blank verse. It was first performed at the Inner Temple on 6 January, 1562. Poems of his were included in Tottel's *Songes and Sonnettes* (1557).

Works:
Cauthen, Irby B., ed. *Gorbuduc, or, Ferrex and Porrex*. Lincoln, Nebraska, 1970.

Studies:
Clemen, W. H. *English Tragedy before Shakespeare: The Development of Dramatic Speech*, trans. T. S. Dorsch. London, 1961.

PEELE, GEORGE (1558?–1597?)
Son of James Peele, salter and clerk of Christ's Hospital, himself a writer of pageants. Educated at Christ's Hospital, and Broadgates Hall and Christ Church, Oxford. B.A. 1577, M.A. 1579. A player himself; in 1583 arranged performances of plays by William Gager at Oxford then probably returned to London and associated with Greene in circle of 'University Wits' (see Greene's *Groats-worth of Wit* [1592]). Worked with the Lord Admiral's Company, later the Queen's, and the Chapel Royal. Many of his plays are lost. *The Merry Conceited Jests of George Peele* (1605) may offer some evidence for biography, but is padded with material from traditional jest books. Wrote pageants as well as five extant plays. His name attached to other lost texts and his authorship detected in others. Died of smallpox.

Works:
Prouty, C. T., gen. ed. *The Life and Works of George Peele*. 3 vols. New Haven, 1952–70.

Studies:
Ashley, L. R. *George Peele*. New York, 1970.
Braunmuller, A. R. 'Characterization through language in the early plays of Shakespeare and his contemporaries' in K. Muir *et al.*, eds., *Shakespeare: Man of the Theatre* (Newark, Delaware, 1982), pp. 128–47.
George Peele. Boston, 1983.
Ewbank (née Ekeblad), Inga-Stina. 'The House of David in Renaissance drama: a comparative study'. *RenD* 8 (1965), 3–40.
'"What words, what looks, what wonders?": language and spectacle in the theatre of George Peele' in G. R. Hibbard, ed., *The Elizabethan Theatre V* (Hamden, Connecticut, 1975), pp. 124–54.
Johnson, Robert C., ed. *Robert Greene, 1945–1965 ... George Peele, 1939–1965*. Elizabethan Bibliographical Supplements 5. London, 1968.
Jones, Gwenan. 'The intention of Peele's "Old Wives' Tale"'. *Aberystwyth Studies* 7 (1925), 79–93.

Montrose, Louis A. 'Gifts and reasons: the contexts of Peele's *Araygnement of Paris*'. *ELH* 47 (1980), 433–61.

Senn, Werner. *Studies in the Dramatic Construction of Robert Greene and George Peele*. Swiss Studies in English, 74. Bern, 1973.

Von Hendy, Andrew. 'The triumph of chastity: form and meaning in *The Arraignment of Paris*'. *RenD* n.s. 1 (1968), 87–101.

PORTER, HENRY (*fl.* 1596 *d.* 1599)

Payments recorded to him in Henslowe's diary on account of Admiral's Men in 1596–7. Meres names him 'the best for comedy amongst us' (*Palladis Tamia*, 1598). Not traceable after 1599 and *The Two Angry Women of Abington* his only extant play. Chambers records identifications with various 'Henry Porters' of the period. Stabbed to death by the playwright John Day.

Works:

Jardine, Michael and John Simons, eds. *The Two Angry Women of Abington*. Nottingham, 1987.

Studies:

Nosworthy, J. M. 'Notes on Henry Porter'. *MLR* 35 (1940), 517–21.

'Henry Porter'. *English* 6 (1946), 65–9.

PRESTON, THOMAS (>1569–1589<)

Educated Eton and King's College, Cambridge. Played there in *Dido* before the Queen and was awarded a pension of £20 p.a. Fellow of King's until 1581. 1584 Master of Trinity Hall, Cambridge; 1589 Vice-Chancellor. Chambers considers it 'incredible' that such a scholar could have been responsible for his only extant play, *Cambises*. Some of his ballads published as broadsides.

Works:

Johnson, R. C., ed. *A Critical Edition of Thomas Preston's 'Cambises'*. Salzburg, 1975.

ROWLEY, WILLIAM (?–1626)

Little is known of his early life except that he was associated with Queen Anne's Men in 1607. Wrote plays for the Duke of York's Men from 1610–15. Acted and wrote for the Princess Elizabeth's Men 1615–19, collaborating with Middleton, Massinger, Ford, Dekker, Webster, and Heywood until 1621. Later wrote for Lady Elizabeth's Men at the Cockpit, and wrote and acted for the King's Men from 1623. Name attached to some fifty plays. His death is alluded to in Jonson's *Staple of News*.

Works:

See under Middleton and Rowley's other collaborators.

Studies:

Stock, C. W. *William Rowley, his All's Lost by Lust*. University of Pennsylvania Publications, Series in Literature and Philology, 13, 1910.

SACKVILLE, THOMAS (1536–1608)
Son of Sir Richard Sackville, first cousin of Anne Boleyn. Perhaps educated at Hart Hall, Oxford and St John's College, Cambridge. A barrister at the Inner Temple. Wrote the Induction to the *Mirror for Magistrates* (1559–63), which was completed by William Baldwin and George Ferrers. Became Lord Buckhurst in 1567 and Earl of Dorset in 1604. Lord Treasurer under both Elizabeth and James. With Thomas Norton (q.v.) wrote *Gorboduc*.

Works:
See Norton, Thomas.

Studies:
Bacquet, P. *Un contemporain d'Elisabeth I: T. Sackville, l'homme et l'oeuvre*. Geneva, 1966.
Swart, J. *Thomas Sackville*. Groningen, 1949.

SHAKESPEARE, WILLIAM (1564–1616)
See Wells, Stanley, ed. *The Cambridge Companion to Shakespeare Studies*. Cambridge, 1986.

SHARPHAM, EDWARD (1576–1608)
Born East Allington, Devonshire. Entered Middle Temple 1594 and died, probably of the plague, the day after he made his will (22 April 1608). Wrote *The Fleer* and *Cupid's Whirligig*, which were performed by the Children of the Revels at the Blackfriars. Drummond noted that Jonson considered Sharpham, Day, Dekker, and Minshew to be all rogues.

Works:
The Fleir. Materialen zur Kunde des älteren Englischen Dramas. Reprinted, Kraus Reprint, Louvain, 1963.
Nicoll, Allardyce, ed. *Cupid's Whirligig*. Waltham Saint Lawrence, 1926.

SHIRLEY, JAMES (1596–1666)
A Londoner by birth, educated at Merchant Taylors' School then St John's College, Oxford and St Catherine's College, Cambridge. 1618 printed a poem 'Eccho'. Sometime an Anglican clergyman in Hertfordshire, and, after converting to Catholicism, a schoolmaster. Patronized by Queen Henrietta Maria, and associated with Massinger, Ford, and others. Later, managed the Werburgh St Theatre in Dublin. Succeeded Massinger as principal dramatist of the King's Men (1640). Accompanied his patron Newcastle in the campaigns of 1642–4. His *Poems* of 1646 appeared under the patronage of Thomas Stanley. His prefatory epistle to the Beaumont and Fletcher folio of 1647 testifies to his admiration of these dramatists. Died soon after the Great Fire of London.

Works:
Gifford, William and Alexander Dyce, eds. *The Dramatic Works and Poems of James Shirley*. 6 vols. London, 1833. Reprinted, New York, 1966.

Studies:

Bas, G. *James Shirley, 1596–1666: dramaturge caroléen*. Service de réproduction des thèses, Université de Lille III. Lille, 1973.

Burner, Sandra A. *James Shirley: A Study of Literary Coteries and Patronage in Seventeenth-Century England*. London, 1989.

Butler, Martin. *Theatre and Crisis 1632–1642*. Cambridge, 1984.

Forsythe, R. S. *The Relations of Shirley's Plays to the Elizabethan Drama*. New York, 1914.

Lucow, B. *James Shirley*. Boston, 1981.

Morton, Richard. 'Deception and social dislocation: an aspect of James Shirley's Drama'. *RenD* 9 (1966), 227–46.

Nason, A. H. *James Shirley, Dramatist: A Biographical and Critical Study*. New York, 1915.

Reed, Robert R. Jr. 'James Shirley and the sentimental comedy'. *Anglia* 73 (1955), 149–70.

Schipper, J. *James Shirley: sein Leben und seine Werke*. Vienna, 1911.

Sensabaugh, G. F. 'Platonic love in Shirley's *The Lady of Pleasure*'. *A Tribute to George Coffin Taylor* (Chapel Hill, 1952), pp. 168–77.

Wertheim, Albert. 'Games and courtship in James Shirley's *Hyde Park*'. *Anglia* 90 (1972), 71–91.

Zimmer, Ruth. *James Shirley: A Reference Guide*. Boston, 1980.

SUCKLING, SIR JOHN (1609–1641)

Son of the Secretary of State, and educated at Trinity College, Cambridge. Admitted to Gray's Inn and inherited large estates from his father. A passionate Royalist who wrote plays as well as lyric poetry. Financed a lavish production of one, *Aglaura* (1637), himself. One of the Sons of Ben [Jonson]. After setting on foot the abortive 'first army plot', fled to Paris where, according to Aubrey, he committed suicide.

Works:

Beaurline, L. A. and T. Clayton, eds. *The Works of Sir John Suckling*. 2 vols. Oxford, 1971.

Studies:

Squire, C. L. *Sir John Suckling*. Boston, 1978.

TARLTON, RICHARD (?–1588)

A clown for the Queen's Men. His only known play (unless he wrote *The Famous Victories of Henry V*) is *The Seven Deadly Sins*, revived by the Admiral's or Strange's Men about 1590. Anecdotes, some probably fictitious, about him were published in *Tarlton's Jests*, 1592?–1611?.

Works:

Halliwell, J. O., ed. *Tarlton's Jests*. London, 1884.

Studies:

Bradbrook, M. C. *The Rise of the Common Player*. London, 1962.

Lawrence, W. J. 'On the underrated genius of Dick Tarleton' in his *Speeding up Shakespeare* (London, 1937), pp. 17–38.

TOMKIS, THOMAS (?1580–?1634)
Entered Trinity College Cambridge 1597. B.A. 1600, M.A. and fellow of the college 1604. Probably wrote *Lingua* (1603?) as well as *Albumazar* (1615) for college performances – the latter was performed before the King – both being founded on Italian models.

Works:
Dick, Hugh G., ed. *Albumazar, a Comedy (1615) by Thomas Tomkis*. University of California Publications in English, no. 13. Berkeley, 1944.
Lingua. Tudor Facsimile Texts. London, 1913.

TOURNEUR, CYRIL (*died* 1626)
Date and place of birth obscure. Only *The Atheist's Tragedy* (*c.*1611) can be confidently attributed to him; author of occasional and satirical poems 1605–13. Employed in the Netherlands, 1613, and as Sir Edward Cecil's secretary in the unsuccessful Cadiz expedition of 1625, whence he was invalided to Ireland, where he died. Although much recent scholarship points to Middleton as being the author of *The Revenger's Tragedy*, critical essays on that play are listed here.

Works:
Parfitt, George, ed. *The Plays of Cyril Tourneur*. Cambridge, 1978.

Studies:
Dollimore, Jonathan. 'Two concepts of mimesis: Renaissance literary theory and *The Revenger's Tragedy*' in James Redmond, ed., *Themes in Drama. 2. Drama and Mimesis* (Cambridge, 1980).
Donovan, Dennis, ed. *Thomas Dekker, 1945–1965 … Cyril Tourneur, 1945–1965*. Elizabethan Bibliographies Supplements 2. London, 1967.
Foakes, R. A. 'The art of cruelty: Hamlet and Vindice'. *ShS* 26 (1973), 21–32.
Marston and Tourneur. Harlow, 1978.
Kaufmann, R. J. 'Theodicy, tragedy and the Psalmist: Tourneur's *Atheist's Tragedy*'. *CompD* 3 (1969–70), 241–62.
Murray, P. B. *A Study of Cyril Tourneur*. Philadelphia, 1964.
Salingar, L. G. 'Tourneur and the tragedy of revenge' in Boris Ford, ed., *The Age of Shakespeare* (rev. edn, Harmondsworth, 1982), pp. 436–56.
Schuman, S. *Cyril Tourneur*. Boston, 1977.
Tucker, Kenneth. *A Bibliography of … John Ford and Cyril Tourneur*. Boston, 1977.

TOWNSHEND, AURELIAN (*fl.* 1601–1643)
Steward to Robert Cecil, friend of Jonson and Herbert. Enjoyed a high literary reputation at court of Charles I. Wrote masques and poems, succeeding Jonson as court masque writer about 1632.

Works:
Brown, Cedric C., ed. *Poems and Masques of Aurelian Townshend*. Reading, 1983.
Chambers, E. K., ed. *Aurelian Townshend's Poems and Masques*. Oxford, 1912.

UDALL, NICHOLAS (1505–1556)
Born in Hampshire, educated at Winchester College, 1517, and Corpus Christi
College, Oxford, where he became a fellow in 1524. In 1526 suspected of Lutheran-
ism. Headmaster of Eton in 1534 but was dismissed for (homosexual?) misconduct in
1541. Perhaps *Ralph Roister Doister* (printed in 1566), the earliest known English
comedy, was acted by Eton boys before then. Held various ecclesiastical offices
before his death (headmaster of Winchester from 1554) and also published scholarly
and theological works.

Works:
See C. W. Whitworth, ed. *Three Sixteenth-Century Comedies*. London, 1984.

Studies:
Egerton, William L. *Nicholas Udall*. New York, 1965.
Plumstead, A. W. 'Satirical parody in *Roister Doister*: a reinterpretation'. *SP* 60
     (1963), 141–54.

WAGER, W[ILLIAM?] (*c.* 1559)
Nothing is known of him except for his authorship of two Protestant morality plays,
The Longer thou Livest, the More Fool thou Art and *Enough is as Good as a Feast*.

Works:
Benbow, R. Mark, ed. *The Longer thou Livest*; and *Enough is as Good as a Feast*.
     London, 1968.

WEBSTER, JOHN (?1580–1625)
Son of a wealthy coach-maker who worked near the Fortune and Red Bull play-
houses. Educated at Merchant Taylors' school and at the Middle Temple. Wrote
tragedies alone and collaborated with many of his contemporaries – Drayton,
Munday, Middleton, Dekker, Heywood, etc. – as well as writing occasional verse.
Worked with others on 'Monuments of Honour', the Lord Mayor's Pageant of 1624.

Works:
Lucas, F. L., ed. *The Complete Works of John Webster*. 4 vols. Rev. edn, London, 1958.

Studies:
Berry, Ralph. *The Art of John Webster*. Oxford, 1972.
Bliss, Lee. *The World's Perspective: John Webster and the Jacobean Drama*. New
     Brunswick, New Jersey, 1983.
Bogard, Travis. *The Tragic Satire of John Webster*. Berkeley, 1955.

Bradbrook, M. C. *John Webster: Citizen and Dramatist*. London, 1980.

Calderwood, James L. '*The Duchess of Malfi*: styles of ceremony'. *EIC* 12 (1962), 133–47.

Dent, R. W. *John Webster's Borrowing*. Berkeley, 1960.

Donovan, Dennis, ed. *Thomas Middleton, 1939–1965; John Webster, 1940–1965*. Elizabethan Bibliographical Supplements 1. London, 1967.

Ekeblad, Inga-Stina. 'Webster's constructional rhythm'. *ELH* 24 (1957), 165–76.

'The "impure art" of John Webster'. *RES* 9 (1958), 235–67.

Forker, C. R. *The Skull Beneath the Skin: The Achievement of John Webster*. Carbondale and Edwardsville, Illinois, 1986.

Gunby, D. C. '*The Devil's Law Case*: an interpretation'. *MLR* 63 (1968), 545–58.

Hunter, G. K. and S. K. Hunter, eds. *John Webster: A Critical Anthology*. Harmondsworth, 1969.

Lagard, F. *John Webster*. 2 vols. Toulouse, 1968.

Morris, Brian, ed. *John Webster*. London, 1970.

Murray, Peter B. *A Study of John Webster*. The Hague, 1969.

Pearson, Jacqueline. *Tragedy and Tragicomedy in the Plays of John Webster*. Manchester, 1980.

WHETSTONE, GEORGE (?1544–?1587)
A Londoner who, after spending his patrimony in riotous living, served in the Netherlands against the Spaniards, 1572–4. Wrote prose translations, pamphlets, occasional verse, and *Promos and Cassandra*, the plot of which resembles that of *Measure for Measure*.

Works:
Promos and Cassandra. Tudor Facsimile Texts. London, 1907.

Studies:
Izard, T. C. *George Whetstone: Mid-Elizabethan Man of Letters*. New York, 1942.

WILKINS, GEORGE (*fl.* 1604–1608)
Nothing is known of him except that he wrote pamphlets and plays for the King's and Queen's Men. His only extant play is *The Miseries of Enforced Marriage*. Parts of *Pericles* (he certainly wrote a novella, *The Painful Adventures of Pericles* [1608]) have been ascribed to him.

Works:
The Miseries of Enforced Marriage. Malone Society Reprint. Oxford, 1963.

WILSON, ROBERT (>1572–1600)
There may have been more than one dramatist of this name. It is attached to a handful of plays and various collaborations. Probably a member of Leceister's company (*c.*1572–81), served with Tarlton in the Queen's Men (1583–*c.*1586), later joining Lord Strange's Men. May have written a Catiline play with Chettle.

Works:
The Cobbler's Prophecy. Tudor Facsimile Texts. London, 1911.
The Three Ladies of London. Tudor Facsimile Texts. London, 1911.
The Three Lords of London. Tudor Facsimile Texts. London, 1912.

Studies:
Cameron, G. M. *Robert Wilson and the Plays of Shakespeare.* Riverton, New Zealand, 1982.

WOODES, NATHANIEL (?)
A Norwich minister, and author of a Protestant allegory, *The Conflict of Conscience* (>1581).

Works:
The Conflict of Conscience. Malone Society Reprint. Oxford, 1952.

Chronological table

This is a full but not complete list of plays of the period 1497–1642. It does not contain entertainments, pageants, masques, school plays, or Latin academic plays. Titles are not always given in full. Moreover, space does not permit even a partial account of either textual revisions or early theatrical history: dates given are those of composition or first performance and no attempt is made to distinguish between these. Asterisked titles can be dated only approximately, revivals and adaptations are not listed, and revisions, authorized and unauthorized (a category which includes 'bad quartos'), are not noted here. When a play is attributed to a particular company, that is the first company which is known to have performed it but not necessarily the company which performed it first; companies associated with a play's subsequent history are not listed. Collaborators are not always listed where the nature of multiple authorship is uncertain. The list does not include plays the texts of which have not survived. For further reference see A. Harbage (rev. edn, S. Schoenbaum and Sylvia Wagonheim), *Annals of English Drama 975–1700*, London, 1989.

Date	Author	Title	Company	Events
1485				Accession of Henry VII
1497	Medwall, Henry	*Fulgens and Lucrece*	Morton's House	
1509				Accession of Henry VIII
1513	Anon.	*Hick Scorner*	?	
1520	Heywood, John?	*The Four P's*	?	Field of the
		Johan Johan	?	Cloth of Gold
		*The Pardoner and	?	(meeting of
	Anon.	the Friar*		Henry VIII and
	Anon.	*Andria*	Closet	François I)
		Johan the Evangelist	?	
1521	Skelton, John	*Magnificence*	?	Diet of Worms condemns Luther for heresy
1527	Rastell, John	*Calisto and Melebea*	?	
1528	Heywood, John	*The Play of the Weather*	?	

419

Date	Author	Title	Company	Events
1530	Anon.	*Pater, Filius, et Uxor*	?	
1533				Act in Restraint of Appeals (severing English ecclesiastical courts from Rome)
1534				Act of Supremacy
1535	Anon.	*Temperance and Humility*	?	Thomas More executed
1536				Pilgrimage of Grace
1538	Bale, John	God's Promises	St Stephen's, Canterbury	
		1 and 2 King John	St Stephen's, Canterbury	
		The Temptation of our Lord	St Stephen's, Canterbury	
		Three Laws of Nature	St Stephen's, Canterbury	
1540	Lindsay, David	A Satire of the Three Estates	Linlithgow, before James V	
	Palsgrave, John	Acolastus	Closet	
1547				Accession of Edward VI
1549				Book of Common Prayer; Kett's rebellion
1550	Anon.	*Nice Wanton	?	
1553	Stevenson, W. (?)	*Gammer Gurton's Needle	Christ's College, Cambridge	Accession of Mary
1554	Udall, N. (?)	*Jacob and Esau	?	Marriage of Mary to Philip II; persecution and burning of Protestants
1555	Anon.	*Jack Juggler	?	Worcester's Men become active
1556				Cranmer executed

Date	Author	Title	Company	Events
1558				Accession of Elizabeth I
1559	Heywood, Jasper	*Troas*	Closet	Warwick's Men become active;
	Phillip, John	*Patient and Meek Grissel	?	Act of Settlement
	Wager, W.	*The Longer thou Livest …	?	
1560	Heywood, Jasper	*Thyestes*	Closet	Geneva translation of Bible
	Ingelend, Thomas	*The Disobedient Child	?	
	Wager, W.	*Enough is as Good as a Feast	?	
1561	Heywood, Jasper	Hercules Furens	Closet	
	Preston, Thomas	*Cambises	Court?	
1562	Norton & Sackville	Gorboduc	Inner Temple	
1563	Neville, Alexander	Oedipus	Closet	Derby's Men become active; 39 Articles define Anglican theology
1564	Blower, Richard	*Appius and Virginia	Westminster Boys (?)	Rich's Men become active
	Jeffere, John (?)	*The Bugbears	?	
1565	Edwards, Richard	*Damon and Pithias	Merton College, Oxford	
1566	Gascoigne, George	Supposes	Gray's Inn	
	Gascoigne, G. & Kinwelmershe, F.	Jocasta	Gray's Inn	
1567	Pickering, John	Horestes	Court (?)	Red Lion playhouse built;
	Studley, John	Hyppolytus	Closet	O'Neill's rebellion in Ireland
	Wager, W. (?)	The Trial of Treasure	?	
	Wilmot, R. etc.	*Gismond of Salerne	Inner Temple	
1568	Anon.	The Marriage of Wit and Science	Court (?)	Mary, Queen of Scots, flees to north of England; Bishops' Bible

Date	Author	Title	Company	Events
1569	Fulwell, Ulpian	*Like Will to Like*	?	Sussex's Men become active; pro-Catholic Rising of the North
	Garter, Thomas	*The Most Virtuous and Godly Susanna*	?	
1570	Preston, T. (?)	*Clyomon and Clamydes*	?	Papal bull ex-communicat-ing Elizabeth
1571	Rudd, Anthony etc.	*Misogonus*	Trinity College, Cambridge	
	Anon.	*New Custom*	?	
1572	Woodes, Nathaniel	*The Conflict of Con-science*	?	Massacre of St Bartholomew's Day
1573				Leicester's Men become active
1575	Gascoigne, George	*The Glass of Govern-ment*	Closet	
	Golding, Arthur	*Abraham's Sacrifice*	Closet	
1576	Wapull, George	*The Tide Tarrieth No Man*	?	The Theatre built
	Anon.	*Common Conditions*	?	
1577	Lupton, Thomas	*All for Money*	?	Strange's Men become active; first Blackfriars, Curtain, and, about this time, playhouse at Newington Butts built
1578	Whetstone, George	*1 & 2 Promos and Cassandra*	Unacted (?)	
1579	Merbury, Frances	*A Marriage Between Wit and Wisdom*	?	Elizabeth's mar-riage to Duc d'Anjou dis-cussed; start of military involve-ment in Dutch rebellion against Spain
1580				Oxford's Men become active
1581	Newton, Thomas	*Thebais*	?	Campion ex-ecuted

Date	Author	Title	Company	Events
	Peele, George	*The Arraignment of Paris	Chapel at court	
	Wilson, Robert	*The Three Ladies of London	?	
1582	Anon.	The Rare Triumphs of Love and Fortune	Derby's at court	Chamberlain's Men become active
1583	Legge, Thomas	*Solymitana Clades	?	Queen's Men become active
1584	Lyly, John	*Campaspe	Oxford's Boys	Oxford's Boys at the Blackfriars;
		*Sapho and Phao	Oxford's Boys	Oath of Association to defend
	Munday, A.	*Fedele and Fortunio	Court	Elizabeth against native or foreign enemies
1585	Lyly, John	*Gallathea	Paul's	Admiral's Men become active
1586	Marlowe & Nashe	*Dido, Queen of Carthage	Chapel (?)	Babington Plot to free Mary, Queen of Scots;
	Anon.	*The Famous Victories of Henry V	Queen's at Bull Inn	Battle of Zutphen
1587	Greene, Robert	*Alphonsus, King of Aragon	Queen's (?)	Rose built; Mary, Queen of
	Kyd, Thomas	*The Spanish Tragedy	Strange's	Scots, executed
	Marlowe, Christopher	*1 Tamburlaine the Great	Admiral's	
1588	Greene & Lodge	*A Looking Glass for London and England	Queen's (?)	Spanish Armada
	Hughes, T. etc.	The Misfortunes of Arthur	Gray's Inn at court	
	Kyffin, Maurice	Andria	Closet	
	Lyly, John	Endymion	Paul's at court	
	Wilson, Robert	*The Three Lords and Three Ladies of London	Queen's	
	Anon.	*The Wars of Cyrus	?	
1589	Greene, Robert	*Friar Bacon and Friar Bungay	Strange's	English attacks on Portuguese coast

Date	Author	Title	Company	Events
	Lyly, John	*Midas*	Paul's	
		*Mother Bombie	Paul's	
	Marlowe, C.	**The Jew of Malta*	Strange's	
	Munday, A.	**John a Kent and John a Cumber*	Admiral's (?)	
	Peele, George	**The Battle of Alcazar*	Admiral's	
	Anon.	**A Warning for Fair Women*	Chamberlain's	
1590	Greene, Robert	**James IV*	Queen's (?)	
		*George a Greene	Sussex's	
	Herbert, Mary	*Antonius*	Closet	
	Kyd, Thomas (?)	**Soliman and Perseda*	?	
	Lyly, John	**Love's Metamorphosis*	Paul's	
	Munday, A. (?)	**Fair Em, the Miller's Daughter*	Strange's	
	Shakespeare, William (?)	*Edward III*	Admiral's (?)	
	Shakespeare, William	**1 Henry VI*	Strange's	
		*2 Henry VI	Strange's	
		*3 Henry VI	Strange's	
		*The Two Gentlemen of Verona	?	
	Wilson, Robert	**The Cobbler's Prophecy*	Court (?)	
	Anon.	**King Leir*	Queen's (?)	
	Anon.	**Mucedorus*	?	
1591	Fraunce, Abraham	*Phillis and Amyntas*	Closet	
	Greene, Robert	**Orlando Furioso*	Queen's and Strange's	
	Peele, George	**Edward I*	Queen's (?)	
	Shakespeare, William	**The Taming of the Shrew*	Queen's (?)	
		*The Comedy of Errors	Strange's (?)	
		*Richard III	Strange's (?)	
		*Titus Andronicus	Strange's (?)	
	Anon.	**Arden of Faversham*	?	
	Anon.	**Jack Straw*	?	
	Anon.	*The Troublesome Reign of King John*	?	
	Anon.	**The True Tragedy of Richard III*	Queen's	

Date	Author	Title	Company	Events
1592	Greene, Robert (?)	*1 Selimus *John of Bordeaux	Queen's Strange's (?)	Plague closes playhouses for two years
	Marlowe, Christopher	*Doctor Faustus *Edward II	Admiral's Pembroke's	Pembroke's Men become active
	Nashe, Thomas	Summer's Last Will and Testament	Whitgift's house (?)	
	Warner, William	*Menaechmi	Closet	
	Anon.	A Knack to Know a Knave	Strange's	
	Anon.	*Thomas of Woodstock	?	
1593	Daniel, Samuel	Cleopatra	Closet	
	Lyly, John	*The Woman in the Moon	?	
	Marlowe, Christopher	The Massacre at Paris	Strange's	
	Peele, George	*The Old Wives Tale *David and Bethsabe	Queen's ?	
	Anon.	*Edmund Ironside	?	
	Anon.	*Guy Earl of Warwick	?	
1594	Heywood, Thomas	The Four Prentices of London	Admiral's	Series of poor harvests begins, leading to
	Kyd, Thomas	Cornelia	Closet (?)	hoarding, riots
	Shakespeare, William	*Love's Labour's Lost	?	
	Yarington, Robert	*Two Lamentable Tragedies	Admiral's (?)	
	Anon.	*Alphonsus, Emperor of Germany	?	
	Anon.	A Knack to Know an Honest Man	Admiral's	
	Anon. ('W.S.')	*Locrine	?	
1595	Munday, A. etc.	*Sir Thomas More	Worcester's (?)	Swan built; Ralegh's voyage
	Shakespeare, William	*Richard II *Romeo and Juliet *A Midsummer Night's Dream	Chamberlain's Chamberlain's (?) Chamberlain's	to Guiana; Tyrone's Irish rebellion

Date	Author	Title	Company	Events
	Anon.	*Caesar and Pompey*	Trinity College, Oxford	
1596	Chapman, George	*The Blind Beggar of Alexandria*	Admiral's	Essex attacks Cadiz
	Greville, Fulke	*Mustapha*	Closet	
	Jonson, Ben	*A Tale of a Tub*	Admiral's (?)	
	Shakespeare, William	*King John*	Chamberlain's	
		The Merchant of Venice	Chamberlain's	
	Anon.	Captain Thomas Stukeley	Admiral's	
1597	Chapman, George	An Humorous Day's Mirth	Admiral's	Second Black-friars built; se-cond armada fails
	Jonson, Ben	*The Case is Altered*	?	
	Shakespeare, William	*1 Henry IV*	Chamberlain's	
		2 Henry IV	Chamberlain's	
		The Merry Wives of Windsor	Chamberlain's	
1598	Brandon, Samuel	The Virtuous Octavia	Closet	Comprehensive Poor Law enacted
	Chettle & Munday	1 & 2 Robin Hood	Admiral's	
	Haughton, William	Englishmen for My Money	Admiral's	
	Jonson, Ben	Every Man in his Humour	Chamberlain's	
	Porter, Henry	*The Two Angry Women of Abingdon*	Admiral's	
	Shakespeare, William	Much Ado about Nothing	Chamberlain's	
1599	Dekker, Thomas	Old Fortunatus	Admiral's	Globe built; Essex in Ireland
		The Shoemaker's Holiday	Admiral's	
	Drayton, M. etc.	1 Sir John Oldcastle	Admiral's	
	Heywood, T. etc.	*1 & 2 Edward IV*	Derby's	
	Jonson, Ben	Every Man out of his Humour	Chamberlain's	
	Marston, John	*Antonio and Mellida*	Paul's	
	Marston, John (?)	*Histriomastix*	Paul's (?)	
	Shakespeare, William	*Henry V*	Chamberlain's	
		Julius Caesar	Chamberlain's	

Date	Author	Title	Company	Events
		*As You Like It	Chamberlain's	
	Anon.	*Club Law	Clare Hall, Cambridge	
	Anon.	*A Larum for London	Chamberlain's	
	Anon.	*Look about You	Admiral's	
	Anon.	*The Pilgrimage to Parnassus	St John's College, Cambridge	
1600	Chettle & Haughton	1 The Blind Beggar of Bednal Green	Admiral's	Fortune built; Gowrie plot against James
	Chettle, Dekker, & Haughton	Patient Grissel	Admiral's	VI of Scotland
	Day, Dekker & Haughton	The Spanish Moor's Tragedy	Admiral's	
	Greville, Fulke	*Alaham	Closet	
	Haughton, William	The Devil and his Dame	Admiral's	
	Marston, John	*Antonio's Revenge	Paul's	
		Jack Drum's Entertainment	Paul's	
	Shakespeare, William	*Hamlet	Chamberlain's	
	Anon.	Lust's Dominion	Admiral's (?)	
	Anon.	*The Maid's Metamorphosis	Paul's	
	Anon.	*1 The Return from Parnassus	St John's College, Cambridge	
	Anon.	*Thomas Lord Cromwell	Chamberlain's	
	Anon.	*The Weakest Goeth to the Wall	Oxford's	
	Anon.	The Wisdom of Dr Dodypoll	Paul's	
1601	Chapman, George	All Fools	Queen's Revels	Essex's revolt, execution; fur-
	Dekker, Thomas	*Satiromastix	Chamberlain's	ther Poor Law amends 1598
	Dekker, Thomas (?)	Blurt, Master Constable	Paul's	and sets pattern for centuries
	Dymock, J. (?)	Il Pastor Fido	Closet (?)	
	Jonson, Ben	*Cynthia's Revels	Chapel	

Date	Author	Title	Company	Events
		*Poetaster	Chapel	
	Marston, John	What You Will	Paul's	
	Percy,	Arabia Sitiens	?	
	William	The Cuckqueans and Cuckolds Errants	?	
	Shakespeare, William	Twelfth Night	Chamberlain's	
	Anon.	Liberality and Prodigality	Chapel	
	Anon.	*The Trial of Chivalry	Derby's	
1602	Chapman, George	*The Gentleman Usher	Chapel	
		*May Day	Chapel	
		*Sir Giles Goosecap	Chapel	
	Chettle, Henry	Hoffman	Admiral's	
	Dekker, Thomas (?)	*The Merry Devil of Edmonton	Chamberlain's	
	Dekker & Webster	*Sir Thomas Wyatt	Queen Anne's	
	Heywood, Thomas	*1 The Fair Maid of the West	?	
		*The Royal King and the Loyal Subject	Worcester's	
	Heywood, Thomas (?)	*How a Man May Choose a Good Wife from a Bad	Worcester's	
	Percy, William	A Country Tragedy	?	
	Shakespeare, William	*Troilus and Cressida	Chamberlain's	
	Anon.	*The Fair Maid of the Exchange	?	
	Anon.	*Timon	Inner Temple (?)	
	Anon.	*Wily Beguiled	Paul's (?)	
1603	Alexander, William	Darius	Closet	Accession of James I; serious
	Heywood, Thomas	A Woman Killed with Kindness	Worcester's	outbreak of plague; 'Main' and 'Bye' plots; Admiral's Men be-
	Jonson, Ben	Sejanus	King's Men	
	Marston, John	*The Malcontent	Queen's Revels	come Prince Henry's Men;

Date	Author	Title	Company	Events
	Middleton, Thomas	*The Family of Love	Admiral's (?)	Chamberlain's Men become
	Percy, William	The Fairy Pastoral	Syon House (?)	King's Men
	Shakespeare, William	*Measure for Measure	King's Men	
	Anon.	*2 The Return from Parnassus	St John's College, Cambridge	
	Anon.	Narcissus	St John's College, Oxford	
	Anon.	Philotus	Closet (?)	
1604	Alexander, William	Croesus	Closet	Worcester's Men become
	Cary, Elizabeth	*Miriam, the Fair Queen of Jewry	Closet	Queen Anne's Men; Queen's Revels become
	Chapman, George	*Bussy D'Ambois	Paul's	active; Hampton Court con-
	Daniel, Samuel	Philotas	Queen's Revels	ference; peace treaty with
	Day, John	*Law Tricks	King's Revels	Spain; negotia-
	Dekker, Thomas (?)	*The London Prodigal	King's Men	tions over Union with Scotland
	Dekker & Middleton	1 Honest Whore	Prince Henry's	begin and con- tinue until 1607
	Dekker & Webster	Westward Ho!	Paul's	
	Heywood, Thomas	*1 If You Know not Me	Queen Anne's	
		*The Wise Woman of Hogsdon	Queen Anne's	
	Marston, John	*The Dutch Courtesan	Queen's Revels	
		*Poetaster or The Fawn	Queen's Revels	
	Middleton, Thomas	*The Phoenix	Paul's	
	Rowley, Thomas	*When You See Me You Know Me	Prince Henry's	

Date	Author	Title	Company	Events
	Shakespeare, William	*Othello	King's Men	
		*All's Well that Ends Well	King's Men	
	Verney, Francis	*Antiope	Trinity College, Oxford	
	Anon.	*The Birth of Hercules	Christ's College, Cambridge (?)	
	Anon.	*Charlemagne	?	
	Anon.	*The Fair Maid of Bristow	King's Men	
	Anon.	*1 Jeronimo	King's Men (?)	
	Anon.	The Wit of a Woman	?	
1605	Chapman, George	*Caesar and Pompey	?Red Bull built;	Gunpowder Plot
		Monsieur d'Olive	Queen's Revels	
		*The Widow's Tears	Queen's Revels (?)	
	Chapman, Jonson, & Marston	Eastward Ho!	Queen's Revels	
	Daniel, Samuel	The Queen's Arcadia	Christ Church, Oxford	
	Dekker, Thomas	*2 Honest Whore	Prince Henry's	
	Dekker & Webster	Northward Ho!	Paul's	
	Heywood, Thomas	If You Know Not Me You Know Nobody	Queen Anne's	
	Middleton, Thomas	*Michaelmas Term	Paul's	
		A Trick to Catch the Old One	Paul's	
	Middleton, T. & ?	A Yorkshire Tragedy	King's Men	
	Shakespeare, William	*King Lear	King's Men	
	Shakespeare & Middleton	*Timon of Athens	King's Men	
	Anon.	*Nobody and Somebody	Queen Anne's (?)	

Date	Author	Title	Company	Events
1606	Armin, Robert	*The Two Maids of More-Clacke*	King's Revels	Whitefriars built
	Barnes, Barnabe	The Devil's Charter	King's Men	
	Beaumont & Fletcher	The Woman Hater	Paul's	
		*Love's Cure	King's Men (?)	
	Day, John	The Isle of Gulls	Queen's Revels	
	Dekker, Thomas	*The Whore of Babylon	Prince Henry's	
	Fletcher & ?	*The Noble Gentleman	King's Men	
	Jonson, Ben	*Volpone	King's Men	
	Marston, John	*Sophonisba	Queen's Revels	
	Middleton, Thomas	*A Mad World My Masters	Paul's	
		The Puritan	Paul's	
		*The Revenger's Tragedy	King's Men	
	Shakespeare, William	Macbeth	King's Men	
		*Antony and Cleopatra	King's Men	
	Sharpham, William	The Fleer	Queen's Revels	
	Wilkins, George	*The Miseries of Enforced Marriage	King's Men	
1607	Alexander, William	*The Alexandraean Tragedy	Closet	King's Revels (boys) at Whitefriars; Plantation (colonization) of Virginia
		Julius Caesar	Closet	
	Beaumont, Francis	*The Knight of the Burning Pestle	Queen's Revels	
	Day, Rowley, & Wilkins	The Travels of the Three English Brothers	Queen Anne's	
	Heywood, Thomas	*The Rape of Lucrece	Queen Anne's	
	Machin, Lewis (?)	*Every Woman in her Humour	King's Revels (?)	
	Marston & Barkstead	*The Insatiate Countess	Queen's Revels	
	Mason, John	*The Turk	King's Revels	
	Middleton, Thomas	Your Five Gallants	Paul's (?)	
	Shakespeare, William	*Pericles	King's Men	

Date	Author	Title	Company	Events
	Sharpham, Edward	*Cupid's Whirligig*	King's Revels	
	Anon.	*Claudius Tiberius Nero*	Closet (?)	
1608	Barry, Lording	*Ram Ally*	King's Revels	King's Men
	Chapman, George	*Byron's Conspiracy*	Queen's Revels	lease
		Byron's Tragedy	Queen's Revels	Blackfriars
	Day, John	*Humour out of Breath*	King's Revels	
	Fletcher, John	*The Faithful Shepherdess*	Queen's Revels (?)	
	Fletcher & Beaumont	*Cupid's Revenge*	Queen's Revels	
	Markham & Machin	*The Dumb Knight*	King's Revels	
	Rowley, William	*A Shoemaker a Gentleman*	Queen Anne's (?)	
	Rowley & ?	*The Birth of Merlin*	?	
	Shakespeare, William	*Coriolanus*	King's Men	
1609	Beaumont & Fletcher	*Philaster*	King's Men	Cockpit
		The Coxcomb	Queen's Revels	(Phoenix)
	Field, Nathan	*A Woman is a Weathercock*	Queen's Revels	built;
				Plantation
	Heywood & Rowley	*Fortune by Land and Sea*	Queen Anne's	(colonization) of Ulster
	Jonson, Ben	*Epicoene*	Queen's Revels	
	Middleton & Rowley	*Wit at Several Weapons*	?	
	Shakespeare, William	*The Winter's Tale*	King's Men	
1610	Beaumont & Fletcher	*The Maid's Tragedy*	King's Men	Petition of Right on
	Chapman, George	*The Revenge of Bussy D'Ambois*	Queen's Revels	impositions; Great Contract
	Daborne, Robert	*A Christian Turned Turk*	?	fails in Parliament
	Heywood, Thomas	*The Golden Age*	Queen Anne's	
	Jonson, Ben	*The Alchemist*	King's Men	
	Shakespeare, William	*Cymbeline*	King's Men	

Date	Author	Title	Company	Events
1611	Beaumont & Fletcher	*A King and No King*	King's Men	Baronetcies sold;
	Cooke, John	*Greene's Tu Quoque*	Queen Anne's	King James's translation
	Dekker, Thomas	**Match Me in London*	Queen Anne's (?)	of Bible; Lady
	Dekker (& Daborne?)	**If It Be Not Good, the Devil Is in It*	Queen Anne's	Elizabeth's Men become active
	Dekker & Middleton	*The Roaring Girl*	Prince Henry's	
	Field, Nathan	**Amends for Ladies*	Queen's Revels	
	Fletcher, John	**Monsieur Thomas*	Queen's Revels (?)	
		*The Night Walker	Lady Elizabeth's (?)	
		*The Woman's Prize	King's Men (?)	
	Heywood, Thomas	**The Brazen Age*	Queen's	
		*The Silver Age	Queen Anne's Men & King's Men	
	Jonson, Ben	*Catiline His Conspiracy*	King's Men	
	Middleton, Thomas	*The Second Maiden's Tragedy*	King's Men	
	Rowley, William	**A New Wonder*	?	
	Shakespeare, William	**The Tempest*	King's Men	
	Tourneur, Cyril	**The Atheist's Tragedy*	King's Men (?)	
1612	'R.A.'	**The Valiant Welshman*	Prince's Men	Prince's Men become active;
	Chapman, George	**Chabot, Admiral of France*	Lady Elizabeth's (?)	Lancashire witches hanged; Prince Henry
	Fletcher, John	**The Captain*	King's Men	dies
	Heywood, Thomas	**1 & 2 Iron Age*	Queen's	
	Webster, John	**The White Devil*	Queen Anne's	
1613	Field & Fletcher	*The Honest Man's Fortune*	Lady Elizabeth's	Prince Henry's become Palsgrave's Men;
	Fletcher, John	**Bonduca*	King's Men	Globe burns

Date	Author	Title	Company	Events
	Fletcher & Beaumont	*The Scornful Lady*	Queen's Revels (?)	down; Elizabeth Stuart marries
	Fletcher & Field (?)	*Four Plays in One*	?	Frederick, Elector Palatine, and
	Middleton, Thomas	A Chaste Maid in Cheapside	Lady Elizabeth's	later King of Bohemia
		No Wit, No Help Like a Woman's	Lady Elizabeth's (?)	
	Shakespeare & Fletcher	Henry VIII	King's Men	
		The Two Noble Kinsmen	King's Men	
	Stephens, John	Cynthia's Revenge	Closet	
	Tailor, Robert	The Hog Hath Lost his Pearl	Apprentices at Whitefriars	
1614	Daniel, Samuel	Hymen's Triumph	?	Second Globe built; Hope
	Fletcher, John	*Valentinian*	King's Men	built; Addled
		Wit Without Money	Lady Elizabeth's (?)	Parliament
	Jonson, Ben	Bartholomew Fair	Lady Elizabeth's	
	Smith, W[entworth?]	*The Hector of Germany*	Tradesmen at Bull and Curtain	
	Webster, John	*The Duchess of Malfi*	King's Men	
	Zouche, Richard	*The Sophister*	Oxford	
1615	Fletcher & Massinger	*Thierry and Theodoret*	King's Men	Porter's Hall built; Earl
	Middleton, Thomas	*More Dissemblers Besides Women*	King's Men	and Countess of Somerset
		The Witch	King's Men	tried for
	'S.S.'	*The Honest Lawyer*	Queen Anne's	Overbury's
	Tomkis, Thomas	Albumazar	Trinity College, Cambridge	murder
1616	Fletcher & Beaumont	*Love's Pilgrimage*	King's Men	Pocohontas arrives in
	Fletcher & Middleton	*The Nice Valour*	?	England
	Jonson, Ben	The Devil is an Ass	King's Men	
	Middleton, Thomas	*The Widow*	King's Men	
	Middleton & Rowley	*A Fair Quarrel*	Prince's	

Date	Author	Title	Company	Events
1617	Brewer, Anthony	*The Lovesick King*	?	James I visits
	Daborne, Robert	*The Poor Man's Comfort*	Queen Anne's	Scotland
	Fletcher, John	*The Chances*	King's Men	
		The Mad Lover	King's Men	
	Fletcher & Massinger	*The Bloody Brother*	King's Men (?)	
	Fletcher, Massinger, & Field	*The Queen of Corinth*	King's Men	
		The Knight of Malta	King's Men	
	Goffe, Thomas	*Orestes*	Christ Church, Oxford	
	Webster, John	*The Devil's Law-Case*	Queen Anne's	
	Anon.	*Stonyhurst Pageants*	Closet (?)	
1618	Field & Massinger	*The Fatal Dowry*	King's Men	Ralegh executed;
	Fletcher, John	The Loyal Subject	King's Men	Synod of Dort; 30
	Fletcher & Massinger	*Beggar's Bush*	King's Men	Years' War begins
	Goffe, Thomas	*The Raging Turk*	Christ Church, Oxford	
	Holiday, Barten	Technogamia	Christ Church, Oxford	
	Middleton, Thomas	*Hengist, King of Kent*	?	
	Middleton, Rowley, & Massinger (?)	*The Old Law*	?	
	Shirley, Henry	*The Martyred Soldier*	Queen Anne's (?)	
	Anon.	*Swetnam the Woman Hater*	Queen Anne's	
1619	Cumber, John (?)	*The Two Merry Milkmaids*	Red Bull company	Queen Anne dies and remnant of her
	Fletcher, John	*The Humorous Lieutenant*	King's Men	company becomes Red Bull
	Fletcher & Massinger	*The Little French Lawyer*	King's Men	(Revels) company; Olden
		Sir John van Olden Barnavelt	King's Men	Barnavelt executed

Date	Author	Title	Company	Events
	Ford, John	*The Laws of Candy	King's Men	
	Goffe, Thomas (?)	*The Careless Shepherdess	Christ Church, Oxford (?)	
		The Courageous Turk	Christ Church, Oxford	
	Rowley, William	*All's Lost by Lust	Prince's	
	Anon.	*Nero	?	
1620	Dekker & Massinger	The Virgin Martyr	Red Bull company	*Mayflower* arrives in Massachusetts Colony
	Fletcher, John	*Women Pleased	King's Men	
	Fletcher & Massinger	*The Custom of the Country	King's Men	
		*The Double Marriage	King's Men	
		*The False One	King's Men	
	May, Thomas	The Heir	Red Bull company	
	Middleton & Rowley	The World Tossed at Tennis	Prince's	
	Anon.	*The Costly Whore	Red Bull company (?)	
1621	Dekker, Ford, & Rowley	The Witch of Edmonton	Prince's	Attack on monopolies; impeachment revived
	Fletcher, John	*The Island Princess	King's Men	
		*The Pilgrim	King's Men	
		*The Wild Goose Chase	King's Men	
	Massinger, Philip	*The Maid of Honour	Lady Elizabeth's	
	Middleton, Thomas	*Women Beware Women	King's Men (?)	
	Middleton & Webster	*Anything for a Quiet Life	King's Men	
	Anon.	*The Faithful Friends	?	
1622	Dekker, Thomas	The Noble Spanish Soldier	Admiral's (?)	
	Fletcher & Massinger	The Prophetess	King's Men	
		The Sea Voyage	King's Men	
		The Spanish Curate	King's Men	

Date	Author	Title	Company	Events
	Markham & Sampson	*Herod and Antipater	Red Bull company	
	Massinger, Philip	*The Duke of Milan	King's Men	
	Middleton & Rowley	The Changeling	Lady Elizabeth's	
	Rowley, William (?)	*A Match at Midnight	Red Bull company	
	Anon.	*The Two Noble Ladies	Red Bull company	
1623	Dekker, Thomas	*The Welsh Ambassador	Lady Elizabeth's (?)	Prince Charles and Duke of Buckingham
	Dekker & Ford	The Spanish Gypsy	Lady Elizabeth's	travel to Spain, negotiate over
	Fletcher, John	The Wandering Lovers	King's Men	marriage of Infanta
	Fletcher & Rowley	The Maid in the Mill	King's Men	
	Mabbe, James (?)	*The Captive Lady	?	
	Massinger, Philip	The Bondman	Lady Elizabeth's	
1624	Davenport, Robert	The City Nightcap	Lady Elizabeth's	Statute against
	Drue, Thomas	The Duchess of Suffolk	Palsgrave's	Monopolies
	Fletcher, John	Rule a Wife and Have a Wife	King's Men	
		A Wife for a Month	King's Men	
	Heywood, Thomas	The Captives	Lady Elizabeth's	
	Massinger, Philip	The Parliament of Love	Lady Elizabeth's	
		The Renegado	Lady Elizabeth's	
		*The Unnatural Combat	King's Men	
	Middleton, Thomas	A Game at Chess	King's Men	
	Webster, John	*Appius and Virginia	?	
1625	'J.D.'	*The Knave in Grain	Red Bull	Accession of Charles I; mar-
	Davenport, Robert	*A New Trick to Catch the Devil	Queen Henrietta's (?)	riage to Henrietta Maria of France; Queen

Date	Author	Title	Company	Events
	Fisher, Jasper	*Fuimus Troes	Magdalen College, Oxford	Henrietta's Men become active; serious outbreak of plague; English attack on Cadiz repulsed
	Fletcher & Massinger	*The Elder Brother	King's Men	
	Heywood, Thomas	*The English Traveller	Queen Henrietta's	
		*The Escapes of Jupiter	?	
	Massinger, Philip	A New Way to Pay Old Debts	Queen Henrietta's	
	Sampson, William	*The Vow Breaker	?	
	Shirley, James	The School of Compliment	Lady Elizabeth's	
	Webster & Rowley	*A Cure for a Cuckold	?	
	Anon.	*The Partial Law	Closet	
1626	Fletcher & ??	The Fair Maid of the Inn	King's Men	Remnant of Prince's Men forms Red Bull company; Forced Loan controversy
	Hemming, William	*The Jews' Tragedy	?	
	Jonson, Ben	The Staple of News	King's Men	
	Massinger, Philip	The Roman Actor	King's Men	
	May, Thomas	Cleopatra, Queen of Egypt	?	
	Shirley, James	The Maid's Revenge	Queen Henrietta's	
		*The Wedding	Queen Henrietta's	
	'J.W.'	The Valiant Scot	?	
	Anon.	Dick of Devonshire	?	
1627	Davenant, William	The Cruel Brother	King's Men	Start of ineffective English intervention (at Isle of Rhé, La Rochelle) on behalf of Huguenots
	Massinger, Philip	The Great Duke of Florence	Queen Henrietta's	
	May, Thomas	*Antigone, the Theban Princess	Unacted	
	Randolph, T.	*Plutophthalmia Plutogamia	Trinity College, Cambridge (?)	

Date	Author	Title	Company	Events
1628	Davenant, William	*Albovine, King of the Lombards*	Unacted	Petition of Right; assassination of Buckingham
	Davenport, Robert	*King John and Matilda*	Queen Henrietta's	
	Ford, John	The Lover's Melancholy	King's Men	
		The Queen	?	
	Gomersall, Robert	*Ludovick Sforza*	Unacted (?)	
	May, Thomas	Julia Agrippina, Empress of Rome	?	
	Reynolds, Henry	Aminta	Closet	
	Shirley, James	The Witty Fair One	Queen Henrietta's	
	Anon.	*Philander, King of Thrace*	?	
1629	Brome, Richard	The Lovesick Maid	King's Men	Beginning of 11 year period without meeting of parliament; Salisbury Court built
		The Northern Lass	King's Men	
	Carlell, Lodowick	*The Deserving Favourite*	King's Men	
	Clavell, J. (?)	*The Soddered Citizen*	King's Men	
	Davenant, William	The Just Italian	King's Men	
		The Siege	King's Men (?)	
	Ford, John	*The Broken Heart*	King's Men	
	Jonson, Ben	The New Inn	King's Men	
	Massinger, Philip	The Picture	King's Men	
	Shirley, James	The Grateful Servant	Queen Henrietta's	
	Anon.	*Hierarchomachia*	?	
1630	Brome, Richard	*The City Wit*	King's Revels	Peace treaties with Spain and France
	Heywood, Thomas	*2 The Fair Maid of the West*	Queen Henrietta's	
	Randolph, Thomas	Amyntas	King's Revels	
		The Muses' Looking Glass	King's Revels	
	Sidnam, Jonathan	*Filli de Sciro*	Closet	
		Il Pastor Fido	Closet	
	Wilson, Arthur	*The Inconstant Lady*	King's Men	

Date	Author	Title	Company	Events
1631	Brome, Richard	*The Queen's Exchange*	King's Men (?)	Prince Charles's
	Dekker, Thomas	*The Wonder of a Kingdom*	Queen Henrietta's	Men become active
	Mabbe, James	*The Spanish Bawd*	Closet	
	Marmion, Shackerly	*Holland's Leaguer*	Prince Charles's	
	Massinger, Philip	*Believe as You List*	King's Men	
		The Emperor of the East	King's Men	
	Shirley, James	*The Contention for Honour and Riches*	Privately acted (?)	
		The Humorous Courtier	Queen Henrietta's	
		Love's Cruelty	Queen Henrietta's	
		The Traitor	Queen Henrietta's	
	Wilson, Arthur	*The Swisser*	King's Men	
1632	'T.B.'	*The Country Girl*	King's Men (?)	Cockpit-in-Court converted
	Brome, Richard	*The Novella*	King's Men	
		The Weeding of the Covent Garden	King's Men (?)	
	Ford, John	*Love's Sacrifice*	Queen Henrietta's	
		'Tis Pity She's a Whore	Queen Henrietta's	
	Hausted, Peter	*The Rival Friends*	Queens' College, Cambridge	
	Jonson, Ben	*The Magnetic Lady*	King's Men	
	Massinger, Philip	*The City Madam*	King's Men	
	Percy, William	*Necromantes*	Closet (?)	
	Randolph, Thomas	*The Jealous Lovers*	Trinity College, Cambridge	
	Shirley, James	*The Ball*	Queen Henrietta's	
		Changes	King's Revels	
		Hyde Park	Queen Henrietta's	
1633	Cockain, Aston	*Trappolin Creduto Principe*	?	Laud becomes Archbishop of Canterbury;

Date	Author	Title	Company	Events
	Cowley, Abraham	*Love's Riddle	Unacted	Charles visits
	Ford, John	*Perkin Warbeck	Queen Henrietta's	Scotland
	Heywood, Thomas	*A Maidenhead Well Lost	Queen Henrietta's	
	Marmion, Shackerly	*A Fine Companion	Prince Charles's	
	Massinger, Philip	The Guardian	King's Men	
	Montague, Walter	The Shepherd's Paradise	Court	
		The Launching of the Mary	?	
	Nabbes, Thomas	Covent Garden	Queen Henrietta's	
	Shirley, James	The Bird in a Cage	Queen Henrietta's	
		The Gamester	Queen Henrietta's	
		The Young Admiral	Queen Henrietta's	
	Wilson, Arthur	The Corporal	King's Men	
1634	Brome & Heywood	The Late Lancashire Witches	King's Men	
	Davenant, William	Love and Honour	King's Men	
		The Wits	King's Men	
	Glapthorne, Henry	*Albertus Wallenstein	King's Men	
	Heywood, Thomas	Love's Mistress	Queen Henrietta's	
	Massinger & Fletcher (?)	Cleander	King's Men	
		A Very Woman	King's Men	
	Nabbes, Thomas	*Tottenham Court	Prince's Men (?)	
	Peaps, [William (?)]	*Love in its Ecstasy	Unacted	
	Rutter, Joseph	*The Shepherd's Holiday	Queen Henrietta's	
	Shirley, James	The Example	Queen Henrietta's	
		The Opportunity	Queen Henrietta's	
1635	Brome, Richard	*The New Academy	King's Revels (?)	

Date	Author	Title	Company	Events
		The Queen and Concubine	King's Revels	
		The Sparagus Garden	King's Revels	
	Cartwright, William	*The Ordinary	Christ Church, Oxford (?)	
	Davenant, William	News from Plymouth	King's Men	
		The Platonic Lovers	King's Men	
	Ford, John	*The Fancies Chaste and Noble	Queen Henrietta's	
	Glapthorne, Henry	The Lady Mother	King's Revels	
	Heywood, Thomas	*A Challenge for Beauty	King's Men	
	Jones, John	*Adrasta	Unacted	
	Jordan, Thomas	*Money is an Ass	King's Revels (?)	
	Killigrew, Henry	The Conspiracy	King's Men	
		*The Prisoners	Queen Henrietta's	
	Kirke, John	*The Seven Champions of Christendom	Prince Charles's (?)	
	Marmion, Shackerly	*The Antiquary	Queen Henrietta's	
	Nabbes, Thomas	Hannibal and Scipio	Queen Henrietta's	
	Richards, Nathaniel	Messalina, the Roman Empress	King's Revels	
	Rider, William	*The Twins	King's Revels (?)	
	Shirley, James	The Coronation	Queen Henrietta's	
		The Lady of Pleasure	Queen Henrietta's	
	Anon.	*Love's Changelings' Change	Closet (?)	
	Anon.	Wit's Triumvirate	?	
1636	Carlell, Lodowick	*1 & 2 Arviragus and Philicia	King's Men	
	Cartwright, William	The Royal Slave	Christ Church, Oxford	
	Glapthorne, Henry	The Hollander	Queen Henrietta's	
	Killigrew, Thomas	*Claracilla	Queen Henrietta's	

Date	Author	Title	Company	Events
		*The Princess	King's Men (?)	
	Massinger, Philip	The Bashful Lover	King's Men	
	May, Thomas	The Old Couple	?	
	Shirley, James	The Duke's Mistress	Queen Henrietta's	
	Strode, William	The Floating Island	Christ Church, Oxford	
	Wilde, George	Love's Hospital	St John's College, Oxford	
1637	Berkeley, William	*The Lost Lady	King's Men	Beeston's Boys, Queen's Men
	Brome, Richard	The English Moor	Queen's	and, in Dublin, Ogilby's Men
	Carlell, Lodowick	*The Fool would be a Favourite	Queen's (?)	become active; Werburgh Street Theatre built in
		*Osmond the Great Turk	Queen's (?)	Dublin; Ship-money case
	Cartwright, William	*The Lady Errant	Privately acted	
	Glapthorne, Henry	*The Ladies' Privilege	Beeston's Boys	
	Jonson, Ben	*Mortimer his Fall	Unacted	
		*The Sad Shepherd	Unacted	
	Mayne, Jasper	*The City Match	King's Men	
	Neale, Thomas	The Ward	Unacted	
	Rutter, Joseph	*1 The Cid	Beeston's Boys	
	Shirley, James	The Royal Master	Ogilby's Men	
	Speed, J.	The Converted Robber	St John's College, Oxford	
	Suckling, John	Aglaura	King's Men	
		*The Sad One	Unacted	
	Anon.	*The Wasp	King's Revels	
1638	Baylie, Simon	*The Wizard	?	Solemn League and Covenant
	Brome, Alexander (?)	*The Cunning Lovers	Beeston's Boys	(Scotland) launched

Date	Author	Title	Company	Events
	Brome, Richard	*The Antipodes*	Queen's	
		The Damoiselle	Beeston's Boys (?)	
	Carlell, Lodowick	*1 & 2 The Passionate Lovers*	King's Men	
	Cartwright, William	*The Siege*	Unacted(?)	
	Davenant, William	*The Fair Favourite*	King's Men	
		The Unfortunate Lovers	King's Men	
	Ford, John	*The Lady's Trial*	Beeston's Boys	
	Glapthorne, Henry	*Argalus and Parthenia*	Beeston's Boys	
		Wit in a Constable	Beeston's Boys	
	May, Charles	*Grobiana's Nuptials*	St John's College, Oxford	
	Mayne, Jasper	*The Amorous War*	?	
	Mead, Robert	*The Combat of Love and Friendship*	Christ Church, Oxford	
	Nabbes, Thomas	*The Bride*	Beeston's Boys	
	Rawlins, Thomas	*The Rebellion*	King's Revels	
	Rutter, Joseph	*2 The Cid*	Unacted (?)	
	Salusbury, Thomas	*Love or Money*	Privately acted	
	Shirley, James	*The Constant Maid*	Ogilby's Men, Dublin (?)	
		The Doubtful Heir	Ogilby's Men, Dublin	
	Suckling, John	*The Goblins*	King's Men	
	Anon.	*The Fairy Knight*	?	
1639	Brome, Richard	*The Lovesick Court*	Prince Charles's (?)	First Bishops' War
		A Mad Couple Well Matched	Beeston's Boys (?)	
	Cockain, Aston	*The Obstinate Lady*	?	
	Davenant, William	*The Spanish Lovers*	King's Men	
	Drue, Thomas (?)	*The Bloody Banquet*	Beeston's Boys (?)	
	Freeman, Ralph	*Imperiale*	Closet (?)	
	Hemming, William	*The Fatal Contract*	Queen Henrietta's	
	Lower, William	*The Phoenix in her Flames*	Unacted (?)	

Date	Author	Title	Company	Events
	Nabbes, Thomas	*The Unfortunate Mother*	Unacted	
	Sharpe, Lewis	*The Noble Stranger*	Queen's	
	Shirley, James	The Gentleman of Venice	Ogilby's Men, Dublin (?)	
		The Politician	Ogilby's Men, Dublin (?)	
		1 St Patrick for Ireland	Ogilby's Men, Dublin	
	Suckling, John	*Brennoralt*	King's Men	
1640	Brome, Richard	*The Court Beggar*	Beeston's Boys	Second Bishops' War; Short
	Burnell, Henry	*Landgartha*	Ogilby's Men, Dublin	Parliament; Long Parliament summoned at
	Cavendish & Shirley	*The Country Captain*	King's Men	Oxford
	Chamberlain, Robert	*The Swaggering Damsel*	Beeston's Boys (?)	
	Glapthorne, Henry (?)	*Revenge for Honour*	?	
	Gough, John	*The Strange Discovery*	Closet (?)	
	Habington, William	The Queen of Aragon	Amateurs at Court	
	Harding, Samuel	*Sicily and Naples*	Unacted (?)	
	Sandys, George	Christ's Passion	Closet	
	Shirley, James (?)	The Arcadia	Queen Henrietta's	
		The Imposture	King's Men	
	Anon.	*The Cyprian Conqueror*	Closet (?)	
	Anon.	*The Ghost*	?	
1641	Brome, Richard	A Jovial Crew	Beeston's Boys	Star Chamber abolished;
	Cavendish, William	*The Variety*	King's Men	Strafford attainted;
	Denham, John	*The Sophy*	King's Men	Laud impeached
	Jordan, Thomas	The Walks of Islington and Hogsdon	Red Bull company (?)	
	Killigrew, Thomas	*The Parson's Wedding*	King's Men	
	Quarles, Francis	*The Virgin Widow*	Privately acted	

Date	Author	Title	Company	Events
	Shirley, James	*The Brothers*	King's Men	
		The Cardinal	King's Men	
	Tatham, John	*The Distracted State*	Red Bull company (?)	
	Wild, Robert	*The Benefice*	Cambridge	
1642	Cowley, Abraham	*The Guardian*	Trinity College, Cambridge	Theatres closed; royal standard raised; battles of
	Jaques, Francis	*The Queen of Corsica*	Unacted (?)	Edgehill, Turnham Green
	'J.S.'	*Andromana*	Unacted (?)	
	Shirley, James	*The Court Secret*	Unacted	
		The Sisters	King's Men	

Index of English plays, masques, entertainments, and other dramatic forms, by author

Anonymous plays are grouped alphabetically at the end of this index.

Index of English plays, masques, entertainments, and other dramatic forms

General index

Only more-than-incidental mentions are indexed here; English plays and other dramatic forms are separately listed. There are two group entries, for theatre companies (where entries include a company's alternative names) and for theatres.

CAMBRIDGE COMPANIONS TO LITERATURE